Maria Montessori

PEDAGOGICAL ANTHROPOLOGY

PEDAGOGICAL ANTHROPOLOGY

By

MARIA MONTESSORI
AUTHOR OF "THE MONTESSORI METHOD"

TRANSLATED FROM THE ITALIAN BY
FREDERIC TABER COOPER

WITH 163 ILLUSTRATIONS AND DIAGRAMS

GYAN

Published by

GYAN

Gyan Publishing House
5, Ansari Road
Daryaganj, New Delhi-110002
Phone: 011-47034999, 9811692060
E-mail: books@gyanbooks.com

Distribution Network
gyanbooks.com
India, USA, Canada, UK, Australia, France

ISBN : 978-81-212-6262-0 (PB)
First Published, 1913

2nd Impression 2022

Printed at: Gyan Press, Delhi.

PEDAGOGICAL ANTHROPOLOGY
Author: MARIA MONTESSORI

PEDAGOGICAL ANTHROPOLOGY

BY

MARIA MONTESSORI

AUTHOR OF "THE MONTESSORI METHOD"

TRANSLATED FROM THE ITALIAN BY

FREDERIC TABER COOPER

WITH 163 ILLUSTRATIONS AND DIAGRAMS

TO

MY MOTHER

RENILDE STOPPANI

AND MY FATHER

ALESSANDRO MONTESSORI

ON THE OCCASION OF THE FORTY-FIFTH ANNIVERSARY
OF THEIR UNCLOUDED UNION, I DEDICATE THIS
BOOK, FRUIT OF THE SPIRIT OF LOVE AND
CONTENTMENT WITH WHICH THEY
HAVE INSPIRED ME

PREFACE

For some time past much has been said in Italy regarding Pedagogical Anthropology; but I do not think that until now any attempt has been made to define a science corresponding to such a title; that is to say, a method that systematises the positive study of the pupil for pedagogic purposes and with a view to establishing philosophic principles of education.

As soon as anthropology annexes the adjective, "pedagogical," it should base its scope upon the fundamental conception of a possible amelioration of man, founded upon the positive knowledge of the laws of human life. In contrast to general anthropology which, starting from a basis of positive data founded on observation, mounts toward philosophic problems regarding the *origin of man*, pedagogic anthropology, starting from an analogous basis of observation and research, must rise to philosophic conceptions regarding the *future destiny* of man from the biological point of view. The study of congenital anomalies and of their biological and social origin, must undoubtedly form a part of pedagogical anthropology, in order to afford a positive basis for a universal human hygiene, whose sole field of action must be the school; but an even greater importance is assumed by the study of *defects of growth* in the normal man; because the battle against these evidently constitutes the practical avenue for a wide regeneration of mankind.

If in the future a scientific pedagogy is destined to rise, it will devote itself to the education of men already rendered physically better through the agency of the allied positive sciences, among which pedagogic anthropology holds first place.

The present-day importance assumed by all the sciences calculated to regenerate education and its environment, the school, has profound social roots and is forced upon us as the necessary path toward further progress; in fact the transformation of the outer environment through the mighty development of experimental sciences during the past century, must result in a correspondingly *transformed man;* or else civilisation must come to a halt before the obstacle offered by a human race lacking in organic strength and character.

The present volume comprises the lectures given by me in the University of Rome, during a period of four years, all of which were diligently preserved by one of my students, Signor Franceschetti. My thanks are due to my master, Professor Giuseppe Sergi who, after having urged me to turn my anthropological studies in the direction of the school, recommended me as a specialist in the subject; and my free university course for students in the Faculty of Natural Sciences and Medicine was established, in pursuance of his advice, by the Pedagogic School of the University of Rome. The volume also contains the pictures used in the form of lantern slides to illustrate the lectures, pictures taken in part from various works of research mentioned in this volume. Acknowledgment is gratefully made to the scientists and scholars whose work is thus referred to.

I have divided my subject into ten chapters, according to a special system: namely, that each chapter is complete in itself—for example, the first chapter, which is very long, contains an outline of general biology, and at the same time biological and social generalisations concerning man considered from our point of view as educators, and thus furnishes a complete organic conception which the remainder of the book proceeds to analyse, one part at a time; the chapter on the pelvis, on the other hand, is exceedingly short, but it completely covers the principles relating to this particular part, because they lend themselves to such condensed treatment.

Far from assuming that I have written a definitive work, it is only at the request of my students and publisher that I have consented to the publication of these lectures, which represent a modest effort to justify the faith of the master who urged me to devote my services as a teacher to the advancement of the school.

MARIA MONTESSORI.

CONTENTS

(The figures in parenthesis refer to the number of the page)

INTRODUCTION

MODERN TENDENCIES OF ANTHROPOLOGY AND THEIR RELATION TO PEDAGOGY

CHAPTER I

CERTAIN PRINCIPLES OF GENERAL BIOLOGY

THE FORM AND TYPES OF STATURE

THE STATURE

THE WEIGHT

CHAPTER II

CRANIOLOGY

CHAPTER III

THE THORAX

CHAPTER IV

THE PELVIS

CHAPTER V

THE LIMBS

CHAPTER VI

THE SKIN AND PIGMENTS

MORPHOLOGICAL ANALYSIS OF CERTAIN ORGANS (STIGMATA)

CHAPTER VII

TECHNICAL PART

THE PERSONAL ERROR

CHAPTER VIII

STATISTICAL METHODOLOGY

CHAPTER IX

THE BIOGRAPHIC HISTORY OF THE PUPIL AND HIS ANTECEDENTS

CHAPTER X

THE APPLICATION OF BIOMETRY TO ANTHROPOLOGY FOR THE PURPOSE OF DETERMINING THE MEDIAL MAN

INTRODUCTION

THE MODERN TENDENCIES OF ANTHROPOLOGY AND THE RELATION THAT THEY BEAR TO PEDAGOGY

Human Hygiene

The Old Anthropology.—*Anthropology* was defined by Broca as "the natural history of man," and was intended to be the application of the "zoological method" to the study of the human species.

As a matter of fact, as with all positive sciences, the essential characteristic of Anthropology is its "method." We could not say, if we wished to speak quite accurately, that "Anthropology is the study of man"; because the greater part of acquirable knowledge has for its subject the human race or the individual human being; philosophy studies his origin, his essential nature, his characteristics; linguistics, history and representative art investigate the collective phenomena of physiological and social orders, or determine the morphological characteristics of the idealised human body.

Accordingly, what characterises Anthropology is not its subject: *man;* but rather the method by which it proposes to study him.

The selfsame procedure which zoology, a branch of the natural sciences, applies to the study of animals, anthropology must apply to the study of man; and by doing so it enrolls itself as a science in the field of nature.

Zoology has a well-defined point of departure, that clearly distinguishes it from the other allied sciences: it studies the *living animal.* Consequently, it is an eminently synthetic science, because it cannot proceed apart from the *individual,* which represents in itself a sum of complex morphological and psychic characteristics, associated with the species; and which furthermore, during life, exhibits certain special distinguishing traits resulting from instincts, habits, migration and geographical distribution.

Zoology consequently includes a vast but well-defined field. Fundamentally, it is a *descriptive* science, and when the general character of the individual living creatures has been determined, it proceeds to draw comparisons between them, distinguishing genus and species, and thus working toward a *classification*. Down to the time of Linnaeus, these were its limits; but since the studies of Lamarck and Charles Darwin, it has gone a step further, and has proceeded to investigate the *origin* of species, an example that was destined to be followed by botany and biology as a whole, which is the study of *living things*.

When anthropology attained, under Broca, the dignity of a branch of the natural sciences, the evolutionary theory already held the field, and man had begun to be studied as an animal in his relation to species of the lower orders. But, just as in zoology, the fundamental part of anthropology was *descriptive;* and the description of the morphology of the body was divided, according to the method followed, into *anthropology*, or the method of *inspection*, and *anthropometry*, or the method of measurements.

By these means, many problems important to the biological side of the subject were solved—such, for instance, as racial characteristics—and a classification of "the human races" was achieved through the evidences afforded by comparative studies.

But the descriptive part of anthropology is not limited to the inspection and measurement of the body; on the contrary, just as in zoology, it is extended to include the *habits* of the individual living being; that is to say, in the case of man, the language, the manners and customs (data that determine the *level of civilisation*), emigration and the consequent intermixture of races in the original formation of nations, thus constituting a special branch of science properly known by the name of *ethnology*.

In this manner, while still adhering rigorously to zoological methods, anthropology found itself compelled to throw out numerous collateral branches into widely different fields, such as those of linguistics and archæology; because man is a *speaking animal* and a *social animal*.

One strictly anthropological problem is that of the origin of man, and its ultimate analogy with that of the other animal species. Hence the comparative studies between man and the anthropoid apes; while palæontological discoveries of *pre-human* forms, such as the pithecanthropus, were just so many arguments calculated to bring the human species within the scheme of a *biological philosophy,* based upon evolution, which held its own, for nearly half a century, on the battle-ground of natural sciences, under the glorious leadership of Darwin.

Yet, notwithstanding that it offered studies and problems of direct interest to man, anthropology failed to achieve popularity. During that half century (the second half of the Nineteenth), which beheld the scientific branches of biology multiply throughout the entire field of analytical research, from histology to biochemistry, and succeeded especially in making a practical application of them in medicine, Anthropology failed to raise itself from the status of a pure and aristocratic, in other words, a superfluous science, a status that prevented it from ranking among the sciences of primary importance. As a matter of fact, while zoology is a required study in the universities, Anthropology still remains an elective study, which in Italy is relegated to three or four universities at most. The epoch of materialistic philosophy and analytical investigation could naturally hardly be expected to prove a field of victory for *man,* the intelligent animal, and nature's most splendid achievement in construction.

The impressive magnificence of this thought, that bursts like pent-up waters from the results of positive research into *man* considered as a *living* individual, was forced to await the patient preparation of material on which to build, such as the gathering of partial and disorganised facts, which were accumulated through rigorous and minute analyses, conducted under the guidance of the experimental sciences. It was in this manner that anthropology slowly evolved a method and, by doing so, raised itself to the rank of a science, without ever once being utilised for practical purposes or recognised as *necessary* as a supplemental or integral element of other sciences.

One branch of learning which might have utilised the important scientific discoveries regarding the antiquity of man, his nature considered as an animal, his first efforts as a labourer and a member of society, is pedagogy.

What could be more truly instructive and educative than to describe to children that first heroic Robinson Crusoe, primitive man, cast away on this vast island, the earth, lost in the midst of the universe? Mankind, weak and naked, without iron, because it still remained mysteriously hidden in the bowels of the earth, without fire because they had not yet discovered the means of procuring it; stones were their only weapons of defense against the ferocious and gigantic beasts that roared on all sides of them in the forests. The rude, splintered stone, the first handiwork of intelligent man, his first instrument and his first weapon, could be prepared solely from one kind of mineral, of which the local deposit began to fail—a state of things which, let us suppose, occurred on some ocean island. Thereupon the men constructed a small boat from the bark of trees, and sped over the waters, in search of the needed stone, passing from island to island, with scanty nourishment, without lights in the night-time, and without a guide.

These marvelous accounts ought to be easily understood by children, and to awaken in them an admiration for their own kinship with humanity, and a profound sense of indebtedness to the mighty power of labour, which to-day is rendered so productive and so easy by our advanced civilisation, in which the environment, thanks to the works of man, has done so much to make our lives enjoyable.

But pedagogy, no less than the other branches of learning, has disdained to accept any contribution from anthropology; it has failed to see man as the mighty wrestler, at close grips with environment, man the toiler and transmuter, man the hero of creation. Of the history of human evolution, not a single ray sheds light upon the child and adolescent, the coming generation. The schools teach the history of wars—the history of disasters and crimes—which were painful necessities in the successive passages through civilisations created by the labour and slow perfectioning of humanity; but civilisation itself, which abides in the evolution of labour and of thought, remains hidden from our children in the darkness of silence.

Let us compare the appearance of man upon the earth to the discovery of the motive power of steam and to the subsequent appearance of railways as a factor in our social life. The railway has no limits of space, it overruns the world, unresting and unconscious, and by doing so promotes the brotherhood of men, of nations, of business interests. Let us suppose that we should choose to remain silent about the work performed by our railways and their social significance in the world to-day, and should teach our children only about the accidents, after the fashion of the newspapers, and keep their sensitive minds lingering in the presence of shattered and motionless heaps of carriages, amid the cries of anguish and the bleeding limbs of the victims.

The children would certainly ask themselves what possible connection there could be between such a disaster and the progress of civilisation. Well, this is precisely what we do when, from all the prehistoric and historic ages of humanity, we teach the children nothing but a series of wars, oppressions, tyrannies and betrayals; and, equipped with such knowledge, we push them out, in all their ignorance, into the century of the redemption of labour and the triumph of universal peace, telling them that "history is the teacher of life."

Modern Anthropology: *Cesare Lombroso and Criminal Anthropology. The Anthropological Principles of Moral Hygiene.*—The credit rests with Italy for having rescued Anthropology from a sort of scientific Olympus, and led it by new paths to the performance of an eminent and practical service.

It was about the year 1855 that Cesare Lombroso applied the

anthropological method first to the study of the insane, and then to that of criminals, having perceived a similarity or relationship between these two categories of abnormal individuals. The observation and measurement of clinical subjects, studied especially in regard to the *cranium* by anthropometric methods, led the young innovator to discover that the mental derangements of the insane were accompanied by morphological and physical abnormalities that bore witness to a profound and congenital alteration of the entire personality. Accordingly, for the purposes of *diagnosis*, Lombroso came to adopt a *somatic* basis. And his anthropological studies of criminals led him to analogous results.

The method employed was in all respects similar to the naturalistic method which anthropology had taken over from zoology; that is to say, the *description* of the individual subject considered chiefly in his somatic or corporeal personality, but also in his physiological and mental aspect; the study of his responsiveness to his environment, and of his habits (*manners and customs*); the grouping of subjects under *types* according to their dominant characteristic (*classification*); and finally, the study of their *origin*, which, in this case, meant a sociological investigation into the genesis of degenerate and abnormal types. Thus, since the principles of the Lombrosian doctrine spread with a precocious rapidity, it is a matter of common knowledge that criminals present anomalies of form, or rather morphological deviations associated with degeneration and known under the name of *stigmata* (now called *malformations*), which, when they occur together in one and the same subject, confer upon him a wellnigh characteristic aspect, notably different from that of the normal individual; in other words, they stamp him as belonging to an inferior type, which, according to Lombroso's earlier interpretation, is a reversion toward the lower orders of the human race (negroid and mongoloid types), as evidenced by anomalies of the vital organs, or internal animal-like characteristics (pithecoids); and that such stigmata were often accompanied by a predisposition to maladies tending to shorten life. Side by side with his somatic chart, Lombroso painstakingly prepared a physio-pathological chart of criminal subjects, based upon a study of their sensibility, their grasp of ideas, their social and ethical standards, their thieves' jargon and tattoo-marks, their handwriting and literary productions.

And, by deducing certain common characteristics from these

complex charts, he distinguished, in his classic work, *Delinquent Man*, a variety of types, such as the *morally insane*, the *epileptic delinquent*, the *delinquent from impulse or passion* (irresistible impulsion), the *insane delinquent*, and the *occasional delinquent*.

In this way, he succeeded in classifying a series of types—what we might call *sub-species*—diverging from the somatic and psycho-moral charts of normal men. But the common bio-pathological foundation of such types (with the exception of the last) was *degeneration*. We may well agree with Morselli that, in many parts of his treatise, Lombroso completed and amplified Morel, whose classic work, *A Study of the Degeneration of the Human Species*, was published in France at a time when Lombroso had hardly started upon his anthropological researches.

Both of these great teachers based their doctrine upon a naturalistic concept of man, and then proceeded to consider him, through all his anomalies and perversions, in relation to that extraneous factor, his environment. Morel, indeed, considers the *social* causes of degeneration, that is to say, of progressive organic impoverishment, as more important than the individual phenomena; they act *upon posterity* and tend to create a human *variety* deviating from the normal type. Such causes may be summed up as including whatever tends to the organic detriment of civilised man: such (in the first rank) as *alcoholism*, poisoning associated with professional industries (metallic poisons), or with lack of nutriment (pellagra), conditions endemic in certain localities (goitre), infective maladies (malaria, tuberculosis), denutrition (surménage). It may be said that whatever produces *prolonged suffering*, or whatever we class under the term *vices*, or even the neglect of our duties, chief among which is that of *working* (parasitism of the rich), or any of the causes which *exhaust*, or *paralyse*, or *perturb* our normal functions, are causes of degeneration, of impoverishment of the species.

Such is the doctrine which underlies the etiological concept of abnormal personality in psychiatry as well as in criminology, or points the way to its bio-social sources.

Accordingly, just as general Anthropology sought to investigate the origins of races or that of the human species in the very roots of life, so criminal Anthropology searches the origins of defective personality in its social surroundings.

The ethical problems which are raised by such a doctrine

cannot fail to be of interest to us. The Lombrosian theories, by raising these problems, have not only shaken the foundations of penal law, but have even brought about a moral renovation of conscience. We will leave to the jurists the great civic labor resulting from having brought the *individual* as well as the *crime* under consideration, in relation to the social phenomenon of delinquency—in other words, of having substituted an anthropological for a speculative attitude. Whether the delinquent should be cured, or simply isolated, or even subjected to punishment; whether the prison should be transformed into an asylum for the criminal insane; whether the penal laws should be reformed on principles of a higher order of civil morality: these are problems which interest us only secondarily.

What does interest us directly as educators is the necessity of *laying our course* in accordance with the standard of social morality which such a doctrine reveals and imposes upon us: since it is our duty to prepare the conscience of the rising generation. And, furthermore, to consider whether the organisation of our schools and of their methods is in conformity with such social progress.

If we cast a general glance at social ethics, from the primitive beginnings of human intercourse, we witness the *evolution of the vendetta*. There was, first, the individual vendetta. It was a form of primordial *justice*, with which were associated the sentiments of dignity, honour and solidarity; the injured party avenged himself by slaying; and the family of the slain retaliated by a new vendetta against the family of the slayer; and thus from generation to generation the tragic heritage continued to be handed down. Even now, in certain districts of civilised countries there exist survivals of these primitive forms of justice. In such cases, the slayer is held to be, not only *honourable* but *virtuous*. Analogously, in course of time, the individual vendetta, regulated by special formalities, developed into the *duel* for a point of *honour*.

At a more advanced period, in the course of the organisation of society, the task of vengeance was taken away from the individual, and the social administration of justice was established. Thereafter, the act of an offender was *punished* by the people collectively, and the victims of the act had no other recompense from society than that of a sense of satisfied hatred.

But throughout all civil progress, from the most primitive forms of society down to our own times, there persisted, as a fundamental principle, the concept of *vengeance*, coupled with the two great moral principles, individually and collectively, of human society: *honour* and *justice*. The naturalistic concept introduced by the Lombrosian doctrine, namely, *living man* entering as a concrete reality into the midst of abstract moral principles, shatters this association of ideas, and by so doing prepares the way for a new order of things—which is not a progess of evolution, but the beginning of an epoch. Vengeance disappears in the new conception of the defense of society and of an active campaign for the progress of humanity; and it ushers in an epoch of redemption and of solidarity, in which all limitations of human brotherhood are swept away.

The theories of Morel and Lombroso have resulted in calling the attention of civilised man to all the types of the *physiologically inferior;* the mentally deficient, epileptics, delinquents; shedding light upon their pathological personality, and transforming into interest and pity the contempt and neglect that were formerly the portion of such creatures. In this way science has accomplished in their behalf a work analogous to that of certain saints on behalf of lepers and sufferers from cancer in the middle ages. At that epoch, and even down to the beginning of modern times, the sick were abandoned to themselves and languished, covered with sores, in the midst of the horrors of infection; lepers were universally shunned, and their bodies decomposed without succor. It was only when these miserable beings began to awaken pity, in the place of loathing and repulsion, and to attract the charity of saints, instead of spreading panic among egoists and cowards, that the *care* of the sick began upon a vast scale, with the foundation of hospitals, the progress of medicine, and later of hygiene.

To-day those purulent plague-spots of the middle ages no longer exist; and infection is being combated with progressive success, in the triumph of physical health.

Yet, we are standing to-day on the selfsame level as the middle ages, in respect to moral plague-spots and infections; the phenomenon of *criminality* spreads without check or succor, and up to yesterday it aroused in us nothing but repulsion and loathing. But now that science has laid its finger upon this moral fester, it demands the cooperation of all mankind to combat it.

Accordingly we find ourselves in the epoch of *hospitals* for the morally diseased, the century of their treatment and cure; we have initiated a social movement toward the triumph of *morality*. We educators must not forget that we have inaugurated the *epoch* of *spiritual health;* because I believe that it is we who are destined to be the true *physicians* and *nurses* of this new *cure*. From the middle ages until now, the science of medicine has slowly been evolving for us the principles required to guarantee our bodily health; but we know very well that while cleanliness and hygiene are *signs* of civilisation, it is its moral standard that establishes its level.

This moral solidarity is something which it is our duty to understand thoroughly, if we wish to undertake the noble task of educators in the Twentieth Century, which was prepared in advance by the intensive intellectual activity of the century of science.

Granting the social phenomenon of *crime,* we ought to ask ourselves: where does the fault lie? If we are to acquit the individual criminal of responsibility, it falls back necessarily upon the social community through which the *causes of degeneration* and disease have filtered. Accordingly, it is we, every one of us, who are at fault: or rather, we are beginning to awaken to a consciousness that it is a *sin* to *foster* or to *tolerate* such social conditions as make possible the suffering, the vices, the errors that lead to physiological pauperism, to pathology, to the degeneration of posterity. The idea is not a new one: all great truths were perceived in every age by the elect few; the fundamental principles of the doctrine of Lombroso are to be already found in Greek philosophy and in that of Christ; Aristotle, in his belief that there is some one particular organism corresponding to each separate manifestation of nature, foreshadows the concept of the correspondence between the morphological and psychic personality; and St. John Chrisostom expounds the principle of moral solidarity in the collective responsibility of society, when he says: "you will render account, not only of your own salvation, but of that of all mankind; whoever prays ought to feel himself burdened with the interests of the entire human race."

Now, if it is not yet in our power to achieve a social reform based on the eradication of degenerative causes—since society can be perfected only gradually—it is nevertheless within our power to *prepare the conscience* for acceptance of the new morality, and by *educational* means to help along the civil progress which science has revealed to us. The honest man, the worthy man, the man of honour, is not he who avenges himself; but he who works for something outside himself, for the sake of society at large, in order to purify it of its evils and its sins, and advance it on its path of future progress. In this way, even though we fail to prepare the material environment, we shall have prepared *efficient men.*

In addition to this momentous principle of social ethics, the Lombrosian doctrines confront us squarely with the philosophic question of liberty of action, the controverted question of Stuart Mill, namely that of "free will." The libertarians admit the freedom of the will as one of the noblest of human prerogatives, on which the responsibility for our acts depends; the determinists recognise that the act of volition obeys certain predetermined *causes.* Now the Lombrosian theories find these *causes,* not after the fashion of the Pythagoreans, in cosmic laws or astrology, but in the *constitution of the organism,* thus serving as a powerful illustration of that *physiological determinism,* under whose guidance modern positive philosophy draws its inspiration.*

In the case of criminality, the actions of the degenerate delinquent are dependent upon a multiplicity of internal factors, that are almost necessarily governed by special predispositions. But, also in accordance with the Lombrosian doctrine, there are external factors which concur in determining acts of volition, factors relating to the environment, studied in accordance with rather vast conceptions: the actions of the individual are determined in advance by that social intercourse in which the great phenomena of any given civilisation have their necessary origin—phenomena such as crime, prostitution, the grade of culture accessible to the majority, the character of industrial products, the limits of general mortality. Now, just as there are necessary fluctuations in the tables of mortality, so also there are fluctuations in the quantity and quality of those individual phenomena that are looked upon as crimes: and in the one case no less than in the other, those who are predisposed are the ones in whom occurs the necessary outbreak of phenomena having their origin in society.

This constitutes in criminology, as well as in psychiatry, the resultant of all etiological concepts, pertaining to the interpretation of individual phenomena. It is precisely the same concept as that so exhaustively demonstrated by Quételet, with the aid of European statistics, in his *Social Physics,* and it has come to represent in

* From a work by E. MORSELLI: *Cesare Lombroso and Scientific Philosophy.*

modern science that fundamental concept which was to be found in all the great religions, of the dependence of the individual upon a governing force that is superior to him. This interpretation of individual phenomena cannot be ignored in the great problems of education; because the more literally we interpret the doctrine here set forth, just so much the less trust must be placed in the efficacy of education as a modifying influence upon personality, while it will acquire new importance as a co-worker in the interpretation of social epochs and individual activities, over which it should exercise a watchful guidance.

But meanwhile it is of interest to us to note how the anthropological movement, introduced with great simplicity of method, without any scientific or philosophical preconceptions, has led the investigations of psychiatry into vast and unsuspected fields of social ethics, bringing into practice fundamental reforms, analogous to those relating to penal law.

Achille De Giovanni and Physiological Anthropology; Anthropological Principles of Physical Hygiene.—Another practical development of anthropology is that instituted by Professor De Giovanni, who has introduced into his medical clinic at Padua the anthropological method in the clinical examination of patients. He applies the well-known naturalistic procedure, namely, the discription of individuals, their classification into types, according to common fundamental characteristics, and the etiological study of their personality. But while Lombroso took note of malformations solely in relation to other symptoms of degeneration, De Giovanni has established a strictly physiological basis for his investigations. Accordingly, he considers the human individual in his entirety, as a *functionating organism,* and he regards all inharmonious bodily proportions as signifying a necessary predisposition to certain determined forms of illness. With this end in view, he does not concern himself about single malformations, such for example as prognathism, the frontal angle, etc., but rather with the general relations of development between the bust which contains the organs essential to vegetative life, and the limbs; and from the external morphology of the bust, determined by measurements, he seeks to establish the reciprocal relations in development within the visceral cavities: "the proportions of the human body depend upon the development of its organs; and equally with its proportions, the whole physiological strength of the body depends upon its organs taken collectively." Whoever has a defective chest capacity not only possesses a smaller allowance of organs fitted for respiration and circulation of the blood, but as a result of such anomaly of development he is also predisposed to attacks of special maladies, such for example as chronic catarrh of the bronchial tubes or pulmonary tuberculosis. Whoever, on the contrary, is over-developed in abdominal dimensions, will be subject to disturbances of the digestive system and of the liver. In his classic work, *Morphology of the Human Body*, De Giovanni proceeds to elaborate a doctrine of temperaments, and of their several predispositions to disease, the tendency of which is to transfer the basis of medicine from a study of diseases to that of the individual patients, and to revive in modern days the ancient concepts of the Greek school of medicine, which from the time of Hippocrates and Galen drew up admirable charts of the fundamental physical types. In place of the ancient classification of temperaments into *nervous, sanguine, bilious* and *lymphatic,* we have to-day as substitutes, according to the school of De Giovanni, morphological types that are very nearly equivalent, and in which the predominant disorders are respectively diseases of the heart, the nervous system, the liver and the lungs.

In short, the result of this theory has been to establish an internal factor of predisposition to disease, analogous to that established by Lombroso as a predisposition to the phenomena of crime. And even here the mesogenic factors, that is, the influence of environment, must be taken into consideration: but environment acts equally upon all individuals: nearly everyone encounters, in his surroundings, that nerve-strain which leads to cardiac disorders and to neurasthenia; almost everyone encounters the bacilli of tuberculosis; the causes of general mortality are dictated by the very conditions of civilisation. But among the vast majority who pass unharmed along the insidious paths of adaptation, only a few fall victims to the particular disease to which some special anomaly of their organism predisposes them. In this way we can understand how it happens that certain ones have reason to dread a cold that will develop into bronchitis, and others on the contrary must guard themselves from errors in diet which will lead to intestinal disorders.

The part of De Giovanni's theory which is of special interest is that which leads to a consideration of the *ontogenetic development in relation* to the anomalies of the physio-morphological personality: "At every epoch of life this principle is applicable: Namely, that the reason for a special predisposition to disease is to be found in a special organic morphology. The individual is in a ceaseless state of transformation, and consequently at different periods of his life he may show a susceptibility to different diseases." A person who is predisposed to suffer continually from some complaint during his adult years, was usually unwell during the greater part of his childhood, although from some other disease; and with this as a basis, a scientific system of observation could speak prophetically regarding the physio-pathological destiny of a child. It is known, for example, that children subject to scrofula are predisposed to arrive at maturity with an undeveloped chest and a tendency to pulmonary tuberculosis.

From our point of view as educators, the doctrine of temperaments, and of their respective predispositions to disease, offers a deep interest, the nature of which is made evident by the author of the theory himself: for he points out that the period of childhood is the one best fitted in which to combat the abnormal predispositions of the organism, wisely guiding its development, to the final end of achieving an ideal of health, which depends upon the harmony of form and consequently of functions, in other words, upon the full attainment of physical beauty.

Here also, as in the Lombrosian doctrines, etiology fulfils the lofty task of throwing light upon the causal links between the bio-sociologic causes and the congenital anomalies of the physiological personality. The hereditary tendencies to disease, the errors of sexual hygiene, especially those regarding maternity, reveal to us the principal causes of that accumulation of imperfections that oppress and deform the average normal human being. It is because of such errors and such ignorance that hardly any of us attain that harmonic beauty that would render us immune to the treacheries of environment, and enable us to achieve, in the triumphant security of good health, our normal biological development.

It is not too much to say, that it is etiology which, applied to the Lombrosian doctrines, reveals the *faults of society*, the *sins of the world*, and, applied to the theories of De Giovanni, reveals its *errors;* and that from the two together there results a sort of ethical guide leading toward the supreme ideal of the *purification of the world* and the *perfectionment of the human species.* These are ideals which were in part cherished by the Greeks, who made their system of education the basis of their physical development. Such physiological doctrines are precisely what we also need to round out our plan for a *moral education.*

Giuseppe Sergi and Pedagogic Anthropology: Anthropological Bases of Human Hygiene.—It is also an Italian to whom we owe that practical extension of anthropology that leads us straight into the field of pedagogy. It was my former teacher, Giuseppe Sergi, who, as early as 1886, defended with the ardor of a prophet the new scientific principle of studying the pupils in our schools by methods prescribed by anthropology. Like the scientists who preceded him, he was thus led to substitute (in the field of pedagogy) the human individual taken from actual life, in place of general principles or abstract philosophical ideas.

As a matter of fact, while the doctrines of Lombroso and De Giovanni are profoundly reformatory, they nevertheless offer us nothing more substantial than certain new ideals of morality and social improvement. But the really practical field in which these ideals might in a large measure be realised is the *school.*

What progress would result for humanity if, on the basis of these new ethical principles, we contented ourselves with transforming our prisons into insane asylums? Such scanty fruit might well be compared to the mercy of that mediæval lordling who, out of consideration for a gentleman, commuted his sentence from hanging to decapitation. And scanty fruit would also be reaped by the science of medicine if, in its new anthropological development, it should content itself merely with diagnosing the personality of the patient, in addition to the disease; that is to say, for example, if, instead of telling a patient that his attack of bronchitis would be cured within twenty days, it should go on to predict, on the basis of the morphology of his body, that he would infallibly fall ill every year, until such time as pulmonary tuberculosis should put a fatal ending to his days.

On the contrary, behind the light of ideality that shimmers through and across these doctrines, we perceive our plain duty to trace out a path that will lead to a regeneration of humanity. If some practical line of action is to result, it will undoubtedly have to be exerted upon *humanity in the course of development,* in other words, at that period of life when the organism, being still in the course of formation, may be effectively directed and consequently corrected in its mode of growth.

Accordingly, the possible solution of the most momentous social problems, such as those of criminality, predisposition to disease, and degeneration, may be hoped for only within the limits of that space which society sets aside for guiding the new generations in their development.

In the school, we have hitherto retained, almost as a principle of justice, a leveling uniformity among the pupils: an abstract equality which seeks to guide all these separate childish individualities toward a single type which cannot be called an idealised type, because it does not represent a standard of perfection, but is on the contrary a non-existent philosophical abstraction: the *Child.* Educators are prepared for their practical services to childhood, by studies based upon this abstract infantile personality; and they enter upon their active work in school with the preconception that they must discover in every pupil a more or less faithful incarnation of the said type; and thus, year after year, they delude themselves with the idea that they have understood and educated *the child.* Now, this supposed uniformity cannot exist in the children of a human race so varied that it can produce, at the selfsame time, a Musolino* and a Luccheni,* a Guglielmo Marconi and a Giosue Carducci. All the different social types of men who labor with their hands and with their brains, the transformers of their environment, the producers of wealth, the directors of governments, equally with the undistinguished crowd of parasites, the enemies of society, all lived together in childhood, sitting side by side, upon the same school benches.

It was in 1898 that the first Italian Pedagogical Congress was held in Turin, and was attended by about three thousand educators. Under the spur of a new passion, that made me foresee the future mission and transformation of a chosen social class, setting forth upon a glorious task of redemption—the class of educators—I attended the Congress. I was at that time an interloper, because the subsequent felicitous union between medicine and pedagogy still remained a thing undreamed of, in the thoughts of that period. We had reached the third day of our sessions, and were all awaiting with interest an address by Professor Ildebrando Bencivenni, who was announced to speak upon the theme of "The School that

*Musolino was a brigand, and Luccheni an anarchist and regicide.

Educates." The discussion of this subject was expected to constitute the substantial work of the Congress, which seemed to have been called together chiefly in order to solve the problem of the greatest pedagogic importance: *how to give a moral education.* It was that very morning, just as the session was opening, that the frightful news burst upon us like a thunderbolt, that the Empress, Elizabeth of Austria, had been assassinated, and that once again an Italian had struck the blow! The third regicide in Europe within a brief time, that was due to an Italian hand!

The entire public press was unanimously stirred to indignation against the educators of the people; and as a demonstration of hostility, they all absented themselves that day from participating in the Congress.

There was something approaching a tumult in the ranks of teachers; inasmuch as they felt themselves innocent, they protested against the calumny of the newspapers in thus unjustly holding them responsible.

Amid the intense silence of the assembly, Bencivenni delivered a splendid discourse regarding the reform of educative methods in the school. Next in order, I took the platform and, speaking as a physician, I said: It will be all in vain for you to reform the methods of moral education in our schools, if you do not bear in mind that certain individuals exist, who are the very ones capable of committing such unspeakable deeds, and who pass through school without ever once being influenced in any manner by education. There exist various categories of abnormal children, who will fruitlessly go through the same grade over and over again, disturbing the routine and discipline of the class: and in spite of punishments and reprimands, they will end by being expelled without having learned anything at all, without having been modified in any manner. What becomes of these individuals who, even in childhood, reveal themselves as the future rebels and enemies of society? Yet we leave such a dangerous class in the most complete abandonment. Now, it is useless to reform the school and its methods, if the reformed school and the reformed methods are still going to fail to reach the very children who, for the protection of society, are most in need of being reached! Any method whatever suffices to fit a sane and normal child for a useful and moral life. The reform that is demanded in school and in pedagogy is one that will lead to the protection of *all* children during their years of development, including those who have shown themselves refractory to the environment of social life.

Thus I laid the first stone toward the education of mentally deficient children and the foundation of special schools for them. The work which followed forms, I think, the first historic page of a great regeneration in the whole class of teachers and of a profound reform in the school; a question so momentous that it spread rapidly throughout all Italy and was followed by the establishment of institutes and classes designed expressly for the deficient; and, most important of all, by the universal conviction which it carried, it also constituted the first page of pedagogy reformed upon an anthropological basis.

This is precisely the new development of pedagogy that goes under the name of *scientific:* in order to educate, it is essential to know those who are to be educated. "Taking measurements of the head, the stature, etc." (in other words, applying the anthropological method), "is, to be sure, not in itself the practice of pedagogy," says Sergi, in speaking of what the biological sciences have contributed to this branch of learning during the nineteenth century, "But it does mean that we are following the path that leads to pedagogy, because we cannot educate anyone until we know him thoroughly."

Here again, in the field of pedagogy, the naturalistic method must lead us to the study of the separate subjects, to a description of them as individuals, and their classification on a basis of characteristics in common; and since the child must be studied not by himself alone, but also in relation to the factors of his origin and his individual evolution—since every one of us represents the effect of multifold causes—it follows that the etiological side of the pedagogical branch of modern anthropology, like all its other branches, necessarily invades the field of biology and at the same time of sociology.

Among the types which it will be of pedagogic interest to trace in school-children, we must undoubtedly find those that correspond to the childhood of those abnormal individuals already studied in Lombroso's *Criminal Anthropology*, and in De Giovanni's *Clinical Morphology*.

Nevertheless, it is a new study, because the characteristics of the child are not those of the adult reduced to a diminutive scale, but they constitute *childhood* characteristics. Man changes as he grows; the body itself not only undergoes an increase in volume, but a profound evolution in the harmony of its parts and the composition of its tissues; in the same way, the psychic personality of the man does not grow, but evolves; like the predisposition to disease which varies at different ages in each individual considered pathologically. For all those anomalous types which to-day are included under the popular term of *deficients*, for the pathological weaklings who reveal symptoms of scrofula or rickets, there is no doubt that special schools and methods of education are essential. We teachers would like, through educative means, to counteract the ultimate consequences of degeneration and predisposition to disease: if criminal anthropology has been able to *revolutionise the penalty* in modern civilisation, it is our duty to undertake, in the school of the future, to *revolutionise the individual.* And by achieving this ideal, pedagogic anthropology will to a large extent have taken the place of criminal anthropology, just as schools for the abnormal and feeble, multiplied and perfected under the protection of an advanced civilisation, will in a large measure have replaced the prisons and the hospitals.

We owe to the intuitive genius of Giuseppe Sergi the conception of a form of pedagogic anthropology far more exact in its methods of investigation than anything which had hitherto been foreshadowed. This master takes the ground that a study of abnormal and weakly children is a task of absolutely secondary importance. What is imperative for us to know, he claims, is *normal humanity,* if we are to guide it intelligently toward that biological and moral perfection, on which the progress of humanity must depend. If general pedagogy is destined to be transformed under a naturalistic impulse, this will be effected only when anthropology turns its investigations to the normal human being.

Educators are still very far from having a *real knowledge* of that collective body of school-children, on whom a uniformity of method, of encouragement and punishment is blindly inflicted; if, instead of this, the child could be brought before the teacher's eyes as a *living individuality*, he would be forced to adopt very different standards of judgment, and would be shaken to the very depths of his conscience by the revelation of a responsibility hitherto unsuspected.

Let us take one or two examples; let us consider, among the pupils, one child who is very poor.

Studied by the anthropological method, he is revealed, in every personal physiological detail, as an inferior type. The child of poverty, as Niceforo has well shown, is an inferior in stature, in cranium, in weight, in muscular and intellectual strength; and the malformations, resulting from defects of growth, condemn him to an æsthetic inferiority; in other words, environment, mode of living, and nutrition may result in modifying even the relative *beauty* of the individual. The normal man may bear within him a germ of physical beauty inherited from parents who begot him normally, and yet this germ may not be able to develop, because impeded by environment. Accordingly, physical beauty constitutes in itself a class privilege. This child, weak in mind and in muscular force, when compared with the child of wealth, grown up in a favorable environment, shows less attractive manners, because he has been reared in an atmosphere of social inferiority, and in school is classed as a pariah. Less good looking and less refined, he fails to enlist the sympathy which the teacher so readily concedes to the courteous manners of more fortunate children; less intelligent himself, and unable to look for help from parents who, more than likely, are illiterate, he fails to obtain the encouragement of praise and high credit marks that are lavished upon stronger children, who have no need of being encouraged. Thus it happens that the down-trodden of society are also the down-trodden in the school. And we call this justice; and we say that demerit is punished and merit is rewarded; but in this way we make ourselves the sycophants of nature and of social error, and not the administrators of justice in education!

On the other hand, let us examine another child, living in an agreeable environment, in the higher social circles; he possesses all the physical attraction and grace that render childhood charming. He is intelligent, smiling, gentle-mannered; at the cost of small effort he gives his teacher ample satisfaction by his progress, and even if the teacher's method of instruction happens to be somewhat faulty, the child's family hasten privately to make up for the deficiency. This child is destined to reap a harvest of praise and rewards; the teacher, egotistically complacent over the abundant fruit gathered with so little effort, and the moral and æsthetic satisfaction derived from the fortunate pupil, gives him unmeasured affection and smooths his whole course through school. But if we study the rich, intelligent, prize-winning child carefully, we find that he, too, is not perfect in his anthropological development; he is too narrow-chested. This is the penalty of the rich and the studious; every privilege brings its own peril; every benefit contains a snare; every one of us to-day, without the light of science, runs the risk of diminishing our physiological equilibrium, by living in an environment that contains so many defects. The child of luxury, living continually indoors, diligently studying in his well-warmed home, under his mother's vigilant eye, is impeding the development of his own chest; and when he has completed his growth and his education, will find himself with insufficient lungs; his physical personality will have been permanently thrown out of equilibrium by a defective environment. This highly cultured man may some day find himself urged on to big endeavour; his intelligence will create vast ideals, but he will not have at his disposal the physical force that is so strictly associated with the power to draw from the surrounding air a sufficient quantity of oxygen by means of respiration. The spirit is ready, but the flesh is weary; and all his ambitious hopes may be shattered in the very flower of life by pulmonary tuberculosis, to which he has himself created an artificial predisposition.

It is our duty to understand the individual, in order to avoid these fatal errors; and to arise to higher standards of justice, founded upon the real exigencies of life—guided by that spirit of love which is essential to the teacher, in order to render him truly an educator of humanity.

Love is the essential spirit of fecundity whose one purpose is to beget life. And in the teacher, love of humanity must find expression through his work, because the very purpose of love is to create something. Accordingly, this spirit of fecundity ought to produce the teacher's *mission*, which to-day is the mission of reforming the school and accepting the proud duty of universal motherhood, destined to protect all mankind, the normal and abnormal alike. This is a reform, not only of the school, but of society as a whole, because through the redeeming and protective labours of pedagogy, the lowest human manifestations of degeneration and disease will disappear; and, more important still, it will make it henceforth impossible for normal human beings, conceived from germs that promise strength and beauty, little by little to lose that beauty and strength along the rough paths of life, through which no one has hitherto had the knowledge to guide them.

"In the social life of to-day an urgent need has arisen," says our common master, Giuseppi Sergi, "a renovation of our methods of education and instruction; and whoever enrolls himself under this standard, is fighting for the regeneration of man."

Enrico Morselli and Scientific Philosophy.—Among the names of Italian scientists that must be called to mind, in discussing the modern developments of anthropology, a special lustre attaches to that of Enrico Morselli, who has earned the right to call himself the critic, or rather, the philosopher of anthropology. Notwithstanding that he has made his name famous in the vast field of psychiatry, this distinguished Genoese practitioner has found time to assimilate the most diverse branches of science and the most widely separated avenues of thought, qualifying himself as a *critic*, and systematising experimental science on the lines of scientific philosophy.

His great work, *General Anthropology*, is developed on synthetic lines, embracing in a single scientific system all the acquired knowledge of the past two centuries, and may rightfully be called the first treatise on philosophic anthropology. While the experimental sciences, by collecting and recording separate phenomena, were gradually preparing, throughout the nineteenth century, a great mass of analytical material, chosen blindly and without form, they apparently engendered a new trend of thought positively hostile to philosophy: the *odium antiphilosophicum*, as Morselli calls it. And conversely, the speculative positivism of Ardigo remained throughout its development a stranger to the immediate sources of experimental research, and adhered strictly to the field of pure philosophy. It remained for Morselli to perceive that the scientific material prepared by experimental science was in reality philosophical material, for which it was only necessary to prepare instruments and means in order to systematise it and lead it into the proper channels for the construction of a scientific philosophy.

Throughout the whole period of his intellectual activity, Morselli sought to unite experimental science and philosophy, by taking his content from the former and his form from the latter. To gather and catalogue bare facts could not be the scope of science; such labour could result only in sterilising the mind. "The human mind," says Morselli, "does not stop at the objective study of a phenomenon and its laws; it wants also to fathom their nature; the *how* does not content it, but it must also have the *wherefore.*" It must mount from facts to synthesis, constantly achieving a new and fuller understanding. But what determines the content of philosophy is not speculative thought, but facts that have been collected *objectively.* Such is the view of Enrico Morselli, expressed in the introduction to his *Review of Scientific Philosophy:* "We think the moment has come for professional philosophers to allow themselves to be convinced that the progress of physical and biological sciences has profoundly changed the tendencies of philosophy; so that it is no longer an assemblage of speculative systems, but rather the synthesis of partial scientific doctrines, the expression of the highest general truths, derived *solely* and *immediately* from the study of facts. On the other hand, we hope also that in every student of the separate sciences, whether pure or applied, the intimate conviction will take root that no science which applies the method of observation and experiment to the particular class of phenomena which form its subject, can call itself fully developed so long as it is limited to the collection and classification of facts. Scientific dilettantism of this sort must end by sterilising the human mind, whose natural tendency is to advance from observed phenomena by successive stages to the investigation of their partial laws, and from these to the research of more and more general truths. But philosophy, thus understood, can never confine itself within the dogmatism of a system, but rather will leave the individual mind free to make constant new concessions, in the pursuit of the truth.

"The human mind is condemned to search forever, and perhaps never to find, the ultimate solution to the eternal problem which it offers to itself; accordingly, let it keep itself *at liberty* to accept to-day as probable, a solution which further researches or newly discovered facts will compel it to reject to-morrow in favor of another. We must admit that in philosophic concepts there is a constant evolution, or rather natural selection, thanks to which the strongest concepts, those best constituted, those that are fitted to make use of scientific discoveries with the broadest liberality, are predisposed to prove victorious or at least to hold their own for a long time in the struggle."*

It is this *liberty* that makes it possible for us to pursue experi-

* From a study by Prof. E. Troilo, *Enrico Morselli as a Philosopher.* In the volume by MORSELLI, MILAN: VALLARDI, 1906.

mental investigations, without fear that our brains may become sterile. And by liberty we mean the readiness to accept new concepts whenever experience proves to us that they are better and closer to the truth which we are seeking. Even though the absolute truth were never reached, the experimental method is the path most likely to lead us toward it step by step.

Accordingly, what we should demand of investigators is not a creed, a philosophic system, but *"the objective method in their researches and in the sources of their inductions."* For this is the way to train the workers and philosophers of experimental science.

And the same lines must serve us for building up a philosophy capable of shaping a regenerated method of pedagogy.

The Method

The determining factor in anthropology is the same that determines all experimental science: the *method.* A well-defined method in natural science applied to the study of living man offers us the scientific content, which we are in the course of seeking.

The content bursts upon us as a surprise, as the result of applying the method, by means of which we make advances in the investigation of truth.

Whenever a science prescribes for itself, not a content but a method of experimenting, it is for that reason called an *experimental* science.

It is not easy for those who come fresh from the pursuit of philosophic studies to adapt themselves to this order of ideas. The philosopher, the historian, the man of letters prepare themselves by assimilating the *content* of one particular branch of learning; and thereby they define the boundaries of their individual knowledge and close the circle of their individual thought, however vast that circle may be.

Indeed, the elaboration of human thought, the series of historic deeds, the accumulated mass of literature, may offer immense fields; but after the student has little by little assimilated them, he cannot do otherwise than contain them within him precisely as they are. Their extent is limited by the centuries that cover the history of civilised man, and it is invariable, since it exists as a work accomplished by man.

Experimental science is of an entirely different sort. We must look upon it as a *means* of investigation into the field of the infinite and the unknown. If we wish to compare it to some branch of learning that is universally familiar, we may say that an experimental science is similar to *learning to read.* When as children we learn to read, we may, to be sure, estimate the effort that it costs us to master a mechanical device; but such a mechanical device is a means, it is a magic key that will unlock the secrets of wisdom, multiply our power to share the thoughts of our contemporaries, and render us dexterous in despatching the practical affairs of life.

Thus considered, *reading* is a branch of learning that has no prescribed limits.

It is our duty to learn to read the *truth,* in the book of *nature;* I. by collecting separate facts, according to the objective method; II. by proceeding methodically from analysis to synthesis. The subject of our research is the individual human being.

1. *The Objective Collecting of Single Facts.*—In the gathering of data, our science makes use of two means of investigation, as we have already seen: observation or *anthroposcopy;* and measurement or *anthropometry.* In order to take measurements, we must know the special *anthropometric instruments* and how to use them; and in making observations, we must treat ourselves as instruments, that is, we must divest ourselves of our own personality, of every preconception, in order to become capable of recording the real facts *objectively.* For since our purpose is to gather our facts from nature and await her revelations, if we allowed ourselves to have scientific preconceptions, we might distort the truth. Here is the point which distinguishes experimental science from a speculative science; in the former, we must banish thought, in the latter we must build by means of thought. Accordingly *at the moment when we are collecting our data,* we must possess no other capacity than that of knowing how to collect them with extreme exactness and objectivity.

Accordingly we need a *method* and a mental preparation, that is, a *training* which will accustom us to divest ourselves of our own personalities, in order to become simple *instruments of investigation.* For instance, if it were a question of measuring the heads of illiterate children and of other children of the same age, who are attending school, in order to learn whether the heads of educated children show greater development, we need not only to know how to use the *millimetric scale* and the cranial calipers which are the instruments adapted to this purpose; we need not only to know the *anatomical points* at which the instruments must be applied in the manner established by the accepted method; but we need in addition to be *unaware*, while taking the measurements, whether the child before us at a given moment is educated or illiterate because the preconception might work upon us by suggestion and thus alter the result. Or again, to take what in a certain sense is an opposite case, and nevertheless analogous, we may undertake a research into some absolutely unknown question, as for instance, what are the psychic characteristics of children whose development has kept fairly close to the normal average, and of those whose anthropological measurements diverge notably from the average: in such a case we ought to measure all the children, make the required psychological tests separately, and then compare the results of the two investigations.

A woman student in my course, last year, undertook precisely this sort of investigation, namely, to find out what was the standing in school of children who represent the normal average anthropological type, that is to say, those whose physical development had been all that was to be desired: and she found that normal children are *vivacious* (happy), *very intelligent*, but *negligent;* and consequently their number never includes the *heads of the classes*, the *winners of prizes.*

In addition to gathering *anthropological data*, which requires a special *technique* of research, we need to know how to proceed to interpret them.

We are no longer at the outset of our observations. No sooner was the method established, than there were a multitude of students in all parts of the world capable of objective research, that is to say, of anthropological investigations. The sum total of all these researches forms a *scientific patrimony*, which needs to be known to us, in order that our own conclusions may serve to complete those of other investigators, who have preceded us, and thus form a contribution to science.

In other words, there have already been certain *principles* established and certain *laws* discovered, on an experimental basis; and all this forms a *true* and fitting content of our science. It will serve to *guide* us in our researches, and to furnish us with a *stand-*

ard of comparison for our own conclusions. Thus, for example, when we have measured the stature of a boy of ten, we have undoubtedly gathered an individual anthropological fact; but in order to interpret it, we must know what is the average stature of boys of ten; and the average will be found established by previous investigators, who have obtained it from actuality, by applying the well-known method of measuring the stature, to a great number of individuals of a specified race, sex, and age, and by obtaining an average on the basis of such research.

Accordingly, we ought to *profit from* the researches of others, whenever they have been received, as noteworthy, into the literature of science. Nevertheless, the patrimony which science places at our disposition must never be considered as anything more than a *guide*, an expression of universal collaboration, in accordance with a uniform method. We must never *jurare in verba magistri*, never accept any master as infallible: we are always at liberty to *repeat* any research already made, in order to verify it; and this form of investigation is part of the established method of experimental science. One fundamental principle must be clearly understood; that we can never become anthropologists merely by reading all the existing literature of anthropology, including the voluminous works on kindred studies and the innumerable periodicals; we shall become anthropologists only at the moment when, having mastered the method, we become investigators of *living human individuals.*

We must, in short, be *producers*, or nothing at all; assimilation is useless. For example, let us suppose that a certain teacher has studied anthropology in books: if, after that, he is incapable of making practical *observations* upon his own pupils, to what end does his theoretical knowledge serve him? It is evident that theoretic study can have no other purpose than to guide us in the interpretation of data gathered directly from nature.

Our only book should be the living individual; all the rest taken together form only the necessary means for reading it.

2. *The Passage from Analysis to Synthesis.*—Assuming that we have learned how to gather anthropological data with a rigorously exact technique, and that we possess a theoretic knowledge and tables of comparative data: all this together does not suffice to qualify us as interpreters of nature. The marvellous reading of this amazing book demands on our part still other forms of prepara-

tion. In gathering the separate data, it may be said that we have learned how to *spell,* but not yet how to read and interpret the sense. The reading must be accomplished with broad, sweeping glances, and must enable us to penetrate in thought into the very synthesis of life. And it is the simple truth that *life* manifests itself through the living individual, and in no other way. But through these means it reveals certain general properties, certain laws that will guide us in grouping the living individuals according to their common properties; it is necessary to know them, in order to interpret individual differences dependent upon race, age, and sex, and upon variations due to the effort of adaptation to environment, or to pathological or degenerative causes. That is to say, certain general principles exist, which serve to make us *interpreters of the meaning,* when we read in the book of life.

This is the *loftiest* part of our work, carrying us above and beyond the individual, and bringing us in contact with the very fountain-heads of life, almost as though it were granted us to materialise the unknowable. In this way we may rise from the arid and fatiguing gathering of analytical data, toward conceptions of noble grandeur, toward a *positive philosophy of life;* and unveil certain secrets of existence, that will teach us the moral norms of life.

Because, unquestionably, we are *immoral,* when we disobey the laws of life; for the triumphant rule of life throughout the universe is what constitutes our conception of beauty and goodness and truth—in short, of divinity.

The technical method of proceeding toward synthesis, we may find well defined in biology: the data gathered by measurement can be grouped according to the statistical method, be represented graphically and calculated by the application of mathematics to biology: to-day, indeed, *biometry* and *biostatistics* tend to assume so vast a development as to give promise of forming independent sciences.

The *method* in biology, considered as a whole, may be compared to the microscope and telescope, which are instruments, and yet enable us to rise above and beyond our own natural powers and come into contact with the two extremes of infinity; the infinitely little and the infinitely large.

Objections and Defences.—One of the objections made to pedagogical anthropology is that it has not yet a completely defined content, on which to base an organic system of instruction and reliable general rules.

It is the *method* alone that enables us to be eloquent in defence of pedagogic anthropology, against such an accusation. For the accusation itself is the embodiment of a conception of a method differing widely from our own: it is the accusation made by speculative science, which, resting on the basis of a content, refuses to acknowledge a science that is still lacking and incomplete in its content, because it is unable to conceive that a science may be essentially summed up in its method, which makes it a means of revelation.

How could we conceive of the *content* of pedagogic anthropology otherwise than as something to be derived by the experimental method from the observation of *school-children?* And where could we conceive of a possible laboratory for such a science, if not in the school itself? The *content* will be determined little by little, by the application of the anthropological study to school-children in the school, and never in any other manner.

Now, if it were necessary to await the completion of a content before proceeding to any practical application, where could we hope to get this content from—especially since we look for no help either from speculative philosophy or divine revelation?

When a *method* is applied to any positive science, it results in giving that science a new *direction,* that is to say, a new avenue of progress: And it is precisely in the course of advance along that avenue that the content of the science is formed: but if we never made the advance, the science would never take its start. Thus, for example, when the microscope revealed to medicine the existence of micro-organisms, and bacteriology arose as the positive study of epidemiology, it altered the whole procedure in the cure and prophylaxis of infective maladies. Prior to this epoch people believed that an epidemic was a scourge sent by divine wrath upon sinners; or else they imagined it was a miasma transported by the wind, which groves and eucalyptus trees might check; or they pictured the ground ejecting miasmatic poisons through its pores:—and humanity sought in vain to protect itself with bare-foot processions and religious ceremonies, attended by jostling throngs and cruel flagellation; or else they betook themselves to the shade of eucalyptus trees, in the midst of malarial lowlands. Entire cities were destroyed by pestilence, and malarial districts remained uncultured deserts, because entire populations, in the brave effort to perform their work, were destroyed by successive impoverishment of the blood.

It is bacteriology that has put to flight this darkness of ignorance that was the herald of death, and has created the modern conditions of environment, which, by a multitude of means, defend the individual and the nation from infective diseases; so that to-day civilised society may be said to be advancing toward a triumph over death.

But the microbes have not all of them been discovered; bacteriology and general pathology are still very far from having completed their *content.* If we had been obliged to wait for such completion, we should still be living quite literally in the midst of mediæval epidemics; or, to state the case better, where in the world would the science of medicine ever have attained its new content? For it has been building it up, little by little, *by directing medicine upon a new path.* It was the introduction of this new method of investigating the patient and his environment that experimentally reaped the fruit of new etiological discoveries, and new means of defence: the microscope became perfected because it came into universal use in practice; bacterial cultures owe their perfectionment to the fact that they became the common means of investigation for the purpose of diagnosis; just as tests in clinical chemistry have become perfected through practical use. Without which, who would ever have perfected the microscope, or the science of bacteriology? In a word, whence are we to get the content of any positive science, if not from practical application?

A direction and an applied method represent a triumph of progress; and in progress, a *content* cannot have defined limits. We do not know its goal; we know only that at the moment when it finds its goal, it will cease to be *progress.*

It is many years since medicine abandoned the speculative course, and we see it to-day hourly enriching itself with new truths; its triumphal march is never checked, and it moves onward toward the invasion of future centuries. In the wake of its progress, that frightful phenomenon which we call *mortality* tends to fall steadily to a lower level; giving rise to the hope that through future progress it will cease to be the mysterious, menacing fate, ever watchful and ready to sever the invisible threads of human life. These threads are to-day revealing themselves as the resistant fibres of a fabric; because, humanity by engaging collectively in the audacious search after truth, and by thus protecting the interests of each individual through the common interests, has succeeded in offering a powerful resistance to the mysterious sheers.

Accordingly, we may say that the substitution to-day of an anthropological development of pedagogy, in the place of a purely philosophical and speculative trend, does not offer it merely an *additional content*, an auxiliary to all the other forms of teaching on which it now comfortably reposes; but it opens up new avenues, fruitful in truth and in life; and as it advances along these avenues, regenerated from its very foundations upward, it may be that pedagogy is destined to solve the great problem of human redemption.

The Method to be Followed in These Lectures

Lastly, just one more word regarding the didactic method that I intend to follow, in delivering this course of lectures. From the purpose already stated, it follows that this Course in Anthropology must be eminently practical. Of the three weekly lectures, only one will be theoretical; that is to say, only one in which I shall expound the *content* of our science; a second lecture will treat of the *technique of the method;* that is to say, I shall devote it to describing the practical way of gathering anthropological data, and how we must study them and re-group them in order to extract their laws; and finally, the third lecture will be *practical and clinical;* I shall devote it to the collection of anthropological data from human subjects, and little by little I shall try to work toward the individual study of pupils, until we reach the compilation of biographic charts. At the lectures of the third type, we shall have present subjects who will be, for the most part, normal, but some of them will be abnormal, and all will be drawn from the elementary schools of Rome.

Finally, in further illustration of our course, we shall make excursions, visiting certain schools that offer some particular interest from our scientific point of view; to the end that we may supply what is lacking and what is needed to complete a University Course in Scientific Pedagogy, namely a "Pedagogical Clinic," where pupils of the widest variety of types might be educated, and where it might be possible to lay practical foundations of a far-reaching reform in our schools.

Accordingly, I shall repeat myself three times, in these lectures; first, by setting forth the scientific content, secondly, by expounding the methods of investigation, and thirdly, by applying in practice what I have already taught in theory. The didactic method of repeating the same instruction under different forms, is also a feature of scientific pedagogy, because it represents the method by which positive science must be taught and acquired; and furthermore, it is the method that deserves to be applied wherever instruction of any sort is to be given.

Hitherto, we have not learned how to study; we know only, or at least the majority of us do, how to absorb the contents of books. The only true student is the scientist, who knows how to *advance slowly;* we educators on the contrary plunge in a dizzy, headlong rush, through all acquirable knowledge. To study is to look steadily, to stand still, to assimilate and to wait. We should study for the sake of creating, since the whole object of taking is to be able to give again; but in this giving and taking we ought not to be mere instruments, like high-pressure suction pumps; in work of this sort we ought to be *creators*, and when we give back, to add that part which has been *born and developed* within us from what we acquired. It is wise to give our acquired knowledge time not only to be assimilated but also to develop freely in that fertile psychic ground that constitutes our innermost personality. In other words: assimilate by every possible means, and then *wait.*

In order to start from a point of established knowledge, let us consider what is meant by *meditation:* to meditate means to isolate one's thoughts within the limits of some definite subject, and wait to see what that subject of its own accord may reveal to us, in the course of assimilation. The Jesuits succeeded in winning souls merely by encouraging the people to meditate; meditation opened up an unsuspected inner world, which fascinated the type of person accustomed to flit lightly in thought across a multitude of diverse matters; and under the spell of such fascination, their consciences could attribute to nothing less than some occult power, what was really the application of a great pedagogic principle.

There is a great difference between reading and meditating: we may read a voluminous novel in a single night; we may meditate upon a verse of Scripture for an entire hour. Anyone who reads a novel in a night undoubtedly squanders his physical powers, like a wind that passes over arid ground; but one who meditates assimilates in a special manner that surprises the meditator himself, because he feels something unforeseen coming to life within him, just as though a seed had been planted in fertile soil and, while remaining motionless, had begun to germinate. Accordingly, the act of holding acquired knowledge within ourselves for a period of time results in self-development; superficial learning, on the contrary, means the exhaustion of our personal resources. We become steadily more exhausted and more inefficient, through too much study; and instead, we ought to become all the time more flourishing and more robust, if we studied in the proper way: and this is because we squander our psychic powers, instead of acquiring new energy. The consequence of this mistaken method is that we rapidly forget all that we have learned. Everything is acquired at the cost of effort; what we need is to labor patiently, in order to acquire in the real sense. To-day it is the fashion to study in order to enter upon that particular business or profession that is destined to be our life's work; what we ought to do instead, is to devote our energies to the conquest of thought and the elevation of the spirit.

The didactic method that I am trying to illustrate is not a new one; it dates back to the first precursors of scientific pedagogy. Half a century ago, a marvellous work on pedagogy, based on similar principles, was issued from the press; it was the method elaborated by Séguin, based on thirty years of practical experience in the education of idiotic children. Such a system cannot be foreign to the interests of schools intended for average, normal children, because it is not a specialised method, like that for deaf-mutes or for the blind. Being designed for the mentally deficient, this method applies to any class of undeveloped beings who are striving to grow bigger; we may even apply it to ourselves, and thereby increase our own mental stature. In short, pedagogically considered, it is a rational method.

Perhaps it is already familiar to a good many of you; but an example or two will serve to illustrate it. Let us suppose that we have to impart a lesson in history to a deficient pupil: first of all, a picture is shown him, representing an historic fact; then the same fact will be shown him in as many different ways as possible—through the cinematograph, for example. Finally it will be acted on the stage; and in this case, it is the children themselves who prepare the setting and endeavor, to the best of their ability, to impersonate the historic figures. Now, it is precisely at the moment when they are reproducing the scene that these children *feel it,* and it is only then that they *learn.* But this is not peculiar to deficient children: the same path is the common path for all; it is necessary for all of us to assimilate mentally and to feel, before we can say: I have learned. If there is a latent tendency in the mind of a normal child to love historic happenings, then he will love them, and thus reveal to his teacher one of his intimate and secret tendencies; in other words, we shall have developed a taste, of which the hidden germs already existed. Perhaps it was in some such way that Sabatier succeeded in realising the environment and the life of St. Francis of Assisi.

Let us suppose, again, that we have to teach a child what is meant, in geography, by a mountain, a lake, or an island. According to Séguin's method, we should take the child out into the garden, and make him construct a miniature mountain with earth, a lake with water, etc., than make him trace their geographical outline with chalk, then make him paint them in oils or water-colours, so that in the end he will have, as the result of his handiwork, a little monument, so to speak, of the acquired lesson. It is only after a child has worked that he begins to learn and to be interested. Does not everyone know that, as between the one who receives, and the one who confers a favor, it is the latter who cares the more, because he has done something? The next step is to take the pupil to the top of some hill, so that he may see with his own eyes the things that we have taught him in the garden and through the medium of work; and in the silent contemplation of nature, it may happen that a normal child will hear the call of her mysterious voice, and reveal a dormant tendency to become some day, perhaps, a geographer, or an explorer, like the Duke of the Abruzzi; or perhaps he will feel that lure of nature which, some day or other, when he reaches maturity, will lead him to investigate the secrets of the earth and of meteorological phenomena, even to the point of such heroic sacrifice as was exemplified by Professor Matteucci, during the eruption of Vesuvius.

Repeating the same things over and over, keeping the mind fixed upon the selfsame lesson, teaching how to reproduce objects by the work of the hands, bringing the pupil into direct contact with the object that he is desired to study, such is the true way to enable him to learn. The man who has been educated according to this method has not fruitlessly expended his energy in fatiguing study; he has preserved his forces unimpaired; indeed, if anything, they are all the sounder and more flourishing. By such a system of education, we launch upon the world a sturdy generation, imbued with that living energy, that constitutes the one and only mainspring that really makes the world move.

Accordingly this is the method that we shall follow: studying, repeating, working experimentally: the subject of our study is humanity; our pupose is to become teachers. Now, what really makes a teacher is love for the human child; for it is love that transforms the social duty of the educator into the higher consciousness of a *mission*.

The Limits of Pedagogical Anthropology

In concluding this preamble, it may be well to define the form of study and the purposes of pedagogical anthropology; in order to distinguish it clearly from general anthropology and from the allied branches of applied anthropology (criminal and medical anthropology).

Pedagogical anthropology, like all the other branches of anthropology, studies man from the naturalistic point of view; but, unlike general anthropology, it does not concern itself with the philosophic problems related to it, such, for instance, as the origin of man, the theories of monism or polygenism, of emigration, and classification according to race; problems which, as everyone knows, are difficult of solution, and which constitute the pivot on which biological anthropology revolves. Thus, for example, bacteriology has its origin in biology, in so far as it has certain orders of living organisms for the subject of its research; but it well nigh ignores the problems of biological philosophy associated with them, such as the origin of living matter and of the primitive cell; the fixity or variability of monocellular species; the possibility of life in the isolated nucleus (the microbe), or in the isolated protoplasm (the monera), but it devotes itself to the direct study of microscopic organisms, both in themselves alone and in their influence upon their environment; in short, bacteriology has for its purpose the acquirement of that practical knowledge necessary for a successful campaign against the causes of infective maladies, and for rendering infected districts sanitary. In much the same way, pedagogical anthropology, considered as a form of study, departs from general anthropology. It studies man from two different points of view: his *development* (ontogenesis), and his *variations.*

Since many causes concur in producing variations in the individual during his development (social causes, pathological causes, etc.), we have to take into consideration, and frequently invoke the aid of subsidiary sciences (sociology, pathology, hygiene). *Variations* constitute the most important subject of inquiry in pedagogic anthropology, just as *fixed characteristics* constitute the essential matter of research in general anthropology: because the latter endeavours, by the help of fixed characteristics, to trace back to the origin of species, while the former tries, through the help of variable characteristics, to discover a way for the future perfectionment of the human species and the individual: indeed, this is precisely what constitutes the practical purpose of its application to pedagogy.

In comparison with criminal and medical anthropology, pedagogic anthropology differs substantially in its declared intentions. These other two kindred branches endeavour to *diagnose* the personality of the individual; we must admit that both psychiatry and general medical practice profit by the application of anthropology to the extent of securing greater accuracy in diagnosis and prognosis; but whenever the study of a patient's *personality* sheds light upon decisions of this sort, it generally follows that the personality is fixed and unalterable. For instance, when, in medical practice an individual *constitution* is shown to be fatally predisposed to certain definite diseases, that is precisely one of the cases where medical *treatment* is most impotent; and the same may be said when, in the practice of criminal law we find a defendant whose personality is profoundly degenerate. It follows that the application of these new anthropological methods is substantially diagnostic; furthermore, they are limited to special classes of human beings, to those who are physiologically the most impoverished, such as criminals and the diseased. Pedagogic anthropology, on the contrary, embraces *all humanity;* but it pays special attention to that part of it which is psychologically superior: the normal human being. Its purpose is none the less diagnostic; but it regards diagnosis as constituting a *means*, and not merely indicating an end; because the end projected by pedagogic anthropology is a far-reaching and rational system of *hygiene*.

More than that, the proposed system is the one true one, a hygiene that pays more attention to the man himself than to his environment; striving to perfect him in his physiological functions, or to correct any tendency to abnormal and pathological deviations.

It follows that, in pedagogic anthropology, the direction taken by the naturalistic study of man is predominantly *physiological*.

In the same manner as the other two kindred branches of anthropology, this branch which has joined forces with pedagogy has severed connection with the original parent stock of general anthropology, and abandoned its dogmatisms and to a large extent its phraseology.

Criminal anthropology, for example, shows great daring and scant accuracy in its affirmations and its researches; and to a large extent it has acquired a nomenclature of its own; and medical anthropology lays down laws that general anthropology never took into consideration, and neglects to bestow particular attention upon the *head*, which formed the object of fundamental research in general anthropology.

In the same way, pedagogic anthropology has had to emancipate itself from the general science from which it has sprung, in order to proceed unhampered along the practical line of research, which consists essentially in a study of the pupil and the compilation of biographic charts, from which a fund of material will result, destined to enrich the scientific content of this branch of learning.

But since the study of the pupil must not be morphological alone, but psychological as well, it is necessary for anthropology to invoke the aid of experimental psychology, in order to achieve its purpose. Now it is essential to psychology, no less than to pedagogic anthropology, to study the reactions of the physiological and psychical personality of the child in the environment which we call *school*. Consequently it is reserved for the teacher to make a large contribution to these two parallel sciences, which are coming to assume the highest social importance.

It follows further that pedagogic anthropology differs from the other two allied branches in its practical applications; the progress of criminal and medical anthropology requires, as a matter of fact, only the labors of *medical specialists;* in the case of pedagogic anthropology there is equally a need of *medical specialists*, to whom the *diagnosis* and the *treatment* of abnormal pupils must be entrusted, as well as the *hygiene* of their development; but in addition to these, the teachers also are summoned to a vast task of observation, which, by its continuity, will supplement and complete the periodic observations of the physician.

Furthermore, the *teacher* will acquire under the guidance of anthropology certain practical rules in the art of educating the child; and it is this especially that makes the anthropological and psychological training of the modern teacher so necessary.

The school constitutes an immense field for research; it is a "pedagogical clinic," which, in view of its importance, can be compared to no other gathering of *subjects* for study. Thanks to the system of compulsory education, it gathers to itself every living human being of both sexes and of every social caste, normal and abnormal; and it retains them there, throughout a most important period of their growth. This is the field, therefore, in which the *culture of the human race* can really and practically be undertaken; and the joint labour of physician and teacher will sow the seed of a future *human hygiene*, adapted to achieve perfection in man, both as a *species* and as a *social unit.*

CHAPTER I

CERTAIN PRINCIPLES OF GENERAL BIOLOGY

In order to *understand* the practical researches that must be conducted for anthropological purposes, it is necessary to have an adequate preparation in the science of biology. The *interpretation* of the data that have to be gathered according to technical procedure, demands a *training;* and this training will form our subject in the theoretic part of the present volume. The limits, however, not only of the book itself, but of pedagogic anthropology as well, preclude anything more than a simple general outline; but this can be supplemented by those other branches of study which are either collateral to it or constitute its necessary basis (*i.e.*, general biology, human anatomy and physiology, hygiene of environment, general anthropology, etc.).

The Material Substratum of Life

The Synthetic Concept of the Individual in Biology

According to the materialistic theories of life, of which Haeckel is the most noted supporter, *life* was derived from a form of matter, protoplasm, which not only has a special chemical composition, but possesses further the property of a constant molecular movement of scission and redintegration; vital metabolism or interchange of matter, by which the molecules are constantly renewed at the expense of the environment.

It was Huxley who defined protoplasm as the *physical basis* of life; and, as a matter of fact, life does not exist without protoplasm.

But Schultze and Haeckel carried this doctrine further, to the point of maintaining that a minute particle of protoplasm was all that was needed to constitute life; and that such a particle could be formed naturally, whenever the surrounding conditions were favorable, like any other inorganic chemical substance; and in this way the materialists endeavoured, with great ingenuousness, to maintain the *spontaneous origin* of life. And when Haeckel thought that he had discovered the *moneræ* or living cells composed of a single particle of protoplasm, he held that these were the first species to have appeared on earth.

But the further researches of physiologists and the improvements in the technique of the microscope proved that protoplasm does not exist independently in nature; because living cells are always a combination of protoplasm and a nucleus. If the nucleus is extracted from a radiolarium, the latter mortifies, and the protoplasm also dies; if an *amœba* is severed in such a manner that one part contains nucleus and protoplasm and the other protoplasm alone, it will be found that the latter part mortifies and dies, while the first part continues to live. If an infusorium is divided in such a way that each of the separate sections contains a part of the nucleus and a part of the protoplasm, two living infusoria are developed similar to the original one. Experiments of this kind, to which Verworn has given high authority, serve to prove that life does not exist except in cells divisible into protoplasm and nucleus. Further discoveries confirm this theory, as for instance the presence of a nucleus in hemacytes or red blood corpuscles, which were formerly believed to be instances of anuclear cells; and the discovery of protoplasm in microbes, which had formerly been considered free nuclei.

Now, when we have an independent living cell, it represents an *individual,* which not only has, as à general feature, this primitive complexity of parts, but also certain special characteristics of *form,* of reaction to environment, etc., that mark the *species* to which this particular living creature belongs.

Accordingly, we cannot assert, without committing the error of confining ourselves to a generic detail, that life originates in protoplasm or in a combination divisible into protoplasm and nucleus; we should say that *life* originates in living *individuals;* since, aside from abstract speculation, there can be no other material substratum of life.

Such a doctrine is eminently *synthetic,* and opens the mind to new conceptions regarding the *properties* that *characterise* life.

Formerly when life was defined as a form of matter (protoplasm) subject to constant movement (metabolism), only a single general property had been stated; for that matter, even the stars consist of matter and movement; and, according to the modern theory of electrons, atoms are composed of little particles strongly charged with electricity and endowed with perennial motion. Accordingly, these are universal characteristics, and not *peculiar* to life; and *metabolism* may be regarded as a *variation* of such a property, which is provoked by, or at least associated with the phenomenon of life.

The properties which are really characteristic of life have been summed up by Laloy in two essential groups; *final causes* and *limitations of mass*, or, to use a term more appropriate to living organisms, *limitations of form and size.*

The term *final causes* refers to a series of phenomena that are met with only where there is life, and that tend toward a definite purpose or *end.* Living organisms take nutriment from their environment, to the *end* of assimilating it, that is, transforming it from an inert, indifferent substance into a substance that is a living part of themselves.

This phenomenon is undoubtedly one of the most characteristic. But there are still other forms of *final cause,* such for example as the transformation of the fertilised ovum into the fully developed individual, predetermined in its essential characteristics, such as form, dimensions, colour, activities, etc. There are ova that to all appearances are exactly alike; the human ovum itself is nothing more than a simple cell composed of protoplasm and nucleus, measuring only a tenth of a millimeter ($= \frac{1}{250}$ inch); yet all these ovum cells produce living organisms of the utmost diversity; yet so definitely predetermined that, if we know to what species the ovum belongs, we are able to predict how many bones will compose the skeleton of the animal destined to develop from it, and whether this animal will fly or creep upon the ground, or rise to take a place among those who have made themselves the lords of the earth. Furthermore, knowing the phases of development, we may predetermine at what *periods* the successive transformations that lead step by step to the complete development of the individual will take place.

Another form of *final cause* is seen in the *actions* of living creatures, which reveal a *self-consciousness;* a consciousness that even in its most obscure forms guides them toward a destined *end.*

Thus, for example, even the infusoria that may be seen through a microscope in a drop of water, chasing hither and thither in great numbers, avoiding collision with one another, or contending over some particle of food, or rushing in a mass toward an unexpected ray of light, give us a keen impression of their possession of consciousness, a dim glimmering of self-will, which is the most elementary form of that phenomenon that manifests itself more and more clearly, from the metazoa upward, through the whole zoologic scale: the *final cause* of psychic action.

Again, in multicellular organisms there are certain continuous and so-called *vital* phenomena, which some physiologists attribute to cellular consciousness: for example, the leucocytes in the blood seem to obey a sort of glimmering consciousness when they rush to the encounter of any danger threatening the organism, and ingest microbes or other substances foreign to the blood; and it is also due to a phenomenon that cannot be explained by the physical laws of osmosis, that the erythrocytes or red blood corpuscles and the plasma in the blood never interchange sodium salts for those of potassium; and lastly the cells of each separate gland seem to *select* from the blood the special substances that are needed for the formation of their specific products: saliva, milk, the pancreatic juice, etc.

Still another manifestation of *final cause* is the tendency exhibited by each living individual to make a constant struggle for life, a struggle that depends upon a minimum expenditure of force for a maximum realisation of life, thanks to which life multiplies, invades its environment, adapts itself to it, and is transformed.

Another fundamental synthetic characteristic of life is the limitation of *form and size* that is a fixed and constant factor in the characteristics of each species; the body of the living individual cannot grow indefinitely.

Living creatures do not increase in quantity by the successive *accumulation* of matter, as is the case with inorganic bodies, but by *reproduction*, that is, the multiplication of individuals.

Through the phenomenon of reproduction, life has a share in the eternity of matter and of force, that is, in a universal phenomenon. But what distinguishes it is that the individual creatures produced by other living individuals form, each one of them, an *indivisible element* in which life manifests itself; and this element is *morphologically fixed* in the limits of its form and size.

The peculiarities which are attributed to the chemical action of protoplasm are of an analytic character, so far as they concern the fundamental characteristics of life. The constant interchange of matter, namely, *metabolism*, constitutes undoubtedly a phenomenon peculiar to living matter, protoplasm; but protoplasm *does not exist* apart from living organisms. And what constitutes its chief characteristic is that, when brought into contact with it, inert substances are assimilated, *i. e.*, they become like it, or rather, are transformed into *protoplasm;* mineral salts such as the nitrates or nitrites of sodium and potassium are transformed in the case of plants into living plasma capable of germinating either into a rose bush or a plane tree or a palm, and inert organic substances such as bread or wine are transformed into human flesh and blood. So that the phenomenon of *assimilation* outweighs, as a characteristic of life, the molecular chemical action through which it is accomplished. Since *metabolism* does not occur in nature as a chemical phenomenon, and cannot be produced artificially, but is found only in the matter composing living organisms, it follows that life is the cause of this form of dynamic action, and not that this dynamic action is the cause of life.*

Even the latest theory, developed especially by Ludwig in Germany—that protoplasm contains a separate *enzyme* for each separate function appointed to a particular task—amounts to nothing more than an analysis of the living organism.

The Formation of Multicellular Organisms

We cannot say that the *cell* is the element of life, because, in an absolute sense, it is not alive; it lives only when it *constitutes an individual.* Even the brain cells, the muscular fibres, the leucocytes, etc., are cells; but they *do not live independently;* their life depends upon the living individual that contains them. We may, however, define the cell as the means, the morphological material, out of which all living organisms are formed: because, from the algæ to the orchids, from the cœlenterata up to man, all complex organisms are composed of an accumulation of those microscopic little bodies that we call cells.

The manner of union between the cells in the most primitive *living colonies,* whether vegetable or animal, is analogous to that followed in the segmentation of the ovum in its ontogenetic (*i.e.*, individual) development.

*See further, as to these fundamental ideas: Laloy, *L'Évolution de la Vie. Petite Encyclopédie du XX Siècle;* Claude Bernard, *Leçons sur les Phènomènes de la Vie;* Le Dentu, in *La Matière Vivante, et Théorie nouvelle de la Vie;* Luciani, *Fisiologia Umana,* in the first chapter: "Material Substratum of Vital Phenomena."

But the *manner of construction* differs notably, as between *animal* and *vegetable* cells.

Vegetable cells, on the one hand, have a resistant and strongly protective membrane; animal cells, on the contrary, have either a very thin membrane or none at all. Vegetable cells, as though made *venturesome* by their natural protection, proceed to invade their environment in colonies—in other words, the cells dispose themselves in series of linear ramifications—witness the formation of primitive algæ; and analogously the expansion of the higher types of vegetation into their environment, with branches, leaves, etc. And just as though the vegetable cell acquired self-confidence because it is so well protected, it becomes stationary and strikes its roots into the soil.

To this same fact of cellular protection must be attributed the inferior sensibility and hence the permanent state of obscured consciousness in vegetable life.

This protection against the assaults of environment, and the consequent lack of sensibility, constitute from the outset an inferior stage of evolution.

Animal cells have an entirely different manner of forming themselves into colonies; acting as though they were *afraid*, they group themselves in the form of a little sphere, enclosing their environment within themselves, instead of reaching out to invade it; and subsequent developments of the animal cell consist in successive and complex *invaginations*, or formations of layers, one within another—instead of ramifications, after the manner of vegetable cells.

Accordingly, if we advance from that primitive animal type, the volvox, consisting of a simple group of cells arranged spherically, like an elastic rubber ball, to the cœlenterata, we meet with the phenomenon of the first invagination, producing an animal body consisting of *two layers* of cells and an internal *cavity*, communicating with the exterior by means of a pore or mouth. The two layers of cells promptly divide their task, the outer layer becoming *protective* and the inner *nutritive;* and in consequence of their different *functions*, the cells themselves *alter*, the outer layer acquiring a tougher consistency, while the inner remains soft in order to absorb whatever nutriment is brought by the water as it passes through the mouth. In this way, there is a division of labor, such that all the external cells protect not only themselves, but the whole organism; while the internal cells absorb nutriment not only for themselves but for the others. This is the simplest example of a process that becomes more and more complex in the formation of higher organisms; in adapting themselves to their work, the cells become greatly modified (formation of tissues) and perform services that are useful to the entire organism. And at the same time, because of the very fact that they have been differentiated, they become dependent upon the labors of others, for obtaining the means of subsistence. Similar laws seem to persist even at the present day in the formation of *social organisms*, in human society.

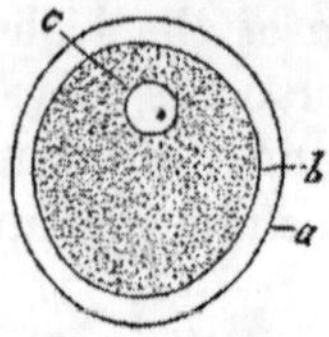

FIG. 1.—Human Ovum, Magnified. *a*. Vitelline membrane; *b*. Vitellus; *c*. Germinal Vesicle.

During the development of the embryo, all animals pass through similar phases; and to this man is no exception.

He traces his origin to an ovum-cell formed of protoplasm, nucleus and membrane, measuring only a tenth of a millimetre, yet vastly large in comparison with the spermatic cell destined to fertilise it by passing through one of the innumerable pores that render the dense membrane penetrable.

After the ovum-cell is fertilised, it constitutes the *first cell* of the new being; that is, it contains *potentially* a *man*. But as seen through the microscope, it is really not materially any-

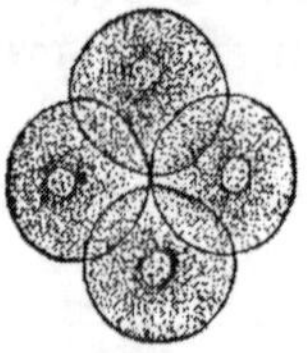

FIG. 2.—First Segmentation of a Fertilised Ovum.

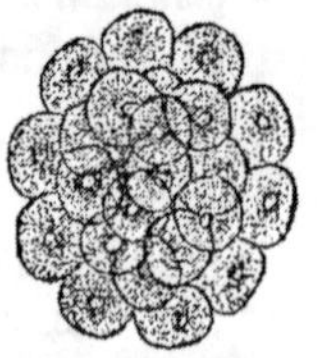

FIG. 3.—A Morula as seen from the Outside.

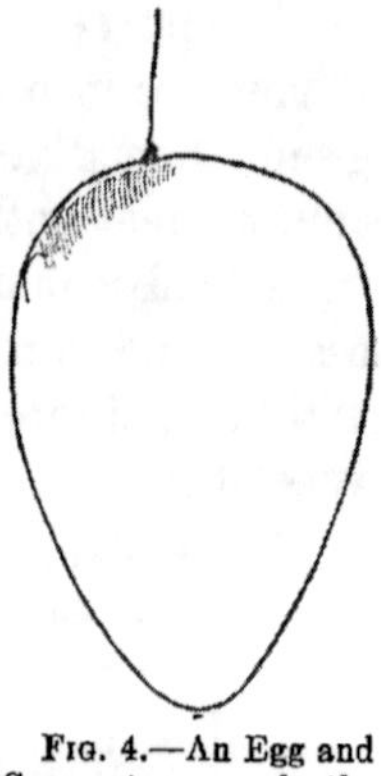

FIG. 4.—An Egg and Spermatozoon of the same Species, about to Fertilise It. Note the difference in the proportional size of the two cells.

thing more than a microscopic cell, undifferentiated, and in all things similar to other independent cells or to fertilised ovarian cells belonging to other animals. That which it contains, namely, *man*, often already predetermined not only in *species*, but in individual characteristics—as, for instance, in degenerative inferiority—is certainly not there in *material* form.

At an early stage of the embryo's development, it exhibits a form analogous to that of the volvox; namely, a hollow sphere, called the *morula;* and subsequently, by the process of invagination, two layers of cells, an inner and an outer, are formed, together with the first body cavity, destined to become the digestive cavity, and also a pore corresponding to the mouth.

This formation has received the name of *gastrula* (Fig. 10, facing page 72), and the two layers of cells are known as the *primary layers,* otherwise called the *ectoderm* and the *entoderm.* To these a third intermediate layer is soon added, the *mesoderm.* These three layers consist of cells that are not perceptibly differentiated from one another; but *potentially* each and every one contains its own special *final cause.* In each of the three layers, invaginations take place, furrows destined to develop into the nervous system, the lungs, the liver, the various different glands, the generative organs; and during the progress of such modifications, corresponding changes take place in the elementary cells, which become differentiated into *tissues.* From the ectoderm are developed the nervous system and the skin tissues; from the entoderm, the digestive system with its associate glands (the liver, pancreas, etc.); from the mesoderm, the supporting tissues (bones and cartilage) and the muscles. But all these cells, even the most complex and specialised, as for example those of the cerebral cortex, the fibres of the striped muscles, the hepatic cells, etc., were orginally *embryonic* cells—in other words, simple, undifferentiated, all starting on an equal footing. Yet every one of them had within it a predestined end that led it to occupy, as it multiplied in number, a certain appointed portion of the body, in order to perform the work, to which the profound alterations in its cellular tissues should ultimately adapt it.

Like children in the same school, these embryonic cells, all apparently just alike, contain certain dormant activities and destinies that are profoundly different. This unquestionably constitutes one of the properties of life, namely, the *final cause;* it is certainly associated intimately with *metabolism* and *nutrition,* considered as a means of *development* and not as a cause. Upon *metabolism,* however, depends the more or less complete attainment of the *final cause* of life. In man, for example, strength, health, beauty, on the one hand, degeneration on the other, stand in intimate relations with the *nutrition* of the embryo.*

The Theories of Evolution.—At the present day, there is a general popular understanding of the fundamental principles involved in the mechanical or materialistic theories of evolution which bear the names of Lamarck, Geffroy-Saint-Hilaire, and more especially the glorious name of Charles Darwin.

According to these theories, the environment is regarded as the chief cause of the evolution of organic forms. Charles Darwin, who formulated the best and most detailed theory of evolution, based it on the two principles of the *variability* of living organisms, and *heredity*, which transmits their characteristics from generation to generation. And in explanation of the underlying cause of evolution, he expounded the doctrines of the *struggle for existence* and the *natural selection* of such organic forms as succeeded to a sufficient degree in adapting themselves to their environment.

Whatever the explanation may be, the substantial fact remains of the *variability of species* and the successive and gradual transition from lower to higher forms. In this way, the higher animals and plants must have had as antecedents other forms of *inferior species*, of which they still bear more or less evident traces; and in applying these theories to the interpretation of the personalities of human degenerates, he frequently invoked the so-called principle of *atavism*, in order to explain the reappearance of atavistic traits that have been outgrown in the normal human being, certain anomalies of form more or less analogous to parallel forms in lower species of animals.

There are other theories of evolution less familiar than that of Darwin. Naegeli, for instance, attributes the variability of species to *internal*, rather than external causes—namely, to a spontaneous activity, implanted in life itself, and analogous to that which is witnessed in the development of an individual organism, from the primitive cell up to the final complete development; without, however, attributing to the progressive alterations in species that predestined final goal which heredity determines in the development of individual organisms.

The internal factor, namely life, is the primary cause of *progress* and the *perfectionment* of living creatures—while environment

* Consult: HAECKEL, *Anthropogenie;* E. PERRIER, *Les Colonies animales et la Formation des Organismes;* RICHET, *L'Effort vers la Vie, et la Theorie des Causes finales.*

assumes a secondary importance, such as that of *directing* evolution, acting at one time as a stimulus toward certain determined directions of development; at another, permanently establishing certain useful characteristics; and still again, effacing such forms as are unfit.

In this way the external causes are associated with evolution, but with very different effects from those attributed to them by Darwin, who endowed them with the creative power to produce new organs and new forms of life.

Naegeli compared the internal forces to invested capital; it will draw a higher or lower rate of interest, according as its environment proves to be more or less favourable to earning a profit.

The most modern theory of evolution is that of De Vries, who, after having witnessed the spontaneous and unforeseen transformations of a certain plant, the Œnohtera Lamarckiana, without the intervention of any external phenomenon, admitted the possibility of the unexpected occurrence of other new forms, from a preexistent parent form—and to such phenomena he gave the name of *mutations*.

It is these *mutations* that create new species; the latter, although apparently unheralded, were already *latent* in the germ before they definitely burst into life. Consequently, new species are formed potentially in the germinating cells, through spontaneous activity.

The characteristics established by *mutations* are hereditary, and the species which result from them persist, provided their environment affords favourable conditions, better suited to them than to the preexisting parent form.

Accordingly new species are *created* unexpectedly. De Vries draws a distinction between mutations and variations, holding that the latter are dependent upon environment, and that in any case they constitute simple *oscillations of form* around the normal type determined in each species by mutation.

Species, therefore, cannot be transformed by external causes or environments, and the mechanism of transformation is not that of a succession of very gradual variations, which have given rise to the familiar saying: *natura non facit saltus.* On the contrary, what produces stable characteristics is a *revolution* prepared in a latent state, but unannounced in its final disclosure. A parallel to this is to be found, for example, in the phenomena of *puberty* in its relation to the evolution of the individual.

Now, when a species has once reached a fixed stability as regards its characteristics, it is *immutable*, after the analogy of an individual organism that has completed its development; henceforth its further evolution is ended. In such a case, the oscillations of variability are exceedingly limited, and adaptation to new environments is difficult; and while a species may offer the appearance of great strength (*e.g.*, certain species of gigantic extinct animals), it runs the risk of dying out, because of a lower potentiality of adaptability; or, according to the theory of Rosa, it may even become extinct spontaneously.

Accordingly it is not the fixed species that continue the process of *evolution*. If we compare the tree of life to a plant, we may imagine evolution as soaring upward, sustained by roots far below; the new branches are not put forth by the old branches, but draw their sustenance from the original sources, from which the whole tree draws its life. When a branch matures and flowers, it may survive or it may wither but it cannot extend the growth of the tree.

Furthermore, the new branches are always higher up than the old ones; that which comes last is the highest of all.

Thus, the species which are the *latest* in acquiring a stable form are the highest up in the biological scale, because the privilege of carrying forward the process of evolution belongs to those species which have not yet become fixed. An apparent weakness, instability, an active capacity for adaptation, are consequently so many signs of *superiority*, as regards a potential power of evolution—just as the nudity and sensibility of animal cells, for example, are signs of superiority, as compared with vegetable cells—and of man, as compared with the lower animals.

In order to show that the inferiority of a species is in proportion to its precocity in attaining fixed characteristics, Rosa conceived the following striking comparison. Two animals are fleeing, along the same road, before an advancing flood. One of the two climbs to the top of a neighboring tree, the other continues in its flight toward a mountain. As the level of the water rises, it threatens to isolate and engulf the animal now stalled upon the tree; the other animal, still fleeing toward the heights, reaches, on the contrary, a higher and more secure position.

The animal on the tree stands for an inferior species that has earlier attained a fixed form; the other represents a higher species that has continued to evolve; but the animal upon the mountain never was on the tree at all, because, if he had mounted it and become caught there, he would have lost his chance of continuing on his way. In other words, the *higher* species never was the *lower* species, since the characteristics of the latter are already fixed.

Some eloquent comparisons might be drawn from the social life of to-day. We are all of us spurred on to choose as early as possible some form of employment that will place us in a secure and definite place at the great banquet of existence. The idea of continuing to follow an indefinite and uncertain path, leading upward toward the heights is far less attractive than the safe and comfortable shelter of the shady tree that rises by the wayside. The same law of inertia applies to every form of life. Biological evolution bears witness to it, in the *forms* of the different species; social evolution, in the *forms* of the professions and trades; the evolution of thought, in the *forms* of the different faiths. And whoever first halts in any path of life, the path of study, for instance, occupies a lower place than he who continues on his road.

The salaried clerk, armed only with his high-school certificate, has an assured income and the pleasures of family life, at a time when the physician, with an independent profession, is still struggling to establish a practice. But the obscure clerk will eventually hold a social position below that of the physician; his income will always be limited, while the physician may acquire a fortune. Now, the clerk, by *adapting* himself to his bureaucratic environment, has acquired certain well-defined characteristics; we might even say that he has become a representative type of the *species*, clerk. And the same will be true of the physician in his independent and brilliant life as high priest of humanity, scientist and man of wealth. Both men were high-school students, and now they are two widely different social types; but the physician never represented the type of clerk; or, in other words, he did not have to be a clerk before he could be a physician; on the contrary, if he had been a clerk, he never could have become a physician. It is somewhat after this fashion that we must conceive of the sequence of species in evolution. It follows that man never was an anthropoid ape, nor any other animal now living around us. Nor was the man of the white race ever at any time a negroid or a mongolian. Consequently, the theory is untenable which tries to explain certain morphological or psychic malformations of man, on the principle of atavism—because no one can inherit if he is not a descendant.

So, for example, reverting to our previous comparisons, if the animal on the mountain should climb a tree, or if the physician should become pedantic, this would not prove that the animal from the mountain was once upon a time the animal in the tree, nor that the physician recalled, by his eventual pedantry, certain by-gone days when he was a clerk.

The theories of evolution seemed for a time to illumine and definitely indicate the origin of man. But this illusion has so far resulted only in relegating to still deeper darkness the truth that the biologists are seeking. We do not know of whom man is the son.

Even the earlier conceptions regarding the mechanics of evolution are essentially altered. The mystery of the origin of species, like that of the mutability of forms, has withdrawn from the forms that are already developed, and taken refuge in the *germinal cells;* these cells in which no differentiation is revealed, yet in which the future organism, in all its details, exists in a potential state; in which, we may even say, *life exists independent of matter*, are the real *laboratorium vitæ.* The individual, in developing, does nothing more than *obey,* by fulfilling the potentiality of the germs.

The direction of research has shifted from the individual to its germs. And just as the early Darwinian theories evolved a *social ethics,* seemingly based upon the facts of life, to serve as a guide in the *struggle for existence,* so in the same way, to-day, there has arisen from the modern theories a new *sexual ethics,* founded upon a biologic basis.

The Phenomena of Heredity.—The most interesting biological researches of to-day are in regard to the hereditary transmission of characteristics.

To-day the phenomena of heredity are no longer absolutely obscure, thanks to the studies of Mendel, who discovered some of its laws, which seemed to open up new lines of research prolific in results. Yet even now, although this field has been invaded by the most illustrious biologists of our time, among others, De Vries, Correns, Tschermack, Hurst, Russell, it is still in the state of investigation. Nevertheless, the *general trend* of researches relative to Mendel's laws is too important to permit of their enlightening first steps being neglected by Anthropology.

The first phenomena observed by Mendel, and the ones which led him to the discovery of the laws of heredity which bear his name, were revealed by a series of experiments conducted with peas.

Exposition of the Phenomena of Hybridism.—If two strains of peas are crossed, one of them having red flowers and the other white flowers, the result in the first generation is, that all the plants will have red flowers, precisely similar to those of one of the parent plants.

Accordingly, in hybridism, the characteristic of one of the parents completely hides that which is antagonistic to it in the other parent. We call this characteristic (in the case cited, the red flowers), *dominant;* in distinction to the other characteristic which is antagonistic to the first and overcome by it; namely, the *recessive* characteristic (in the present case, the white flowers). This is the law of prevalence, and constitutes Mendel's first law, which is stated as follows:

Mendel's First Law: "When antagonistic varieties or characteristics are crossed with each other, the products of the first generation are all uniform and equal to one of the two parents."

This result has been repeatedly reached in a host of researches, which have experimentally established this phenomenon *as a law.*

Thus, for example, if we cross a nettle having leaves with an indented margin, with a nettle having leaves with a smooth margin, the product of the first generation will all have leaves with indented margins, and apparently identical with the parent plant having indented margins, in other words, having the characteristic that has proved itself the dominant one (Russell).

These phenomena discovered by Mendel have been observed in many different species of plants, such as wheat, Indian corn, barley and beans.

They have also been verified in certain animals, such as mice, rats, rabbits, caveys, poultry, snails, silk-worms, etc. One of the most typical experiments was that of Cuénot, who, by crossing ordinary mice with jumping mice, obtained as a result a first generation composed wholly of normal mice; the characteristic of jumping was thus shown to be recessive.

Notwithstanding that the first generation is apparently in every way similar to the parent with the dominant character, there is in reality a difference.

Because, if we cross these hybrids *together*, we meet, in the second generation, with the following phenomenon: to every three individuals possessing the dominant character, one is born having the recessive character. To go back to Mendel's first example, that of the peas with red flowers (dominant) and with white flowers (recessive), we find, by crossing together the hybrids of the first generation, that for every three plants with red flowers, there is one plant with white flowers.

And similarly, the crossing of hybrid nettles with indented leaves will result in a second generation composed of three plants with indented leaves to every one with smooth-edged leaves (see Fig. 5).

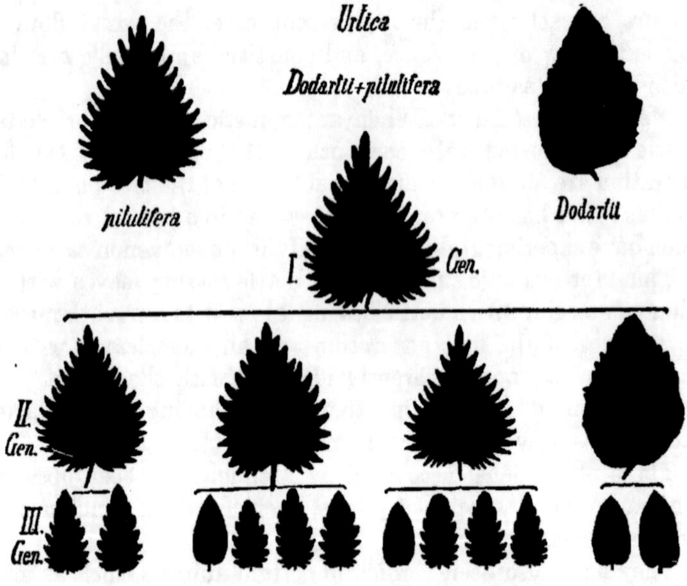

Fig. 5.

That is, the characteristics which belonged to the first two parents all survive, even though in a latent form, in the descendants; and they continue to differentiate themselves in well established proportions. In one offspring out of four, the characteristics of the grandfather, which have remained dormant in the father, once more reappear. This intermittent heredity of characteristics, that are passed from grandfather to grandson, overleaping the father, is one of the best-known laws of *pathological heredity* in man; and it is called *atavistic heredity,* to distinguish it from *direct heredity,* which denotes the transmission from parent to offspring. But no explanation had ever been found for this sort of phenomenon. Undoubtedly, it must be connected with the phenomena of Mendelism.

Accordingly, in the second generation Mendel's second law has been established, the *law of disjunction,* which is stated as follows:

Mendel's Second Law: "In the second generation obtained by reciprocal fertilisation of the first hybrids, three quarters of the offspring will exhibit the dominant character, and one quarter the recessive"

Mendel's Hypothesis, Designed to Explain the Phenomena of Heredity.—Mendel's great service is to have conceived a hypothesis that seems to have disclosed the key adapted to unlock all the secrets of heredity.

While the body of an individual is the resultant of forces so mutually exclusive that the appearance of one characteristic means the disappearance of its antagonist; *in the development of the sexual cells the two antagonistic characters are distributed in equal proportion.* That is to say, one-half of the male cells contain the dominant character, and one-half the recessive; and the same holds true for the female cells. The characters of the two parents, in other words, never *merge* in the reproductive cells, but are distributed *in equal measure,* independently of the question whether they are dominant or recessive. Thus for example: in the case already cited of the first hybrid generation of the peas with red flowers, in every one of the plants, without distinction, half the pollen has potentially the red character and half has the white; and in the same way the female cells have, half of them a red potentiality and half of them a white. Such hybrids of the first generation, therefore, although apparently similar to the parent with red flowers, *differ in their germinative powers,* which are not made apparent in the individual. And the same may be said of hybrid nettles with indented leaves, etc.

Granting Mendel's hypothesis, we have on the one hand pollen and on the other seed ready to come together in every manner included within the range of possible combinations; the *individual* is, in its characteristics, nothing else than the product of a combination which must necessarily manifest itself in accordance with the well-known mathematical laws of *probability*.

For instance, let us proceed to diagram the possible disposition of the sexual cells of the hybrids of peas, all of them having red flowers. In terms of percentage, they will give, out of every hundred, fifty red and fifty white.

P = pollen; *O* = ova; *R* = red, dominant; *w* = white, recessive:

The possible number of combinations between the pollen grains and the ova are four; namely, *RR*, *Rw*, *wR*, *ww*. But where a dominant characteristic encounters a recessive (*Rw*, *wR*), the recessive disappears, to make way in the individual for the dominant characteristic alone. The definitive result is three individuals of dominant character, to one of recessive character.

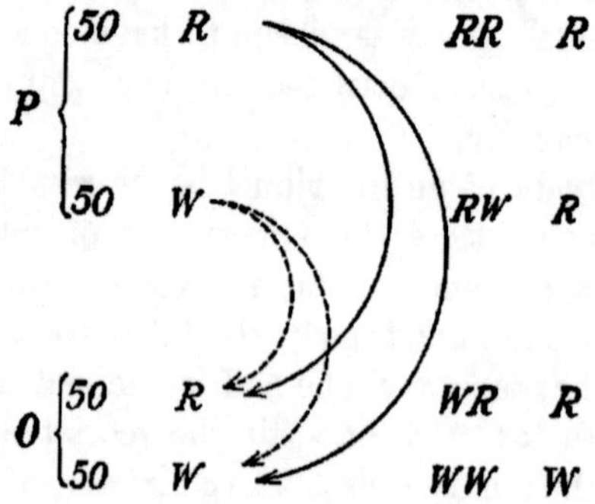

Fig. 6.

Nevertheless, the hybrids of dominant character are not all equal among themselves. Those belonging to the combination *RR*, indeed, are *permanent* in character and in all respects alike, and they reproduce the original red-flower progenitor. The other red-flower hybrids, belonging to the groups *Rw* and *wR* are, on the contrary, similar to the hybrids of the first generation and contain reproductive cells differentiated in character; such hybrids, if reciprocally fertilised, will again give three dominant offspring to every one recessive; that is, they will obey the law of disjunction. The hybrids belonging to the fourth group, on the contrary, are constant, like those of the first group, and are permanently of recessive character; and they will reproduce the original progenitor with white flowers.

The same results may be attained with nettles with smooth

and indented leaves, and with all other types of plant and animal life that obey the laws of Mendelism.

The figure given actually represents the third generation of nettles; from a combination corresponding to *RR*, there result only indented leaves, and from another combination corresponding to our *ww* there result only smooth-edged leaves, and from the two mixed groups there come three offspring with indented leaves to every one with smooth leaves.

It is possible to represent, by means of a general diagram, the mathematical succession of characteristics in hybrids, after the following manner; denoting the dominant character by *D*, and the recessive by *r*.

In each successive generation, provided the fertilisation takes place only between uniform individuals, as indicated in the diagram, and as may be effected by actual experiment with plants,

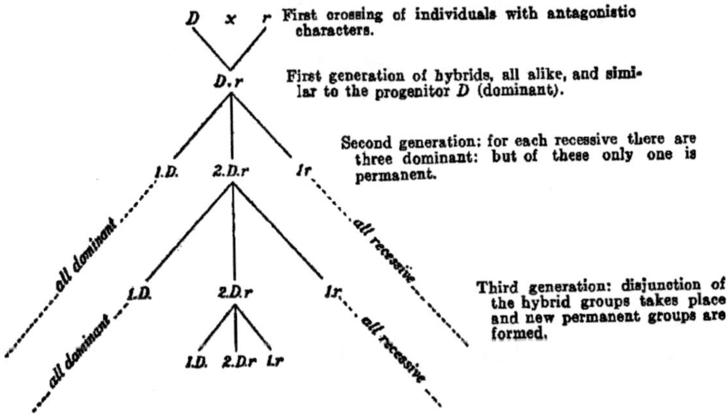

FIG. 7.

groups identical with the original progenitors will continue to be formed, through successive disjunction of the hybrids; the sexual phenomenon operating in obedience to the laws of probability.

An effective experiment, that anyone may repeat for himself, is the one originated by Darbishire. He took two boxes, typifying respectively the male and female organ, and placed in them black and white disks of equal size, so distributed that each box contained fifty disks of each colour. After mixing these disks very carefully, he proceeded to take *at random* one disk at a time alternately from each box; and he piled up each pair of disks in such a manner that the black ones should be on top and the white underneath. The result was that for every three black disks on top of the piles there was one white disk; but of the black groups one consisted of two black disks, while in the other two the lower disk was white. This is simply one of the many games dependent on the laws of probability.

Now, supposing that instead of one, there are two characteristics that are in antagonism; in that case, we have the occurrence of double hybridism (dihybridism).

Let us take the strains of peas already considered, but let us choose for observation the character of their seed. One of the plants has round seed and yellow cotyledons; and the other angular seed and green cotyledons. These two characteristics, therefore, are both inherent in the seed; condition of surface (rough, smooth), and colour (green, and yellow).

After fertilisation, Mendel's first law, that of the prevalence of the dominant character, will operate, and all the plants of the first generation will have round seed and yellow cotyledons. Hence these are the dominant characteristics, which we will represent by capital letters: R (round), Y (yellow), to distinguish them from the recessive characteristics, which we will designate with small letters: a (angular), and g (green).

According to Mendel's hypothesis, all these hybrids with round seed and yellow cotyledons, contain sexual cells of opposite potentialities, numerically equal and corresponding to the antagonistic characters of the parent plants. That is, they must have in their pollen grains and their ovarian cells all the possible combinations of their different potentialities.

They should produce in equal quantities:

pollen grains (P) with	round	seed and	yellow	cotyledons:	$R\ Y$
	"	"	green	"	$R\ g$
	angular	"	yellow	"	$a\ Y$
	"	"	green	"	$a\ g$
ovarian cells (O) with	round	"	yellow	"	$R\ Y$
	"	"	green	"	$R\ g$
	angular	"	yellow	"	$a\ Y$
	"	"	green	"	$a\ g$

The total number of combinations that may result is sixteen; that is, each one of the four combinations of pollen may unite with any one of the ovarian cells; thus constituting four groups of four. And these groups represent the combinations (of pollen and ova) capable of producing individuals:

$RY - RY = RY$	$aY - RY = RY$
$RY - Rg = RY$	$aY - Rg = RY$
$RY - aY = RY$	$aY - aY = aY$
$RY - ag = RY$	$aY - ag = aY$
$Rg - RY = RY$	$ag - RY = RY$
$Rg - Rg = Rg$	$ag - Rg = Rg$
$Rg - aY = RY$	$ag - aY = aY$
$Rg - ag = Rg$	$ag - ag = ag$

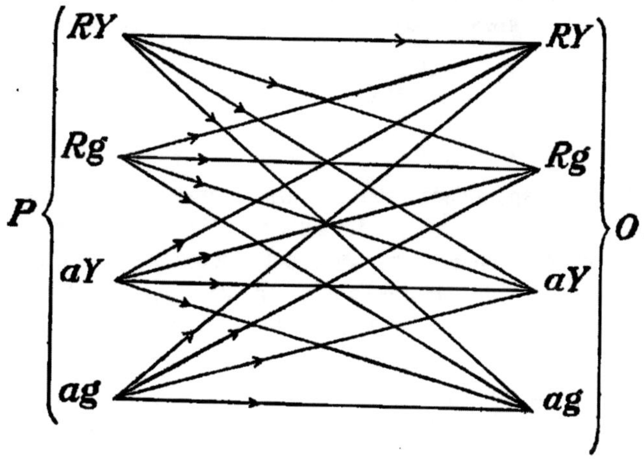

FIG. 8.

Every time that a dominant characteristic encounters a recessive one (R with a or Y with g), it overpowers and hides it: consequently the results of the different combinations are quite definitely limited as determining forms of different individuals. In fact, the results of the sixteen combinations are as follows:

RY	RY
RY	RY
RY	aY
RY	aY
RY	RY
Rg	Rg
RY	aY
Rg	ag

That is to say, the only forms which occur are the following:

R Y, *R g*
a Y, *a g*

whose relative probability of occurrence is:

R Y......9 times in 16 = 56.25%
R g......3 times in 16 = 18.75%
a Y......3 times in 16 = 18.75%
a g......1 time in 16 = 6.25%

Now, as a result of actual experiment, the forms obtained show the following relative percentage:

	Results of experiments with plants	according to the combinations and laws of probability
R Y	56.5%	56.25%
R g	19.75%	18.75%
a Y	18.2%	18.75%
a g	5.8%	6.25%

The correspondence between these figures is close enough to warrant the acceptance of Mendel's hypothesis as the true interpretation of the phenomena that are shown to take place within ths sexual cells; the germinal cells of the hybrid contain potentialities belonging to one or the other only of the parents, and not to both; one-half of the cells contain one of these potentialities, and the other half the other potentiality.

But in the phenomena of hybridism, we have seen the results of another fact which determines Mendel's third law; the *Law of the Independence of Characteristics*.

That is, that while the original progenitors had angular seed and green cotyledons, and round seed and yellow cotyledons, certain hybrid plants inherited the round seed of the one and the green colour of the other; or the angular seed of the one and the yellow colour of the other. In the same way, it may happen, for example, that the colour of one plant may combine with the height of another, etc. That is, that each separate characteristic of the progenitor is independent and may combine with the characteristics of the other progenitor—even to the point of separating the colour from the form, as in the case cited.

What we find in hybrids, then, is not a separation into two types of generative cells, considered as united and complex entities; but every separate germ cell may *break up* into as many different potentialities as there are separate characteristics in the individual;

and that, too, not only as regards the separate minute parts of the individual body, but, within the same organ, as regards the shape, colour, character of the surface, etc.

Such phenomena of Mendelism cannot as yet be generalised; yet it has already been established by a host of experiments that a great number of characteristics obey the laws of Mendel, such, for example, as the character of the hair or plumage; the gradations of colour, the abundance or absence of hair; physical malformations, such as cerebral hernia in poultry; the character of locomotion, as in the jumping mice: and even normal physiological attributes connected with the epoch of maturity in certain plants.

But the manner in which the dominant character asserts itself is not always uniform. There are times when a *fusion* of antagonistic characters takes place. Thus, for example, when two varieties of the *mirabilis jalapa* are crossed, one having red flowers and the other white, a fusion of the colours takes place in the first generation, and *all* the plants have pink flowers. In the second generation we get, for every plant with red flowers, two with pink flowers and one with white. That is, the law of disjunction has again asserted itself, but the individual hybrids merge their antagonistic attributes, which remain, nevertheless (as their differentiation proves), separate one from the other in the sexual cells.

Another phenomenon observed in individual hybrids is the *intermingling* of characteristics. For instance, there are cases where the flowers of a hybrid produced by a plant with red flowers and another with white are *variegated* with red and white stripes.

Accordingly, the transmission of antagonistic attributes through the individual may be divided into three different methods:

Transmission {
- Exclusive.
- By fusion.
- By intermingling.

In the first case, the character of one of the parents is transmitted intact; in the second, the formation of a new characteristic results, constituting a form more or less nearly midway between those from which it comes and whose fusion it represents; in the third case (which is very rare and seems to obey Mendel's laws in quite an uncertain way), the result is a *mosaic* of the fundamental attributes.

Of special interest to us are the two first methods of hereditary transmission of characteristics. Even before Mendel's discoveries, anthropologists had observed that in the intermixture of races certain human attributes remained *distinct* while others *merged.* In the first case they called the individuals *hybrids,* and in the second case they called them *metics.* Take, for example, the colour of the skin when black and white merge in the so-called *mulatto.*

Other characteristics, instead of merging, intermingle, as for instance those that are internal or related to the skeleton, and those that are external or related to the soft tissues and the skin. It may happen, for example, that where one race has an elongated head and black hair and another has a round head and blond hair, the result of their union will be hybrids with elongated heads and blond hair or *vice versa.* Similarly, if one of the parents is tall of stature and fair complexioned, and the other of short stature with a dark skin, these characteristics may be interchanged in the hybrids. A very common occurrence, as regards the colour of the hair, is the *fusion* of blond and brunette into chestnut; while parents with chestnut hair may have either fair-haired or dark-haired children. In his book entitled *Human Races and Varieties,* Sergi says in regard to hybridism: "It is impossible to ignore human hybridism, which, for that matter, has been demonstrated under various forms by all the anthropologists; America, in itself alone, offers us a true example of experimental anthropology in regard to this phenomenon. Already the result of investigations shows that human hybridism is multiform among all the peoples of the earth; but what is best known of all is the exchange of external characteristics and their intermingling with the internal; that is, the combination of external characteristics of one type with internal characteristics of another type. It is easy, for instance, to find cases in which a certain colour of skin and hair, with the special qualities proper to them, are found combined with peculiarities of the skeleton that do not rightfully belong to types of that particular colouring, and *vice versa;* and this same phenomenon may be observed regarding certain separate attributes, and not all of them—such as the stature, or the face with its outer covering of soft tissues, or the shape of the skull alone.

"If we observe our European populations, that call themselves a white-skinned race, but whose whiteness has many different gradations, we are convinced of the great *intermixture* of characters, and, what is more, a varied mixture resulting in a great variety of individual types, consisting of characters differing widely from one another. It requires a very accurate and very minute analysis to distinguish the different elements that are found in the composition of ethnic characters in individuals and peoples. Undoubtedly these intermixtures and combinations of character differ in their constituent elements and in the number of such elements in the different nations, according to whether we study those of the south, or the centre, or the north of Europe; and this results from different degrees of association with mongrel races.

"But a more important fact, and one that seems to have escaped the attention of anthropologists, is the *absence of fusion* of internal and external characteristics in the product of such intermixture. We find only a positional relationship between the different ethnic elements, a syncretism or superposition of characteristics, and a consequent *readiness to disunite and form other unions.* This phenomenon has already been demonstrated in America, on a mass of evidence; but it is apparent also in Europe, among the peoples that are seemingly most homogeneous, if by careful observation we *separate the characteristics* that constitute the ethnic types; and not only the types, but the individuals belonging to the different peoples."

And in the following passage, Sergi expresses himself still more clearly:

"From my many observations, it follows, further, that human hybridism, or meticism, as others choose to call it, is a syncretism of distinct characteristics of great variety, and that these do not modify the skelital structure or the internal characteristics, excepting by way of individual variation; it may happen that separate parts of the skeleton itself acquire characteristics peculiar to themselves. The stature, the chest formation, the proportion of the limbs, may all be in perfect correlation and be united with external characteristics of diverse forms, as for instance with different forms of cranium, or the cranium may be associated with different facial forms, and conversely. Furthermore, the *forms adapted separately* and in part in hybrid composition *remain unvaried in their typical formation.* The face retains its typical characteristics in spite of its union with different forms of cranium; and similarly the cranium preserves its architectural structure when combined with different types of face. The stature maintains its proportions in spite of combinations with diverse cranial and facial types, and in spite of varied colours of skin and hair."

The foregoing page, that I have borrowed from this masterly investigator, is most eloquent testimony that, in regard to the phenomena of hybridism, man also comes within the scope of Mendel's laws. There is something wonderful in the power of observation and intuition shown by Sergi, who, running counter to the convictions of the majority of anthropologists, arrived through these conclusions at a *truth* the key to which was destined to be discovered later on through studies, very far removed from anthropology, such as were pursued by the botanists Mendel and De Vries. While Mendel was led by his *experiments* to the discovery of the laws based upon his ingenious hypothesis, Sergi was drawn simply by *observation* to conclusions that to-day are confirmed by experience. And from difficult observations of *single characteristics taken separately*, Sergi demonstrated, in his ingenious studies, their *persistence* through innumerable generations; while, through the identification of separate characteristics, he achieved that brilliant analysis of the races which revealed to his anthropological insight that the European varieties of man originated among the peoples of Africa and Asia. Unquestionably, the laws of Mendel confirm what hitherto were considered, in the scientific world of Europe, simply as the individual hypotheses of Sergi, but which American anthropologists recognise and welcome as a scientific truth, brilliantly observed and expounded by the Italian anthropologist.

Thus, through single characteristics, through *particularities*, we may read the origins of races; and recognise which are the constant characteristics and which the transitory ones.

Accordingly, let us keep these principles in mind, as we proceed further in our investigation of the phenomena of heredity.

Mendel's laws, however much they may be discredited or illuminated by further experience, serve in the meanwhile to give an absolutely new conception of the individual and to shed light upon many obscure problems relating to heredity.

The individual is the product of a combination of germ potentialities, which, in the case of hybrids (and consequently always in the case of man, who is the product of racial intermixture), meet in accordance with the mathematical laws of probability. One might almost conceive of a *formula*, or, better yet, a calculation, in accordance with which the *individual* resulting from any given germs might be predetermined; if it were not for the fact that the calculations would become infinitely complicated through the multiplication of characteristics. With only ten pairs of characteristics it is already possible to form upward of 1024 kinds of germinal cells and these give rise to 1,000,000 different combinations.

Furthermore, through the law of dominant characteristics, the combinations of germs would produce in the descendants 1000 varieties distinguishable by their external appearance, and 60,000 differing only internally, that is, in their germinal cells.

There remains, however, one general principle: the individual contains not only his personal attributes, but also other attributes which belonged to his ancestors, and which are latent in him, and may reappear in his descendants. Consequently, if the individual is a hybrid, he must be interpreted *not only through himself alone, but through the history of his family;* and the characteristics which he may transmit are not those of his own body, but those of his origin.

The individual body is nothing more than a "temporary expression" of those germinal characteristics which have united to give it consistency; but the complex transmission of characteristics rests wholly with the germinal cells. The problem of heredity is transferred from the individual and from the series of individuals, who are simple and transitory products of combinations, to the sexual cells and their potentialities. And this is unquestionably an absolutely new scientific concept, and a *revolutionary* one as well, capable of drawing in its wake a lengthy evolution of thought. Since the *germinal potentialities* determine the single characteristics, they may be considered as the *atoms* of the biologist. "The field of investigation," says Bateson, "does not appear to differ greatly from that which was opened to the students of chemistry at the beginning of the discovery that chemical combinations are governed by definite laws. . . . . In the same way that the chemist studies the properties of every *chemical substance,* the characteristics of organisms ought to be studied, and their composition determined." (*First Report*, p. 159).

This brings us to two widely diverse facts that demand consideration: first, the subdivision of antagonistic characteristics in the germinal cells that form, so to speak, the atomic and chaotic substratum of characteristics—characteristics that combine according to the mathematical laws of probability; and, secondly, the *dominance* of characteristics, or else their fusion, which, independently of anything that may happen in the germinal cells, serves to determine and define the individual.

What sort of characteristics are the dominant ones?

According to the latest researches of Mendelism, the dominant characteristics are those acquired latest in the course of evolution, in other words, the *youngest*, or, if you prefer, the *most highly evolved*. Accordingly, in hybrids, the most perfected characteristics and forms are the ones that triumph in the end.

This is quite a new principle. Hitherto it was held that the *pure* species or race was the most perfect; and the hybrid or bastard was under a cloud of contempt. And, as a matter of fact, the first crossings of different races may result in some combinations lacking in harmony, and calculated to sanction the old-time conception of the æsthetic inferiority of the bastard.

But it is necessary to leave time for new generations and further crossings, in order that *all of the more highly evolved characteristics* may unite and end by triumphing in reciprocal harmony. This the followers of Mendel cannot yet give us, because it would require decades or centuries, according to the species, to produce experimentally such æsthetic forms of hybridism.

But in the human race we have an experiment already accomplished, which actually shows us the *æsthetic triumph* achieved in the region where the races have for the greatest length of time been crossed and recrossed, through the agency of the most ancient civilisation: the Europeans surpass in physical beauty the people of any other continent; and the Neo-Latin races, the most ancient hybrids of all, seem to be nearing the attainment of the greatest æsthetic perfection. In fact, when I was engaged in compiling an anthropological study of the population of Latium, in accordance with Sergi's principles, and was making a most minute examination of all the different characteristics and their prevalence, as a possible basis for a delineation of the fundamental racial types, I found that complete beauty is never granted to any one race, but distributed among different races: "as a result of my labours, I find perfect artistic proportion as to certain facial features, in a race having inferior hands and feet; and, *vice versa*, I find facial irregularities in the race having the smallest extremities, and the most artistically proportioned hands. What we now consider as standards of human beauty, and delight in bringing together artificially in a single figure in a work of art, are found in nature scattered and distributed among different races." (See *Physical Characteristics of Young Women of Latium*, p. 69.)

Upon the combination of all the different points of beauty in a single individual depend Quételet's biological theories of the medial man (l'homme moyen), lately revived and extensively developed by Viola. The new importance acquired by the reconstruction of the *medial man* is due precisely to the fact that the new method of reconstructing him is by bringing together all the single characteristics taken separately and worked out mathematically according to the laws of individual variations that behave precisely like those of probability. (See *Biometry and the Theory of the Medial Man.*)

Viola considers, in its relation to the physiological laws of *health*, the combination in a single individual of the maximum number of average characteristics, which at the same time are the characteristics numerically prevalent in individuals (dominant characteristics?). The man who accumulates the greater number of average characteristics, escapes diseases and predisposition to disease; he is consequently sounder and more robust and *handsomer*. De Giovanni, on the contrary, through an ingenious conceit, bestows the name of *morphological combination* upon the union in a single individual, of parts that are mutually inharmonic and incapable of performing their normal functions together, in consequence of which such an individual's morphological personality is predisposed to special maladies.

Accordingly the meeting and union of germinative potentialities may be either more or less propitious; as for instance the result sometimes produced by the combination of a platyopic (broad) face and an aquiline and extremely leptorrhine (narrow) nose; in other words, combinations that are discordant from the æsthetic standpoint, but harmless as regards health; or again, there may be a lack of harmony between the internal organs, incompatible with a healthy constitution. There may even exist malformations due to the meeting of forms that clash violently; each of which parts may be quite normal, when considered by itself, but cannot adapt itself to the other parts with which it is united.

It is as though the dominant characteristic in respect to an organ had been overpowered by another, which ought on the contrary, in this special case, to have been recessive.

It is precisely on this question of the dominance of characteristics that the researches of the Mendelists are at present being expended. It has been observed in the course of experiments that there exist certain special *correlations between potentialities*, in consequence of which certain characteristics must always go together; as, for example, when two characteristics, having once been united, must continue to recur together, although they each exist separately. These laws, which are not yet clearly determined, may serve to explain the final harmony of the sum total of individual attributes.

But in general the *dominance* of characteristics is not absolute, but subject to many causes of variation, associated with environment. Thus, for example, just as a change in nutrition of a young plant will result in a different height, it is also possible in the mechanics of reproduction that the original relations of germs may be altered by external causes, and the dominant characteristics be made recessive.* Many deviations are attributable to the influences that act upon the germinative cells of hybrids, after the latter have already been determined in their potentiality; thus for example when certain germinal cells are less resistant during maturation; or again when *combinations* between potentialities are difficult to achieve. That is to say, there may exist certain phenomena associated with environment, thanks to which Mendel's natural laws concerning the dominance of characteristics may become inverted.

Another fact of great significance is this: that, in the course of extensive experimental plantings, for the purpose of verifying the laws of Mendel, a widespread sickliness and mortality occurred among cryptograms, at the expense of the plants of recessive character; which would go to prove that a lower power of resistance accompanies the appearance of recessive characteristics. The dominant characteristics accordingly are not only the most highly evolved, but they also possess a greater power of resistance. So that, to-day, the dominance of the strong tends through the workings of the phenomena of Mendelism, to do away, little by little, in the course of generations, with characteristics that are

* CORRENS: *Concerning the Laws of Heredity.*

weak or antiquated. This has an important bearing upon human pathology, because it opens the way to hope for a possible regeneration in families branded with hereditary disease.

The germinal potentialities that contain beauty and strength seem predestined to that predominance which will achieve the triumph of life in the individual. To learn the laws of the union, in one individual and definitive unity, of the infinite dominant and recessive potentialities that must encounter one another in the mysterious labyrinth in which life is prepared—therein lies the greatest problem of the present day.

It is that which should constitute our guiding purpose.

Form and Types of Stature

The Form.—Fundamental Cannons regarding the Form.—Types of Stature, Macroscelia and Brachyscelia; their physiological Significance.—Types of Stature in relation to Race, Sex, and Age.

A few years ago, when anthropology first began to be studied, the skull was taken as the point of departure; because in the analytical study of the human body it represents the principal part. Indeed, the same thing was done by Lombroso, when he applied anthropology to the practice of psychiatry and later to the study of criminals. It is a matter of fact that degenerative stigmata of the gravest significance are to be found associated with the skull; and this he could not fail to take into account, because of its bearings upon criminal anthropology.

But to-day anthropology is reaching out into vaster fields of science and striving to develop in diverse directions, such as those of physiology and pathology; and revolting from the collection of degenerative details, it undertakes to study normal man in regard to his external form as related to his functional capacity, or else the man of abnormal constitution, who in his outward form reveals certain predispositions to illness; and starting on these lines, it proposes to investigate principally the metamorphoses of growth, through the successive periods of life.

From this new point of view, it is not any single malformation, but the individual as a whole in the exercise of his functions, who assumes first importance. The study of the cranium (formerly so important as to be the basis of a special science, craniology), becomes only one detail of the whole. As a matter of fact, the brain, which is what gives the cranium its importance, is not only the immediate organ of intelligence, but it is also the psychomotor organ; and as such exercises control over all the striped muscles, and is morphologically associated with the development and the functional powers of the whole body.

It follows that, the larger the body, the bigger brain it needs to control it, independently of the question of intelligence. Therefore the first point of departure should be eminently synthetic, and should include the morphological personality considered as a whole.

One of the properties of living bodies is that of attaining a determinate development, whose limits, both in regard to the *quantity of its mass* and the *harmony of its form*, are defined by that biological final cause which is implanted in the race and transmitted by heredity. Consequently every living creature has determinate limits: and these constitute a fundamental *biological* property.

The causality of such limits has not yet been determined by scientific research; nevertheless it is a phenomenon over which we must pause to meditate. If the philosopher pauses to contemplate the immensity of the ocean from the sea shore, marvelling that the interminable and impetuous movement of the waves should have such exact and definite limits that it cannot overpass by so much as a metre the extreme high-water line upon the beach, we may similarly pause to meditate upon the material limits that life assumes in its infinitely varied manifestations.

From the microbe to the mammal, from the lichen to the palm, all living creatures have inherited these limits, which permit the zoologist and the botanist to assign to each a *measure* as one of its descriptive attributes.

This is the first attribute which we must take into consideration in the study of anthropology: namely, the *mass* of the body, and together with the mass, its morphological *entirety*. The Italian vocabulary lacks any one word which quite expresses this idea, [and in this respect English is scarcely more fortunate*]. The stature which represents to us the most synthetic measure of the body in its entirety (a measure determined by the vertical linear distance between the level on which the individual's feet are placed, up to the top of his head as he stands erect), does not

* Translator's note.

represent the entire body in the sense above indicated. It may rather be considered as a *linear index* of this entirety. The French language, on the contrary, possesses the word *taille*, which may be rendered in Italian by the word *taglia* [and in English by the word *form* *], provided that we understand it to signify the conception of the whole *morphological personality*.

No single measurement can express the form; the weight of the body, indeed, may give us a conception of the *mass* but not of the *shape;* and the latter, if it needs to be determined in all its limits, requires a series of measurements, mutually related, and signifying the reciprocal connection and harmony of the parts with the whole; in other words, a *law*. We may establish the following measurements as adapted to determine the form, in other words, as *fundamental laws:* the *total stature*, the *sitting stature*, the *total spread of the arms*, the *circumference of the thorax*, and the *weight*. Of these measures, the two of chief importance are the stature and the weight, because they express the linear index and the volumetric measure of the entire body. The other measurements, on the contrary, analyse this entirety in a sweeping way: thus, the sitting stature, in its relation to the total stature, indicates the reciprocal proportions between the *bust* and the *lower limbs;* the perimeter of the chest records the transverse and volumetric development of the bust; and the total spread of the arms denotes a detail that is highly characteristic in the case of man: the development of the upper limbs, which, while they correspond to organs of locomotion in the lower animals, assume in the case of man higher functions, as organs of labour and of *mimic* speech.

Such measurements constitute a *law*, because they are in constant mutual relationship, when the normal human organism has reached complete development. The stature, in fact, is equal to the total spread of the arms; the circumference of the thorax is equal to one-half the stature, and the sitting stature is slightly greater than the perimeter of the chest. As regards the weight, it cannot be in direct proportion to any linear measure; nevertheless, an empirical correspondence in figures has been noted that may be recorded solely for the purpose of aiding the memory: the normal adult man usually weighs as many kilograms as there are centimetres in his stature, over and above one metre (for

* Translator's note.

instance, a man whose height is 1.60 metres will weigh 60 kilograms, etc.).

To make these laws easier to understand, we may resort to signs and formulæ. Thus, if we denote the stature by *St*, the total spread of the arms by *Ts*, the circumference of the thorax by *Ct*, the essential or sitting stature by *Ss*, and the weight by *W*, we may set down the following formulæ, which will result in practice in more or less obvious approximations:

$$St = Ts;\ Ct = \frac{St}{2};\ Ct = Ss$$

And for the weight, the following wholly empirical formula:

$$W = Kg(St - 1\text{ m.}).$$

Stature.—Among all the measurements relating to the form, the principal one is the stature. It has certain characteristics that are essentially human. What we understand by stature is the height of a living animal, when standing on its feet. Let us compare the stature of one of the higher mammals, a dog for instance, with that of man. The stature of the dog is determined essentially by the length of its legs, while the spinal column is supported in a horizontal position by the legs themselves. Such is the attitude of all the higher mammals, including the greater number of monkeys, notwithstanding that these latter are steadily tending to raise their spinal column in an oblique direction, in proportion to the lengthening of their fore-limbs, which serve them as a support in walking—a form of locomotion half way between that of quadrupeds and of man. Man alone has permanently acquired an erect position, that renders the bust (= sum of head and trunk) vertical, and leaves the upper limbs definitely free from any duty connected with locomotion, thus attaining the full measure of the human stature, which is the sum of the bust and the lower limbs. Thus, we may assert that one fundamental difference between man and animals consists in this: that in animals the spinal column does not enter into the computation of stature; while in man, on the contrary, it is included in its entirety. Consequently, in man the stature assumes a characteristic and fundamental importance, because part of it (that part relating to the bust) represents, as a linear index, all the organs of vegetative life and of life in its external relations.

If we examine the human skeleton in an erect position (Fig. 9), it shows us the varying importance of the different parts of its structure, according as they are destined to protect, or simply to sustain. At the top is the skull, an enclosed bony cavity; and this arrangement indicates that it is designed to contain and protect an organ of the highest importance. By means of the occipital foramen, this cavity communicates with the vertebral canal, also rigourously closed, that is formed by the successive juxtaposition of the vertebræ. Such protective formation is in accord with the high physiological significance and the delicate structure of the organs of the central nervous system, which represent the supreme control over physiological life and over the psychic activities of life in its external relations. Below the skull, the structure of the skeleton is profoundly altered; in fact, the framework of the thorax is a sort of bony cage open at the bottom; still, the external arrangement of the bones renders them highly protective to the organs they enclose, namely, the lungs and the heart—physiological centres, whose perpetual motion seems to symbolise the rhythm and consequently the continuity of life.

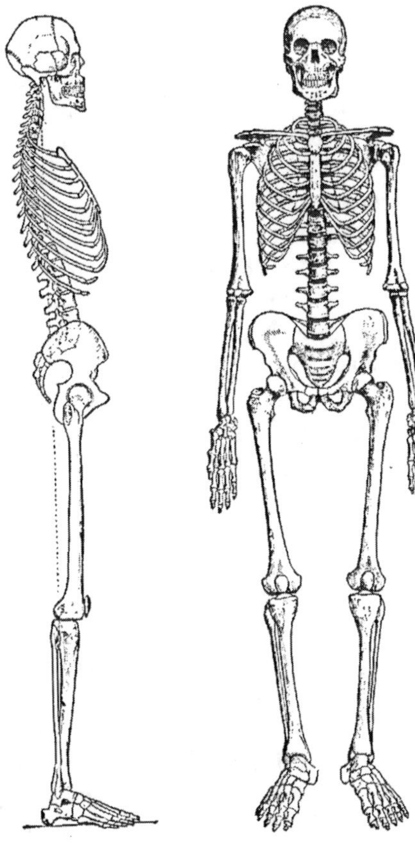

FIG. 9.

Continuing to descend, we come to a sort of hollow basin, the pelvis, which seems merely to contain, rather than protect, the abdominal organs: the intestines, kidneys, etc. Such a structure seems to be in accord with the minor physiological importance of these organs, whose function (digestion) is periodic and may be temporarily suspended, in defiance of physiological stimuli, without suspension of life. In the lower part of the skeleton, on the contrary, the arrangement between the soft and bony tissues is inverted: the long bones of the limbs constitute the inner part; and they are covered over with thick, striped muscles, organs of mechanical movement for the purpose of locomotion. Here the function of the skeleton is exclusively that of support, and in its mechanism it represents a series of levers.

Accordingly, the structure of the skeleton also shows us how the stature is composed of parts that differ profoundly in their physiological significance; life as a *complete whole*, the *living man*, is contained within the *bust*, which holds the organs of the individual, vegetative life; those of life in relation to its environment, and those of life in relation to the race, namely, the organs of reproduction.

Deprived of arms and legs, man could still live; the limbs are nothing more than appendages at the service of the bust, in all animals; they serve to *transport* the bust, that is, the part which constitutes the real living animal, which without the limbs would be as motionless as a vegetable, unable to go in pursuit of nourishment or to exercise sexual selection.

The embryos of different animals, of a dog, a bat, a rabbit and of man (as may be seen in Fig. 11) show that the fundamental part of the body is the spinal column, which *limits* and *includes* the whole animal in the process of formation.

If we next examine the embryonic development of man, as shown in Fig. 13, we may easily see how the limbs develop, at first as almost insignificant appendages of the trunk, remaining hidden within the curve of the spinal column; and even in an advanced stage of development (15th week), they still remain quite accessory parts in their relation to the whole.

Having established these very obvious principles, we may ask ourselves: of two men of equal stature, which is physiologically the more efficient? Evidently, that one of the two who has the shorter legs.

In other words, it is of fundamental importance to determine the reciprocal relation, in the stature, between the bust and the

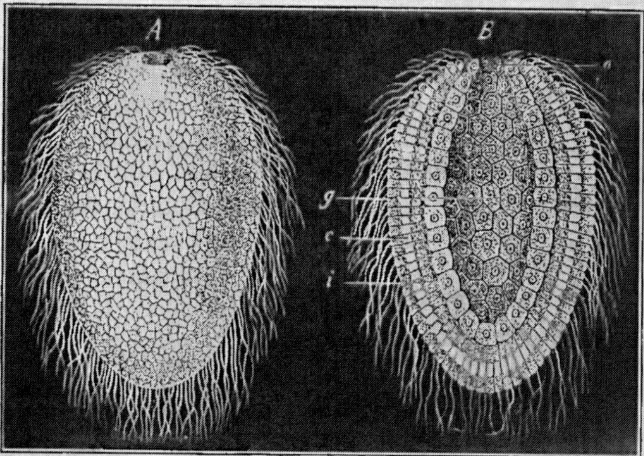

Fig. 10.—Gastrula of a sponge.

External surface. Internal section.

(Showing the inner and outer primary layers, and the mouth orifice.)

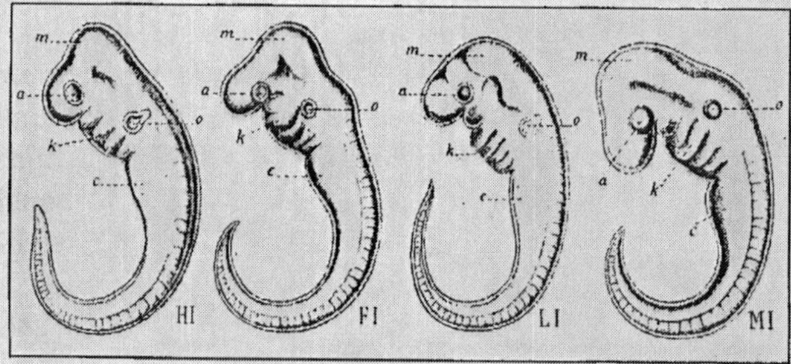

Fig. 11.

Dog. Bat. Rabbit. Man.

(From the work by E. Haeckel: *Anthropogeny.*)

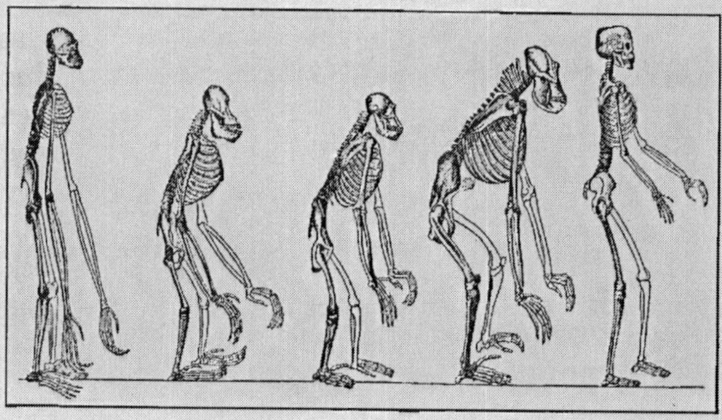

Fig. 12.

Four skeletons of anthropoid apes. Man.

lower limbs, that is, between the *height of the bust* and the *total height of the body.*

The height of the bust was called by Collignon the *essential stature,* a name that indicates the biological significance of this measurement. It may, however, also be called the sitting stature, from the method of taking the measure, which equals the vertical distance from the level on which the individual is seated to the top of his head. The other is the total stature.

Accordingly, in anthropology we may define the physiological efficiency of a man by the relation existing between his two statures,

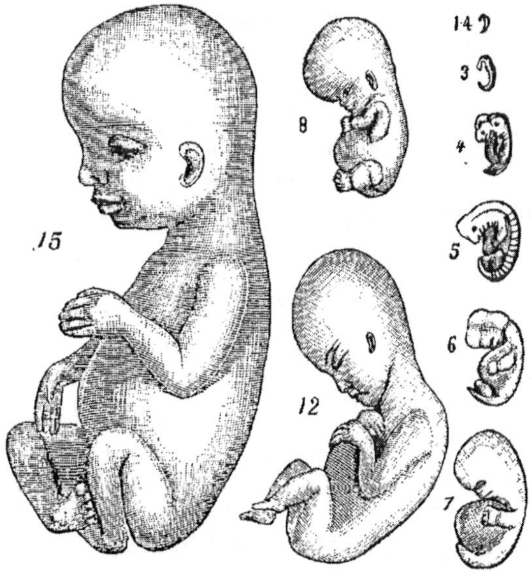

FIG. 13.
14 days, 3 weeks, 4 weeks, etc. (natural size).

the total and the essential. If we reduce the total stature (which for the sake of brevity we will call simply the *stature*) to a scale of 100, we find that the essential stature very slightly exceeds 50, oscillating between 53–54; yet it may fall to 47 and even lower, or it may rise above 56. In such cases we have individuals of profoundly diverse types, whose diversity is essentially connected with the proportional differences between the several parts of their stature.

Hence, we may distinguish the *type of stature;* understanding by this, not a measure, but a *ratio between measures,* expressed by a number; that is, "*the type of stature is the name given to the ratio between the essential stature and the total stature reduced to a scale of* 100." The *number* resulting from this ratio, since it indicates the ratio itself, is called the *index of stature* (See "Technical Lessons: on the Manner of Obtaining and Calculating the Indexes"). Manouvrier has distinguished the type with short limbs and preponderant trunk, by the name of *brachyscelous;* and those of the opposite type, that is, with long legs, by the name of *macroscelous;* reserving the term *mesatiscelous* to designate the intermediate type.

These types differ not only in the reciprocal relation between the two statures, but in all the recognised *laws of the form.* The brachyscelous type has a circumference of chest in excess of half the stature, because the trunk is more greatly developed in all its dimensions; and the total weight of the body exceeds the normal proportion in relation to the stature. The contrary holds true of the macroscelous type; their trunk, being shorter, is also narrower, and the circumference of the chest can never equal one-half the stature, while the total weight of the body is below the normal.

Canons of Form

Passing next to a consideration of the total spread of the arms, since there is an evident correspondence between the upper and lower limbs, it follows that in the brachyscelous type the total spread is less than the stature, while in the macroscelous it surpasses it to a greater or less degree, according to the grade of type; the two types consequently differ in the level reached by the wrist, when the arms are allowed to hang along the sides of the body.

This is a very interesting fact to establish, since at one time it was held that excessive length of arm was an atavistic feature, in other words, an anthropoid reminder. To-day, since the old interpretation of the direct descent from species to species has been abandoned in the light of modern theories of biological evolution, we can no longer speak of *atavistic revivals.* It is true that the anthropoid apes, as may be seen in Fig. 13, have extremely long forelimbs, and that man is characterised by the shortness of his arms, free to perform work and obedient instruments of his brain. But if it happens that certain individual men have excessively long arms, even if they should coincide with an inferior capacity for work and social adaptation, such a simple coincidence must not be interpreted by the laws of cause and effect. The modern theories of evolution tend to admit between the anthropoid apes and man, only a common origin from lower animals not yet fixed in a determined species. So that in phylogenesis men are not considered as the children or grandchildren of apes, but rather their brothers or cousins of a more or less distant degree; and their resemblance must be attributed to a parallel evolution.

Consequently, it is not possible to speak of *direct transmission* of characters.

Therefore, we must interpret an excessive length of arm, or an excessive shortness, after the same fashion, namely, in its relation to the *type of stature*, or to the established *canons of the form*—in other words, as a detail of individual human types.

Let us sum up the three canons in the following table:

Mesatisceles	Brachysceles	Macrosceles
$St = Ts$	$St > Ts$	$St < Ts$
$Ss = \frac{St}{2}$	$Ss > \frac{St}{2}$	$Ss < \frac{St}{2}$
$Ct = \frac{St}{2}$	$Ct > \frac{St}{2}$	$Ct < \frac{St}{2}$
$W = K(St - 1\text{ m.})$	$W > K(St - 1\text{ m.})$	$W < K(St - 1\text{ m.})$

From these measurements are derived certain types of *individuality* which we may now describe in detail.

The *brachyscelous type* has an excess of bust, consequently a preponderance of *vegetative life;* the great development of the abdominal organs tends to make a person of this type a *hearty eater*, a man addicted to all the pleasures of the table; his big heart, abundantly irrigating the body, keeps his complexion constantly highly coloured, if not plethoric. We can almost see this man of big paunch, corpulent, with an ample chest, fat, ruddy, coarse, and jolly; an excess of nutriment and of blood-supply are favourable to the ready accumulation of adipose tissue, and as the body constantly grows heavier it steadily becomes more difficult for the undersized legs to support it; so that inevitably this man will tend to become sedentary, and he will select a well-spread table as his favourite spot for lingering. Whatever elements of the *ideal* the world contains, will escape the attention of this type of man, who is far more ready to understand and engage in *commerce*, which leads by a practical way to the solution of the material problems of life.

In the other *type*, on the contrary, the macroscelous, the organs of vegetative life are insufficient and the central nervous system is defective. Such a man feels, even though unconsciously, that the abdominal organs are incapable of assimilating sufficient nutriment, and that his lungs, unable to take in the needed quantity of oxygen, render his breathing labourious. His small heart is inadequate for circulating the blood through the whole body, which consequently retains an habitual pallor; while the nervous system is in a constant state of excitation. We can almost see this man, so tall and thin that he seems to be walking on stilts, with pallid, hollow cheeks and narrow chest, suffering from lack of appetite and from melancholia; nervous, incapable of steady productive work and prone to dream over empty visions of poetry and art. The man of this type is quite likely to devote his entire life to a platonic love, or to conceive the idea of crowning an ideal love by committing suicide; and so long as he lives he will never succeed in escaping from the anxieties of a life that has been an economic failure.

It is interesting to examine the types of stature from different points of view: such, for example, as the height of stature, the race, the sex, the age, the social conditions, the pathological deviations, etc.

The Types of Stature According to the Height of the Total Stature.—There exists between the bust and the limbs a primary relation of a *mechanical* nature, already well known, even before Manouvrier directed the attention of anthropologists to the types of stature. When one individual is very tall and another is very short, the consequence of this fact alone is that the taller of the two has much longer limbs as compared with the shorter. This is because, according to the general laws of mechanics, the bust *grows less than the limbs* and is *subject to less variation.*

But notwithstanding this general fact, other conditions intervene to determine the comparative relations between the two portions of the stature. Indeed, Manouvrier exhibits, within his own school, specimens of equal stature but of different types; and furthermore, he notes that the inhabitants of Polynesia are of tall stature and have a long bust, while negroes, who are also of tall stature, have a short bust.

Types of Stature According to Race.—Among the characteristics of racial types, present-day anthropology has included the reciprocal proportions between the two statures. This means that the medium type in the different races is not always contained within the same limits of fluctuation in regard to stature: but some races are brachyscelous, others are macroscelous, and still again others are mesatiscelous. The most brachyscelous race is the Mongolian, prevalent in the population of China; the most macroscelous is the Australian type that once peopled Tasmania. Other races, as for example the negroid, while in a measure macroscelous, approach nearer to the mesatiscelous type, characteristic of the population of Europe. Let us examine the psycho-ethnic characters of these various peoples. The Chinese are the founders of the most ancient of all oriental civilisations, and have established themselves in a vast empire, solid and stable in its proportions, as well as in the level of its civilisation. It would seem as though the Chinese people, having accomplished the enormous effort of raising themselves to a determined civic level, were no longer capable of advancement. Individually, they have a singularly developed spirit of discipline, and are the most enduring and faithful workers; it is well known that in America the Chinese Mongolian does not fear the competition of labourers of any other race, because no others can compete with him in parsimony, in simple living, and in unremitting toil.

The Tasmanians constituted a people that was considered as having the lowest grade of civilisation among all the races on earth. Even English domination failed to adapt them to a more advanced environment, and their race was consequently scattered and destroyed.

Accordingly, we find associated with extreme macroscelia (Tasmanians) an incapacity for civic evolution; and with the corresponding extreme of brachyscelia an insuperable limitation to civic progress. Consequently, the triumph of man upon earth cannot bear a direct relation to the volume of the bust, or in other words, we cannot assume that the man most favourably endowed on the physiological side is the one who has the largest proportion of viscera. As a matter of fact, the conquering race, the race which has set no limit to the territory of its empire nor to the progress of its civilisation, is composed of white men, whose type of stature is mesatiscelous, that is to say, representative of *harmony* between its parts. This conception will serve us in establishing a fundamental principle in morphological biology: namely, that perfectibility revolves around a centre, which represents a perfect equilibrium between the various parts constituting an organism. Hence, in order to determine the deviations of the individual type, we must always start from those central data, which represent, as the case may be, *normality* or perfection.

Even among the populations of Europe, and within the Italian people themselves, fluctuations occur in the degree of mesatiscelia, approaching to a greater or less degree the eccentric forms of brachyscelia or macroscelia; and such fluctuations are an attribute of race.

We should draw a distinction between a people and a race. The term *race* refers exclusively to a biological classification, and corresponds to the *zoological species*. On the other hand, we mean by a people a group of human individuals bound together by political ties. Peoples are always made up of a more or less profound intermixture of races. It is well known that one of the most interesting and difficult problems of ethnology is that of tracing out the original types of races in peoples that represent an intermixture centuries old. Without entering too deeply into this question, which lies outside of our present purpose, it will suffice to point out that in the people of Italy it is possible to trace types of races differing from one another, yet so closely related as to render them apparently so similar that they might almost be regarded as a single race.

Now, in an anthropological study of mine on the young women of Latium, I succeeded in tracing, within the confines of that region, different racial types that show corresponding differences in degrees of mesatiscelia. Thus, for example, in Castelli Romani there exists in an almost pure state a dark-haired race, short of stature, slender, elegantly modelled in figure and in profile, and showing within the limits of mesatiscelia a brachyscelous tendency, in contrast with another race, tall, fair, massive, of coarse build, which within the limits of mesatiscelia shows a macroscelous tendency, and which is found in almost pure groups around the locality of Orte, that is, on the boundaries of Umbria. It is interesting to note the importance of researches in ethnological anthropology conducted in small centres of habitation. If it is still possible to trace out groups even approaching racial purity, they will be found only in localities offering little facility to emigration and to the consequent intermixture of races. The fact that we still find in Castelli Romani types so nearly pure, is due to the isolation of this region, which up to yesterday was still in such primitive and rare communication with the capital as to permit of the survival of brigandage. On the contrary, in localities that have attained a higher civic advancement, and in which the inhabitants are placed in favourable economic and intellectual conditions, the facilities of travel and emigration will very soon effect an alteration in the anthropological characters of the race. Hence it would be impossible, in a cosmopolitan city like Rome, to accomplish any useful studies of the sort that I accomplished in the district of Latium, and which led me to conclude that in the small and slender race of Castelli Romani we may trace the descendants of the ancient conquerors of the world: descendants that belong to one variety of the great Mediterranean race, to whom we owe the historic civilisations of Egypt, Greece and Rome.

It would seem that this race, disembarking on the coast of Latium, must have driven back, among the Apennines, the other race, blond and massive, whose pure-blooded descendants are still found in numerical prevalence at Orte, an ancient mediæval town and a natural fortress from the remotest times, through its fortunate situation on the crown of a rocky height, that easily isolates it from the surrounding country (see the ancient history of the town of Orte).

Accordingly, within the limits of mesatiscelia, it appears that the race which in early times won the victory was the more brachyscelous, *i.e.*, the one which had the larger bust, and consequently the larger brain and vital organs. In other words, within the limits of normality, brachyscelia is a physiologically favourable condition.

Variations of Type of Stature According to Social Conditions.—Independently of race, and from such a radically different point of view as that of the *social condition*, or adaptation to environment, we may still distinguish brachyscelous and macroscelous types. Brachysceles may readily be met with among the labouring classes, habituated from childhood to hard toil in a standing position, thus interfering with a free development of the long bones of the lower limbs; while the macroscelous type will be found among the aristocratic classes, whose members, spending much time sitting or reclining, give the long bones an opportunity to attain their growth (mechanical theories of stature). Without stopping to discuss the suggested causes of such differentiation in types, we may nevertheless point out that the brachyscelous type is eminently useful to society, constituting, one may say, the principal source of economic production, while the macroscelous and unproductive type settles comfortably down upon the other like a parasite. But the progress of the world is not due to the labouring class, but to the men of intellect, among whom the prevailing type is the medium, harmonic type, with mesatiscelous stature.

Types of Stature in Art.—The existence of these different individual types, which combine a definite relationship of the parts of stature with the complete image of a well-defined individuality, was long ago perceived by the eye, or rather by the delicate intuition of certain eminent artists. These immortalised their several ideals, investing now the one type and now the other with the genius of their art. Thus, for example, Rubens embodies in his Flemish canvases the brachyscelous type, robust and jovial, and usually represents him as a man of mighty appetite revelling in the pleasures of the table.

Botticelli, on the contrary, has idealised the macroscelous type, in frail, diaphanous, almost superhuman forms, that seem, as they approach, to walk, shadow-like, upon the heads of flowers, without bending them beneath their feet and without leaving any trace of their passage. Accordingly, these two great artists have admirably realised, not only the two opposite types of stature, but also the psychic and moral attributes that respectively belong to them. But it was not granted to these artists to achieve the supreme glory of representing perfect human beauty in unsurpassed and classic masterpieces. The art of Greece alone succeeded in embodying in statues which posterity must admire but cannot duplicate, the medial, normal type of the perfect man.

Variations of Stature According to Sex.—It is not always necessary to interpret the type of stature in the same sense. Even from an exclusively biological standpoint, it may lend itself to profoundly different interpretations.

Thus, for example, the type of stature varies normally according to the sex. Woman is more brachyscelous than man; but the degree of brachyscelia corresponds to a larger development of the lumbar segment of the spinal column, which corresponds to the functions of maternity.

In fact all the various segments of the spinal column show different proportions in the two sexes.

As we know, the spinal column consists of three parts; the cervical (corresponding to the neck), the thoracic (corresponding to the ribs), and the abdominal, including the os sacrum and the coccyx.

Now, Manouvrier, reducing the height of the spinal column to a scale of 100, expresses the relations of these different parts in the two sexes as follows:

Segments	Men	Women
Cervical	22.1	23.9
Thoracic	58.5	55.4
Lumbar	11.4	23.7
Sacro-coccygeal	7.9	6.7

In woman the thoracic segment is shorter and the abdominal is longer than in man; but the total sum in woman is relatively greater in proportion to the whole stature.

In a case like this we have no right to speak of a morphological or psychosocial superiority of type; nor would a fact of this sort have any weight, for example, in establishing the anthropological superiority of woman. Nevertheless, it may be asserted that, if the day comes when woman, having entered the ranks of social workers, shall prove that she is socially as useful as man, she will still be, in addition, the mother of the species, and for that reason preeminently the greater producer.

Now, it is beyond question that this indisputable superiority is in direct relation with the type of stature. But without insisting unduly on a point like this, we should note the connection between the brachyscelous type and the tendency shown by women to accumulate nutritive substances, adipose tissue; consequently, as compared with man, she is the more corpulent—as are all brachysceles as compared with macrosceles.

Types of Stature at Different Ages.—Another factor that influences the types of stature is the *age;* or rather, that biological force which we call *growth.*

Growth is not an augmentation of volume, but an alteration in form; it constitutes the *ontogenetic* evolution, the development of the individual. The child, as it grows, is transformed. If we compare the skeleton of a new-born child with that of an adult, we discover profound differences between the relative proportions of the different parts. The child's head is enormously larger than that of the adult in proportion to its stature; and similarly, the chest measure is notably greater in the child. If we wish to compare the fundamental measurements of the new-born infant with those of the adult, we get the following figures, on a basis of 100 for the total stature:

		Adult	Child at birth
Total stature = 100	Essential stature.......	52	68
	Perimeter of thorax....	50	70
	Height of head.........	10	20

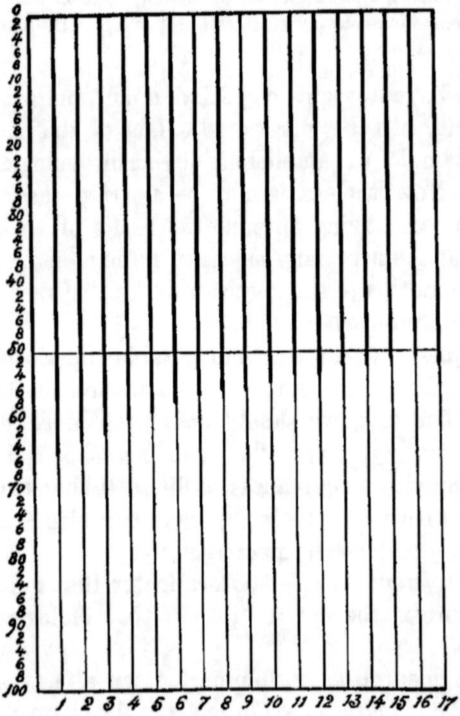

FIG. 14.

Accordingly, the child has to acquire, in the course of its growth, not only the dimensions of the adult, but the harmony of his forms; that is, it must reach not only certain determined limits of dimension, but also a certain type of *beauty*.

Among the fundamental differences between the new-born child and the adult one of the first to be noted is the reciprocal difference of proportion between the two statures. The child is ultrabrachyscelous, that is, he presents a type of exaggerated brachyscelia, calling to mind the form of the human fœtus, in which the limbs appear as little appendages of the trunk. In the course of growth, a successive alteration takes place between the reciprocal proportions of the two parts, so that the lower limbs, growing faster than the bust, tend to approach the total length of the latter. Godin has noted that during the years before puberty the lower limbs acquire greater dimensions, as compared with the bust, than are found in the fully developed individual; in other words, at this period a rapid growth takes place in the long bones of the lower limbs, and accordingly at this period of his life the individual passes through a stage of the macroscelous type. Immediately after puberty, there begins, in turn, an increase in the size of the bust, which regains its normal excess over the lower limbs, thus attaining the definite normal type of the adult individual. After the age of 17 years, by which time these metamorphoses have been completed, the individual may increase in stature, but the proportions between the parts will remain unaltered. In Fig. 14 we have a graphic representation of the relative proportions between the height of the bust and the length of limbs at different ages, the total stature being in every case reduced to 100. The upper portion of the lines represents the bust, and the lower portion the limbs, while the transverse line corresponding to the number 50 indicates one-half of the total stature. From such a table, it is easy to see how the bust, enormously in excess of the limbs at birth, gradually loses its preponderance.

It was drawn up from the following figures calculated by me:

TYPES OF STATURE ACCORDING TO AGE IN YEARS

At birth	1	2	3	4	5	6	7	8	9	10	11	12	13	14	15	16	17
68	65	63	62	60	59	57	56	55	55	54	53	53	52	52	51	51	52

Godin furnishes the following figures, relating to the type of stature at the period preceding and following puberty:

RATIO OF SITTING STATURE TO TOTAL STATURE REDUCED TO SCALE OF 100 (GODIN)

Age....	13 1/2	14	14 1/2	15	15 1/2	16	16 1/2	17	17 1/2
Ratio...	52	52	51	51	51	52	52	52	52

Hrdlicka has calculated the index of stature for a thousand white American children and a hundred coloured, of both sexes, and has obtained the following figures, some of which, based upon an adequate number of subjects, (10–13 years) are what were to be expected, while others, owing to the scarcity of subjects (under 6 and above 15 years) are far less satisfactory:

PROPORTION BETWEEN THE SITTING STATURE AND THE TOTAL STATURE

(American Children)

Age in years	Number of subjects of each age	Males, white	Females, white	Number of subjects of each age	Males, coloured	Females, coloured
3	—	—	—	1	60.8	59.5
4	—	—	—	1	—	58.9
5	2	57.4	57.3	3	57.3	57.9
6	15	56.6	57.4	5	55.9	55.6
7	38	56.3	57.2	5	54.9	55.4
8	56	55.9	56.2	13	55.1	53.3
9	62	55.2	55.9	25	54.2	54.1
10	98	54.6	54.2	12	54.9	53.7
11	99	54.0	55.0	12	52.8	53.8
12	93	53.5	54.1	10	57.7	54.0
13	86	52.9	53.8	13	52.9	51.9
14	53	52.7	54.1	7	52.3	51.8
15	20	53.1	53.7	6	51.7	53.0
16	9	52.0	55.0	2	53.0	—
17	3	52.2	54.7	—	—	—

Which goes to prove (in spite of the inaccuracies due to the numerical scarcity of coloured subjects of any age) that the females are more brachyscelous than the males; and that the blacks are more macroscelous than the whites.

The above table of indices of stature was worked out by Hrdlicka from the following measurements:

SITTING STATURE

Age in years	Males, white	Females, white	Males, coloured	Females, coloured
3	—	—	476	476
4	—	—	—	534
5	551	576	597	571
6	595	608	616	607
7	631	621	630	625
8	644	635	659	671
9	672	663	679	680
10	684	687	697	695
11	711	718	718	703
12	728	734	797	792
13	751	770	737	767
14	764	809	787	808
15	777	825	753	819
16	839	824	795	—
17	864	850	—	—

TOTAL STATURE

Age in years	Males, white	Females, white	Males, coloured	Females, coloured
3	—	—	783	839
4	—	—	—	906
5	961	1004	1044	985
6	1051	1060	1101	1091
7	1120	1086	1147	1127
8	1152	1130	1196	1260
9	1212	1187	1251	1257
10	1248	1267	1271	1295
11	1315	1304	1360	1307
12	1362	1357	1381	1467
13	1420	1431	1392	1477
14	1449	1495	1505	1559
15	1462	1535	1455	1545
16	1615	1498	1500	—
17	1654	—	—	—
18	—	1554	—	—

The following chart, prepared by MacDonald, on the growth of the total stature and the sitting stature of male white children, born in America, gives a very clear idea of the rhythm of each of the two statures. The sitting stature increases quite slowly, and its greatest rate of growth is immediately after puberty (from 15 to 17 years) (Fig. 15)

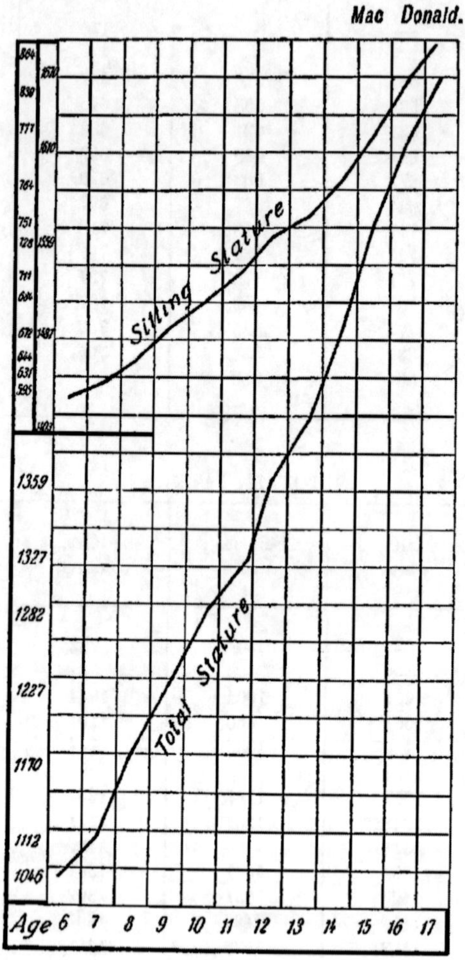

Fig. 15.

Lastly, in order to make this phenomenon still more clear, I have reproduced an illustration given by Stratz, consisting of a series of outlined bodies of children representing the proportions of the body at different stages of growth; and not only the proportions between the bust and the lower limbs, but also between the various component parts of the bust, as for instance the head and trunk. The transverse lines indicate the changes in the principal levels: the head, the mammary glands, and the bust (Fig. 16).

The different types of stature at different ages deserve our most careful consideration, yet not from the point of view already set forth regarding the different types in the fully developed individual. In the present case for instance, we cannot say of a

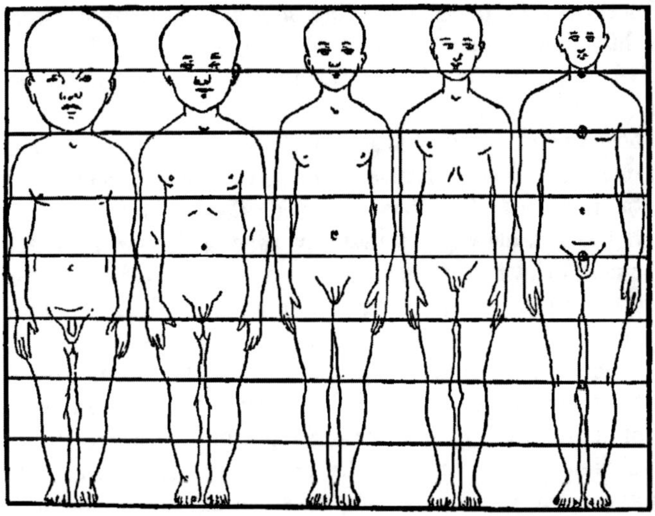

FIG. 16.

youth of sixteen that, because he is macroscelous he is a weakling as compared with a boy of ten who is brachyscelous; nor that a new-born child represents the maximum physical potentiality, because he is ultra-brachyscelous. Our standards must be completely altered, when we come to consider the various types as stages of transition between two normal forms, representing the evolution from one to the other. At each age we observe not only different proportions between the two fundamental parts of the stature, but physiological characteristics as well, biological signs of predispositions to certain determined maladies, and psychological characteristics differing from one another, and each typical of a particular age. From the purely physical and morphological point of view, for example, a child from its birth up to its second year, the period of maximum brachyscelia and consequent visceral predominance, is essentially a *feeding* animal. After this begins the development of psychic life, until finally, just before the attainment of full normal proportions, the function of reproduction is established, entailing certain definite characteristics upon the adult man or woman. In accordance with its type of stature, we see that the child from its birth to the end of the first year shows a maximum development of the adipose system together with a preponderance of the digestive organs; while the adolescent, in the period preceding puberty, shows in accordance with his macroscelous type of stature, and reduction in the relative proportion of his visceral organs, a characteristic loss of flesh.

These evolutionary changes in the course of growth having been once established, it remains for us to consider the individual variations. The alterations observed at the various ages, or rather, the notable characteristics of each age, serve as so many fundamental charts of the normal average child; and we may consider each successive type of stature, from the new-born infant to the adult man, in the same light as we do the average type of the mature mesatiscelous type. In the case of the latter, we found that both above and below the medium stature, there were a host of individual types departing more or less widely from it, and tending toward brachyscelia on the one hand and toward macroscelia on the other, thus constituting the oscillations of type in the individual varieties. Similarly, in the case of the medium type of each successive age we may find brachyscelous or macroscelous individuals whose complex personal characteristics may be compared to those already observed in the adult, and may be summed up as follows: that the macroscele is a weakling; and that the brachyscele may be, according to the degree of variation, either a robust individual or an individual that has been arrested in his morphological development, and retained the type of a younger age.

Pedagogic Considerations.—From the above conclusion, we may deduce certain principles that can be profitably applied to pedagogy, especially in regard to some of the methods suited to our guidance in the physical education of children. Let us begin with the happy comparison drawn by Manouvrier, who describes an imaginary duel with swords between a macroscelous and a brachyscelous type. The duel, according to social conventions, must take place under equal conditions: hence the seconds take rigorous care in measuring the ground, the length of the swords, and determine the number of paces permitted to the duelists. But since they have forgotten the anthropologic side, the conditions are not entirely equal: by having a longer arm, the macroscele is in the same position as though he had a longer sword; and because he has a greater development of the lower limbs, the established number of strides will take him over a greater space of ground than his adversary. Consequently, the conditions as a matter of fact are so favourable to the macroscele, that is, to the weaker individual, that the latter has a greater chance of victory. The brachyscele might, to be sure, offset this by a different manœuvre depending on his superior agility; but both he and the macroscele were trained in the same identical method, which takes into consideration only the external factor, the arms of defence, and the immutable laws of chivalry.

Well, something quite similar happens in the duel of life, which is waged in school and in the outside social environment. We ignore individual differences, and concern ourselves solely with the *means* of education, considering that they are just, so long as they are equal for all. The fencing-master, if he had been an anthropologist, might have counteracted the probability that the stronger pupil would be beaten by the weaker, by advising the brachyscele always to choose a pistol in place of a sword, or by teaching him some manœuvre entirely different from that which affords the macroscele a favourable preparation for fencing. And in the same way, it is the duty of the school-teacher to select the *arms* best adapted to lead his pupil on to victory.

That is, the teacher ought to make the anthropological study of the pupil precede his education; he should prepare him for whatever he is best adapted for, and should indicate to him the paths that are best for him to follow, in the struggle for existence.

But, aside from general considerations, we may point out that something very similar to the above-mentioned duel takes place in school when, in the course of gymnastic exercises, we make the children march, arranging them according to their total height.

We expect them to march evenly and walk, not run, yet we do not trouble to ask whether their legs are of equal length. When we wish to know which of our pupils is the swiftest runner, we start them all together, macrosceles and brachysceles alike, neglecting to measure their lower limbs, the weight of their bodies, the circumference of their chests. Then we say "bravo!" to the macroscele, that is, the pupil who is most agile but at the same time the weakest, and we encourage him in a pride based upon a physiological inferiority. When we practise exercises of endurance, we find that certain children weary sooner, suffer from shortness of breath, and frequently drop out of the contest, in which the victory is reserved for others. The latter are the brachysceles, who have big lungs and a robust heart at their disposal. In this case we say "bravo!" to the brachysceles. Then we try to arouse a noble rivalry between the two types, encouraging emulation, and holding up before the brachyscele the example of the macroscele's agility, and before the macroscele the example of the brachyscele's endurance—and perhaps we reward the two types with different medals. Such decisions by the teacher evidently have no such foundation in justice as he supposes; the diverse abilities of the two types of children are associated with the constitution of their organisms. A modern teacher ought instead to subject the brachyscelous child to exercises adapted to develop his length of limb, and the macroscelous to gymnastics that will increase the development of his chest; and he will abstain from all praise, reward, exhortation and emulation, that have for their sole basis the pupil's complete anthropological inefficiency.

"*The judgment passed by the teacher in assigning rewards and punishments is often an unconscious diagnosis of the child's anthropological personality.*"

Similar unconscious judgments are exceedingly widespread. Manouvrier gives a brilliant exposition of them in the course of his general considerations regarding the macroscelous and brachyscelous types. A brachyscelous ballet-dancer, all grace and endurance in her dancing, thanks to the strength of her lungs, can never be imitated in her movements by a macroscelous, angular woman, with legs ungracefully long. The latter, on the contrary, wrapped in a mantle, may become the incarnation of a stately matron, extending her long arms in majestic gestures. Yet it often happens that the stately actress envies and seeks to imitate the grace of the dancer, while the latter envies and emulates the grave dignity of the actress.

In any private drawing-room the same thing occurs, in the shape of different advantages distributed among persons of different types. *There are some gestures that are inimitable because they are associated with a certain anthropologic personality.* Every one in the world ought to do the things for which he is specially adapted. It is the part of wisdom to recognise what each one of us is best fitted for, and it is the part of education to *perfect* and *utilise* such predispositions. Because education can *direct* and *aid* nature, but can never transform her.

Manouvrier is constantly observing how the macroscelous and brachyscelous types are adapted to *different kinds* of social labour; thus, for example, the macroscele will make an excellent reaper, because of the wide sweep of his arms, and he is well adapted to be a tiller of the soil; while the brachyscele, on the contrary, will succeed admirably in employment that requires continuous and energetic effort, such as lifting weights, hammering on an anvil, or tending the work of a machine.

In the social evolution now taking place, the services of the macrosceles are steadily becoming less necessary; intensive modern labour requires the short, robust arm of the brachyscele. Such considerations ought not to escape the notice of the teacher, who sees in the boy the future man. He has the high mission of preparing the duelists of life for victory, by now correcting and again aiding the nature of each. And the first point of departure is undoubtedly to learn to know, in each case *le physique du role.*

Abnormal Types of Stature and General Principles of Biological Ethics

Abnormal types of stature in their relation to moral training.—Macroscelia and brachyscelia in pathologic individuals (De Giovanni's hyposthenic and hypersthenic types).—Types of stature in emotional criminals and in parasites.—Extreme types of stature among the extrasocial classes: Nanism and gigantism.

Let us start from a picture traced in the course of the preceding lessons; the types of stature as related to race. The Chinese, being brachyscelous, ought to be hearty eaters; instead, they are the most sparing people on earth. Such parsimony, equally with religion and social morality, may be considered as a racial obligation. The whole life of the Chinese is founded upon duty:

fidelity to religion, to the laws, to the spirit of discipline, to the spirit of *sacrifice*, which always finds the Chinese citizen ready to die for his ethics and for his country, are strong characteristics of these invincible men. Their whole education rests solely upon a *mnemonic* basis; and their laws, which are highly democratic, make it possible for anyone to rise to the highest circles, provided he can pass the competitive examinations. In other words, the laws aid in the *natural* selection of the really strong, and regard favouritism as a crime against the State. On such individual and national virtues is founded the survival of the race and of the massive empire. If tomorrow the Chinese should renounce his creed, become a *glutton*, a pleasure-seeker, and follow the instincts of nature, he would be advancing in mighty strides on the path that leads to death. Accordingly, what we call *virtue* may have a biologic basis, and represent the *active force* that tends to correct the defects of nature.

We can conceive of a *type* of man, whose *life* is associated with sacrifice; and whose path of evolution is necessarily limited, first because his personality is imperfect, secondly because a part of his individual energy is necessarily expended in *conquering*, or if you prefer, in *correcting* his own nature. Evolution ought to be free; but instead, such a type is necessarily in bondage to *duty*, which stops its progress. Accordingly, the civilisation of China remains the civilisation of China; it cannot invade the world.

The European on the contrary has no such racial virtues; whatever virtues he has are associated with transitory forms of civilisation, and are ready to succeed one another on the pathway of unlimited progress. The race can permit itself the luxury of not being virtuous on its own account; its biological conditions are so perfect, that they have reached the *fullness of life*. If *virtue* is the goal of the Chinese, happiness is the goal of the European. The *race* may indulge freely in the joys of living; and dedicate its efforts solely to the *unlimited progress of social civilisation*, and to the conquest of the entire earth.

The Tasmanian, on the other hand, sparing by nature, lacking sufficient development of the organs of vegetative life, avoids every form of civilisation, and precipitates himself, an unconscious victim, upon the road to death. His natural parsimony, the scantiness of his needs, have prevented him from ever feeling that *spur* toward struggle and conquest which has its basis in the necessities of life. Neither virtue, nor felicity, nor civilisation, nor survival were possible to that race, whose extermination began with the first contact with European civilisation. Hence we may draw up a table that will serve to make clear certain fundamental ideas that may prove useful guides along our pedagogic path:

Biological types	Brachysceles	Mesatisceles	Macrosceles
Races and peoples...	Chinese.	Europeans.	Tasmanians.
Civilisation.........	Stable civilisation, but limited.	Changeable civilisation, with unlimited powers of evolution.	Outside the pale of civilisation.
Psycho-moral types..	High ideal of virtue and sacrifice.	Happiness.	Insensibility.

We ought to strive for the supreme result of producing men who will be *happy;* always keeping clearly before us the idea that the happy man is the one who may be spared the effort of thinking of himself, and dedicate *all* his energies to the unlimited progress of human society. The preoccupation of *virtue*, the *voluntary sacrifice* are in any case forces turned back upon themselves, that expend upon the individual energies that are lost to the world at large; nevertheless, such *standards of virtue* are necessary for certain inferior types. There exist, besides, certain individuals in rebellion against society, outcasts whose lives depend upon the succor of the strong, or may be destroyed by their adverse intervention, but in any case have ceased to depend upon the will of the individuals themselves.

Between two inferior types the one with the better chances is the one with the larger chest development; apparently, in the case of biological deviations, *melius est abundare quam deficere.*

Accordingly, let us draw up a chart. Human perfectionment tends toward *harmony.* If we wish to represent this by some symbolic or intuitive sign, we could not do so by a mere line; because perfection is not reached by the quantitative increase of favourable parts; robustness, for instance, cannot be indefinitely increased by augmenting the degree of brachyscelia; nor can intelligence be increased by augmenting the volume of the head; but perfection is approached, in the race and in the individual, through a *central harmony*. It is accordingly in the direction of this centre that progress is made; and whoever departs furthest from this centre, departs furthest from perfection, becomes more eccentric, more untypical, and at the same time also loses the psycho-moral potentiality to attain the highest civic perfection.

In Fig. 17, we have a graphic representation in three concentric circles.

Let us begin by considering the middle circle, that of the abnormals. Here we have inscribed, as psycho-moral and physio-pathological traits, abstemiousness, *anti-social tendency, predisposition to disease.* Abstemiousness represents a *corrective*, without which the individual tends toward an anti-social line of action and contracts diseases. Abstemiousness is present within the circle of abnormal human beings, as a more or less attainable ideal; but it must be regarded as the pedagogic goal, when the problem arises of educating an untypical class of individuals. In other words, there are certain abnormal individuals who, if they are not to turn out criminals, must exercise a *violent corrective influence over their psycho-physical personality*, and they must be trained to do so; for it is an influence unknown to the normal man, who not only has no inclination to commit a crime, but recoils from doing so, and on the contrary may arise to degrees of moral perfection that are inconceivable to the abnormal man. Consequently, in order to maintain a relatively healthy condition, certain abnormal individuals are constrained to submit themselves to a *severe hygienic régime throughout their entire life;* a régime useless to the normal man, who indulges naturally in all the pleasures which are consistent with the full measure of physical health, and which remain forever unknown, and unattainable, to the abnormal individual organically predisposed to disease.

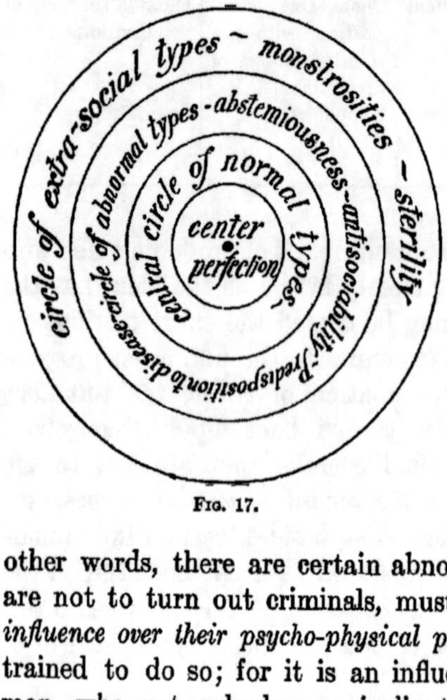

FIG. 17.

Such self-restraint we may call the *culte of virtue*, a necessity only to certain categories of men; and we may also call it the *virtue of inferior individuals.* It applies and is limited almost wholly to the individual.

Meanwhile, there is the normal man's high standard of virtue, which is an indefinite progress toward moral perfection; but the path it follows lies wholly in the direction of society collectively, or toward the biological perfectionment of the species. In life's attainment of such a triumph, man both feels and is *happy* rather than *virtuous.*

The separation between the circles, or rather between the different categories of indviduals, the normal and the abnormal, is not clear-cut. There always exist certain imperceptibly transitional forms, between normality and abnormality; and furthermore, since no one of us is ideally normal, no one who is not abnormal in *some one thing,* it follows that this "some one thing" must be corrected by the humbling practice of self-discipline. At the same time it is rare for a man to be abnormal in all parts of his personality; in such a case he would be outside the social pale, a monstrosity; the high, collective virtues can, therefore, even if in a limited degree, illuminate the moral life of the abnormals. St. Paul felt that it "is hard to kick against the pricks"; and the *picciotto* of the Camorra feels that he is obeying a society that protects the weak.

It is a question of *degree.* But such a conception must lead to a separation in *school* and in method of education, for the two categories of individuals.

Abnormal Types According to De Giovanni's Theory

Certain very important pathological types have been distinguished and established in Italy by De Giovanni, the Paduan clinical professor who introduced the anthropological method into clinical practice. Through his interesting studies, he has to-day fortunately revived the ancient theory of temperaments, explaining them on a basis of physio-pathological anthropology.

De Giovanni distinguishes two *fundamental types;* the one *hyposthenic* (weak), the other *hypersthenic* (over-excitable); these two types obey the following rules: morphologically considered, the hyposthenic type has a total spread of arms greater than the total stature and a chest circumference of less than half the stature: these data alone are enough to tell us that the type in question is *macroscelous;* as a matter of fact, the chest is narrow and the abdomen narrower still. De Giovanni says that, owing to the scant pulmonary and abdominal capacity the organs of vegetative life are inadequate; the heart is too small and unequal to its function of general irrigator of the organism; the circulation is consequently sluggish, as shown by the bluish net-work of veins, indicating some obstacle to the flow of blood.

The type is predominantly lymphatic, the muscles flaccid, with a tendency to develop fatty tissues, but very little muscular fibre; there is a predisposition to bronchial catarrh, but above all to pulmonary tuberculosis. This *hyposthenic type,* which corresponds to the *lymphatic temperament* of Greek medicine, is in reality a macroscelous type somewhat exceeding normal limits and therefore physiologically inefficient and feeble.

The following is De Giovanni's description:

Morphologically.—Deficient chest capacity, deficient abdominal capacity, disproportionate and excessive development of the limbs; insufficient muscularity.

Physiologically.—Insufficient *respiration,* and consequent scanty supply of oxygen (a form of chronic asphyxia of internal origin), insufficient *circulation,* because the small heart sends the blood through the arteries at too low a pressure; and this blood, insufficiently oxygenated, fails to furnish the tissues with their normal interchange of matter, and therefore the assimilative functions in general all suffer; finally, the venous blood is under an excessive pressure in the veins, the return flow to the heart is rendered difficult and there results a tendency to venous hyperemia (congestion of the veins), even in the internal organs. This is accompanied by what De Giovanni calls *nervous erethism* (in contradistinction to *torpor*), which amounts to an abnormal state of the central nervous system, causing predisposition to insanity and to various forms of neurasthenia (rapid exhaustion, irritability).

This type is especially predisposed to maladies of the respiratory system, subject to bronchial catarrh recurring annually, liable to attacks of bronchitis, pleurisy, and pneumonia, and easily falls victim to *pulmonary tuberculosis.*

Here are a few cases recorded by De Giovanni.* (It must be

* De Giovanni, *Op. cit.*, p. 236. Cases referring to the first morphologic combination.

borne in mind that the total spread of the arms, *Ts*, ought to equal the total stature, *St.* The measurements are given in centimetres.)

F. M.—*St* 147; *Ts* 151.—Extremely frail; frequent attacks of hemorrhage of the nose; habitually pale and thin. Certain disproportions of the skeleton, hands and feet greatly enlarged; extreme development of the subcutaneous veins. *Pulmonary tuberculosis.*

A. M.—*St* 161; *Ts* 193.—Nervous erethism; from the age of twelve subject to laryngo-bronchial catarrh; every slight illness accompanied by fever; habitually thin. *Pulmonary tuberculosis.*

F. M.—*St* 150; *Ts* 150; *Ct* 67.—Lymphatic, torpid, almost chronic bloating of the abdomen. Enlargement of the glands; scars from chilblains on hands and feet. *Primary tuberculosis of the glands, secondary tuberculosis of the lungs.*

A. M.—*St* 172; *Ts* 179.—Extreme emaciation, heart singularly small. *Chronic bronchial catarrh.*

If it is important for us, as educators, to be acquainted with this type in the adult state, it ought to interest us far more during its *ontogenesis,* that is, during the course of its individual evolution.

Since, in the process of growth, man passes through different *stages,* due to alteration in the relative proportions of the different organs and parts, it follows that this hyposthenic type correspondingly alters its *predisposition to disease.* Its final state, manifested by various defects of development, gave unmistakable forewarnings at every period of growth.

In early infancy symptoms of rickets presented themselves, and then disappeared, like an unfulfilled threat: dentition was tardy or irregular; the head was large and with persistent nodules. This class, as a type, is weak, sickly, easily attacked by infectious diseases, tracoma, purulent otitis.

When the first period of growth is passed, *glandular* symptoms begin, with liability to sluggishness of the lymphatic glands (scrofula) or persistent swelling of the lymphatic ganglia of the neck. This is supplemented by bronchial catarrh, recurring year after year; finally intestinal catarrh follows, accompanied in most cases by loss of appetite.

Such conditions are influenced very slightly or not at all by medical treatment.

During the period of *puberty, cardiopalmus* (palpitation of the heart) is very likely to occur, often accompanied by frequent and abundant epistasis, or by the occurrence of slight fever in the evening, and by blood-stained expectorations, suggestive of tuberculosis. The patient is pale (oligohæmic), very thin, and shoots up rapidly (preponderant growth of the limbs); he is subject to *muscular asthenia* (weakness, exhaustibility of the muscles) and to various forms of nervous excitability.

These symptoms also (some of them so serious as to arouse fears, at one time of rickets and at another of tuberculosis), are all of them quite beyond the reach of medical treatment (tonics, etc.).

Now, a fact of the highest importance, discovered by De Giovanni, is that of *spontaneous corrections*, that is, the development of *compensations* within the organism, suited to mitigate the anamolous conditions of this type, and hence the *possibility of an artificial intervention* capable of calling forth such compensations. Such intervention cannot be other then *pedagogic;* and it should consist in a rational system of gymnastics, designed in one case to develop the heart, in another the chest, in another to modify the intestinal functions or to stimulate the material renewal of the body; while every form of over-exertion must be rigorously avoided.

"I think that we should regard as an error not without consequences what may be seen any day in the gymnasiums of the public schools, where pupils differing in bodily aptitude, and with different gymnastic capacity and different needs are with little discernment subjected to the same identical exercises, for the same length of time.

"And day by day we see the results: there are some children who rebel outright against the required exercise which they fear and from which they cannot hope to profit, because it demands an effort beyond their strength. Some have even been greatly harmed; so that one after another they abandon these bodily exercises, which if they had been more wisely directed would assuredly have bettered their lot.

"Experience also teaches that one pupil may be adapted to one kind of exercise and another to another kind. Accordingly a really physiological system of gymnastics requires that *those*

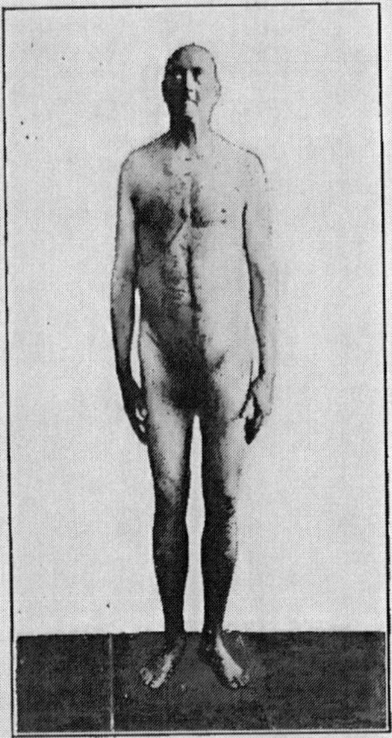

Fig. 18.

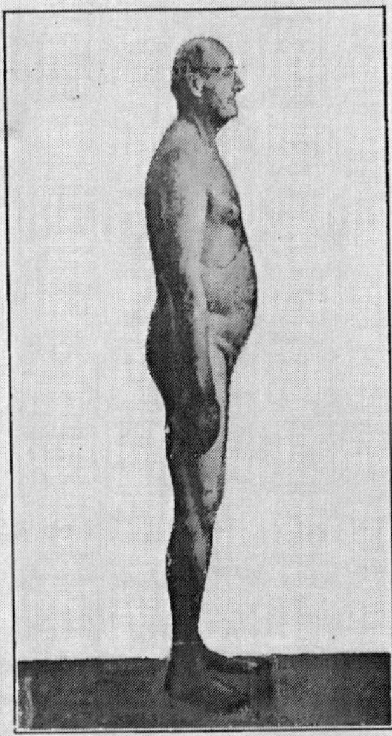

Fig. 19.

Brachyscelous type (from Viola).

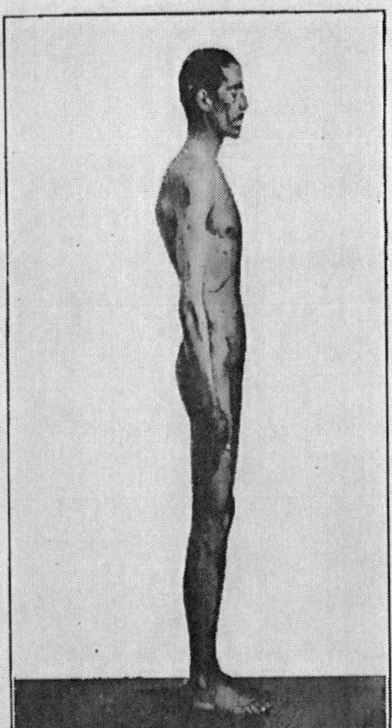

Fig. 20.

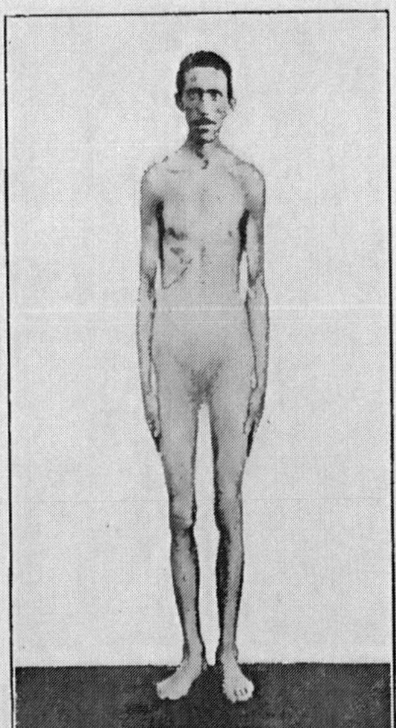

Fig. 21.

Macroscelous type (from Viola).

movements and those exercises which are least easily performed should be practised according to special methods, until they have strengthened the less developed functions, without ever causing illness or producing harmful reactions.*"

So that the final results are an improvement in the morphological proportions of the organism, and consequently a correction and improvement in the relative liability to disease.

The other fundamental pathological type described by De Giovanni is the *hypersthenic* (second morphological combination), corresponding in part to the *sanguine* temperament of Greek medicine, and in part to the *bilious* temperament. In this type the total spread of the arms is generally less than the stature, and the perimeter of the chest notably exceeds one-half the stature. Consequently we are dealing with the *brachyscelous* type.

This type has a greatly developed thorax, a *large heart,* an excessive development of the intestines; hence he is a hearty eater, subject to an over-abundance of blood; he is over-nourished, the ruddy skin reveals an abundant circulation, there is an excess of adipose tissue and a good development of the striped muscles. Such a constitution accompanies an *excitable, impulsive, violent* disposition, and conduces to diseases of the heart. "This type is characterised in general by robustness and a liability to disorders of the central circulatory system."†

But there are still other forms of disease that await the individuals of this class, such for example as disorders affecting the interchange of organic matter (diabetes, gout, polysarcia = obesity) and attacks of an apoplectic nature. In the case of acute illness individuals of this class suffer from excess of blood and may be relieved by being bled. They are readily liable to bloody excretions.

Here are a few cases illustrating this *morphological combination,* which is characterised by an exorbitant chest development (it must be borne in mind that the circumference of the thorax, *Ct,* should equal one-half the stature, *St*).

P. A.—*St* 156; *Ct* 93.—Endocarditis; insufficient heart-action.

Z. C.—*St* 168; *Ct* 95.—Cerebral hyperemia of an apoplectic nature. Hypertrophy of the left ventricle of the heart. *Polysarcous* (gluttonous) *eater.*

* De Giovanni, *Op. cit.*

† De Giovanni, *Op. cit.*

B. G.—*St* 166; *Ct* 104.—Diabetic, obese, subject to diabetic ischialgia (neuralgia), frequent recurrence of gravel in the urine. *Tendency to excesses of the table.*

D. G.—*St* 160; *Ct* 96.—Polysarcia, the first symptoms of which appeared in early youth. At the age of sixteen, suffered from all the discomforts of obesity. Shows atheroma (fatty degeneration) of the aorta, irregular heart-action, hypertrophy and enlargement of the heart.

In this brachyscelous type it may happen either that the whole trunk (that is, both the thoracic and abdominal cavities) is in excess, or else that the excessive development is confined to the abdomen. This latter case is very frequent, and may easily be found even in early childhood. Such children are hearty eaters, are very active and, for this reason, the pride and joy of their parents. Nevertheless, there are many signs that should give warning of constitutional defects; constant digestive disturbances (diarrhœa), frequent headaches, pains in the joints, apparently of a rheumatic character, tendency to pains in the liver which is excessively enlarged; excess of adipose tissue; a tendency to fall ill very easily, of maladies that are almost always happily overcome (but the truly robust person is not the one who recovers from illness, but the one who *does not become ill*), and finally an excessively lively disposition, irritability and above all, *impulsiveness.*

Such individuals ought, like the macrosceles, to live under the necessary and perpetual tyranny of a hygienic régime, adapted to correct or to diminish the morbid predispositions associated with the organism. A special dietetic, a regular hydrotherapic treatment, a moderate gymnastic exercise designed to *direct* the child's motive powers, and thus to prepare the *man* for that form of existence to which it is necessary for him to subject himself, if he does not wish to shorten his own life, or at least his period of activity—all these things are so many duties which the *school* ought in great part to assume.

In this way we have briefly considered the *abnormal* types of brachyscelia and macroscelia, which by their very constitution are *predisposed* to incur special and characteristic forms of disease, which may be avoided only by subjecting the organism to a special hygienic regimen. *Men cannot all live according to the same rules.*

Types of Stature in Criminals

In these latter times, some very recent researches have been made by applying De Giovanni's method to the anthropological study of criminals, especially through the labours of Dr. Boxich. He has found that the great majority of parasitic criminals, thieves for example, are macrosceles. They exhibit the stigmata already revealed by Lombroso: great length of the upper limbs, with elongated hands; furthermore, a narrow chest and a small heart, insufficient for its vital function; such individuals are singularly predisposed to pulmonary tuberculosis, and hence in their physical constitution they are already stamped as organisms of inferior biological value—having little endurance and almost no ability as producers—consequently they are forced to live as they can, that is like parasites, profiting by the work of others. On the contrary, the great majority of criminals of a violent character present the brachyscelous type: the thorax is greatly developed, the heart hypertrophic, the arterial circulation superabundant. This class of criminals, including a large proportion of murderers, have a special tendency to *act from impulse*, corresponding to their large heart which sends an excess of blood pulsing violently to the brain, obscuring the psychic functions; or, in the speech of the people, such a man has "lost his reason," "the light goes from the eyes when the blood goes to the brain."

Here are some notes regarding these two different types: we will select as measures of comparison the stature and the weight, bearing in mind that in the macrosceles the weight is scanty and that the opposite is true of the brachysceles, while normally there ought to be a pretty close correspondence betwen the weight in kilograms and the centimetres of stature over and above one metre.

Types of Non-violent Criminals (*Parasites*)

Case No. 24.—*St.* 168; *Wt.* 56. Farm steward, three years' sentence for theft. Pallid complexion, visible veins, scant muscles. Heart small and weak, pulse feeble and slow.

Case No. 34.—*St.* 175; *Wt.* 61. Baker, comfortable financial circumstances, has received a number of sentences for theft, amounting altogether to ten years. Is twenty-four years of age. Cyanosis of the extremities (bluish tinge, due to excessive venous circulation). Cardiac action feeble. Scant muscles.

Case No. 43.—*St.* 156; *Wt.* 51. Peasant. Straitened circumstances. Four years' sentence for theft. Rejected by the army board for defective chest measurement. Dark complexion. Extensive acne. Scant muscles. Bronchial catarrh. Has had hemoptysis (spitting of blood). Cardiac action weak. Pulse very feeble.

Case No. 52.—*St.* 173; *Wt.* 66. Book-binder. Prosperous circumstances. Four years' sentence or thereabouts, for theft; age, twenty-four. Conjunctivitis and blepharitis from early childhood. Frontal and parietal nodules prominent. Muscles scant; cardiac action weak; lymphatic glands of the neck enlarged.

The following is an example of the typical thief:*

St. 162; *Wt.* 46.—Exceedingly small heart, feeble cardiac action. Suffers from chronic bronchial catarrh. Cranial nodules very prominent. Began as a small child to steal in his own home, and since then has received sentence after sentence for theft, up to his present age of twenty-nine.

Types of Violent Criminals (*Assault, Mayhem, Homicide*)

Case No. 54.—*St.* 157; *Wt.* 62. Peasant. Good financial circumstances. Condemned to thirty years in prison for homicide. Well-developed muscles. Blood vessels congested. Strong heart action; the pulsation extends as far down as the epigastrium. Ample pulse.

Case No. 60.—*St.* 156; *Wt.* 70. Shoemaker. Bad financial circumstances. Condemned to fifteen years' imprisonment for homicide, after having been previously convicted three times for theft. The chest circumference exceeds one-half the stature by 11 centimetres. Subject to frequent pains in the head. Good muscles. Corpulent. Full pulse. (It should be noticed that the florid complexion, accompanying this type of stature, persists in spite of straitened circumstances!)

Case No. 85.—*St.* 168; *Wt.* 70. Turner in iron. Comfortable circumstances. Sentenced to thirty years in prison after one previous conviction for criminal assault. Ruddy complexion. Veins not visible. Abdomen very prominent. Gastrectasia

*Boxich, *Contribution to the Morphological, Clinical and Anthropological Study of delinquents.*

(dilation of the stomach). Entire cardiac region protuberant. Laboured breathing. Cardiac action abundant.

Hence we perceive, in the etiology of crime, the importance of the organic factor, connected directly with the lack of harmony in the viscera and their functions, and consequently accompanied by special morbid predispositions.

As a result of this line of research, criminality and pathology are coming to be studied more and more in conjunction. For that matter, it was already observed by Lombroso that in addition to the various external malformations found in criminals, there were also certain anomalies of the internal organs, and a widespread and varied predisposition to disease. In short, his statistics reveal a prevalence of cardiac maladies and of tuberculosis in criminals, as well as a great frequency of diseases of the liver and the intestines.

Extreme or Infantile Types, Nanism and Gigantism, Extra-social Types

Whenever the disproportion between the bust and the limbs surpasses the extreme normal limits, the whole individual reveals a complex departure from type. Thus, for example, in connection with extreme *brachyscelia,* there exists a characteristic form of nanism (dwarfishness), called *achondroplastic nanism,* in which, although the bust is developed very nearly within normal limits, the limbs on the contrary are arrested in their growth so as to remain permanently nothing more than *little appendages* of the trunk. This calls to mind the fœtal form of the new-born child, and the resulting type, because of this morphological coincidence, is classed among the infantile types.

Achondroplastic nanism is associated with a *pathological* deformity due to fœtal rickets. It is not only the child after birth, but the fœtus also which, during its intrauterine life, may be subject to diseases. Rickets (always a localised disease, usually attacking some part of the skeleton) in this case fastens upon the enchondral cartilages of the long bones. As we know, the long bones are composed of a body or *diaphysis* and of extremities or articular heads, the *epiphyses.* Now, these different parts, which form in the adult a continuous whole, remain separate throughout the fœtal and the immediate post-natal period: so that the heads of the humerus and the femur, for example, in the case of the new-born child, are found to be joined to the *diaphysis* by cartilages (destined to ossify later on), which are the chief seat of growth of the bones in the direction of length. Well, in these cases of pre-natal rickets, the union of the bony segments takes place prematurely, and since the bones can hardly grow at all in length, they develop in thickness, and the result is that the limbs remain very short and stocky. Meanwhile the bust, the bones of which have in no way lost their power of growth, develops normally.

Now, these dwarfs, who have abundant intelligence, because they have the essential parts of stature in their favour, constituted the famous jesters of the mediæval courts, whose misfortune served to solace the leisure hours of royalty. Paolo Veronese went so far as to introduce a dwarf buffoon, of the achondroplastic type, into his famous painting, *The Wedding at Cana.*

Conversely, in connection with an exaggerated *macroscelia,* we have gigantism.

Ordinarily, a giant has a bust that is not greatly in excess of normal dimensions. The limbs, on the contrary, depart extremely from the normal limits, in an exaggerated growth in the direction of length: so much so that the bodies of giants present the appearance of small busts moving around on stilts.

Nevertheless, many different forms of gigantism occur. The pathology of this phenomenon is quite complex; but we can not concern ourselves with it here. It is a scientific problem of no immediate utility to our pedagogic problems. Dwarfs and giants, whatever their type and their pathological etiology, constitute extra-social individuals, who have been at all times excluded from any possibility of adaptation to useful labour, and employed, whether in the middle ages or in the twentieth century, to a greater or less extent as a source of amusement to normal beings, because of their grotesque appearance, either at court or in the theatres, or in moving pictures, or (in the case of giants) as figures suited to adorn princely or imperial gateways. These individuals are as completely independent of the social conditions of the environment in which they were born as if they were extraneous to humanity. In relation to the species, they are *sterile.*

From the biological side, a consideration of these types serves merely as an illustration of an important law: *the essential part of the organism* (the vertebral column) is *less variable* than the accessory parts (the limbs).

Summary of the Types of Stature

According to the relative development of bust and limbs we have distinguished three types, the macrosceles, the brachysceles and the mesatisceles, within their respective limits of oscillation.

Since the type of stature gives us a proportion between the different parts of an individual, it constitutes a fundamental criterion for a morphological judgment of the personality. That is, it leads to a diagnosis of the individual constitution, with which are associated not only the "character" but also certain predispositions to disease.

A knowledge of these *types* shows us the necessity we educators are under of taking into consideration the individual pupils, each of whom may have separate needs, tendencies and forms of development; and of demanding separate *schools*, in which even the *methods of moral education* must differ. Because men are not only not all adapted to the same forms of work, but they are not even all adapted to the same standards of *morality*. And since it is our duty to assume the task of aiding the *biological development* and the *social adaptation* of the new generations, it will also be part of our task to *correct* defective organisms, and at the same time to correct the types of mental and moral inferiority.

In the following chart we may summarise the points of view from which we have studied the types of stature:

SYNOPTIC CHART

Types of stature	Macrosceles.......		long legs, short bust.
	Brachysceles......		short legs, long bust.
Variations in types of stature	Normal	Race	Mongols (brachysceles).
			Tasmanians (macrosceles).
			Dark Mediterranean race (mesatisceles tending toward brachyoscelia).
			Blond race (mesatisceles tending toward macroscelia).
		Sex	Woman more brachyscelous.
			Man more macroscelous.
		Age	Childhood brachyscelous.
			Old age macroscelous.

SYNOPTIC CHART—*Continued*

Variations in types of stature	Pathologically abnormal.	De Giovanni's hyposthenic types.	Macrosceles predisposed to tuberculosis.
		De Giovanni's hypersthenic types.	Brachysceles predisposed to diseases of the heart.
	Criminals.	Macrosceles.........	parasites.
		Brachysceles........	violent.
	Infantile types	Achondroplastic nanism.	
		Gigantism.	

Summary of the Scientific Principles Illustrated in the Course of our Discussion

Biological Laws.—a. Growth is not only an augmentation in volume, but also an evolution in form.

b. The more essential parts vary less than the accessory parts in the course of their transformations.

The Index.—The index is the mathematical relation between the measurements belonging to the same individual, and as such it gives us an idea of the *form;* since the form is determined by the relations between the various parts constituting the whole.

The Stature

While the figure and the type of stature tend to delineate the *individual* considered by himself, the different measurements considered separately may guide us in our study of individuals in their relation to the race and the environment.

Among the measurements of the *form,* we will limit ourselves to a study of the *stature* and the *weight,* which serve to give us respectively the linear index of development and the volumetric estimate of the body taken as a whole. We shall reserve the study of the other measurements, such as the total spread of the arms and the perimeter of the thorax, until we come to the analytical investigation of the separate parts of the body (limbs, thorax).

The *stature* is expressed by a *linear measure* determined by the distance intervening in a vertical direction between the plane on which the individual is standing in an erect position and the top of his head.

It follows that the *stature* is a measurement determined by the *erect position;* on the other hand, when a man is in a recumbent position, what we could determine would be the *length* of body, which is not identical with the stature.

In fact, a man on foot, resting his weight upon articulations that are elastic, and therefore compressible, is a little shorter than when he is recumbent.

If we examine the skeleton (see Fig. 9), we discover that the single synthetic measure that constitutes the stature results from a sum of parts that differ greatly from one another. To be specific, it is composed of the long and short bones of the lower limbs; of flat bones, such as the pelvis and the skull; of little spongy bones, such as the vertebræ; all of which bones and parts obey different laws in the course of their growth. Furthermore, intervening between these various bones are *soft*, elastic parts, known as the articulations, which, starting from below, succeed each other in the following order:

1. *Calcaneo-astragaloid*, between the *calcaneus* and the superimposed *astragalus*.
2. *Tibio-astragaloid*, between the *astragalus* and the superimposed *tibia*.
3. Of the *knee*, between the *tibia* and the *femur*.
4. Of the *hip*, between the *femur* and the *os innominatum*.
5. *Sacro-iliac*, between the *os iliacum* and the *sacrum*.
6. *Sacro-vertebral*, between the *sacrum* and the *last lumbar vertebra*.
7. Of the *vertebræ*, consisting of 23 intervertebral disks, that is to say interposed between the vertebræ, which include the following: 5 *lumbar*, 12 *thoracic*, 7 *cervical*.
8. *Occipito-atloid*, between the first cervical vertebra, called the *atlas* and the *os occipitale* of the cranium.

Accordingly, there are *thirty* articulations in all; and of these, 23 are the intervertebral disks, which constitute, taken together, a fourth part of the complex height of the vertebral column.

Furthermore, the height of the body cannot be considered simply the *sum* of the component parts, since these are not superimposed in a straight line. As a matter of fact, if we examine the vertebral column, we see that it is not straight as in the case of animals, but exhibits certain curves that are characteristic of the *human species*, and must be taken into consideration in their relation to the *erect position*. In fact, the vertebral column presents two curvatures, the one *lumbar*, and the other *cervical*, which together give it the form of an S. These curvatures are *acquired* along with the *erect position*, and are not innate; one of the points of difference between the skeleton of the new-born child and that of the adult is precisely this, that the former has a *straight* vertebral column.

A fact of no small importance to note, since in the *course of growth* a certain *determined* form of normal curve, and no other, ought to establish itself; otherwise, *abnormal deviations* in the vertebral column will become established. And for the very reason that it is *plastic* and *destined* to assume a *curve*, the vertebral column may very easily be forced into exaggerating or departing from its morphological destiny. In such a case, the resulting stature would be *inferior* to what it should normally have been.

Accordingly, the stature is the resultant of the sum of *anatomical parts* and of *morphological conditions*.

Hence it is a *linear index* not only of *biological man*, that is, of man considered in relation to his racial limitations; but also of social man, that is, of man as he has developed in the struggle for adaptation to his environment.

The limits of stature, according to race. Stature is an anthropological datum of great *biological* value, since it is a definite *racial* characteristic and is preserved from generation to generation by *heredity*. The first distinguishing trait of a race is the height of the body in its natural erect position. It is also the first characteristic that strikes us when a stranger comes toward us for the first time. And that is why we make it the leading descriptive trait: a person of tall, or of low stature. If, for a moment, we should picture to ourselves the legend of Noah's Ark—quite incredible, because emigration and embarkation of all the known species would have required more than a century of time (it is enough merely to think of the embarkation of the tortoises and the sloths!), and the necessity of an ark as big as a nation, what must inevitably have struck Noah and his sons would have been the *stature* of the individuals belonging to each separate species.

The *stature* is the linear index of the limit of mass.

Among the human races the variations in stature are included between fairly wide oscillations: coming down to facts, the average stature of the Akkas is 1.387 m. (4 ft. 6 1/2 in.) for the males; and that of the Scotchmen of Galloway is 1.792 m. (5 ft. 10 1/2 in.). Accordingly between the average heights of the two races that are considered as the *extremes*, there is a difference of 40 cm. (15 3/4 in.); but since the averages are obtained from a complex mass of normal measurements, some of which are *above* and others necessarily *below* the average itself, we may assert that the "*normal human individuals*" may differ in stature to an extent of more than half a metre; the oscillations of normal individuals on each side of the racial average being estimated at about 10 cm. (3.937 in.).

If we should see a little Akka 4 ft. 4 in. (1.33 m.) in height alongside of a Scotchman 6 ft. (1.83 m.) high we should say "a *dwarf* beside a *giant*." But such terms are *pathological* and should never be employed to indicate *normal individualities.* As a matter of fact dwarfs and giants are as a class extra-social and sterile; normal individuals, on the contrary, represent the physiopsychic characteristics of their respective races. Consequently we may say that normal people have a *low stature,* or a *high stature;* or if it is a question of extremely low stature (such as that of the Akkas) we may make use of the term *pigmies* or of the *pigmy race,* in speaking of such individuals. Sergi has proved the existence, among the prehistoric inhabitants of Europe, of various pigmy races.

In the field of anthropology the scientific terminology ought always to be based upon certain determined limits. The authorities indicate the normal extremes of individual stature, beyond which we pass over the into realm of *pathology,* incompatible with the survival of the species; and even in the pathological cases they determine the extreme limits, obtained from the individual monstrosities that have actually existed in the course of the centuries, and that seem to indicate the furthest limits attained by the human race.

Deniker, in summing up the principal authorities, assigns the following limits:

Statures less than 1.25 m.	Normal statures, range of oscillations among the races						Statures from 2 m. upward
	Lowest individual extreme	Exceptionally low individual stature	Extreme low racial average	Extreme high racial average	Exceptionally high individual stature	Highest individual extreme	
Nanism	1.25 m.	1.35 m.	Akkas 1.387 m.	Scotchmen of Galloway 1.792 m.	1.90 m.	1.99 m.	Gigantism

The pathological extremes that would seem to indicate the limits of stature compatible with human life would seem to be on the one hand the little female dwarf, Hilany Agyba of Sinai, described by Jaest and cited by Deniker,* 15 inches high (0.38 m.—the average length of the Italian child at birth is 0.50 m. = 19 1/2 in.), and on the other, the giant Finlander, Caianus, cited by Topinard†, 9 ft. 3 1/2 in. in height (2.83); the two extremes of human stature would accordingly bear a ratio of 1:7. On the other hand, Quételet‡ gives the two extremes as being relatively 1:6—namely, the Swedish giant who was one of the guardsmen of Frederick the Great, and was 2.523 m. tall (8 ft. 3 in.); and the dwarf cited by Buffon, 0.43 m. in height (16 3/4 in.).

When there is occasion for applying the terms *tall* or *low* stature to individuals of our own race, it is necessary at the same time to establish limits that will determine the precise meaning of such terms. Livi§ gives as the average stature for Italians 1.65 m. (5 ft. 5 in.), and speaking authoritatively as the leading statistician in Anthropology, establishes the following limits:

STATURE OF ITALIANS (LIVI)

Averages Determining The Terminology of Stature

1.60 m. and below, low statures.	1.65 m. and all between 1.60–1.70, mean statures	1.70 m. and above, tall statures.

The individual extremes among the low statures tend to approach the average stature of the Japanese race (1.55 m.), and those among the high statures approach the Anglo-Saxon average (the Scotch = 1.79 m.)

There is much to interest us in studying the *distribution* of statures in Italy.

In Livi's great charts, he has marked in *blue* those regions where the prevailing percentage of stature is high (1.70 m. and upward), and in red those where the low statures prevail (1.60 m. and below; and the varying intensity of colouration indicates the greater or lesser prevalence of the high or low statures.

* Deniker, *Races et peuples de la terre.*
† Topinard, *Elementi di Antropologia.*
‡ Quételet, *Proporzioni medie (mean Proportions).*
§ Livi, *Antropometria Militare (Military Anthropometry).*

Thus it becomes evident in one glance of the eye that tall statures prevail in northern Italy and low statures in the south; while the maximum of low stature (indicated by the most intense red) is found in the islands, and especially in Sardinia.

In the vicinity of the central districts of Italy (the Marches, Umbria, Latium) the two colours fade out; this indicates that here all notable prevalence of stature, either tall or low, ceases; consequently we have here, as the prevailing norm, the mean stature (1.65 m.).

Anyone wishing to analyse the natural distribution of stature, has only to study these charts by Livi, which are worked out with great minuteness. If a study of this sort, extending over the entire peninsula, seems too great an undertaking, it is at least advisable for a teacher to acquaint himself with the *local distribution* of stature; in order that when it becomes his duty to judge of the stature of pupils in his school he will have the necessary idea regarding the *biological* (racial) *basis* on which so important an anthropological datum can oscillate.

Livi's charts, based upon the male stature, correspond almost perfectly with my own regional charts based upon the *average statures* of the women of Latium. Both Livi and I find that in the region of Latium the tall statures prevail north of the Tiber, especially toward the confines of Umbria; while the lowest statures are found in the neighbourhood of the valley of the Tiber, toward the sea (Castelli Romani). That is to say, the stature becomes lower from north to south, and from the mountains toward the sea. Furthermore, there exist certain nuclei of pure race, such as at Orte and in Castelli Romani, where we may find the extremes of average stature, which for women are found to be 1.61 m. at Orte, and 1.47 m. at Castelli Romani; while the extreme individual statures, according to my figures, oscillate between 1.42 m (Castelli) and 1.70 m (Orte). It would be helpful to the teachers of Rome and Latium, if they would acquire some idea regarding the racial types of the district, by studying my work on the *Physical Characteristics of the young Women of Latium*, which is the only work on regional anthropology taken directly from life that so far exists in anthropologic literature.*

The Stature in Relation to Sex.—It is sufficient to point out that the stature varies normally between the sexes, so that the average

* MONTESSORI, *Caratteri fisici delle giovani donne del Lazio.*

figures differ by about 10 centimetres (nearly 4 in.) in the direction of a lower stature for woman.

Variations in Stature Through the Different Ages

Nothwithstanding that growth is an evolution, it manifests itself also by an *absolute augmentation of mass;* and the linear index of such augmentation is given by the *growth in stature,* or by its variations at different ages.

This exceedingly important measurement ought to be taken in the case of all pupils; and undoubtedly in the course of time anthropometry will form a part of our school equipment; because, by following the increase of stature in a child, we follow his physical development.

In Chapter VII, in which the technique of the stature is discussed, there is a graphic representation of the annual increase of stature in the two sexes; the upper parabolic line refers to the male sex, and the lower one to the female. On the vertical line are marked the measures of growth, from the base upward, and on the horisontal line the ages. All the dotted vertical lines which rise from the horizontal, each corresponding to a successive year of life, and stop at the parabolic line, represent the relative proportion of stature from year to year; while the parabola which unites the extremities of such lines may be regarded as a line drawn tangent to the top of the head of an individual through the successive periods of his life.

If we analyse this table, we find that the greatest increase in stature takes place during the first year; in fact, a child which at birth has an average length of body of 0.50 m. for males, and 0.48 m. for females (the new-born child does not have *stature,* but only *length of body,* since it has not yet acquired an erect position) has by the end of the first year augmented the length of body by 20 centimetres, which gives an average length of 0.70 m. In no other year of life will the stature acquire so notable an increase; it is very important for mothers to watch the growth of the child during this first year of its life; and the following figures may be useful for comparison:

It will be seen that the maximum increase takes place during the first four months—especially in the first month (4 cm. = 1.57 in.) the rate diminishing from this point up to the fourth month (2 cm. = 0.78 in.), after which the monthly increase remains steadily at one centimetre (0.39 in.).

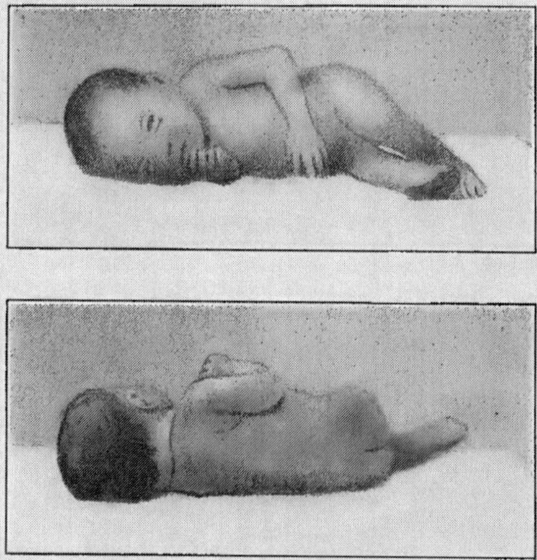

FIG. 22.—New-born child, seen from in front and from behind. (Stratz.)

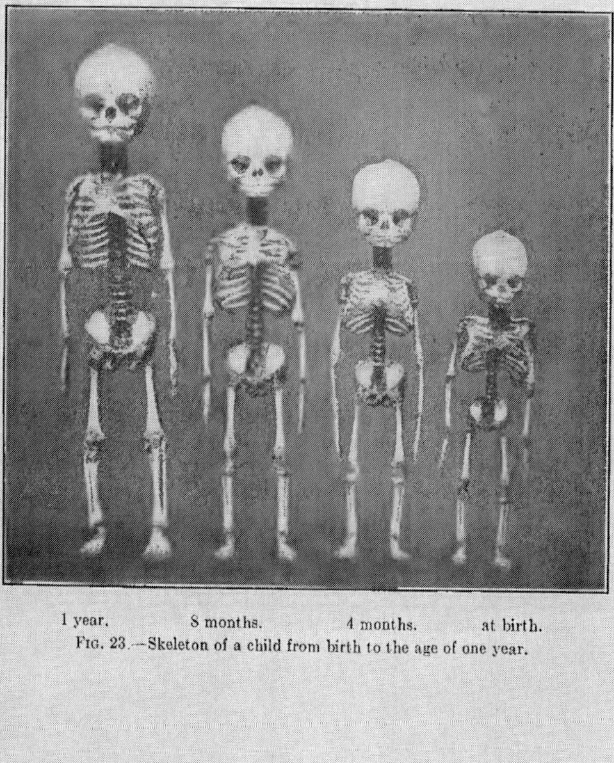

1 year. 8 months. 4 months. at birth.

FIG. 23.—Skeleton of a child from birth to the age of one year.

GROWTH IN LENGTH OF BODY DURING THE FIRST YEAR OF LIFE
(FROM FIGUEIRA)

Age in months	Length of body in metres	Monthly increase
0	0.50	0
1	0.54	4
2	0.57	3
3	0.60	3
4	0.62	2
5	0.63	1
6	0.64	1
7	0.65	1
8	0.66	1
9	0.67	1
10	0.68	1
11	0.69	1
12	0.70	1

The same facts appear from the combination picture given by Stratz, showing an infant's skeleton at four-month intervals from birth to the end of the first year.

During the second year of life, the increase in stature is about one-half that of the preceding year, that is, about 10 cm. (4 in.), so that at the end of the second year the child attains a height of about 80 cm. (31 1/2 in.). After this, the annual increase diminishes in intensity (see "Figures of the increase of stature according to Quétélet and other authors," in the technical part, Chapter VII), as is shown by the horizontal dotted lines, which, starting from a vertical line at points corresponding to the height of various statures, represent by the intervals of space between them the successive growth from year to year.

This increase is not regular, but proceeds by periodic *impulses* that in early childhood seem to recur at intervals of three years.

Thus for example the increase

between 0– 3 years of age is successively 20, 10, 6 cm.
between 3– 6 years of age is successively 7, 6, 5 cm.
between 6– 9 years of age is successively 7, 6, 5 cm.
between 9–12 years of age is successively 6, 4, 3 cm.

Accordingly we have a *triennial rhythm*, decreasing throughout the whole period of childhood; the maximum increase is in the first triennium, the second and third periods of three years correspond exactly, while the last period shows a lowered rate of increase.

At this point the period of approaching puberty begins (13 years for boys), after which the rate of increase becomes more rapid than it had been during the second or third period, attaining its maximum during the years 13–15; to be specific, the rate from 13 to 18 is successively 4, 8, 7, 5, 6, 3 cm.

When the period of puberty is ended (18 years), the rate of growth is much slower; in fact, during the two following years (18 to 20) it hardly attains one centimetre.

Nevertheless, the stature continues to increase up to the twenty-fifth year; according to Quétélet's figures, the average male stature at the age of eighteen is 1.70 m. (in Belgium) and at twenty-one it is 1.72 m.

From twenty-five to thirty-five the stature remains stable; this is the adult age, the full attainment of maturity; at the age of forty the period of involution insensibly begins, and after fifty in the case of women, and sixty in the case of men, the stature begins insensibly to decrease; a decrease which becomes more marked with the advance of age, corresponding to an anatomical diminution of the soft parts interposed between the bones in the sum of parts that make up the stature; more especially the intervertebral disks; and in connection with this phenomenon the vertebral column tends to become more curved.

According to Quétélet's figures, at the age of eighty the average male stature is 1.61 m. (5 ft. 3 2/5 in.), a stature corresponding to that of the age of sixteen.

Accordingly, the variations in stature throughout the different periods of life are neither a *growth* nor an *evolution*, but a *parabolic curve,* including *evolution and involution.* This curve represents the true *human stature;* the measurements taken successively from year to year representing nothing more than transitory *episodes* in the individual life.

Man, as he really is, we may represent by portraits taken successively from time to time, from his birth until his death: the occasional photograph which it is the custom to have taken represents nothing; following no rule, it seizes a fugitive instant in the life of an individual, who is never a fixed quantity but is constantly in transition during the whole course of his existence. So that the habit of taking a picture annually on a child's birthday is an excellent one if we wish to preserve a true likeness; and this practice is recommended in pedagogic anthropology, when it is desired to preserve the biographic history of the pupil.

It is interesting to study, side by side with the growth of stature and the marked rhythms and periods that constitute its laws, the phenomenon of general mortality in its relation to age.

Lexis gives the following curve of general mortality: the horizontal line marks the years and the vertical line the corresponding number of deaths, while the curved line shows the *progress* of mortality, and the highest points in the curve indicate the maximum mortality. It is highest of all during the first year and in general during early childhood, and is steadily lowered to a point corresponding to the ages from ten to thirteen, after which it rises again.

Let us examine the curve up to this point, since it has a bearing upon our school work. We can prove that the *maximum mortality*

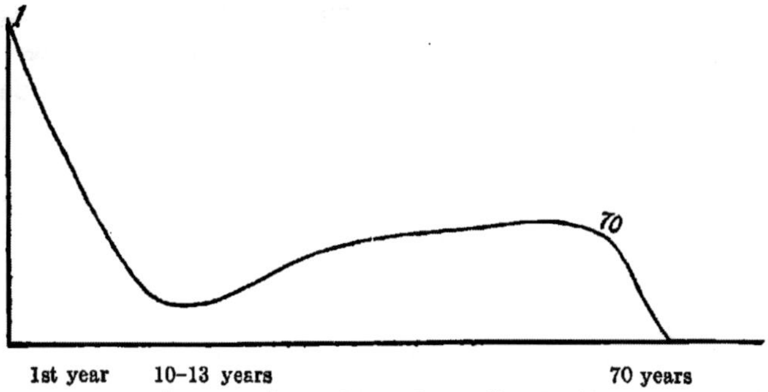

FIG. 24.—Curve of general mortality (Lexis).

corresponds to the maximum individual growth; in other words, an organism in *rapid evolution* is exposed to death, its powers of immunity to infective diseases are weakened; it constitutes what in medical parlance is known as a *locus minoris resistentiæ*.

In that period of *calm* in growth, which would seem to be a *repose* preceding the evolution of puberty, mortality is at the lowest; only to rise again rapidly *during the period of puberty;* while the rise becomes less rapid after the eighteenth year, notwithstanding that after that age mankind in general are exposed, in their struggle for existence, to many causes of death that did not exist during the preceding years. Toward the age of seventy the line of mortality attains another apex, because the age of *normal death* is reached; after which it drops precipitously because of the lack of survivers.

From these facts we may deduce certain very important principles that throw useful light upon pedagogy: there are certain *ages at which even the strong are weak;* and their weakness is of such a nature that it *exposes the individual to death.*

Now, whenever the phenomenon of *mortality* occurs it is always an indication of *impoverishment in the survivors.* For example, of every one person that dies, many persons have been ill who have recovered from their illness; but there are still many others who, although they did not actually fall ill, were weakened even though they passed through the peril unharmed.

In short, for each death, which represents a *final disaster*, there are many victims. And whenever there is a rise in the phenomenon of mortality in connection with any one age, it is our duty to give special attention to those individuals who are not only weak in themselves, but whom the *social causes affecting* them tend to weaken still more and push onward toward illness and death. Whenever there are many deaths, there are undoubtedly also *many sufferers.*

Now, in pedagogy we have no criterion to guide us in this matter of *respecting the weaknesses characteristic of the various ages,* as, for example, that of early infancy and of the age of puberty.

With the most cruel blindness we punish and discourage the lad who, having reached the age of puberty, no longer makes the progress in his studies that rendered him the brilliant champion during the period of physiological repose in his growth; and instead of regarding this as a psychic indication of a great physiological transformation that it is necessary to protect, we urge on the organism to *enforced effort,* without even suspecting that, in proportion to the degree of resistance of our pupil, we may be doing our share to induce in him a permanent weakness, or an arrest of development, or disease and death.

Our responsibility as educators is great, because we have the *threads of life* entrusted to our care; man represents a continuous transition through successive forms, and each following period has been prepared for by the one preceding.

Whenever we have the misfortune to concur in *weakening a child,* we touch that parabolic line traced in the graphic chart of stature, and standing as an index of the life of the body, and we give it a shock throughout its whole length; it may either be shattered or be brought down to a lower grade.

But the life of an individual does not contain merely that *individual alone;* the cycle of the stature with its violent period of puberty and the perfect physiological repose corresponding to the years from 25 to 36, or even 45, indicates the *eternity of the individual in the species:* his maturity for reproduction. Man in his progress through the different levels of height, as indicated on the graphic chart of stature, does not pass through them without reproducing himself, save in exceptional cases; he commences the ascent alone, but in his descent he attains the majesty of a creator who leaves behind him the immortal works of his own creation. Well, even the capacity of *normal reproduction,* and of begetting a strong species, is related to the *normal cycle of life:* whoever weakens a child and puts a strain upon the threads of its existence, starts a vibration that will be felt throughout posterity.

The parabolic cycle of stature shows us which is the most favourable period for the reproduction of the species; it is undoubtedly that period that stands at the highest apex of the curve, and at which the organism has reached an almost absolute peace, as if forgetful of itself, in order to provide for its eternity. When it has completed its period of *evolution,* during which the organism shows that it has not yet matured; and before the commencement of involution, in which period the organism is slowly preparing for departure—that is the moment when man *may* or rather *ought* to procreate his species.

Careful forethought not to produce immature or feeble fruit, will form part of the coming man's regard for his posterity. A new moral era is maturing, that is giving birth to a *solidarity,* not only between all living beings, but including also those future beings who are as yet unborn; but for whose existence the living man of to-day is preparing through his care of his own strength and his own virtue. To have intentionally begotten a son better than himself will be a proud victory for the man who has attained the higher sexual morality; and such pride will be no less keen than that of the artist, who by perfecting his marvelous talents has created a masterpiece.

The statistics collected by Quételet demonstrate that "too precocious marriages either occasion sterility or produce children that have a smaller probability of living."

They prove furthermore that the number of children who die is largest in marriages contracted at the age of sixteen or earlier, and becomes lowest among the children born of marriages contracted between the years of 29 and 32. During these years also the parents are most fertile: as is shown by the following tables:

SANDLER'S FIGURES BASED ON THE FAMILIES OF ENGLISH PEERS

Age of parents at marriage	Percentage of deaths of children before attaining marriageable age	Average births to each marriage	Percentage of births to each death
15 years..........	35	4.40	0.283
16–19 years........	20	4.63	0.208
20–23 years........	19	5.21	0.188
24–27 years........	12	5.43	1.171

Age at the time of child's birth	Percentage of deaths to each birth	Average number of births in one year of marriage
16 years..................	0.44	0.46
17–20 years...............	0.43	0.50
21–24 years...............	0.42	0.52
25–28 years...............	0.41	0.55
29–32 years...............	0.40	0.59

The results of a recent research show that famous men have hardly ever been the first-born, and that the great majority were begotten of parents who were at the time between the ages of 25 and 36 years.

Variations of Stature with Age, According to the Sexes.—The general laws of the growth and involution of stature are pretty nearly the same for the two sexes. The female stature, beginning at birth, averages throughout life somewhat less than the male.

But since the development of puberty takes place earlier in woman than in man, the female child manifests the characteristic increase in stature at an earlier age than the male; consequently at that age (about eleven) she overtakes him, and for the time being both boy and girl are equal in stature. But as soon as the boy enters upon the period of puberty, he rapidly surpasses the girl, and his stature henceforth steadily maintains a superiority of about ten centimetres (nearly four inches), as is shown by the deviations between the two parabolic curves, representing the variations of stature in the two sexes. Even the involution of stature occurs precociously in women, as compared with man.

Variations in Stature due to Mechanical Causes of Adaptation to Environment

Variations due to Mechanical Causes. Transitory and Permanent Variations. Deformations.—The individual stature is not a fixed quantity at all hours of the day; but it varies by several millimetres under the influence of mechanical causes connected with the habits of daily life. In the morning we are slightly taller than at night (by a fraction of a centimetre): in consequence of remaining on foot a good deal of the time during the day, our stature is gradually lowered. This is contrary to the popular belief that "while we stand up our stature grows."

As a matter of fact, in the erect position the soft tissues that form part of the total stature are under constant pressure; but being elastic, they resume their previous proportions after prolonged rest in a horizontal position.

Consequently at night, especially if we have taken a long walk, or danced, we are shorter than in the morning after a long sleep; the act of stretching the limbs in the morning completes the work of restoring the articular cartilages to their proper limits of elasticity. Nevertheless, according to the mechanical theory accepted by Manouvrier, persons who are habituated from childhood to stand on foot much of the time (labourers) interfere with the free growth of the long bones in the direction of length and at the same time augment the growth in thickness; hence the skeleton is rendered definitely shorter in its segments as well as in its bones (*i.e.*, a shallower pelvis, shorter limbs, etc.). The result is a stocky type with robust muscles: the *europlastic type*, which is found among labourers. On the contrary, a person who spends much time reclining on sofas among cushions, and taking abundant nutriment, is likely to tend toward the opposite extreme; bones long and slender, the skeleton tall in all its segments, the muscular system delicate; this is the *macroplastic* or aristocratic type. According to Manouvrier, when a person has a long, slow convalescence after a protracted infectious malady such as typhoid, recumbent much of the time and subjected to a *highly nutritive* diet, it may happen, especially if he has reached the period of puberty at which a rapid osteogenesis naturally takes place in the cartilages of the long bones, that he will not only become notably taller, but will even acquire the macroplastic type.

The macroplastic type is artistically more beautiful, but the europlastic type is physiologically more useful.

It is not only the erect position that tends to reduce the stature, but the sitting posture as well. In fact, whether the pelvis is supported by the lower limbs or by a chair, the intervertebral disks are in either case compressed by the weight of the bust as a whole. If, for example, children are obliged, during the period of growth, to remain long at a time in a sitting posture, the limbs may freely lengthen, while the bust is impeded in its free growth, and the result may be an artificial tendency toward macroscelia. This is why children are more inclined than adults to throw themselves upon the ground, to lie down, to cut capers, in other words to restore the elasticity of their joints, and overcome the compression of bones and cartilages. Accordingly, such variations of stature recur habitually and are *transitory*, and since they are associated with the customary attitudes of daily life, they are *physiological*.

But if special causes should aggravate such physiological conditions, and should recur so often as not to permit the cartilages to return completely to their original condition, in such a case *permanent variations* of stature might result, and even *morphological deviations* of the skeleton. For example, a porter who habitually carries heavy weights on his head, may definitely lower his stature; and in the case of a young boy, the interference with the growth of the long bones through compression exerted from above downward, may produce an actual arrest of development of the limbs and spinal column, presenting all the symptoms of rickets. Witness certain consequences of "child-labour" chief among which must be mentioned the deformities of the *carusi* [victims of child-labour, who from an early age toil up the succession of ladders, bearing heavy burdens of sulphur from the mines below.*] in the Sicilian sulphur mines.† As a general rule, all *cramped positions that are a necessary condition of labour, if they surpass the limits of resistance and elasticity of* the human frame, and especially if they operate during periods of life when the skeleton is in process of formation, result in deformities, and when the skeleton is deformed, the

* Translator's note.

† Fig. 25 and those following it, dealing with deformities resulting from labour, are taken from Picraccini's great work, *The Pathology of Labour*.

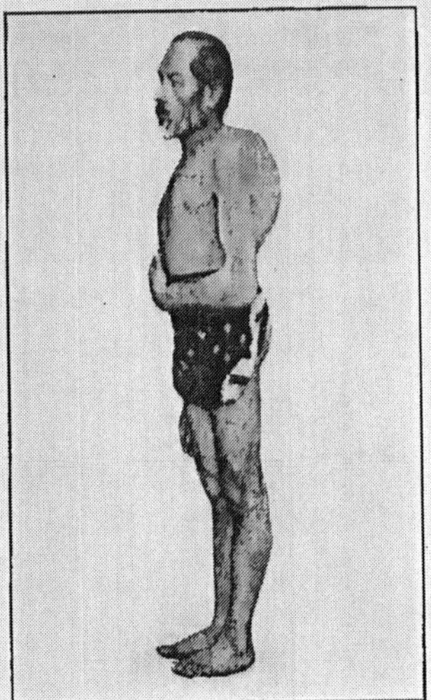

FIG. 25.—Vincenzo Militella of Lercara, a Sicilian *caruso*.

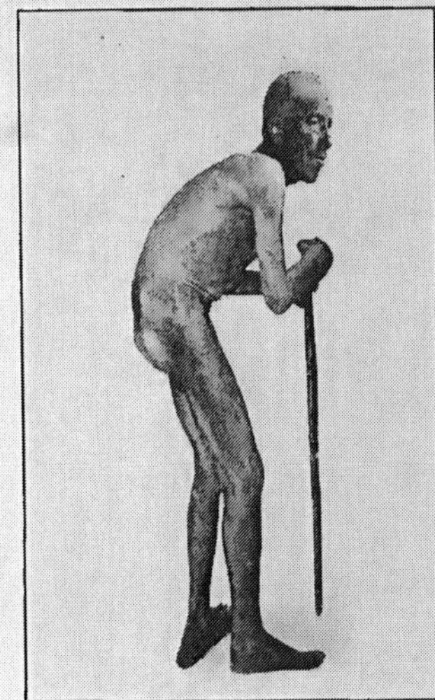

FIG. 26—Aged field labourer.

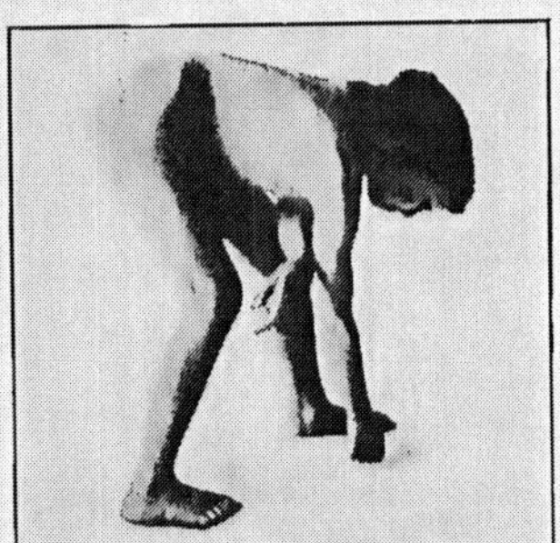

FIG. 27.

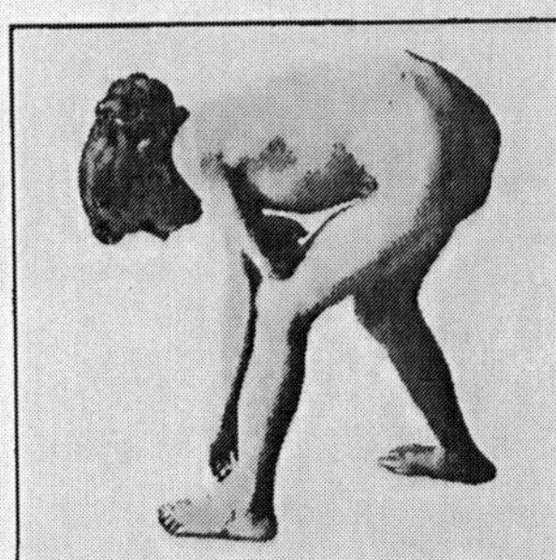

FIG. 28.

Attitude of woman working in the rice fields as seen from the right and left sides.

FIG. 29.—A gang of eight workers in the rice fields.

internal organs and hence the general functional powers of the whole organism, suffer even greater alteration.

Consider the postures that miners must endure, or as Pieraccini phrases it, their "disastrous attitudes."

The transport galleries are ordinarily too low to permit a man of average height to walk erect; along these galleries little transport-wagons are run by hand, excepting where the carrying is done on the backs of the men themselves.

"Even in the front of the advance tunnels and in the galleries that are being worked, miners are to be seen in the most incongruous attitudes. These anomalous positions of the body maintained throughout long hours of toil react upon the functional action of the heart and lungs, upon the stomach and intestines in the proper performance of their tasks, and result in producing hernia, varicose veins and eventually deformities of the skeleton (vertebral column, thorax)."*

Field labourers also (Fig. 26) become permanently deformed, with diminution of stature, from remaining too long bent over in the act of hoeing or reaping. But a still more painful labour is that of the women in the rice fields during the period when the weeding is done.

The position necessitated by this work requires a strained and prolonged dorsal flexion of the vertebral column, accompanied by a strain on the lower dorsal nerves; great *elasticity* is required to endure a position so painful and so apt to induce *lumbago;* only young women can endure it, and even they become deformed, and suffer seriously from anemia, intestinal maladies and diseases of the uterus, which predispose them to abortion or sterility (Figs. 27, 28, 29).

Stone breakers also contract painful diseases and deformities from their work. They are constantly bowed over their task, performing a rhythmic, alternating movement of flexion, extension and torsion of the trunk upon itself, while at the same time there is a slight undulation in a backward and forward direction, accompanying the rising and falling of the arm holding the hammer. These movements of extension and flexion of the trunk involve the whole vertebral column, while the pelvis remains practically motionless. "At the end of the day they rise from their task bowed over and they walk home bowed over, holding the ver-

* Pieraccini, *Op. cit.*

tebral column rigid; any attempt to force the trunk into an erect position is extremely painful. In the morning they return to their work with their loins still aching." And among these stone breakers there are young men, some of them mere boys! And when we think that these injurious *attitudes* are coupled with malnutrition, we must realise the extent of the organic disaster that accompanies diminution of stature as a result of adaptation to labour.

We are naturally horrified at such conditions enforced upon a certain portion of humanity; and we pray for a time to come when machinery will have universally replaced human labour, in transportation, in stone-breaking, and in reaping, and when children will be spared from hard and deforming toil.

But how is it that while we are so sympathetic regarding conditions at a distance from us, we remain unconscious of similar conditions, that are close beside us, and of which we are the directors, the cruel enforcers, the masters?

In the near future, I hope that people will tell with amazement, as if citing a condition of inferior civilisation, how the school children, up to the opening of the twentieth century represented one category of those "deformed by prolonged and enforced labour in injurious positions!"

Such studies in *school hygiene* as deal with the type of school benches, designed to minimise the danger of deformities of the vertebral column in children—will, I hope, be regarded by the coming generations with the most utter amazement! And the school benches of to-day will find their place in *museums*, and people will go to look at them as if they were relics of bygone barbarism, just as we now visit the collections from old-time insane asylums, of series of complicated instruments of wood and iron that in bygone centuries were considered *necessary* for maintaining discipline among the insane.

What in the world would we say, if somebody should propose, in order to obviate the deformities and physiological injuries of labourers, that certain mechanisms should be applied to them individually for the purpose of diminishing the harm? Imagine a law being proposed, to the effect that all miners should be obliged to wear trusses, to keep their viscera from breaking loose, as a result of prolonged compression! What would we think of such reforms and such a path toward an orthopedic state of society?

Our way toward progress and higher civilisation is a very

different one. To remove man from torturing toil that twists the bones and undermines the health—such is the goal that it is our duty to set before us!

For the deformed vertebral column is the *extreme* sign of a great accumulation of evils; the internal organs are correspondingly affected with disorders fatal to the entire organism; but even greater is the corresponding harm done to the human soul! What we want is not only that the bones shall not be thrown out of their eurhythmic harmony, but that the souls of the labourers shall be freed from the inhuman yoke of slavery (progress can consist solely in a radical alteration of the *form of labour*).

So far as concerns the school, which is not limited to a few categories of human beings, but is extended to *all, by requirements of law*, is it not possible for us to adopt a different attitude of mind?

The established fact that the pupils may even deform their skeletons in the course of their work, goes to prove that this work contains some *error in principle* that is fatal to successive generations; and so long as this principle is maintained, we may assert *a priori* that even if, with the help of school benches as complicated and as costly as orthopedic machines, we should succeed in checking the deformation of the vertebral column, we should fail to check the deformation of the soul. Because whoever is condemned to labour that deforms is a slave.

And as a matter of fact we employ coercive means, "rewards and punishments," to enforce upon children a condition that in their eyes amounts to serving their first sentence.

It is not the school bench, but the *method* that needs reforming; it is not the ligaments of the spinal column, but *human life in evolution* that we ought to respect, and *lead toward the attainment of perfection!* Amid the many banners of liberty that have been raised in these latter times, one is still missing—one which we ought to seize upon as the standard of our cause: the liberty of the new generation, which is groaning in the slavery of compulsory education, upon iron-bound benches, emblematic of chains!

I foresee, in a radical reform of pedagogic methods, the practical possibility of taking as guiding principles the *individual liberty of the pupil* and a *reverential regard for life.* And I affirm this all the more loudly, because I have applied such a method with indisputable success in the "Children's Houses," obtaining prodigious results in the health and happiness of the children, perfect discipline in the classes, marvelously rapid progress in studies, and a surprising awakening of souls, a passionate love for the work.

Variations Due to Adaptation in Connection with Causes of Various Kinds— Social, Physiological, Physical, Psychic, Pathological, Etc.

Physiology and Social Conditions.—*Nutrition.*—One of the effects of environment, of the highest importance in its relation to the development of stature, is nutrition. In order to attain the maximum development as biologically determined by heredity in a race, sufficient nutriment is the first necessity. It is a familiar fact that material or physiological life consists essentially in the exchange and *renewal of matter*, or in *metabolism*, which is also a renewal of vital force.

The living molecules are continually breaking up, thus expressing in an active form forces that had accumulated in a potential form, and eliminating the rejected matter; only to form again by means of new matter, containing potential forces. This breaking up and renewal constitutes the material of life, that never pauses in its molecular movement; the cessation of renewal of matter is death, that is, scission without reparation; consumption without renewal; and consequently a rapid disintegration of the body. Living matter consists in metabolism, and is consequently directly related to the nutritive substances which renew the elements necessary for continual redintegration.

We may disregard certain individual potentialities, of a purely biological nature, and that are capable of manifesting vital forces of varying degrees of intensity: but it may be asserted as beyond question that every living being, if he is to live according to his biological destiny, has need of sufficient nutrition. This is not the same as saying that the food determines the life of an individual in its final development, in the sense that by eating in excess one may attain the stature of a giant, or an imbecile become intelligent or a man of talent become a genius. We all bear within us, in that fertilised germ that constituted the first cell of our organism, predetermined biological conditions, on which depend the physical limits of our body, as well as those of our psychic individuality. But in order that this germ may develop in accordance with its potentiality, it is necessary that it shall obtain the requisite material from its environment. Because otherwise—and here the relation is direct—neither the volumetric development nor the morphological development can be accomplished, nor the psychic potentiality express itself; in other words, the stature will be undersized, in a body defrauded of the degree of beauty potential in the germ, and the muscular forces, in common with those of the brain, will remain at a level of development below that which nature had intended. Consequently, to deprive children of their requisite nutriment is *stealing* from life, it is a *biological crime.*

While we live, we must eat; and while we labour, that is, while we expend the vital forces, it is necessary to repair them. The schools should establish a system of luncheons for the pupils; this is a principle that has already been generally recognised and is already bearing fruit.

There was a time when a good appetite was regarded as a *low material instinct;* it was also the time when people sang the praises of *spirituality,* but actually indulged in banquets of Lucullian lavishness. The vice of the palate and the physiological need of nourishment were included under one and the same disdain.

To-day science has shed its light upon the true conception of nutrition and holds it to be the *first necessity* of life, and consequently the first social problem to be solved.

From this point of view, food is not a vulgar material thing, nor the dinner-table a place of debauchery. Indeed, there is nothing which affords better proof of immateriality than the act of eating. In fact, the necessity of eating is itself a proof that the matter of which our body is composed does not endure but passes like the fleeting moment. And if the substance of our bodies passes in this manner, if life itself is only a continual passing away of matter, what greater symbol of its immateriality and its spirituality is there than the dinner-table?

". . . the bread is my flesh and the wine is my blood; do this in remembrance of what life really is."

Something similar to this is being accomplished to-day by science in regard to the sexual relations. We are accustomed to consider the sexual instincts as something contemptible, material and low, praising abstinence, and leaving these instincts wholly out of consideration in the course of education, as though they were something degrading, or even shameful. And undoubtedly our sexual abuses are shameful, and shameful also is the barbaric tolerance of the masses regarding prostitution, seduction, illegitimacy and the abandonment of new-born children. It is criminal abuse that makes us despise sexual relations, just as at one time excesses of the table made us despise nutrition. But the day will come when science will raise to the dignity of a new sexual morality the physiological function which to-day is considered material and shameful—and that comprehends the most sublime of human conceptions. In it are to be found the words which ancient races deposited in their religious tabernacles: creation, eternity, mystery. And in it are also to be found the most sublime conceptions of modern races: the destiny of humanity, the perfectionment of the human species.

Accordingly, we must to-day regard the serving of food in the schools as a necessity of the first order; but it is well, in introducing it into the schools, to surround it with that halo of gladness and of high moral significance that ought to accompany all manifestations of life. The *hymn to bread,* which is a human creation and a means of preserving the substance of the human body, ought to accompany the meals of our new generations of children. The child *develops* because the substance of his body passes away, and the meals that he eats symbolise all this: furthermore, they teach him to think of the vast labour accomplished by men who, unknown as individuals, cultivate the earth, reap the grain, grind the flour, and *provide* for all men and for all children. Where they are and who they are, we do not know; the bread bears neither their name nor their picture. Like an impersonal entity, like a god, humanity provides for all the needs of humanity: and this god is labour. If the child is destined some day to become himself a labourer, who produces and casts his products to humanity without knowing who is to receive his contribution toward providing for humanity, it is well that as he lifts his food to his lips he should realise that he is contracting a debt toward society at large, and that he must give because he takes; he must "forgive debts as his have been forgiven"; and since life is gladness, let him send forth a salutation to the universal producing power: "Our Father, give us our daily bread!"

The Providence of human labour rules over our entire life; it gives us everything that is necessary. The God of the Universe, in whose train come cataclysms, is not more terrible than the god, Humanity, that can give us War and Famine. While we give bread to the child, let us remember that man does not live by bread alone: because bread is only the material of his fleeting substance.

The system of furnishing meals in school constitutes a chapter of *School Hygiene* that cannot directly concern us. Nevertheless, there are three rules of this hygiene which should be borne in mind: Children should never, in any case, drink wine, alcoholic liquors, tea or coffee—in other words, stimulants, which are poisons to their childish organisms. On the other hand, children need *sugar*, because sugar has a great formative and plastic power; all young animals have sweetish flesh because their muscles, in the course of development, are extremely rich in sugar. The method of giving sugar to children should be as simple as possible, such, for instance, as is endorsed by the very successful English system of hygiene for children, which recommends freshly cooked fruits, sprinkled with sugar or served with a little syrup. But the substantial nourishment for young children should consist of *soup* or *broth* served hot, since heat is as essential as sugar for organisms in the course of evolution.

The English recommend soups made of cereals and gluten, in which it is never necessary to use soup stock, just as it is never necessary to use meat in children's diet.

That nutrition has a noteworthy influence upon growth, and therefore upon the definitive limits of stature, is exhaustively proved by statistics.

In his brilliant studies of the poorer classes, Niceforo has collected the following average statures:*

Age	Stature (in centimetres)	
	Children	
	Rich	Poor
7 years	120	116
8 years	126	122
9 years	129	123
10 years	134	128
11 years	135	134
12 years	140	138
13 years	144	140
14 years	150	146

*Alfredo Niceforo, *Les classes pauvres* (the poorer classes).

from which it appears that, in spite of the strong biological impulse given by the attainment of *puberty,* the children of the poor continue to show a stature lower than that of the well-to-do. Aleš Hrdlička has compiled the following comparative table of the poor or orphaned children received into the asylums, and the pupils of the public schools in Boston:

Stature of American children: (1) In asylums; (2) in Boston public schools

Boys

Age in years	5	6	7	8	9	10	11	12	13	14	15	16
(1)	971	1088	1172	1163	1234	1261	1315	1367	1424	1452	1518	—
(2)	1060	1120	1176	1223	1272	1326	1372	1417	1477	1551	1599	1665

Girls

(1)	—	—	1101	1158	1204	1289	1290	—	—	1398	—	—
(2)	1052	1109	1167	1221	1260	1315	1366	1452	1492	1532	1559	1567

Even after reaching the adult age these differences are maintained, as may be shown by the following statistics taken from various authorities:

Average statures obtained from soldiers (in centimetres)

Italians		English		French	
Students and professional men	167	Professional men	175	Students	169
Tradesmen	165	Merchants	172	Domestics	166
Peasants	164	Peasants	171	Day labourers	165
		City employees	169		

from which it appears that while in Italy the class of labourers having the lowest stature is the peasant class, which lives under the most deplorable economic conditions, in England on the contrary it is the workers in the cities who live under worse economic conditions than the peasantry, it being well known that the English peasant is the most prosperous in the agricultural world.

According to Livi, it is nutrition which causes the differences of average stature that are usually to be found between different social classes, and those between the inhabitants of mountains and of plains, or between the dwellers on the mainland and on the islands. In general the mountain-bred peasants have a *lower* stature than those of the plains; and this is because the means of procuring food are fewer and harder in mountainous regions.

Similarly, the islanders, because of less ready means of communication, have less likelihood than those on the mainland of obtaining adequate nutrition.

The same may be said regarding the differences found between the statures of cultured persons and of the illiterate, to the disadvantage of the latter (the poorer classes).

Students show the tallest stature of all, because they have in their favour the joint effect of the two chief factors of environment that influence this anthropological datum: *mechanical causes* and *nutrition*. A sedentary life, and above all a hearty diet both contribute to the tall stature of students, doctors, and members of the liberal professions. In this respect, the average figures of all the authorities agree, as appears from the following tables:*

LIVI: 256,166 ITALIAN SOLDIERS

Professions and callings	Average stature in centimetres
Students and professional men	166.9
Small shopkeepers and the like	165.0
Peasants	164.3
Blacksmiths	165.0
Carpenters	165.1
Masons	164.8
Tailors and shoemakers	164.5
Barbers	164.3
Butchers	165.7
Carters	164.4
Bakers	164.7
Day labourers in general	164.4

* Taken from Livi: *On the Development of the Body in relation to the profession and the social condition.* Rome, Voghera, 1897.

ROBERT AND RAWSON: 1935 ADULT ENGLISHMEN

Professions and employments	Average stature in centimetres
Professional men	175.6
Merchants and tradesmen	172.6
Peasants and miners	171.5
City labourers	169.2
Sedentary workmen	167.4
Prisoners	168.0
Insane	166.8

OLORIZ: 1798 CONSCRIPTS FROM THE CITY OF MADRID

Professions and employments	Average stature in centimetres
Liberal professions	163.9
Including:	
Students	164.0
Other professions	161.1
Workmen employed in the open air	160.7
Workmen employed in closed rooms	159.8
Including:	
Tailors, hatters and the like	159.0
Shoemakers	158.9

Conditions of nutrition, which are always accompanied by a combination of other hygienic conditions all tending toward the same effects, have also an influence upon the development of puberty.

Puberty is retarded by malnutrition. As a result of an inquiry made among the inmates of the Pia Barolo Society, which offers an asylum to reformed prostitutes, Marro* records that out of ninety rescued girls only those above the age of fourteen had begun to menstruate: notwithstanding that the normal period for the development of puberty in Italian women is between the years of twelve and thirteen. Furthermore, among the girls above the age of fourteen, menstruation had not yet begun in all cases; on the contrary, a large proportion of them still failed to show the phenomena of puberty:

* MARRO, *Puberty*.

Age in years	Whole number	Number menstruating
14–15	11	4
15–16	11	7
16–17	11	8
17–18	8	7

All the rest (thirty in number) menstruated for the first time after the age of eighteen.

Among those in whom menstruation had appeared earlier, the order of appearance was as follows:

Years..........	10	11	12	13	14	15	16	17
Number........	1	3	4	5	12	17	9	5

When we consider that we are dealing with *rescued* girls, we may conclude that direct sexual stimulus does not facilitate the normal development of puberty, but on the contrary, in conjunction with other causes, *retards it.* Accordingly, we must not confound the *normal development of the organism* with its disorders: whatever aids the natural development of life is useful and healthy. There may be conditions *unfavourable* to the development of puberty, which are favourable to the development of sexual vices (see, further on, the other causes influencing puberty, and moral conditions in colleges).

In his work above cited, Marro compares his figures obtained from the Pia Barolo Society with those of Dr. Bianco* taken from 78 young girls in city institutes representing young women in easy circumstances:

Date of first menstruation	Girls in the Pia Barolo Society. Percentage	Girls in city institutes for the wealthy classes. Percentage
10 years..................	1.7	——
11 years..................	5.3	1.3
12 years..................	7.1	13.3
13 years..................	8.9	18.7
14 years..................	21.4	29.3
15 years..................	30.3	20.0
16 years..................	16.0	8.0
17 years..................	8.9	4.0

* Cited by PAGLIANI, *Human Development, according to age, sex, etc.*

It should be noted that the cold climate of Turin retards puberty (see below): but the above table clearly shows the precocious puberty of young women in easy circumstances; in the great majority, in fact, it occurs between the ages of twelve and fourteen, with thirteen for the average; on the other hand, the majority for reformed prostitutes is between fourteen and sixteen, with fifteen for the average.

Besides labour and nutrition, there are other factors that contribute to the development of stature (which we regard as an index to the entire mass of the body). Such factors are:

Physical Conditions—Heat, Light, Electricity

Thermic Conditions.—Among the physical conditions which may have an influence upon the stature, the *thermic* conditions ought to receive first consideration.

It is a principle demonstrated by nature that organisms in the course of evolution have need of heat. Even the invertebrates, as for example the insects, develop during the heat of summer; and the eggs of the higher vertebrates such as the birds, develop their embryo by means of the maternal warmth. In placental animals the development throughout the whole embryonic period takes place within the maternal womb, in the full tide of animal heat. In order to preserve life in premature babies, that is, in those born before the expiration of the physiological term of nine months, *incubators* have been constructed, an oven-like arrangement in which the child may be maintained at a temperature considerably higher than would be possible in the outside air; the term is also specifically used of the structures in which fertilised hens' eggs are kept during the required period of time until the chickens are hatched.

Accordingly it is a principle taught us by nature that organisms in the course of evolution have need of heat. The most luxuriant vegetation, the most gigantic animals, the most variegated birds belong to the fauna and flora of the tropics.

How is this physiological law, which nature expresses in such broad, general lines, to be interpreted by us in the environment of the school? It is well known that in this regard there are two conflicting opinions. There are some who would go to excessive lengths in protecting small children from the cold, by dressing them entirely in woolen garments and keeping their apartments well heated; others on the contrary assert that the *physiological struggle of adaptation* to the cold invigorates the infant organism, and they advise that the child's body should never be completely protected, as for example that the legs should always be left bare, that the child should be lightly clad, that his apartments should not be heated, etc.

Furthermore, it used to be held in the pietistic schools, and still is to some extent, that *warmth* had a demoralising influence, inasmuch as it tended to enervate both mind and body.

We educators cannot fail to be interested in such a discussion. As often happens in physiological arguments, the two opposite contentions each contain a part of the truth. In order to get at the truth of the matter, it is necessary to distinguish two widely separated facts: on the one hand, *physiological exercise in the form of thermal gymnastics*, and on the other, the *development of organisms in a constantly cold environment.*

To live constantly warm, protected either by clothes or by artificial heat, so that the organism remains always at a constant temperature, is not favourable to growth, because it deprives the organism of the physiological exercise of adapting itself to variations in external temperature, an exercise which stimulates useful functions. By perspiring in summer, we cleanse our system of poisonous secretions, and by shivering in winter we give tone to our striped muscles and to our internal organs, as is proved by our gain in appetite. Anyone who wishes to be kept on ice in summer and to transform his apartment into a hot-house in winter, robs himself of these advantages and enfeebles his system.

The apparent *comfort* is not in this case a real physiological enjoyment but a *weakness of habit* that is accompanied by a loss of physiological energy. What makes us robust is a rational exercise of all our energies. *Thermal gymnastics* is consequently useful. It consists in exposing a healthy, resistant organism to changes in temperature, trusting to our physiological resources for the means of defense. Thus, for example, a child who is well fed and well protected from the cold for many hours of the day in the well-heated family apartment, can go out with bare legs into the snow; and doing so will make him more robust. In the same way, the ancient Romans exposed themselves in their hot baths to the steadily increasing temperature of the *calidarium,* up to the point of 60 degrees (140 Fahrenheit), and then still perspiring flung themselves into a cold plunge. And it is a familiar fact that afterward they held lavish banquets in these same baths. Such exercise which in classic times gave vigour to the race that made itself master of the world may be summed up as follows: "*Thermic gymnastics*" of organisms "well nourished and strong."

Our own boatmen also throw themselves into the river in mid-winter, half nude, and half nude they ply their long poles. They expose themselves to the cold, in the same way that they might raise a weight of many pounds with their robust arms, for *gymnastic exercise.*

But all this differs radically from living continually in a cold temperature. It is a very different thing from the life of a child of the lower classes, who goes bare-foot in winter, clad in a few scant rags, half frozen in his wretched tenement, and unable to obtain sufficient nourishment to develop the needed heat-units. He is already deficient in bodily heat because of malnutrition, and the effects of cold are cumulative. In this case it is not a question of *thermic exercise* but of a permanent *deprivation of heat,* in individuals who are already suffering from an *insufficient development of heat-units.* Consequently the organism is enfeebled—it grows under unfavorable conditions—and the result is a permanent diminution of development. Whoever grows up, exposed to cold after this fashion, has, in the average case, a lower stature than those who grow up in the midst of warmth, or in the practice of that healthful exercise which constitutes the ideal: *thermic gymnastics.*

The contradictory ideas that are held as to the efficacy of heat in regard to growth, are due to a large extent to a prejudice which amounts to this: heat is effective in promoting the evolution of life as a whole, and consequently the development of that part of life that is centred in the organs of reproduction; from which comes the well-nigh antiquated theory that artificial heat should be banished from the schools, as one of the factors leading to immorality! It is true that *warmth* accelerates the development of puberty; but who is there in this twentieth century who can still conceive the idea that it is a moral act to silence the forces of nature? Good nourishment also leads to a more precocious puberty; and the same is true of the repeated psychic stimulus produced by various forms of intellectual enjoyment, by conversation, and by social intercourse with individuals of the opposite sex. Accordingly, if it were a moral act to retard the development of puberty and to produce a general impoverishment of sexual life, the moral measures to be taken in education would be cold, malnutrition, and the isolation of the sexes in the schools, which, as a matter of fact, form the stumbling-block of environment in our colleges. But it is well known that all this leads on the contrary to moral and physical degeneration! As has already been said, the normal physiological development stands in counterdistinction to immoral habits; consequently, whatever is an aid to physiological development is in its very nature moral.

In warm climates the first manifestations of puberty occur precociously in man as well as in woman; and with them come all the transformations that are associated with puberty, among others the rapid increase of stature. In cold climates, on the contrary, such manifestations are more tardy. The women of Lapland are latest of all to develop. With them, menstruation begins only at eighteen, and they are incapable of conceiving under the age of twenty, while the period of the menopause (involution of sexual life) is correspondingly early; in other words, the entire period of sexual life is shortened. Furthermore, the fertility of the women of Lapland is low; they cannot conceive more than three children. But if these same women leave Lapland and make their home in civilised countries, as for example in Sweden, they have a more precocious sexual life, as well as longer and more fertile, and altogether quite similar to that of the Swedish women.*

Cabanis† notes that even in cold climates, when young girls spend much of their time in the vicinity of stoves, menstruation begins at about the same age as in women who live on the banks of the Ganges—as is the case with the daughters of wealthy Russians, whose development is quite precocious. In Arabia, in Egypt, and in Abyssinia the women are frequently mothers at the age of ten, menstruation having begun at the eighth year. It is even said that Mahomed married Radeejah when she was only five and that he took her to his bed at the age of eight. The religious laws of India permit the marriage of girls when they are eight years old.

* RACIBORSKI, cited by MARRO, *Puberty*.
† *Idem.*

Consequently it is true that *heat* has an influence upon the development of the organism independently of other influences; in fact, heat acts both in the form of *climate*, that is, in a natural state, and also in an artificially warmed environment. It is also one of the causes of the different degrees of growth in *stature* through the successive seasons (see below).

In conclusion: it is enjoined upon us, as a hygienic necessity, to heat the schools in winter, especially the schools for the poorer classes; it means more than increased vigour, it may even mean giving *life* to some who otherwise would pine away from deprivation of heat-units, a condition most unfavourable to organisms in the course of evolution.

Photogenic Conditions.—Light also has a perceptible influence upon growth: it is a great physiological stimulant. At the present day, physical therapy employs *light baths* for certain forms of neurasthenia and partial enfeeblement of certain organs; and some biological manifestations, such as the pigments—and similarly the chlorophyl in plants and the variegated colouring of birds—receive a creative stimulus from light.

Light contains in its spectrum many different colours, which act quite differently upon living tissues; the ultra-violet rays, for instance, kill the bacilli of tuberculosis and sometimes effect cures in cases of cancer. Psychiatrists and neuropaths have demonstrated that many colours of light have an exciting effect, while others, on the contrary, are sedative.

Hence there has arisen in medicine a vast and most interesting chapter of *phototherapy*.

In regard to the phenomena of growth, it has been noted that certain coloured lights are favourable to it, while certain others, on the contrary, diminish or arrest it, as the red and the green.

Phototherapy ought to concern us as educators, especially in regard to schools for the *benefit* of nervous children: a periodic sojourn in a room lit by *calming colours* might have a beneficent effect upon epileptic, irritable, nervous children, in place of the debilitating hot bath, or, worse yet, the administration of bromides; while light-baths would be efficacious for weak and torpid children.

But for normal children we must consider the light of the sun as the best stimulant for their growth. A sojourn at the sea-shore, so favourable to the development of children, is now believed to owe its beneficial effects to the fact that the child, playing half naked on the sea-shore, bathes more in the sunlight than he does in the salt water. Gymnastics in the sun, while the body is still only half dry, is what the younger generations should practise on a large scale, if they would bring about the triumph of physiological life.

We must not forget this great principle when, by planning home work for the pupils, we practically keep them housed during the entire day, keeping them for the most part employed in writing or reading; in other words, using their sense of sight, which, if it is to be preserved unharmed, demands a *moderate light.* The eye ought to rest its muscles of accommodation, and the whole body be exposed to the full light of the sun during the greater part of the day. Let us remember that often the children of the poor live in a home so dark that even in full mid-day they are obliged to light a lamp! Let us at least leave them the light of the street, as a recompense for wretchedness that is a disgrace to civilisation!

According to certain experiments conducted in Rome by Professor Gosio, the light of the sun has an *intensive* effect upon life. Living creatures reared in the solar light grow and mature *earlier,* but at the same time their life is shortened; that is, the cycle of life is more intense and more precocious; conversely, in the shade the cycle of life is slower, but of longer duration. A plant matures more quickly in the sun, but its stature is lower than that of a plant in the dark, which has grown far more slowly, but has become very tall and slender and lacking in chlorophyl. Similarly, as is well known, the women in tropical countries attain a precocious puberty, while conversely those of the North attain it tardily; and this fact must be considered in relation to the influence of the sun. A life passed wholly in the sunlight would be too intense; an organism that is exposed a few hours each day to the rays of the sun is invigourated; the interchange of matter (metabolism) is augmented; all the tissues are beneficially stimulated. For this reason sun baths are employed for paralytic and idiot children, and consist in exposing the body of the child, reclining upon its bed and with its head well protected, to the direct rays of the sun for several hours a day; this treatment is found to be most efficacious in giving *tone* to the tissues and improving the general condition of the system.

Variations in the Growth of Stature According to the Seasons.—One proof of the beneficent influence of heat and sunlight upon the growth of the organism, is afforded by the variations in the rate of growth according to the seasons. Every individual grows more in summer than in winter. Daffner gives the following figures relative to the increase in stature according to the seasons:

Number of subjects	Age in years	Stature in centimetres			Increase in centimetres		
		October	April	October	Winter	Summer	Entire year
12	11–12	139.4	141.0	143.3	1.6	2.3	3.9
80	12–13	143.0	144.5	147.4	1.5	2.9	4.4
146	13–14	147.5	149.5	152.5	2.0	3.0	5.0
162	14–15	152.5	155.0	158.5	2.5	3.5	6.0
162	15–16	158.5	160.8	163.8	2.3	3.0	5.3
150	16–17	163.5	165.4	167.7	1.9	2.3	4.2
82	17–18	167.7	168.9	170.4	1.2	1.5	2.7
22	18–19	169.8	170.6	171.5	0.8	0.9	1.7
6	19–20	170.7	171.1	171.5	0.4	0.4	0.8

In the "Children's Houses," I require a record of stature to be made month by month in the case of every child, the measurement being taken on the day corresponding to the day on which he was born in the month of his birth; in addition to which I keep a record of the total annual increase.

The ages of these children vary between three and four years, and they all belong to the poorer social classes.

MONTHLY AVERAGE INCREASE IN STATURE
IN THE "CHILDREN'S HOUSES"
(In millimetres)

Cold months			Warm months		
December	January	February	May	June	July
4	3	4	7	8	8

Another factor of growth is

Electricity.—One of the most interesting discoveries of recent date is that of the influence of terrestrial electricity upon the growth of living organisms.

A series of experiments were made, by isolating cavies (a species of small Indian pig) from terrestrial electricity, and as a result they were found to be retarded in growth and to develop very imperfectly, much as though they had been suffering from rickets. In short, they manifested an arrest of organic development.

If, in electro-therapy, an electric current is applied to the cartilages of the long bones in children whose limbs have apparently been arrested in development, the result is a rapid increase in length, amounting to a luxuriant *osteogenesis.*

Since we know that the electric current can stimulate the nerve filaments and the fibres of the striped muscles when they have been rendered inactive from the effects of paresis or even of paralysis, we realise that *electricity* can exert an influence over the entire physiological life of an organism. We live not only upon nutriment, air, heat, and light, but also upon a mysterious, imperceptible force, that comes to us from the mother earth.

In addition to the biological potentialities which control the development of every individual, all living creatures owe something of themselves to their environment.

Space.—An empirical contention, without scientific value, but nevertheless of some interest, is that there is an ultimate *relationship* between the dimensions of living bodies and the *territorial space,* that is, the environment in which they are destined to live. In view of the innumerable varieties of living creatures, such an assertion would seem to be utterly unfounded. But as a matter of fact we see that while inorganic bodies can increase indefinitely in dimension, living creatures are limited in form and size. This fact undoubtedly has some primal connection with properties innate in corporeal life itself; in fact, in order to attain its appointed end, life requires the services of certain very small microscopic particles called *cells.* But the aggregations and combinations of cells in living organisms are also limited in their turn, and no matter how willingly we would attribute the greatest share of causation to biological facts, nevertheless, as always happens in life, we cannot wholly exclude *environment.*

Both animals and men that are bred on vast continents (Chinese, Russians) have tended to produce races of powerful and giant build: in islands, on the contrary, the men and the animals are of small size; it is sufficient merely to cite the men and the little donkeys of Sardinia, the small Irishmen who furnish jockeys for the race-track, and the small Irish horses or *ponies* that serve as saddle-horses for the children of the aristocracy the world over.

There is a harmony of associations, as between the container and the contained, between environment and life, notwithstanding that as yet science has not made serious investigations in regard to it.

Voltaire, in his *Micromega,* avails himself of this intuitive conception to create the material needed for his satire; he talks amusingly of the inhabitant of the planet Sirius, who was eight leagues in height and at four hundred years of age was still in school, while the inhabitant of Saturn was a mere pigmy in comparison, being scarcely a thousand rods tall—in fact, the inhabitants of Saturn could not be otherwise than pigmies in comparison, since Saturn is barely nine hundred times larger than the earth.

Gulliver makes use of similar standards in his *Travels,* which are read with so much delight by children.

Psychic Conditions.—*Psychic Stimuli.*—Accordingly many chemical and physical factors associated with the environment concur in aiding *life* in its development. From the light of the sun to the electricity of the earth, the whole environment offers its tribute to life, in order to cooperate in life's triumph. But, in the case of man, in addition to these widely different factors, there is still another distinctly human factor that we must take into consideration and that we may call the *psychic stimulus of life:* We may scientifically affirm the Bible statement that "man does not live by bread alone."

Without reverting to the basic physiological explanations of the emotions, as given by Lange and James, we may nevertheless assert that sensations of pleasure stimulate the renewal of bodily tissues and consequently promote health, happiness, and strength; while, on the contrary, painful events produce physiological effects depressing to the tone of the nervous system and to the metabolic activity of the tissues.

But it is precisely these metabolic phenomena that hold the key of life, and an organism in the course of evolution depends directly upon them. This problem concerns pedagogy in a very special way: when we have given food to the children in our schools, we have not yet completed our task of *nourishing* these children; for the phenomena of nutrition which take place in the hidden recesses of their tissues are very different from a simple intestinal transformation of aliments, and are influenced by the psychic conditions of the individual pupil.

Great workers not only need abundant nutriment, but they require at the same time a series of stimuli designed to produce "pleasure." The pleasures of life, necessary to human existence, include more than *bread*. In the history of social evolution there exist, side by side with the *productions* of *labour*, an entire series of *enjoyments*, more or less elevated, that constitute the *stimului* to production, and hence to evolution, and more profoundly still, to life itself.

The further man evolves and the more he produces, the more he ought to multiply and perfect his means of *enjoyment*.

Without stimuli, nutrition would grow less and less till it ended in death. Every-day experience in the punishment of criminals gives us proof of this. Confinement to a solitary cell is nothing else than a complete deprivation of psychic stimuli. The prisoner does not lack *bread*, nor air, nor shelter from the elements, nor sleep; his whole physiological life is provided for, in the strict material sense of the word. But the bare walls, the silence, the isolation from his fellow men in utter solitude, deprive the prisoner of every stimulus, visual, oral and moral.

The consequences are not merely a state of hopelessness, but a real and actual *malnutrition* leading to tuberculosis, to anemia, to death from atrophy. We may affirm that such a prisoner *dies slowly of hunger due to defective assimilation;* the solitary cell is the modern donjon, and far more cruel than the one in which Ugolino died within a few days, so much so that solitary confinement, being incompatible with life, is only of short duration.

Labour, love, and sensations apt to stimulate ideas, that is, to nourish the intelligence, are necessities of human life.

This is further proved by observations made regarding the development of puberty. Psychic stimuli may render such development precocious, and, on the contrary, their absence may retard it. Jean Jacques Rousseau relates in *Émile* that at Friuli he encountered young people of both sexes who were still undeveloped, although they were past the usual age and were strong and robust, and this he attributed to the fact that "owing to the simplicity of their customs, their imagination remained calm and tranquil for a longer time, causing the ferment in their blood to occur later, and consequently rendering their temperament less precocious."*

Recent statistical research confirms the intuitive observation of that great pedagogist; the women in the environs of Paris attain puberty nearly a year later than those who live in the city; and the same difference is observed between the country districts around Turin and those of the city itself.

All this goes to prove the fact of psychic influence upon physiological life: psychic excitation, experienced with *pleasure*, by developing healthy activities, aids the development of physical life.†

These principles must be taken under deep consideration when it comes to a question of directing the *physiological growth* of children. Fenelon relates a fable about a female bear who, having brought into the world an exceedingly ugly son, took the advice of a crow and licked and smoothed her cub so constantly that he finally became attractive and good-looking. This fable embodies the idea that *maternal love* may modify the *body of the child*, aiding its evolution toward a harmony of form by means of the first psychic stimuli of caresses and counsel.

Nature has implanted in the mother not only her milk, the material nourishment of her child, but also that absolutely altruistic love which transforms the soul of a woman, and creates in it moral forces hitherto unknown and unsuspected by the woman herself—just as the sweet and nourishing corpuscles of the milk were unknown to the red corpuscles of her blood. Accordingly, the nature of the human kind protects the *species* through the mother in two ways, which together form the complete nutrition of man: aliment and love. After a child is weaned, it obtains its aliment from its environment in more varied forms; and it also obtains from its environment a great variety of psychic stimuli, calculated not only to mould its psychic personality, but also to bring its physiological personality to its full development.

* ROUSSEAU, *Émile*, cited by MARRO.

† It should be noted that sexual precocity or vice retards the development of puberty, while healthful psychic stimuli are favourable to it. Hence it was a right instinct that led us to give the name of sin and vice to what retards the normal development of life, and virtue and honour to what is favourable to it.—Author's note.

I have had most eloquent experience of this in the "Children's Houses" in the San Lorenzo quarter of Rome. This is the poorest quarter in the city, and the children are the sons and daughters of day labourers, who consequently are often out of work; illiteracy is even yet incredibly frequent among the adults, so much so that in a very high percentage of cases at least one of the parents is unable to read. In these "Children's Houses" we receive little children between the ages of three and seven, on a time schedule that varies between summer, from nine to five, and winter, from nine to four.

We have never served food in the school; the little ones, all of whom live in their own homes, with their parents, have a half hour's recess in which to go home to luncheon. Consequently we have not *in any way influenced their diet.*

The pedagogic methods employed, however, are of such sort as to constitute a gradual series of psychic stimuli perfectly adapted to the needs of childhood; the environment stimulates each pupil individually to his rightful psychic development according to his subjective potentiality. The children are *free* in all their manifestations and are treated with much cordial affection. I believe that this is the *first time* that this extremely interesting pedagogic experiment has ever been made: namely, to *sow the seed* in the consciousness of the child, leaving free opportunity, in the most rigourous sense, for the spontaneous expansion of its personality, in an environment that is *calm,* and warm with a sentiment of affection and peace.

The results achieved were *surprising:* we were obliged to remodel our ideas regarding child psychology, because many of the so-called instincts of childhood did not develop at all, while in place of them unforeseen sentiments and intellectual passions made their appearance in the primordial consciousness of these children; true *revelations* of the sublime greatness of the human soul! The intellectual activity of these little children was like a spring of water gushing from beneath the *rocks* that had been erroneously piled upon their budding souls; we saw them accomplishing the incredible feat of despising *playthings,* through their insatiable thirst for knowledge; carefully preserving the most fragile objects of the lesson, the tenderest plants sprouting from the earth—these children that are reputed to be vandals by instinct! In short, they seemed to us to represent the childhood of a human race more highly evolved than our own; and yet they are really the same humanity, marvelously guided and stimulated through its own natural and free development!

But what is still more marvelous is the astonishing fact that all these children are so much improved in their general *nutrition* as to present a notably different appearance from their former state, and from the condition in which their brothers still remain. Many weakly ones have been organically strengthened; a great many who were lymphatic have been cured; and in general the children have gained flesh and become ruddy to such an extent that they look like the children of wealthy parents living in the country. No one seeing them would believe that these were the offspring of the illiterate lower classes!

Well, let us glance over the notes taken upon these children at the time when they first entered the school; for the great majority, the same note was made: need of tonics. Yet not one of them took medicine, not one of them had a change of diet; the renewed vigour of these children was due solely to the *complete satisfac-*

tion of their psychic life. And yet they remain in school continually from nine till five through eleven months out of the year! One would say that this was an excessively long schedule; yet what is still more surprising is that during all this period the children are continually *busy;* and even more remarkable is the report made by many of the mothers to the effect that after their little ones have returned home they continue to busy themselves up to the hour of going to bed; and lastly—and this seems almost incredible—many of the little ones are back again at school by half past eight in the morning, tranquil, smiling, as though blissfully anticipating the enjoyment that awaits them during the long day! We have seen small boys become profoundly observant of their environment, finding a spontaneous delight in new sensations. Their stature, which we measure month by month, shows how vigourous the physiological growth is in every one of them, but particularly in certain ones, whose blood-supply has become excellent.

Such results of our experiments have amazed us as an unexpected *revelation* of nature, or, to phrase it differently, as a *scientific discovery.* Yet we might have foreseen some part of all this had we stopped to think how our own physical health depends far more upon happiness and a peaceful conscience than upon that material substance, bread!

Let us learn to know *man,* sublime in his true reality! let us learn to know him in the tenderest little child; we have shown by experiment that he develops *through work, through liberty, and through love;* hitherto, in place of these, we have stifled the splendid possibilities of his nature with irrational toys, with the slavery of discipline, with contempt for his spontaneous manifestations. Man lives for the purpose of learning, loving and producing, from his earliest years upward; it is from this that even his bones get their growth and from this that his blood draws its vitality!

Now, all such factors of physiological development are *suffocated* by our antiquated pedagogic methods. We prevent, more or less completely, the development of the separate personalities, in order to keep all the pupils within the selfsame limits. The perfectionment of each is impeded by the common level which it is expected that all shall attain and make their limit, while the pupils are forced to *receive* from us, instead of producing of their own accord; and they are obliged to sit motionless with their minds in bondage to an iron programme, as their bodies are to the iron benches.

We wish to look upon them as machines, to be driven and guided by us, when in reality they are the most sensitive and the most superb creation of nature.

We destroy divine forces by slavery. Rewards and punishments furnish us with the needed scourge to enforce submission from these marvelously active minds; we encourage them with rewards! to what end? to winning the prize! Well, by doing so we make the child lose sight of his real goal, which is knowledge, liberty and work, in order to dazzle him with a prize which, considered morally, is vanity, and considered materially is a few grains of metal. We inflict punishments in order to conquer nature, which is in rebellion, not against what is good and beautiful, not against the purpose of life, but against us, because we are tyrants instead of guides.

If only we did not also punish sickness, misfortune and poverty!

We are breakers-in of free human beings, not educators of men.

Our faith in rewards and punishments as a *necessary means* to the progress of the children and to the maintainence of discipline, is a fallacy already exploded by experiment. It is not the material and vain reward, bestowed upon a few individual children, that constitutes the psychic stimulus which spurs on the multifold expansions of human life to greater heights; rewards degrade the grandeur of human consciousness into vanity and confine it within the limits of egotism, which means perdition. The stimulus worthy of man is the joy which he feels in the consciousness of his own growth; and he grows only through the conquest of his own spirit and the spread of universal brotherhood. It is not true that the child is incapable of feeling a spiritual stimulus far greater than the wretched prize that gives him an egotistical and illusory superiority over his companions; it is rather that we ourselves, because already degraded by egotism, judge these new forces of nascent human life after our own low standards.

The small boys and girls in our "Children's Houses" are of their own accord distrustful of rewards; they despise the little medals, intended to be pinned upon the breast as marks of distinction, and instead they actively search for objects of study through which, without any guidance from the teacher, they may model and judge and correct themselves, and thus work toward perfection.

As to punishments, they are depressing in effect, and they are inflicted upon children who are already depressed!

Even in the case of those who are adult and strong, we know that it is necessary to encourage those who have fallen, to aid the weak, to comfort those who are discouraged. And if this method serves for the strong, how much more necessary it is for lives in the course of evolution!

This is a great reform which the world awaits at our hands: we must shatter the iron chains with which we have kept the intelligence of the new generations in bondage!*

Pathological Variations.—Among the factors that may have a notable influence upon the stature are the pathological causes. Aside from those very rare occurrences that produce gigantism, it may be affirmed that pathological variations result in general in an arrest of development. In such a case it may follow that an individual of a given age will show the various characteristics of an individual of a younger age; that is, he will seem younger or more childish.

In such a case the stature has remained on a *lower* level than that which is normal for the given age; and this in general is the most obvious characteristic, because it is the index of the whole inclusive arrest of the physical personality. But together with the diminution of stature, various other characteristics may exist

* Compare *The method of Scientific Pedagogy applied to infantile education in the "Children's Houses,"* MONTESSORI: Casa Editr. Lapi, 1909.

that also suggest a younger age; that is, the entire personality has been arrested in its development.

It follows, in school for example, that such pathological cases may *escape* the master's attention; he sees among his scholars a type that is apparently not abnormal, because it does not *deviate* from the common type, in fact is *quite like* other children; but when we inquire into its age, then the anomaly becomes evident, because the actual age of this small child is greater than his apparent age.

A principle of this sort announced in these terms is perhaps too schematic; but it will serve to establish a clear general rule that will guide us in our separate observations of a great variety of individual cases.

This form of arrested development was for the first time explained by Lasegue, who introduced into the literature of medicine or rather into nosographism, the comparative term of *infantilism*.

Infantilism has been extensively studied in Italy by Professor Sante de Sanctis, who has written notable treatises upon it. I have taken from his work *Gli Infantilismi*, the following table of *fundamental* characteristics necessary to constitute the *infantile type*.

1. Stature and physical development in general below that required by the age of the patient.
2. Retarded development or incomplete development of the sexual organs and of their functions.
3. Incomplete development of intelligence and character.

In order to recognise infantilism, it is necessary to know the dimensions and morphology of the body in their relation to the various ages, and to bear in mind that in young children sexual development either has not begun or is still incomplete.

Dimensions and Morphology of the Body at the Various Ages.—What we have already learned regarding stature will give us one test in our diagnosis of infantilism: the increase of stature and the transformations of *type of stature* concur in establishing the dimensions and the morphology of the body (See Stature, Types of Stature, Diagrams).

A sufferer from infantilism will have, for example at the age of eleven, a stature of 113 centimetres and a statural index of 56, while the average figures give:

Age	Stature	Index
7 years	111	56
8 years	117	55
9 years	122	55
10 years	128	54
11 years	132	53

Consequently, in such a case the eleven-year-old patient would have the appearance of a child of seven, not only in stature but also in the relative proportions of his body. (And if we examined him psychically, we should probably find his speech was not yet perfected, that he showed a tendency toward childish games, a mental level corresponding to the age of seven or thereabouts; in school the child would be placed in the first or second elementary grade.)

Accordingly the anthropological verdict of infantilism must not be based upon limits of measurement alone, but also upon the *proportions* of the body. Every age has its own morphology.

Now, such changes are found not only in the reciprocal relations between the bust and the limbs, but also between the various parts of the bust, as we shall see when we come to an analytical study of the morphology of the head, the thorax and the abdomen; the detailed anthropological examination of the individual patient will furnish us with further accompanying symptoms helpful in establishing a diagnosis. Further on we shall give a summarised table of the morphology of the body from year to year (laws of growth); and of the most notable and fundamental psychological characteristics of the different years of childhood; so that a teacher may easily derive from it at a glance a comprehensive picture that will aid in a diagnosis of the *age*, and hence of the arrest of development, in subjects suffering from infantilism.

Before entering upon the important question of pathogenesis in its relation to infantilism, I will reproduce a few biographic notes of *infantile types*, taken from various authorities:

Giulio B. was brought to the clinic because of his continued love for toys, notwithstanding his age. At seventeen and a half he retained the manners, the games and the language of a child of between ten and twelve. In appearance, he gave the impression of being between thirteen and fourteen, and was as well proportioned as a lad of that age. His stature was 1.45 meters (at thirteen the average stature is 1.40 m. and at fourteen it is 1.48 m.; while at seventeen it ought to be 1.67 m.) and his weight was 39 kilograms (at fourteen the weight is 40 k. and at seventeen it is 57 k.). His appearance was lively, intelligent, but on the whole childish. His genital organs were like those of a boy of twelve (Fig. 30). The patient understood all that was said to him, he could read, write and sing, but could not apply himself to any serious occupation; he did not read the papers, but would amuse himself by looking at pictures in illustrated books; he could play draughts, but was equally pleased when playing with children's toys. During his stay at the clinic he was several times punished for childish pranks: he filled his neighbour's chamber vessel with stones, and amused himself by making little paper boats and sailing them in the urine, etc. He was employed as a page at an all-night café; his age permitted him to perform this work forbidden to children, while his appearance rendered him fitted for the task. When questioned discreetly regarding his sexual functions, or rather his sexual incapacity, he understood at once, and expressed in a childish way his deep regret, because he had heard it said that "that was why they wouldn't let him serve in the army."

Vittorio Ch. Is twenty-two years old and looks about eight or ten. Stature 1.15 metres (average stature for the age of seven being 1.11 m.; for eight, 1.17 m.). Has no beard, nor any signs of virility; genital organs like those of a child. His intelligence is alert, but does not surpass that of a boy of ten. He speaks correctly, can read, write and sing; plays draughts, but does not disdain children's toys, and prefers looking at pictures in illustrated books to reading the daily papers. After the death of the patient, it was found, as a result of the autopsy, that the epiphyses of the long bones had not yet united with the diaphyses, and that the bones of the skull were still as soft as those of a child (Fig. 31).

Here is another case, taken from Moige:*

It is the case of a young working girl, presenting all the appearance of a child of twelve or fourteen; she had not yet attained puberty, although she was thirty years of age. No external sign gave evidence that she was undergoing the sexual transition that should give her womanhood. Her breasts were reduced to the

* MOIGE, *Nouvelle Iconographie de la Salpêtrière*, 1894.

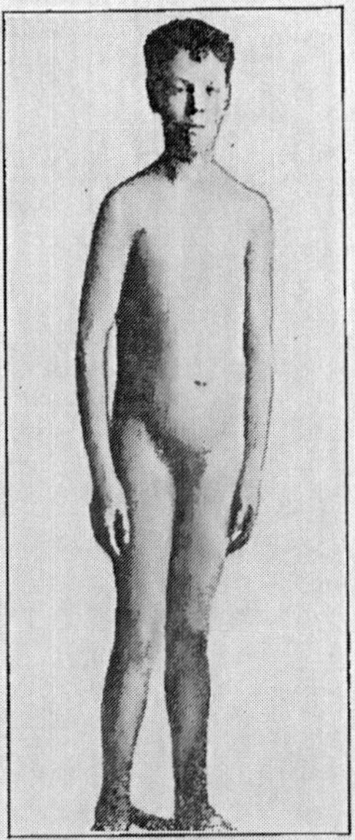

Fig. 30.—Boy, seventeen and one-half years old.

Fig. 31.—Young man, twenty-two years old.

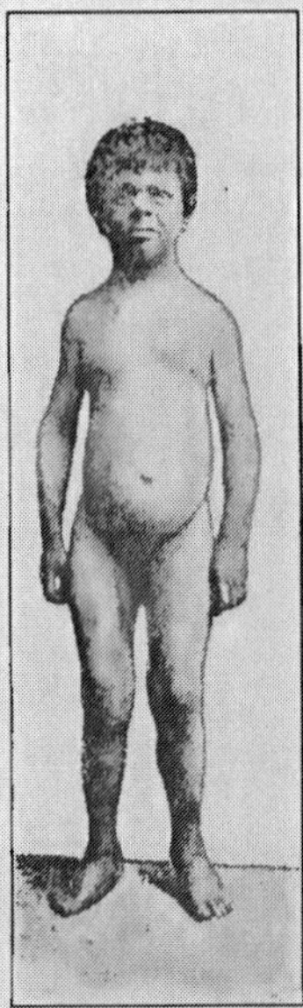

Fig. 32.—Idiotic cretin, age 20 years, stature 1,095 m.

Fig. 33.—An example of myxedematous infantilism.

Fig. 34.—A group of cretins in the valley of Aosta (Piedmont). The alteration of the thyroid gland is of endemic origin.

mere nipple, as in infancy. Her voice was weak. This woman was hysterical and subject to frequent attacks of convulsions. Her mental condition remained infantile. She was gentle, docile, timid and apprehensive; she was destitute of coquetry or sense of shame.

"Renato L.,* age twenty-nine; stature 1.30 m. (average stature at the age of ten, 1.28 m.; at eleven, 1.32 m.) weight, 32 kilograms (average weight, age of twelve, 31 k.). It appears from his history that he developed normally up to the age of nine, after which period an arrest of development occurred, both physical and psychic. An arrest of the genital organs dates back also to early childhood. His intelligence is that of a backward child; he has never been able to read or write, but can count up to 1000. He has never been able to learn a trade, but shows some talent for drawing.

His criminal instincts seem to be especially developed. He spends whole hours, turning over the leaves of popular illustrated novels, and whenever he comes across a picture representing a homicide or an assassination, he utters loud exclamations of delight. He has only one passion, tobacco, and only one object of adoration, Ravachol. Very violent, extremely irritable; when he is angry, he would kill someone, if, as he says, "he had the strength for it." Although, as a rule, he docilely obeys the orders given him, it is because he is "afraid of being scolded." His ideal is to be able some time to obtain refuge in the Hospice de Bicêtre.

From De Sanctis's work, *Gli Infantilismi*, I obtain the following data, that are very suggestive on the anthropological side, regarding a case of infantilism observed by the professor in his asylum-school for defective children, in Rome.

Vincenzo P., seven years of age. Father in good health and of good character. Mother small, thin, weak, underfed; has had nine children, of which five are living, all feeble. Vincenzo was born in due time, birth regular; had five wet-nurses; cut his teeth at the normal intervals; began to walk at the end of the second year and to speak at the end of the first. According to his mother, all went well until the fourth year. At this period, Vincenzo became very troublesome and ceased to "grow taller." Later on he was sent to the communal school, but the director of the school

* Apert, *Op. cit.*

in the Via Ricasoli, seeing how undersized and backward he was, sent him to the Asylum-School for defective children.

In appearance the child is eurhythmic, excepting that the head appears a little *too big* in proportion to the rest of his body; but it is not of the hydrocephalic type (an infantile characteristic). He is slightly asymmetric, the postero-inferior portion of the right parietal bone being more depressed than that of the left (infantile plagiocephaly).

Measurements		Age at which the measurements of Vincenzo would be normal
Of the child	Normal measurements at the age of seven	
Stature, 0.870 m.	1.10 m.	Three years, stature, 0.864 m.
Weight, 12.400 kg.	20.16 kg.	Two years, weight, 12 kg.
Circumference of chest, 0.507 m.	0.55 m	Four years, circumference of chest, 0.505 m.
Vital index, 59	Vital index, 54	Two years, vital index, 59.

The bust is *greatly developed* in comparison with the lower limbs, which are unquestionably short. (The sitting stature was not taken, but this note, recorded from simple observation, reminds us of the enormous difference between the indices of stature at the age of two or three and at the age of seven: Index at two years = 63; at three = 62; at seven = 56.)

But although we lack the index of stature, we may make use of the vital index, which is given by the proportion between the circumference of the chest and the stature, and consequently gives us an index of the morphology of the bust in its relation to the whole personality; thus we find that the vital index corresponds in the present case to that of a child of two, as is also true of the weight, so that we may deduce that the index of stature was probably about 62–63.

He shows no impairment as to external sensations; on the other hand, internal sensations, such as satiety, illness, etc., are blunted. His power of attention seems sufficient, both at play and in school and when questioned. Neither does his memory show anything abnormal. Emotionally, he is below the normal level; he says that he is afraid of thunder; occasionally he shows annoyance when disturbed; but it is equally certain that he never becomes angry, never turns pale and never blushes, as the result of any excitement. He is of an indifferent disposition and is passive in manner; he is good natured, or rather, a certain degree of apathy makes him appear so.

All things considered, his mental development may be described as that of a three-year-old child; only that he differs from children of that age in his lack of vivacity and in his complete development of articulate speech (it should be noted, in regard to the diagnosis of age made by so distinguished a psychologist as De Sanctis, that he judged the child to have a psychic development corresponding to the age of three years; while we, studying the general measurements of the body, determined that they correspond to three different ages, namely, two, three and four the average of which is precisely three; while the *stature*, which is the index of development of the body as a whole, corresponds almost exactly to that average of three years (0.870 m., 0.864 m.).

Pathogenesis of Infantilism.—At this point it might be asked: Why do we grow? We hide the mechanism of growth under very vague expressions: biological final causes, ontogenetic evolution, heredity. But, if we stop to think, such expressions are not greatly different from those which they have replaced: the divine purpose, creation.

In other words, a causal explanation is lacking. But positive science refuses to lose itself in the search after final causes, in which case it would become metaphysical philosophy. Nevertheless, it may pursue its investigations into the genesis of phenomena, whenever the results of experiments permit it to advance.

So it is in the case of growth; certain relatively recent discoveries in physiology have made it possible to establish relations between the development of the individual and the functions of certain little glands of "internal secretion." Now, the discovery of these relations is certainly not a causal explanation of the phenomenon of growth, but only a profounder analysis of it.

Hitherto, we have considered the organism in regard to its chief visceral functions: in speaking of macroscelia and of brachyscelia, we considered the different *types* in relation to the development of the organs of vegetative life and the organs of external relations: the central nervous system, the lungs, the heart, the digestive system. Our next step is to enter upon the study of certain little organs, which were still almost ignored by the anatomy and physiology of yesterday. These organs are glands which, unlike other glands (the salivary glands, the pancreas, the sudoriferous glands, etc.), are lacking in an excretory duct, through which the juices prepared for an immediate physiological purpose might be given forth; and in the absence of such excretory tubes, their product must be distributed through the lymphatic system, and hence imperceptibly conveyed throughout the whole organism.

One of these glands, the one best known, is the *thyroid*; but there are others, such, for example, as the *thymus*, situated beneath the sternum, or breast-bone, and much reduced in size in the adult; the *pineal gland* or hypophysis cerebri, situated at the base of the encephalon; the *suprarenal capsules*, little ear-shaped organs located above the kidneys. Up to a short time ago, it was not known what the functions of such glands were; some of them were regarded as atavistic survivals, because they are more developed in the lower animals than in man, and consequently were classed with the vermiform appendix as relics of organs which had served their functions in a bygone phylogenetic epoch and remain in man without any function, but on the contrary represent a danger through the local diseases that they may develop. The cerebral hypophysis was in ancient times regarded as the *seat of the soul.*

These glands are very small; the largest is the thyroid, which weighs between thirty and forty grams (1 to 1 $\frac{3}{8}$ oz.); the suprarenal glands weigh four grams each (about 60 grains); the hypophysis hardly attains the weight of one gram.

The importance of these glands began to be revealed when antiseptic methods rendered surgery venturesome, and the attempt was made (in 1882) to remove the thyroid gland. After a few weeks the patient operated on began to feel the effects of the absence of an organ necessary to normal life: effects that may be summed up as, extreme general debility; pains in the bones and in the head; an elastic swelling of the entire skin; enfeebled heart action, and anemia; and on the psychic side, loss of memory, taciturnity, melancholy. After the lapse of some time the patient showed such further symptoms as the shedding of the cuticle of the skin, whitening of the hair and *facies cretinica.*

But when Sick undertook to operate upon the thyroid of a child of ten, the deleterious effects of interrupting the above-mentioned function of the gland manifested itself in an *arrest of development;* at the age of twenty-eight the patient operated on by Sick was a cretin (idiotic dwarf) 1.27 metres tall (average stature at age of ten = 1.28 m.). Since that time certain diseases have been recognised that call to mind the condition of patients who have undergone an operation for removal of the thyroid glands, and in which the subjects have suffered from *hypothyroidea,* or insufficient development of the thyroid.

Such individuals were characterised by *nanism,* solid edema of the skin, arrest of psychic development, and absence of development of puberty; this malady has taken its place in medical treatises under the name of myxedema; and, when serious, is accompanied by *nanism* and myxedematous idiocy. But in *mild cases* it may result in a simple myxedematous infantilism.

The other glands of internal secretion are also associated with the phenomena of growth. First in importance is the *thymus* which is found highly developed in the embryo and in the child at birth, and thereafter diminishes in volume, until it almost disappears after the attainment of puberty. In the psychological laboratories of Luciani, at Rome, the first experiments were conducted upon dogs, for the purpose of determining what alterations in growth would result as a consequence of the removal of the thymus. The dogs thus operated on were weak; furthermore they became atrophied, accompanied by roughness of the skin and changes in pigmentation. After this, experiments were made in the Pediatric Clinic at Padua, under the direction of Professor Cervesato, in the application of thymic organotherapy (that is, the use of animal thymus as medicine) with notable success in the case of atrophic children (infantile atrophy occurs in early infancy; this form is known popularly in Italy as the "monkey sickness." Nursing children become extremely thin, cease to grow in length, the little face becomes elongated and skeleton-like, and is frequently covered with a thick down).

Stoppato also obtained analogous results in infantile atrophy and anemia. Hence it is evident that the very rapid growth in the embryo is associated with the functional action of the thymus. And this is also true of the very rapid growth during the first years of a child's life.

The pituitary gland, or cerebral hypophysis, has also functions associated with the general nervous tone and trophism (or nourishment) of the tissues, and especially of the osseous system. There is a disease known as acromegalia (Marie's disease) which is characterised by an abnormal and inharmonic growth of the skeleton, especially in the limbs and the jaw; the hands and feet become enormously enlarged, while the jaw lengthens and thickens (an unhealthy formation on which the common people of Italy have bestowed the name of "horse sickness," because of the appearance assumed by the face). Such patients complain of general and progressive debility of their psychic activities. In such cases, an autopsy shows an alteration of the pituitary gland, often due to malignant tumors (sarcoma).

The suprarenal capsules also bear a relation to general trophism and particularly to the pigmentation of the skin. It was already noted by Cassan and Meckel that the negro races show a greater volumetric development of the suprarenal capsules; when in 1885 Addison for the first time discovered a form of disease associated with alterations of the suprarenal capsules, characterised by an intensely brown colouration of the skin (bronzed-skin disease), general debility of the nervous and muscular systems, progressive anemia and mental torpor; the malady ends in death. In the case of animals operated on for physiological experiments, not one of them has been able to survive.

Some interesting observations have been made by Zander on the connection between the development of the nervous system and the suprarenal glands. He found that there was an insufficient development of these glands in individuals having teratological (monstrous) misshapements of the brain, as in the case of hemicephalus (absence of one-half the brain), cyclops, etc.

There exists between all the ductless glands, or those of internal secretion, an organic sympathy: in other words, if one of them is injured the others react, frequently to the extent of assuming a vicarious (compensating) functional action.

What their functional mechanism is, that is, whether the secretions act as formative stimulants or enzymes, ferments of growth, or whether as antitoxines to the toxines elaborated by various organs in the process of regression, is a question still controverted and in any case cannot enter within the limits of our field.

It is enough for us to know that the general growth of the organism and its morphological harmony, depend not only as regards the skeleton, but equally in relation to the cutaneous system and its pigmentation, the development of the muscles, the heart, the blood, the brain, and the trophic functions of the nervous system, upon some formative and protective action of all these little glands of "internal secretion," with which are associated the *psychic activities* and even the life itself of each individual, as though within the embryonic crucible there must have been certain substances that acted by stimulating the genetic forces and directing the trophism of the tissues toward a predetermined morphology.

To-day it is held that even the *mother's milk* contains these formative principles, or *enzymes*, suited to stimulate the tissues of her own child in the course of their formation; consequently, it produces results which no other milk in all nature can replace.

Alterations in these glands of "internal secretion" may therefore produce an arrest of development—and, in mild cases, forms of infantilism. But the gland which in this connection is of first importance is the *thyroid*.

Now there is one form of arrest of the trophic rhythm of growth which may be due to *hereditary causes* effecting the formative glands (myxedematous infantilism), or to exceptional causes occurring in the individual himself in the course of formation, either at the moment of conception, or at some later moment, as may happen even during the period of infancy (dystrophic infantilism of various origin).

In all these cases, however, according to Hertoghe, the exceptional causes, deleterious to growth, would first of all exercise their influence upon the glands of internal secretion and especially upon the *thyroid*.

In order to make clear, in connection with such complex pathological problems, the cases which are important from the point of view of pedagogy and the school, let us divide them into:

Myxedematous infantilism, due to congenital insufficiency of the thyroid gland from hereditary causes, and

Dystrophic infantilism, associated with various causes deleterious to individual development—and acting secondarily upon the glands of internal secretion (syphilis, tuberculosis, alcoholism, malaria, pellagra, etc.).

Myxedematous infantilism is characterised by short stature, by excessive development of the adipose system, and by arrest of mental development (including speech). Such *infantiles* very frequently have a special morphology of the face, that suggests the mongol type, and characteristic malformations of the hands (little fingers atrophied). When treated with extracts of the thyroid glands of animals, they improve notably; they become thinner, they gain in stature, their mentality develops to the extent of permitting them to study and to work. Certain mongoloids treated by De Sanctis in the Asylum-School at Rome were improved to the point of being able to attend the high-school and therefore were restored to their family and to society as useful individuals—all of which are facts that are of singular importance to us as educators! Medical care working hand in hand with pedagogy may save from parasitism individual human beings who otherwise would be lost. We ought to be convinced from such evidence of the necessity of *special schools* for deficients, wholly separated from the elementary schools, and where *medical care* combined with a specially adapted pedagogic treatment may transform the school into a true "home of health and education." The plan of a "school with a prolonged schedule of hours," including two meals and a medical office, as was conceived and organised by Prof. Sante de Sanctis in Rome, has been proved to answer admirably to this social need; because without wholly removing the children from their families, and therefore without exposing them to the disadvantages of a boarding school, it provides them with all the assistance necessary to their special needs.

Dystrophic Infantilism.—Given a case of infantilism, discoverable by the teacher through the general measurements of the body and psychic examination, it is interesting to investigate the deleterious *causes.*

It may be the result of *poisoning,* as for example from *alcohol.* Alcohol has such a direct influence upon the arrest of development that in England jockeys are produced by making the lads drink a great deal of alcohol. Children who drink alcohol *do not grow in stature,* and similarly the embryo grows in a less degree when the mother indulges in alcohol during pregnancy; some Swiss women deliberately resort to this means, in order that a smaller child may lessen the pain of child-birth. But alcohol not only diminishes the stature, but destroys the harmony of the different parts; that is, in the development of the body it arrests both the volumetric and the morphological growth. Furthermore, alcohol produces in children an arrest of mental development. An acquaintance with this principle of hygiene should be looked upon by the teacher less as a piece of special knowledge than as a *social duty*. From the point of view of the educator, the fight against alcoholism should have no assignable limits! It would be vain for him to perfect his didactic methods in order to *educate* a *child that drank wine or other still worse alcoholic liquors*. It would be better if the efforts which he meant to dedicate to such educative work could be all turned to a *propaganda* directed toward the parents of such children, or toward the children themselves, to induce them to abstain from so pernicious a habit!

We may also consider in the category of *poisonings* certain chronic maladies which act upon the organism with special toxic (poisonous) effects. In the foremost rank of such maladies belongs

Syphilis.—This disease is ranked among the principal causes of *abortion;* in other words, the fœtus which results from a syphilitic conception lacks *vitality*, and often fails to complete the cycle of intrauterine life. But even granting that the fœtus survives and attains its complete development, the child after birth *grows* tardily, and very often remains an *infantile*. It is well known that syphilis has been transmitted to new-born infants at the time of birth, in consequence of which these infants may in turn transmit syphilis to their wet-nurses. In such cases they are really *sick* and need medical treatment from the hour of their birth. Just as in the adult patient, syphilis has several successive stages, an acute primary stage, with plain manifestations of hard ulcers, erythema diffused over the skin of the entire body, glandular infiltrations, etc., and then secondary and tertiary manifestations that eventually become chronic and exhibit almost imperceptible symptoms; so in the case of children, syphilis may be transmitted in various degrees of virulence. In the acute stage the result will be abortion or the child will be still-born, or else the new-born child will plainly exhibit ulcerations and erythema, but at other periods of the disease, the child may bear far less evident signs of its affliction, as for instance a special form of corrosion in the enamel of its teeth; the *cervical pleiades* or enlargement of certain little lymphatic glands like the beads of a rosary, distinguishable by touch in the posterior region of the neck; certain cranial malformations (prominent nodules on the parietal bones, Parrot's nodes); and in the child's whole personality an under-development

11

in respect to its age. In cases like these the teacher's *observations* may be of real social value, because the child has shown no symptoms of such a nature as to cause the parents to have recourse to a physician, and it is the child's *scholarship* (using the word in the broad sense of the *way in which the child reacts in the environment of school,* the profit he derives from study, etc.) that may reveal an abnormal development to an intelligent teacher.

The first indication is a *stature below what is normal at a given age.* Such observations ought to be obligatory upon teachers who are in sympathy with the new ideas, for they alone can be the arbiters of the rising generations. It is being said on all sides, to be sure, with optimistic assurance that argues a deficiency of critical insight and common sense, that an adequate *education of the mothers* ought to enlighten all women in regard to the laws of growth in children and the abnormalities that are remediable. But of what class of mothers are we supposed to be speaking? Certainly not of the great mass of working women and illiterates! certainly not of the women who have been constrained to hard toil from childhood up, and later on condemned to abortion because of such unjust labor, while their spirit is brutalized and their memory loses even the last lingering notion of an alphabet! It will always be easier and more practical, in every way, to enlighten twenty-five thousand teachers regarding these principles than to enlighten many millions of mothers; not to mention that if we wished to enlighten these mothers in a practical way regarding the principles of the hygiene of generation, we should still have to invoke the services of that very class whose assigned task in society is precisely that of educating the masses!

The teacher can and should learn at least how to *suspect* the presence of hereditary syphilis in his pupils, in order to be able to invoke the aid of the physician, leaving to the latter the completion of the task, namely, the eventual cure. It is well known that iodide of potassium and its substitutes, especially if used at an early stage, can *cure* syphilitic children and therefore save innocent boys and girls from eventual definite arrest of development and from all the resultant human and social misery.

Another cause that is deleterious to development is

Tuberculosis.—Although it has now been demonstrated that tuberculosis is not hereditary, as an active disease—that is, we cannot inherit in our organism localised colonies of the tuberculosis bacillus, because the bacilli cannot pass through the placenta into the fœtus during the period of gestation—nevertheless a *predisposition* to infection from the bacillus can be inherited.

A predisposition which consists in a special form of weakened resistance of the tissues, rendering them incapable of immunity, and a skeletal formation which is distinguished by a narrowness of the chest, and a consequent smallness of lungs, which, being unable to take in sufficient air, constitute a *locus minoris resistentiæ* (locality of less resistance) to localisation of the bacilli. Now, since our environment is highly infected by the bacilli of tuberculosis, we must all necessarily meet with it, we must all have repeatedly received into our mouths and air passages Koch's bacilli, alive and virulent; and yet the strong organism remains immune, while the weak succumbs. Consequently those who are predisposed by heredity are almost fated to become tuberculous, and in this sense the malady presents the appearance of being truly hereditary. But such organic weakness in a child predisposed to tuberculosis is manifested not only by possible attacks of various forms of the disease localised in the glands (scrofula) or the bones, but also by a *delayed development of the whole personality.*

Now, the environment of school and the educative methods still in vogue in our schools, not only are not adapted to correct such a predisposition, but what is more, the school itself *creates* this predisposition! In fact, the sitting posture—or rather, that of stooping over the desk, to write—and the prolonged confinement in a closed environment, impede the normal development of the thorax and of all the physical powers in general. Many a work on pedagogic anthropology has already shown that the *most studious scholars,* the *prize-winners,* etc., have a wretched chest measure, and a muscular force so low as to threaten ruin to their constitutions.

Consequently, children who are predisposed to tuberculosis ought unquestionably to be *removed* from our schools and cared for and educated in favourable environments. While we are still impotent in the face of fatalities due to this deplorable disease, we are not ignorant of the means needed to save a predisposed child and transform him into a robust and resistant lad. Such knowledge, to be sure, was applied to *mankind* only as a second thought; for the first men to apply and then to teach such means of defence were the owners of cattle and the veterinaries. The owners of cattle discovered that if a calf was born of a tuberculous cow, it could be saved and become an excellent head of cattle, if only it was subjected to a very simple procedure; the calf must be removed from its mother and given over to be nursed by another cow in the open country; and it must remain in the open pastures for some time after it its weaned.

By taking similar precautions in the case of children, it has been shown that the son of a tuberculous woman, if entrusted to a wet-nurse in the *open country*, and brought up on an abundance of nourishing food until his sixth year in the freedom of the fields, can be made as robust as any naturally sound child. From this we get the principle of *schools in the open air*, or of *schools in the woods*, or *on the sea-shore*, for the benefit of weak, anemic children, predisposed to tuberculosis. Such a sojourn constitutes the "School-Sanatorium," the lack of which is so grievously felt by the parents of feeble children, and that might so easily be instituted in our mild and luxuriant peninsula, so rich in hillsides and sea-coast!

Malaria.—One of the chief causes of mortality and of biological pauperism in many regions of Italy is *malaria*. This scourge rages even to the very gates of Rome. The country folk of these abandoned tracts pine away in misery and at the same time in illiteracy, while their blood is impoverished by disease, and a notable percentage of the children are *victims of arrested development*.

These unfortunates, forgotten by civilisation, are destined to roam the fields, bearing with them, till the day of their death, a deceptive appearance of youth, and an infantile incapacity for work, an object-lesson of misery and barbarity! Among the means of fighting malaria, the spread of civilisation and the school ought to find a place. Even the quinine given freely by the government is distributed with difficulty among these unhappy people, brutalised by hunger and fever; and some message from civilisation ought to precede the remedy for the material ill. A far-sighted institution is that of Sunday classes founded by Signor Celli and his wife in the abandoned malarial districts. In these classes, the teachers from elementary schools give lessons every Sunday, spreading the principles of civic life, at the same time that they distribute quinine to the children.

If we stop to think that wherever malaria is beaten back, it means a direct conquest of fertile lands and of robust men, and hence of wealth, we must realise at once the immense importance of this sort of school and this sort of struggle, which may be compared to the ancient wars of conquest, when new territories and strong men constituted the prize of battles won, and the grandeur of the victorious nations.

Pellagra.—Pellagra is still another scourge diffused over many regions of Italy. It is well known that this disease, whose pathological etiology is still obscure, has some connection with a diet of mouldy grain. Pellagra runs a slow course, beginning almost unnoticed in the first year, with a simple cutaneous eruption, which the peasants sometimes attribute to the sun. The second year disturbances of the stomach and intestines begin, aggravated by a diet of spoiled corn; but it is usually not until the third year that pellagra reveals itself through its symptoms of great nervous derangements, with depression of muscular, psychic and sexual powers, together with *melancholia*, amounting to a true and special form of psychosis (insanity) leading to homicide, even of those nearest and dearest (mothers murdering their children) and to suicide.

This established cycle of the disease is not invariable. Instead of representing successive *stages*, these symptoms may often be regarded merely as representing the *prevailing* phenomena in various forms of pellagra; in any case, it constitutes a malady that runs a slow course during which the same patient is liable to many relapses. While the malady is running its course, the patients may continue their usual physiological and social life, and even *reproduce* themselves. So that it is not an infrequent case when we find mothers, *suffering from pellagra*, nursing an offspring generated in sickness and condemned to manifold forms of *arrested development, both physical and mental.*

Against a disease so terrible that it strikes the individual and the species, it is now a matter of common knowledge that there is an exceedingly simple remedy: it consists in a strongly nitrogenous diet (*i. e.* meat) and that, too, only temporarily. In fact, in the districts where the pellagra rages, various charitable organisations have been established, among others the economic *kitchens* for mothers, which by distributing big rations of meat effect a cure, within a few months, not only of the sick mothers but of their children as well.

The real battle against pellagra must be won through *agrarian reforms:* but in the meantime the local authorities could in no small degree aid the unhappy population with their counsel, by enlightening the peasants regarding the risks they run, as well as by informing them of the various forms of organised aid actually established in the neighbourhood and often unknown to the public or feared by them, because of the ignorance and prejudice with which they are profoundly imbued!

Pauperism, Denutrition, Hypertrophy.—We may define all the causes hitherto considered that are deleterious to growth, as *toxical dystrophies,* since not only alcohol, but the several diseases above discussed—syphilis, tuberculosis, malaria, pellagra—produce forms of chronic intoxication. But besides all these various forms of dystrophics, we may also cite cases of infantilism due purely to defective nutrition, and family poverty. Physiological misery may produce an arrest of growth in children.

But just as denutrition associated with pauperism (social misery, economic poverty, lack of nourishment) may cause an organism in course of development to arrest its processes of evolution through lack of material, the same result is equally apt to be produced by any one of a great variety of causes liable to produce organic denutrition, physiological poverty.

For example, too frequent pregnancies of the child's mother, which have resulted in impoverishing the maternal organism, causing deficiency of milk, etc.

Infant Illnesses.—In the same way, organic impoverishment is caused by certain maladies of the digestive system which impede the normal assimilation of nutritive matter: dysentery, for instance; and the effects may be still more disastrous if symptoms of this kind are accompanied by feverish conditions, as in typhus.

There are cases, however, in which the arrest of development is not to be attributed to some wasting disease, or to the denutrition resulting from it; but rather to some acute illness occurring in early childhood (pneumonia, etc.), after which the child ceased to progress in accordance with his former obviously normal development.

Anangioplastic Infantilism.—Another form of infantilism is associated with a malformation of the heart and blood-vessels, that is to say, the heart and aorta together with the entire circulatory system are of small dimensions; the calibre of the arteries is less than normal. In such a case the restriction of the entire vascular system and the scantiness of circulation of the blood constitute an impediment to the normal growth of the organism.

Although in such cases the explanation of the cause of the phenomenon is purely mechanical, nevertheless such abnormality of the heart and veins is to be classed as a teratological (monstrous) malformation, determined by original anomalies of the ductless glands, similar to what is found in cases of cephalic and cerebral monstrosities.

In this form of infantilism the patient shows not only the usual fundamental characteristics already noted, but also symptoms of *anemia* as obstinate to all methods of treatment as *chlorosis* is; in addition to which they often show congenital malformations of the heart, in every way similar in their effects to valvular affections such as may result from pathological causes (chief of which are mitral and aortic stenosis, which consist of a stricture of the valves connected with the left ventricle of the heart).

Accordingly, children who show forms of mitral infantilism are inferior to their actual age not only in their whole psychosomatic appearance, but they are noticeably weak, pale and suffering from shortness of breath and disturbances of the circulation. In such cases, neither pedagogy nor hygiene can counteract the arrest of development; but it is well that the attention of teachers should be called to such cases, in order that cruel errors may be prevented, which would unconsciously do additional harm to individuals already burdened by nature with physiological wretchedness.

In conclusion: The normal growth of the organism is *associated* with the functional action of certain glands known as glands "of internal secretion," such as the thymus and thyroid, first of all, as well as the suprarenal capsules and the cerebral hypophysis.

This group of *formative* glands presides not only over the entire growth of the body, but also over the intimate modeling of its structure; so that a *lesion* or *deficiency* in any of them results not only in nanism and an arrest of mental development, but in various forms of general dystrophy.

That the organism is associated in the course of its transformations with the functional action of specific glands is shown by the *development of puberty*, which consists in a series of transformations of the *entire organism*, but is associated with the establishment of funçtional activity of glands that were hitherto immature: the genital glands (ovaries, testicles). These glands also are functionally in close sympathy with the entire group of formative glands: so much so that, if the glands of internal secretion are injured, the genital glands usually fail to attain normal development (infantilism). Now, the transformations which take place in the organism at the period of puberty might be produced at other periods if the functional action of the generative glands should show itself at a different epoch. That is, these transformations are not associated with the *age of the organism*, but with the development of specific glands. There are cases of the genital glands maturing at abnormal ages; or of local maladies that have hastened the appearance of the phenomena of puberty in children of tender years. A notable case is that described by Dr. Sacchi,* of a nine-year old boy, who had grown normally up to the age of five and a half, both in his physiological organism and in his psychic personality. At the age of five and a half, the child's father noticed a physical and moral alteration; the child's voice grew deeper, his character more serious, and the skeletal and muscular systems grew rapidly, while on certain portions of the body, as for example on the face, a fine down appeared. At the age of seven the child had attained a stature that was gigantic for his age; he was very diligent and studious and did not care to play with his comrades. At nine, he had a stature of 1.45 metres (the normal stature being 1.22), a weight of 44 kilograms (normal = 24); his muscles were highly developed, his powers of traction and compression being equal to those of a man; his chin was covered with a thick beard five centimetres long. When he was examined by a physician, the latter discovered a tumor in the left testicle. After an operation, the child lost his beard and regained his childish voice; his character became more timid and sensitive; he began once more to enjoy his comrades and take part in boyish games. His muscular force underwent a notable diminution.

Rickets.—It is important not to confound any of the various forms of infantilism with *rickets*. Rickets is a well-defined malady whose special point of attack is the osseous system in course of formation; but it leaves the nervous system and the genital system unimpaired. The sufferer from rickets may be a person of intelligence, capable of attaining the highest distinctions in art or in politics; he is normal in his genital powers, so that he is capable of normal reproduction, without, in many cases, transmitting any taint of rickets to his descendants.

* Cited by Marro.

Nevertheless this disease, like all constitutional maladies, occurs only in individuals who are *weakly.*

Among the characteristics of rickets, the one which assumes first importance is *inferiority of stature* in comparison with the normal man. In this connection I quote the following figures from Bonnifay:*

Age	Stature in centimetres	
	Rachitic children	Normal children
11 months	66.5	69.4
2 years	70.7	74.8
2–3 years	75.8	83.0
3–4 years	76.8	91.9
5–6 years	91–93	101.25
6–7 years	105.0	106.8
7–8 years	110.6	115.3
8–9 years	118.4	119.0
9–10 years	121.6	124.4

But together with diminution of stature there exist in rickets various *deformities* of the skeleton, especially in the bones of the cranium, in the vertebral column and in the frame of the thorax; although even the pelvis and the limbs have been known to show the characteristic deformities.

An objective knowledge of the first symptoms of rickets ought to be regarded as indispensable on the part of mistresses in children's asylums, and in any case to form an important chapter in pedagogic anthropology. For it is well known that in the early stages of *rickets* the child may be so guided in its growth as to save it from deformities of the skeleton, even though a definite limitation of the stature may not be *prevented.*

That is to say, that through the intervention of hygiene and pedagogy the rachitic child may be saved from becoming a *cripple* or a *hunchback,* and will simply remain an individual of *low stature;* with certain signs and proportions of the skeleton indicative of the attack through which he has passed. Even in very severe cases it is at least possible to minimize the deformity of the thorax and the curvature of the vertebral column.

* Cited by Figueira, *Semejotica Infantile,* p. 121.

The precursory signs of rickets in a child are: a characteristic *muscular weakness*, frequently accompanied by excessive development of adipose tissue, giving an illusory impression of abundant nutrition; delay in the development of the teeth and in locomotion, which from the very beginning may be accompanied by curvature of the long bones of the legs. The bregmatic fontanelle of the cranium closes later than at the normal period, and is larger than in normal cases, just as the entire cerebral cranium is abnormally developed in volume, while the facial portion remains small, especially in regard to the jaw bones.

One of the most salient characteristics, however, is the peculiar enlargement of the *articular heads* of the long bones, easily recognizable in the size of the *wrists:* the enlargement is also found in the extremities of the ribs, which at their points of union on each side of the sternum form a succession of little lumps, like the beads of a rosary. In conjunction with these characteristics, it is to be noted, at all ages, as appears from the figures given by Bonnifay, that there is a notable *diminution of stature.*

The *treatment* of rickets is *medical* and *pedagogical* combined. Children of this type should be *removed* from the public school, where the school routine might have a fatally aggravating effect upon the pathological condition of such children. In fact, gymnastics based upon marching and exercising in an erect position, together with a prolonged sitting posture, are likely to produce weaknesses of the skeleton and deformities, even where there are no symptoms of rickets!

The establishment of *infant* asylums for rachitic children is one of the most enlightened movements of the modern school. We Italians are certainly not the last to found such institutions, and Padua possesses one of the oldest and most perfect asylums of this sort of which Europe can boast. Asylums for rachitic children ought to have a special school equipment, so far as concerns the *benches* and the apparatus for *medical and orthopedic gymnastics;* furthermore they should be provided with a pharmaceutical stock of remedies suited to building up the osseous system and the organism in general; and a school refectory should be provided, adapted to the condition of the children. The methods of instruction should rigorously avoid any form of *fatigue,* and instead provide the child with psychic stimuli designed to overcome a sluggishness due to the mental prostration to which he is for the most part subject. As regards their situation, these asylums for rachitic children may be advantageously located upon the *sea-coast.*

The Stature of Abnormals.—The name of abnormals is applied to the entire series of individuals who are not normal: hence the categories already considered (infantilism, gigantism, rachitis) are included by implication. The group of abnormals, however, includes besides a long series of other classes, neuropathics, epileptics, and degenerates.

Under the head of abnormals may also be included those who are abnormal in character, such as criminals, etc. It is not irrational to group together the different types of abnormals, for the purpose of anthropological research, in contrast with those who are normal. In America, for instance, such studies are conducted on a large scale, precisely for the purpose of showing the *deviation* of abnormal dimensions of the body from normal dimensions, not only in the definitive development of the body, but also during growth. The abnormals depart from the mean measurements, now rising above and again falling below, as though they were intermittently impelled by the biological impulse of their organism, which at one time manifests a hypergenesis and at another a hypogenesis. A clear illustration of these facts is afforded by MacDonald's diagram (see page 168): the solid line which rises regularly represents the growth in stature of normal individuals; the dotted line which forms a zig-zag, now rising rapidly above the normal line and then falling very much below it, represents the growth in stature of the abnormals. Naturally such a chart must be interpreted by comparison with the standards of mean measurements gathered at successive ages from a large number of different children. It shows that normal children are nearly uniform among themselves, and in relation to the years of their growth: while abnormal children differ greatly one from another and do not accord with the mean stature of the age they represent.

Regarding the stature of *criminals* there can be nothing special to say: *criminals* do not represent an anthropological entity. They belong to a large extent, whenever the criminal act has a psycho-physiological basis, to various categories of *abnormals*. From the victim of rickets to the infantile, to the submicrocephalic, to the ultra-macroscele or ultra-brachyscele, all abnormal organisms may contribute to the number of those predisposed to the social phenomenon of criminality. And it is for this reason that we may say in general that the stature of abnormals is sometimes above and sometimes below the normal, but with a prevailing tendency to fall below.

Moral and Pedagogic Considerations.—The objection may be raised that a medico-pedagogic system of treatment, designed to prevent a threatened arrest of development or to minimise its progressive symptoms, demands on the part of society an excessive effort, out of proportion to the end in view. To cure or ameliorate the condition of the weak may even be regarded as a principle of social ethics that is contrary to nature, whose laws lead inexorably to the selection of the strong and to the elimination of all those who are unfitted for the struggle for life. Sparta has furnished us with a practical example that is very far from the principles which scientific pedagogy is to-day seeking to formulate as a new necessity of social progress.

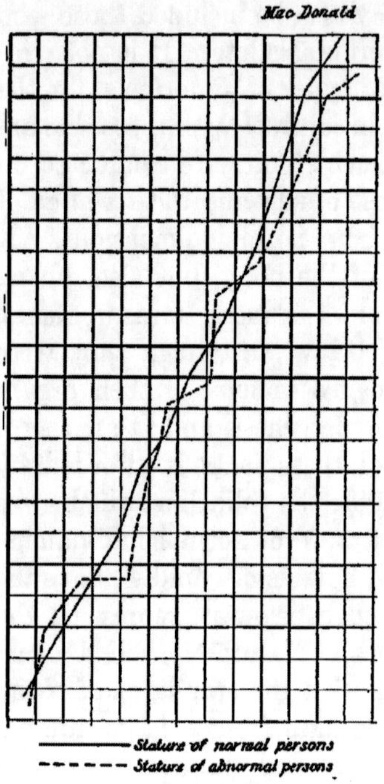

FIG. 35.

But we are too far removed from the triumphant civilisation of Greece, to recur to the authority of her example: the principle sanctioned to-day by modern civilisation, that of "respect for human life," forbids the violent *elimination* of the weak: Mount Taygetus is no longer a possible fate for innocent babes in a social environment the civic spirit of which has abolished the death penalty for criminals. Consequently, since the weak have a right to live, as many of them as naturally survive are destined to become a burden, as parasites, upon the social body of normal citizens; and they furnish a living picture of physiological wretchedness, a spectacle of admonitory misery, inasmuch as it represents an *effect* of social causes constituting the collective errors of human ethics. Ignorance of the hygiene of generation, maladies due to the vices and the ignorance of men, such as syphilis, other maladies such as tuberculosis, malaria and pellagra, representing so many scourges raging unchecked among the people, are the actual causes that are undermining the social structure, and manifesting themselves visibly through their pernicious fruit: the birth of weaklings. To forget the innocent results of such causes, as we forget the causes themselves, would be to run the risk of plunging precipitously into an abyss of perdition. It is precisely these disastrous effects upon posterity that ought to warn us and shed light upon the errors through which we are passing lightly and unconsciously. Accordingly, to gather in all the weaklings is equivalent to erecting a barrier against the social causes which are enfeebling posterity: since it is impossible to conceive that if the existence of such a danger were once demonstrated, society would rest until every effort had been made to guard against the possibility of its recurrence.

In addition to such motives for human prophylaxis, a more immediate interest should lead us to the pedagogic protection of weak children. The establishment of special schools for defective children, sanatarium-schools for tuberculous children, rural schools for those afflicted with malaria and pellagra, infant asylums for rachitic children, is a work of many-sided utility. They constitute a fundamental and radical purification of the schools for normal children: in fact, so long as intellectual and moral defectives and children suffering from infantilism and rachitis intermingle with healthy pupils, we cannot say that there really exist any *schools for normal children,* in which pedagogy may be allowed a free progress in the art of developing the best forces in the human race.

Still another useful side to the question is that of putting a stop to the physiological ruin of individual weaklings. Very small would be the cost of schools for defective children, asylums for the rachitic, tonics, quinine, the iodide treatment, school refectories for little children afflicted with hereditary taints and organic disease: very small indeed, in comparison to the disastrous losses that society must one day suffer at the hands of these future criminals and parasites gathered into prisons, insane asylums and hospitals, in comparison to the harm that may be done by one single victim of tuberculosis by spreading the homicidal bacilli around him. It is a principal of humanity as well as of economy to *utilise* all human forces, even when they are represented by beings who are apparently negligible. To every man, no matter how physiologically wretched, society should stretch a helping hand, to raise him. In North America the following principle has the sanction of social custom: that the task of improving physiological conditions and at the same time of instilling hope and developing inferior mentalities to the highest possible limit constitutes an inevitable human duty.

Accordingly it remains for the science of pedagogy to accomplish the high task of human redemption, which must take its start from those miracles that the twentieth century has already initiated in almost every civilised country: straightening the crippled, giving health to the sick, awakening the intelligence in the weak-minded—much as hearing is restored to the deaf and speech to the mutes—such is the work which modern progress demands of the teacher. Because such straightening of mind and body naturally lies within the province of those who have the opportunity to give succor to the human being still in the course of development; while after a defect has reached its complete development in an individual, no manner of help can ever modify the harm that has resulted from lack of intelligent treatment.

The prevention of the irremediable constitutes a large part of the work which is incumbent upon us as educators.

Summary of Stature

We have been considering *stature* as the linear index of the whole complex development of the body, taking it in relation to two other factors, the one internal or biological, and the other external or social. These two factors, indeed, unite in forming the character of the individual in his final development; and in each of them education may exert its influence, both in connection with the hygiene of generation and through reforms instituted in the school.

In the following table are summed up the different points of view from which we have studied stature in its biological characteristics and in its variations:

- **Varieties of stature**
  - Ethnic varieties and limits of oscillation
    - Stature in different races; extreme limits.
    - Stature of the Italian people; and its geographical distribution.
    - Limits of stature: medium, tall, low.
  - Biological varieties
    - Difference of stature in the sexes.
    - Stature at different ages (growth).
- **Variations in stature**
  - Variations due to adaptation
    - Mechanical
      - Transitory or physiological.
      - Permanent, often accompanied by deformities. (Causes: the attitudes required by the work.)
    - Physiological
      - Nutrition.
    - Physical
      - Heat.
      - Light.
      - Electricity.
    - Psychic
      - Psychic stimuli.
  - Pathological variations
    - Infantilism
      - Myxedematous.
      - Dystrophic
        - from alcohol.
        - from syphilis.
        - from tuberculosis.
        - from malaria.
        - from pellagra.
      - Hypotrophic
        - Denutrition.
      - Anangioplastic
    - Rachitis

Summary of the Scientific Principles Illustrated in the Course of the Exposition of our Subject

When an anthropological datum is of such fundamental importance as the *stature*, its limits of oscillation must be established, and its terminology must be founded upon such limits expressed in figures that have been measured and established by scientists (medium, tall, low).

The stature is the most important datum in pedagogic anthropology, because it represents the linear index of the development of the body, and for us educators is also the *index* of the child's normal growth.

Bio-pathological Laws.—In cases of total arrest of development of the personality (infantilism) the first characteristic symptom usually consists in a diminution of stature in relation to age; the morphological evolution, as well as the psychic, fails to progress in proportion to the *age of the subject;* but it corresponds to the mean bodily proportions belonging to the age which would be normal for the actual stature of the subject.

WEIGHT

The *weight* is a measure which should be taken in conjunction with the stature; because, while the stature is a linear index of the development of the body, the weight represents a *total measure of its mass;* and the two taken together give the most complete expression of the bio-physiological development of the organism.

Furthermore the weight permits us to follow the *oscillations* of development; it provides educators with an index, a level of excellence, or the reverse, of their methods as educators, and of the hygienic conditions of the school or of the pedagogic methods in use.

The fact is, that if a child is ill, or languid, etc., his stature remains unchanged; it may *grow more slowly,* or be arrested in growth; but it can never diminish. The weight, on the contrary, can be lost and regained in a short time, in response to the most varied conditions of *fatigue,* of *malnutrition,* of *illness,* of *mental anxiety.* We might even call it the *experimental datum* of the excellence of the child's development.

Another advantage which the measure of weight has over that of stature is that it may serve as an *exponent of health* from the very hour of the child's birth; while *stature* does not exist in the new-born child, and begins to be formed (according to the definition given) only after the first year of its life, that is, when the child has acquired an erect position and the ability to walk steadily.

Variations.—Weight is one of the measures that have been most thoroughly studied, because it is not a fruit of the recently founded science of pedagogic anthropology; but it enters into the *practice* of pediatricians (specialists in children's diseases) and of obstetricians (specialists in child-birth), while even the general practitioner can offer precious contributions from his experience.

According to Winckel, and practically all pediatricians agree with him, "the weight of a child, if taken regularly, is the best thermometer of its health; it easily expresses in terms of figures what the nursing child cannot express in words."*

The new-born child weighs from three to four kilograms; but oscillations in weight from 2,500 to 5,000 grams are considered normal. Some obstetricians have noted weights in new-born chil-

[1] Cited by FIGUEIRA (Rio Janeiro) in his volume, *Elementi di Semejotica infantile*, 1906. From this volume, which contains the result of the most modern investigations in pediatry, I have taken a number of data regarding the weight of children.

dren that are enormous, true gigantism, which, however, while possible, are altogether exceptional; nine and even eleven kilograms.

The oscillations in weight of the child at birth, within normal limits, may have been determined by general biological factors, as for example the sex (the female child weighing less than the male), and the race (especially in regard to the stature of the parents): but the factors which influence the weight of the new-born child in a decisive manner are those regarding the *hygiene of generation.*

1. "The children which have the greater weight are those born of mothers between the ages of twenty-five and thirty." (Mathews Duncan.) Let us recall what we have said regarding stature; at the end of the twenty-fifth year, that is, at the end of the period of growth, man is admirably ripe for the function of reproduction; and we ought further to recall the views cited regarding the mortality of children conceived at this age which is so favourable to parenthood; and finally the note in regard to celebrated men, almost always begotten at this age.

2. "First-born children have in general a weight inferior to that of those born later (1,729 first-born children gave an average of 3,254 grams: while 1,727 born of the second or subsequent conceptions gave an average of 3,412 gr." (Ingerslevs). Let us remember that celebrated men are scarcely ever the *fiirst-born.*

3. "Very short intervals between successive pregnancies interfere with this *progression* in weight; long intervals on the contrary do not interfere with it" (Wernicke). In other words, too frequent pregnancy is unfavourable to the result of the conception.

4. "Mothers who, at the birth of their first child weigh less than fifty-five kilograms and are under twenty years of age, have children of inferior weight, who are less predisposed to normal growth" (Schafer).

Let us recall what we have said regarding the *form* and the scanty weight in the case of macrosceles; and also in regard to the age of procreation in its relation to stature.

5. "Women who toil at wearisome work up to the final hour give birth to children inferior in weight to those born of mothers who have given themselves up to rest and quiet for some time before the expected birth" (Pinard).

All these considerations which refer to *normal individuals,* represent a series of hygienic laws regarding *maternity,* which may be summed up as follows: excellence in procreation belongs to those mothers who have already attained the age at which the individual organism has completed its development, and before it has entered upon its involutive period; the mother must herself have a normal weight; the pregnancies must be separated by long intervals; and during the last weeks of pregnancy it is necessary that the mother should have the opportunity of complete rest.

The increase in weight of the new-born child during the first days of its life, may constitute a valuable prognostic of the child's life. That is to say, through its successive gains it reveals the vitality, the state of health of this new human being.

Here also the pediatrists can furnish us with valuable experimental data, which serve to formulate the "laws of growth." These are:

1. From the moment of a child's birth, throughout the first two days, it suffers a loss in weight of about 200 grams, due to various causes, such as the emission of substances accumulated in the intestines during the intrauterine life (meconium), and the difficulties of adaptation to a new environment and to nutrition. But by the end of the first week a normal child should have regained its original weight; so that after the seventh day the normal child weighs the same as at the moment of birth.

On the contrary, children born prematurely, or those having at the time of birth a weight below the average, or those that are affected with latent syphilis, or are weak from any other cause whatever, regain their original weight only by the end of the second week.

Accordingly, in one or two weeks the family may form a prognosis regarding future life of the new-born child: a matter of fundamental and evident importance.

Furthermore, an antecedent detail of this sort may be valuable in the progressive history of subjects who, having attained the age for attendance at school, come to be passed upon by the teachers.

To this end, in the more progressive countries, the *carnet maternel*, or mother's note-book, has begun to come into fashion, for the use of mothers belonging to the upper social classes (as, for instance, in England): it consists of a book of suitable design, in the form of an album, and more or less *de luxe* in quality, in which the most minute notes are to be registered regarding the lives of the children from the moment of their birth onward. Various authors, especially in France, now give models for the *maternal registration* of the child's physiological progress; true *biographic volumes* that would form a precious supplement to the *biographic charts* of the schools: and the efforts of the family would round out and complete those of the school for the protection of the lives of the new generations. Such assistance, however, is only an *ideal,* because nothing short of a great and far distant social progress could place *all* mothers (the working women, and the illiterate of Italy) in a position to compile their *carnet maternel.* Auvard advocates, for registering the weight of the child during the first days of its life, a table in which the successive days from the first to the forty-fifth are marked along a horizontal line, while a vertical column gives a series of weights, with 25-gram intervals, covering a range of 700 grams, the multiples of a hundred being left blank, to be determined by the actual weight of the child and filled in by the mother or whoever takes her place.

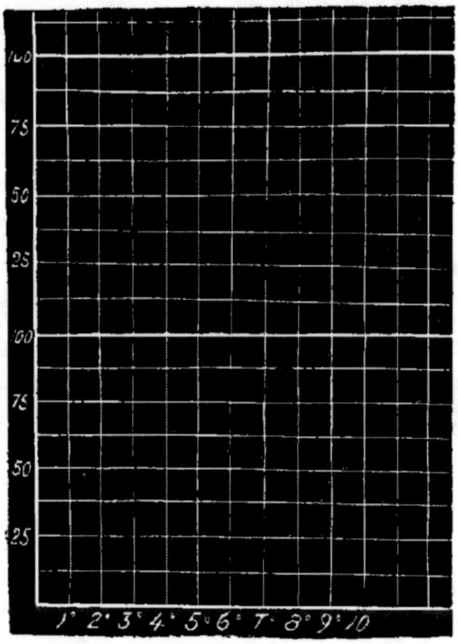

Fig. 36.

In such a table, the graphic sign indicating the changes in weight ought to fall rapidly and rise again to the point of departure by the seventh day, *if the child is robust.*

Another law of growth which may serve as a prognostic document in the child's physiological history is the following:

2. "Children nourished at their mother's breast double their weight at the fifth month and triple it at the twelfth." In other words, before the middle of its first year a healthy child, normally nourished, will have doubled its weight.

On the contrary, "Artificial feeding retards this doubling of weight in children, which is attained only by the end of the first year; so that the weight is not tripled until some time in the course of the second year."

And this gives us pretty safe principles on which to judge of the personality in the course of formation, at an epoch when stature does not yet exist.

Undoubtedly a great moral and social progress would be accomplished through a wide dissemination of very simple and economical *carnets maternels;* which should contain not only tables designed to facilitate the keeping of the required records, but also a statement of the laws of *infant hygiene;* or at least, simple and clear explanations of the significance of such phenomena, in relation to the life and health of the child; and also as to the causes which produce weakness in new-born children; or in other words, advice regarding the fundamental laws of the hygiene of generation. All that would be needed, in such case, would be a progressive exposition by means of the *carnets,* through lessons made as simple and as objective as possible, such as the weighing of small babies, to make the much desired "education of the mothers" both possible and practical.

But without this practical means; without this new sort of syllabarium on hand, to serve as a constant and luminous guide for married women, I do not believe that we shall have much success with the scattered lectures, obscure and soon forgotten, that at present are being multiplied in an attempt to reach the mothers of the lower classes.

In conclusion, I note this last contribution that comes to us from the pediatrists:

3. "There are certain maladies that cause a daily and very notable loss in weight"; they are the intestinal maladies; there may be an average loss of from 180 to 200 grams a day; but even in cases of simple loss of appetite (dyspepsia) the weight may decrease by about 35 grams a day. But when a child suffering from acute febrile intestinal trouble (cholera infantum), loses a tenth of his weight in twenty-four hours, the illness is mortal.

Now from the point of view of the educator this fact ought to be of serious interest, because we very frequently find among the recorded details of sickly children, or those suffering from arrested or retarded development, a mention of some *intestinal* malady incurred in early infancy.

Still one further observation: Meunier has noted a fact of extreme importance: that while children are passing through the period of incubation of an infectious disease, and before they show *any symptoms* likely to cause a suspicion of the latent illness, they sustain a *daily loss in weight*, from the fourth or fifth day after exposure to contagion until the appearance of decisive symptoms. In children between one and four years old, the daily loss is about fifty grams, and the total about 300; but such a loss may rise as high as 700 gr. The most numerous observations were taken in cases of *measles*.

Now, there is no need of explaining the prophylactic imporance of observations such as these! A child who for a period of twenty days is in a state of incubation, is called upon to struggle, with all the forces of immunity that his organism possesses, against a cause of disease which has already invaded him; yet no external sign betrays this state of physical conflict. Consequently, the child's organism *continues* to sustain the customary loss of energy due to the activities of its daily life, and by doing so lessens its own powers of immunity. To prescribe rest, if nothing more, for a child suspected of passing through the period of incubation would in many cases mean the saving of a life, and at the same time would protect his companions from infection, which is communicable even during the period of incubation.

In our biographic records of defective children, which include the great majority of the weakly ones, we find in many cases a *characteristic tendency to relapses* in all kinds of infective diseases, from which they regularly recovered. Such organisms, feeble by predisposition, yet sufficiently strong to recover from a long series of illnesses, were *exhausted in respect to those biological forces* on which the normal growth of the individual depends, by this sort of internal struggle between the organic tissues and the invading microbes. No scheme of special hygiene for children of this type can help us, either in the home or at school; the *daily variations in weight*, on the contrary, might constitute a valuable guide for the protection of such feeble organisms; at the first signs of a diminution in weight, such children ought to be subjected to absolute repose.

The use of the weighing-machine, both at home and in school cannot be too strongly recommended. In America the pedagogic custom has already been established of recording the weight of the pupils regularly once a month; but instead of once a month, the weight ought to be taken *every day*. The children might be taught to take their own weight by means of self-registering scales, and to compare it with that of the preceding day, thus learning to keep watch of themselves: and this would constitute both a physical exercise and an exercise in *practical living.*

The weight may be considered by itself, as a measurement of the body; and it may be considered in its relation to comparative mean measurements given by the authorities; just as it may also be considered, in the case of the individual. in its relation to the stature.

a. The weight, taken by itself, is not a homogeneous or rigorously scientific measurement. In the same manner as the stature, it represents a sum of parts differing from one another, the difference in this instance being that of specific gravity. As a matter of fact, it makes a great difference whether a large proportion of the weight of an individual is adipose tissue, or brain, or striped muscles. Each of the various organs has its own special specific gravity, as appears from the following table:

Specific Gravity		
Tubular bones		1.93
Spongy bones		1.24
Cartilage		1.10
Muscles	from	1.10
	to	1.30
Tendons		1.16
Epidermis	from	1.10
	to	1.19
Hair	from	1.28
	to	1.34
Liver		1.07
Kidneys		1.04
Brain		1.039
Cerebrum		1.036
Cerebellum		1.032
Adipose tissue		0.97

All these specific gravities are low; we weigh but little more than water; and for that reason it is easy for us to swim. But because of the difference in their composition, the *total weight of the body* gives us no idea of its constituent parts.

Take for example the question of increase in weight. We can compare the mean figures given by the authorities with the ascertained weight of some particular child of a given age, so as to keep an empirical check upon the normality of its growth. But since we know that an individual in the course of evolution undergoes profound alterations in the volumetric proportions of the different organs in respect to one another, we cannot obtain from the total weight any light upon this extremely important alteration in proportions. Thus, for example, Quételet gives the following figures of increase in weight for the two sexes:

	Weight			Weight	
Age	Males	Females	Age	Males	Females
9	3.20	2.91	15	46.41	41.30
1	10.0	9.30	16	53.39	44.44
2	12.0	11.40	17	57.40	49.08
3	13.21	12.45	18	61.26	53.10
4	15.07	14.18	19	63.32	—
5	16.70	15.50	20	65.0	54.46
6	18.04	16.74	—	—	—
7	20.16	18.45	25	68.29	55.08
8	22.26	19.82	30	68.90	55.14
9	24.09	22.44	40	68.81	56.65
10	26.12	24.24	50	67.45	58.45
11	27.85	26.25	60	65.50	56.73
12	31.0	30.54	70	63.03	53.72
13	35.32	34.65	80	61.22	51.52
14	40.50	38.10	—	—	—

INCREASE IN WEIGHT OF BODY

ACCORDING TO SUTILS

Age	Weight of body in grams	Increase
At birth	3000	—
1 month	3750	750
2 months	4450	700
3 months	5100	650
4 months	5700	600
5 months	6250	550
6 months	6750	500
7 months	7200	450
8 months	7600	400
9 months	8000	400
10 months	8350	350
11 months	8700	350
12 months	9000	300

But these figures give no idea of the laws of growth that govern each separate organ, and that have been studied by Vierordt. According to this authority, the total weight of the body increases nineteen-fold from birth to complete development. Certain ductless glands, on the contrary, *diminish* in weight in the course of growth; the thymus, for instance, is reduced to half what it weighed originally.

Furthermore, the various organs all differ in such varying degrees, as compared with their respective weights at birth, that it facilitates comparison to reduce the weight of each separate organ to a scale of 1. On this basis we find that when complete development is attained, the eyes weigh 1.7; the brain 3.7; the medulla oblongata (spinal marrow) 7; the liver 13; the heart 15; the spleen 18; the intestines, stomach and lungs 20; the skeleton 26; the system of striped muscles 48.

And these widely different augmentations are not uniform in their progress, nor is the complete development of each organ attained at the same epoch. As a matter of fact, the brain acquires one-half its final weight at the end of the first year of age; the organs of vegetative life attain half their weight at the beginning of the period preceding puberty (eleventh year). To offset the lack of indications regarding such increases in weight, we have a guide in the *morphology* of growth, which reveals how differently the various parts of the body develop.

However empirical it may be from an analytical point of view, the datum of weight is a valuable index, and represents, *taken by itself,* a synthetic anthropological measure of prime importance.

It obeys certain laws of growth which are themselves of great interest; namely, there exist two periods of rapid growth: at birth and during puberty; while at various periods in childhood, between the ages of three and nine, there are alternations of greater and lesser growth analogous to those already noted in relation to stature.

Accordingly, the weight confirms the fact that the organism does not proceed uniformly in its evolution, but passes through *crises of development* during which the forces of the organism are all devoted to its rapid transformation; such periods represent epochs at which the organism is more predisposed to maladies, more subject to mortality and less capable of performing work (compare the observations already made in relation to stature).

Index of Weight.—Accordingly, weight and stature stand in a certain mutual relationship, but the correspondence between them is not perfect. In the study of individual physiological development it is necessary to know the anthropological relation between weight and stature; in other words, the ponderal index. Without this, we cannot get a true idea of the weight of an individual. For instance, if two persons have the same weight, 65 kilograms for example, and one of them has a stature of 1.85 metres and the other of 1.55 m.; it is evident that the first of these two will be very thin, because his *weight is insufficient*, while the second, on the contrary, will have an *excessive weight.*

A stout, robust child will weigh less, in an absolute sense, than an adult man who is extremely thin and emaciated; but relatively to the mass of his body, he will weigh more. Now this relative weight or index of weight, the *ponderal index*, gives us precisely this idea of relative *embonpoint*, of the more or less flourishing state of nutrition that any given individual is enjoying. Hence it is a relation of great physiological importance, especially when we are dealing with children.

The calculation of the ponderal index ought to be analogous to that of other indexes; what has to be found is its relation to the stature reduced to a scale of 100. In this case, however, we find ourselves facing a mathematical difficulty, because *volumetric* measurements are not comparable to *linear* measurements. Consequently it is necessary to reduce the measurement of weight by extracting its cube root, and to establish the following equation:

$$St: \sqrt[3]{W} = 100 : X$$

$$\text{whence } Pi = \frac{100\sqrt[3]{W}}{S}$$

The application of this formula necessitates a troublesomely complicated calculation, which it would be impracticable to work out in the case of a large number of subjects. But as it happens, tables of calculations in relation to the ponderal index already exist, thanks to the labours of Livi* and it remains only to consult them, as one would a table of logarithms, by finding the figure corresponding to the required stature, as indicated above in the horizontal line, and the weight as indicated in the vertical column.

Some authors have thought that they were greatly simplifying

* LIVI: *Antropometria.*

the relation between weight and stature by calculating the proportional weight of a single centimetre of stature and assuming that they had thus reduced the relation itself to a ratio based upon a single linear measurement (one centimetre), analogous to the ratio established by the reduction of the total stature to a scale of 100. But evidently such a calculation is based upon two fundamental errors, namely: first, no comparison is ever possible between a linear measure and a measure of volume; and secondly, the relation which we are trying to determine is that between synthetic measurements, *i.e.*, measurements of the whole, and not of parts.

In the aforesaid method of computing (which is accepted by such weighty authorities as Godin and Niceforo), the number expressing the weight in grams is divided by the stature expressed in centimetres, and the quotient gives the average weight of one centimetre of stature expressed in grams. This method, which sounds plausible, may easily be proved to be fallacious, by the following illustration, given by Livi in his treatise already cited (Fig. 37). The two rectangles *A* and *B* represent longitudinal sections of two cylinders, which are supposed to represent respectively (in *A*) the body of a child so fat that he is as broad as he is long (the rectangle *A* is very nearly square), and (in *B*) that of a man of tall stature and so extremely thin that he very slightly surpasses the child in the dimensions of width and thickness (note the length and narrowness of rectangle *B*). Evidently the ponderal index of *A* is very high and that of *B* is very low. But if we calculate the *proportional weight* of one centimetre of stature, it will always be greater in the man than in the child, and consequently we obtain a relation contrary to that of the ponderal index.

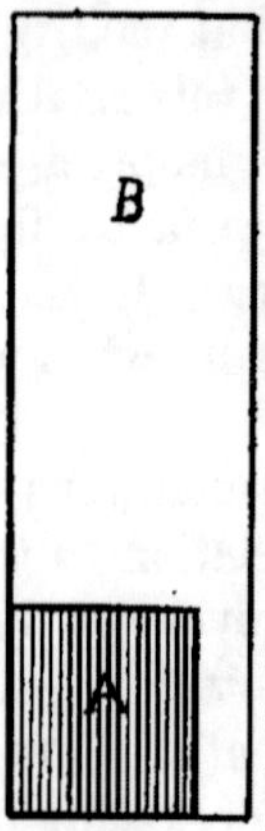

Fig. 37.

Let us make still another counterproof by means of figures; let us take an adult with a stature of 1.70 metres and a weight of 19 kilograms; and a three-year-old child 0.90 m. tall and weighing 55 kg. (the normal weight of a child of four). In the case of the adult one centimetre of stature will weigh $\frac{65000}{170}$ grams = 382 grams; while one centimetre of the child's height will weigh $\frac{15000}{90} = 166$

grams. In other words, one average centimetre of the child's stature weighs less than one centimetre of the adult, as it naturally should, while the ponderal index on the contrary is 23.6 in the case of the adult, and 27.4 in that of the child.

The reciprocal relations between stature and weight vary from year to year. In babyhood, the child is so plump that the fat forms the familiar dimpled "chubbiness," and Bichat's adipose "fat-pads" give the characteristic rotundity to the childish face; while the adult is much more slender. A new-born syphilitic child which, with a normal length of 50 centimetres, weighed only two kg.—and consequently would be extremely thin—would have the same identical ponderal index as an adult who, with a stature of 1.65 m., weighed 100 kg.

The *evolution* of the ponderal index forms a very essential part in the *transformations* of growth; and it shows interesting characteristics in relation to the different epochs in the life of the individual.

In this connection, Livi gives the following figures, for males and for females; from which it appears that at some periods of life we are *stouter*, and at others more *slender;* and that men and women do not have the same proportional relation between mass and stature.

	Indices			Indices	
Age in years	Males	Females	Age in years	Males	Females
0	29.7	29.6	15	23.1	23.4
1	30.9	30.5	16	23.4	23.6
2	28.7	28.9	17	23.1	23.7
3	27.5	27.3	18	23.2	24.1
4	26.5	26.6	19	23.4	24.1
5	25.8	25.6	20	23.5	24.1
6	25.1	24.8	—	—	—
7	24.4	24.1	25	23.7	24.1
8	24.0	23.8	30	23.8	24.1
9	23.5	23.5	40	23.9	24.7
10	23.1	23.2	50	24.3	25.3
11	22.8	23.3	60	24.6	25.3
12	23.1	23.6	70	24.5	24.9
13	23.4	23.5	80	24.4	24.7
14	23.1	23.3	—	—	—

It may be said in general, so far as regards the age, that the following is the established law of individual evolution: during the first year the ponderal index increases, after which it diminishes up to the period immediately preceding puberty (eleventh year for males, tenth year for females), the period at which boys and girls are exceedingly slender. After this, throughout the entire period of puberty, the ponderal index seems to remain remarkably constant, oscillating around a fixed figure. At the close of this period (seventeenth year for males, fourteenth for females), the ponderal index resumes its upward course (corresponding to the period in which the transverse dimensions of the skeleton increase, and in which the individual, as the phrase goes, *fills out*), and it continues to rise well into mature life (the individual *takes on flesh*); until in old age, the ponderal index begins to fall again (the soft tissues shrink, the cartilages ossify, the whole person is shrunken and wasted.)

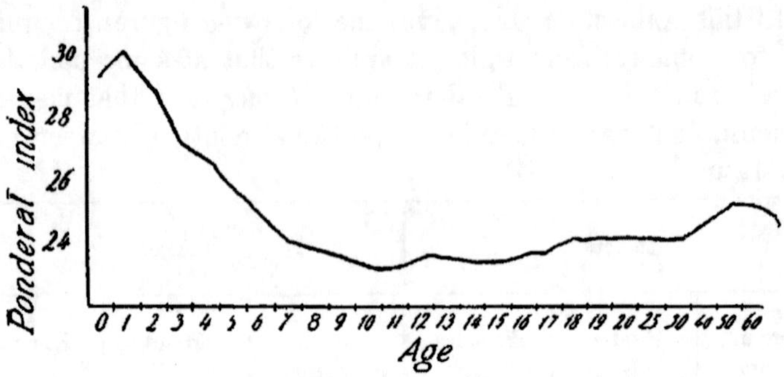

FIG. 38.

Women, during their younger years are on a par with men in respect to the ponderal index, but in later life surpass them, because of woman's greater tendency toward *embonpoint*, since she is naturally stouter and plumper than man, who is correspondingly leaner and more *wiry*.

The following diagram indicates the progressive evolution and involution of the ponderal index throughout the successive stages of life:

The ponderal index has revealed certain physiological conditions in pupils that are extremely interesting. Some authors had already noted that the ponderal index was higher in *well-nourished* children (Binet, Niceforo, Montessori); but last year one of my own students, Signorina Massa, in a noteworthy study of children, all taken from the same social class and quite poor, and who did not attend the school refectory or have the advantage of any other physiological assistance, established the fact that the more *studious* children, the *prize winners*, have a lower *ponderal index* and a *muscular force* inferior to that of the non-studious (negligent) pupils. That the development of the ponderal index stands in some relation to the muscular force, might already have been deduced from the fact that the greatest increase of weight is due, in the evolution of the individual, to the system of striped muscles. Studious children, accordingly, are sufferers from *denutrition through cerebral consumption;* furthermore, they are weakened throughout their whole organism; in fact, I discovered, in the course of researches made among the pupils in the elementary schools of Rome, that the *studious* children, those who *received prizes*, had a *scantier* chest measurement than the non-studious. This goes to prove that school prizes are given at the cost of a useless holocaust of the physiological forces of the younger generations!

That the ponderal index has an eminently physiological significance, is further shown by the following comparative figures between normal and weak-minded children. The stature, which is biologically significant, is lower in the weak-minded; but their ponderal index is greater when they are well fed, as in the asylums in Paris.

Accordingly, the sole cause of the physical inferiority of studious children is *study, cerebral fatigue.*

BIO-PHYSIOLOGICAL DIFFERENCES BETWEEN NORMAL AND WEAK-MINDED CHILDREN

(SIMON AND MONTESSORI: BASED ON CHILDREN FROM 9 TO 11)

Age	Weight in kilograms		Average stature		Ponderal index	
	Weak-minded	Normal	Weak-minded	Normal	Weak-minded	Normal
9	21.0	25.5	1.15	1.24	24	23.9
10	26.5	28.5	1.25	1.30	24	23.6
11	27.0	30.5	1.25	1.33	24	23.6

It should be noted that in the foregoing table the normal children include both the studious and the non-studious.

CHAPTER II

CRANIOLOGY

Having finished the study of general biological questions and of the body considered in its *entirety*, we may now pass on to analyse its separate parts, treating in connection with each of such parts the social and pedagogic questions which may pertain to it.

The *parts* of the body which we shall take under consideration are: the *head*, the *thorax*, the *pelvis* and the *limbs*.

The Head.—When we pass from the body as a whole to a more particularised study of the separate parts, it is proper to begin with the head because it is the most important part of the whole body. The older anthropology, and biological and criminal anthropology as well were very largely built up from a study of the head; a study so vast and important that it has come to constitute a separate branch of science: *craniology.*

The fact is that the characteristics manifested by the cranium are chiefly in the nature of *mutations* rather than *variations*, and consequently the anthropological data relating to the cranium correspond more directly to the characteristics of the species, or in the case of man, to the characteristics of race. Hence they are of special interest to the general study of anthropology. But when these mutative characteristics, which are naturally constant and have a purely biological origin, undergo *alterations*, they are to be explained, not as variations, but as *pathological deviations;* and for this reason criminal anthropology has drawn a very large part of its means of diagnosis of *anomalies* and of *degeneration* from malformations of the cranium.

Furthermore, the cranium together with the vertebral column represents not only the characteristics of species, but also those of the *genus;* in fact, it corresponds to the cerebro-spinal axis, which is the *least variable* part of the body throughout the whole series of vertebrates; just as, on the contrary, the *limbs* represent the *most variable* part. Indeed, if we study separately the cranio-vertebral system and the limbs, through the whole series of vertebrates, we shall discover *gradual* alterations in the former, and sudden wide alterations in the latter. The cerebro-spinal axis (and hence the cranio-vertebral system) shows from species to species certain progressive differences that suggest the idea of a gradual sequence of modifications (from the amphioxus to man) to which we could apply the principle, *Natura non facit saltus:* while the limbs on the contrary, even though they preserve certain obvious analogies to the fundamental anatomic formation of the skeleton, undergo profound modifications—being reduced in certain reptiles to mere rudimentary organs, developing into the wing of the bird, the flying membrane of the bat, and the hand of man.

Since it is not only a characteristic of species and race, but of *genus* as well, the cranium constitutes one of the most *constant* anatomical features. For the same reason it is less subject to *variations due to environment,* and from this point of view offers slight interest to pedagogic anthropology. But since the cranium contains the organ on which the psychic manifestations depend, we have a deep interest in knowing its human characteristics, its *phases of development,* and its normal limits.

Head and Cranium

The term *Head* is applied to the living man; the *Cranium,* from which this branch of science takes its name, is the *skeleton of the head.* The cranium is composed of two parts, which may be virtually separated, in the lateral projection, by a straight line passing through the external orbital apophysis and extending to the auricular foramen, thus separating the facial from the cerebral portion of the cranium. Hence the *cranium* is the skeleton of the head in its entirety, and is divisible into the *cerebral cranium* and the *facial cranium.*

The Cranium.—The cranium is a complex union of a number of flat, curved bones united together by means of certain very complicated arborescent sutures, and forming a hollow osseous cavity of rounded form. I will briefly indicate the bones which form its external contour. On the anterior part is the *frontal* bone, terminated by the suture which unites it to the two parietal bones: the *coronal suture;* while the two parietal bones are joined together by the *median* or *sagittal suture,* which forms a sort of T with the other suture.

On the posterior side is the *occipital bone*, which is also joined to the two parietal bones, by means of the occipital or *lambdoidal* suture. Below the two parietal bones, in a lateral direction, are the *two temporal bones;* and between the temporal and parietal bones are situated the *great wings of the sphenoid.* The main body of the sphenoid is at the base of the cranium. Besides these there is another, internal bone, the *ethmoid.*

The Face.—The skeleton of the face is composed of fourteen bones; some of these are external and lend themselves to measurement; others which are internal and hidden contribute to the completion of the delicate scaffolding of this most important portion of the skeleton. The principal bones of the face are: the two *zygomatic bones* (articulating with the temporal, frontal and maxillary bones); the two nasal bones (articulating with the frontal and with the ascending branch of the maxillary, and uniting above to form the bridge of the nose; this is a bone of great importance in anthropology, because it determines the naso-frontal angle and the formation of the nose); the two upper maxillary bones, or upper jaw (articulating together in front to form the subnasal region; laterally with the zygomatic bones; above with the nasal bones; internally with each other, to form the palate, and posteriorly with the palatine bones); the *mandible* or lower jaw (a single bone, and the only movable bone in the cranium), articulating with the temporal bones by means of a condyle, and the separate parts of which are distinguished as the *body of the mandible* and the *ascendant branches,* which are united to the cranium.

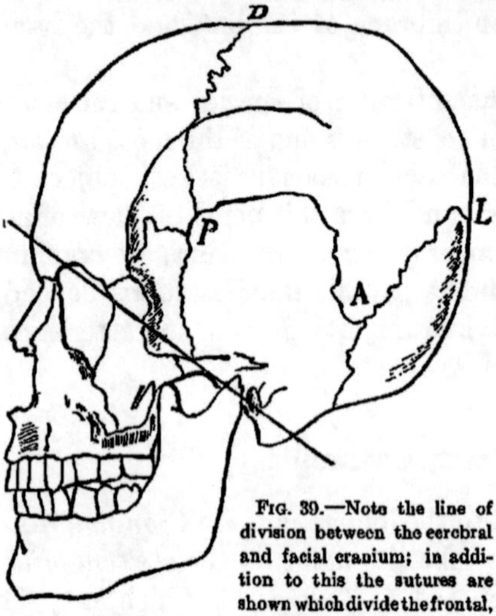

Fig. 39.—Note the line of division between the cerebral and facial cranium; in addition to this the sutures are shown which divide the frontal, parietal, occipital and temporal bones. PD. Coronal Suture; DL. Sagittal Suture: AL. Lambdoidal Suture.

The bones of lesser importance, which are interior and hidden are: the two *lacrymal bones* (situated at the inner angle of the orbitary cavity), the *vomer* or osseous septum of the nose; the two bones in the nose which lie on each side of the vomer and are known as the *turbinated bones* (*concha nasalis*); and the two palate bones (which form the backward continuation of the palatine vault constituted by the maxillary bones).

Human Cranium and Animal Cranium.—The dividing line between the cerebral and facial cranium is of great importance in anthropology, because the relative proportions between these two parts of the cranium form a human characteristic, contrasting widely with the animal characteristics; and they offer a simple criterion for determining the higher or lower type of the human cranium. (Compare in this connection Fig. 40, skulls of the higher mammals and of man.)

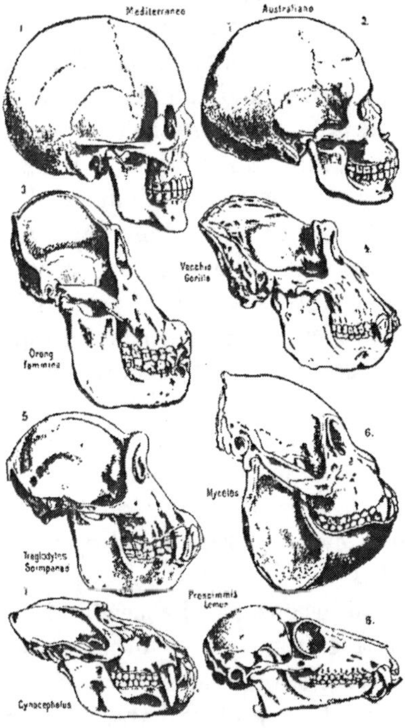

FIG. 40.

The illustration represents a number of different animal skulls; and at the top are two human skulls, the one of an Australian and the other of a European. It will be seen that the proportions between the facial and cerebral portions are very different; in the animals, even in the higher orders such as the *primates* (orang-utan, gorilla, etc.), the *facial* and *masticatory* parts predominate over the cerebral.

One might even say that the skeleton gives us at a glance the characteristic psychological difference; the animal *eats,* man *thinks;* that is, the animal is destined only to vegetate, to feed itself; man is an entirely different species; he has a very different task before him; he is the *creative being,* who, through thought and labour, is destined to subjugate and transform the world.

There are still other characteristic differences between the animal and the human skull. The cerebral cranium of the ape is not only smaller but it is furnished with strong bony ridges, to serve as points of attachment for powerful muscles intended to protect the cranial cavity. The human skull is completely devoid of such ridges; it is perfectly smooth, with delicate contours; it might be described as "frail and naked"; for the word nakedness precisely expresses the *absence* of those defences with which the cranium of the anthropoid ape is so abundantly provided. Accordingly, the human cranium is *undefended* by soft tissues; and even the bony walls themselves are far from thick. If we take a transverse section of the bones of the cranium, we find that they are formed of two very thin layers of bone united by a porous, osseous substance; the external layer is in direct contact with the muscles of the scalp, and the internal layer with the brain. These two layers differ widely in their degree of elasticity: the external layer is so elastic that if it receives a bruising blow (provided this is not so heavy as to surpass its limits of elasticity) it will yield even to the point of touching the inner layer and then spring back to its original position without leaving any perceptible trace of the blow received (this is especially true in the case of infants),* while the inner layer is so unelastic as to appear almost as brittle as *glass:* so much so, for example, that the indirect shock of the same contusion may cause it to splinter into fragments, which may either penetrate the substance of the brain, or produce hemorrhages, or inflammatory reactions in the meninges—and sometimes may constitute the sole cause of epilepsy, and various forms of inflammation of the brain (even resulting in idiocy), and sometimes of meningitis and death.

Contusions on the heads of children, and in general blows resulting from falls or other causes, must be taken into serious consideration, in the history of the individual, even though they have left no profound traces *externally*.

This human characteristic of nakedness, of the *absence* of powerful bodily defences, is not limited to the head alone, but is diffused over the entire morphological organism. Man, considered as an animal, is weak; he is born naked and he remains naked, and destitute of those natural defences which explain the endurance and the survival of other species; neither the fur nor the plumage of mammals and of birds nor the bony shields of reptiles and scales of fishes serve as defences for this vertebrate, who has

* See the application to pathological surgery of this anatomo-physiological condition of the cranium, as given by Tillaux, *Anatomia topografica*.

raised himself to the highest eminence in the zoological scale; neither the muscular strength and powerful teeth of the felines, nor the talons of the birds of prey have been his arms of conquest.

Nevertheless, man who has conquered the earth and overcome all his powerful biological enemies, owes his survival, equally with all other living creatures, to his victory over other animals and over his environment. Wherein lies the special strength of this little, feeble being, who has become the lord of the earth? It lies in his brain. The arms of this conqueror are wholly psychic. It is his intelligence which has prevailed over the might of other animals and enabled him to acquire the means of adapting himself to his environment, or else of adapting his environment to himself. His intelligence, which sufficed him as a weapon with which to achieve victory in the struggle for existence, is also the means which still permits him to continue on the road toward self-perfectionment.

The morphological importance attached by anthropologists to the cerebral cranium depends precisely upon this: that it is the envelope of the *brain*. If we examine the interior of the human cerebral cranium, we find that it has adapted its bony contours so faithfully to those of the soft tissues that it bears the imprint of the various parts of the brain (cerebrum, cerebellum), the convolutions, and even the blood-vessels of the meninges. Accordingly, a study of the cerebral cranium amounts to an indirect study of the brain itself.

Characteristics of the Human Cranium.—The characteristics of the human cranium are all associated with the great development of the volume of the brain. Let us assume that we have an elastic vessel, representing in form an animal cranium, open at the base through an orifice corresponding to the occipital foramen. If we inflate this vessel, it will not only begin to enlarge at the expense of its folds (ridges), and to stretch and distend its walls (thinness and fragility of the cranial bones); but furthermore it will undergo a change in form, acquiring a more pronounced rotundity and *pushing upward* in its anterior part above the face. This part, rising erect above the face, and determined by the volume of the brain, is the *forehead*. Animals do not have an erect forehead; their orbits continue backward in an almost horizontal line, giving them an extremely receding brow. Corresponding to this preponderance of the cerebral portion, the facial portion *retires* below the brow, the mandibles do not extend beyond the anterior axis of the brain, and are so far diminished in volume that they assume, as compared with animals, a new function; in short, the mouth is no longer merely the organ of mastication, but also the organ of speech; its animal part has been spiritualised.

The Evolution of the Forehead.—Inferior Skull Caps; the Skull of the Pithecanthropus; the Skull of the Neanderthal Man. The forehead is so distinctly a human characteristic that mankind has not needed the help of anthropology in order to realise its importance—and as a sign of superiority, nobility or sovereignty, has placed upon the forehead the crown of laurel, or the crown of nobility or kingship.

Has the forehead always been a human characteristic, or have we acquired it little by little? Such a problem is associated with the evolution of the brain. There are in existence certain remains of the skeletons of primitive men, which show them to have possessed a cerebral cranium inferior in volume to that now attained by the human species; and in these remains the forehead is also profoundly different from that of to-day, in that it is much lower and slants backward, while the supraorbital arches are very prominent. Such is the evidence of the "cranial caps," discovered in the early geological strata.

In the tertiary strata of the island of Java, which in that remote epoch of the earth's history must, together with Sumatra, have formed part of the continent of Asia, which is considered as the "laboratory of races," a skull was found by Dubois which raised the problem whether it should be classed as that of an ape superior to those now existing, or of a primitive man. Prior to this discovery, it had been maintained that man did not make his appearance until the quaternary period. This supposed primitive man was called by his discoverer the Pithecanthropus, *pithecanthropus erectus.*

Remains that are unquestionably human occur in the quaternary period, in which however skeletons are very rare, as compared with relics of human labour or social life, relics which are found scattered everywhere throughout Asia and Europe as well (chipped flints). The various remains of skeletons show us skulls much inferior to those of modern man, but superior to that of the pithecanthropus. In treatises of general anthropology reproductions are given of human crania known as the Spy or Neanderthal type, belonging to the epoch when the gigantic mammoth still roamed the earth. The forehead is very low and receding and the orbital arches are enormously developed; while the cerebral capacity calculated from the cranial dimensions is inferior to that of modern man.

Consequently, as the brain increases in volume in the course of the revolution of the race, the cranium not only shows a corresponding volumetric increase, but at the same time *alters its form,* thus producing the *forehead* which little by little rises from a receding to an erect position, and becomes high where it was formerly low, while at the same time the prominent orbital arches disappear. Accordingly, we may consider the forehead as the *skeletal index* of the cerebral volume, and hence of the relative anthropological and intellectual superiority.

In addition to its above-mentioned value, it also furnishes us with a biological principle of much importance: the relation *between the volume and form* of the cranium.

While the volume has a significance that is *relative* to the mass of the body, the significance of the form is *absolute.*

Let us examine these two skulls: normal human skulls of our own epoch; one of the Celtic race (Fig. 46) and the other Sardinian (Fig. 43); that of the Celtic race is much larger and rounder; that of the Sardinian is very much smaller and more elongated.

If we were considering only the *volume,* we might say that it was simply a case of a *microcephalic* and a *macrocephalic:* two terms (microcephaly and macrocephaly) that fall within the province of pathology. On the contrary, these two skulls are normal, but they belonged to individuals characterized by differences of race; the one (small skull) having a low stature; the other (large skull) having a tall stature.

The volume of the head therefore bears a relation to that of the body; the volume has a *relative* significance. But the form in both of them reveals a state of normality; the two skulls have a high and erect forehead, and exhibit in their whole contour a fine and regular development. Therefore the *form* has an *absolute* significance. It even proves to us the *normality* of the volume, a fact which could not be determined by the volume alone.

Another mechanical correspondence between volume and form is disclosed when we compare the skull of a new-born child with that of an adult. The skull of the new-born child is much smaller in volume; but the form shows the relatively enormous volumetric development of the brain; in fact the skull is protuberant and the forehead bulges forward above the face (*front bombé*), while corresponding to this *index* of cerebral development is the enormous preponderance of the cerebral cranium over the facial cranium, which is so small as to be almost reduced to a simple rudiment.

Hence the form by itself alone reveals the infantile character of the cerebral volume, which, in relation to the bulk of the body is of far greater dimensions than in the adult. In fact, if a child simply increased in volume and its growth was not the sum total of a morphological evolution, the adult man would become a monster; his macrocephaly would be so exaggerated that his neck could not sustain the weight of the head (If the relations between the proportions in infancy were maintained through life the adult man would have a head with a perimeter of 130 centimetres, = 4ft. 3in.).

Aside from its mechanical relations to the volume, the *form* has characteristics dependent upon biological factors, such as the *sex* and the *race*. The female cranium in fact has a straighter forehead than the male and the orbital arches are absolutely wanting, while the entire surface of the cranium is smoother and more rounded.

Similarly, the different races exhibit *forms* determined by biological factors and not by mechanical causes—for instance, the degree of dolichocephaly (elongated cranium) and of brachycephaly (short cranium).

Hence the form is life's manifestation not only of the characteristics proper to the species, but also of the mechanical adaptations demanded by the material composing the body.

It may be said that the *volume* and the *form* of the cranium are dependent upon two different biological potentialities: the volume is mainly determined by the cerebral mass; the form, on the contrary, is mainly determined by the bony structure—no matter how completely form and volume coincide in their reciprocal mechanical relations.

That is, the attainment of a given volume of head depends upon the development of the brain; the bone follows this development passively, is the index of it, the skeletal representation of it, but never the determining factor.

At one time it was thought, on the contrary, that a precocious ossification of the cranial cavity would arrest the development of the brain; *microcephaly* was believed to be caused by a precocious

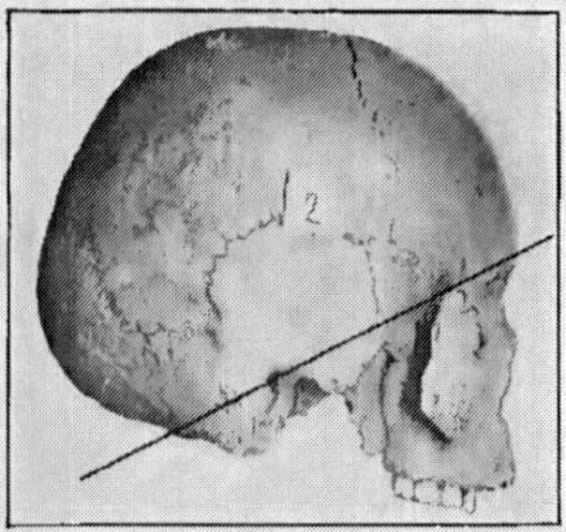

Fig. 41.

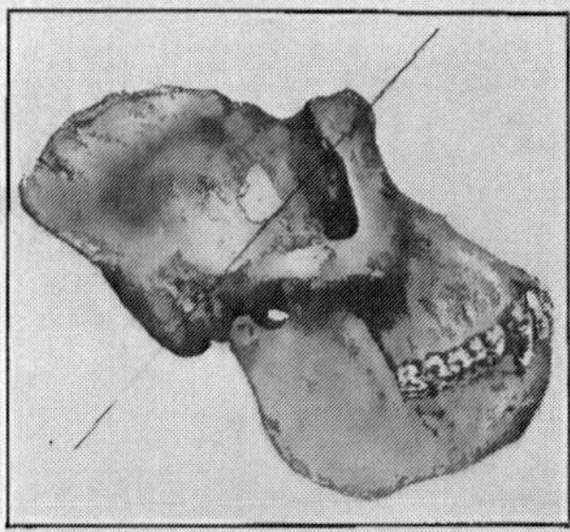

Fig. 42.

Dividing line in human skull, as compared with that of gorilla.

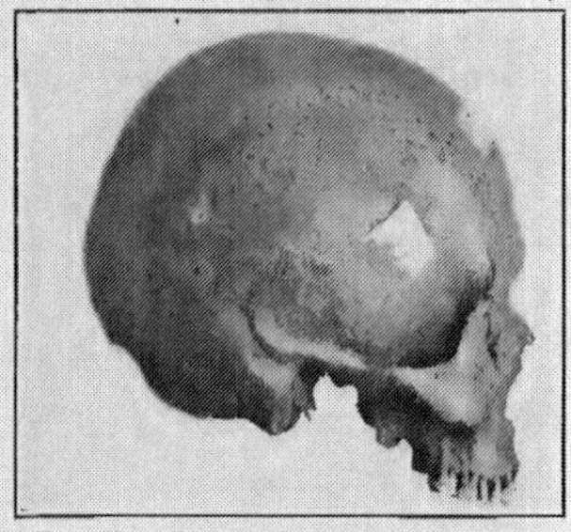

Fig. 43.—Rounded ellipsoidal cranium.

Fig. 44.—Brachycephalic cranium (vertical norm)

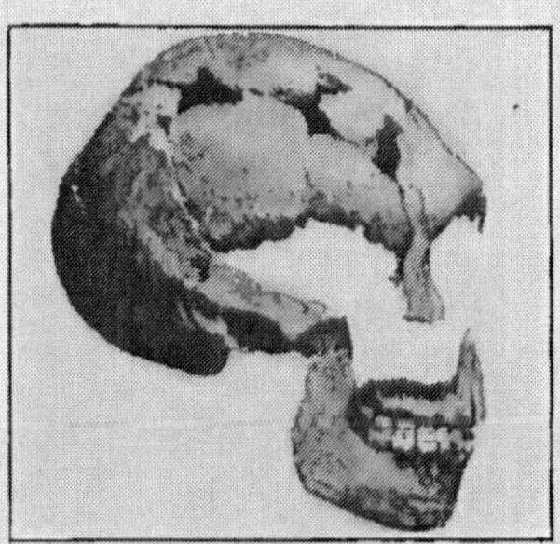

Fig. 45.—Remains of spy cranium.

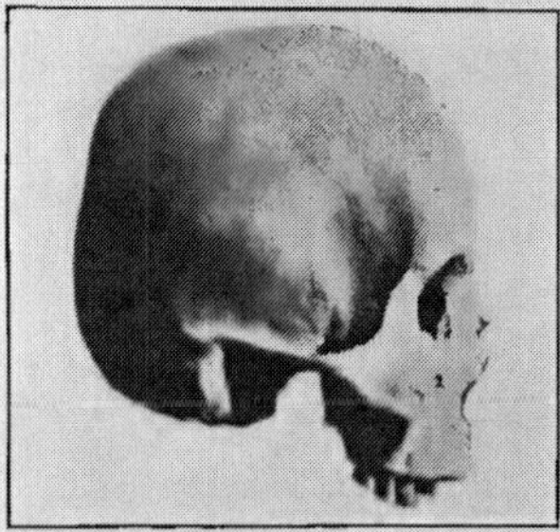

Fig. 46.—Brachycephalic cranium.

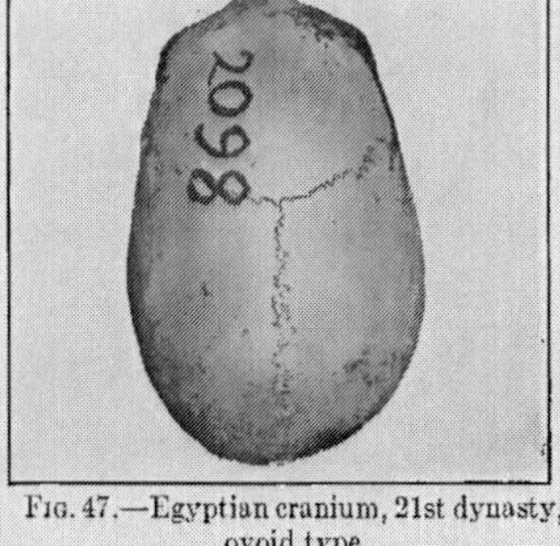

Fig. 47.—Egyptian cranium, 21st dynasty, ovoid type.

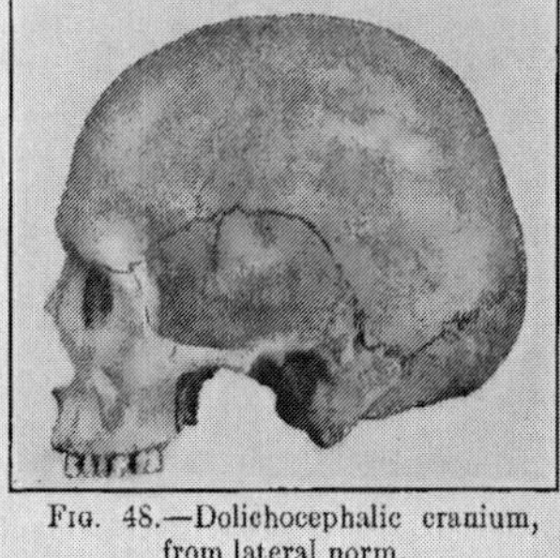

Fig. 48.—Dolichocephalic cranium, from lateral norm.

closing of the sutures of the cranial bones; and there was a certain period when the surgical treatment of microcephaly consisted in the removal of a portion of the cranial bone, in order to allow the brain to develop freely.

But the failure of such attempts afforded additional proof of the fact that the volumetric development of the cranium depends upon the brain alone.

If a precocious or abnormal suture occurs in the cranial bones, there does not follow an arrest of development, but simply a *malformation;* which is precisely in proportion to the potentiality of the brain, which grows less where the suture has been formed, and in compensation grows more than normally where the conditions of the bones permit of cerebral expansion; and a deformity results. Microcephaly on the contrary shows inferiority of form (smallness, receding forehead, etc.), but not *malformation.*

Anomaly of form, therefore, results only from anomaly of skeletal development, and is frequently found in conjunction with a *normal development of the brain.*

Consequently *malformations* of the cranium do not have the grave significance of biological inferiority or of degeneration that they were at one time believed to have; but frequently they must be considered in connection with pathological conditions resulting for the most part in delayed development in the embryo or in early infancy, producing a thickening of the bone, or a partial suturation of the points, or parts, or of the entire suture (punctiform synostosis, partial or total); sometimes the sutures remain unaltered, and the deformation must be attributed to various disturbances connected with the nutrition of the skeleton in the course of intrauterine evolution (hereditary syphilis, denutrition of the mother during pregnancy, etc.). In short, a cranium that is abnormal in form is an indication of pathological occurrences or of physiological errors that have resulted in altering the normal growth of the individual.

There are many anomalies in the form of the cranium, but here we will cite only the two principal ones, because they are the most frequent and most likely to be encountered in individuals whose growth has been retarded (from lack of nutrition) and consequently constitute signs of physiological inferiority often associated with social caste. These two forms are: scaphocephaly and plagiocephaly.

The scaphocephalic cranium (Figs. 51, 52), is characterised by being very narrow and flattened laterally; while the forehead and the occiput project in front and behind, the two parietal bones meet above almost in an angle, so that, if it were turned upside down, the vault of the cranium would have the appearance of the hull of a ship.

The *plagiocephalic* cranium is a cranium which is unsymmetrical in respect to its longitudinal axis; that is, it is not equally developed on the right and on the left.

As a matter of fact, our bilateral symmetry is an ideal standard rather than an absolutely attainable reality; we are all of us a little larger on one side and a little smaller on the other, but to so slight a degree as to escape superficial observation, so that in general we have *apparently* a bilateral symmetry—that is, we appear to be symmetrical according to the testimony of our senses; but a more delicate examination proves that this is not true. Plagiocephaly therefore represents an exaggerated case of a normal fact. Plagiocephaly may be simple or compound; it is simple when the asymmetry is partial; namely, when it is confined to the anterior or posterior portion; it is compound when it is total; and in such case we find a complete diagonal correspondence: for instance, if the right nodule in the frontal region is more prominent, the left nodule is more prominent in the left occipital region, or *vice versa.* In general it may be said that the various forms of *plagiocephaly* are produced by asymmetry of the *nodules* or of the *flattened* surfaces of the cranium. Even in the case of *microcephaly* and of *macrocephaly*, which are substantially anomalies of *volume*, we find corresponding characteristic abnormalities of form. The microcephalic cranium is of inferior type, suggesting that of the ape —in other words, it is a cranium which has mechanically adapted itself to a brain of inferior volume: the macrocephalic cranium, especially if the abnormality is due to *rickets* or to *hydrocephaly*, calls to mind the infantile type of cranium; it has the characteristic bulging forehead, while mechanical adaptation frequently renders it very round (pathological brachycephaly). We will take up this question again when we come to speak in particular of *malformations* and to describe the technical methods of cranioscopy. What more particularly concerns us now is a consideration of the *normal* form of the cranium and its morphological evolution.

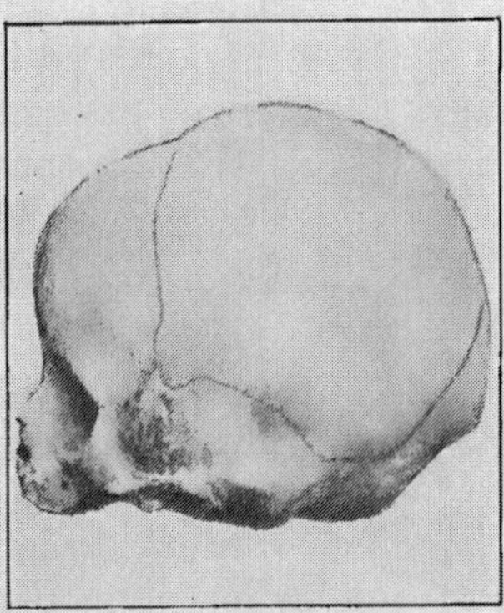

FIG. 49.—Cranium of new-born child (lateral norm).

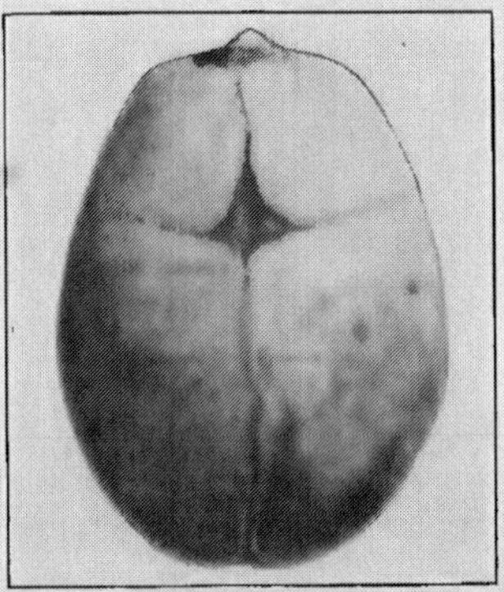

FIG. 50.—Cranium of new-born child (vertical norm).

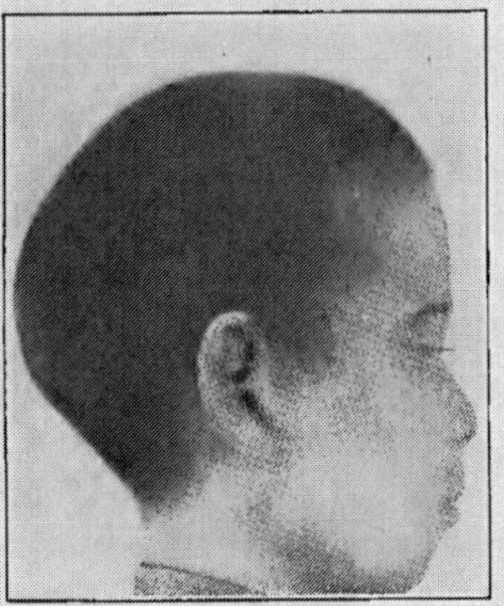

FIG. 51.

FIG. 52.

Scaphocephalic cranium.

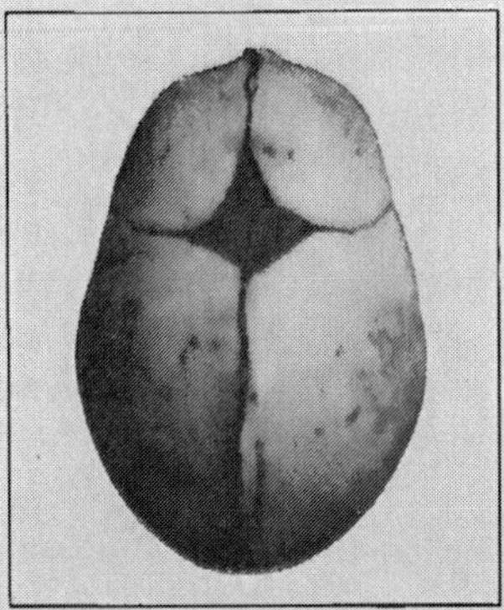

FIG. 53.—Cranium of new-born child seen from above, showing polyhedric contour due to nodules of ossification; fontanelle of the bregma; and suture dividing the two frontal bones.

FIG. 54.—Ellipsoides (classified by Sergi).

The Morphological Evolution of the Cranium through the Different Periods of Life. *Embryogeny. Order of Appearance of the Points of Ossification and of Synostosis of the Sutures.*—In its successive transitions through the different periods of life, the cranium not only acquires successively greater volume, but it assumes forms corresponding to the different grades of morphological evolution. We may group its transformation under five different periods: 1. from conception until birth (embryonic evolution); 2. from birth until the end of the third year (infantile evolution); 3. from three years old until twenty (youthful evolution); 4. from twenty to forty (adult age); 5. from forty to the end of life (involution).

First Period.—In the earliest stages of intrauterine life the cranium consists of a membranous skin, enclosing the primitive cells of nerve tissue constituting the brain; it has a cartilaginous

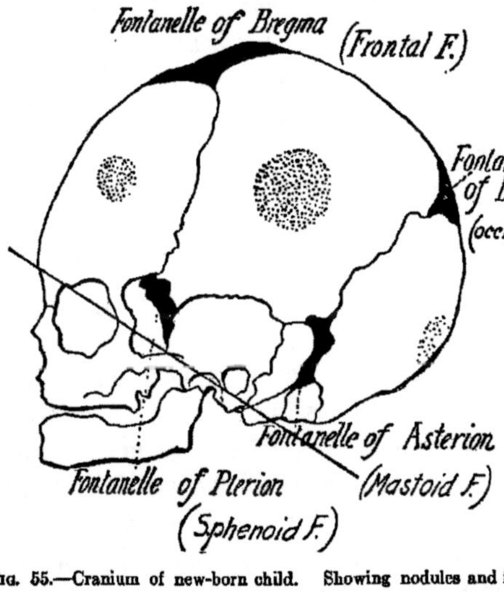

FIG. 55.—Cranium of new-born child. Showing nodules and fontanelles.

basal part, destined later to form the *base* of the skull (basioccipital and basisphenoid bones). But all the rest (the vault or cap of the cranium) remains in a membranous state, so that at this period the head of the embryo has not yet acquired a definite form.

In the second month of intrauterine life the phenomena of ossification have already begun to take place; that is, a fine network has formed, spreading over almost the entire surface, which proceeds to fill up its interstices with calcareous salts. This process, however, is more rapid and more intense at certain points (points of ossification), from which it cannot properly be said that the ossification *radiates*, but rather that at these points the general process is intensified and concentrated. There are five principal points of ossification: two frontal, two parietal and one occipital, which appear clearly defined and projecting like nodules, imparting to the cranium, when seen from above, a pentagonal form, which is the normal form of the infant cranium.

Second Period.—At birth the cranium has not yet completed the process of ossification, nor are the normal number of bones that will eventually compose the adult cranium, as yet definitely determined. Therefore the cranium of the new-born child has three distinct characteristics:

1. It is not yet uniformly rounded, but polyhedral because of the noticeable prominence of the five primitive nodules or centres of ossification (2 frontal, 2 parietal, 1 occipital, Figs. 53, 55).

2. Since the process of ossification of the bones is not yet completed, certain membranous portions or *cranial fontanelles* still remain, which are especially wide at the points where several bones meet. The principal fontanelle is that of the bregma (at the juncture of the two frontal with the two parietal bones, quadrangular). Next comes that of the lambda, which is much smaller (juncture of the two parietal bones with the occipital, triangular), and lastly the fontanelles of the asterion and the pterion, on opposite sides of the temporal bones, the former being situated behind and the latter in front.

3. Since the process of ossification is incomplete, the fusion of bony portions into entire bones, such as they are destined to be when complete development is reached, has not yet been accomplished; that is to say, certain bones of the cranium are still divided into several portions. For example, the frontal bone in the new-born child is composed of two bones, separated by a longitudinal suture that is destined to disappear, and the occipital bone is composed of four parts, namely, the base, the squama and the two condyles (basioccipital, exoccipital and superoccipital bones).

During the first period of three years, while the brain is increasing notably and rapidly in volume, the cranium undergoes various and interesting transformations. The pentagonal form of the cranium tends steadily to become rounder, because the primitive nodules are diminishing, or even disappear, although in this regard many individual varieties result; and the processes of ossification reach their completion. This is the most important period of growth, during which the individual development of the perfect cranial form may be attained, provided the rhythm of growth between the brain and its envelope remains harmonious; or again, certain deformations may be definitely established, owing to the intervention of some pathological condition or a disturbance of nutrition, altering either the internal volume or the normal process of ossification of the bony covering.

The first closing of the fontanelles takes place, in our race, in those of the asterion (posterior to the temporal bones), and next in those of the pterion; and it sometimes happens, as an anomaly of growth that leaves no external trace in the living man, that a little bone is formed, duplicating the shape of the fontanelle itself; such little bones, very common in abnormal crania, are called *Wormian bones*. They may occur in connection with any of the fontanelles, but especially with that of the bregma.

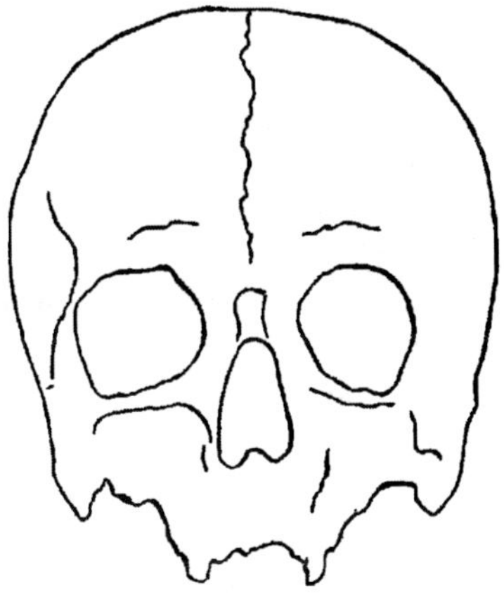

FIG. 56.—Cranium of adult with abnormal medio-frontal suture.

The fontanelle of the lambda generally closes during the first year; and the last of all the fontanelles to close is the largest, which is situated toward the front of the head, at the *bregma*, and is well known, even by the common people, and can easily be felt upon a child's head; it generally closes toward the end of the second year; and its characteristics may furnish valuable indications of abnormality or insufficiency of the child's development. For example, if it diminishes and disappears ahead of time, this may constitute the first symptom of *microcephaly*, or at all events, of submicrocephaly (*i.e.*, a case of microcephaly that is not very pronounced). On the contrary, when this fontanelle remains dilated and delays its normal closing, this is a sign of organic weakness and debilitating disease (cachexia, rickets, myxedema). Furthermore, the fontanelle in question may alter its characteristic appearance in certain forms of sickness. In the case of hydrocephaly it becomes distended, while in enteritis, on the contrary, in which the organism parts with a large proportion of liquid, it becomes depressed.

The *sutures* also undergo notable changes during this period of life. The first to become effaced is the metopic or medio-frontal suture, which is destined to close and form a single bone; by the end of the first year it is obliterated throughout the middle third of its length, and thereafter the process of suturation spreads upward and downward until it is completed at the end of the second year (Welcker, Haeckel, Humphry). Sometimes, however, this suture is not obliterated until very late, and there are anomalous cases where it has remained throughout life, giving the forehead a characteristic form (pronounced frontal nodules and a slight palpable furrow along the medial line of the forehead).

During this same time a fusion has also taken place between the occipital squama and the two lateral or condyloid portions; but the resultant whole still remains separated from the *corpus* or *base* of the occipital bone, which will not become welded into one solid piece with the rest before the age of seven years.

At the age of three, the ossification of the cranial vault has been completed. In place of being depressed and protuberant, as it was at birth, the cranium has grown upward and forward in the frontal region, assuming an almost definitive form; the volume of the cranium has at the same time undergone an exceedingly rapid growth, attaining proportions very near to those of an adult.

From the age of three onward the head grows slowly, and its transformations are much slighter and fewer. The cranial capacity which at birth is 415 cubic centimetres, becomes at the age of three, 1,200, at the age of fifteen, 1,393, and in the adult, 1,400 cu. cm. respectively. Accordingly we might say that at the age of three a sort of *repose* has been established in the growth both of the the brain and of the cranium; this is the age at which an awakening begins in the child of that intelligence which is to put him in touch with the external world, and it is also the age at which he may begin his education in school.

Third Period.—There follows a slow and parallel growth of both brain and cranium. The ossification of the cranium itself reaches completion. At the age of seven the occipital is definitely solidified into a single bone and between the years of fifteen and twenty the body of the sphenoid also becomes welded to the occiput. This process of synostosis begins from the interior of the cranium, and only subsequently manifests itself externally. Consequently, the basilar suture closes at the time when the last large molars, the so-called "wisdom teeth," appear. After this period, the base of the cranium can no longer undergo any sort of growth, and in the case of uneducated persons the complete development of the cranium is definitely accomplished.

Fourth Period.—But in the case of cultured persons, those who form the class of brain-workers, the brain continues to grow, although extremely slowly, up to the age of thirty-five or even forty, thanks to the sutures which still remain completely intact and which still make an expansion of the bony envelope possible.

After this comes the beginning of the

Fifth Period.—The period of involution, during which the synostosis (closing) of all the cranial sutures will successively occur, until in advanced old age the cranium becomes composed of a single bone, just as in the embryo it was formed of a single membrane.

The synostoses which occurred in the early periods had an evolutive significance and were associated with the growth of the body and the intelligence. These later synostoses, on the contrary, have an involutive significance and are associated with the physiological decay of the organism and at the same time with that of the psychic activities.

The first point at which synostosis takes place is in the region of the obelion, that is, near the middle of the suture which unites the two parietal bones; shortly afterward, the fronto-parietal sutures begin to unite along the pterion. At the age of forty-five, the obeliac synostosis has progressed as far as the lambda, and that of the fronto-parietal suture to the bregma; and at fifty the ossification is very nearly accomplished, at least on the right-hand side (according to Broca's series of crania). At seventy the squama of the temporal bone unites with the parietal, and at eighty the entire cranium has become a single bone.

These processes are subject to no small number of individual variations; there have been cases of persons who, although very old, still preserved many of their cranial sutures intact and their psychic activities remained correspondingly alert (men of genius). Conversely, the closing of the sutures sometimes begins as early as the thirty-fifth year. A diagnosis of age, as determined by the skeleton, is consequently only approximate.

During the periods of growth the cranium may exhibit transitory anomalies; it is very common to encounter in the heads of children of the lower social classes, who are consequently subject to denutrition, *malformations* which represent various degrees and forms of *plagiocephaly*, and which subsequently disappear completely, as the development of the cranium advances. Anomalies of form must therefore be judged differently in the case of the child than in that of the adult.

It may even happen that the five primitive nodules persist for a long time and even remain as a definitive form of the adult cranium constituting, according to Sergi, a distinct variety, the *pentagonal* cranium. But this is quite rare. From the frequency with which this form is to be observed in schools attended by children of the poorer classes, it is better to regard it as due to a delay in morphological evolution, which will probably disappear later on.

Normal Forms of the Cranium

We are indebted to Sergi for an exact knowledge of the *normal forms* of the cranium. Such forms are racial characteristics and are *invariable*, as Sergi has succeeded in proving by a comparison of the most ancient forms of the cranium with recent forms. Accordingly this authority takes the cranial formation as the basis for his classification of races. We have no direct interest, so far as concerns the special scope of our own science, in the value of this theory of classification—a theory, by the way, already divined, although very imperfectly and under a different form, by French and German anthropologists. Sergi's studies of cranial forms interest us solely as a diagnostic test of *normality* as compared with *abnormality*. For it is due to these researches that certain forms that used to be considered pathological, have come to be recognised as normal.

The *normal forms* of the cranium may be grouped, according to Sergi, under nine primary varieties, each of which includes *sub-varieties*.

These nine varieties are named as follows:

I. Ellipsoid; II. Ovoid; III. Pentagonoid; IV. Rhomboid;

V. Beloid; VI. Cuboid; VII. Sphenoid; VIII. Spheroid; IX. Platycephalic.

I. *Ellipsoid* (Fig. 58).—This form is recognised by inspecting the cranium according to the vertical norm (see in the chapter on *Technique* the method of cranioscopy).

The cranial contour recalls an ellipse in which no trace of the nodules remains, and in which the occiput is not in the least flattened; while the anterior half of the cranium closely corresponds to the posterior half.

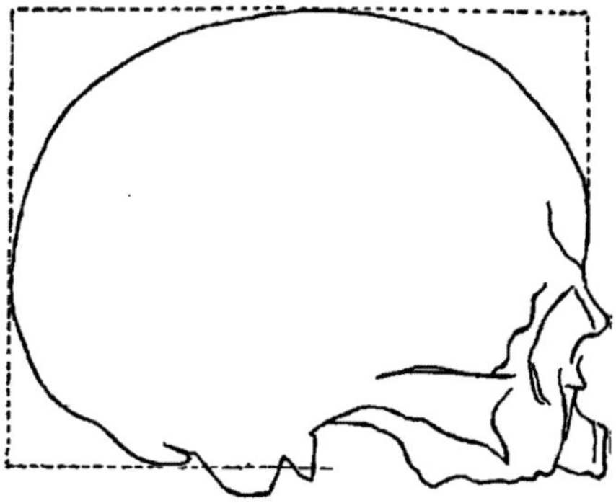

FIG. 57.—*Elliipsoides depressus* cranium.

The sub-varieties are differentiated by their greater breadth and length, by the form and protrusion of the occiput, and also by the height of the cranium measured vertically.

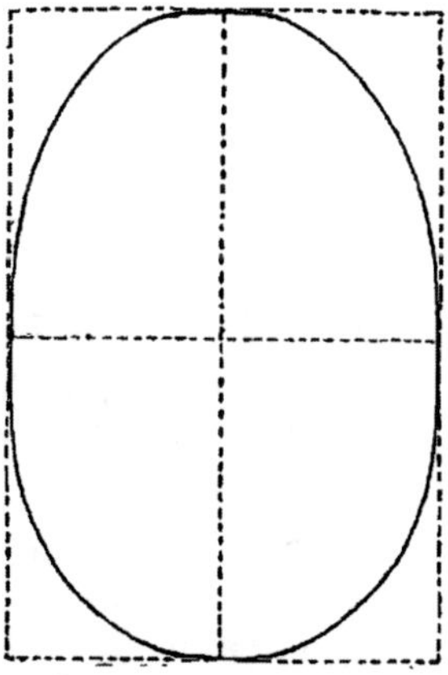

FIG. 58.—Ellipsoid cranium.

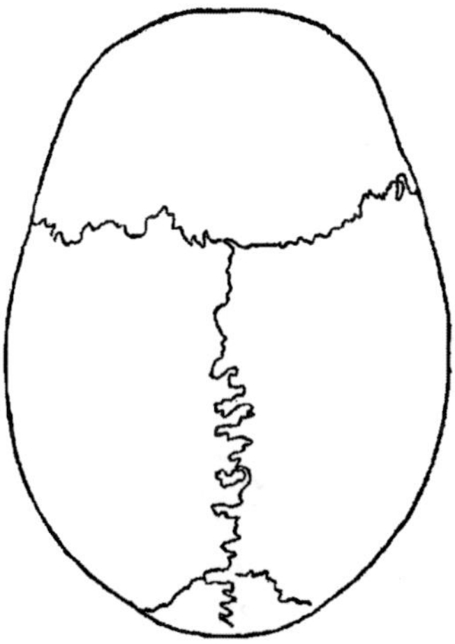

FIG. 59.—Ovoid cranium.

Accordingly, the sub-varieties have a binominal nomenclature indicating, in addition to the fundamental characteristic (variety) the qualitative characteristic of the sub-variety (*e.g., ellipsoides depressus;* compare Fig. 57, showing a cranium seen laterally).

II. *Ovoid.*—This form of cranium, seen from above, is that of an ovoid, with the broader portion corresponding to the parietal bones, at the point where the characteristic embryonal nodules are situated. The protrusions of the parietal bones are apparent

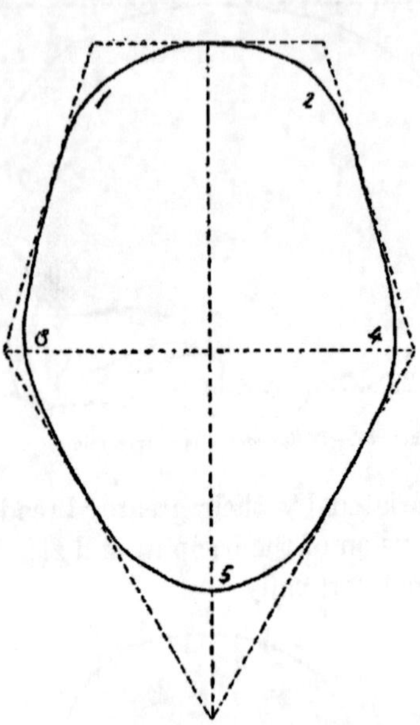

FIG. 60.—Pentagonoid cranium.

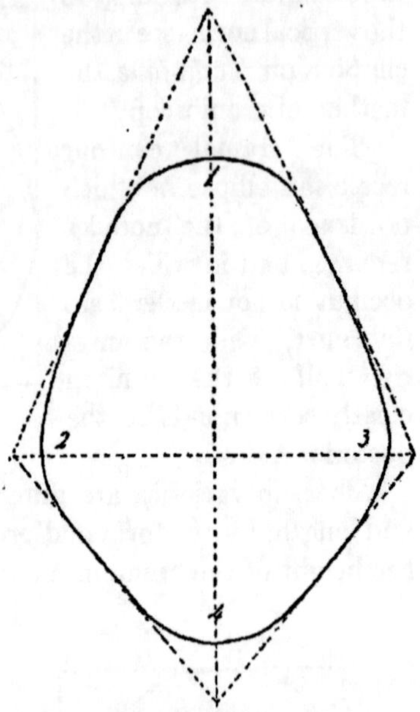

FIG. 61.—Rhomboid cranium.

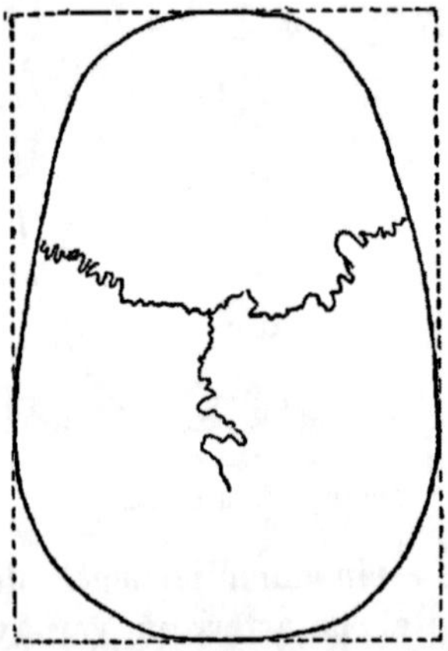

FIG. 62.—Beloid cranium.

(swellings) but not angular (nodules). The occiput protrudes and is broad (Fig. 59).

III. *Pentagonoid.*—In this form, persistent traces of the five primitive embryonal nodules are still plainly visible, giving the contour of the cranium, when seen vertically, the appearance of a pentagon. The protuberances, however, are quite smooth and not pointed, as in the embryonal cranium.

IV. *Rhomboid.*—This form is similar to the pentagonoid, excepting that the parietal breadth is much more notable in proportion to the forehead, which is much narrowed and has lost its nodules.

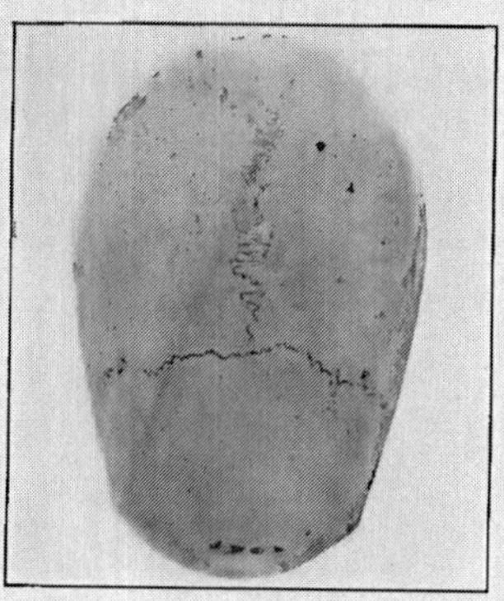

FIG. 63.—Ovoides (classified by Sergi).

FIG. 64.—Pentagonoides acutus (Sergi's collection).

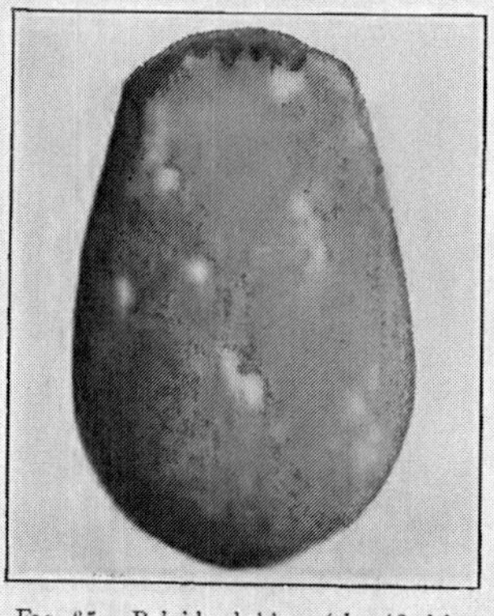

FIG. 65.—Beloides lybicus (classified by Sergi).

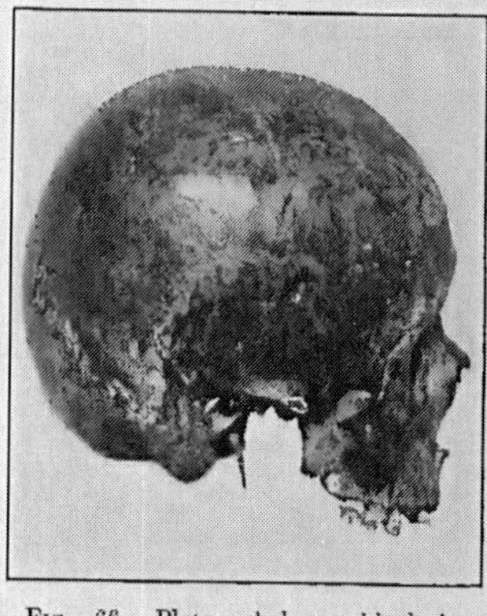

FIG. 66.—Platycephalus orbicularis (classified by Sergi).

FIG. 67.—Platycephalus ovoidalis (classified by Sergi).

FIG. 68.—Spheroidal cranium, vertical norm (Sergi's collection).

V. *Beloid.*—The beloid, or arrow-head cranium is like the ovoid with the occiput more flattened, so that the widest portion is further back than in the ovoid; toward the front it becomes narrower, constituting altogether an admirably shaped type of head.

VI. *Cuboid.*—This form is most clearly perceived when the cranium is seen either sidewise or from the rear. Not only the face, but the lateral and occipital walls as well are flattened; so also is the forehead, which in general is quite vertical.

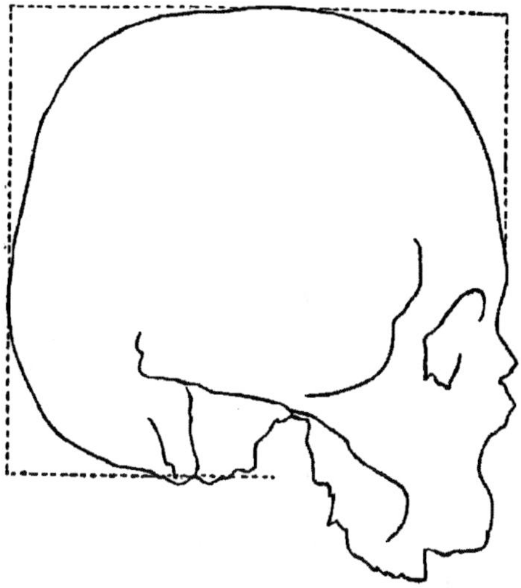

FIG. 69.—Cuboid cranium.

VII. *Sphenoid* (cuneiform).—The broadening between the two parietal bones is usually far back and very evident, while the cranium narrows toward the front. The occiput is flattened.

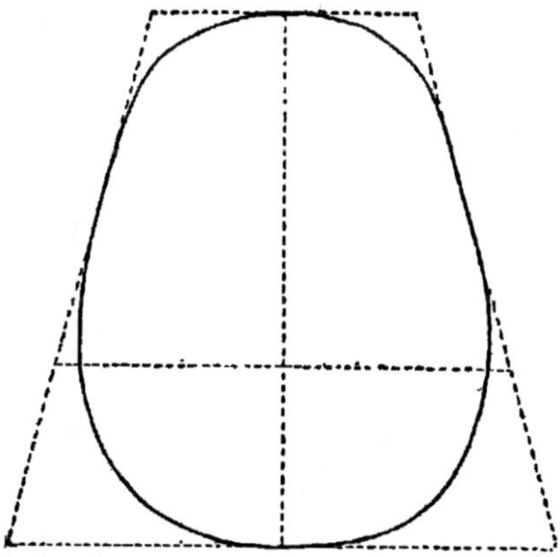

FIG. 70.—Sphenoid cranium.

VIII. *Spheroid.*—Seen vertically, it presents the appearance of a very broad ellipse; all the curves tend to become spherical. The forehead, however, is not notably vertical.

IX. *Platycephalic.*—The fundamental characteristic of this type of cranium is that it is flattened on top, or rather, since such flattening cannot be absolute, the arch of its vault is a segment of a circle of very large diameter (Sergi), with the result that this cranium has the appearance of being very low vertically and very broad laterally. When seen vertically it may present a wide variety of contours, ellipsoid, ovoid, pentagonoid, etc., but its distinguishing characteristic remains that of the flattened vault.

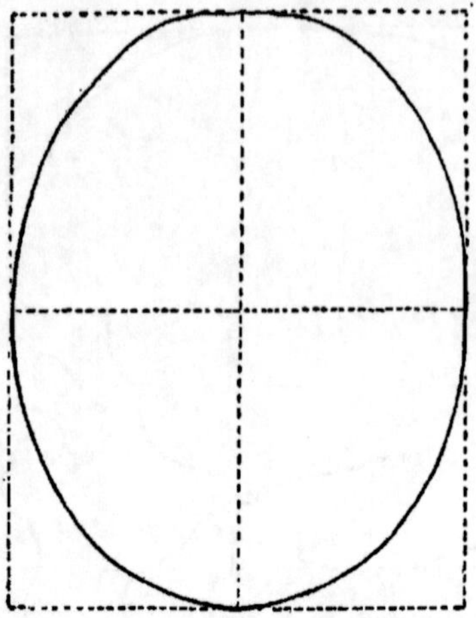

FIG. 71.—Spheroid cranium.

Sub-varieties.—*Sphenoides trapezoides,* or *trapezoid cranium.* Observed from the vertical norm, this form appears as a variety of the *sphenoid;* and when seen laterally it is characterised by the lines of its contour forming a *trapezium.* Starting from the vertex of the cranium one line slants toward the forehead and another toward the occiput, which is very massive. In the figure given below, the quadrangle drawn in solid lines serves to indicate the correct position of the cranium, while the trapezium formed of dotted lines gives us its characteristic form.

Among the forms described by Sergi, are several which were formerly held to be *abnormal,* such, for instance, as the *platycephalic cranium* and the *pentagonoid.* Similarly, when the surfaces of the cranium showed a tendency toward flatness, or when there were cranial protuberances, even though these were destined to disappear, they were regarded as malformations. Before this high authority offered us his guidance, there were certain forms, frequently encountered, that it was difficult to define, for example, the trapezoid cranium, which often presents a notable vertico-

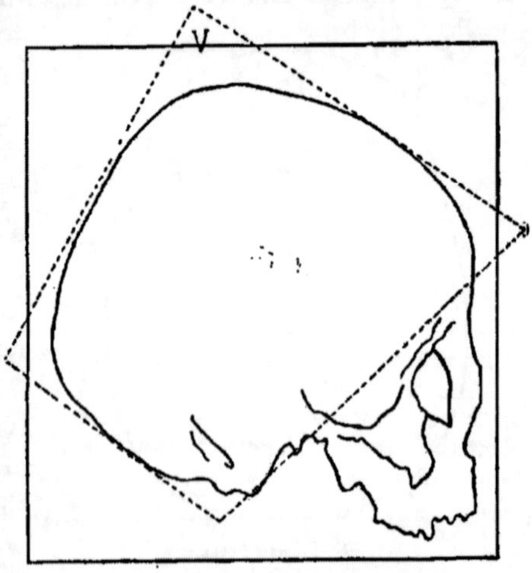

FIG. 72.—Trapezoid cranium.

occipital flattening, with the vertex notably higher than the forehead.

There are also certain forms of cranium having the frontal region more restricted than the parietal region, or slanting down from a much elevated vertex, which have been proved to be *normal forms;* while still another error previously made was that of trying to judge the *forehead* on the criterion of a single model, deviations from which were much too readily relegated to the category of abnormalities. The most regular and beautiful forms, and the ones that are commonest in our racial stocks are the ellipsoid, ovoid and sphenoid. In my work on the women of Latium, precisely one of the points that I noted was the frequent occurrence of certain sub-varieties of the *ellipsoid* and the *sphenoid.*

In order to recognise the *forms of the cranium,* a certain training is necessary which each one must acquire for himself. Observations of the cranium will make it easier to judge of the form in relation to the *head,* at least, when the latter is not too much hidden by the hair, as often happens in the case of young children.

A knowledge of the *normal* forms of the cranium will also guide us in our judgment of many abnormal forms, which very often present the appearance of *exaggerations* of normal types.

Thus, for example, the *acrocephalic* cranium (much raised in the parieto-lambdoideal region and sloping forward toward the brow, while the occipito-lambdoideal region is flattened) recalls the *trapezoid;* and the clinocephalic cranium (in which the coronal suture forms a slight girdle-like indenture and divides the contour of the cranium, when observed along the vertical norm, in two curves, a lesser anterior and a greater posterior curve, resembling a figure of 8) recalls certain varieties of ovoid cranium described by Sergi. This brings us to a principle that is very interesting to establish, namely, that frequently *anomalies* represent *exaggerations* of the racial or family type.

The Cephalic Index

Retzius was the first to take the *cranium* under consideration as a basis for a classification of the human races; and he attempted to determine a concept of its *form* by means of a numerical formula expressing the relation between the length and width of the cranium (cephalic index). Thus he distinguished the races into *brachycephalics,* or those having a short head; and *dolichocephalics,* or those having a long head. Following Retzius, who may be regarded as the founder of craniology, Broca adopted, completed and expanded this method, deriving from the cranium, or rather from the particular character given by the cephalic index, a *key*, as it were, suited to unlocking the intricate mysteries of hybridism among the human races. Consequently the cephalic index was not confined, as regards its importance, within the same limits as all the other indexes, but was raised by the French school, warmly seconded by Italian anthropologists, to the dignity of a fundamental determinant of the *ethnic type*, as definitely as, for example, the vertebral column serves as basis for a classification including all species of vertebrates.

The Germans refused to accept the cephalic index as determining the classification of races; but while seeking to prove themselves independent of it, they continued to regard the *form of the cranium* as a basis of classification (Rütimeyer, von Höller, and to-day Virchow), but without ever having identified, as Sergi has now done, existing *forms* as normal types of race.

The *cephalic index* is obtained by the well-known formula expressing the relation between the *maximum transverse diameter* of the skull (see "Technique") and the *maximum longitudinal diameter* reduced to 100, and is expressed as follows: $Ci = \frac{100d}{D}$ (the cephalic index is equal to a hundred times the lesser diameter divided by the greater; in the present case the lesser diameter is the transverse).

This *proportion between linear measurements* cannot properly sum up the *form* of the cranium. We can, for example, conceive of a microcephalic cranium having a normal *cephalic index*, since the relation between the two maximum diameters necessary for deducing the index, does not tell us, for example, either the dimension of the cranium or the form of the forehead.

If, for instance, we should imagine a photograph of a cranium enlarged a hundred diameters, the reciprocal relations between the length and the width would still remain unchanged.

In order to demonstrate that the cephalic index does not determine the form of the cranium, Sergi makes use of a number of different geometric figures, such as a triangle, an ellipse, a trapezoid inscribed within equal rectangles, and which consequently have an equal base and equal altitude, that is, the same proportion between length and width.

It follows that skulls corresponding more or less closely in shape, trapezoidal, trigonocephalic, ellipsoidal, plagiocephalic, and hence both normal and abnormal, can be expressed by a cephalic index having the same identical figures.

But, although the cephalic index is far from being *descriptive* in regard to the form of the cranium, it constitutes an anthropological datum that has two advantages: 1. It depends upon measurements and is therefore accessible to those who, not being anthropologists, lack the trained eye that can distinguish with careful accuracy the true *forms* of the cranium in their manifold variety. Furthermore, since the measurement of maximum diameters is sure and easy and may be obtained with exactness, regardless of the thickness of the hair, it may be applied in anthropological research to all subjects. 2. The cephalic index, even if it does not give us the form, does give us a fact which has a bearing upon the form, namely, whether the cranium is long or short; in other words, it substantially represents the most real and evident difference between the different types of cranium. And since the cranium has a visibly spheroid form, that is, with smooth and rounding surfaces, and constantly adheres to this generic delineation, the fact of being longer or shorter introduces a definite differentiation into the general and accepted form, and gives a very simple and concise indication of it, that conveys the idea more clearly than a description would.

Granting the *practicality* of this line of research, the cephalic index may also be accepted as an index of form, so long as there is no intention of going deeply into minute differentiations for systematic purposes. Professor Sergi himself, author of the system that forms the basis of the study of cranial forms, urged me to exclude from a practical course in pedagogic anthropology the classification of forms, limiting the concept of form to that included in the cephalic index.

The cephalic index has the additional advantage of having been extensively studied and consequently of having an abundance of mean averages for comparison that are of great practical use. Furthermore, the idea it gives regarding the cranium by means of one simple figure serves to convey certain fundamental principles with great clearness.

In dealing with figures that determine an anthropological datum of such high importance, it is necessary to define its limits and its nomenclature.

Various authors have introduced their own personal classification of the cephalic index, and no small confusion in nomenclature has resulted; so much so that a need was felt of establishing a uniformity of numerical limits and of the relative terminology, in other words, of simplifying the scientific language.

Accordingly, a congress was held at Frankfort in 1885, at which the following nomenclature was established by international agreement:

CEPHALIC INDEX.—*Nomenclature established at Frankfort*

Dolichocephalia = 75 and below
Mesaticephalia = from 75.1 to 79.9
Brachycephalia = from 80 to 85
Hyperbrachycephalia = 85.1 and above.

Previous to this, the most widely varied classifications were in use, and the leading authorities had all introduced into the literature of the subject their own personal classifications. Here are some of the more important:

BROCA:

Dolichocephalics = 75 and below
Subdolichocephalics = from 75 to 80
Subbrachycephalics = from 80 to 83.3
Brachycephalics = 83.3 and above.

RANKE:

Dolichocephalics = 74.9
Mesaticephalics = from 75 to 79.9
Brachycephalics = 80 and above.

KOLLMAN:

Dolichocephalics = 73.9 and below
Mesaticephalics = from 74 to 79.9
Brachycephalics = from 80 to 86.9
Hyperbrachycephalics = 87 and above.

RETZIUS and DAVIS:

Dolichocephalia = 79 and below
Brachycephalia = 80 and above.

TOPINARD:

Dolichocephalics	64	and below = Ultradolichocephalics.
	65, 66, 67, 68, 69	True dolichocephalics.
	70, 71, 72, 73, 74	Subdolichocephalics.

Class	Index	Subdivision
Mesaticephalics	75, 76	True mesaticephalics.
	77	(*Mean average.*)
	78, 79	Submesaticephalics.
Brachycephalics	80, 81, 82, 83, 84	Subbrachycephalics.
	85, 86, 87, 88, 89	True brachycephalics.
	90	and above = Ultrabrachycephalics.

It remains to determine the extreme *limits of oscillation* of the index, both in relation to the normal mean and in relation to the fluctuations of this important ethnic datum in a given population.

Topinard, as we have seen, gives as his mean figures for the extreme normal limits among the human races 64 and 90.

Deniker gives, as his mean averages for the human races, the following figures: For dolichocephaly, 69.4 (natives of the Caroline Islands; Australia); For brachycephaly, 88.7 (the Ayssori of the Transcaucasus; Asia).* But we know that a mean is obtained from figures either greater or smaller than the mean itself, so that the limits of *individual variation* must exceed that of the given figures.

Accordingly the oscillation of the normal cephalic indices may be given as ranging from 70 to 90.

In regard to abnormalities (extreme human limits of the cephalic index) the authorities give 58 for dolichocephaly (scapho-cephaly) and 100 for brachycephaly (in which case the cranium is round and known as *trochocephalic;* it is met with among the insane).

Between oscillations of such extremely wide range in the normal cephalic index, the number chosen as a medial figure to serve the purpose of dividing the dolichocephalics from the brachycephalics is that of 80, which is included within the division of brachycephaly. In spite of the nomenclature established at Frankfort, there is a distinct scholastic advantage, because of the greater simplicity of memorising and fixing the idea, in reverting

* Broca gives, not as mean averages, but as extreme limits, 70.9 for dolichocephalics (Tasmanians) and 90 for brachycephalics (natives of the Sandwich Islands).

to the nomenclature of Retzius, who classes as brachycephalics all crania from 80 upward, and as dolichocephalics all those below 80. It is certainly strange to class all crania from 80 to 90 without distinction as brachycephalics, and then to alter the name and call a cranium with an index of 79.9 a dolichocephalic. It has been found that there is always a slight difference between the index taken from measurements of the *cranium* and that obtained from measurements of the *head*. According to Broca, it is necessary to subtract *two units* from the cephalic index taken from a living person, in order to obtain that of the cranium; thus, for example, if the cephalic index (taken from life) is 80, the cranial index (taken from the skeleton) would be 78. Such differences are due to the disposition of the soft tissues. Consequently, even according to the simple subdivision of Retzius, a person who was brachycephalic during life, would become dolichocephalic after he was dead.

But this is what always happens in biology, whenever we try to establish *definite* limits. Life undergoes an insensible transition through successive limits and forms, and this fact constitutes the grave difficulties and the apparent confusion of biological systems. In determining degrees of difference, it is necessary to have recourse constantly to *special methods*, which teach us to recognise general properties and to use them as a basis in dividing living creatures into separate groups (see in the section on *Method*, "Mean measurements and formation of series in relation to individual variations").

Hence, for mnemonic purposes, we need remember only the single number, 80.

But if we wish to adopt the nomenclature of Frankfort, it is necessary to keep in mind two figures denoting limits, 75 (inclusive) for dolichocephaly, and 80 (inclusive) for brachycephaly.

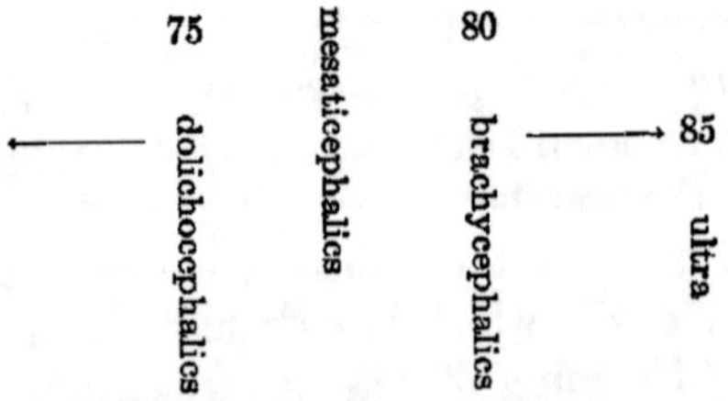

These constitute, as it were, two centres, beyond which, on this side and on that, we may picture to ourselves the *individual variations* drawn up in martial line. In this case, the space between 75

and 80, in other words, the limits of mesaticephaly, may be interpreted as due to oscillations between dolicho- and brachycephaly according to the laws of variability, which is analogous to what takes place in the case of oscillations in the opposite direction (70–75 dolichocephaly; 80–85 brachycephaly). From this point of view, these two numbers, 75 and 80, constitute *median centres* of two different types.

But according to Broca and his school—and this view is accepted by many anthropologists—mesaticephaly should be regarded as constituting a *fusion* of the two other types, the brachy- and dolichocephalic, whence it follows that mesaticephalics would be *hybrids*. Other authorities, on the contrary, exaggerating the conception of the fixity of the cephalic index in a given race, admit the existence of mesaticephalic races.

FIG. 73.

But it has been observed that the greater number of mesaticephalics are to be found in regions where dolichocephaly prevails; in certain districts of Africa, as for example, in Somaliland, not a single brachycephalic exists, yet none the less the mesaticephalics are numerous. Accordingly, mesaticephaly may be classed with *dolichocephaly* and regarded as one of its variations, while it seems to be independent of brachycephaly. Therefore the nomenclature of Retzius may for many good reasons be chosen and adopted in our schools. In conclusion, we shall regard the brachycephalics and dolichocephalics as the two fundamental types; and shall adopt the figure 80, included among the brachycephalics, as the limit of separation. The different grades of dolicho- or brachycephaly are to be determined by *mean averages*, and the oscillations due to individual variations, by *series*.

Hence it is important to determine the *mean average* and the oscillation of the cephalic index for the different races; and this is of interest to us as educators, in order to establish the limits of *normality*.

The practical method of studying the cephalic index is according to geographical distribution.

Here are a few general data of the cephalic index relative to its distribution:

The most dolichocephalic of all peoples are found in Melanesia, Australia, India and Africa. In the Fiji Islands the mean cephalic index is 67; in the Caroline Archipelago it is 69; in various regions of India, 71; that of the Hottentots, 74; of the Bantus, 73. Belonging to the dolichocephalics or mesaticephalics are the populations of the extreme south of Europe (Mediterranean race) and at the extreme north (English, Scotch). On the contrary, the races of western Europe and of central Asia are brachycephalic (Celts, Mongols). The most brachycephalic of all these peoples are met with in the Transcaucasus; their mean average is 88.7. There also exists a notable brachycephalic type in France (Savoyards, 86.9; inhabitants of the upper Loire, 87.4); also in Dalmatia, 80, while the Lapps of Scandinavia are also ultrabrachycephalic, 87.4

On very general lines, it may be said that the dolichocephalics are the Eurafrican races (including the Mediterranean race, with which the first civilisations are associated: Egyptian, Greek and Roman) who migrated from the Mediterranean basin into Europe; and the brachycephalics are the Eurasian races, who on the contrary migrated from continental Asia across western Europe (the Aryans).

As far as regards Italy, its population is by no means evenly constituted. The median index given by Livi for Italy, deduced from observation of more than 29,000 subjects is 80; in regard to regional distribution, the results are shown in the following table:

Piedmont	85.9
Emilia	85.2
Venetia	85.0
Lombardy	84.4
Umbria	84.1
Marches	84.0
Liguria	82.3
Tuscany	82.3
Campania	82.1
Abruzzo and Molise	81.9

Latium	81.0
Basilicata	80.8
Apulia	79.8
Sicily	79.6
Calabria	78.4
Sardinia	77.5

Let us remember that if the cephalic index were measured directly from the cranium, the result would be one or two units less, hence the mean average of the cranial index would be about 78.

The accompanying map represents still more clearly the geographical distribution. The results show that in Piedmont, in Emilia, and in Northern Italy in general the inhabitants are more brachycephalic; while in the south and more especially in the island possessions we find the more dolichocephalic part of the population. The highest degree of dolichocephaly is found in Sardinia.

But if, instead of the cartographic summary herewith reproduced, we could examine the exhaustive one with which Livi has illustrated his great work on Anthropometry, we should discover that the distribution does not follow the great *regional lines;* but that as a matter of fact certain *human groups* exist, isolated like little islands, which have a cephalic index in marked contrast to that of the remaining population of the same region.

Thus, for example, at Lucca, in the midst of a brachycephalic population, there is a pronouncedly dolichocephalic group; and in the midst of the dolichocephalic population of Abruzzo and the neighbouring provinces, there exists at Chieti a strongly brachycephalic group. Besides these and similar groups contrasting with the regional type, there exist a multiplicity of differences, from one successive boundary line to another, so that the *limits of the cephalic index* may be determined with great minuteness in the various regions.

Livi's large charts lend themselves with great clearness to this sort of analytical study, which would be found to be very profitable to teachers.

It is also quite instructive to compare the different charts representing various anthropological data of ethnical importance; such, for example, as that of the distribution of stature and that of the distribution of pigmentation. These data are regarded by anthropologists as attributes of race. Well, in these three charts it is evident at the first glance that there is a notable resemblance in distribution, so much so than an eye untrained to observation would be likely to confuse them. The cephalic index, the stature, the colour of the skin are consequently of almost uniform distribution. Corresponding to the most pronounced brachycephaly, we have the tallest stature and the fairest complexion; corresponding to the most pronounced dolichocephaly, we find instead the lowest stature and the most brunette types. Such an accumulative coincidence, in certain communities, of characteristics, in contrast to those that are found combined in certain other communities, reveal the existence in Italy of *two different races.* One of these races seems to have descended from over the Alps; the other, to have landed on the shores of the Mediterranean. The first belong to the Eurasians; the second to the Eurafricans.

In my work upon the population of Latium, the mean cephalic index obtained by me is 78. The distribution according to the localities studied affords the mean averages noted in the following table, in which I have also recorded the maximums and minimums, and the percentage of brachycephalic and dolichocephalic individuals who contributed to the given means:

CEPHALIC INDEX AMONG THE PEOPLE OF LATIUM
(According to Montessori)

Provinces	Mean cephalic index	Minimum	Maximum	Dolicho-cephalics, per cent.	Brachy-cephalics, per cent.
Rome	78	73	89	63	37
Castelli Romani	76	70	79	100	—
Tivoli	80	76	87	59	41
Velletri	79.5	75	86	50	50
Frosinone	80.7	75	87	43	57
Civitavecchia	78.5	78	80	65	35
Bracciano	77	75	80	65	35
Orte	83.6	75	90	11	89
Acquapendente	79.4	76	81	60	40

The results show a preponderance of brachycephalics or of dolichocephalics in the places where the mean cephalic index is respectively highest for brachycephaly (Orte) or for dolichocephaly (Castelli Romani). Furthermore, the extreme maximum and minimum figures are found to be included in these groups (90 at Orte and 70 at Castelli).

It should be noted that at Castelli Romani the mean average is mesaticephalic (76), notwithstanding the absence of brachycephalics; this average is based on figures showing an extremely pronounced dolichocephaly (ranging to 70!). The groups at Castelli and at Orte also showed characteristics in respect to stature (see page 111); at Orte the mean stature is 1.61 m., with a maximum of 1.70 m. (very tall statures for women), and at Castelli the mean stature is 1.47 m., with a minimum of 1.42 m. (low statures).

Similarly, in regard to pigmentation, I found at Orte a prevalence of blonds, and at Castelli of brunettes. Hence the conclusion may be drawn that at Castelli and at Orte there exist groups of human beings who are of almost pure race, in the midst of a population in which racial types have become attenuated or hidden; but in centres like these we still find persistent testimony as to the ethnic factors that combined to form the people of Latium: the one, a blond, tall, brachycephalic race; the other, dark, small, and dolichocephalic.

The Cephalic Index at Different Ages of Life.—Another quality that renders the cephalic index of great importance is that it remains constant in the course of growth, since the two maximum diameters, the antero-posterior and the transverse, increase at very nearly the same rate, excepting during the earliest years, at which time the length of the cranium increases slightly more than the width. According to some authorities it is in the second year, according to others it is in the fourth or seventh, that the cephalic index becomes constant (Binet, Deniker, Pearson, Fawcette, Ammon, Johannson, and Westermarck).

The following table is one that I have drawn up on the basis of Quételet's figures:

CEPHALIC INDEX

Age	Males	Females	Age	Males	Females
At birth	83	83	11 years	80	79
1 year	80	80	12 years	80	79
2 years	80	80	13 years	80	79
3 years	80	80	14 years	80	79
4 years	79	79	15 years	80	79
5 years	79	79	16 years	80	79
6 years	79	79	17 years	80	79
7 years	79	79	18 years	80	79
8 years	79	79	19 years	80	79
9 years	80	79	20 years	80	79
10 years	80	79	—	—	—

Since it has been observed that the cranium in the course of its growth may assume forms, amounting even to apparent malformations (due chiefly to "bumps," either symmetrical or asymmetrical), which disappear during the evolution of the individual, the *cephalic index*, for *the very reason* that it does not represent a faithful description of the form, gives us precious aid in judging the cranium of the child, because it *accurately determines the proportions between length and breadth* which are destined to persist even in the adult, and hence serve to give, even in infancy, a sure indication of the ethnic type to which the child belongs.

We owe to Dr. Ales Hrdlicka the extremely important graphic chart, which I will proceed to summarise, of the cephalic indices

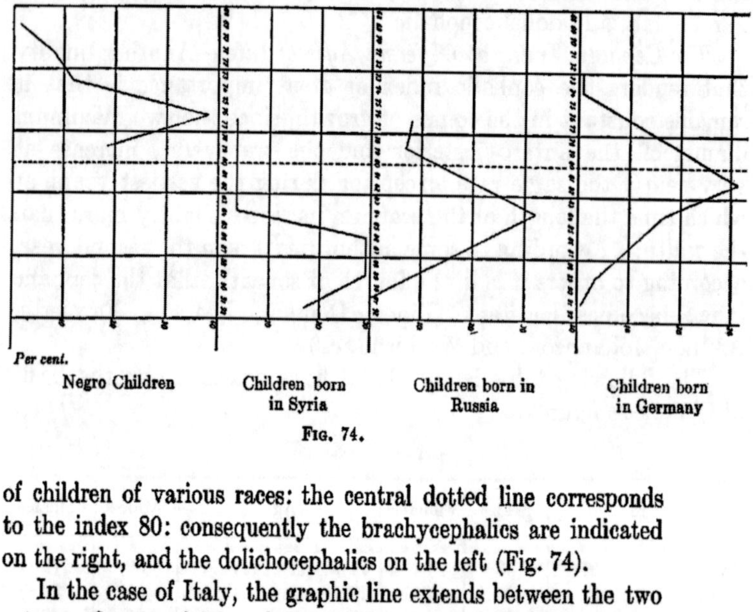

FIG. 74.

of children of various races: the central dotted line corresponds to the index 80: consequently the brachycephalics are indicated on the right, and the dolichocephalics on the left (Fig. 74).

In the case of Italy, the graphic line extends between the two extreme figures of 70 and 90, which are precisely the extreme limits that we have already noted for individual adults, in the case of the women of Latium: moreover, the curve is perceptibly symmetrical, although the brachycephalics are in the majority; a fact already established by Livi's mean averages. One might say that this curve was a graphic representation of Livi's two-colour method in his map of the cephalic index: one-half of Italy is brachycephalic and the other half is dolichocephalic; but since brachycephaly prevails in the northern half, a wider extent of territory is occupied by brachycephalics.

In America, where emigration brings every variety of humanity, the curve is even more symmetrical, and rests on a broader basis, representing widely separated extremes. Ireland also shows a very perceptible symmetry, the population being a mixture of Celts (brachycephalics) and of Scotch (northern blond dolichocephalics).

In Germany there is a prevalence of brachycephalics; we are here approaching the eastern regions from which the Eurasian race came through emigration. Here the Slavs and Celts (brachycephalics who immigrated into Europe at various epochs) are

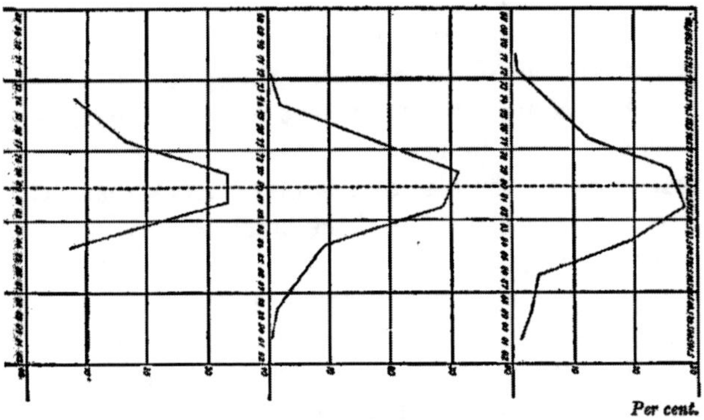

FIG. 74.

intermingled with a notable percentage of dolichocephalics (Teutons).

But in Russia, a region still further east, and similarly in Syria, we find an almost pure race: the curves lie wholly within the field of brachycephaly.

On the contrary, the dark-skinned children given in the last chart, and belonging to African races and tribes of American Indians, are all of them *dolichocephalic.*

According to Binet and other writers, the *cephalic index* and the *cranial volume* are the two anthropological data on which the criterion of *normality* of children's heads must be based.

When we observe a child's head which is apparently malformed, we cannot call it *abnormal;* it is not abnormal unless it has a volume notably too small (submicrocephaly, microcephaly) or too large (rickets, hydrocephaly); and a cephalic index exceeding the normal limits, in other words, *exaggerated* (scaphocephaly, trococephaly, pathological brachycephaly occurring in hydrocephalics).

The Volume of the Cranium

The volume of the cranium owes its importance, as we have already seen, to the fact that the cranium represents the *envelope* of the brain, and is consequently normally determined, as regards its dimensions, by the cerebral volume. Accordingly, in normal cases, when we speak of the cranial volume, we are speaking by implication of the *cerebral volume;* and all anthropological questions regarding the volumetric development of the cranium in reality have reference to the brain.

In abnormal cases, on the contrary, it may happen that the bony covering is not a skeletal index of the brain; in fact, pathological cases may occur analogous to those we have already observed in discussing the etiology of cranial malformations, in which the flat bones of the cranial vault undergo a notable thickening, so that as a result the greater volume of the cranium is due to the increased quantity of bony substance, and not of brain tissue, and is very heavy, so that it readily droops over upon the shoulder: *pachycephalic* cranium.

Another cause for lack of correspondence between the cerebral and the cranial volume may be the abnormal production of cerebro-spinal fluid within the brain: *hydrocephalic* cranium.

The Development of the Brain.—In the earliest period of embryonal life, the brain consists of a single vesicle, the continuation of which forms the spinal marrow: later on, this vesicle divides into three superimposed vesicles which represent respectively the embryonal beginnings of the anterior, middle and posterior brain; continuing their development, the anterior and posterior brains each divide in turn into two other vesicles, so that there result in all five primitive vesicles of the brain, superimposed one upon another (see Fig. 75); the anterior vesicle which is destined to grow enormously, dividing into two parts, right and left, with a longitudinal division, will constitute the cerebral hemispheres;

the second vesicle will constitute the optic thalami; the third vesicle, the corpora quadrigemina; the fourth vesicle, the cerebellum, and the fifth vesicle, the medulla oblongata.

When complete development is attained, the cerebral hemispheres completely cover the other parts of the brain, besides which they themselves are covered over with a multiplicity of folds constituting the *convolutions*. If we take a cross-section of the hemispheres, we find that they consist of an outer layer of *gray* matter formed of nerve cells, and of a central mass of *white* matter, formed of fibres.

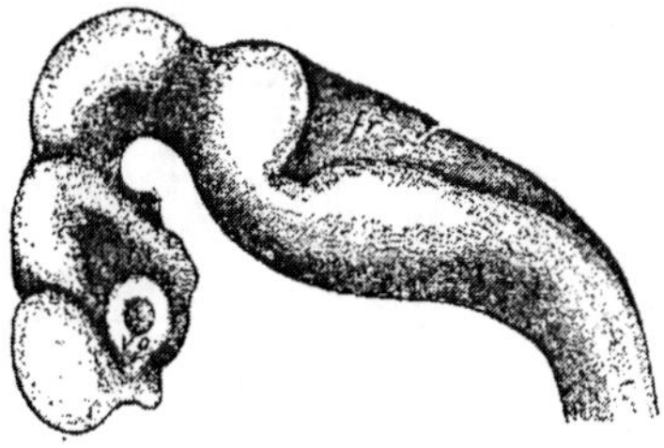

Fig. 75.—Brain of a Human Embryo after the Fourth Week.

The study of the convolutions is quite important from the anthropological standpoint, because their number is not identical in the different branches of the human race, and also because they differ both in number and in arrangement from the convolutions in the brain of the anthropoid apes. But however interesting they may be, considered as differentiating characteristics, we cannot linger over a study of this kind, which has a purely theoretic importance, and for the present cannot be applied in any practical and direct way to our problems of pedagogic anthropology. It will be sufficient to note rapidly that at the present time the study of the *convolutions* has received a new impulse through the labours of certain distinguished investigators, among whom we must once more include Dr. Sergio Sergi. Instead of studying the surface convolutions, Dr. Sergi studies the internal folds which are disclosed by separating the lips of the cerebral fissures; and from these he draws deductions which to a large extent correct those made by previous scientists, in regard to the eventual ancestry of the different species, the marks of biological superiority or inferiority, the differences in the brain due to sex, etc.

The surface fissures which divide the cerebral hemispheres into convolutions are shown in the two accompanying figures (Figs. 76 and 77), the first of which shows the outer side of the hemispheres, and the second the inner side.

15

Of chief importance to us is the arrangement of convolutions and furrows on the outer surface of the hemispheres.

The points to be noted are the following: the two great fissures, Rolando's, running longitudinally, and Silvius's running transversely, which, together with the perpendicular fissure, divide the hemisphere into four lobes: the *frontal* lobe and the *parietal* lobe, situated respectively in front and behind Rolando's fissure; the *temporal* lobe, situated below Silvius's fissure, and lastly, the *occipital* lobe at the posterior apex of the hemisphere.

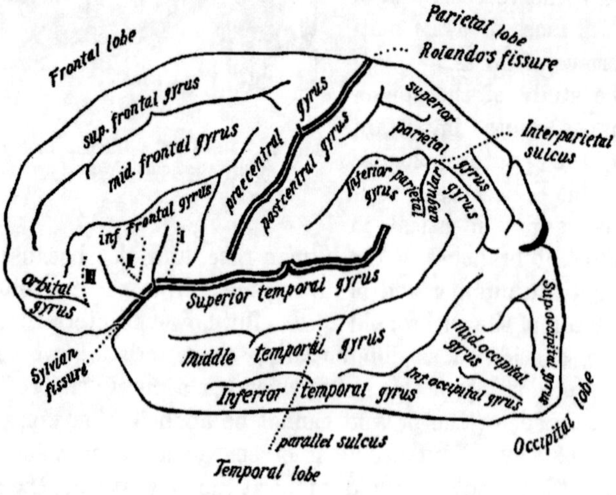

FIG. 76.—Cerebral hemisphere; external face.

In the third frontal convolution are situated Broca's centres, which are believed to be the seat of articulate speech; while along Rolando's fissure, in the ascendant convolutions, is the locality designated by physiologists as the motor centres.

The occipital lobe is the location of the zone of sight; and the temporal lobe, that of hearing.

It is important for us to observe the volume of the brain, and therefore that of the head, in relation to the rest of the body; it is enormous in the embryo; and even at birth and during childhood the head is quite voluminous as compared with the body, as appears from the diagram in Fig. 16, in which a new-born child and an adult man are reduced to the same scale, each retaining his relative bodily proportions. In Fig. 22 a new-born child is shown in two positions: from the front and from behind; the head is very large and the cranial nodules are plainly visible. Figs. 80 and 81 represent the same child at the age of six months and a year and a half; in the first picture the head is still very large as compared with the body, and the forehead protrudes (infantile forehead); in the second, the proportion between head and body has already altered.

A knowledge of the laws governing the growth of the brain is of particular importance in relation to pedagogic anthropology.

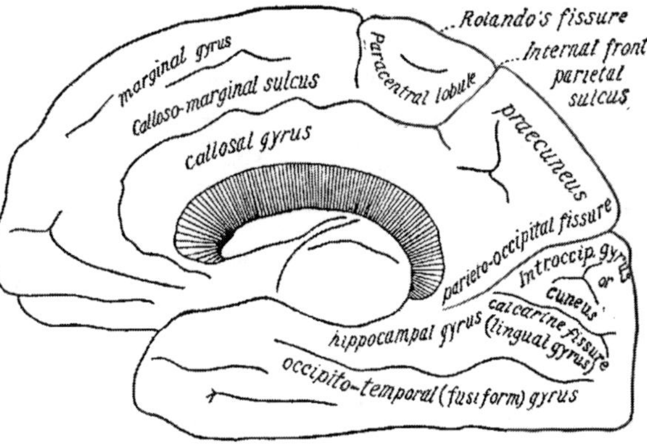

FIG. 77.—Cerebral hemisphere, internal face.

Within the last few years anthropologists have established certain principles that are well worthy of notice:

1. The child's head is normal when its *volume* and *cephalic index* come within the limits of normality (even if the shape appears abnormal: Simon, Binet, etc.).

2. When the volume of the head is too small it frequently indicates psychic deficiency; when it is too large, even up to the age of twenty years, it indicates a predisposition to precocious mortality (see below).

Very frequently when the size of the head is larger than normal and is not due to pathological causes (rickets, hydrocephaly, etc.), it is associated with an excessive development of the brain, and also with an intellectual precocity. A high percentage of this type die before reaching the age of twenty years; and this fact confirms the popular belief that children who are too intelligent or too good cannot live long.

This indication alone ought to be sufficient to prove the pedagogic importance of the cerebral volume.

The researches made by various authors in regard to the growth of the brain are not rigorously in accord as to the *limits of volume:* but they do agree as to the *rhythm of growth.*

Welcker gives the following figures:

WEIGHT OF THE BRAIN IN GRAMS

(According to WELCKER)

Age	Males	Females
At birth	400	360
Two months	540	510
One year	900	850
Three years	1,080	1,010
Ten years	1,360	1,250

Accordingly, the *weight* of the brain is doubled before the end of the first year; according to Massini it is very nearly doubled at the end of the first six months:

MASSINI'S FIGURES AS TO THE WEIGHT OF THE BRAIN

Age	Total weight	Increase	
At birth	352	68	279
First month	420	211	
From first to third month	631		
From third to sixth month	675	44	63
From sixth month to 1 year	694	19	

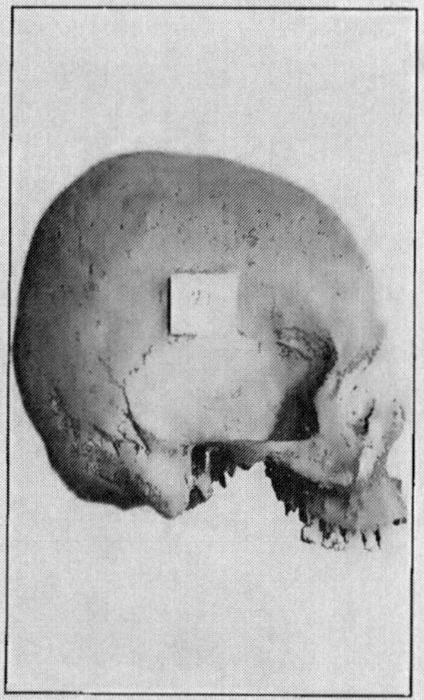

FIG. 78.—Spheroidal cranium lateral norm (Sergi's collection).

FIG. 79.—Sphaeroides typicus (from Sergi's collection).

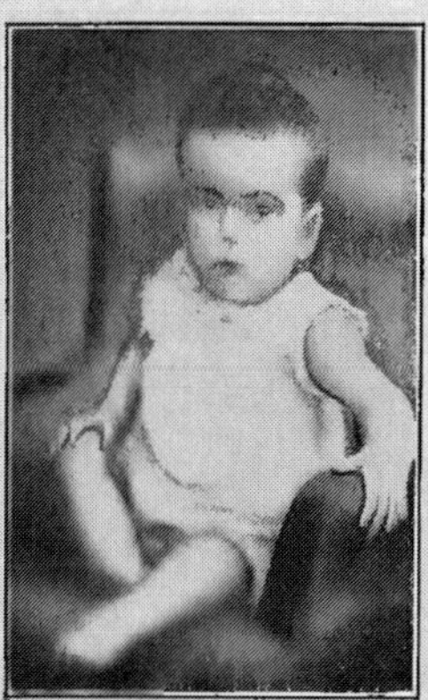

FIG. 80.—A child six months old.

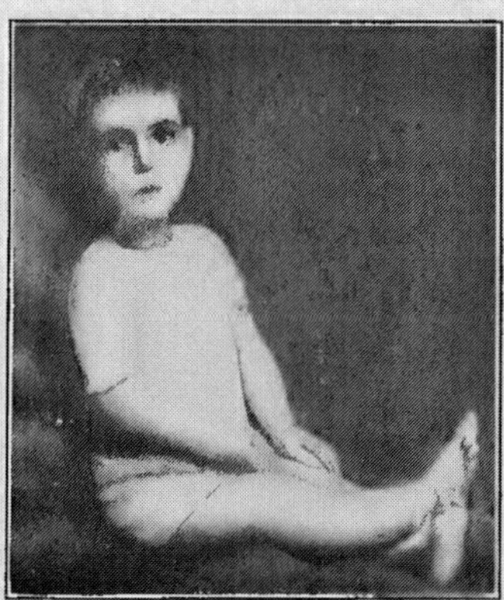

FIG. 81.—The same child a year and a half old.

It follows from these figures that by the end of the sixth month the weight of the brain is already very nearly doubled; but the maximum growth takes place between the ages of one month and three, after which it shows a notable diminution of rate.

But while the weight of the whole body is increased threefold by the end of the first year, that of the brain is very far from being tripled, since the rate of growth is still further diminished during the second six months; in fact even according to Welcker the weight at the end of the first year has little more than doubled.

Accordingly the rhythm of cerebral growth is not identical with that of the increase in weight of the body taken as a whole.

According to Massini, the relation between the cerebral weight and the weight of the body, at the various successive ages, is as follows:

RELATION BETWEEN WEIGHT OF BRAIN AND TOTAL WEIGHT

(According to MASSINI)

Age	Brain	Body	Age	Brain	Body
At birth	1	8	2 years	1	15
First month	1	9	3 years	1	14
From first to third month.	1	9	....	....	....
to sixth month	1	10	....	....	....
one year	1	12	25 years	1	40

In other words, the body grows more rapidly than the brain, and consequently, than the head: a fact which results in the different proportions already noted between head and body.

The rhythm of brain growth considered by itself has been set forth in a most noteworthy and accurate fashion by Boyd, based on the study of about two thousand cases; from the figures given by Boyd, I have calculated the amount of increase from period to period, as well as from year to year, the whole result being set forth in the following table:

RHYTHM OF GROWTH OF BRAIN
(*Males:* According to BOYD)

Age	Weight in grams	Difference for each period	Difference for each year	Relative epoch	Proportion to maximum reduced to 100
At birth................	331	—	—	—	24.2
From birth to 3 months.	493	+162	—	—	36.0
From 3 to 6 months....	603	+110	—	—	44.1
From 6 months to 1 year	777	+174	+446	1st year	56.8
From 1 to 2 years.....	942	+165	+165	2d year	69.0
From 2 to 4 years.....	1,097	+155	+ 77	2d– 4th	80.4
From 4 to 7 years.....	1,140	+ 43	+ 14	4th– 7th	83.4
From 7 to 14 years.....	1,302	+162	+ 23	7th–14th	95.3
From 14 to 20 years.....	1,374	+ 72	+ 12	14th–20th	100.5
From 20 to 30 years.....	1,357	—	—	—	99.3
From 30 to 40 years.....	1,366	+ 9	+ 0.9	30th–40th	99.3
From 40 to 50 years.....	1,352	– 14	– 1.4	40th–50th	98.9
From 50 to 60 years.....	1,343	– 9	– 0.9	50th–60th	98.3
From 60 to 70 years.....	1,315	– 28	– 2.8	60th–70th	96.9
From 70 to 80 years.....	1,289	– 26	– 2.6	70th–80th	95.3
From 80 to 90 years.....	1,284	– 5	– 0.5	80th–90th	94.2

In the above table, the first column of figures gives the *mean average weight* of the brain, obtained by direct observation of individual subjects; while from all the others the rhythm of cerebral growth and involution throughout the successive periods of life may be computed.

We see that the maximum growth takes place in the first years of life, the intensity is greater in the first year than in the second, and greater in the first three months than in those that follow. Already at the end of the first year the brain has surpassed one-half of the maximum weight which the individual is destined to attain in adult life (last column: proportions computed on scale of 100). A notable rate of increase continues up to the age of four, after which it moderates, but receives a new impulse at about the fourteenth year (period of puberty); hence it appears that at this important epoch of life the *brain* not only shares the general rapid growth of the body, but that by the end of the fourteenth year the brain has *already practically completed its development;* in fact, assuming that 100 represents its complete development, the weight of the brain is already 95.3; and at thirty it will be only 99.3.

By studying the above table we can obtain a clear analysis of these phenomena.

For women, Boyd gives the following figures:

THE GROWTH OF THE BRAIN IN WOMEN

(Figures Given by Boyd)

Age	Weight	Proportion to the maximum reduced to 100
At birth	283	22.8
Three months	452	36.5
From 3 to 6 months	560	45.2
From 6 months to 1 year	728	58.8
From 1 to 2 years	844	68.1
From 2 to 4 years	991	80.8
From 4 to 7 years	1,136	91.7
From 7 to 14 years	1,155	93.3
From 14 to 20 years	1,244	100.4
From 20 to 30 years	1,238	100.0
From 30 to 40 years	1,218	98.3
From 40 to 50 years	1,213	97.9
From 50 to 60 years	1,221	98.2
From 60 to 70 years	1,207	97.4
From 70 to 80 years	1,167	94.2
From 80 to 90 years	1,125	90.8

The rhythm of growth of the female brain is analogous to that of the male, except for the more precocious attainment of the maximum weight, which corresponds to the more precocious evolution of the female organism.

It should be noted that in the tables above cited the maximum is actually given as occurring at the age of twenty; and that after this period the weight diminishes again, subsequently increasing up to an age that varies according to the sex. But this maximum at the age of twenty must be considered as one of the false results of mean averages; and it must be explained on the ground that after the twentieth year the death rate has eliminated a series of individuals whose heads were abnormally large, and that a majority of the survivors were those whose whose heads had developed within normal limits.

This fact is further confirmed by Wagner's figures, cited by Broca:

MEAN WEIGHT OF THE BRAIN

(According to Wagner)

Age	Men	Women
Under 10 years	985	1,033
From 11 to 20 years	1,465	1,285
From 21 to 30 years	1,341	1,249
From 31 to 40 years	1,410	1,262
From 41 to 50 years	1,391	1,261
From 51 to 60 years	1,341	1,236
Above 60 years	1,326	1,203

Here again we have a false maximum at twenty, which nature subsequently corrects through mortality.

From such knowledge we obtain certain important rules of hygiene.

The normal brain which exceeds the common limits of volume is not, in an absolute sense, *incompatible* with life. We need only to call to mind certain men of genius who had the brains of a giant.

Accordingly a brain which exceeds the limits *demands of the individual who possesses it* that he shall live according to certain special rules of hygiene. Children and young people who are *too intelligent, too good,* in other words, children of the elite class demand a special treatment, just as much as any other class of beings that pass beyond the bounds of average normality. Parents and teachers ought to be enlightened in regard to these scientific principles; the growth of individuals who are exceptional in regard to their intelligence and their emotions, should be supervised as though it were something precious and fragile. Such individuals are destined to be more subject than others to *infective maladies,* which frequently prove fatal, developing symptoms of meningitis and cerebral affections. Consequently a hygienic life, *psychic repose*, an avoidance of emotional excitement, moderate physical exercise in farm or garden, a prolonged stay in the open country, might be the salvation of children of this type, who often are over-praised and over-stimulated by friends and relatives, and consequently subjected to continual excitement and *surménage* to a degree destructive to their health.

Extreme Individual Variations of the Volume of the Brain.—In regard to individual variations, the authorities give various figures, from which the following have been selected as most noteworthy for their accuracy of research:

NORMAL EXTREMES OF INDIVIDUAL VARIATIONS IN THE VOLUME OF THE BRAIN

Authors	Age: from 20 to 60 years		From 60 to 90	
	Maximum	Minimum	Maximum	Minimum
Calori	1,542	1,024	1,485	1,080
Bischoff	1,678	1,069	1,665	1,080
	Without distinction of age:			
	Maximum		Minimum	
Broca	1,830		1,049	

These figures refer to individuals belonging to European races.

Comparison with the Brains of Apes.—The brain of the great anthropoid apes (Chimpanzee, Orang-utan, Gorilla), whose total weight of body is comparable to that of man, weighs on an average 360 grams, and the greatest weight which it can attain is 420 gr.

Specific Gravity of the Human Brain.—In normal individuals, the average specific gravity is 1.03; in insane persons it is slightly higher: 1.04.

The Relation between the Weight of the Brain and the Cranial Capacity: Figures given by Lebon:

Weight of the brain in grams	Cranial capacity in cubic centimetres
1,450	1,650
1,350	1,550
1,250	1,450
1,150	1,350

Figures given by Manouvrier:

Weight of the brain in grams	Cranial capacity in cubic centimetres
1,700	1,949
1,450	1,663
1,250	1,432
1,000	1,147

Increase in the Volume of the Brain.—Studies regarding the growth of the head, although not yet complete, have gone sufficiently far to give us some useful ideas. In regard to the volume in a general sense, the *cranium in its growth obeys the cerebral rhythm.*

We shall speak in the section on *Technique* of the methods of measuring the head: at present it will suffice to point out that the measurements may be made directly upon the cranium, and the *cranial capacity* calculated directly from the head: and that the *maximum linear measurements* are sufficient to indicate the volume—such measurements being the three maximum diameters, *longitudinal, transverse, and vertical,* and the *maximum circumference.* Even the forehead, as an index of the general volume of the brain, is of interest in researches relating to the volumetric growth of the head.

Regarding the growth of the several cranial dimensions, the most accurate and complete knowledge is furnished by Binet's researches among the school-children of Paris (1902).

This author has made special investigations into the *rhythm* of growth of the cranium and of the face, with special reference to the period of *puberty.* The following are the mean averages obtained by him, relative to the three diameters corresponding to the three maximum dimensions of the head:

MEAN AVERAGES OF CEPHALIC MEASUREMENTS TAKEN UPON CHILDREN OF DIFFERENT AGES

(BINET: *From the schools of Paris*)

Measurement	Kindergartens		Lower primary schools				Upper primary schools		Normal schools
	4 years	5 years	8 years	10 years	12 years	14 years	14 years	16 years	18 years
Antero-post. diameter	169.5	173.9	174.7	177.1	181.5	181.5	185.3	188.3	190.4
Transverse diameter..	140.6	141.7	145	145.7	147.9	150.1	155.5	152.3	156.7
Vertical diameter....	118.8	121.6	122	122.8	127.6	129.7	128.1	131.4	130.8

It is evident that these figures contain inaccuracies, especially in regard to the vertical diameter (where the subsequent two-year period gives a smaller measurement than the preceding) due to the fact that the averages were obtained from an insufficient number of subjects or from subjects differing too widely in intelligence (from schools of different grades). For this reason Binet summarises the differences in growth, that is, the increase in relation to the diameters, under broad groups (six year groups, from four to ten years, and from ten to sixteen), in order to determine whether puberty exerts a sensible influence upon the cranial growth. The result is contained in the following table:

INCREASE OF THE THREE MAXIMUM DIAMETERS OF THE HEAD IN MILLIMETRES FROM FOUR TO EIGHTEEN YEARS OF AGE

Age in years: from — to —	4–6; 6–8; 8–10	10–12; 12–14; 14–16	16–18
Antero-posterior diameter.....	5.6; 0.8; 2.4	4.4; 1.8; 5	2.1
	8.8	**11.2**	
Transverse diameter..........	1.1; 3.3; 0.7	2.2; 3.9; 0.5	4.4
	5.1	6.6	
Vertical diameter............	2.8; 0.4; 0.8	4.8; 2.3; 2.5	0.6
	4.0	**9.6**	

From which it appears that there exists, in regard to the head, a puberal acceleration of growth.

These conclusions of Binet are indirectly confirmed by the researches of Vitale Vitali regarding the development of the forehead in school-children; since it is well known that the forehead represents the index of the general growth of the cerebral cranium.

Vitale Vitali based his observations upon school-children and students between the ages of ten and twenty. He not only measured the width of the forehead (*frontal diameter;* see *Technique*), but also measured its height, obtaining the percentage of its relation to the width (frontal index).

These are his figures:

FRONTAL INDEX AND DIAMETER ACCORDING TO AGE

(VITALE VITALI: RESEARCHES AMONG SCHOLARS AND STUDENTS FROM 10 TO 20 YEARS OLD)

Age	Frontal index	Frontal diameter	Amount of increase
11 years	73.05	107.5	—
12 years	74.11	112.0	4.5
13 years	74.14	112.5	0.5
14 years	74.80	114.4	1.9
15 years	75.67	116.8	2.4
16 years	77.24	120.1	3.3
17 years	77.02	120.6	0.5
18 years	77.36	121.5	0.9
19 years	77.60	122.8	1.3
20 years	77.15	122.1	0.7

Accordingly, between the years of fourteen and sixteen there is a puberal acceleration of growth, accompanied by an elevation of the forehead (high frontal index).

Vitali gives, as extreme limits of the frontal index, 68 and 83.

But in order to give a better illustration of the author's figures, his own words may be quoted: "It appears from our observations that the forehead begins to develop in notable proportions during the fourteenth year, and that the development of the frontal region as compared with the parietal region continues to augment up to the sixteenth year; after this it still increases, but only by a few millimetres, until the end of the sixteenth year. The cephalic development is completed between the sixteenth and eighteenth years. This observed fact is of great importance in relation to the development of the intellect."

The most complete figures at the present time on the growth of the brain, are those of Quételet, which follow its development from birth until the fortieth year. They are summarised in the following table:

INCREASE IN THE CIRCUMFERENCE OF THE BRAIN AND IN ITS THREE MAXIMUM DIAMETERS

(According to Quételet)

Age	Circumference in millimetres		Maximum diameters					
			Antero-post.		Transverse		Vertical	
	Men	Women	Men	Women	Men	Women	Men	Women
At birth	335	335	120	120	100	100	80	80
1 year	440	439	158	157	127	126	105	105
2 years	471	469	168	167	135	134	113	113
3 years	486	483	171	170	137	136	117	115
4 years	496	493	174	173	138	137	119	116
5 years	503	500	176	175	139	138	120	117
6 years	508	505	178	177	140	139	121	117
7 years	513	509	179	178	142	140	122	118
8 years	519	512	180	179	143	141	123	118
9 years	523	515	181	180	144	141	124	119
10 years	527	517	182	180	145	142	125	119
11 years	531	518	183	181	146	142	126	120
12 years	535	519	184	181	147	143	127	121
13 years	539	520	185	182	147	143	128	122
14 years	543	521	186	182	148	144	129	123
15 years	547	523	186	183	149	144	130	124
16 years	551	525	187	183	150	145	130	125
17 years	555	528	188	184	151	145	130	125
18 years	561	531	189	184	152	146	131	126
19 years	563	533	190	185	153	146	131	126
20 years	564	535	191	185	153	147	131	126
25 years	564	537	191	186	153	147	131	127
30 years	564	538	191	186	153	147	131	127
40 years	564	538	191	186	153	147	131	127

It appears from the foregoing table that after the twenty-fifth year the growth of the cranium practically ceases in all directions. In regard to the rhythm of growth, the problem is rendered clearer by the following table, which gives the annual increase:

ANNUAL INCREASE IN THE MAXIMUM CRANIAL MEASUREMENTS IN MALES

(From Figures Given by Quételet)

Age	Circumference	Antero-post. diameter	Transverse diameter	Vertical diameter
1	105	38	27	25
2	31	10	8	8
3	15	3	2	4
4	10	3	1	2
5	7	2	2	1
6	5	2	1	1
7	5	1	1	1
8	6	1	1	1
9	4	1	1	1
10	4	1	1	1
11	4	1	1	1
12	4	1	1	1
13	4	1	1	1
14	4	1	1	1
15	4	1	1	1
16	4	1	1	1
17	4	1	1	1
18	4	1	1	1
19	4	1	1	1
20	1	1	1	1

It appears from the above table that the total growth of the cranium takes place to a notable extent during the early years of life; as regards the diameters, the longitudinal diameter grows faster during the first few months than the transverse; but after the first year, the two maximum diameters which determine the cephalic index increase in very nearly the same proportion (constancy of the cephalic index throughout life). The vertical diameter on the contrary undergoes a relatively much greater increase than the two others, since, although much shorter than the transverse, it nevertheless overtakes and surpasses it in its absolute annual increase.

This corresponds to the fact that the first two diameters are indexes of growth relative to the base of the cranium, while the vertical diameter is the index of expansion of the cranial vault, which more directly follows the growth of the brain and elevates the forehead as it pushes upward.

Quételet's figures, however, fail to show in the rhythm of growth that puberal acceleration which has been observed to take place in the growth of the brain. This contradicts the researches of Vitali and also those of Binet.

Similar studies have been made a number of times during the last few years, especially in America, but with English tables of measurement, and with little uniformity in the results obtained by the different investigators.

Among the most recent and most complete figures should be cited those of Bonnifay* in which however the measurement of the vertical diameter is lacking, or in other words the third element needed, in conjunction with the dimensions of length and breadth, to give the volumetric factors.

CRANIAL MEASUREMENTS AT DIFFERENT AGES

(According to BONNIFAY)

Age from — to —	Absolute figures			Amount of increase		
	Circumference	Antero-posterior diameter	Transverse diameter	Circumference	Antero-posterior diameter	Transverse diameter
Birth to 15 days........	343.9	116.3	93.4	—	—	—
15 days to 2 months....	368.7	126.3	99.1	24.8	10.0	5.7
3 months to 4 months.	388.8	132.7	106.0	20.1	6.4	6.9
6 months to 1 year....	429.8	145.4	118.2	41.0	12.7	12.2
1 year to 2 years....	459.7	154.3	129.3	29.9	8.9	11.1
2 years to 3 years....	473.5	161.9	133.3	13.8	7.6	4.0
3 years to 4 years....	487.4	166.2	136.3	13.9	4.3	3.0
4 years to 5 years....	495.7	169.9	138.3	8.3	3.7	2.0
5 years to 6 years....	497.8	171.9	140.4	2.1	2.0	2.1
6 years to 7 years....	504.4	172.8	141.1	6.6	0.9	0.7
7 years to 8 years....	511.6	175.2	143.7	7.2	2.4	2.6
8 years to 9 years....	514.1	176.1	144.3	2.5	0.9	0.6
9 years to 10 years....	514.7	176.4	144.2	0.6	0.3	0.9
10 years to 11 years....	519.8	177.1	146.6	5.1	0.7	2.3
11 years to 12 years....	521.1	177.5	145.7	1.3	0.4	0.1
12 years to 13 years....	529.7	180.1	147.8	8.6	2.6	1.2
13 years to 14 years....	533.1	178.1	148.5	3.4	—	0.7
14 years to 17 years....	548.8	182.4	152.2	15.7	2.3	3.7
22 years to 27 years....	549.1	186.6	153.2	0.3	4.2	1.0

*BONNIFAY, *On the development of the Head from the point of view of cephalometrical measurements taken after birth.* Thesis, Lyons, 1897.

Among the linear measurements of the cranium, the one which serves to give the most exact index of volume is the *maximum circumference.*

This index, nevertheless, is not a perfect one, in the same sense that the *stature*, for instance, is a perfect index in respect to the body, because in the case of the cranium another element enters in: the form. The cranial circumference of an extremely brachycephalic cranium (almost circular) may contain a larger surface (and consequently include a larger volume), than a maximum circumference of the same identical measure, which belongs to an extremely dolichocephalic cranium (approaching the shape of an elongated ellipse). This may be easily understood if we imagine a loop of thread laid out in the form of a circle: if we pull it from two opposite sides, the enclosed area diminishes until it finally disappears as the two halves of the thread close together, while the length of the thread itself remains unaltered.

Nevertheless, the maximum circumference still remains the linear index best adapted to represent the *volume*; indeed, the authorities take its proportional relation to the stature as representing the reciprocal degree of development between head and body at the different successive ages.

Here are the figures which Daffner gives in this connection:

DEVELOPMENT OF THE STATURE AND OF THE CEPHALIC PERIMETER FROM BIRTH TO THE AGE OF ELEVEN YEARS

Males				Females			
Number of subjects	Age	Stature in centimetres	Cranial perimeter, centimetres	Number of subjects	Age	Stature in centimetres	Cranial perimeter, centimetres
65	At birth	51.17	34.58	65	At birth	50.27	34.23
11	1.55	74.18	46.74	10	1.39	77.20	46.45
30	2.43	85.32	48.03	30	2.45	83.48	47.23
53	3.34	91.88	49.20	49	3.43	89.97	47.73
112	4.43	96.64	49.55	81	4.50	96.07	48.37
244	5.42	103.21	50.21	208	5.40	100.61	48.76
234	6.41	106.49	50.73	179	6.37	104.92	49.87
30	7.30	114.47	51.66	25	7.36	117.36	50.38
28	8.38	112.10	51.97	24	8.41	121.58	50.72
27	9.40	128.41	52.38	30	9.40	126.76	51.10
21	10.34	129.12	52.24	28	10.40	130.00	51.08
20	11.42	135.84	52.50	31	11.46	137.04	51.42

DEVELOPMENT OF THE STATURE AND OF THE CEPHALIC PERIMETER BETWEEN THE YEARS OF 13 AND 22

Number of subjects	Age	Stature in centimetres	Cephalic perimeter in centimetres
13	13.39	147.92	52.83
24	14.50	149.21	53.53
20	15.38	163.55	54.34
41	16.43	162.53	53.34
35	17.36	167.93	55.89
26	18.35	171.65	54.91
15	19.40	172.97	55.48
6	20.05	173.97	56.50
342	21.02	168.00	55.37
171	22.22	168.08	55.62

One very important research made by Daffner is in reference to the maximums and minimums that are normal for each successive age. This is extremely useful for the purpose of diagnosing the *morphological normality in relation to the age.* He naturally bases his figures upon subjects studied by him personally, who altogether form an aggregate number of 2,230, and are not always sufficiently numerous when distributed according to their ages. Nevertheless, in the great majority of groups, especially those including the younger children, the number of subjects is sufficient and even superabundant.

At all events, Daffner's researches may serve as a valuable guide in the researches that lay the foundation for diagnosis; and every future investigator will find it an easier task, under such guidance, to make his own contribution to it and to correct those inaccuracies which (for certain epochs) are to be attributed to an insufficient number of subjects.

Daffner distinguishes, for each year, a *maximum* and a *minimum* both for the stature and for the cephalic perimeter; but since the person having the maximum stature does not always have the maximum cephalic perimeter, and *vice versa,* the author indicates, in connection with the maximum and minimum figures, the other of the two measurements which, as a matter of fact, corresponds to them in each given case.

Individual Variations

MAXIMUMS AND MINIMUMS OF STATURE AND OF CRANIAL CIRCUMFERENCE

Age	Measurements S. = Stature Cc. = Cranial circumference	Maximum (M.) and minimum (m.) in millimetres	Measurements occurring in combination with the M. or m. measurements
	Males from birth to the age of eleven years		
At birth	Cranial circumf.	M. = 372	(S. = 625).
		m. = 326	(S. = 500).
	Stature	M. = 550	(Cc. = 369, 365, 354).
		m. = 480	(Cc. = 343, 341, 337).
1 year	Cranial circumf.	M. = 491.	
		m. = 456.	
	Stature	M. = 805	(Cc. = 491).
		m. = 680	(Cc. = 456).
2 years	Cranial circumf.	M. = 506	(S. = 855).
		m. = 462	(S. = 800).
	Stature	M. = 920	(Cc. = 496).
		m. = 785	(Cc. = 467).
3 years	Cranial circumf.	M. = 521	
		m. = 462	(S. = 915).
	Stature	M. = 995	(Cc. = 521, 501).
		m. = 795	(Cc. = 472).
4 years	Cranial circumf.	M. = 530	(S. = 1035).
		m. = 465	(S. = 900).
	Stature	M. = 1090	(Cc. = 510).
		m. = 835	(Cc. = 499, 481).
5 years	Cranial circumf.	M. = 527	(S. = 1070).
		m. = 481	(S. = 930).
	Stature	M. = 1173	(Cc. = 519).
		m. = 920	(Cc. = 495).

Note.—═══ indicates that the number of subjects is abundant.
▬▬▬ indicates that the number of subjects is sufficient.
········ indicates that the number of subjects is scarce.

MAXIMUMS AND MINIMUMS OF STATURE AND OF CRANIAL CIRCUMFERENCE—*Continued*

Age	Measurements S. = Stature Cc. = Cranial circumference	Maximum (M.) and minimum (m.) in millimetres	Measurements occurring in combination with the M. or m. measurements
6 years..........	Cranial circumf...	M. = 532........	(S. = 1090).
		m. = 481........	(S. = 1045).
	Stature..........	M. = 1163.......	(Cc. = 517).
		m. = 950........	(Cc. = 495).
7 years..........	Cranial circumf...	M. = 541........	(S. = 1232).
		m. = 502........	(S. = 1156, 1223).
	Stature..........	M. = 1276.......	(Cc. = 527).
		m. = 1092.......	(Ca. = 514).
8 years..........	Cranial circumf...	M. = 542........	(S. = 1207, 1292).
		m. = 496........	(S. = 1158).
	Stature..........	M. = 1375.......	(Cc. = 537).
		m. = 1099.......	(Cc. = 497).
9 years..........	Cranial circumf...	M. = 548........	(S. = 1333).
		m. = 507........	(S. = 1250).
	Stature..........	M. = 1383.......	(Cc. = 546).
		m. = 1185.......	(Cc. = 522).
10 years.........	Cranial circumf...	M. = 553........	(S. = 1303).
		m. = 497........	(S. = 1270).
	Stature..........	M. = 1372.......	(Cc. = 538).
		m. = 1218.......	(Cc. = 534).
11 years.........	Cranial circumf...	M. = 543........	(S. = 1350).
		m. = 505........	(S. = 1307).
	Stature..........	M. = 1466.......	(Cc. = 542).
		m. = 1300.......	(Cc. = 513).

FEMALES FROM BIRTH TO THE AGE OF ELEVEN YEARS

Age.	Measurements S. = Stature Cc. = Cranial circumference	Maximum (M). and minimum (m.) in millimetres	Measurements found in combination with the M. or m. measurements	Observations
At birth.	Cranial circumf. .	M. = 372...	(S. = 500).	(The most frequent S. was 550 mm. combined with Cc. = 357, 337).
		m. = 324...	(S. = 480).	
	Stature.........	M. = 565...	(Cc. = 355).	
		m. = 475...	(Cc. = 333, 325).	
1 year...	Cranial circumf. .	M. = 486...	(S. =	
		m. = 450...	(S. = 750, 740).	
	Stature.........	M. = 810...	(Cc. = 486).	
		m. = 705...	(Cc. = 455).	
2 years. .	Cranial circumf. .	M. = 495...	(S. = 850).	
		m. = 448...	(S. = 810).	
	Stature.........	M. = 910...	(Cc. = 491).	
		m. = 720...	(Cc. = 464).	
3 years. .	Cranial circumf. .	M. = 501...	(S. = 865).	
		m. = 457...	(S. = 870).	
	Stature.........	M. = 1015..	(Cc. = 473).	
		m. = 810...	(Cc. = 476).	
4 years. .	Cranial circumf. .	M. = 510...	(S. = 1050).	
		m. = 455...	(S. = 920, 870).	
	Stature.........	M. = 1060..	(Cc. = 507).	
		m. = 860 ..	(Cc. = 461).	
5 years. .	Cranial circumf. .	M. = 515...	(S. = 1035).	
		m. = 462...	(S. = 905).	
	Stature.........	M. = 1140..	(Cc. = 492).	
		m. = 875...	(Cc. = 481).	
6 years. .	Cranial circumf. .	M. = 522...	(S. = 1020).	(The maximum S. was found in a child of 6 years and 11 months; the next highest stature was 1177 mm., Cc. 512; another little girl of 6 years and 11 months had S. = 1099; Cc. = 507).
		m. = 460...	(S. = 965).	
	Stature.........	M. = 1221..	(Cc. = 516).	
		m. = 920...	(Cc. = 489).	
7 years. .	Cranial circumf. .	M. = 524...	(S. = 1215).	
		m. = 479...	(S. = 1185).	
	Stature.........	M. = 1270..	(Cc. = 513).	
		m. = 1058..	(Cc. = 499).	

FEMALES FROM BIRTH TO THE AGE OF ELEVEN YEARS—*Continued*

Age	Measurements S. = Stature Cc. = Cranial circumference	Maximum (M.) and minimum (m.) in millimetres	Measurements found in combination with the M. or m. measurements	Observations
8 years..	Cranial circumf..	M. = 542...	(S. =).	
		m. = 484...	(S. =).	
	Stature..........	M. = 1328..	(Cc. = 542).	
		m. = 1082..	(Cc. = 484).	
9 years..	Cranial circumf..	M. = 526...	(S. = 1272).	
		m. = 493...	(S. = 1306).	
	Stature.........	M. = 1325..	(Cc. = 520).	
		m. = 1173..	(Cc. = 499).	
10 years.	Cranial circumf..	M. = 533...	(S. = 1291).	
		m. = 476...	(S. = 1204).	
	Stature.........	M. = 1403..	(Cc. = 530).	
		m. = 1153..	(Cc. = 506).	
11 years.	Cranial circumf..	M. = 537...	(S. = 1420).	(The next higher S. was 1495, with a Cc. of 529).
		m. = 478...	(S. = 1284).	
	Stature.........	M. = 1464..	(Cc. = 512).	
		m. = 1255..	(Cc. = 497).	

EXTREMES BETWEEN THE AGES OF 13 AND 22 YEARS
(The figures here given are less exact, because of the great scarcity of subjects)

Age	Measurements S. = Stature Cc. = Cranial circumference	Maximum (M.) and minimum (m.) in millimetres	Measurements that occur in conjunction with M. and m. measurements
13 years.........	Cranial circumf...	M. = 554........	(S. =).
		m. = 492........	(S. =).
	Stature..........	M. = 1715.......	(Cc. = 554).
		m. = 1345.......	(Cc. = 492).
14 years.........	Cranial circumf...	M. = 564........	(S. = 1560).
		m. = 515........	(S. = 1555).
	Stature..........	M. = 1630.......	(Cc. = 537).
		M. = 1405.......	(Cc. = 526).
15 years.........	Cranial circumf...	M. = 567........	(S. = 1575).
		m. = 526........	(S. = 1570).
	Stature..........	M. = 1795.......	(Cc. = 566).
		m. = 1450.......	(Cc. = 534).

EXTREMES BETWEEN THE AGES OF 13 AND 22 YEARS—*Continued*

Age	Measurements S. = Stature Cc. = Cranial circumference	Maximum (M.) and minimum (m.) in millimetres	Measurements that occur in conjunction with M. and m. measurements
16 years	Cranial circumf.	M. = 566	(S. = 1675).
		m. = 519	(S. = 1460).
	Stature	M. = 1807	(Cc. = 561).
		m. = 1330	(Cc. = 532).
17 years	Cranial circumf.	M. = 582	(S. = 1757).
		m. = 507	(S. = 1610).
	Stature	M. = 1759	(Cc. = 560).
		m. = 1561	(Cc. = 555).
18 years	Cranial circumf.	M. = 565	(S. = 1785).
		m. = 522	(S. = 1702).
	Stature	M. = 1930	(Cc. = 557).
		m. = 1604	(Cc. = 536).
19 years	Cranial circumf.	M. = 578	(S. = 1707).
		m. = 541	(S. = 1693).
		M. = 1823	(Cc. = 545).
	Stature	m. = 1637	(Cc. = 549).
20 years	Cranial circumf.	M. = 594	(S. = 1671).
		m. = 551	(S. = 1780).
	Stature	M. = 1832	(Cc. = 560).
		m. = 1629	(Cc. = 552).
21 years	Cranial circumf.	M. = 590	(S. = 1700).
		m. = 512	(S. = 1590).
	Stature	M. = 1790	(Cc. = 581).
		m. = 1570	(Cc. = 571).
22 years	Cranial circumf.	M. = 595	(S. = 1730).
		m. = 510	(S. = 1650).
	Stature	M. = 1790	(Cc. = 576).
		m. = 1570	(Cc. = 548).

Nomenclature Relating to Cranial Volume. Anomalies.—(In regard to the method of directly measuring or calculating the cranial capacity, and of taking and estimating the measurements of the skull, see the section on *Technique.*)

Limits.—The cranial capacity, according to Deniker, has normally such a wide range of oscillation that the minimum is fully doubled by the maximum, the limits being respectively 1,100 and 2,200 cubic centimetres—these figures, however, including men of genius. Furthermore, the mean average capacity oscillates between limits that change according to race—not only because the cerebral volume may of itself constitute an ethnic characteristic (superior and inferior races) with which the *form of the forehead* is usually associated, but also because the cranial volume bears a certain relation to the *stature*, which is another factor that varies with the race.

Deniker gives the following mean averages of oscillations:

Europeans.	from 1,500 to 1,600 cu. cm.
Negroes.	from 1,400 to 1,500 cu. cm.
Australians, Bushmen.	from 1,250 to 1,350 cu. cm.

The average difference of cranial capacity is 150 cubic centimetres less in woman than in man.

The following nomenclature for oscillations in cranial capacity was established by Topinard, based upon the figures and methods of Broca:

Macrocephalic crania.	from 1,950 cu. cm. upward
Large crania.	from 1,950 to 1,650 cu. cm.
Medium or ordinary crania	from 1,650 to 1,450 cu. cm.
Small crania.	from 1,450 to 1,150 cu. cm.
Microcephalic crania	from 1,150 cu. cm. downward

To-day, however, the terms *macrocephalic* and *microcephalic* have come to be reserved for *pathological* cases. Virchow has introduced the term *nanocephalic* to designate normal crania of very small dimensions; while Sergi has adopted a binomial nomenclature, calling them *eumetopic* microcephalics, which signifies *possessed of a fine forehead:* since, as we have seen, it is precisely the shape of the forehead which determines normality. And in place of *macrocephalic*, we have for very large normal crania the new term *megalocephalic*.

Pathological terminology includes the following nomenclature: macrocephaly, sub-macrocephaly, sub-microcephaly, microcephaly

Microcephaly may fall as low as 800 cubic centimetres; macrocephaly may rise as high as 3,000 cubic centimetres, and at these extremes the volume alone is sufficient to denote the anomaly. But in many cases the volume may fall within the limits of normality; in such cases it is the *pathological form* and an examination of the patient which lead to the use of the term sub-microcephalic in preference to that of nanocephalic, etc.

The volume, taken by itself, if it is not at one of the extreme limits, is not sufficient to justify a verdict of abnormality.

The terms macro- and microcephalic are, in any case, quite generic, and simply indicate a morphological anomaly, which may include many widely different cases, such, for example, as rickets, hydrocephaly, pachycephaly, etc., all of which have in common the morphological characteristic of *macrocephaly*.

In rickets, for instance, macrocephaly may occur in conjunction with a normal or even supernormal intelligence (Leopardi). Microcephaly, on the contrary, could never occur combined with normal intelligence, since it is a sign indicative of *atrophy of the cerebro-spinal* axis and diminution or, as Brugia phrases it, dehumanization of the individuality.

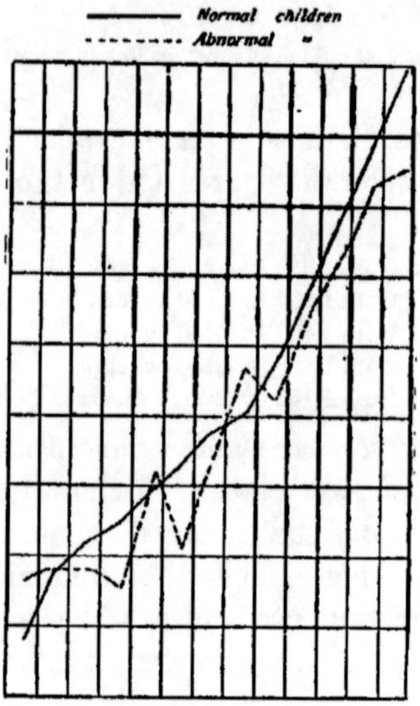

FIG. 82.—Growth of Cranial Circumference.

In all the widely varied series of pathological and degenerate individuals who are included under the generic names of "deficients" and "criminals," there is a notable percentage of crania that are abnormal both in volume and in form; the percentage of crania with normal dimensions is less than that of the crania which exceed or fall below such dimensions, and among these there is a preponderance of *submicrocephalic* crania: a morphological characteristic associated with a partial arrest of cerebral development, due to *internal causes* and manifested from the earliest period of infant life.

The accompanying chart (Fig. 82) demonstrates precisely this fact. It represents the growth of the cranium in normal and in abnormal children. The abnormal are at one time superior and at another inferior to the normal children; but their general average shows a definite inferiority to the normal. Lombroso established the fact that among adult criminals there is an *inferiority* of cranial development, frequently accompanied by a stature that is normal, or even in excess of normality.

Quite recently, Binet has called attention to a form of *sub-*

microcephaly acquired through external causes, which is of great interest from the pedagogic point of view. Blind children and those who are deafmutes have, up to the seventh or eighth year, a cranium of normal dimensions, but by the fourteenth or fifteenth year the volume is notably below the normal, and this stigma of inferiority remains permanently in the adults. This fact, which is of very general occurrence, is attributed by Binet to a deficiency of sensations, and consequently a deficiency of certain specific cerebral exercises.

This whole question has a fundamental interest for us as educators, because it affords an indirect proof that *cerebral exercise develops* the brain, or in other words, that education has a physical and morphological influence as well as a psychic one.

This question, coupled with that of the influence of *alimentation* upon the development of the head, leads to the conclusion that a two-fold nutriment is necessary for the normal development of man: *material* nutriment and nutriment of the *spirit.*

It follows that education must be considered from two different points of view: that of the progress of civilisation, and that of the perfectionment of the species.

In regard to variations of cranial volume, just as in the case of variations of stature, there are a number of different factors which may be summed up in such a way as to afford us certain determining characteristics of *social caste.* Delicate questions these, which we may sum up in a single question equally delicate, that lends itself to a vast amount of discussion; namely, what is the relation between the *volume* of the brain and the development of the intellect?

Individual Variations of Cerebral (and Cranial) Volume. Relation between the Development of the Cerebral Volume and the Development of the Intelligence.—The series of arguments in reference to the *cerebral volume* ought to be considered independently of the biological and biopathological factors which we have up to this point been considering; namely, race, sex, age, degeneration and disease.

That is to say, in normal individuals, other conditions being equal, volumetric differences of the brain may be met with, analogous to those other infinite individual variations, in which nature expresses her creative power, even while preserving unchanged the general morphology of the species.

It is due to this fact that the innumerable individuals of a race, while all bearing a certain resemblance to one another, are never any two of them identically alike.

Variations of this sort, which might be called biological individualisations, are in any case subject to the most diverse influences of environment, which concur in producing individual varieties.

This is in accordance with general laws which are applicable to any biological question whatever, but that in our case assume a special interest. There are certain men who have larger or smaller brains; and there are men of greater or of less intelligence. Is there a quantitative relation between these two manifestations, the morphological and the psychic?

Everyone knows that this is one of those complicated, much discussed questions that spread outside of the purely scientific circles and become one of the stock themes of debate among classes incompetent to judge; consequently it has been colored by popular prejudice, rather than by the light of science. It is well that persons of education should acquire accurate ideas upon the subject.

If the volume of the brain should be in proportion to the intellectual development, argues the general public, what sort of a head must Dante Alighieri have had? He would have had to be the most monstrous macrocephalic ever seen upon earth. And on the basis of this superficial observation, they wish to deny any quantitative relation whatever between brain and intelligence. And yet it is this same general public that keeps insisting: Woman has less intelligence than man, *because* she has a smaller brain.

A single glance up and down the *zoological scale* suffices to show that throughout the whole animal series a greater development of brain is accompanied by a correspondingly greater development of psychic activity; and that there is a *conspicuous* difference between the human brain and that of the higher animals (anthropoid apes), corresponding to the difference between the level of man's psychic development and that of the higher mammals; and this justifies the assertion that, *as a general rule*, there is a quantitative relation between the brain and the intellect.

This suggests the thought that the perfect development of this delicate *instrument*, the brain, demands a variety of harmonious material conditions, among others the *volume*, in order to render possible the conditions of psychic perfection.

From this premise, we may pass on to a more particularised study of the *material conditions* essential to the superior type of brain. The volume is the quantitative index; but the *quality* may be considered from various points of view, which may be grouped as follows:

I. *The General Morphology of the Brain* in reference to:

(*a*) The harmonious, relative volumetric proportions between the lobes of the brain (namely, the proportion between the frontal, parietal, temporal and occipital lobes). It was formerly believed that a superior brain ought to show a prevalence of the frontal lobes, since a lofty forehead is a sign of intellect; but it was afterward established that there is no direct relation between the development of the forehead and the development of the frontal lobes; a higher forehead results from a greater volume of the entire cranial contents; the superior brain, on the contrary, is that in which no one lobe prevails over another, but all of them preserve a reciprocal and perfect harmony of dimensions.

(*b*) The form, number and disposition of the cerebral convolutions, and of the folds of the internal passage (Sergio Sergi).

(*c*) The form, number and disposition of the cells in the cortical strata of the brain, and the proportion between the gray matter and the white, that is to say, between the cells and fibres; in short, the histological structure of the brain.

II. The *Chemistry* of the brain:

(*a*) The chemical composition of the substances constituting the brain, which may be more or less complicated. (Recent studies of the chemical evolution of living organisms have demonstrated that the atomic composition is far more complex in the higher organisms.)

(*b*) The intimate interchange of matter in the cerebral tissues, in connection with their nutrition.

(*c*) The chemical stimuli coming from the so-called glands of internal secretion (thyroid, etc.).

All these conditions concur in determining the *quality* of the cerebral tissues. In its ontogenetic evolution, for example, the brain does not merely increase in volume, and its development is not limited to attaining a definite morphology; but its intimate structure and its chemical composition as well must pass through various stages of transition before attaining their final state. We know, for example, that the myelination of the nerve fibres takes place upward from the spinal marrow toward the brain, and that the pyramidal tracts (voluntary motor tracts) are the last to myelinate, and hence the last to perform their functions in the child.

The consistence of the cerebral mass and its specific gravity also differ in childhood from that of the adult state. The evolution of the brain is therefore a very complex process; and this process may not be fully completed (for instance, it may be completed in volume, but not in form or chemical composition, etc.).

Consequently, just as in the case of volume, there may be various qualitative conditions, such as would produce organic inferiority.

But supposing that qualitatively the evolution has been accomplished normally, where there is greater cerebral volume, is there a correspondingly greater intellect?

At this point it is necessary to take into consideration another series of questions regarding the brain considered as a *material organ,* and having reference to the relation between the volume of the *brain* and that of the *stature.*

The brain must govern the nerves in all the *active parts* of the body, especially the striped muscles, which perform all voluntary movement. Consequently the cerebral volume must be in proportion, not only to the intellectuality, but also to the *physical activity.*

Evidently, a greater mass of body demands a greater nervous system to give it motive power.

The biological law is of a general nature: if the brain of a rat weighs 40 centigrams, that of an ox weighs 734 grams, and that of an elephant 4,896 grams.

"*The absolute volume of the brain increases with the total volume of the body.*"

But this correspondence is not proportional. There are two facts that alter the proportions. One of these is that the mass of the body increases faster than the brain, throughout the biological series of species, so that the smaller the body the greater the proportional quantity of brain. Just the opposite from what was found to hold true for the absolute weight.

It may be affirmed as a biological law that "*the relative volume of the brain increases as the size of the body diminishes.*" For instance, the tiny brain of a rat is a 43d part of the total volume of its body; the brain of an ox, on the contrary, is a 750th part. Consequently we may say that the little rat has relatively a far larger brain than the huge ox.

And the same thing holds true among men; those of small build have a proportionately larger brain than those of large build.

A second fact which alters the absolute proportion between the volume of brain and the volume of body has reference to the "*functional capacity*" of the active parts. The muscles which are capable of the best activity and the greatest agility are the ones more abundantly stimulated through their nerves than those which are capable only of slow and sluggish action. The same may be said of the organs of sensation; the more highly the sensibility is developed, the larger are the corresponding nerves, and consequently the greater is the corresponding quantity of cerebral cells. Accordingly the animal which is nimblest in its movements, and most capable of sensations has in proportion to this greater *functional activity* a greater cerebral volume. In this same way we may explain the enormous difference in relative brain volume between the extremely active, sensitive and intelligent little beast which we call the rat, and the sluggish and stupid animal which we call the ox. Consequently this *functional activity* has a correspondingly greater volume of brain, without a correspondingly greater volume of the various highly sensitized organs. In such a case it may be stated as a general law that "*the relative volume of the brain is in direct proportion to the intelligence* (*or, more broadly, to the functional activity*), *while the absolute volume is in direct relation to the total mass of the body.*"

Man has a cerebral volume of 1,500 cubic centimetres, a volume equal to a fortieth part of the whole body. Consequently he has a brain twice the actual size of that of the ox, while considered in its relation to bodily bulk, he has more brain than the smallest rat (man $= \frac{1}{40}$; rat $= \frac{1}{43}$). A volume so far exceeding the proportions found in animals, is beyond doubt directly related to *human intelligence.*

Relation between Cerebral and Intellectual Development in Man.—This ends our examination of the generic question of the relation between cerebral volume and intellect.

Granting these biological principles, and wishing to apply them to normal man, let us go back to our first question: "Do persons of greater intelligence have a greater cerebral volume, and consequently a larger head?"

There is an extensive literature upon this question, the tendency of which is to decide it affirmatively.

Parchappe has made a comparative study between writers of recognized ability and simple manual workers, and has found that the former have a development of the head notably in excess of the latter.

Broca took measurements, in various hospitals, of the heads of physicians and male nurses, and found a greater development of head in the case of the physicians.

Lebon made a study of cranial measurements in men of letters, tradesmen, the nobility and domestic servants, and found the maximum development among the men of letters and the minimum among the servants. The tradesmen, who at all events are performing a work of social utility, stand next to the men of letters; while the aristocrats show some advantage over the domestics. Bajenoff took his measurements from famous persons on the one hand and from convicted assassins on the other, and found a greater head development among the former.

Enrico Ferri has made similar researches among soldiers who have had a high-school education and those who are uneducated, and has found a more developed cranium among the educated soldiers.

I also have made my own modest contribution to this important question, by seeking to determine the difference in cranial volume between the school-children who stand respectively at the head and foot of their class, and have found among children of the age of ten a mean cranial circumference of 527 millimetres for the more intelligent and of only 518 millimetres for the less intelligent.

Similar results were obtained by Binet in his researches among the elementary schools of Paris. He found among children of the age of twelve that the brightest had a mean cranial circumference of 540 millimetres and those at the foot of their class a mean of only 530 millimetres. The following table gives a parallel between these various cranial measurements:

CRANIAL MEASUREMENTS (in Millimetres)*

Binet.......... Children in the elementary schools of Paris, from 11 to 13 years of age
Montessori.... Children in the elementary schools of Rome, from 9 to 11 years of age

Measurements	Binet's figures			Montessori's figures		
	Pupils chosen for intelligence	Pupils chosen as backward	Difference	Pupils chosen for intelligence	Pupils chosen as backward	Difference
Maximum circumference of cranium.	540	530	+10	527	518	+9
Length of cranium...	181	177	+4	180	177	+3
Breadth of cranium..	150.4	146.2	+4.2	143	140	+3
Height of cranium...	123.3	124	−0.7	130	127	+3
Minimum frontal diameter.	104	102	+2	99	98	+1
Height of forehead...	46	45.5	+0.5	57	56	+1

By calculating the cranial capacities according to Broca's method, I obtained:

Cranial capacity { in the best pupils chosen........... 1557 cu. cm.
in the worst pupils chosen......... 1488 cu. cm. }

From all these manifold researches above cited, we can reach no other conclusion than that individuals of greater intelligence have a larger quantity of brain; or else that individuals with a greater quantity of brain are more intelligent.

There is a subtle distortion of this principle, which many sociological anthropologists have taken as their starting-point, especially in Germany, in their attempt to establish a biological basis for the Schopenhauerian theories of Friedrich Nietzsche.

According to these, the persons who have acquired high social positions are biologically superior (possessing a greater cerebral mass), and the same may be said of conquering races as compared with the conquered. Differences in caste are to be explained in the same way, and on this ground nature sanctions the social inferiority of woman.

This is a question of the greatest importance, which merits a vast amount of discussion.

*Montessori, *Sui caratteri antropometrici in relazione alle gerarchie dei fanciulli nelle scuole*, p. 51. ("Anthropometric characteristics in relation to the grading of children in schools").

What Sort of Man is the Most Intelligent?—Straightway, a first serious objection suggests itself: What sort of persons are the most intelligent? Are they really those who have attained the higher academic degrees and the most eminent social positions? Consequently, is the Prime Minister more intelligent than the Assistant Secretary of State, and the latter more intelligent than the Head of a Department, and he again than the door-keeper?

Are literary productions and the acquisition of laurels reliable tests of intelligence? Is this man a doctor because he is more intelligent, and that man a hospital attendant because he is less intelligent?

It is evident that there exist in the social world certain privileges of caste, which may raise to the pinnacle of literary glory or to a clamorous notoriety certain persons who owe their rise to favoritism and trickery; or at least, so-called "literary fame" must be dependent upon the possibility of getting writings published, which another man perhaps would have had no way of bringing before the public so as to make them known and appreciated; just as, on the other hand, there are men of genius who are destined to feel their inborn intelligence suffocating under the cruel tyranny of existing economic conditions, which punish pauperism with obscurity and hold protection and favours at a distance.

A thousand various conditions of our social environment hinder powerful innate activities from finding expression and attaining elevated social positions. Now, when we start to measure these different categorics of persons, shall we measure the more or the less fortunate individuals, those more or those less favoured by economic conditions of birth and environment, or shall we measure those persons who are actually the more and the less intelligent?

And even in school can we be sure that the child whom we judge the most intelligent is actually so? Studies in experimental psychology made in quite recent times of men whose works justify their being placed in the ranks of geniuses, have shown that these men of genius were never, in their school-days, either at the head of their class, or winners of any competitions. Consequently, we have not yet learned the means of *judging intelligence.*

If we stop to think of the way in which the intelligence of pupils was judged up to only a few years ago, according to pedagogic methods that were a remnant of the pietistic schools, this will help us to form some idea. The more intelligent ones were those best able to recite dogmatic truths from memory. And even to-day we have not advanced very far above that level.

As a general rule that pupil is considered the most intelligent who best succeeds in echoing his teacher and in modeling his own personality as closely as possible upon that of his preceptor.

This fact is so well known that it has come to be utilised as one of the clever tricks for obtaining higher marks even in university examinations, and for winning competitions; it is known that the prize is reserved for the student who can repeat most faithfully and proclaim most eloquently the master's own ideas.

Here is precisely one of the most fundamental problems offered by scientific pedagogy: how to diagnose the human intelligence, and distinguish the person who is intelligent from the person who is not. A difficult task, or rather a difficult problem.

The Influence of Economic Conditions upon the Development of the Brain.—Certain factors, due to environment, exert an influence upon the development of the cerebral volume; this fact opens up another whole series of interesting questions.

Among the factors due to environment, the leading place is held by *nutrition,* dependent upon economic conditions.

Niceforo contends that among the various social classes, those who can obtain the best nourishment have the greatest development of brain, and consequently of head. He offers in evidence the figures summarised in the following table:

CIRCUMFERENCE OF THE HEADS OF

Boys of the age of	Rich	Sons of small tradesmen and clerks	Poor
11 years	534.9	529.7	524.8
12 years	537.1	530.3	524.9
13 years	537.8	532.4	528.6
14 years	545.4	533.3	528.4

In short, there is a gradation of cranial volume corresponding to the economic status in society. This is a condition easy to understand: we simply find repeated in this particular the same thing that we have already seen happen to the body as a whole; the organism in its entirety and consequently each separate part

17

of it—if it is to develop in accordance with its special biological potentiality and so attain the limits of finality set for it—must receive nourishment. It is only natural that children who, during their period of growth, are deprived of sufficient and suitable nutrition should remain inferior in development to those who had the advantage of an abundance of the proper kind of food. The influence of the economic factor is indisputable. Consequently, reverting once more to the studies above cited, may we not conclude that the man of letters, the physician, the person of distinction have a greater development of head than the manual labourer, the hospital attendant, the illiterate, simply because it was their good fortune to obtain better nutriment, through belonging to the wealthy social classes?

The Influence of Exercise upon Cerebral Development.—The second interesting question is in reference to the influence which *exercise* may have upon the development of the brain. As early as 1861 Broca investigated this question in a classic work: *De l'influence de l'éducation sur le volume et la forme de la tête* ("The influence of education on the volume and form of the head), in which he arrived at the following conclusion: that a suitable exercise (intellectual culture, education, hygiene) does have an influence on the development of the brain, in the same way as with any other organ, as, for example, the striped muscles, which gain in volume and strength and beauty of form through gymnastic exercise. "Consequently," exclaims Broca enthusiastically, "education not only has the power of rendering mankind *better;* it has also the marvellous power of rendering man superior to himself, of enlarging his brain and perfecting his form!"

"Popular education means the betterment of the race."

Accordingly we might say, relying on the above-mentioned studies, that the man of letters, the physician, the person of distinction have a more highly developed head than the manual workman, the hospital attendant and the illiterate, because they exercised their brain to a greater extent, and not because they were more intelligent. This, however, is a question which differs profoundly from that which we were previously considering, nutrition, because in this case exercise, in addition to developing the organ, gives its own actual and personal contribution to the intelligence.

Therefore, we are able to be creators of intelligence and of brain tissue, which in turn becomes the creative force of our civilisation. A system of instruction which, in place of over-straining the brain, should aid it to develop and perfect itself, stimulating it to a sort of autocreation, would truly be, as Broca says, "capable of rendering man superior to himself." This is what is being sought by scientific pedagogy, which has already laid the foundation of "cerebral hygiene."

We are still very far to-day from realising this highest human ambition! We do not yet know the basic laws of the economy of forces that would lead to a stimulation of the human activities to the point of creation; on the contrary, we are still at a primitive period, in which many of the environing conditions interfere, to the point of preventing the human germ to attain its natural biological finality. In short, we know how to obtain artificially an arrest of development; but we have not yet learned the art of aiding and enriching nature!

The Influence of the Biological Factor upon Cerebral Development.—What conclusion ought we to reach from what has been said up to this point? Upon what does the cerebral volume depend, in all its individual variations, resting on the common biological bases of race, normality and sex? Is individual variation due solely to causes of environment, such as nutrition and exercise? And does it follow that it is not dependent upon *biological potentialities* more or less pronounced in separate individuals—in short, upon different degrees of intelligence?

In the presence of such a multiplicity of questions we must proceed, not to a selection but to a sum. Every biological phenomenon is the result of a number of factors. The development of the brain depends in precisely the same way as the development of the whole body or of a single muscle, upon the combined influence of biological factors determining the *individual variability*, and of factors of environment, principal among which are nutrition and exercise. A suitable diet aids growth, and so also does a rational exercise; but underlying all the rest, as a *potential* cause, is the biological factor which mysteriously assigns a certain *predestination* to each individual. The environment may combat, alter, and impede what nature "had written upon the fertilised ovum;" but we cannot forget that this *scheme*, pre-established by the natural order of life, is the principal factor among them all, the one which determines the "*character of the individual.*"

Now, on the basis of this influence of the biological factor upon the cerebral development, we may affirm that: to greater intelligence there corresponds a brain more developed in volume. What gives us proof of this is the brain of the exceptional man—of men of genius, who frequently have heads of extraordinary volume.

Persons of high celebrity, and not those, for example, who have become known through some recent discovery in the field of positive science—since a piece of good fortune may coincide with a normal cranial volume—but the true creative geniuses who have left the deep imprint of themselves upon their immortal works, have generally had a cerebral volume that was truly gigantic: the poetic brain of the great Schiller weighed 1,785 grams, that of Cuvier, the naturalist, 1,829 grams, that of the great statesman, Cromwell, 2,231 grams, and lastly, that of Byron, 2,238 grams. The brain of the normal man weighs about 1,400 grams.

Consequently, these are extraordinary volumetric figures that could not be acquired, either by much eating, or by being educated according to the scientific means of the most advanced pedagogy; they are due to the extraordinary biological potentiality of the man of genius.

In these extraordinary heads the exceptional volume is combined with a characteristic form: they always have a more than normal development of the forehead. Even in the course of biological evolution, as we have already seen, in the higher species a greater cerebral volume has a correspondingly broader and more erect forehead. If we examine portraits of men of genius, what strikes us chiefly in them is the high and spacious brow, as though men of genius, in comparison with the rest of us, were representatives of a superior race. But if the portrait shows the face taken in profile, it will be easily observed that the *direction* of the forehead is not vertical, but even slightly recessive; that is, it preserves the characteristic male form, with the vault slightly inclined backward and the orbital arches slightly pronounced.

The Pretended Cerebral Inferiority of Woman.—One final argument, which is of interest to us, is the great question of the relation between cerebral volume and intelligence in woman. Because, as you know, there is a very widespread belief of long standing that is confirmed in the name of science: that woman is biologically, in other words totally, inferior, that the volume of her brain is condemned by nature to an inferiority against which nothing can prevail. Just as our perfected pedagogy, excellent alimentation and improved hygienic conditions could never endow a normal man with the brain of a genius, in the same way, so it is said, it is impossible ever to augment the size of the brain of woman, who is necessarily condemned to resign herself to remain in that state of social inferiority to which she is now reduced and from which she would in vain attempt to emancipate herself.

Names as famous as that of Lombroso* which are associated with the progress of positive science, lend the weight of their authority to this form of condemnation! And it is not easy to do away with this sort of prejudice, which has slowly been disseminated among the people under the guise of a scientific theory. But to-day there are scientists who have been impelled to make certain extremely minute, impartial and objective studies, without any preconception on the subject—such men as Messedaglia, Dubois, Lapique, Zanolli, and Manouvrier—who, by calculating the cerebral mass, at one time in comparison with the whole body, at another with the surface of the body, and still again with the various active or skeletal parts of the organism—have arrived at an opposite conclusion: namely, that they can demonstrate a greater development of brain in woman. Among these scientists it gives me pleasure to name before all others Manouvrier—one of the most gifted anthropologists of our day—who has devoted twenty years to an exceedingly minute study of this problem. Here in brief outline are his method of procedure and his conclusions. That the cerebral volume should be considered in its relation to the stature is a familiar principle; but a comparison between man and woman based solely upon such a proportion, continues to maintain the cerebral inferiority of woman. Have we, however, the right to compare a volumetric measure (the cerebral mass) with a linear measure (the stature)? Such a comparison is a mathematical error, as we have already technically proved. Accordingly we find that Manouvrier compares the brain with the mass of the whole body, its entire bulk; and he analyzes this entire bulk, considering separately its active parts, without troubling himself about their functional potentiality. He deduces from them certain figures and proportions; more than that, he forms a sort of index, which might be called the "index of sexual mass," between woman (minor mass) and man, reduced to a scale of 100—which

* LOMBROSO (who died while this book was in press) defended the principle of the innate inferiority of woman and regarded her, in comparison with man, as a case of infantile arrest of development.

may be summed up in an equation: man : 100 = woman : the following percentual analyses:

Stature and weight of body	88.5
Weight of brain	90.0
Weight of skeleton (femur)	62.5
CO_2 exhaled in twenty-four hours	64.5
Vital capacity (at age of eighteen)	72.6
Strength of hands	57.1
Strength of vertical traction	52.6

Hence it is evident, that, in comparison with her actual organic mass, woman differs from man far more than is indicated by the differences in stature and in bodily weight.

Instead of taking all these various separate mean measurements, let us take one single comprehensive mean resulting from them: woman: man = 80 : 100; there we have the proportion. Now, Manouvrier proceeds to reduce all the separate measurements of man from 100 to 80, and calculates how much brain man would lose if he were reduced to a mass having feminine limits; he finds that the loss would be 172 grams. Woman on the contrary has only 150 grams of brain less than man. Consequently the cerebral volume of woman is superior to that of man!

This is an anthropological superiority which is further revealed in the more perfected form of the cranium, insomuch as woman has an absolutely erect forehead and has no remaining traces of the supra-orbital arches (characteristics of superiority in the species).

Thus, we have a contradiction between existing anthropological and social conditions: woman, whom anthropology regards as a being having the cranium of an almost superior race, continues to be relegated to an unquestioned social inferiority, from which it is not easy to raise her.

Who is Socially Superior?—But here again we may ask, as we did regarding the question of intelligence: What constitutes social superiority? And in our social environment who is superior and who is inferior?

Social superiority, like moral superiority, is the product of evolution. In primitive times when men, in order to live, were limited like animals to gathering the spontaneous fruit of the earth, according to the poetry of the biblical legend, and according to what sociology repeats to-day, the superior man was the one of largest stature, the giant. People paid him homage because he was the most imposing, without troubling themselves to ask whether,

Fig. 83.—Leptoprosopic face.

Fig. 84.—Chameprosopic face.

Fig. 85.—Lina Cavalieri.

Fig. 86.—Maria Mancini.

or not, he might be insane. In this way Saul was the first king. When the time came that men were no longer content to live on the spontaneous fruit of the earth, but were forced to till the soil, then a new victory was inaugurated, the victory of the more active and intelligent man. David killed Goliath. This great Bible story marks the moment when the superiority of man came to be considered under a more advanced and spiritual aspect. When the men who cultivated the earth began to feel the need of other neighbouring lands and became conquerors, then the soldier was evolved, until in the middle ages there resulted such a triumph of militarism that the nobles alone were conquerors in war; and the persons who to-day would be called superior, the men of intellect, the poets, were considered as feeble folk, despicable and effeminate. In our own times, now that the great conquests of the earth have been made and the victorious people consequently brought into harmony, the moment has come for conquering the environment itself, in order to wring from it new bread and new wealth. And this is the proud work of human intelligence which creates by aiding all the forces of nature and by triumphing over its environment; thus to-day it is the man of intelligence who is superior. But it seems as though a new epoch were in preparation, a truly human epoch, and as though the end had almost come of those evolutionary periods which sum up the history of the heroic struggles of humanity; an epoch in which an assured peace will promote the brotherhood of man, while morality and love will take their place as the highest form of human superiority. In such an epoch there will really be superior human beings, there will really be men strong in morality and in sentiment. Perhaps in this way the reign of woman is approaching, when the enigma of her anthropological superiority will be deciphered. Woman was always the custodian of human sentiment, morality and honour, and in these respects man always has yielded woman the palm.

Face and Visage

The Limits of the Face.—The face is that part of the head which remains when the cranial cavity is not considered. To attempt to separate accurately, in the skeleton, the facial from the cerebral portion would involve a lengthy anatomical description; for our purpose it is enough to grasp the general idea that the face is the portion *situated beneath* the forehead, bounded in front by the curves of the eyebrows, and in profile by a line passing in projection through the auricular foramen and the external orbital apophysis (Fig. 39, page 188).

It is customary during life to consider the entire anterior portion of the head as constituting one single whole, bounded above by the line formed by the roots of the hair, and below by the chin. This portion includes actually not only the face but a *portion of the cerebral cranium as well*, namely, the forehead; it bears the name of the *visage* and is considered under this aspect only during life.

Human Characteristics of the Face.—One characteristic of the human cranium, as we have already seen (Fig. 40), as compared with animals, is the decrease in size of the face, and especially of the jaw-bones in inverse proportion to the increase of the cranial volume.

"Man," says Cuvier, "is of all living animals the one that has the largest cranium and the smallest face; and animals are stupider and more ferocious as they depart further from the human proportions."

In man, the cranium, assuming that graceful development which is characteristic of this superior species, surmounts the face, which recedes below the extreme frontal limit of the brain.

The different races of mankind, however, do not all of them attain so perfect a form; in some of them the face protrudes somewhat in advance of the extreme frontal limit, and in such cases we say that it is prognathous.

Thus the relations in the reciprocal development between cranium and face are different in animals and in man; as they also are in the various human races. Cuvier gives some idea of these proportions by comparing the European man with animals, by means of the following formulas which he has obtained by calculating approximately the square surface of a middle section of the head:

Cranium : face =	
European man (cranium four times the size of the face)	4 : 1
Orang-utan and chimpanzee	3 : 1
Lower monkeys	2 : 1
Carnivora	1 : 1
Ruminants	1 : 2
Hippopotamus	1 : 3
Horse (the reverse of man)	1 : 4
Whale	1 : 20

Fig. 87.—Portrait of the *Fornarina* (Raphael Sanzio) Rome: Barbarini gallery.

Fig. 88.—Triangular face.

Fig. 89.—Ellipsoidal face.

Fig. 90.—Long ovoid face.

But no general law, no systematic connection can be deduced from such relative proportions. They serve only to demonstrate a characteristic.

Upon this characteristic depends preeminently the *beauty* of the human visage. If we are considering the *visage* from its æsthetic aspect and wish to compare it with the muzzle of animals, we may say that in regard to its proportions it is as though the muzzle had been forced backward from its apex, while the cranium had swelled, through the increase of its vertical diameter. The muzzle is formed of the two jaws alone, on the upper of which the nose is located horizontally; there is neither forehead nor chin along the vertical line of the visage. As the jaws recede and the cranium augments, the forehead rises, the nose becomes vertical, and when the mandible has retreated beyond the frontal limit, the wide yawning mouth has been reduced in size, while a new formation has appeared below it—the chin. By this, I am trying merely to draw a comparison which I trust will be of service by suggesting a didactic method of illustrating the reduction of an animal's muzzle to human proportions. Whatever forms a part of the *visage* bears the morphological stamp of humanity: the forehead, the erect nose and the entire region of the mandible, which contains the principal beauty of the human face.

The narrow opening of the lips, mobile because so richly endowed with the muscles that unite in forming it, is quite truly the charming and gracious doorway of the organs of speech, which by shaping the internal thought into words are able to give it utterance; while the winning *smile* allures, captivates and consoles, thereby accomplishing an eminently *social* function; and sociability is inseparable from humanity.

The animal mouth, on the contrary, is the organ for seizing food, the organ of mastication, and, in felines, a weapon of offence and a means of destruction.

Tarde says: "The mandibles seem to shape themselves in accordance to the degree of intelligence; they become more finely modeled in proportion as the two social functions of speaking and smiling acquire a greater importance than the two individual functions of biting and masticating."

And Mantegazza says: "Cruelty has localised its imprint around the mouth, perhaps because killing and eating are two successive moments of the same event."

The Normal Visage

The visage is that part of the body which is preeminently human; being richly endowed with muscles, it represents the "mirror of the soul," through the expressions that it assumes according to the successive sentiments, passions and transitions of thought. The visage is a true mine of individual characteristics, by which different persons may be most easily and clearly distinguished from one another; while at the same time it bears the stamp of the most general characteristics of race, such as the form, the expression, the tone of complexion, etc., in consequence of which the face has hitherto held the first place in the classifications of the human races.

Even the peoples of ancient times, such as the Egyptians, made a physiognomical study of individual characteristics, founding a sort of empirical science that sought to read from the physiognomy the sentiments of the soul, the tendencies of character and the destiny of man. The visage also contains the greatest degree of attraction and charm, constituting that physical and spiritual beauty by which one person arouses in others feelings of sympathy and love. Oriental women cover their faces with thick veils through modesty, because the face reveals the entire feminine individuality, while the rest of the body reveals only the female of the human species, a quality common to all women.

The visage includes many important parts, which, by developing differently alter the physiognomy; the forehead, index of cerebral development, surmounts the face like a crown, revealing each individual's capacity for thought; furthermore, the visage contains all the organs of specific sense: sight, hearing, smell and taste, and hence all the "gate-ways of intelligence."

The organs of mastication, whose skeleton consists of the maxillaries and the zygomata which reinforce and anchor the upper maxillary, are the parts that constitute by far the greater portion of the facial mass. In fact, their limits (breadth between the two zygomata; breadth between the external angles of the mandible, chin) are the determining factors of the contour and general form of the face, which is completed by the soft tissues.

Forms of Face.—The first distinction in facial forms is that which is made between *long* or *leptoprosopic* faces and *short* or *chameprosopic* faces. Figs. 83 and 84 (facing page 258) represent two faces

FIG. 91.—Tetragonal face (parallelopipedoidal).

FIG. 92.—Pentagonal leptoprosopic face.

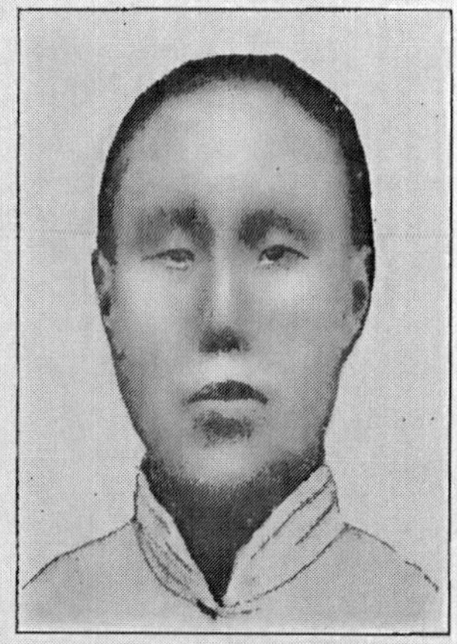

FIG. 93.—Pentagonal mesoprosopic face.

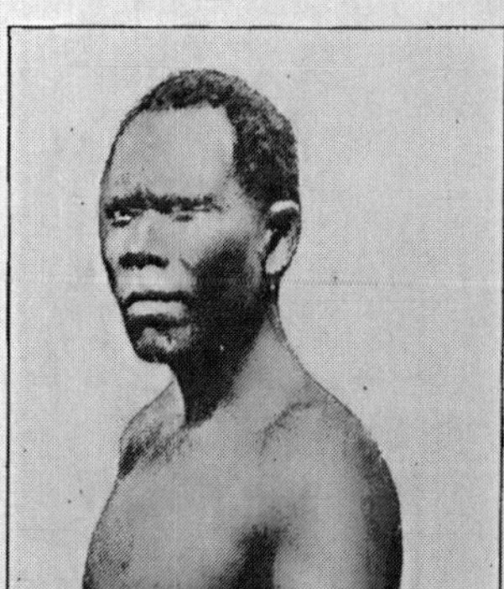

FIG. 94.—Face of inferior type prominence of the maxillary bones (prognathism).

having the same identical breadth between the zygomata or cheek-bones; the profound difference between them is due to their different height or length of visage.

The precise relation between height and breadth constitutes the *index of visage,* which is analogous to the index that we have already observed for the cranium.

Normally there is a correspondence in form between the cranium and the face; dolichocephalics are also leptoprosopic; and brachycephalics are chameprosopics; normally, also, mesaticephaly is found in conjunction with mesoprosopy; but owing to the phenomena of hybridism or pathological causes (rickets), it may also happen that such correspondence is wanting; and that we have instead, for instance, a leptoprosopic face with a brachycephalic cranium or *vice versa.*

Accordingly, *long* and *short* faces are characteristics of race almost as important as the cephalic index. But leptoprosopy and chameprosopy are not in themselves sufficient to determine the *form* of the face. On the contrary, in the case of living persons it is necessary also to take into consideration the *contour of the visage,* which contains characteristics relating to race, age and sex. The races which are held to be inferior have *facial contours* that are more or less angular; those that are held to be superior have, on the contrary, a rotundity of contour; men have a more angular facial contour, in comparison with that of women; while children have a contour of face that is distinctly rotund.

The angularities of the face are due to certain skeletal prominences, owing either to an excessive development of the zygomata (cheek-bones), or to a development of the maxillaries, which sometimes produce a salience of the lower corners of the mandible, and at others a prominence of the maxillary arch (prognathism).

Accordingly, the facial contours may be either rounded or angular, and that, too, independently of the facial type; because in either case the visage may be either *long* or *short.*

Depending upon the rounded facial contours, the visage may be distinguished as ellipsoidal or oval; we may meet with faces that are *long, short* or *medium ellipsoids* (leptoprosopic, chameprosopic, mesoprosopic faces), even to a point where the contour is almost circular: the *orbicular face.* Similarly, the oval faces may be classified as *long, short* and *medium ovals.* The so-called typical *Roman visage* is mesoprosopic, with an ellipsoidal contour. The faces of Cavalieri and of the *Fornarina* (Figs. 85, 87), celebrated for their beauty, are mesoprosopic ovals—and the exceptionally beautiful face of Maria Mancini is a mesoprosopic ellipse (Fig. 86).

Countenances with rounded and mesoprosopic contours belong to the Mediterranean race, and the more closely they come to the *mean average* of that type and to a *fusion* of contours, the more *beautiful* they are.

Faces with angular contours may be: *triangular* (due to prominence of the cheek-bones, or zygomata, and of the chin); *tetragonal*, further subdivided into *quadrangular* (chameprosopic) and parallelepipedoidal (leptoprosopic, due to prominence of zygomata and corners of mandible); and polygonal, which may be either *pentagonal*, formed by the protrusion of the zygomata, the angles of the mandible, and the chin; or hexagonal, formed by protrusion of the frontal nodules, the zygomata and the angles of the mandible.

There may occur, in certain types of face, a very notable prevalence of one part over another, so much so as to produce sharply differentiated and characteristic physiognomies. Thus, for example, a prevalence of forehead characterises the higher and superior type of the *man of genius* (compare the portrait of Bellini or of Darwin). On the other hand, a prevalence either of the cheek-bones, or the lower jaw, or the angles of the mandible, together with an accompanying powerful development of the masticatory muscles, produce three different types, all of them chameprosopic, which represent, in respect to the face, inferior racial types, differing from one another, but which are frequently met with (at least to a noticeable extent) even among our own people, as types of the lower-class face, precisely because of the preponderance of the coarser features.

Combined with the general type of face, there are certain specified particulars of form of the separate parts; as, for example, in the case of the ellipsoid or ovoid types of mesoprosopic face, which seem to have attained the most harmonic *fusion* of characteristics, and consequently the highest standard of beauty, the eyes are very large and almond-shaped (the *Fornarina*, Maria Mancini, Cavalieri); angular faces are characterised by a narrow, slanting eye, through all the degrees down to that of the Mongolian; faces of low type have an eye characterised less by its form than by its smallness. The nose also shows differences; it is long and narrow

Fig. 95.—Hexagonal face.

Fig. 96.—Tetragonal face (square).

Fig. 97.—Faces of inferior type (cheek bones prominent).

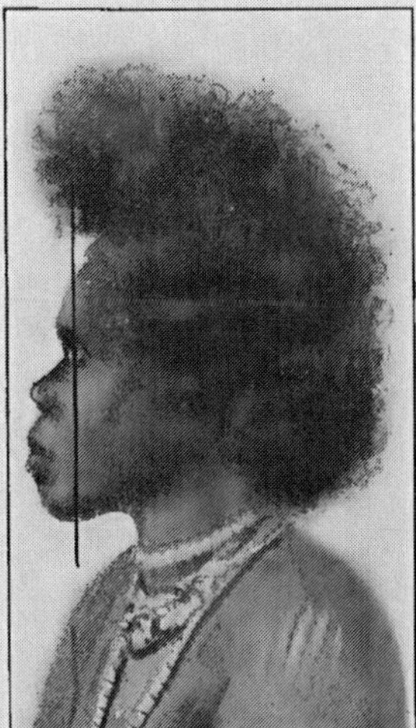

Fig. 98.

(leptorrhine) in the more leptoproscopic faces, and short, broad and fleshy (platyrrhine, flat-nosed) in chameprosopic faces, especially in the *lower types;* in mesoprosopic faces it assumes its proper proportions, and occurs as the last detail or crowning touch of harmony in the perfect faces of the above-mentioned women.

When one starts to make the first draft of an ornamental design, it often happens that the proportional relations are based upon certain *geometric figures* that might be called the skeleton of the ornamental design that is being constructed from them. Accordingly, when an artist wishes to judge of the harmony of proportions in a drawing, a painting, or a statue, he often reconstructs with his eye a geometrical design that no longer exists in the finished work, but that must have served in its construction. In short, there exist certain secret guiding lines and points which the eye of the observer must learn to recognise, to trace and to judge.

This is the way that we should proceed in studying the facial profile.

Let us take or assume a person with the head *orientated* (*i.e.*, with the occipital point resting against a vertical wall, and the glance level). The line uniting the point of the tragus (the little triangular cartilage projecting from the auricular foramen), with the juncture between the nasal septum and the upper lip, ought, in the case of an æsthetically regular face, to be *horizontal.* We may call this line the line of *orientation.* If it proves not to be horizontal, but oblique, slanting either forward (long nose) or backward (short nose), this in itself denotes an irregularity which is plainly perceptible, even to the casual observer. But it is only in exceptional cases that this line is not horizontal; its horizontality constitutes the *norm,* in our hybrid races.

Naturally, it is horizontal only when the head is *orientated* in the manner above stated. Hence in normal cases its horizontality is an *index* of the orientation of the head. The orientated head is perfectly upright; and the line in question marks its *level.*

Everyone knows that this position of the head is known as that of "attention" and constitutes the position which formerly only soldiers, but now school children as well, must assume as a sign of salutation and respect toward their superiors. It is also the anthropologically normal attitude (as we may see in statuary).

And it is a known fact that it is a position exceedingly difficult to assume intentionally with absolute accuracy.

In fact, it corresponds to an attitude which has to be called forth by some inward stimulus of emotion, and for this reason I would call it the "fundamental psychological line." The man who is conscious of his own dignity, or who hopes for his own redemption; the man who is free and independent involuntarily holds his head orientated.

It is not the vain man, or the proud man, or the dreamer, or the bureaucratic official, whose head assumes this *involuntary horizontal level* that is characteristic of the most profound sentiments known to humanity; persons of such types hold their heads slightly raised and the line shows a slight backward slant.

The man who is depressed and discouraged, the man who has never had occasion to feel the deep, intimate and sacred thrill of human *dignity*, has on the contrary, a more or less forward slant in the psychological line of orientation.

Look at Fig. 99, which shows a very attractive group of *Ciociari* or Neapolitan peasants.

The man, or rather the beardless youth who is just beginning to feel himself a man, and therefore hopes for independence, holds his head proudly level; but the very pretty woman seated beside him holds her head gracefully inclined forward. For that matter, this is woman's characteristically *graceful* attitude. She never naturally assumes, nor does the artist ever attribute to her the proud and lofty attitude of the level head. But this graceful pose is in reality nothing else than the pose of slavery. The woman who is beginning to struggle, the woman who begins to perceive the mysterious and potent voice of human conflict, and enters upon the infinite world of modern progress, raises up her head—and she is not for that reason any the less beautiful. Because beauty is enhanced, rather than taken away, by this attitude which to-day has begun to be assumed by all humanity: by the laborer, since the socialistic propaganda, and by woman in her feministic aspirations for liberty.

Similarly in the school, if we wish to induce little children to hold their heads in the position of orientation, all that is necessary is to instil into them a sense of liberty, of gladness and of hope. Whoever, upon entering a children's class-room, should see their heads assume the level pose as if from some internal stimulus of

FIG. 99.—A group of Roman peasants.

renewed life, could ask for no greater homage. This, and nothing else, is certainly what will form the great desire of the teacher of the future, who will rightly despise the trite and antiquated show of formal respect, but will seek to touch the souls of his pupils.

To return to our lines, it follows that the level orientation is the true human position for the head; it ought never to be abased nor carried loftily, because man ought never to make himself either slave or master; it is the *normal line,* because it should be that of the accustomed attitudes; because man cannot normally be perpetually meditating, with his gaze upon the ground, as if forgetful of himself and of his social ties; nor can he forever gaze at the heavens, as though drawn upward by some supernal inspiration. The normal attitude is that of the thinking man, who cannot lean either in the one direction or the other, because he is so keenly conscious of being in close connection with all surrounding humanity; and he looks with horizontal gaze toward infinity, as though studying the path of common progress.

Now, if from the *metopic* point of the forehead, we drop an imaginary perpendicular to the line of orientation, it ought to form, in projection, a tangent to the point of attachment of the nostrils. Observe the two lines traced on the profile of Pauline Borghese.

This line, if prolonged, passes slightly within the extreme angle of the labial aperture, and forms the limit of the chin (see the portrait of Cavalieri, Fig. 101). In this case the profile is eurignathous.

When the line does not pass in the aforesaid manner, but the facial profile protrudes beyond it, we have a case of *prognathism,* which may be total, when the whole face projects; maxillary when the mandibles project, nasal when it is only the nose that projects, and mental (or *progeneism*) when it is only the chin that protrudes.

Figures 98, 100 and 103 represent forms of normal prognathism (related to race, Figs. 98, 100), and of pathological prognathism (Fig. 103, form associated with microcephaly). These two microcephalic profiles call to mind the muzzle of an animal; there is no erect forehead, the orbital arch forming the upward continuance; the nose is very long and almost horizontal to the protruding jaw; the fleshy lips constitute in themselves the anterior apex of the visage; while the chin recedes far back beneath them.

But leaving aside these exceptional profiles, which serve by their very exaggeration to fix our conception of *prognathism,* let us examine the series of profiles in Fig. 100, which include some forms more or less peculiar, and others that are more or less customary, of prognathism; forms that serve to characterise the physiognomy.

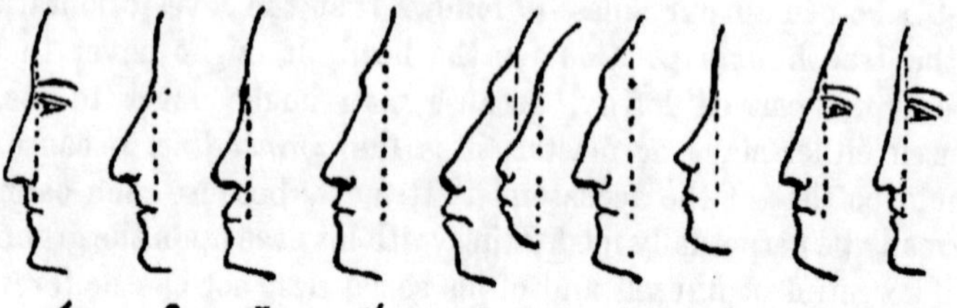

1 2 3 4 5 6 7 8 9 10

FIG. 100.—(1) Orthognathous face; (2) prognathism limited to the nasal region; (3) prognathism limited to the sub-nasal region; (4) total prognathism, including the three regions, supra-nasal, nasal and sub-nasal; (5) exaggerated total prognathism, accompanied by mandibular prognathism; (6) the same in a child; (7) very marked prognathism, but due entirely to the prominence of the supra-nasal section, resulting in an apparent orthognathism (male of tall stature); (8) opposite type to the preceding: pronounced prognathism not extending to the supra-nasal region (feminine type); (9) misunderstood Greek profile (incorrect) resulting in a notable prognathism; (10) correct Greek profile, *i.e.*, conforming to that of Greek statues, and incompatible with prognathism.*

Manouvrier, analysing the forms of prognathism from the point of view of physiognomy and cerebral development, notes that varieties 4 and 5 seem to him to correspond to a more or less serious cerebral development; variety 2, very frequent in France and more particularly, according to the author, among the Jews, is not incompatible with a high cerebral inferiority. Variety 3, more frequent in the feminine sex, is found in conjunction, sometimes with a weakly skeletal system, and frequently with rickets and cretinism; nevertheless, Beethoven showed an approach to this profile.

Variety 4 indicates on the contrary an extremely vigorous development of the skeleton, with the qualities and defects commonly associated with great physical strength; variety 7 is regularly associated with tall stature; in fact, in this case the prognathism is determined by excessive development of the frontal bone-sockets.

It is this development, prevalent in the male sex, that renders sub-nasal prognathism much rarer in man. As a matter of fact, the feminine type of prognathism shown in No. 8 is not greater in degree than the male type, No. 7. Variety 9 shows us a form of *prognathism in art*, due to a false interpretation of the Greek profile; it is commonly believed that in the Greek profile the frontal line is a continuation of that along the bridge of the nose, and hence we frequently meet with commemorative medals, etc., bearing the monstrous profile shown in No. 9, with pronounced prognathism and receding forehead. The true *Greek* profile is shown in No. 19, but we can better analyse it by studying the profile of the Discobolus (Fig. 105) and of Antinoous (Fig. 106).

* The above elucidation and illustrations of the face are taken from MANOUVRIER, *Cephalométrie Anthropologique.*

Fig. 101.

Fig. 102.—Head of Pauline Bonaparte Borghese (Rome, Borghese Museum).

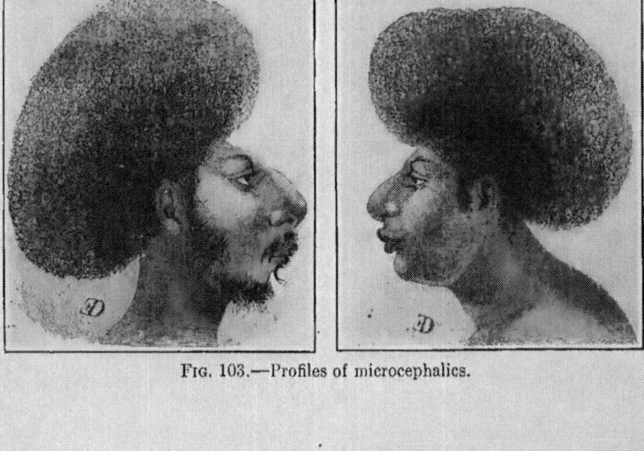

Fig. 103.—Profiles of microcephalics.

The lines of the facial angle have been traced upon the profile of the Discobolus, but the profile of Antinoous has been left untouched, in order that we may trace the same lines upon it in imagination, and thus judge of its perfect beauty (facing page 270).

Let us first examine these two Greek profiles, without stopping to analyse their separate characteristics, but considering them from the more general point of view of the facial profile in general. Reverting, instead, for our analytical study to the schematic figure shown in Fig. 104, we see that it also shows the line of the facial profile, that of orientation and the vertical, and that these lines form certain right-angled triangles; the right angle *MPA* is not the facial angle, any more than the corresponding angle shown in the Discobolus is the facial angle. It is said that Greek art considered the right angle as the perfect facial angle; but that is not true. In order to obtain the facial angle it is necessary to draw a third line (*MS*) which extends from the metopic point to the point of attachment of the nasal septum to the upper lip; this is the line of the facial profile, and the angle *MSA* is the facial angle. It is never a right angle (see the Discobolus), but it approaches very closely to a right angle. Let us examine the triangle *MPS*, bounded by the vertical, the line of profile and the line of orientation; it is right-angled at *P*. Hence, the sum of its other two angles must be equal to one right angle; but the upper angle, corresponding to the nasal aperture, is of only 15°, and consequently the facial angle is 75°. The facial angle of the Discobolus also, like that of Antinoous, like that of the *normal human visage*, is 75°.

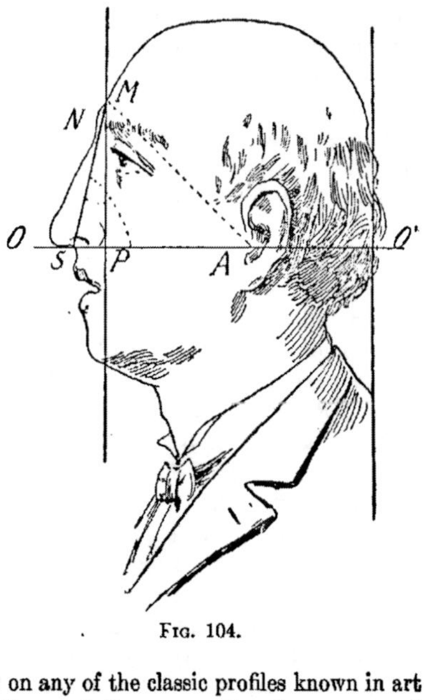

Fig. 104.

Examine further this Fig. 104; in it the line of the facial profile, extending from the metopion to the septo-labial point also passes through the point corresponding to the attachment of the base of the nose (nasion).

The figure is schematic; but anyone who will trace it in imagination upon the profile of Cavalieri, or on that of the seated woman in the group of Neopolitan peasants, or on any of the classic profiles known in art as the Roman profile, will find that the nasal line, connecting the supra- and sub-nasal points, coincides with the line drawn from the sub-nasal point to the metopion. But if we observe the Greek profile of the Discobolus, we shall find that the line of profile does not coincide with the base of the nose, but passes behind it.

This is the real characteristic difference between the *Roman* and the *Greek* profile: in the Greek profile, the root of the nose is attached further in front of the metopico-subnasal line, and this is due to the special form of the Greek forehead, which, instead of being slightly flattened at the glabella, as in the equally beautiful Roman forehead, is rounded to such a degree that the transverse section of the forehead follows a circular line. Hence, it results that the metopic region of the forehead is more prominent and the nose straight, and hence also the line of the forehead is a perceptible continuation of that of the nose (compare the Antinoous). This unique and essential difference between the Greek and the Roman profile has not hitherto been pointed out, so far as I am aware; it is indicated by just one of the facial lines, the one which forms an angle of 75° with the line of orientation. I had an opportunity to observe these differences in my study of the women of Latium, which I pursued side by side with a study of the statues in the museums of Rome, under the guidance of distinguished art specialists; nevertheless, they had none of them ever defined by mathematical lines the sole difference between the two classic types.

The habit of tracing these imaginary lines renders us far more keen in recognising any and every degree of prognathism, even the least perceptible, and any other imperfection of the profile, than the most complicated system of goniometry would make us. For instance, examine the profile of Pauline Borghese; it is certainly not prognathous, since the vertical line reveals a most impeccable orthognathism. But let us trace the nasal line: it meets the vertical line before reaching the metopic point; in order to meet it at this point, the nose would have had to be narrower from front to back; in that case the profile of Pauline Borghese would have been a perfect Roman profile; but the imperial stigma of the Napoleonic house deprived the beautiful princess of the privilege of perfect classic beauty.

In my studies of the women of Latium, in addition to the Greek and Roman forms of profile which are very frequent (the former distinguished by the morphological peculiarity of having no definite naso-frontal angle nor metopic flattening of the forehead) I found a third profile, less frequent yet quite characteristic, among the representatives of the Mediterranean (Eurafrican) race. It is worthy of note (Figs. 107, 108).

First of all, the forehead has a slight transverse depression along its middle line, and the mandible is slightly elongated; but if we draw our imaginary vertical line from the extreme forward point of the brow, we find that none of the forms of prognathism is involved, and that the auriculo-subnasal line is horizontal. This is the type that has been described by Sergi as Egyptian; and the young woman, shown in profile, really does suggest a reincarnation of the proud beauty of the daughters of Pharoah; the somewhat fleshy lips and the form of the eyes, not almond-like, but very wide and horizontal, complete the characteristics of the type immortalised in Egyptian art.

In the normal profile two forms can be distinguished which are associated with the two general forms of leptoprosopic and chameprosopic face, and hence also with the dolichocephalic and brachycephalic forms of cranium. In the one case, the features are more elongated and seem to be more depressed laterally, with the result that the profile is more refined, the visage narrower, along the longitudinal line; in this case the profile is *proopic* (as, for example, in the aforesaid Egyptian profile and in the elongated ovoidal English face, Fig. 90); aristocratic faces of

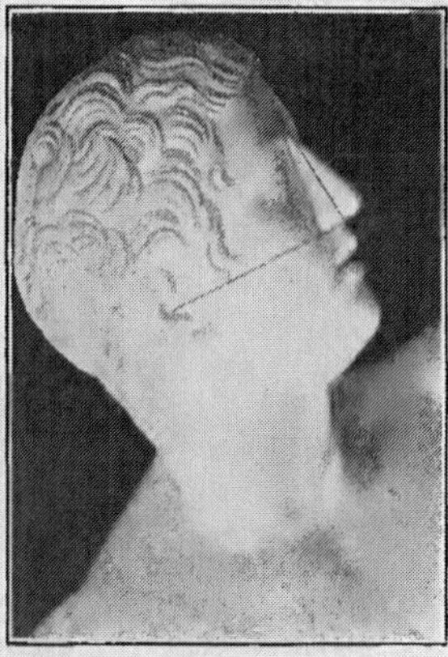

FIG. 105.—The Discobolus by Miron (Rome, Vatican Museum).

FIG. 106.—Head of statue known as the *Capitoline Antinoous* (Rome, Capitoline Museum).

FIG. 107.

FIG. 108.

the finer type are proopic. On the other hand, broad faces are anteriorly flattened to such an extent that the flatness shows even in the profile: *platyopic profile.*

These general forms are associated with certain special forms of the separate organs.

Thus, for example, in proopic faces the palate is narrow, long and high; in platyopic faces, on the contrary, it is broad, low and flat; and the teeth corresponding to them may present a widely different appearance (long, narrow teeth; broad teeth).

Low Types and Abnormal Forms.—Low types, as we have already noted, depend upon the development of the face in its least noble parts (those of mastication); prominence of the cheek-bones and maxillary angles, great development of the upper and lower jaw (prognathism). These conditions are frequently accompanied by a low, narrow, or receding forehead, indicating a scanty cerebral development. Lombroso found a great prevalence of similar forms among criminals; but recent studies have disclosed the fact that such forms of facial development are in some way related to the environment in which the individual has developed, so much so that, on the basis of these morphological characteristics, we might almost succeed in delineating the physiognomies distinguishing the different *social castes.* In fact, while the aristocratic face is ellipsoidal and proopic, that of the peasant is characterised by a pronounced wideness between the cheek-bones, and that of the city labourer by a peculiar development in the height of the mandible. Thus the peasant has a broad face, and the city workman a somewhat elongated face, with very pronounced maxillary angles.

A real and important abnormality which indicates a deviation from every type of race or caste is *facial asymmetry* or *plagioprosopy,* analogous to plagiocephaly, and frequently associated with it.

It is necessary, however, in the case of the face, to distinguish instances of *functional asymmetry,* due to unequal innervation of the muscles in the two sides of the face; either from some cerebral cause, or from some local cause affecting the facial nerves. In such cases, the trophic state of the muscles and their contractibility being unequal, there is a resultant asymmetry, especially evident in the play of facial expression.

This form of asymmetry must necessarily be limited to the soft tissues and be due to a pathological cause; consequently it should not be confounded with the asymmetry due to a different skeletal development of the two sides of the face, an abnormality analogous to plagiocephaly, which is met with among degenerates as a stigma of congenital malformation. We owe to Brugia a most admirable method for demonstrating the high degrees of facial asymmetry which sometimes reach such an extreme point as to give the two halves the appearance of having formed parts of two different faces. This is precisely what Brugia shows by the aid of photography, uniting each half with a reversed print of itself, making the two prints coincide along the median line. The result is that every asymmetric face gives two other faces formed respectively from one of the two inequal halves, and presenting profoundly different aspects.

Other abnormalities are revealed by the *facial profile.* They are due either to total or partial prognathism (already analysed), or to orthognathism, where the facial angle equals or exceeds a right angle; such a profile occurs in cases of *hydrocephaly* or of *macrocephaly* in general, usually resulting from infantile arrest of development.

The Evolution of the Face.—The human countenance, that is so marvellously beautiful in our superior hybrid races, passes, during its embryonal life, through many forms that are very far removed from such perfection.

Figures 110, 111, and 112 represent the evolution of the face in animals and in man: and the complete evolution of a woman's face from the embryo during the first weeks of its formation to the attainment of old age.

The embryonal face, as may be seen even better in animals than in man, is surmounted by the brain divided and differentiated into its superimposed primitive vesicles; furthermore, it consists of one single, widespread cavity, at the sides of which may be discerned two diminutive vesicles or bulbs, which are offshoots of the brain and constitute the first rudiments of the eyes. In studying a more advanced stage of development, we may note in what constitutes the upper lip of this wide facial cavity, two *nasal ducts* or furrows, which are the first indications of the nose.

The principal differentiation which takes place in the face consists of the development from its two lateral walls on left and right, of two thin plates or laminæ that advance across the cavity itself, in its anterior portion, and proceed to unite in a median ridge, the *raphe palati;* this constitutes the formation of the palatine vault, which is destined permanently to divide the single cavity into two cavities—an upper or nasal, and a lower or buccal cavity. If this process of formation is not completed, the result is a grave abnormality, the cleft palate, popularly known in Italy as a "wolf's throat," and consisting in the fact that the nasal and buccal cavities to a greater or less extent open into each other; this abnormality, due to an arrest of embryonic development, is almost always accompanied by a hare-lip.

Simultaneously with the formation of the palatine vault, another and vertical septum is formed, which divides the upper cavity into two halves, right and left. This division, however, is limited to the anterior portion; the three cavities thus formed have no such division in the rear, but all three open into the gullet or œsophagus, which represents the only relic of the single original cavity.

The maxillary bones are formed in a manner analogous to that of the nasal and palatal septa, through extroversions destined to become ossified.

It is not until later that the *external nose* is formed (middle of the second month of embryonal life).

After this, the evolution of the embryo becomes evidently a *perfectionment* and a *growth*, rather than a transformation.

In the *new-born child* the face is extremely small in comparison with the cerebral cranium.

If we compare the head of an adult with that of an infant, and draw the well-known line of separation between the facial and the cerebral cranium, the difference in the reciprocal proportions between the two parts at once becomes apparent. The infant's face seems like a mere *appendix* to its cranium; and the mandible is especially small; in fact, very young children remain much of the time with their mouth open and the under lip drawn back behind the upper.

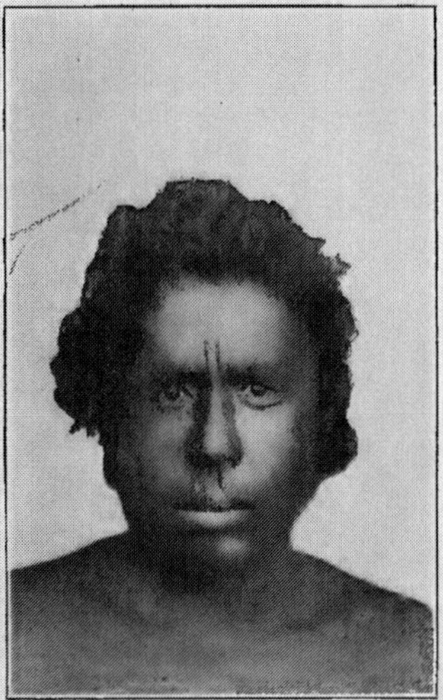

FIG. 109.—Face of inferior type. Prominence of angles of jaw (Gonia).

FIG. 110.

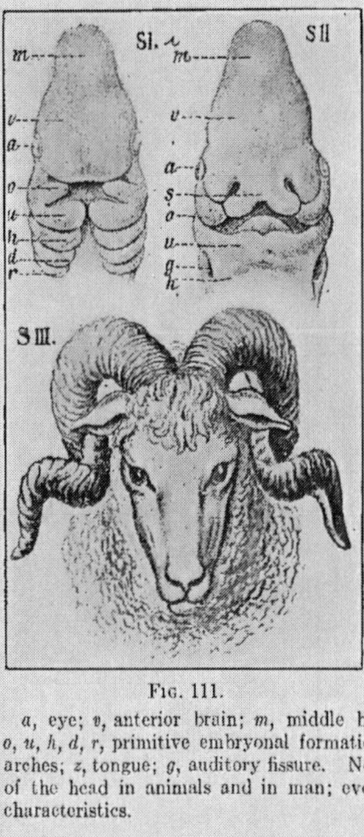

FIG. 111.

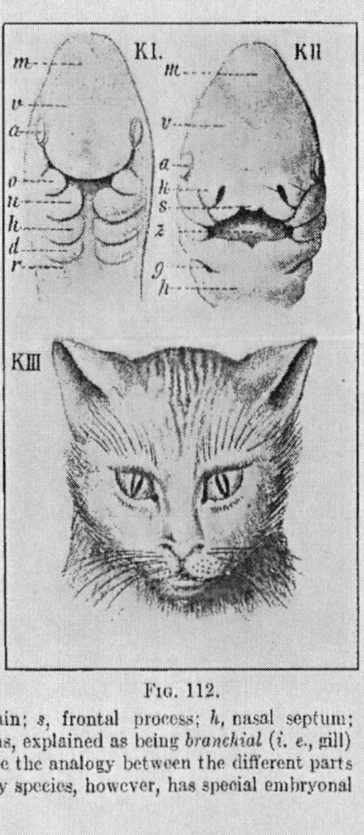

FIG. 112.

a, eye; *v*, anterior brain; *m*, middle brain; *s*, frontal process; *h*, nasal septum; *o*, *u*, *h*, *d*, *r*, primitive embryonal formations, explained as being *branchial* (*i. e.*, gill) arches; *z*, tongue; *g*, auditory fissure. Note the analogy between the different parts of the head in animals and in man; every species, however, has special embryonal characteristics.

Consequently, the growth of the face obeys laws and rhythms differing from those of the cranium, in comparison to which the face is destined to assume very different proportions by the time that the adult age is reached. The face grows *much more* than the cranium.

In its characteristic infantile form, the face is quite round (short and broad), and, when the child is plump, it often happens that at birth the face is broader than it is long. Seen in profile it is *orthognathous*, and this orthognathism endures throughout early infancy, because the profile still remains in retreat behind the plane of the protruding forehead; *i.e.*, the facial angle exceeds a right angle, and the mandibular region is further back than the nasal (compare profile of infant).

In the course of growth it may be said in a general way that the facial index diminishes; that is, the numerical proportion between width and height becomes lowered as the face lengthens; while the facial angle changes from somewhat more than a right angle to a right angle, and finally to an acute angle of 75°.

In order to obtain an exact idea of the transformations of the face, children should have their pictures taken, full face and profile, on every birth-day, as is already customary in England for the purposes of the *carnet maternel*, the "mother's note-book."

In the illustrations facing this page we have portraits of the same person taken at successive ages (Figs. 113, 114, 115, 116), *i.e.*, at the age of six months, one year and a half, seven, and lastly twelve years; it will be seen that the face has steadily lengthened.

In this case the individual happens to be noticeably leptoprosopic; but observe the rotundity of the infantile face at the age of six months.

An analogous observation may be made in the case of the girl represented in Figs. 118 and 119, at the age of ten months and thirteen years respectively.

Even in the case of abnormal children the same law holds good; an examination of the three pictures of an incurable idiot boy, taken at the ages of six, eleven, and sixteen years (Figs. 121, 122, 123 facing page 276), shows that the face, from being originally rotund has become elongated.*

We owe to Binet the most exact and complete studies that exist in anthropologic literature on the subject of the growth of the face. He has made a great number of facial measurements, both of children and young persons of the male sex, from four to eighteen years of age, taking the measurements at intervals of two years. The measurements chosen by Binet are all the possible distances that will serve to give the various widths of the face, the distance of the ear from the various points of the profile, and the heights of the various segments; namely (for an exact understanding of these measurements, see section on *Technique*), auriculo-mental diameter, auriculo-nasal diameter, auriculo-subnasal diameter, auriculo-ophryac diameter, auriculo-metopic diameter, frontal diameter, biauricular diameter, bizygomatic diameter, length of nose, length of chin, subnasomental distance, height of forehead.†

* From Thulié, *Le Dressage des jeunes dégénérés*, page 633.

† Binet, *Le croissance du crâne et de la face chez les normaux entre 4 et 18 ans.*

Binet's conclusions are as follows: the growth of the whole head may be divided into three rhythms: that of the cerebral cranium, that of the face apart from the nose, and that of the nose.

If the total development of the cerebral cranium from the fourth to the eighteenth year shows a proportion of 12 per cent., the facial development shows an increase of 24 per cent. and that of the nose 39 per cent. Consequently the face increases twice as much as the cranium, and the nose three times as much. In the growth of the face, however, the transverse dimensions must be distinguished from the longitudinal dimensions, because the *facial index* varies greatly according to the age. The width of the face follows very nearly the same rhythm as the cranium, never exceeding the latter's proportional increase; the length of the face, on the contrary, follows the special rhythm of the growth of the face, which lengthens far more than it broadens.

If we consider the distances of the various points in the profile from the auricular foramen, we find that these distances show a greater increase in proportion as the points in question are further from the forehead and nearer to the chin.

The central section (the nose) and the mandible are the portions which contribute most largely to the increase in length of the face.

While in the case of the cranium there is a *very slight*, and often imperceptible puberal acceleration of growth, the puberal transformations of the head are, on the contrary, most notable in respect to the face.

The entire region of the upper and lower jaws, but more especially the lower, undergoes a *maximum increase during the period of puberty*.

In regard to the nose, its rapid growth begins at the time immediately preceding puberty; that is, it undergoes a *prepuberal maximum increase*. When a boy is about to complete his sexual development, the nose begins to gain in size.

The puberal growth of the mandible has long been a familiar fact, and bears a relation to the development of the sexual glands.

A special characteristic noted by Binet and by myself is that the height of the lower jaw in boys who have reached the prepuberal stage is greater in the boys who are least intelligent; just as in the case of these boys the nose is less leptorrhine and the face less broad. This means that at the period of puberty the most

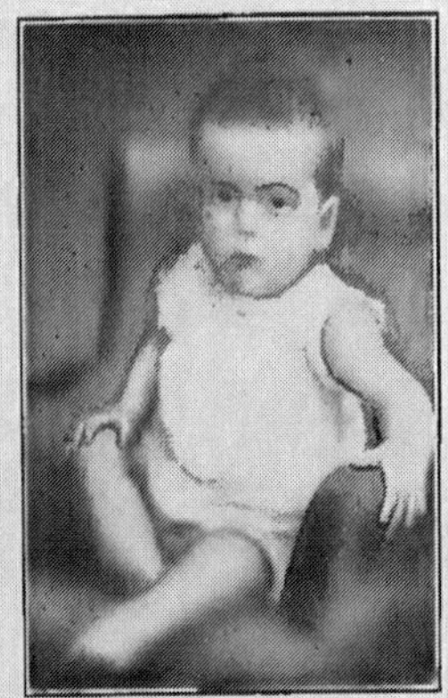

FIG. 113.—A child at six months.

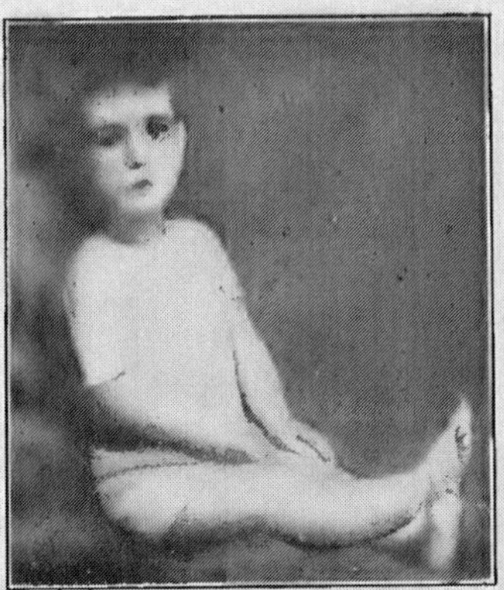

FIG. 114.—The same child at a year and a half.

FIG. 115.—A seven-year-old boy.

FIG. 116.—The same boy at the age of twelve.

intelligent boys not only have a greater development of head, but also certain distinctive facial characteristics. They should have, for instance, a more ample forehead, a broader face, especially in the bizygomatic diameter (between the cheek-bones), and a leptorrhine nose (infantile leptorrhine type). The backward boys, on the contrary, have a longer face, accompanied by a higher mandible and a flat or "snub" nose. Here are the comparative figures:

FACIAL MEASUREMENTS

Binet.......Children from the elementary schools of Paris from 11 to 13 years of age
Montessori..Children from the elementary schools of Rome from 9 to 11 years of age

Measurements	Binet's figures			Montessori's figures		
	Brightest pupils	Backward pupils	Difference	Brightest pupils	Backward pupils	Difference
Minimum frontal diameter	104	102	2	99	98	1
Height of forehead........	46	45.5	0.5	57	56	1
Mento-subnasal distance..	62	64.6	2.4	54	56	2
Bizygomatic diameter.....	124.8	122.9	1.9	109	107	2
Bigoniac diameter........	93.5	92.1	1.4	87	86	1

COMPARATIVE FACIAL MEASUREMENTS OBTAINED FROM THE BRIGHTEST AND THE MOST BACKWARD PUPILS IN THE SCHOOLS OF ROME (MONTESSORI)

Measurements and indices in millimetres	Brightest pupils	Backward pupils	Difference
Height of mandible..............	34 mm.	36 mm.	2 mm.
Length of nose..................	47 mm.	45 mm.	2 mm.
Width of nose...................	28 mm.	29 mm.	1 mm.
Nasal index.....................	59 mm.	64 mm.	5 mm.

These results would seem to prove that there are high and low *infantile* types of face, analogous, let us say, to types of social caste; and in school life they correspond to the castes of the *intelligent* and the *backward* pupils.

Intelligent children tend to preserve the infantile form of face more intact (broad and short) or rather, if we extend our researches to pupils who have reached the pre-puberal age, we may conclude that intelligent pupils develop according to the normal laws—the growth is confined to the nose; backward children invert the order of growth—the lower jaw is already enlarged before the nose has even begun the acceleration of puberal growth. This difference remains permanent in the adult, and we have in consequence *low* types of face characterised by a flat nose and heavy lower jaw.

Facial Expression.—The study of the human face cannot be limited to a consideration of the form alone; because what gives character to it is the *expression.* Internal thought, sensory impressions and all the various emotions produce responsive movements of the facial muscles, whose contractions determine those *visible phenomena* corresponding to the inner state of mind.

The teacher ought to understand facial expression, just as a physician must train himself to recognise the *facies* corresponding to various diseases and states of suffering. The study of expression ought to form a part of the study of psychology, but it also comes within the province of anthropology, because the habitual, life-long expressions of the face determine the wrinkles of old age, which are distinctly an anthropological characteristic.

The facial muscles may be divided into two zones: one of which comprises the frontal and ocular region, and the other the buccal region; corresponding to which are the two upper and lower branches of the frontal nerve.

Accordingly we may speak of a frontal or higher zone of expression and of an oral or lower zone.

The expressions of pure thought (attention, reflection) group themselves around the forehead; those of emotion, on the contrary, call forth a combined action of both zones, and frequently irradiate over the entire body. But as a general rule the man of higher intelligence has a greater intensity of frontal expression, and the man of low intelligence (uneducated men, peasants, and to a much greater degree, imbeciles, idiots, etc.) have a predominance of oral expression.

In children the frontal zone has slight mobility, and the oral zone has a preponderance of expression; infantile expression, however, is diffuse and exaggerated and is characterised by *grimaces.* Undoubtedly there are certain restraining powers, which develop in the course of time and serve to limit and definitely determine the facial expressions.

FIG. 117.—Profile of a child.

FIG.—118. A child of ten months.

FIG. 119.—The same, 13 years old.

As for the mechanics of expression, they consist of the facial nerve, and the surface muscles stimulated by it, which are: the *frontal muscle*, which covers the entire forehead and merges above into the epicranial aponeurosis; the *superciliary muscle* extending transversely along the superciliary arch and concealed by the *orbicular muscle of the eyelids* (*m. orbicularis palpebrarum*), which surrounds the eye-socket like a ring; the *pyramidal* muscle (*m. pyramidalis nasi*), which is connected with the point of origin of the frontal muscle at the inner angle of the eyebrow, and separates below into four symmetrical fasciæ, two of which are attached to the *ala* or wing of the nose, and the other two to the upper lip.

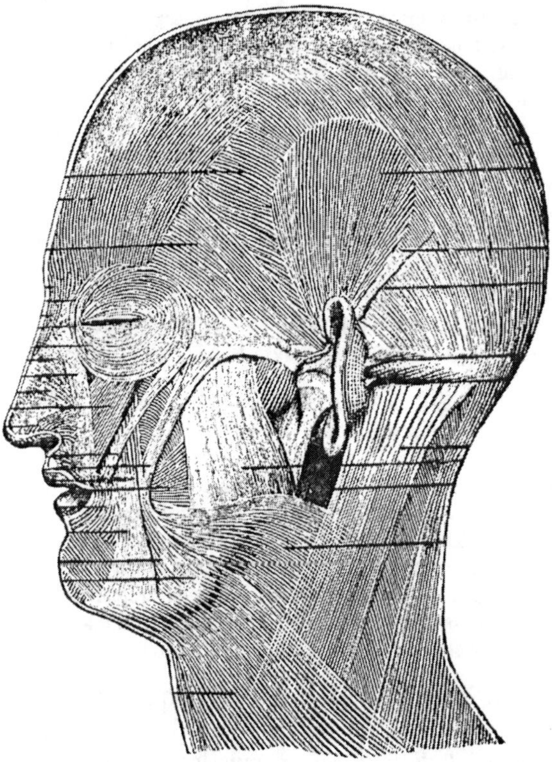

FIG. 120.—The Muscles of the Head and Face.

A group of very delicate muscles controlling the sensitive movements of the wings and septum of the nose (*m. compressor narium*, *m. depressor alæ nasi*, *m. levator alæ nasi*, *anterior* and *posterior*, and *m. depressor septi*) have their points of attachment around the nasal *alæ* (just above the upper incisor and canine teeth). There is a great wealth of muscles surrounding the mouth; no animal, not even the anthropoid ape, is equipped with so many muscles; it is due to them that the human mouth is able to assume such a great variety of positions. The greater number of these muscles are arranged like radii around the mouth; and there is one which, unlike the rest, surrounds the oral aperture like a ring.

The radiating muscles, descending from the sides of the nose down along the chin are: the levator muscle of the upper lip (*m. levator labii superioris*, starting from the bony margin below the infraorbital foramen); the levator muscle of the angle of the mouth (*m. levator anguli oris*, starting from the fossa of the upper maxilla); the large and small zygomatic muscles (starting from the anterior surface of the malar bones); the risorial muscle (*m. risorius*), the smallest of all the facial muscles, which has its origin in the soft surface tissues (aponeurosis parotido-masseterica); the depressor muscle of the mouth angle (*m. depressor anguli oris*, or *m. triangularis*) originating on the lower margin of the maxilla; the depressor muscle of the lower lip or quadratus muscle of the chin (*m. quadratus labii inferioris* or *quadratus menti*, also originating on the lower maxilla); the levator muscle of the chin (*m. levator menti*) between the two *musculi quadrati*, also has its origin in the lower maxilla; the buccinator muscle, hidden beneath the preceding, has its origin behind the molar teeth in the alveolar process of the two maxillæ, and extends horizontally, terminating in the two lips, in such a manner that its two fasciæ partly cross, so that the upper fasciæ of the muscle starting from the mandible extend to the upper lip, and the lower fasciæ of the muscle starting from the maxilla extend to the lower lip. Consequently the contraction of this muscle stretches the angles of the mouth in a horizontal direction only; it is the most voluntary of all the muscles, and plays a greater part than the others in forced laughter; in consequence it robs this movement of its characteristic charm.

Lastly we must note the *orbicular* muscle of the lips (*m. orbicularis oris* or *sphincter oris*), which constitutes the fleshy part of the lips and surrounds the oral aperture like a ring.

The contraction of these muscles produces antagonistic motorial action; for instance, the orbicular muscle tends to close the mouth into a circular orifice; the various muscles which radiate from the corners of the mouth (especially the buccinator) tend, on the contrary, to enlarge and stretch it in a transverse direction; certain muscles tend to raise the mouth, and others to lower it. Accordingly, there results a *play* between the muscles of expression and upon their continual antagonism depend the changing expressions of the human countenance.

Here are a few of the principal facial expressions, described in a masterly manner, and for the first time, by Charles Darwin:*

Expression of Sorrow.—The muscles that are principally brought into play are the superciliary, the frontal and the triangular or depressor muscles of the lips; the eyebrows are furrowed, being drawn upward by the action of the frontal muscle; this, however, cannot contract completely because drawn downward laterally by the superciliary muscles, and hence the forehead wrinkles only at its middle point and together with the slanting eyebrows assumes a shape that suggests three sides of a quadrilateral.

* Charles Darwin, *The Expression of Emotions in Man and Animals.*

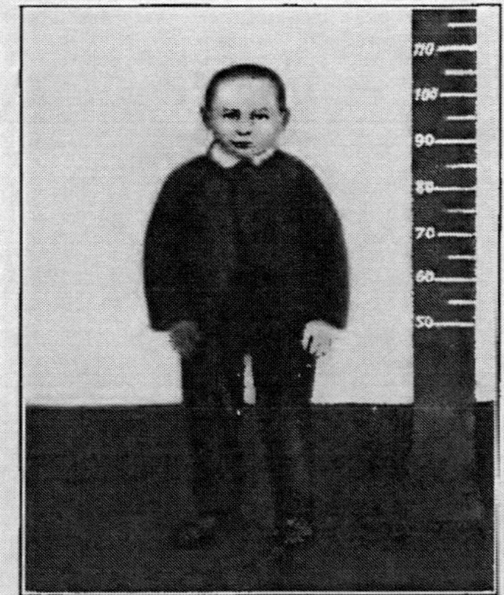

FIG. 121.—A six-year-old boy.

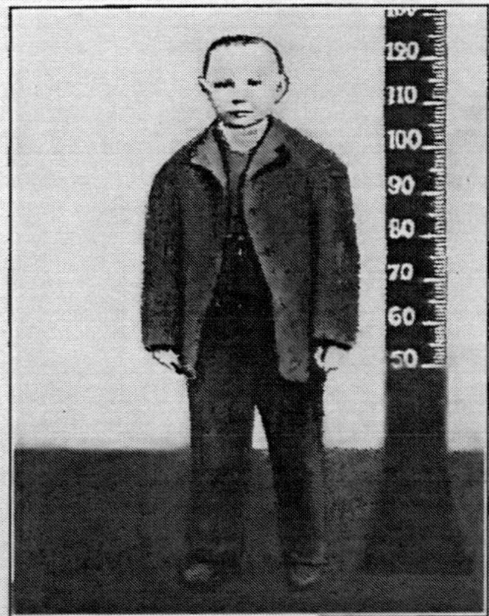

FIG. 122.—The same, eleven years old.

FIG. 123.—The same, sixteen years old.

Simultaneously there is a drooping of the corners of the mouth, which, when exaggerated in infancy, forms the characteristic and charming *grimace* of a child who is on the point of crying. Accordingly, sorrow draws the frontal zone upward, and the labial zone downward; in other words, it *lengthens* the face.

Expression of Pleasure.—On the contrary, *laughter* and *happiness* shorten the face; all the muscles are brought into play that stretch the corners of the mouth, as well as those which raise the upper lip, in consequence of which the upper teeth are disclosed.

The frontal zone remains in repose; excepting that there is a contraction of the orbicular muscle of the eyelids, especially in its lower portion; the lower lid is drawn upward and the skin is puckered at the external angle of the eye; the lachrymal gland is compressed, the circulation of blood stimulated, as always results from every expression of joy, the secretion of the gland is increased, and consequently a few tears are readily shed. The eye, grown smaller and half hidden, shines brilliantly, because moistened from without and irrigated from within by an abundant flow of blood.

Expression of Various Emotions: Anger.—During *anger* the superciliary muscles prevail in exceedingly energetic action, drawing the forehead strongly downward, wrinkling it vertically, and also producing transverse wrinkles on the nose. In the labial zone the orbicular muscle is intensely active, and the lips contract. When anger endures for a long time, the condition above described diminishes in intensity, leaving only a slight frown, while the closed lips protrude in tubular form. An expression usually described by the terms, to *sulk* or *pout*.

This is the way in which little children express their displeasure; and the pouting lips sometimes rise clear to the tip of the little nose, in sign of proud defiance. This form of grimace is common to the children of every race: it has been observed in the children of Hottentots and Chinese, as a sign of prolonged anger and ill humor.

Hence the contraction of the mouth is a characteristic sign of anger; and when the emotion is very strong, even the masticatory muscles may enter into play, causing a *grinding of the teeth.*

Surprise.—In *surprise*, on the contrary, the entire labial zone is in repose, and there is complete and free contraction of one muscle alone, the frontal; consequently it produces longitudinal lines across the entire forehead, uplifting the eyebrows, which passively follow the elevation produced by the frontal muscle, forming two arches around which the wrinkles of the forehead form themselves in parallel lines. The eyes in consequence are stretched to their widest. The oral zone is so far relaxed that the lower jaw droops in obedience to gravity and the mouth gapes open: *bouche béante.* Sometimes a less intense degree of surprise fails to do away with the contraction of the orbicular muscle of the lips, which, without being actively contracted, but simply because relieved from the interference of antagonistic muscles, closes the mouth in a rounded or tubular aperture.

This same facial expression, which is a very striking one, exists in all races.

When children are still too young to contract the frontal muscle completely, they show surprise by a gaping mouth, and a puckering of the entire forehead, in place of the transverse furrows.

Expression of Thought.—In addition to the expressions of the emotions, the authorities describe those due to thought, and give special consideration to the expression of *external* or sensory *attention,* and *internal attention* (reflection, meditation). The young child is capable of intense sensorial attention, which is manifested especially in visual attention.

I have been able to make many observations in the "Children's Houses," where children two or three years old take part in games that demand attention, comparison, and the exercise of reason, without tiring their minds or encountering any great difficulty. These children wrinkle their foreheads and hold their mouths slightly open.

This is the expression also noted by Darwin, and the one which notoriously produces those vertical lines in the middle of the forehead, known as the *lines of thought.*

When these children are obliged to make an effort of thought or when they are for any reason troubled and anxious, slight contractions pass across their foreheads, like a continuous succession of broken shadows (Darwin).*

It should be noted that in any case a contraction of the eyebrows during intellectual work denotes *effort,* a *difficulty* to be overcome. Pure thought, by itself alone, produces no such contractions.

* Charles Darwin, *Op. cit.*

The contemplative man, absorbed in profound meditation, shows a face overspread with serenity, due to muscular repose; the gaze is fixed upon the void, and the head, as though no longer sustained by the relaxed muscles, is inclined forward.

If his eyes retain steadfastly the same original direction, even after the body has dropped forward, they give the impression of being turned on high. Such is the expression of the man sunk in profound thought, so long as his thought follows an uninterrupted course.

But when a difficulty arises, see how he begins to knit his brow. It is the difficulty which has arisen, and not the course of his thoughts, that has produced this muscular reaction.

The movement is similar to what occurs in the case of any difficulty to overcome, as, for instance, the threading of a needle.

Consequently the wrinkles of thought are the wrinkles of the *fatigue of thought.*

The mystics, who are purely contemplative thinkers, and not solvers of difficulties, have a forehead without lines. Similarly in art, the faces of the Madonna or of the Saints have an intense expression of thought in their gaze, but the serene countenance shows neither contractions nor lines.

De Sanctis* has made some interesting observations regarding the facial expression of the mentally deficient. They have a singular difficulty in contracting the frontal muscle even at the age of eleven or twelve years; even when urged by example and command, they frequently do not succeed in contracting the forehead. Labial expression, on the other hand, is much more developed, and frequently attention is indicated by a contraction of the orbicular muscle of the lips into a circle; and surprise is shown in the same way.

In general, however, what characterises the face of the imbecile, the idiot, the epileptic, is its *immobility:* hypomimia or amimia.

There are, however, frequent cases of cerebrophlegia (a progressive malady of the brain occurring during the early years of childhood), in which exaggerated contractions of the face occur as the result of the least mental effort. The French give the name of *grimaciers* to children who show such symptoms; from pathological causes they exhibit a hypermimia that transforms their facial expressions into grimaces. Furthermore, there are certain

* Sante de Sanctis, *La Mimica del Pensiero* (The Expression of Thought).

degenerate children in whom the muscular reactions do not correspond to the normal expression of their feelings; for example, they exhibit sorrow when they mean to show attention, etc. In such cases the play of the opposite and contradictory facial muscles has become perverted: *dismimia.*

One of the most frequent occurrences among the abnormal is asymmetry of the facial expressions; the muscles contract more on one side of the face than on the other. This symptom, however, in a mild degree, is met with also in normal persons.

From what has been said, it is evident that for the examination of the face we must depend, if not exclusively, at least far more upon anthroposcopy than upon anthropometry; and since the minute description required is too difficult and too lengthy a task, especially as regards the *facial expressions* (which are so characteristic of the individual) it is necessary in pedagogic anthropology to resort to photography.

The instantaneous photograph, in all progressive countries, is already within the reach of mothers. It ought also to form part of the equipment of our schools.

The Neck

The neck is a part which is anatomically of much importance, but not of equal importance from the anthropological side. The skeleton of the neck is formed of the seven cervical vertebræ. Notwithstanding that in all the higher vertebrates the neck is constituted of the same number of vertebræ, it can assume the most varied dimensions, all the way from the giraffe to the whale. Similarly, at the different ages of man it is at one time barely indicated and almost wanting altogether, as in the new-born child, and again long and flexible, as in the lovely women of some of the higher races.

Godin has observed that the maximum increase of the neck takes place between the fourteenth and sixteenth year, *i.e.*, at the epoch of puberty; but at the fourteenth year it undergoes such a rapid increase that it surpasses proportionally the puberal increase of the total stature.

This is shown in the following table:

PROPORTION OF LENGTH OF NECK TO THE STATURE REDUCED TO 100

Age in years:	13½	14	14½	15	15½	16	16½	17	17½
Proportions:	10	12	10	10	10	10	10	10	10

Consequently the proportion between neck and stature is a datum that tends strongly to remain a *fixed* quantity. The result, however, is different if we study the proportion between the neck and the vertebral column as a whole.

PROPORTION OF LENGTH OF NECK TO THE TRUNK REDUCED TO 100

Age in years:	13½	14	14½	15	15½	16	16½	17	17½
Proportions:	34	35	34	35	35	35	35	35	34

Accordingly it is about one-third of the trunk.

The circumference of the neck is also taken, for it shows whether the neck is *slender* or *thick;* and this often bears a relation to the degree of development of the thyroid gland.

In my work upon the women of Latium I have shown that the small, dark women have a longer and more flexible neck than those who are fair and of tall stature. Therefore this is a racial difference, similar to the difference we have already noted for *types of stature.* The macrosceles have a long and slender neck, and the opposite is found in the case of the brachysceles; consequently, a very long neck is an indication of a weak constitution.

CHAPTER III

THE THORAX

We have already had occasion to point out, in connection with the *types of stature,* the importance of the thorax.

The relation of the thoracic perimeter (circumference of the chest) to the total stature (see chapter on *Technique*) was called by Goldstein the *index of life,* in order to indicate that the organic resistance of any individual depends upon the proportional relation between the thorax and the whole body; whoever has a narrow chest is liable to pulmonary tuberculosis, and in his physiological entirety is a weakling (see chapter on *Macroscelous and Brachyscelous Types*).

Anatomical Parts.—Anatomically the thorax is determined in height by the twelve dorsal or thoracic vertebræ, which are characterised by having a transverse apophysis, which articulates with the twelve pairs of ribs, forming the *thoracic cage,* or chest.

The first seven pairs of ribs articulate in front, by means of cartilages, with the lateral margins of a flat bone, the sternum or breast-bone, which is formed of three pieces: the *manubrium* uppermost, then the *corpus,* then, lowest of all, the *ensiform* (sword-shaped) *process.*

The manubrium and the corpus form, at their juncture, an angle more or less marked, according to the individual, and the lateral articulation of the second rib corresponds to this angle. In the new-born child the sternum is a cartilage with points of ossification arranged longitudinally like the beads of a rosary. The seventh vertebra articulates laterally at the point at which the ensiform process is attached to the corpus of the sternum. The next three ribs (8th, 9th and 10th) are articulated together and with the seventh by means of cartilaginous arches; the last two pairs of ribs (11th and 12th) are free or *floating.* At the top, the thoracic cage is reinforced by the *thoracic girdle,* which serves also to afford articulation for the upper limbs, and which consists of the *clavicles,* in front, and of the scapulæ, behind. The clavicles are long bones placed in an almost horizontal position above the thorax, and they determine the *width* of the chest; at the inner extremity they articulate with the manubrium of the sternum and at the outer extremity they are attached to the acromial process of the scapulæ. The scapulæ are flat bones which are attached to the posterior surface of the thoracic frame, on which they are freely movable, covering a tract extending from the second to the seventh rib. At their upper and outer extremity they are provided with two bony processes; namely, the *acromion,* already mentioned, which contains the points of maximum width of the shoulders, and the *coracoid process,* which terminates anteriorly and, together with the acromion, overhangs the articulation of the humerus with the body of the scapula.

Powerful muscles clothe the thoracic frame, serving partly in the movements of respiration and partly in the movements of the upper limbs. It may suffice to mention, among the muscles situated posteriorly, the *cucullaris,* the great dorsal (*m. longissimus dorsi*), the rhomboids of the scapulæ (*m. rhomboidus major* and *minor*), and the *serratus posterior* of the ribs; anteriorly, the large and small pectoral and the great *serratus;* beside which there are the intercostal muscles, extending from rib to rib and taking part in the movements of respiration. But the most important muscle is the *diaphragm,* which completely closes the thoracic cavity, rising into it in a convex vault and separating it from the abdomen; this constitutes the most active of all the muscles which participate in the movements of respiration. The thoracic cavity, thus determined, encloses the two most important viscera of vegetative life—the heart and the lungs.

The heart is a muscle shaped like a pear or cone, having its base turned upward, and its apex or point turned downward and outward toward the left, corresponding to the fifth intercostal space; it is divided, as is well known, into four cavities, and constitutes the *great motor power* of the circulation of the blood. The lungs are two in number, right and left, and surround the heart, completely filling the thoracic cavity. The lungs are divided into superimposed *lobes,* three in the right and two in the left lung; they are composed essentially of infinitely small ramifications of the bronchi, resolving into tiny series of chambers, the *pulmonary alveoli* or air-cells. These alveoli, consisting of a single layer of extremely small cells, are surrounded by a dense network of capillary tubes, through which takes place the interchange of oxygen and carbon dioxide. It has been calculated that if we should estimate and sum up the internal surfaces of the pulmonary alveoli, or, what comes to the same thing, if we should spread out and join together the alveolar walls of the lungs, they would have a superficial area of 200 square metres. This area might be compared to the foliage of a great human tree (respiratory surface).

Physiological and Hygienic Aspect.—The importance of the thorax is physiological, because it contains the highly important viscera of vegetative life; but this importance is especially associated with the lungs. The lungs are the organs that acquire the oxygen from the outside environment, and this oxygen, when taken up by the hemoglobin in the blood, will serve to oxygenate the tissues of the entire organism, and thus aid in the processes of cellular metabolism. A large supply of oxygen stimulates this interchange of matter, not only because the organism as a whole is enriched in the substance essential to this process (oxygen), but because the heart responds to the increased activity of the lungs by more energetic pulsations calculated to set the blood circulating in far greater quantities. It is no exaggeration to say that our whole physiological life is enclosed within the thorax, because the digestive system does nothing more than prepare a blood that is unfitted to irrigate the tissues for the purpose of supplying them with nutriment; it is only after this blood has passed through the lungs that it is transformed into *oxygenated blood* and is adapted to assimilation. Consequently the intestines prepare nothing more than the *raw material*, and it is the lungs which perform the service of perfecting it; while the heart drives it through its circuit into contact with all the tissues of the organism.

Whoever has inadequate lungs is for that reason alone a person who necessarily receives insufficient nutriment (thin and weak macroscele), and frequently is also a melancholiac. Melancholia accompanies every form of physiological decadence. On the contrary, persons with ample lungs are generally serene of spirit and joyous. In fact, the emotion of joy is at the same time both the cause and the consequence of an active circulation of oxygenated blood (florid or ruddy complexion).

Certain experiments conducted with birds have proved that if free oxygen is introduced under an air-bell in which the birds have been enclosed, they gradually become more and more excited, singing and fluttering as if possessed by a frensy of joyousness. It is a fact that we often rid ourselves of a fit of melancholy by taking a walk in the open air; persons possessed of good lungs feel within themselves a vital potentiality that perceptibly aids them to make what we call an "effort of will"; when sorrow befalls them, or over-exertion has exhausted their strength, persons of this type feel some force spring up within them that seems to give them fresh hope and courage. It is their oxygenated blood, which neither weariness nor depression of spirit can stay in its luxuriant course; the man of weak lungs, on the contrary, is mentally depressed, because his physiological life has slowed down; and, instead of aiding him, it is his physiological life which demands of him a genuine effort of will to reestablish its equilibrium.

Accordingly, those persons who have a well-developed chest are certainly the healthiest and the happiest.

But this is not the only pulmonary function; the lungs are also the *organs of speech.* In fact, while speech is manufactured in the brain and the cerebral nerves that stimulate the organs of the spoken word, it requires also its "driving power," that is to say, air, in order to obtain utterance; and it is the lungs to which singers and speakers alike owe the physical strength of their voice. Even the respiratory rhythm has a great influence upon speech.

The spoken word requires a most complicated mechanism, and among the details of this mechanism, by no means the least important are the acts of *inspiration,* by which the air is received into the lungs, and of *expiration,* by which it is expelled, simultaneously with all the other movements producing speech. Indeed, we know that when speech is further complicated by the act of singing, it becomes necessary to *study special rules* for breathing; in short, to *educate the voice.*

Now, why do we not also educate the voice for its ordinary task of the spoken language? Speech is one of the marvels that characterise man, and also one of the most difficult spontaneous creations that have been accomplished by nature. Through the voice, the lawyer defends the innocent, the teacher educates the new generations, the mother recalls her erring son to the path of virtue, lovers unite their souls, and all humanity interchanges ideas. If intelligence is the triumph of life, the spoken word is the marvellous means by which this intelligence is manifested.

We trouble ourselves to educate the voice only for the purpose of singing, and neglect the spoken word. We do not stop to think that *singing* appeals only to the senses and emotions, while speech appeals to the emotions and the intellect, and therefore charms and at the same time convinces.

Anyone who has heard that wonderfully gifted speaker, Ofelia Mazzoni, expounding our great poets to the labouring classes at the People's University in Milan, rousing the slumbering intelligence of the working man, will understand what an immense educative force we are neglecting.

In a century in which we speak of an intellectual reawakening and a brotherhood of man, we have forgotten the *voice!* Yet in this new era of humanity that is learning brotherly love and striving for peace, the voice plays a part analogous to that of the trumpet-call in the centuries consecrated to war.

As a matter of fact, our schools so far neglect defects of speech that it is not uncommon to hear a stammerer undergoing examinations for a degree in jurisprudence. The fact that an otherwise cultured man lisps or stammers is treated by us as quite an indifferent matter, just as among savage tribes a king may have unclean nails without anyone observing the fact.

Yet it is now known that stammering may usually be cured by a systematic training in the art of breathing.

Respiratory gymnastics ought to constitute one of the principal courses of instruction in schools for children. I have introduced it into the "Children's Houses," among children between the ages of four and six, combining it with a special instruction in written language (letters of the alphabet), designed to *educate the movements* of the organs of speech, without worrying or tiring the children, and this method has borne such good results that our little ones, by the time they are five years old, have lost nearly all their defects in pronunciation.

Spirometry.—The *pulmonary capacity* may be measured directly by means of an instrument called the *spirometer;* the breath must be strongly expelled through a tube opening into a hollow cylinder, thus raising a graduated piston contained in it; and, by reading the figure indicated on the piston-rod, we learn the volume of air expelled from the lungs.

Such an instrument is better adapted for use by adults than by children; and if it should ever come to be introduced into the schools, it should not in any case be used below the elementary grades.

The person who is going to measure the capacity of his lungs by means of the spirometer, begins by drawing in an unusually deep or *forced inhalation;* then, after holding his breath for a moment, he proceeds to expel into the rubber tube all the air in his lungs, in a *forced exhalation.* In an exercise of this sort, all the difficulties of respiratory gymnastics are successively surmounted —inspiration, respiratory pause, expiration.

In fact, in accomplishing the *forced inspiration,* all the pulmonary alveoli must be dilated to the maximum extent, and at the same time the thorax must reach its *maximum dilation.* This is a very different matter from normal inspiration, which does not completely dilate the alveoli. As a matter of fact, the *tidal air* or *air of respiration, i.e.,* the air taken in and expelled in each normal respiration, is about 500 cubic centimetres; but the sum total of air habitually contained in the lungs is made up of two quantities: first, that which may be emitted by a *forced expiration,* the *supplemental or reserve air,* amounting to 1,600 cubic centimetres; and secondly, the air which cannot ever be emitted, because no amount of effort could completely expel all the air from the lungs; *residual air* or *respiratory residuum* amounting to 1,200 cubic centimetres. To recapitulate, the average pulmonary capacity is the sum of the following average quantities of air:

Residual air, or *respiratory residuum* (which can never be expelled from the lungs)	= 1200 cu. cm.
Respiratory reserve (which can be expelled by a forced expiration)	= 1600 cu. cm.
Tidal air	= 500 cu. cm.
Complementary air (which can be drawn in by a forced inspiration)	= 1670 cu. cm.

Accordingly, the total pulmonary capacity is about 5,000 cubic centimetres, or five litres. But in normal respiration, the capacity is less, *i.e.,* about 3,300 cubic centimetres, the air due to a forced inspiration not being included.

Therefore, in each normal respiration a half litre of pure air (assuming that it is pure) is introduced and mingled with the vitiated air already within the lungs; and since, in expiration, a third only of this 500 cubic centimetres is eliminated, it follows that 166 cubic centimetres are mingled with the 3,300 cubic centimetres; in other words, that only one-tenth of the air is renewed in each *normal* act of respiration.

A very energetic forced *inspiration* may draw into the lungs, in addition to the customary 500 cubic centimetres, an additional 1,670 cubic centimetres of pure air, *complementary air*. In this case the lungs contain upward of 5,000 cubic centimetres of air.

The *forced expiration* which follows upon this extra deep inhalation *purges* the lungs of the vitiated air which has formed there. In this way we complete an exercize that is eminently hygienic.

Now, these spirometric movements are fraught with difficulties: 1. The forced inspiration, deep enough to extend the alveoli, may be more or less complete. If a cloth wrung out in cold water is laid across the shoulders, the *inspiration* which follows as a result of reflex action is far deeper than that produced by an act of will; this proves that the lungs can be dilated to a point beyond that which seems to us to be the extreme limit, and therefore that *with practice* we may learn to dilate our lungs still further.

2. When the attempt is made to *hold the breath* after a forced inspiration, almost everyone at the first trials will allow more or less of the air to escape; that is, they will discover themselves incapable of controlling their own organs of respiration; therefore, a gymnastic exercise for acquiring such control is necessary. This is the exercise which will make us masters of the movements required to produce vocal sounds at pleasure.

3. A slow expiration so controlled as to give time for the air to penetrate into the spirometer, is accomplished, though somewhat unevenly, the first few times, and is perfected with practice.

It results from the above that: 1. We take in less air than we are able to take in; 2. part of this air is lost outside the spirometer; consequently the spirometer registers a pulmonary capacity below that which the lungs actually have; and we shall find that, with *practice*, the volumetric figure will successively augment. But the pulmonary capacity has not augmented in proportion; it is only that *practice has perfected* the respiratory movements. Accordingly, the spirometer may serve as an instrument to test the progress made in respiratory gymnastics, and, in the case of those who have *already become skilful in its use*, it becomes a really valuable instrument for measuring the respiratory capacity.

When we remember that a portion of the air, *i.e.*, 1,200 cubic centimetres, never issues from the lungs, it follows that the *respiratory capacity* is less by 1,200 cubic centimetres than the *pulmonary capacity,* which, as we have seen, is on an average upward of 5,000 cubic centimetres (5,370) in the adult man. Hence, the spirometer directly measures the *respiratory capacity,* and only indirectly the pulmonary capacity.

When women measure their lungs by means of the spirometer, they have difficulty in registering 2,000 cubic centimetres, and men have difficulty in attaining 2,600 cubic centimetres. Instead of which, a man ought to be able to register between 3,800 and 4,000 cubic centimetres.

What keeps the lungs healthy is an abundant aeration with air rich in oxygen, and not impure with carbon dioxide and other poisonous gases. When the pulmonary air-cells are insufficiently dilated, they are predisposed to attack by the bacillus of tuberculosis. Indeed, pulmonary tuberculosis usually begins at the *apexes of the lungs,* which are less thoroughly aerated, and also usually attacks persons with narrow chests. The *treatment* of tuberculosis is eminently a *fresh-air treatment;* tuberculous patients may be benefited and even cured in a remarkable percentage of cases (50 per cent.) if they are exposed day and night to the open air. In this way the relation between free respiration and pulmonary health is demonstrated.

In America at the present time the hygienic rule of sleeping at night, winter and summer, with the windows open, is gaining ground, and even the practice of sleeping in the open air. And the various forms of *sport* also have the beneficial effect of bringing those who indulge in them into a healthy contact with fresh air, which civilised man has shown a fatal tendency to abandon.

The same exercise which dilates the lungs (the contents) also dilates the thorax (the container). The result is that man ends by acquiring the thorax corresponding to his vocation, or in other words, a thorax corresponding to the life that he leads in consequence of the form of work to which he devotes himself. Shepherds in mountain districts and mountain peasants have the largest thorax, notwithstanding, as we have seen, that they are more scantily nourished. In cities, the maximum average circumference of chest is found among the cart-drivers, and the minimum among university students and in general among those who have grown up in an inclosed environment, with the thorax artificially cramped by the position assumed while writing or reading at a desk; yet this is the class of persons who have abundant nutriment.

Consequently, we find a division of air and bread between different social castes; those who have air, do not have bread, and they possess large lungs, out of proportion to bodies which, being under-fed, have been unable to grow; and those who have bread do not have air, and they possess lungs that are insufficient for the needs of bodies that have grown under the influence of abundant nutrition. Consequently, all civilised men are physiologically out of equilibrium, and their physical health is lessened. But those who suffer most from this loss of equilibrium are the *studious* class, who have nourished themselves upon hopes and opened their minds to great ideas, and deluded themselves into undertaking big enterprises; but in real action they find that they are weak, and that they easily fall into discouragement and depression, and when their will-power forces them onward, their organism responds with nervous prostration and melancholia.

It is a sad fact that at the present day the best energies of man reach maturity possessed of insufficient lungs, and consequently liable to break down in health, energy and strength.

A large part of the *studious* class, such, for instance, as the teachers, are at the present day devoting themselves to a form of work which is not a pulmonary exercise, but pulmonary *destruction.*

We must remember that healthy exercise of the lungs should take place in the open air, and consists of indrawn breaths deep enough to *dilate* the air-chambers. Instead of this, the teacher *speaks,* which means that he makes *forced expirations,* during many hours in an enclosed environment and in an assemblage of persons who, for the most part, are far from clean. The bacillus of tuberculosis finds in the teacher its favourite camping-ground. In fact, statistics indicate that the maximum mortality from tuberculosis is among teachers; higher even than among nurses. It is really distressing to think of the ignorance of hygiene in which our schools are even yet steeped, so that they seem forgetful of the body, in their pursuit of a spirit that eludes them and that, as a matter of fact, is not being educated in anything approaching a rational manner.

When we enter a class-room, we see rows of benches constructed like orthopedic machines, to the end that the vertical columns of the pupils shall not be distorted during their enforced labour; and the thought arises: this is the spot in which the teacher becomes a consumptive for the sake of transforming the children into hunchbacks. What is the reward of so great a sacrifice? What sort of a preparation in ideals and in character are they giving to the new generations through such disastrous means? What are the obstacles which they are being taught, through so much suffering, to surmount and to conquer? What, in short, is the spiritual gain achieved at the cost of so great an impoverishment of the body?

The answering silence that greets these questions indicates that we have a great mission to accomplish.

Anthropological studies made upon pupils have demonstrated that school-children rarely attain a sufficient chest development. I also have made my modest contribution, proving that the brightest scholars, the prize-winners, etc., who, as a general rule, also enjoy an advantage in social position, have a *narrower chest measure.* Among the children that are recognised as the brightest in their classes, I have been able to distinguish two categories: those who are exceptionally intelligent, and those who are exceptionally studious; the former have a better chest development than the latter.

Signorina Massa, one of my pupils at the University, in the course of kindred studies made among pupils of a uniform social grade (the poorer classes) observed that the *best* and *brightest* scholars, etc., have a chest circumference and a muscular strength notably inferior to the children who are not studious. There can be no doubt that an assiduous application to the study table impoverishes the organism and above all impedes the normal development of the thorax. This fact has a really overwhelming importance. Study the tables of mortality in Italy for infective diseases, *i.e.*, those diseases in which mankind meets the assault of the microscopic invader either with a strong constitution, or with one already predisposed to defeat. The most dreaded diseases, such as diphtheria, typhoid, measles and scarlet fever are all grouped together under a mortality oscillating between five and twenty-five thousand deaths a year. But bronchitis and pneumonia each cause a mortality that ascends to between seventy and eighty thousand deaths; in this group it is evident that we must take into consideration, not only the infected environment, but also the organic predisposition. Every man and woman has been prepared, by their years in school, to have in the form of a narrow chest and an insufficient development of the organs of respiration, a *locus minoris resistentiæ.* Whoever talks of the *war against tuberculosis* ought first of all to investigate the school and its pedagogic methods.

Anthropological Aspect. *Growth of the Thorax.*—In the course of its growth the thorax undergoes an evolution, not only in itself, but also in its relation to the vertebral column.

The nature of the transformations undergone by the skeleton of the trunk in relation to its different parts is substantially as follows: in the child at birth the vertebral column is straight, and the thorax is higher up than in the adult; the pelvis, on the contrary, slants forward and downward. In the adult the vertebral column is curved in the form of an S, showing the two familiar dorsal-lumbar curves, and the axes of the thorax and pelvis are more perceptibly horizontal; in short, in the course of growth a *descent of the thorax* has taken place, together with a *rotation* of the pelvis (Fig. 124).

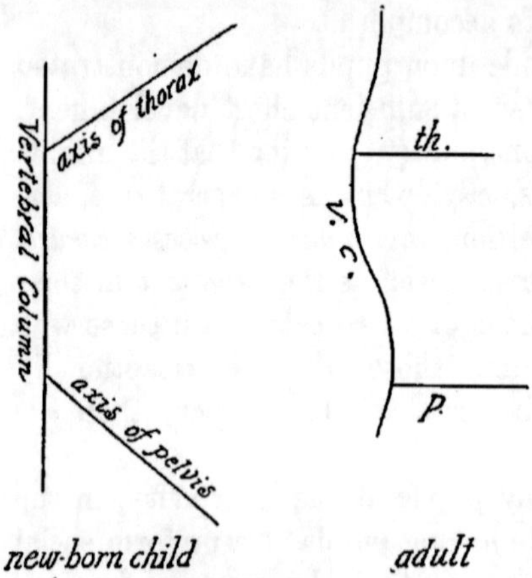

Fig. 124.

A. *Descent of the Thorax.*—This is the chief of these characteristics: the thorax descends in the course of its growth.

In the new-born child the upper edge of the manubrium of the sternum is in juxtaposition to the body of the first dorsal vertebra, while in the adult it is situated on a level with the lower edge of the second vertebra.

Even the tendinous arch of the diaphragm has shifted, being lowered by the space of a vertebra; it is situated between the eighth and ninth vertebræ in the child at birth, and between the ninth and tenth in the adult.

The outside characteristics are in correspondence with this fact; the shoulders descend in the course of growth. In the adult, the acromia or points of the shoulders are on a lower level than the incisura or cleft in the sternum (which is visible at the anterior base of the neck, and may be felt as an indented half-moon); while in the new-born child, on the contrary, the shoulders are higher up than the upper extremity of the sternum.

Another external characteristic of the descent of the thorax is the change in position of the nipples at successive ages; the mammary papillæ of the adult correspond to the level of the lower extremity of the sternum, and are situated respectively at the central points of the two halves of the thorax; in the new-born child, on the contrary, the mammary papillæ are further apart and higher up.

These characteristics of the *descent* of the thorax are fully established in the period of puberty and are of great importance, since, if not completed, they indicate cases of arrest of development or *infantilism*.

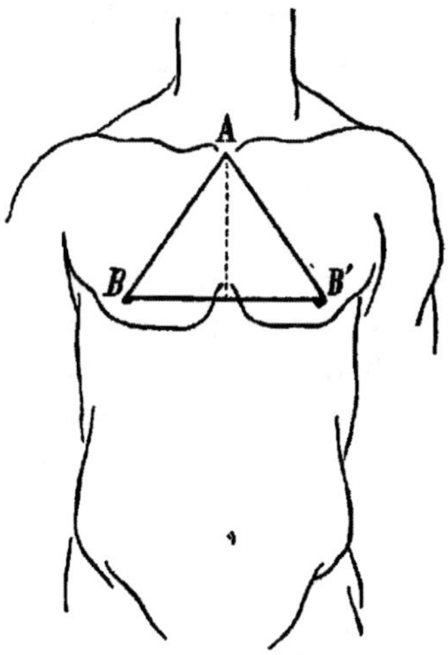

FIG. 125.—A = vertex of triangle; B B' = extremities of base, corresponding to the two nipples.

Quételet has made a study of the *triangulation* of the thorax (Fig. 125).

If the two nipples and the sternal incisura are connected by straight lines inclosing an isosceles triangle ABB', the length of the base in the new-born child is 70 millimetres, and that of the sides BA, $B'A$ is 54 millimetres, and the height 41 millimetres.

In the adult the dimensions are as follows: $BB' = 197$ millimetres; AB, $AB' = 184$ millimetres; and the height $= 155$ millimetres. Comparing the measurements of the child at birth with those of the adult, we find that the base in the adult is 2.81 times, and the side 3.41 times that of the child; in other words, the sides of the triangle increase far more than the base, and its height in the adult (representing very nearly the entire height of the sternum), is 3.78 times that in the new-born child. Consequently, in the course of its transformation the thorax not only descends, but it is also lengthened in the adult, as compared with the form that it had at birth.

B. *Dimensions of Thorax in Relation to Stature.*—Besides its *descent*, there is a second transformation of the thorax, in regard to its volumetric relations to the rest of the body. The perimeter of the thorax and the circumference of the head are pretty nearly equal in the new-born child; if anything, the circumference of the thorax is *a trifle less* than that of the head; but when it equals it, this is a sign of *robustness.* In the majority of cases it is not until the second year or thereabouts that the two circumferences become equal. If, however, such unequality should still persist after the child had entered upon the third year, it would constitute a sign of *rickets* (head too large, chest too narrow).

As to the relations between the thoracic circumference and the stature, it is found that in the child at birth the thoracic circumference exceeds one-half the stature by about 10 centimetres. If the difference is less than 8 centimetres it is a sign of feeble constitution, if it is greater than 10 (for instance, 11 centimetres) it is a sign of great robustness.

This difference disappears little by little; at the age of five years it is already reduced to between 4 and 5 centimetres; at the age of fifteen, the period of puberty, it has wholly disappeared, and the well-known relation between the stature and the circumference of the thorax has become established; the thoracic circumference is equal to one-half the stature (see chapter on *Form*), and this constitutes Goldstein's *vital index:*

$$Vi = \frac{100Tc}{S}$$

As early as 1895, Pagliani published some studies of children, which reveal the *physiological* importance of the dimensions of the thorax; watching the lives of infants whose measurements he took at the foundling asylum, he observed that the *mortality* of infants is quite rare when they exceed the above proportions between circumference of chest, head, and stature.

From a study of 452 infants, Fraebelius has drawn the following conclusions:

I. Mortality 21 per cent.; circumference of thorax greater than half the stature by 9.10 centimetres; circumference of thorax less by 1.5 centimetres than perimeter of cranium.

II. Mortality 42.9 per cent.; circumference of thorax greater by 7 centimetres than one-half the stature; circumference of thorax less by 2.8 centimetres than circumference of cranium.

III. Mortality 67.5 per cent.; circumference of thorax greater by 4.5 centimetres than one-half the stature; circumference of thorax less by 4.7 centimetres than the cranial circumference.

The thorax in children of five years and upward ought to be larger by a few centimetres (not more than from 4 to 5) than one-half the stature.

C. *Transformations of the Thorax Considered by Itself: Alterations in Shape.*

Thoracic Index.—Lastly, the thorax changes its shape in the course of growth. In the new-born child it is very prominent in front, and narrow laterally; in the adult, on the contrary, it is more flattened in its antero-posterior dimension and wider transversely. Consequently the transformation consists in a notable difference in the proportion between the width and depth of the chest, that is, between the antero-posterior and the transverse diameters (see chapter on *Technique*). This proportion constitutes the *thoracic index*, which is expressed by the following formula:

$$Ti = \frac{100A\text{-}PD}{TD}$$

and this formula gives an idea of the *shape* of the thorax.

In the child at birth the antero-posterior diameter is very nearly equal to the transverse; accordingly, the index, at birth, oscillates between 90 and 100.

In the adult, however, the thoracic index is on an average 75; the transverse diameter therefore increases much more than the antero-posterior diameter. According to Quételet, while the transverse diameter multiplies three-fold in the course of its growth, the antero-posterior merely doubles (2.36); in addition to this the thorax also lengthens, as we have already seen.

Proportion, Shape and Dimensions of the Thorax.—In the adult normal man we find the following proportions: The distance between the mammary papillæ is about equal to the antero-posterior diameter of the thorax (hence the papillæ indicate the depth of chest) and is also perceptibly equal to one-half the breadth of the shoulders (measured between the two acromia), which, by the way, is the maximum transverse dimension of the skeleton.

This maximum dimension (the biacromial distance) may be regarded as an index of the skeletal development; and Godin takes its proportion to the *transverse thoracic diameter* (the horizontal distance between the two vertical lines drawn from the armpits, in the plane of the mammary papillæ, see Chapter VII, *Technique*) in order to estimate the proportional relation between the skeleton and the organs of respiration. Since in the course of growth the thorax *broadens*, that is, the transverse diameter increases more than the antero-posterior, we should expect to find that in the course of evolution, the difference between the transverse development of the skeleton and the lateral development of the thorax steadily diminishes.

It happens, on the contrary, that from the age of ten years onward, during the whole puberal development, the transverse diameter of the thorax steadily becomes less, as compared with the breadth of the shoulders, so much so that if the difference was at first 97 millimetres, it becomes finally 116 millimetres. According to Godin, this indicates that the thorax does not obey the harmonic laws of the development of the skeleton as a whole, but that, owing to causes of adaptation (the school!) it remains definitely inferior to the development which it might have attained, and consequently results in throwing the organism *out of its physiological equilibrium.* In fact, if we make men raise their arms, especially men of the student class, a certain hollowness, which is æsthetically displeasing, is revealed along the sides of the thorax. This deficiency is corroborated, according to Godin's studies, by his observation of another correspondence in the measurements of the thorax. In addition to the customary measurements, Godin introduced, besides the well-known and classic *thoracic perimeter*—which is the circumference taken in the horizontal plane passing through the nipples—two other circumferences: one of them higher up, the *subaxillary circumference,* which includes a large proportion of the pectoral and dorsal muscles; and the other lower down, the *submammary circumference,* which determines solely the measurement of the thoracic skeleton, since the intercostal muscles are practically the only ones which descend to this level. These two circumferences are to be considered together, according to Godin, as expressing the relation between the organs of respiration and the muscular mass. In complete repose, the subaxillary circumference is much greater than the submammary; but at the moment of *maximum inspiration* the latter should become equal to the former; hence, the difference between the submammary circumference in repose and during inspiration furnishes an indirect index of the *respiratory capacity,* and the subaxillary circumference is a test of individual capacity. Godin notes that inspiration *almost never* succeeds in attaining an equality between the two circumferences.

Shape of the Thorax.—In regard to the shape, which stands in relation to the *thoracic index*, it is found to vary according to individual *types;* in fact the index itself, although showing a mean average of 75, oscillates between the extremes of 65 and 85. As a general rule, the brachycephalic races have a deeper thorax, *i.e.*, having a cross-section of more rounded form; the dolichocephalics, on the contrary, have a more flattened thorax in the antero-posterior direction (these races, such as the negroes, are more predisposed to contract pulmonary tuberculosis). Consequently there is a correspondence in *type* between the head and the thorax. In the measurements taken by me among the women of Latium the results show that the brachycephalics had an average depth of thorax amounting to 188 millimetres and the dolichocephalics only 181 millimetres, while the transverse diameters were very nearly equal: 241 millimetres in the brachycephalics, and 240 millimetres in the dolichocephalics. Hence, the resultant thoracic index of 78 for the brachycephalics and 75 for the dolichocephalics.

Such differences in the index indicate also differences in the formation of the thorax: that it is more or less flattened in the dolichocephalics, and more prominent in the brachycephalics. There is a corresponding diversity of form in the breasts of the women: the dolichocephalic races have more elongated breasts (pear-shaped), the brachycephalics more rounded.

The shape of the thoracic section is at the present time taken into careful consideration, especially in medicine, because it is apt to reveal predispositions to diseases.

It may be obtained by the aid of the cyrtometer (see chapter on *Technique*). At the present day, however, exceedingly complicated instruments have been constructed, which, by the aid of recording indexes, give a direct representation of the shape of the thoracic perimeter, together with its modifications and respiratory oscillations.

Since these instruments are, for the present, very far removed from widespread practical use, we may adopt as an excellent method for determining the shape and, at the same time, the dimensions of the thorax, that of Maurel, in his research regarding "the square surface of the thoracic section."

Having determined the anthropometric points, Maurel passes strips of metal (stiff enough to retain the shape given them) around the thorax, after the fashion of a tape-measure, first around one half, and then around the other.

Next he places these metal strips (*still retaining the shape given them* by contact with the thorax), upon a sheet of especially prepared paper, marked in squares, and traces upon it the *inner outline of the strips.*

The two halves must be made to coincide in such a manner as to reproduce faithfully the thoracic section, both in form and in dimension.

By adding up the squares contained within the outline we obtain the area of the section.

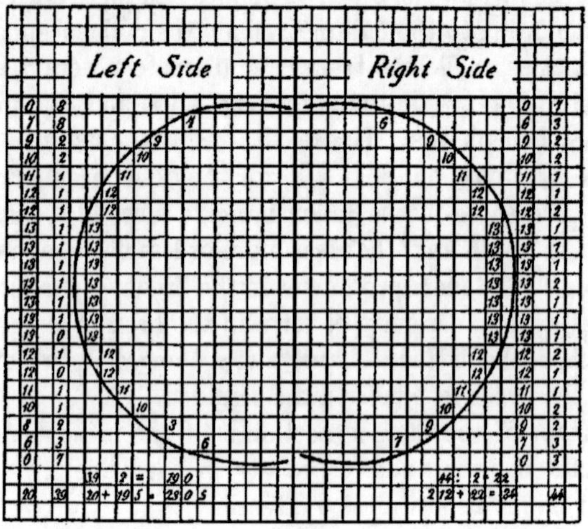

FIG. 126.

This method is the only really rational method for studying the thorax; and its simplicity, practicality and graphic representation recommend it as a valuable aid to pedagogic anthropology.

There is, for example, an abnormal form of thorax, which I have very often met with in deficient children. It consists in an exaggerated curve of the posterior costal arches, which consequently form a very sharp angle with the vertebral column, which is notably indented, while the sternum is also depressed in a groove, and occupies a plane posterior to that of the ribs. The section of the thorax, in this case, approaches the form of a figure 8; and the thoracic perimeter would not represent the true measurement because it would include the empty spaces left by the front and back depressions. The thoracic index would also give a false idea of the facts, because the antero-posterior diameter would be nowhere so short as at the centres of measurement for this diameter.

The only method for representing the true shape and area of this type of thorax is that employed by Maurel.

Anomalies of Shape.—In addition to the preceding anomaly, very frequent in degenerates, and associated with a *deficient development of the lungs* and with physical weakness, there are numerous other anomalies. Among others, those that principally deserve attention are the funnel-shaped or *consumptive thorax,* in which the longitudinal diameter is excessive; the thoracic frame is greatly elongated and the ribs descend to a very low level; this type of thorax is frequent in neuropathic women, and, according to Féré, is associated with degeneration.

The opposite form is the *barrel-shaped thorax,* in which the prevailing diameter is the antero-posterior; it is very prominent and is frequently met with in persons who are subject to forms of asthma, maladies of the heart, etc.

The *bell-shaped* thorax is similar to the preceding, but is characterised by an accompanying exceptional brevity of the longitudinal diameter, which causes it to resemble the infantile thorax (arrest of morphological development).

The *grooved* thorax is the one described above as common among the mentally deficient.

A considerable importance attaches to a form of thorax distinguished by the *shortness of the clavicles,* in consequence of which the chest remains flat, paralytic or *flat thorax* (*habitus phthisicus*). The flattened appearance is due to the fact that the chest cannot rise in front, and the shoulders, being cramped by the shortness of the clavicles, curve forward, while the scapulæ stand out from the plane of the back and spread themselves like wings (scapulæ alatæ). I have met with this form in deficients, accompanied by such *laxity of articulations,* that it was possible to grasp the points of the shoulders and draw them together until they very nearly met in front.

This form of thorax is characteristically predisposed to pulmonary tuberculosis, and is frequently met with in the macroscelous types.

The commonest deformities of the thorax are those associated with *rachitis.*

One of the forms regarded as being rachitic in origin is the *keel-shaped thorax,* in which the sternum is thrust forward and isolated along its median line, like the keel of a boat.

But the thoracic deformities due unquestionably to rickets are of the well-known types that go popularly under the name of *hunchback,* and are accompanied by curvatures of the vertebral column. The first admonitory symptoms are shown by the so-called *rachitic rosary, i.e.,* by the small swellings due to enlargement of the ends of the ribs at their point of attachment to the sternum. Subsequently, the softened ribs become misshapen in various ways, especially from the fourth rib downward, the upper ribs being fastened and sustained by the thoracic girdle and by the muscles. The curvatures of the vertebral column which accompany rickets are *scoliosis* or lateral deviation (frequent in school-children) and *kyphosis,* or deviation in a backward curve; for the most part these two curvatures occur together, so that the vertebral column is thrust outward and at the same time is twisted to one side: *kypho-scoliosis.*

Pedagogical Considerations.—The following considerations are the natural sequence of what has been said above. Deficiency of the thorax is one of the *stigmata* left by the school, which in this way tends to make the younger generations feeble and physiologically unbalanced.

The exaggerated importance which is given to the *school benches* for the purpose of avoiding deformities of the vertebral column deserves to be put aside and forgotten, as an aberration of false hygiene. The bench will not prevent restriction of the thorax; before reaching the critical point which the improved school bench is intended to prevent, many impoverishments of the organism, fatal to robustness and health, and often to *life itself* (predisposition to tuberculosis!) have been incurred; and there is no other remedy to obviate them than a *reform in pedagogic methods.* The admonitory fact that neglected, despised, half-starved children have an enormous *advantage* in the development of the thorax over the more intelligent children who are well-fed and carefully guarded, and solely because the former are free to run the streets, ought to point the direction in which we should look for means of helping the new generations hygienically. They have need of free movement and of air. The recreation rooms which tend to keep the children of the street shut up indoors even during recess are taking from the children of the people the sole advantage that still remained to them. Try to realize that these children are obliged to sleep in dark, crowded environments, and that every night, during the period of sleep, they suffer from such acute poisoning by carbon dioxide that they frequently awaken in the morning with severe pains in the head. The life of the streets is their salvation. We condemn children to death, under the delusion that we are working for their moral good; a perverted human soul may be led back to righteousness; but a consumptive chest can never again become robust. Let those who talk of education and morality and similar themes be sure that they are benefactors and not executioners, and let those who wish to do good seek the light of science.

Curvatures of the vertebral column, such as lordosis and kyphosis, cannot be considered solely in relation to the thorax, but in relation to the pelvis as well, because, especially in lordosis, the lumbar vertebræ are also involved, while the pelvis also suffers a characteristic deformity.

CHAPTER IV

THE PELVIS

Anatomical Note.—The five lumbar, the five sacral and the four coccygeal vertebræ constitute the lumbar and sacro-coccygeal section of the vertebral column.

The *sacrum*, formed by the union of the five sacral vertebræ, appears in the adult in the form of a bone that narrows rapidly from above downward in a general curve whose convex side is turned inward. The coccyx has the importance of being a real and actual caudal appendage, reduced in man to its simplest ana-

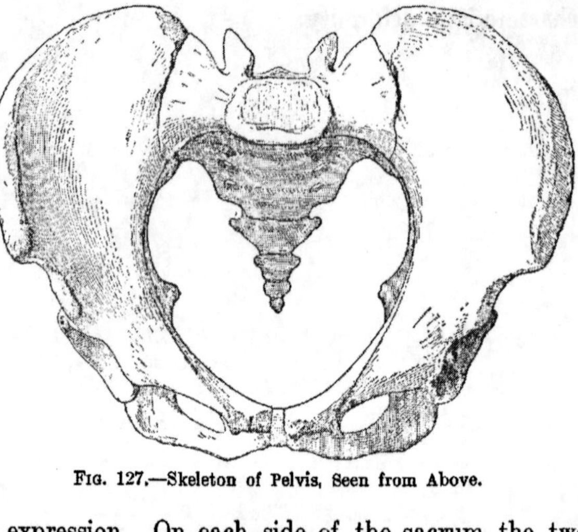

FIG. 127.—Skeleton of Pelvis, Seen from Above.

tomical expression. On each side of the sacrum the two ossa innominata or hip-bones are attached, constituting a sort of massive girdle (cinctura pelvica), serving as point of attachment for the lower limbs, while at the same time it sustains the entire weight of the body and the abdominal viscera. These two bones are made up of three separate parts: an upper part, very broad and rather thin (the ilium, which constitutes the flank or hip), one in front (the os pubis), and a third behind, quite massive, and shaped like the letter V (the ischium). The two ossa innominata and the os sacrum form the pelvis or pelvic basin, a broad cavity with bony walls that are by no means complete, within which are a portion of the digestive organs and a considerable part of the organs belonging to the genito-urinary system. The pelvis supports the vertebral column and is in turn supported by the lower limbs, in quite marvellous equilibrium.

The maximum sexual differences of the skeleton are in relation to the pelvis; in woman the iliac bones form a far ampler basin; in man, the pelvis is higher and more confined and formed of more solid bones; but it is not broader. But where the difference is most apparent is in the pelvic *aperture* (see Fig. 127) which divides the pelvis into two parts, the upper or great pelvis and the lower or small pelvis. This aperture has distinguishing marks that differ widely between the sexes; in woman it is rounder, in man it is more elongated from front to back and is narrowed toward the pubis. One of the most important points of measurement in anthropology and in obstetrics is the extreme anterior apex of the superior border of the ilium or *crista iliaca antero-superior*. The woman in whom this dimension (the bis-iliac) is less than 250 millimetres cannot give birth naturally; similarly the woman who has a prominent os pubis (due to rachitis) will owe the attainment of maternity to the intervention of surgery, and perhaps even of the Cæsarean operation.

There are also many ethnical differences in the pelvis: brachycephalics (the mongolian race) have a broader and shallower pelvis than the dolichocephalics, who, on the contrary, have a deeper and narrower pelvis (the negroes). The same thing is met with, notwithstanding its intermixture, in our own race: blond, brachycephalic women have a wider pelvis than brunette, dolichocephalic women.

Accordingly, cranium, thorax and pelvis correspond in one and the same ethnic type.

The abdomen extends from the arch of the diaphragm to the lower extremity of the pelvis. It contains all the viscera of alimentation: the digestive system together with the glands belonging to it; the liver and pancreas, besides the renal system and, in women, the organs of generation (uterus and ovaries). The diaphragmatic arch, having its convex side uppermost, enters the thoracic frame as far as the first dorsal vertebra. The intestinal mass is more noticeable and prominent in persons having a narrow pelvis; in children, for example, the abdomen is very prominent.

Growth of the Pelvis.—In the skeleton of the new-born child the pelvis differs from that of the adult in two particulars: *height* and *direction.* The pelvis is low in the new-born child and higher in the adult. The central axis is more oblique from front to back (in the higher mammals the axis of the pelvis is almost central); in the adult, on the contrary, this axis tends to straighten up, to the point of becoming nearly vertical, in relation, that is, to the erect position of man. Hence in the course of growth the pelvis not only becomes proportionally higher, but it undergoes a rotary movement around the cotyloid axis; this movement has the effect of elevating the pubis and bringing the ischium forward.

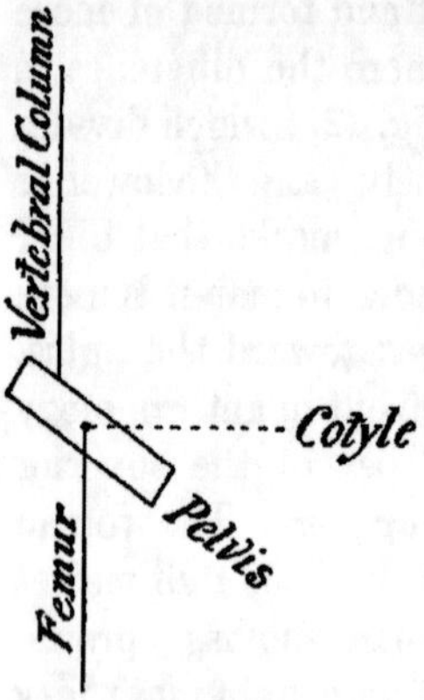

FIG. 128.

The vertebral column rests upon the sacrum, which is the retrocotyloid portion of the pelvis, and its pressure tends mechanically to straighten the pelvis (see diagram, Fig. 128). This process of straightening has certain limits, and is dependent upon the *form of curvature* of the vertebral column; if this is exaggerated, as in lordosis, the weight is thrown further forward, almost over the cotyles; consequently, the elevation of the pelvis is not properly accomplished (low pelvis found in lordotics). If, on the contrary, the lumbar curvature is wanting or reversed (kyphosis), the pressure of the column is thrown backward and the straightening up of the pelvis is exaggerated (high pelvis found in kyphotics). Independently of pathological deformities, there are various forms of lumbar curvature in the vertebral column that are normal oscillations, or oscillations acquired through adaptation.

An exaggerated lumbar curvature or saddle-back is found in children accustomed to carry heavy loads upon their shoulders; a diminished curvature is found in children constrained to remain in a sitting posture for many hours a day. The sitting posture tends to cancel the lumbar inward curve; consequently, while children are in school they are promoting the elevation of their pelvis.

The elevation of the pelvis proceeds rapidly at the fifteenth year, during puberty, when the muscular masses become more solid.

A woman is not fitted for motherhood, even if physically developed, so long as her pelvis has not rotated normally. But if the rotation is exaggerated (due to prolonged sitting posture during years of growth), this is very unfavourable to normal childbirth. In rickets, associated with kyphosis, there is a form of exaggerated rotated pelvis (pubis high). The laborious "modern" childbirth, and the dangerous childbirth in the case of women who have devoted much time to study, must be considered in connection with these artificial anomalies. *Free movement* and gymnastics have for this reason, in the case of women, an importance that extends from the individual to the species.

CHAPTER V

THE LIMBS

THE study of the limbs is of great importance, because, although it is the special province of the bust to contain the organs of vegetative life, it is the limbs which render it useful. In fact, it is the lower limbs which control our locomotion and the upper limbs which execute the labour of mankind.

One characteristic of man, equally with that of standing in an erect position, supported only on the lower limbs, is the independence of the upper limbs, which are raised from the ground and relieved of the function of locomotion—a function that still continues in all other mammals, excepting the anthropoid apes, whose upper limbs are extremely long and barely escape the earth, and serve the animal merely as an aid and a support in walking. The birds, although supported on their hind limbs alone, nevertheless have their fore limbs assigned to the sole office of wings for the transportation of their bodies.

Consequently, the free and disposable upper limb, peculiar to mankind, would seem to mark a new function in the biologic scale —human labour.

Anatomy of the Skeleton of the Limbs.—In contrast to the bust, the limbs have an internal skeleton, adapted solely to the function of support (not of protection). The bones are covered with masses of striped muscles, which have as their special function voluntary movement, that is to say, obedience to the brain.

The upper and lower limbs correspond numerically, and the arrangement of the bones is analogous; and this holds true for all the higher vertebrates. The nearest bones, those that are attached to the trunk, are single in all four limbs. Then, just as though branching out, they next double in number, and then multiply successively as we approach the extremities of the limbs. Thus the forearm and the lower leg have two bones, and the hands and feet have many.

In the upper arm we have the *humerus*, in the thigh the *femur*, in the forearm the *ulna* and *radius* (the ulna is situated on the same side as the little finger and the radius on that of the thumb), in the lower leg the *tibia* and *fibula*. Then come the many short bones (eight in the carpus and seven in the tarsus) which in the hand form the wrist or *carpus*, and in the foot the ankle or instep, the *tarsus*. These are followed by other long bones (five in the hand and five in the foot), which constitute the *metacarpus* and *metatarsus*, and these in turn by the long bones of the *phalanges* (fingers and toes), which grow successively smaller toward the extremities and are successively named *proximal*, *middle* and *distal phalanges* (*phalangettes*). These last are missing in the thumb and the big toe. In conjunction with the last phalanges, the fingers and toes are protected by nails.

The Growth of the Limbs.—Recent studies, conducted principally by Godin in France, author of the classic work upon growth, have demonstrated that the long bones of the limbs obey certain special laws of biologic growth.

While a long bone is growing in length it does not grow in width or thickness, and while it is increasing in thickness it does not gain in length; hence the lengthening of the bones takes place in alternate periods; during the period of repose relative to growth in length, the bone gains in thickness.

I have already explained, in connection with the stature, that we owe the growth of the long bones to a variety of formative elements, the cartilages of the epiphyses, which control the growth in length of the long bones, and the enveloping membrane of the body of the bone, the periosteum, which presides over the growth in thickness.

The above mentioned alternation in the growth of the bones must therefore be attributed to an alternation in the action of these various formative elements of the bones.

In the case of two successive long bones (for example, the humerus and radius, the femur and tibia, the metacarpus and phalanges, etc.), they alternate in their growth; while one of them is lengthening, the other is thickening; consequently the growth of a limb in length is not simultaneous in all the bones, but takes place alternately in the successive bones. During the time when the growth devolves upon the longest bone, the limbs show the greatest rate of increase in length, and when, on the contrary, it devolves upon the shortest bone, the growth is less; but in either case it continues to grow.

The growth of the long bones of the limbs proceeds by alternate periods of activity and repose, which succeed each other regularly.

These periods of activity and repose occur inversely in each two successive bones.

The periods of repose from growth in length are utilised for gain in thickness, and reciprocally. The long bones lengthen and thicken alternately, and not simultaneously.

It is only at the age of puberty (fifteenth year) that a complete simultaneity of growth takes place, after which epoch the growth in stature and length of limb diminishes, yielding precedence to that of the vertebral column.

When the complete development of the bodily *proportions* is attained (eighteenth year), the length of the lower limbs is equal to one-half the stature.

When the upper limbs are extended vertically along the sides of the body, the tip of the middle finger reaches the middle point of the thigh, while the wrist coincides with the ischium (hip-bone). The total spread of the arms is, on an average, equal in length to the stature.

The proportions between the lower limbs and the bust, resulting from the attainment of complete individual development, determine the types of stature: *macroscelia* and *brachyscelia.* Since the order of growth as between the two essential portions of stature is now determined, we are able to interpret macroscelia as a phenomenon of infantilism (arrested development of the bust).

Malformations. Excessive Development of the Nearer and Remoter Segments.—But there are other proportions that are of interest to us, within the limbs themselves. Even between the nearer and remoter portions of the limbs there ought to be certain constant relations (indices) that constitute differential characteristics between the various human races and between man and the ape. If the humerus or upper arm is taken as equal to 100, the radius or forearm is equal to 73 in the European, while in the negro it is equal to about 80. Furthermore, it is a well-known fact that excessive length of the forearm is an ape-like characteristic.

Consequently, the measurement of the segments of the limbs is important, and it is made with a special form of calipers; when the index of the segments deviates from the accepted normal figure, this constitutes a serious *anomaly,* frequently found in degenerates, and it often happens that an excessive development of the remoter segments, the bones of the extremities, explains the excess of the total spread of the arms over the stature, unassociated with the macroscelous type.

Absence of Calf.—In addition to this fundamental deviation from normality, there are other malformations worthy of note that may occur in the limbs. Such, for example, is a deficiency or absence of the calf of the leg. The well-turned leg, which we admire as an element of beauty is a distinctive human trait most conspicuous among the races that we regard as superior. Among the more debased negro races the leg is spindling and without any calf; furthermore, it is well known that monkeys have no calves, and still less do they exist among the lower orders of mammals.

Flat Feet.—Another important malformation relates to the morphology of the feet. Everyone knows the distinctive curve or arch of the foot, and the characteristic imprint which it consequently leaves on the ground. Sometimes, however, this arch is missing, and the sole of the foot is all on the same plane (flat foot). The dark-skinned natives of Australia have flat feet as one of their racial characteristics; in our own race it constitutes an anomaly that is frequent among degenerates. Flat feet may also be acquired as the result of certain employments (butler, door-keeper, etc.), which compel certain individuals to remain much of the time on foot. But in such cases the deformity is accompanied by a pathological condition (neuralgic symptoms and local myalgia). Like all malformations, this may have special importance in connection with infantile hygiene (the position of the pupil, the work done by the children, etc.).

Opposable Big Toe.—Another malformation combined with a functional anomaly, that is never met with as a deformity resulting from adaptation, is the opposable big toe. Sometimes the big toe is greatly developed and slightly curved toward the other toes, and capable of such movement as to give it a slight degree of opposability; hence the foot is prehensile. This characteristic, regularly present in monkeys, is so far developed in certain degenerates as to make it possible for them to perform work with their feet (knitting stockings, picking up objects, etc.); so that this class of degenerates, who are essentially parasites, solve the problem of supporting themselves by trading on the curiosity of the public, so that, by straining a point, we might bestow upon them the title of *foot labourers.*

Loose and Stiff Joints.—Anomalies may also occur in connection with the articulation of the joints. It sometimes happens that they are extremely loose and weak, and allow the bones an excessive play of movement; and, if the lower limbs are thus affected, it increases the difficulty of maintaining equilibrium when standing erect or walking. On the other hand, it may happen that the articulations are too stiff, and consequently render many movements difficult, especially if through an anomalous development of the outer coating of the bone, it results in congenital ankylosis.

Curvature of the Legs.—A special importance attaches to certain alterations undergone by the heads of the bones which contribute to the formation of the knee, because of the curvature of the leg which results from them (rachitis, paralysis). The leg may become bowed outward or inward; when it is bowed inward (knock-knees, *genu valgum*), the knees strike together in walking; when, on the contrary, it is bowed outward, the result is bow-legs (*genu varum*), known popularly in Italy as "legs of Hercules," a deformity which in a mild degree may also result from the practice of horse-back riding.

Club-foot (*Talipes*).—Other deviations from the normal position occur in connection with the foot. Certain paralytic children (Little's disease) walk on the fore part of the foot (*talipes equinus*, "horse's foot"); in some cases the foot is also turned inward, and consequently such children cross their legs as they walk (*talipes equino-varus*).

The Hand

Cheiromancy and Physiognomy. The Hand in Figurative Speech. The High and Low Type of Hand.—The hand is in the highest degree a human characteristic. It is man's organ of grasp and of the sense of touch, while in animals these two functions are relegated to the mouth. The hand has always claimed the attention not only of scientists but of all mankind without distinction. Attempts have been made to discover the secrets of human personality from the hand, and a whole art has been built up, called *chiromancy*, which endeavours to read from the hand man's destiny and psychic personality, just as *physiognomy* was the art of interpreting the character from the face.

Chiromancy was an accredited art as far back as the days of ancient Greece, and it also had a great vogue in the middle ages; while to-day it is out of date and superseded, or perhaps is destined to rise again in some new form, just as physiognomy has risen again in the study of "expressions" of the face and the imprints which they leave behind them. Scientists also have made the hand the object of their careful consideration; and the result of their researches shows that the hand really does contain individual characteristics that are not only interesting but, up to a certain point, are revelations of personality. A written word, a clasp of the hand, may furnish documents for the study of the individual. Graphology, for instance, is naturally related to the functional action and to the characteristics of the hand itself. Gina Lombroso has recently made a study of the *hand-clasp* in its relation to character; when a haughty person offers his hand, he has the appearance of wishing to thrust you from him; the miser barely offers the tips of his fingers; the timid man yields a moist and chilly hand to your touch; the loyal friend makes you feel the whole vigor of his hand in its cordial pressure.

In the gesture we have an individual form of linguistic expression. Consequently, man reveals himself, not alone through his creative part, the head, but also through its obedient servant, the hand. "The hand is gesture, gesture is visible speech, speech is the soul, the soul is man, the soul of man is in the hand."

Furthermore, we can judge from the hand whether a man is fitted for work or not; and it is to work that the hand owes its human importance. The first traces of mankind upon earth are not remains of skeletons, but remains of work—the splintered stone. The whole history of social evolution might be called the history of the hand. To say that the hand is the servant of the intelligence is to express the truth in too restricted a way, because the intelligence is nourished and developed through the products of the hand, as by degrees the work of the latter transformed the environment. Hence, the history of our intellectual development, like that of our civilization, is based upon the creative work evolved by the collaboration of hand and head. And so, in the orphan asylums, we have the children sing the hymn to the hand, which is a hymn to labuor and to progress:

> "Our hand is good for every task."

All the solemn acts of life require the cooperation and sanction of the hand. We take oath with the hand; marriage is performed by uniting the hands of the bridal pair; in proof of friendship or to seal a compact, we clasp hands. The word *hand* has come to be often used in a symbolic sense in many expressive phrases possessing a social and moral significance: "Take heed that the hand of the Lord does not fall upon you;" "Pilate washed his hands;" "to put oneself into another's hands;" "to have a lavish hand;" "to sit with idle hands" or "with the hands in the pockets;" "one hand washes the other;" "to have a hand in the pie;" "to turn one's hand to something;" "to lend a final hand;" "to speak with the hand on the heart;" "to believe the evidence of one's hands," etc.

And this high and symbolic significance given to the hand dates back even to bible times:

Solomon says: "The length of days is in her right hand; and in her left hand riches and honour" (*Prov.* 3, 16).

And Moses: "Therefore shall ye lay up these my words in your soul and bind them for a sign upon your hand" (*Deut.* 11, 18).

Attempts have recently been made to describe the "psychological types" of the human hand. Zimmermann, for instance, studies two types of hand: the *high type*, delicate, small, slender, with rounded, tapering fingers, and convex nails; a hand which would indicate a fine sensibility, delicate and refined sentiments, a well balanced mind, a high degree of intelligence, a strong and noble character. And there is the *low type*, coarse, short and stocky, with thick fingers and flat nails; an index of sluggish sensibilities, vulgar sentiments and a low order of intelligence, a weak will and apathetic character.

In accordance with the theories of mechanics, the type of hand has been considered in relation to its organic use and morphological adaptation. In general, the hand used in the coarser forms of work is of the low type; the high type of hand is that required for nimble and fine movements, in which there is need of the successive concurrence of all those delicate little groups of muscles which are able to act independently and thus give to this organ the marvelous and subtle variety of movements which distinguish it. In regard to dimensions, the large, heavy hand would betoken use, and the little hand *disuse*. Therefore, the small hand may be considered as a stigma of parasitism, a distinction which at the present day has lost its nobility. Excepting in so far as the "brain workers," who make themselves useful without employing their hands, may still show a distinctive smallness of these members.

We should not, however, adhere solely either to the psychological theory of the hand, or to the theory of adaptation; it is necessary to consider the characteristics of the hand from several different points of view.

Dimensions.—The dimensions of the hand bear a constant relation to the stature and to certain partial dimensions of the body, while the various parts of the hand preserve constant reciprocal proportions.

As far back as in the time of Vitruvius it was known that the human hand is related to the stature in the proportion of 10 to 100. This is a very important fact to know, because the proportion varies in the inferior races and in the anthropoid apes, the descent in the scale showing a corresponding increase of length of hand relatively to the stature. Thus, for example, in the Mongolian races the proportional length of the hand is 12.50, and in the higher apes it equals 18. Consequently too long a hand is in itself an anomaly that indicates a low type of man; it is to be classed with those anomalies that were formerly regarded as atavistic reversions, phenomena of absolute retrogression in the biological scale.

Relations between the Hand and the other Dimensions of the Body.—The closed fist, taking the extreme outside measurement between the metacarpo-phalangeal articulations, corresponds to the breadth of the heart.

The length of the hand corresponds to the height of the visage, and also to the distance intervening between the sternal incisura and the auricular foramen; it is also equal to the distance between the two nipples, and therefore also corresponds to the depth of the chest.

There may be hands which are either excessively large or much too small, and that are really marks of degeneration. An excessive volume of these members is called *megalomelia,* and an excessive smallness *oligomelia.*

We may encounter an extremely small hand quite as often in the son of an alcoholic labourer as in the son of a degenerate aristocrat; frequently men whose parents were mentally deficient have small, delicate, almost effeminate hands.

The Proportions between the Various Segments of the Hands.—The length of the middle finger, measured from the digito-palmar *plica* or fold, ought to equal the length of the palm.

Hence the index of the palm should be the proportion between the length of the palm itself and the length of the middle finger. This proportion is of importance because it has certain human characteristics; as a matter of fact, in the anthropoid apes the metacarpus is much longer than the fingers and the palm has a far lower index than that of man. In degenerates (thieves) the hand is frequently narrow and long.

The Proportions of the Fingers.—If the first and second articulations of the fingers are flexed, leaving the third extended, we find that the extremity of the middle finger reaches to the point where the *thenar* and *hypothenar* eminences (fleshy prominences at base of palm) are nearest to each other.

This basic point is only approximate and serves to tell us whether the middle finger is normal. The middle finger serves as a measure for the others, as follows:

The *index-finger* reaches to the base of the nail of the middle finger.

The *thumb*, to the middle of the first phalanx of the middle finger.

The *ring finger*, to the middle of the nail of the middle finger.*

The *little finger*, to the third articulation of the ring finger.

It often happens that the development of the ulnar side of the hand—the little finger, or both little and ring finger together—is defective. Sometimes the little finger is not only extremely small, but a special malformation renders it shorter still when the hand is open; the second phalanx remains flexed, and cannot be extended. Combined with the shortness of such fingers there is also an extreme slenderness—*cubital oligodactylia*. It is a far rarer thing to find similar anomalies in the case of the index-finger. The thumb, on the contrary, is sometimes extremely short, in consequence of which it has slight opposability.

Functional Characteristics.—What characterises the functional action of the human hand is the opposability of the thumb. There ought to be a perfect movement of opposability of the thumb in respect to all the other fingers; but many imbecile children accomplish this movement imperfectly. The mobility of the thumb is associated with a group of muscles situated at its base which forms the great tenar eminence of the palm, opposite which, in corre-

* Many authorities maintain that the normal relation between the index and ring finger is the reverse of that given above; abundant examples occur in favor of each of these views.

sponding relation to the little finger is the small hypotenar eminence. An insufficient development of these palmar eminences represents a serious malformation, which entails functional disturbances. The hand of the monkey is flat.

The Nails.—We have already seen that in the high type of hand the nails should be convex and long, and that in the low type, on the contrary, they are short and flat.

The normal nail should extend to an even level with the finger-tip. Manual labour should normally serve the purpose of keeping the nails worn down; but we, who are not hand-labourers, must use the scissors, in order to maintain the normal state.

For, if they were not worn down, the nails would attain an enormous length, like the nails of certain kings of savage tribes, who as a badge of authority have such long nails that their hands are necessarily kept motionless; these kings must in consequence be waited on, even for the smallest need, and actually become the slaves of their own nails, which might be shattered by any sudden movement on the part of their royal possessor. Long nails, therefore, are a sign of idleness, while at the same time they demand a great deal of attention. Accordingly, let us repudiate the fashion of long nails.

As a form of anomaly, we sometimes meet with nails of such exaggerated length that they have the aspect of claws—*onycogryposis;* or, again, an almost total absence of nails, which are reduced to a narrow transverse strip—this characteristic is often found in idiots, and is aggravated by the fact that from childhood such persons have had the habit of "biting their nails."

Sometimes the nails are exceedingly dense, or actually consist of several superimposed layers, so rich in pigment that they lose their characteristic transparency.

This condition is due to trophic disorders of the nails.

Teratology and Various Anomalies.—There are certain monstrosities that sometimes occur in connection with the hand, such as *hexadactylism and polydactylism,* or hands with six or more fingers; or else hands with less than five fingers—*syndactylism.* There may even be a congenital absence of a phalanx, with a consequent notable shortness of the finger—*brachydactylism.*

Another sort of anomaly frequently found in deficients consists of an excessive development of the interdigital membrane, to the extent of giving the hand the appearance of being web-fingered.

An anomaly of minor importance consists in a distortion of the fingers; the little finger has one of its phalanges turned backward. All the fingers ought to be in contact throughout their whole length, and not leave open spaces between them.

Lines of the Palms.—The lines of the palms, which used to be of so much importance in chiromancy, are now taken into consideration even in anthropology, being studied in normal and abnormal man, and also in the hands of monkeys. The lines of the palms are three in number. The one which follows the curve of the tenar eminence is known in chiromancy as the line of life, and, if long, deep and unbroken, was supposed to denote good health and the prospect of a long life; in anthropology it is called the *biological line.* The second crease, which ought to meet the former between the thumb and the index-finger, is the line of the head, or *cephalic line,* and in chiromancy its union with the line of life was supposed to denote a well-balanced character.

The line highest up, which begins between the index- and middle finger and extends to the extreme margin of the palm, is the line of the heart or the *cardiac line,* which in chiromancy is supposed to indicate the emotional development of the individual. These lines taken together form a semblance of the letter M, and are characteristically and gracefully curved. It is considered as an anomaly, to be met with among degenerates and even in mongoloid idiots, to lack any of these lines (numerical reduction) or to have their arrangement distinctly horizontal, and reminiscent of the hand of the monkey.

If we trace backward in the zoological scale, we find as a matter of fact that to begin with, there were no lines in the palms, and then there appeared a single crease high up, such as we still find in the Cebus. In the human hand Carrara has recently made a study of these anomalies, distinguishing several types. In the first type there is a single transverse furrow. In the second type there are two furrows which, however, follow a definitely straight and horizontal direction and consequently are parallel. In a third type a single transverse furrow is associated with a very deep longitudinal furrow running from the carpus to the base of the index- and middle finger—a form that Carrara has found only in criminals. Nevertheless, many idiots exhibit a similar longitudinal furrow, due to a peculiar development of the palmar aponeurosis.

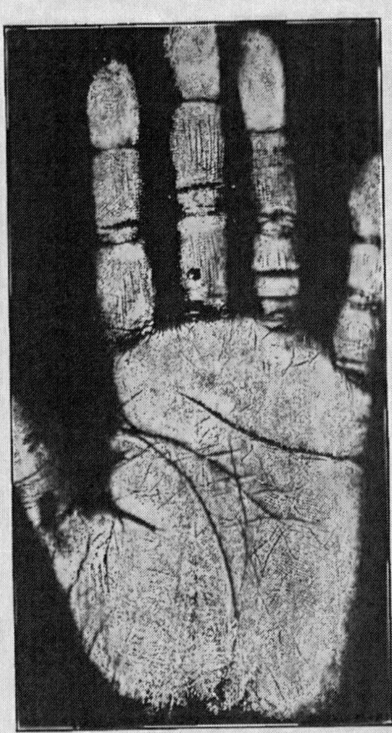

Fig. 129.—Imprint of human hand, showing papillary lines on palm and fingers.

The disposition of the furrows in the palm is not strictly symmetrical in the two hands; in fact, it is said in chiromancy that the right hand represents our natural character, and our left hand the character which we have acquired in the course of living.

Papillary Lines.—For some time past the papillary lines have been attracting the attention of students, in regard to their earliest appearance (in the zoological scale), their disposition and complications. They were already spoken of by Malpighi and Purkinje. Alix has investigated the first appearance, in the animal scale, of these lines in the thoracic and pelvic limbs, and concludes: "The greater or lesser development of the papillary lines seems to bear a relation to the higher or lower position of the group to which the animal belongs, the perfection of its hand and the degree of its intelligence."

Morselli has studied the disposition of these lines in monkeys. We know that the papillary lines bear a relation to the exquisite delicacy of the sense of touch. The primates (higher apes) have on their finger-tips patterns that are far simpler than our own, resembling geometric figures, among which the principal ones are the triangle, the circle, and forms resembling the cross-section of an onion. In the normal human hand, on the contrary, it should be impossible to distinguish any closed figure. The resulting designs, which are very fine and complicated, are not uniform on all the fingers, but differ from finger to finger in proportion to the degree of evolution in a given hand. For example, there is a certain uniformity of design in cases of arrested mental development (imbeciles, epileptics, etc.). This variety of designs produces individual characteristics which are utilized in criminal anthropology for purposes of identification; hence, it is highly important to be able to take impressions of the papillary lines.

Professor Sante de Sanctis has quite recently invented a practical method of preserving papillary imprints by the aid of photography.

CHAPTER VI

THE SKIN AND THE PIGMENTS

Pigmentation and Cutaneous Apparatus.—The outer covering of the body possesses an importance that is not only physiological, as a defense of the living animal, but biological and ethnical as well. In fact, the covering of the body frequently constitutes a characteristic of the species, and we may say that it constitutes to a large extent the æsthetics of coloration, supplementing that of form. In the covering of the body there are in general certain appendages which include the double purpose of defense and attraction, as, for example, the scales of fishes, the quills of the porcupine, the marvellous plumage of certain birds, the furry coat of the ermine. Man, on the contrary, is almost completely deprived of any covering of the skin, and is conspicuous among all animals as the most defenseless and naked. Consequently, the characteristics of the skin itself, quite apart from any covering, assume in man a great ethnic importance, especially as regards his pigmentation. In fact, it is well known that the fundamental classifications of the human races due to Blumenbach and Linnaeus are based upon the cutaneous pigmentation (white, black, yellow races, etc.). This is because it is a recognised fact that the pigmentation is biologically associated with race, and hence inalterable and hereditary, in the same way, for example, as the cephalic index; although we must not forget the modifications of pigment through phenomena due to adaptation to environment. This would lead us into scientific discussions which would here be out of place, since they have no immediate importance to us as educators. It may suffice to indicate that the distribution of racial colour should not be studied in relation to temperature and the direction of the sun's rays, but rather in connection with the history of human emigration; because, while as a matter of fact it is true that there are races at the equator which are darker and races near the poles which are fairer, it is also true that the Esquimaux, for instance, are a dark race, while in Lybia there are types of ashen blond, which is the palest blond in the whole range of human pigmentation.

The pigment is distributed throughout the skin, the cutaneous appendages and the iris.

In the skin, the distribution is not uniform, there being some regions of the body that have more, and some that have less; it is localised in the Malpighian mucous layer, *i.e.*, the granular, germinative layer of the epidermis, which rests directly upon the papillæ of the derma or corium.

The derma, being abundantly supplied with blood-vessels, if seen by itself would appear red; but this color, due to the blood, is concealed to a greater or less extent by the epidermis, according as the latter contains more or less pigment. In the iris of the eye and in the piliferous appendages of the skin, among which we must, from the anthropological point of view, give chief place to the hair of the head, the pigment tends to accumulate, producing a constantly deeper shade.

Pigmentation constitutes an eminently descriptive characteristic, and consequently, in all attempts to determine it, must be subject to all manner of oscillations in judgment on the part of the observer; yet, because it also constitutes an ethnical characteristic, it deserves to be determined with precision. To this end we have in anthropology *chromatic charts,* corresponding not only to the various shades of the skin, but also to those of the piliferous appendages and of the iris. They consist of a graduated series of colour-tones extending over the entire possible range of the real colours of pigmentation in human beings; and every gradation in tone has a corresponding number. When we wish to use the charts practically, for the purpose of determining accurately the precise degree of pigmentation of a given person's hair, we need only to compare the tone of the hair with the colours of the chart, and, having identified the right one, to note the corresponding number. For instance, we may record: "Pigmentation of hair =34 Br. (*i.e.*, No. 34 in Broca's table). Or, again, if we are making a more complex study of all the children in a certain school, we may say: "The chestnut tones (35, 42, 43 Br.) constitute 87 per cent., the remaining percentage consists of the blond shades (36, 37, 46 Br.). And in the case of the skin and the iris the procedure is analogous. By this means the investigation is objective and accurate.

As a rule, the three pigmentations are determined in accordance with a reciprocal correspondence. The light colourings, as well as the dark, generally go together; *i.e.*, a person having blond hair has also light eyes and a fair skin, and *vice versa*—in other words, the entire organism has either a greater or less accumulation of pigment in all its centres of pigmentation. Furthermore, these anthropological characteristics are accompanied by others of equal ethnical importance, such as the stature, the cephalic index, etc.; and all of them combine to determine an ethnic type in all its complex morphology.

In this, as in all other anthropological data, it is necessary to determine the limits between which it may oscillate. In the races of mankind, the colour of the skin ranges from a black brown to a gray brown, to brick red, to yellow, and to white; but among the population of Italy, and among Europeans in general (excepting certain localised groups, like the Lapps, etc.), the variation is confined within the limits of the so-called white tones, that is, from brunette to a sallow white, a rosy white, or a florid red, with each of which tints there are special corresponding grades of pigmentation for hair and eyes, and also, on broad, general lines, different ethnical characteristics oscillating within our normal limits of stature and cephalic index.

All of which may be summarised in the following table:

Pigmentation			Stature	Cephalic index
Skin	Hair	Iris		
Brunette	Black	Black	Medium or low	Dolichocephalic,
Yellow-white Pink-white	Light chestnut and blond.	Chestnut and blue.	Medium or high	Brachycephalic
Florid red	Red	Gray	(Outside of ethnical characteristics: the red colour of the hair is abnormal)	

in which we have also included the abnormal colour of red hair, which plays a part in the actual colour scale of Italian pigmentation: not, however, as a racial characteristic, but rather as a deviation.

In addition to the oscillation of limits, we should also study in any given population the geographic distribution of a definite anthropological datum. This must also be done in the case of the pigments. Among Livi's splendid charts, there is one regarding the distribution of the brunette type in Italy. From this it appears that the greatest prevalence of the brunette type is in Sardinia and Calabria, and that in general there is a prevalence of the dark types in the southern districts; while the lowest percentage of brunnettes is found in Piedmont, Lombardy and Venetia, and in general the number of brunettes is less in northern and central Italy.

The relative distribution of other ethnical data should be noted, such as the stature and the cephalic index, in the corresponding charts.

By combining these results, we find that in the north of Italy the prevalent type is blond, brachycephalic, and of tall stature; while in the south it is a dark, dolichocephalic type, of low stature. This is what I succeeded in showing in my work upon the women of Latium, in which I sought to complete the details of these two ethnic types. In Latium there is a prevalence of the dark, dolichocephalic type of low stature, a type that is still almost pure at Castelli Romani; this type is fine, slender and delicate in formation, and corresponds to Sergi's Mediterranean stock, to which are due the great Egyptian and Græco-Roman civilisations. The other race is blond, tall and brachycephalic, and has only a scanty representation in southern Latium, but is prevalent in an almost pure form in the neighborhood of Orte. This type is much coarser and more massive in its formation, with a euriplastic skeleton, and corresponds to Sergi's Eurasian race that immigrated from the continent.

***

In general, we may say that it is foreordained in our biological destiny not only what form, but also what colouring we ought to attain in the course of our individual evolution, when we finally arrive at mature development.

The Pigments during Growth.—In the course of individual evolution, it is not only the form that becomes modified, but the pigments as well. We know, for example, that children are more blond than adults. Transformations in regard to the pigments occur, however, more especially at the period of puberty.

Pigmentation of the Hair.—The colour of the hair becomes darker in the course of growth, changing from light chestnut to dark, from blond to light chestnut, from dark to black, from light auburn to fiery red. Sometimes this darkening of the hair is accompanied by a change in tone (from blond to chestnut); at other times it consists in an *intensification* of the original colour through an increase of pigment, which *fixes* and *defines* a colour that was previously indefinite.

In children who were ill or ailing during their early years, in other words, weakly children (through denutrition, exhausting illnesses, overexertion), this phenomenon is imperfectly achieved, just as their growth as a whole is imperfectly achieved. The consequence is that these weaklings retain a paler and less decided pigmentation, which explains the fact that statistics show a greater proportion of frail, rachitic, tuberculous and mentally deficient persons among the blonds than among the brunettes; but it is among that class of blonds whose light colour represents an arrest of development (suppressed brunettes).

Social conditions also exert an influence upon the colour of the hair; a larger number of blonds and of lighter and more indefinite blonds are to be found in the schools for the poor than in those for the rich; also a larger number in country schools, where the poverty is greater, than in city schools. Consequently we may conclude that there are two classes of blonds: that which is associated with a racial type, and that which is the consequence of arrested development. The first type has a vivid, uniform and decisive colour tone, accompanied by physiological rebustness; the second is indefinite in colour tone and lacks uniformity—for example, the more exposed parts of the body are paler, and the hair varies in tone, some locks showing greater intensity of colour than others. This is especially noticeable in frail young girls from the country, where the sun discolours the surface layer of hair. In this connection it should be remembered that in those geographical regions where the rays of the sun are most nearly perpendicular, the pigments are, on the contrary, darker and that the skin becomes bronzed under the ardent kiss of the sun. But while the sun intensifies the tints that are strong with life, it destroys those that are weak and moribund, just as it does in the case of lifeless fabrics, which become bleached out by the action of the solar light.

Accordingly the pigments give us an important test for judging the robustness of the body; the blonds who are the product of arrested development of brown tones that have not been attained because of weakness, are frail in health and physical resistance, which is the basis of the popular belief that vigorous wet-nurses must be brunettes.

As a matter of fact, in our own population of Latium the brunette type prevails over the blond by a percentage of 86 per cent.; and it may be that a blond Roman wet-nurse is a weakly creature, just as a Roman red wine is in all probability a white wine that has been coloured.

***

Pigmentation of the Iris.—In regard to the coloration of the eyes, a change often takes place at puberty which is the opposite to that already noted in regard to the hair: *the eyes become more uniformly light;* this happens in the majority of cases.

In the coloration of the eyes it is necessary to distinguish two factors, the *uvea* and the *pigment.*

The iris has a fundamental and uniform light colour (due to the *uvea*) which oscillates, according to the individual, between blue and greenish.

In this layer the pigment is deposited; it may be more or less intense in tone, shading from yellow to a dark maroon.

When the pigment is wanting or is very scant, the fundamental blue or greenish colour of the uvea is apparent.

In little children the pigment is distributed over the uvea in a manner by no means uniform, in little masses or spots that are usually of a mixed colour, so that the colour of the iris in infancy may be uncertain. At puberty a uniform distribution of the pigment already accumulated takes place; but rarely an intensification. Hence the colour becomes more decided, but not deeper, as Godin has recently succeeded in proving.

Pigmentation of the Skin.—In the colouring of the skin it is necessary to distinguish between that which is due to the blood and that which is due to the pigment.

The blood, whose colour shows transparently through the layers of the epidermis, produces the various pinkish tones.

The pigment, deposited in all races of mankind under the Malpighian layer, produces the various brownish tones. The quantity of cutaneous pigment is a constant *racial* factor—a hereditary factor. Nevertheless, in certain individuals, it may be influenced by external agents (sunshine, heat) which tend to cause it to vary; such alterations produce *individual varieties,* and also variations in coloration of the skin between the covered parts of the body and those exposed to the sun or to atmospheric action in general; these variations, one and all, are not hereditary.

At puberty the pigment is increased in certain portions of the body in connection with the generative functions which become established at that time. Besides this, the general pigmentation is intensified; children are whiter than adults.

The Skin and the Hair during the Evolution of the Organism.—In the case of the hair also, the pigment does not remain a constant quantity throughout the different periods of life. Grey hair is a normal sign of the decadence of an organism which has entered upon its involution. As is well known, the hair of the head, the beard, and in general all the piliferous appendages turn white, beginning in the regions where the hair is most abundant, *i.e.*, on the head. In some men, however, the hairs of the beard are the first to turn grey; this is not perfectly normal, it is an *inferior* manner of growing old. A German proverb says, that he who works much with the head (the thinking class) turns grey first in his hair, and that he who works much with his mouth (the hearty eater) turns grey first in his beard.

The skin also gives manifest signs of decadence in the form of *wrinkles.* These serve up to a certain point as documentary evidence of the life which the individual has led and the *high* or *low type* to which he belongs. Just as in the case of grey hair, it is the class of thinkers who have the most wrinkles on their forehead; those who were given over to baser passions, such as called for labial rather than frontal expression, have on the contrary, more wrinkles around the mouth. We know how the peasant class has a veritable halo of wrinkles around the mouth.

Thinkers, on the contrary, have a single vertical furrow in the middle of the forehead: the line of thought. The transverse lines on the forehead are parallel and unconnected.

Faces with precocious wrinkles may be met with, even in children (denutrition, mental anxiety, dystrophic conditions); and conversely, there are faces which have been preserved unwrinkled up to an advanced age (especially in the case of women of the aristocracy, in whom it may happen that neither suffering nor mental effort has left its traces on their lives).

Pigmentation of the Hair.—This anthropological datum merits special consideration, since it plays so large a part in the æsthetics of the human body; and also preserves certain constant characteristics that serve to differentiate the races. In a study of the hair it is necessary to consider the *quantity*, the *disposition* and the *form*. Abundant, strong, sleek hair is in physiological relation to robustness of body. Thin hair, on the contrary, or hair that is easily extirpated at the slightest pull, or dry hair, indicate insufficient nutrition, which may also be connected with dystrophic or pathological conditions (hereditary syphilis, cretinism).

The normal disposition of the hair is characteristic, but it may assume a number of individual variations, as has recently been shown by Dr. Sergio Sergi, son of our mutual instructor Giuseppe Sergi (Sergio Sergi, *Sulla disposizione dei capelli intorno alla fronte*—"The disposition of the hair upon the forehead"—Acts of the Società di Antropologia, Vol. 13, No. 1).

The hair, after forming a single whorl or *vortex*, corresponding to the *obelion*, flows over the forehead in either two or three divisions, the *lines of the parting* (either lateral lines or a single central line) corresponding to the natural divisions of the flowing hair. Across the forehead the hair ceases at the line of *the roots*, which crowns the face cornice-like; it is a sinuous line and rises at the sides in two points, corresponding to the natural partings of the hair. The hair stops normally at the boundary-line of the forehead, which together with the face forms the *visage*, leaving bare that part which in man corresponds to that portion of the frontal bone that rises erect above the orbital arches, *i.e.*, the human portion of the forehead.

The form of the hair is an ethnical characteristic. Among our European populations the extreme forms are wanting, namely, *smooth* hair (stiff, coarse, sparse hair peculiar to the red and yellow races, such as the American Indian, Esquinaux, Samoyed and Chinese), and *kinky* hair (wooly hair, curling in fine, close spirals, such as is found in all its variations among the Australians and the African negroes). Consequently, we cannot use the words *smooth* or *kinky* for the purpose of qualifying the forms of hair found in our populations.

We may, however, meet with *straight* hair (not *smooth*), or *curly* hair (not *kinky*). In addition to these forms, which among us represent the extremes, there are also two other forms—namely, *wavy* hair (in ample curves) and *spiral* hair (forming much narrower curves, the so-called ringlets). Corresponding to these various qualities of hair, there are essential differences in the physical structure of the stem or shaft of the hair itself. If we make transverse sections of hair and examine them under the microscope, we find that the resulting geometrical figures are not all equal: the forms of the sections oscillate between rounded and ellipsoidal forms. Furthermore, there are races in which we may find hair having a circular section (*smooth* hair) and there are others in which we may find, on the contrary, an extremely elongated elliptical section (*kinky* hair); in the first case the hair is a long, bristly cylinder; in the second, it is a ribbon with a tendency to roll up.

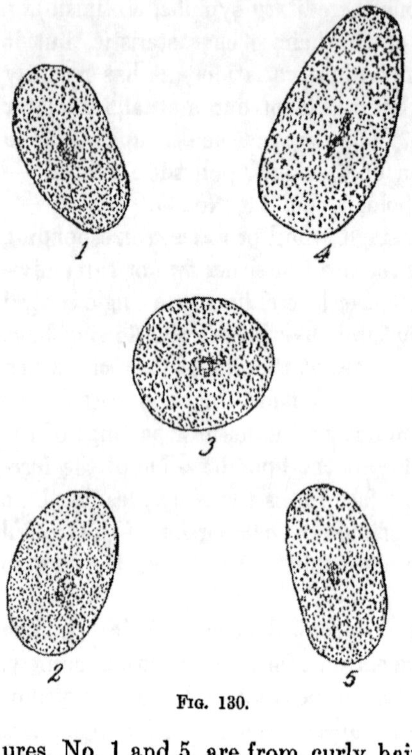

FIG. 130.

In general, the straighter the hair is, the nearer its cross-section approaches a perfect circle; and the more curly it is, the nearer its cross-section approaches an elongated ellipse. The accompanying examples are drawn from the results of my own study of the women of Latium; they represent five microscopic preparations. The figure in the middle (No. 3) represents *straight* hair; the two figures, No. 1 and 5, are from curly hair; No. 2 is wavy hair, and No. 4, close-curled hair, or ringlets. Thus we see how widely the sections of hair differ according to the relative degree of curliness; and conversely, how identical the two sections, Nos. 1 and 5 are, both of them taken from equally curly hair, although from different heads. Straight hair has an almost circular section, although, slightly elliptical; this proves that really straight hair does not exist; in fact, even when it attains the maximum degree of smoothness, it retains a tendency to curl, which is shown, if in no other way, by the readiness with which it acquires a waviness, if habitually kept braided. There is no other section so perfectly circular as that of the red races, thus demonstrating the bristle-like rigidity of the smooth type of hair. Wavy hair is that which, in the form of its section, approaches most nearly to straight hair; it is a slightly elongated ellipse (No. 2).

Anomalies relating to the Pigment, the Skin and the Piliferous Appendages: Pigment and Skin.—There are certain congenital anomalies of the skin, occasionally to be met with, among which I make note of the following principal ones:

a. *Anomalies due to Hypertrophy of the Pigment and the Corium: Ichthyosis.*—The surface of the skin presents large, raised, irregular patches of various dark colours tending to maroon.

b. *Anomalies due to Hypertrophy of the Pigment:*

1. *Nœvi Materni:* dark isolated spots (moles, birth-marks).

2. *Freckles:* small, light brown spots, no larger than the head of a pin, scattered over the body, principally on the chest and face.

3. *Melanosis:* the entire skin has a dark appearance, similar to that of the lower races of mankind, but especially on the face and hands.

c. *Anomalies due to Atrophy of the Pigment. Albinism.*—The skin presents an appearance of milky whiteness; even the hair is white, and the iris of the eye is red.

Wrinkles.—The wrinkles of the face are deserving of attention, as being a detail of noteworthy importance. In regard to wrinkles, two points should be noted; a. precocity; b. anomalies.

a. *Precocity of Wrinkles.*—This is an indication of rapid involution, and is frequently met with in degenerates. Idiotic children often show a flabby, shrivelled skin, overstrewn with a multitude of wrinkles that give them the aspect of little old men.

b. *Anomalies:* the following are to be specially noted:

1. Transverse wrinkles on the nose, frequent in flat-nosed idiots.

2. Wrinkles on the forehead; in normal persons these are interrupted and broken, they are not quite parallel, nor perfectly horizontal, nor very deep.

In degenerates it is frequently noticed that the wrinkles on the forehead form one continuous horizontal line, extending completely across it; sometimes it is so deep that it seems to divide the forehead transversely into two parts. The various wrinkles, straight and unbroken, are quite parallel.

3. The zygomatic (cheek-bone) wrinkles and the wrinkles around the mouth are extremely deep in mentally defective adult and aged persons, and also in criminals, whose facial expression is especially active in the region of the nose and mouth, which constitute the least contemplative portion of the face.

Anomalies of the Hair.—1. *Quantity.*—The quantity of hair may be excessive—*polytrichia*, a mark of degeneration easily to be met with among delinquents and prostitutes; or there may be a scarcity of hair—*atrichia*, among neuropaths, feeble-minded and cretins. Sometimes, precocious baldness occurs, as a result of defective nutrition of the skin.

FIG. 131.—Showing various types of the line of roots of the hair.

2. *Disposition.*—We should note: a. the line of roots of the hair; b. the vortices.

a. *Line of Roots.*—This may be situated *too far down* upon the forehead, in which case it gives a false impression of a low forehead, or *too far back*, in which case it gives a false impression of a high forehead.

Note in addition the form of the line of roots; it ought to be, as we have already said, sinuous; sometimes, on the contrary, this line is straight, and forms a uniform curve, without sinuosity, across the forehead (imbeciles); at other times it descends in a peak at the middle point of the forehead.

b. *Vortices.*—Normally, there ought to be one central whorl or vortex over the sinciput.

Abnormally it may happen:

That the vortex is misplaced—above, below or laterally;

That the vortex is double;

That there are also vortices along the frontal line of roots, or near this line.

3. *Form.*—It sometimes happens that we find in degenerates forms of hair that are normal in inferior races, *i.e.*, smooth hair, or kinky, wooly hair.

Grey Hair.—Sometimes in the case of degenerates or those suffering from dystrophy, a precocious greyness occurs (grey-haired young men, children with white hair); or a partial congenital greyness (clumps of white hair). No form of grey hair, however, should be confused with albinism.

Anomalies relating to the Eyebrows and the Beard. The Eyebrows.—Various anomalies may occur, in respect to the quantity of hair, and the form of the eyebrows.

The hairs may be too abundant or too scanty.

The form may be *oblique,* in degenerate mongoloid types.

A notable anomaly consists in a union of the eyebrows, which meet and form an unbroken line across the region of the glabella. The "united eyebrows" constitute a grave sign of degeneration, and are popularly regarded in Italy as a mark of the "*jettatura*" or "evil eye."

Beard.—It may be very thick or very thin. Too thick a beard is important, especially if the hairs are also abundant on the cheeks and even on the forehead, a characteristic that is frequently accompanied by an abundant growth of hair over the entire body (general hypertrichosis).

A thin beard and moustache may constitute a normal characteristic in certain races, such as the Kaffirs and other African negro tribes; as also in the Chinese. In our own race, on the contrary, it is an abnormal characteristic, which has been interpreted as a sexual inversion (feminism) and is met with frequently among thieves.

Morphological Analysis of Certain Organs (stigmata)

In our morphological analysis of certain organs, we shall have occasion to enumerate a number of separate *malformations,* to the study of which criminal anthropology has devoted much attention. Since many of these are met with in children, we will make a rapid enumeration of them, but must keep in mind that the ability to distinguish the abnormal form from the normal requires practice in the actual observation of subjects, while mere verbal descriptions may lead to false and confusing impressions.

SYNOPTIC CHART

Eyes	position	
	rima palpebrarum or eye-slit	high type low type
	size of eye-ball	macrophthalmia microphthalmia exophthalmia
	sclerotic coat	
	foramina (pupils)	miosis mydriasis anisocoria
Ears	asymmetries	position form
	malformations	Wildermuth's ear embryonal ear Morel's ear handle-shaped ear crumpled ear canine ear, etc.
Nose	types	leptorrhine platyrrhine mesorrhine
	anomalies	flat crooked trilobate
Buccal apparatus	lips	simian mouth negroid mouth hair lip, etc.
	teeth	number dimensions form diastemata irregular position
	tongue	macroglossia microglossia
	palate	ogival (pointed arch) cleft

Generalities.—Passing on to a more minute study of form, we shall have to invade the field of human æsthetics. The proportions of the body are all determined, in respect to their harmony; and especially admirable is the harmony existing between the principal parts of the human physiognomy. Artists know that in a regular face the length of the eye is equal to the interocular distance, or to the width of the nose, while the latter stands to the width of the mouth in a ratio of 2 to 3. The length of the external ear remains, at all ages, exactly equal to the sum of the width of the two eyes.

The eyes and the external ears grow but little, consequently they are relatively quite large in children. The nose and mouth, on the contrary, grow much more, and hence appear quite small in infancy. The growth of the face, like that of the whole body, is an evolution.

Among all the harmonies of the human body, that which can undergo the greatest numbers of alterations in the course of its evolution is the reciprocal harmony between the parts of the face. There are more children than grown persons with beautiful faces, because the efforts of adaptation to environment, or congenital biological causes, or pathological causes may easily alter the evolution of the face.

We will take a rapid glance at the principal morphological anomalies likely to be encountered in connection with the face.

All the malformations that we are about to enumerate are still included under the generic name of *stigmata*, and they may be *degenerative stigmata* (congenital anomalies), *pathological stigmata* (acquired through disease), or *stigmata of caste* (caused by adaptation to environment).

Anomalies relating to the Eye.—The eyes may be too far apart (usually in broad, square faces of the Mongolian type), or too near together (for the most part in long narrow faces, with a hooked nose).

Rima Palpebrarum (Eye-slit).—A straight, narrow slit (low type); an oblique slit (Mongolian eye).

Size of Eye-ball.—The eye-ball may be too large (*macrophthalmia*) and hence often protrudes from the socket (*exophthalmia*); or it may be too small and deep-sunken (*microphthalmia*), or asymmetrical in size (one eye-ball larger than the other).

Direction.—*Strabism* (inward, outward, monolateral, bilateral).

Sclerotic Coat.—It may be injected with blood (delinquents), or partly covered over by an abnormal development of the semilunar *plica* or fold of the palpebral conjunctiva.

Pupillary Foramina.—The two foramina of the pupils ought to be equal in size, circular and with a clearly marked contour. But under various conditions of age and ill health the size as well as the equality of the pupils may vary.

As regards the size of the pupils:

When the pupillary foramina are too small, this constitutes *miosis*—a condition frequently found in certain serious nervous diseases (locomotor ataxia, paralytic dementia), and in chronic opium poisoning; it is frequent in meningitis. In old persons miosis is a normal condition.

When, on the contrary, the foramina of the pupils are too large, this constitutes *mydriasis* (poisoning from atropine, intestinal diseases, etc.).

In addition to these, there is *anisocoria*, when the two foramina are unequal (neurasthenia, chronic alcoholism, first stage of paralytic dementia).

Form of the Pupillary Foramen.—It is not always round, sometimes it is oval (cat's-eye). Frequently the form of the pupil is permanently altered as the result of a surgical operation.

Thus, the contour of the pupil may be broken instead of clear cut; in verifying this phenomenon it is important to inquire whether the subject has suffered from any progressive disease of the iris, such as might produce the same condition.

Anomalies of the Ear.—While in the case of animals the external ear is greatly developed, movable and detached from the cranium, in man it is reduced in size, immovable and attached to the cranium. Two measurements are taken of the ear, the length and the width, and by means of the usual formula we obtain the index of the ear, which for the European race is about 54 per cent. This index has a certain importance because we find that the proportion of width to length steadily increases as we descend through the inferior human races, down to the ape, and the same increase continues if we descend through the different grades of the simian order.

This is to a large extent a result of the fact that, in the descent from man to ape, the lobule of the ear, which is essentially a human form, steadily diminishes, until it finally disappears.

From this it may be concluded that there exist minute zoological differences other than generic between man and animals. As to malformations of the human ear, which may consist of shortness or absence of the lobule (formerly interpreted as a simian inheritance) they are to-day attributed to physiological causes. An abundant circulation produces an ample and *fleshy* lobe; in oligohæmic constitutions (deficiency of blood) the lobe is delicate, pale and even atrophied. Brachysceles often have a big lobe, and macrosceles, predisposed to phthisis, often have no lobe.

In regard to the external ear we should observe:

1. *Symmetry.*—The ears should be symmetrical:

a. In respect to their position.

b. In respect to the more or less pronounced divergence of the ears from the cranium.

c. In respect to their form.

a. *Position.*—We must look for this form of asymmetry by observing the cranium according to the occipital norm. The asymmetry may be caused by one of the ears being placed *too high up* or *too far back* in respect to the other, or both asymmetries may occur together.

b. The asymmetry due to divergence is observed from two norms, the facial and the occipital.

c. Asymmetry of *form* is perceived by observing successively the two external ears according to the lateral norms; their morphological aspect should correspond on the two sides.

2. *Anatomy and Malformations of the External Ear.*—A preliminary anatomical note is necessary. The external ear consists of various parts, which were first studied and named by Fabricius of Acquapendente:

1. *The Helix.*—This is the outermost fold of the ear; it takes its origin above the auricular foramen in a root starting from the inside of the concha and rises upward, to descend again describing a regular helix; and it terminates in the *lobule.* At the point where the helix bends downward to form the descending branch, a small cartilaginous formation can be discerned by the sense of touch; this is the *Darwinian tubercle.*

2. *The Antihelix.*—This originates in two roots under the ascending branch of the helix and terminates in the *antitragus;* it is a cartilaginous formation.

3. *The Auricular Fossa.*—This divides the helix from the antihelix.

4. *The Tragus.*—This is a little triangular cartilaginous formation situated

in front of the auricular foramen. Between the tragus and the antitragus is the *intertragical fossa.*

5. *The Concha.*—This is the concavity, the internal fossa of the auricle, which leads to the channel of the internal ear.

Instances may be found of *malformation* of each and all of these various parts of the ear, which may be excessively developed, or almost wanting, or altered in form.

The Helix.—The overfolding of the cartilage may be wanting, leaving the margin of the auricle straight; this form is met with in the Mongolian race, but among us it is a malformation (Morel's ear). It is a more serious malformation if it occurs combined with excessive development of the Darwinian tubercle; in this case the auricle assumes a really animal-like aspect ("canine ear").

The helix may originate within the concha from a root so prolonged that it divides the concha itself into two parts, an upper and a lower.

The helix may be greatly developed and sharply divergent from the cranium—handle-shaped ear; or it may be bent at an angle at the upper outer margin—*embryonal ear.*

The *lobule* is, as we have already said, an essentially human formation, and as though man were conscious of this fact and proud of it, it is customary in all races to adorn it with ear-rings, to such an extent that in India and in Cochin-China the lobe is burdened with ornaments of great weight, in consequence of which it has continued to develop until it almost touches the shoulder.

The lobule may be attached to the cheek (sessile lobule).

The antihelix may be so developed as to rise in front of the helix—*Wildermuth's ear.*

Another important malformation connected with the ear, which is commonly found in idiots, is a prolongation and restriction of the intertragical fossa into a fissure (*fissura intertragica*). The tragus ought normally to exceed the antitragus in dimensions.

Anomalies of the Nose.—The nose presents very numerous individual varieties, even among normal individuals. In the European race we distinguish the straight nose (Italian), the aquiline, the retroussé (French), the sinuous, etc. But in all these forms one characteristic remains more or less constant: the aperture of the nostrils is long and narrow, or rather its length exceeds its width (the nostrils are thin and mobile, the skeleton of the nose projects above the plane of the face). In the other races of mankind, on the contrary, two other types of nose are distinguished in respect to this characteristic: 1. The aperture of the nostrils is round (the nostrils themselves are fleshy, the base of the nose somewhat flattened)—*mesorrhine nose,* characteristic of the Mongolian race, and found repeatedly in mongoloid idiots; 2. the aperture of the nostrils is broadened, *i.e.,* the width exceeds the length (the nose is flattened and almost level at the base, and furrowed for the most part with transverse wrinkles, the nostrils are exceedingly fleshy and immobile—*platyrrhine nose,* peculiar to the African and Australian races. Corresponding to the external form of the nose there is also a difference in the skeleton in relation to the *piriform aperture* and the naso-labial duct; the external form of the nose is really dependent upon the skeleton (consequently, the above-mentioned nomenclature applies also to the piriform aperture of the cranium (see *Skeleton of the face*). The flat nose is found as a malformation in idiots, and is usually accompanied by prognathism.

Other important malformations relating to the nose are the development of a tubercle at the tip—*trilobate nose,* frequent in *low types of idiots;* and the *tip of the nose bent sideways* (usually toward the left); this form occurs in leptorrhine noses and is considered to be a stigma of criminality (thieves).

Anomalies relating to the Buccal Apparatus.—Malformations occur in relation to the lips, the teeth, the tongue and the palate.

The Lips.—The European type of lips is well known both as regards their proportions and their lines of contour which determine the distinctive form.

Sometimes this graceful modeling is wanting; the contour of the lips is formed of almost horizontal lines, the oral aperture is very wide, and has the appearance, especially when laughing, of being edged by a perfectly uniform, narrow line, thus resembling the mouth of a monkey.

At other times we meet with thick, fleshy lips, slightly pendulous, like those of the black races, especially the Hottentots and Australians; it is a malformation frequent among idiots, and occurs together with prognathism and the flattened nose.

Another notable form is that in which the lips are not only thick and fleshy, but the internal tissues are so abnormally developed that they protrude from the oral orifice in a slight prolapsus; this form of lips is quite characteristic of myxedematous idiots. Finally, we may meet with the so-called hare-lip, or lip divided in the middle, signifying an arrest of embryonal development and frequently accompanied by a cleft palate and a double uvula (see *Development of the face*).

The Teeth.—There is nothing new to tell of the characteristic forms of the teeth—the incisors, the canines, the premolars, and the molars—nor of their regular placement in a single row corresponding to the curve of the maxilla and the mandible. I shall therefore merely give the two dental formulæ corresponding to the two dentitions of man.

First dentition, or "milk teeth":

$$\underset{\text{incisors}}{\frac{2-2}{2-2}} \quad \underset{\text{canines}}{\frac{1-1}{1-1}} \quad \underset{\text{premolars}}{\frac{2-2}{2-2}} = 20 \text{ teeth}$$

Second or final dentition:

$$\underset{\text{incisors}}{\frac{2-2}{2-2}} \quad \underset{\text{canines}}{\frac{1-1}{1-1}} \quad \underset{\text{premolar}}{\frac{2-2}{2-2}} \quad \underset{\text{molars}}{\frac{3-3}{3-3}} = 32 \text{ teeth}$$

In relation to the teeth there are a great number of anomalies which may occur, in number, in position, in size and form, and these anomalies are so frequent that we may say the *smile* stigmatizes the degenerate. Frequently it is the most evident stigma of the whole face; so much so that this same smile which adds so much charm to the normal human countenance becomes ugly and repulsive in degenerates.

Anomalies in Number of Teeth.—Sometimes there are more than 32 teeth, owing to the presence of certain *supernumerary teeth;* these will be found to occur

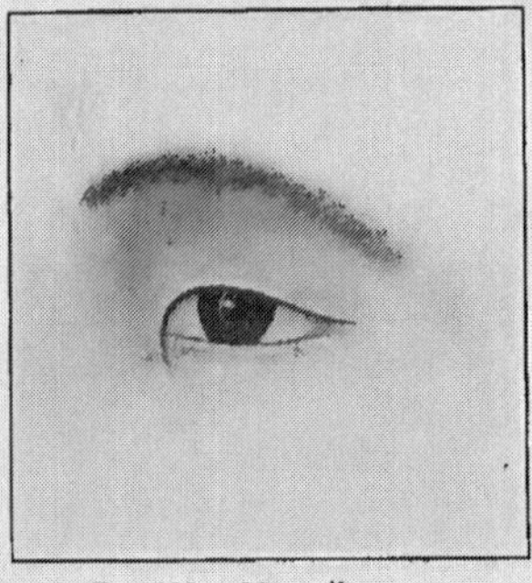

FIG. 132.—Mongolian eye.

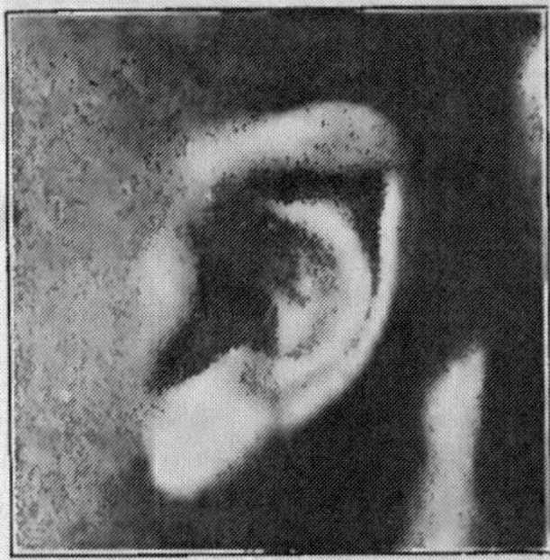

FIG. 133.—Embryonal ear.

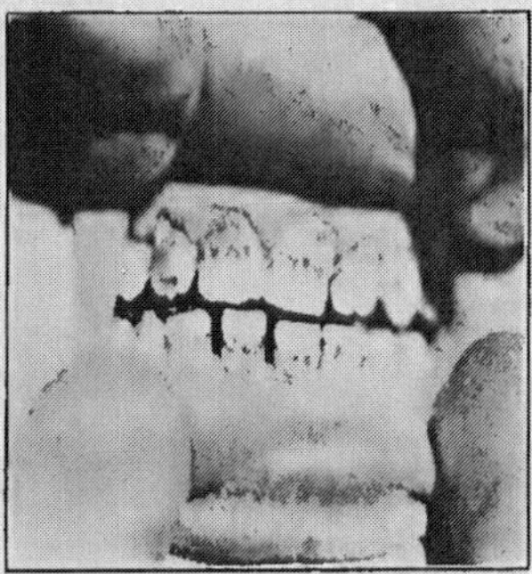

FIG. 134.—Decayed teeth.

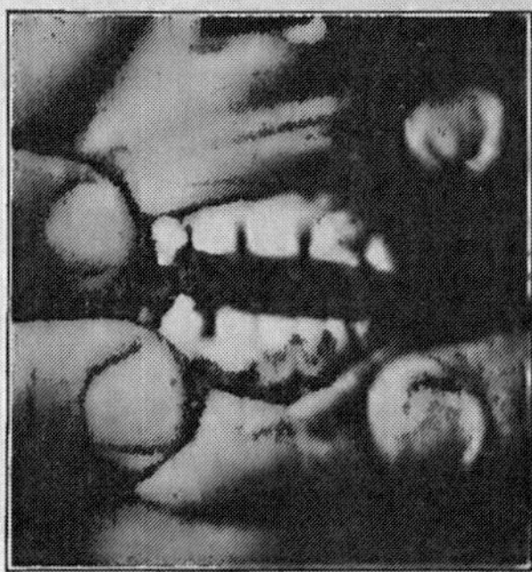

FIG. 135.—Worn-down teeth.

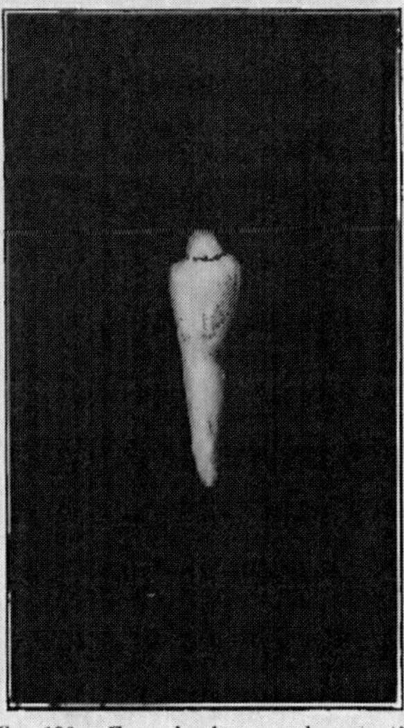

FIG. 136.—Example of a worn-down tooth.

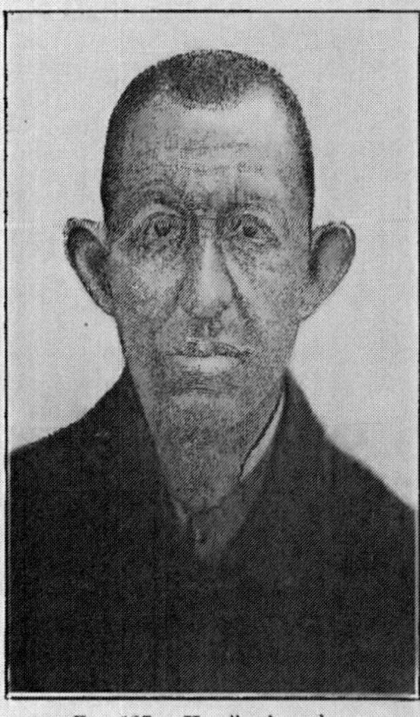

FIG. 137.—Handle-shaped ears.

most frequently in the case of the canines, next in that of the incisors, and lastly in that of the premolars.

Sometimes the number of teeth is less than 32, in which case it is necessary to distinguish two cases of very different significance: First, the last molars ("wisdom teeth") may be wanting; secondly, some of the other teeth may be wanting (incisors, canines, or premolars). The last molar is of no use whatever to man, because it does not enter into the service of mastication, and it is tending to disappear. We may even predict that the day is coming when mankind will no longer have wisdom teeth, and the human dental formula will be as follows:

$$\underset{\text{incisors}}{\frac{2-2}{2-2}} \quad \underset{\text{canines}}{\frac{1-1}{1-1}} \quad \underset{\text{premolar}}{\frac{2-2}{2-2}} \quad \underset{\text{molars}}{\frac{2-2}{2-2}} = 28 \text{ teeth}$$

The absence of useful teeth, on the contrary, is a grave sign of degeneration, and one which leaves wide spaces between two adjacent teeth (wide diastemata).

The *diastema*, or space left between adjacent teeth, is of great importance. There are various causes for this stigma. Besides the one already mentioned, due to congenital absence of a tooth (broad diastema), another recognized cause is an *anomalous placing* of the teeth (narrow diastema). The significance of this is not always the same: for example, the diastema between two upper incisors indicates a very slight anomaly of embryonal development, and, some people think, gives a sympathetic charm to the smile. On the contrary, a diastema occurring at the side of a canine tooth signifies a congenital malformation.

At other times such anomalous spaces may be due to the fact that the teeth have remained small, or happen to have worn away laterally and present an almost filiform or thread-like aspect (diastemata due to microdontia resulting from syphilis or various dystrophic conditions).

The *form* of the teeth demands consideration next in order of importance. Sometimes we encounter cases of teeth that are all nearly alike in form; they have lost that morphological differentiation which already existed in the anthropoid apes; there is an insensible transition from the incisors, all exactly equal in form and dimensions, to the premolars, which also present the same appearance, passing over a tooth which it would be difficult to define either as incisor or premolar (the canine tooth). Usually in such uniform dentition there are slight diastemata.

This condition, however, is not frequently met with; it is much more usual to find this anomaly occurring only in part; the incisor teeth are all equal, or else the canine resembles an incisor or a premolar. In combination with this characteristic, it often happens that there is a diastema next to the canine.

In regard to size, the teeth may be too large, *macrodontia*, or too small, *microdontia*.

Microdontia may be due to a true and actual arrest of development of the teeth (white teeth, small and narrow, often all very much alike), or to a kind of *corrosion* of the teeth due to congenital dystrophism (syphilis). In this case the teeth are ground down and *worn away* either horizontally or laterally (filiform teeth), or again the cutting edge of the tooth is not horizontal in the two upper canines, but oblique, so that the teeth have the appearance of being broken.

Often the teeth are furrowed transversely with yellow streaks corresponding to a lack of development of the enamel.

Finally, the teeth may present various anomalies of position, which may be grouped under three heads:

a. Narrow teeth, so placed as to leave slight intervals between them.

b. Isolated teeth, planted outside the common line, or else transversely instead of horizontally.

c. The dentition does not follow the regular curved line, but shows various sinuosities, usually bending in at the point corresponding to the canine tooth.

The Tongue.—The tongue may present morphological anomalies of great importance, since they are the cause of many defects of speech. Sometimes the tongue is too big—*macroglossia*, in which case it cannot move freely within the buccal cavity and even finds difficulty in remaining within the mouth, but projects between the lips, contributing in no small measure to giving the face an imbecile expression. At other times it is too small—*microglossia*.

A deficient or excessive development of the lingual frenulum may also interfere with the movements of the tongue (tongue-tie).

The Palate.—It is a frequent experience to meet with idiots having an *ogival* or gothic-arched palate, with the vault much curved and narrow, such as is met with in animals and similar in section to a gothic window. A special bony ridge or crest may also occur along the *raphe* or median line. Lastly, the palatine vault may be divided in two (cleft palate), a form frequently accompanied by a double uvula; this stigma may also be one of the causes of defective speech, so frequently met with in deficient children.

The palate normally presents a diversity of forms: Narrow and high, or broad and low—forms associated with the general type of head (dolichocephalic, high palate; brachycephalic, low palate) and especially with the type of face, as we have already seen in treating of the latter.

Importance of the Study of Morphology.—The study of morphology is of high importance in biology, and even more so in anthropology. And since the organism is a harmonic whole, in which the parts and their functions are closely interrelated, any external anomaly leads us to assume that there are corresponding anomalies of the internal organs, and hence, functional anomalies; hence also, in man, psychic anomalies. And conversely, if perfection of form has been attained, it leads us to assume that the entire organism is perfect in its internal organs as well, and in its complex physical and psychic functional action.

"Assure yourselves and one another," says Lelut in his *Cadre de philosophie et de l'homme*, "that wherever you see a change in the body, you will have to search for a corresponding change in the intelligence. Assure yourselves that you will have to establish this correlation throughout the entire scale, from the lowest degradations of imbecility to the highest achievement of genius, from the clearest and strongest mentality to that which is most profoundly and irremediably disordered."

This correlation between the morphological and the psychic personality must be sought throughout the entire scale of human variations, from the genius to the most degraded of imbeciles, from the strongest and most upright character to that which is most profoundly perturbed. Hence morphology constitutes a fundamental part in the study of human personality.

The principle of this aforesaid correlation was at first exemplified in the field of biological science only by abnormal persons, whose noticeable deviations from the customary limits, both in the external form of the body and in their psychic manifestations, gave proof of the phenomenon by exaggerating it. In his classic work, *Traité des dégénérescences*, Morel asserts that "the study of physical man cannot be isolated from the study of moral man." But in our own day, the theory has been marvellously illuminated and popularised by Cesare Lombroso, and precisely on its pathological side.

The Lombrosian theories were so rapidly popularised even before they were fully matured, that it seemed as though the spirit of the times was ripe to receive them, and had awakened to greet the new order of thought, after having long slumbered over the old; thus they wrought a revolution in the field of law and morality, and even laid a foundation for the erection of a new pedagogy.

Or to state it better, they again brought to light certain principles of truth that had been understood even from the most ancient times. For the principles proclaimed by Lombroso are in their general line certainly nothing new nor suddenly derived from a study of modern civilization; the belief that a physical stigma represents a moral stigma is exceedingly ancient. In the Bible we find Solomon saying: we may read the heart in the face. Homer describes the malignant Thyrsites as having a narrow forehead and ferret-like eyes. Caesar feared only those conspirators who were pale and lean. In the Middle Ages there was a law which held that in case of doubt as to which of two men was guilty, the uglier looking one should be hanged. And this same principle has been established from time immemorial in the current wisdom of the people, as is demonstrated by proverbs, which are like laws graven upon stone, and have been gathered experimentally through the repeated observation of successive generations. The proverbs tell us of the physical stigmata of the wicked: "Beware of those who bear the mark of God;" "The bristles prove the brute." Even in art, degenerative stigmata are introduced to represent the malevolent. The satyrs are represented as being of the microcephalic type. The devil was formerly represented as having goat's feet and a tail; Michelangelo pictures him with a narrow, receding forehead and pointed ears.

To-day all this is shown to be true. The truth, and sometimes the intuitive semblances of truth in their relation to outward phenomena, have the most ancient and diffuse history, because, since they always existed, they were analogously interpreted by the intelligence of man. And this is proved by the glorious discoveries of positive science, which we may trace back to far distant foreshadowings; what was in danger of being lost has been born again with an overpowering fertility. The great theories of Darwin regarding evolution were already perceived by Herodotus. The cycle of indestructible material, proclaimed by Greek philosophy, formed the palpitating heart of the teachings of Giordano Bruno; and in our day it formed the fascinating halo of materialism which illuminated the face of my own teacher, Jakob Moleschott.

Now, the fact that it is not new demonstrates that the Lombrosian theory explains phenomena which really exist, since they came under the observation of man from the earliest times. And the fact that this theory has become popularised tells us that the times were ripe to fertilise its renovating principles into practical action. For where is it that we find the triumphant success of science? The attainment of its most profound purposes? We find it wherever science achieves something that is practical and useful for all mankind. Because, so long as anything is merely perceived or looked into, or even deeply studied, it never attains the apogee of its scientific glory and dignity unless it finds some means of benefiting and ameliorating humanity.

Lombroso grasps a principle and turns it into a benefit; and he sends it broadcast throughout human society, to purify society of the spirit of personal vengeance.

Garibaldi redeems an oppressed people and saves the oppressors from the burden of being unjust and tyrannical, through a work of humanity which has no national boundary; Lombroso, by means of his new scientific and moral principle, effects a world-wide redemption of a despised and outcast class, and saves us from the iniquitous burden of social vengeance. Two great deeds of heroism, one of the heart and the other of the brain; two great works of redemption.

Nevertheless, the principle of a morphological and psychic relationship was not wholly wanting in examples of practical application. Not, however, in the case of man; but in regard to animals it had been utilised for a long time back. For instance, when a horse cannot be broken by ordinary methods, the veterinary is called in, and he either discovers some ailment and prescribes a treatment, or else he studies the conformation of the forehead and the nasal bones, and if they are abnormal, he declares that the horse is absolutely untameable. In India the natives are afraid of the solitary elephant with a narrow forehead, for they know that he is ferocious.

To-day we know that many children who can be taught nothing in the public schools are really sick children, in whom anomalies of character coincide with morphological anomalies; and we are beginning to replace the old custom of blind and brutal punishment with a personal interest that leads us to invoke the aid of the physician and to establish special schools for the mentally deficient.

We may say that this new and reforming principle of pedagogics and the school, which transforms punishment into medical care and creates special educational institutions which are at the same time sanatariums, constitutes the pedagogical application of the Lombrosian theories and accomplishes that social task which was foreordained to emanate from the lofty brain of Lombroso.

In its special application to pedagogics, anthropology aids in the difficult task by its diagnosis between the *normal* and the *abnormal* child.

But the contribution of anthropology to pedagogics is vastly wider than this. In this restricted sense of diagnosis, it accomplishes, to be sure, a complete reform of the penal sciences, but it is very far from doing like service to the science of pedagogy.

Scientific pedagogy must concern itself before all and above all, with *normal* individuals, in order to protect them in their development under the guidance of biological laws, and to aid each pupil to adapt himself to his social environment, *i.e.*, to direct him to that form of employment which is best suited to his individual temperament and tendencies.

In this new task, anthropology not only studies the individual, but also gives real and personal contributions to the solution of many pedagogic problems; among others, that relating to study after school hours; to rewards and punishments; to physical training, elocution, etc.; while, by regarding the children as the *effects* of biological and social causes, it establishes new and enlightening standards of morality and justice, and reveals to educators responsibilities not hitherto conceived. It will suffice to call to mind the fact that the most studious children, and therefore those who receive the greatest amount of praise and prizes, show a deficiency in weight, in chest development, and in muscular force; consequently, a physiological impoverishment the blame for which must be attributed to an ignorance of hygiene and of anthropology, such as still persists throughout the whole field of pedagogy; an ignorance which leads the teacher to encourage by his praises the impoverishment of the best forces that reveal themselves in the school (the most intelligent and studious children) in an age when social industries, multiplied and grown to a giant size, demand the cooperation of a vigorous race, and to inspire by rewards and praise a sentiment of superiority and of vanity in an age that is dominated by the sentiment of universal equality and brotherhood.

The teacher ought, on the contrary, to appoint himself the defender of the race, and to demand, among his other rights, that of making such social reforms and such reforms in the school and in pedagogics as may be necessary to the accomplishment of his purpose, which is the attainment of the highest degree of civilisation and of prosperity.

But this subject would lead us to repeat principles on which we have already insisted; it will suffice to reassert that the tendency of anthropology is undoubtedly toward a reform in the school and the opening of a new era in pedagogy.

The Significance of the So-called Physical Stigmata of Degeneration.—We have studied so many congenital malformations and pathological deformations that a synthetic statement of their significance becomes necessary. All the more so, because certain principles in this connection, already widely circulated among the general public, have now been rejected by science.

One of these principles refers to the so-called *atavism* and formed part of the original Lombrosian doctrines: but blessed is the scientist who is obliged to correct himself, for that means that his brain is still fertile.

Certain morphological anomalies call to mind forms of the inferior races and species, from which, according to the original Darwinian doctrine of evolution, the human species had descended in a direct line: hence the term "*atavistic survival.*" It will suffice to mention the receding forehead that calls to mind the Neanderthal cranium, the long simian arms, the prognathism distinctive of the inferior human races and of animals, microcephaly which suggests the crania of anthropoid apes, the mongoloid eyes and protruding cheek-bones, which recall the yellow races; the "canine" ear, the wooly or smooth hair, polytrichia, the dark skin, etc.

Now, all this assemblage of stigmata which went under the name of *atavistic*, or *absolute retrogression*, were held to be in almost direct relation to *degeneration*.

Degeneration was supposed to revive in us forms that had been superseded in the course of evolution, and hence also psychic states that had also been superseded in the history of the human race; it is well known that, according to Lombroso, a criminal might be defined as a savage, a barbarian born among us, yet still having within him his particular instincts of theft and slaughter.

To-day, since the original interpretation of the Darwinian theory has been discarded, with it have fallen all those deductions which medicine and sociology were in too great haste to draw, in order to make scientific application of them.

In conclusion, the principle remains firmly established of a correlation between physical and psychic anomalies, which forms the very essence of the Lombrosian theory. What science wishes to-day to correct is the *atavistic* interpretation of stigmata and of types of degenerates. This takes nothing away from the brilliant record of Lombroso, who interpreted biological and pathological phenomena in the selfsame light that shed glory upon Ernest Haeckel, namely, the Darwinian theory. In the first enthusiasm of that luminous flame which had wrought a reawakening of thought throughout all Europe and the civilised world Lombroso tried to explain *according to the letter* what could properly be explained only according to the spirit; that is to say, in accordance with a very broad principle (evolution and the successive formation of species) which had been divined but not yet demonstrated.

We ought to have recourse, in interpreting congenital (degenerative) malformations to explanations analogous to those in the case of acquired deformations, *i.e.*, to pathological explanations.

We find ourselves in all these cases in the presence of pathological phenomena affecting either the *species or the individual.* On the strength of analogies shown by certain malformations, the tendency to-day is to consider them as "*arrests of development*" or phenomena of *infantilism,* such, for example, as macrocephaly, macroscelia, nipples or shoulders placed too high, nose tending to flatness, handle-shaped ears, etc.—a whole series of stigmata which go by the name of *stigmata of relative retrogression.*

Meanwhile there are other malformations which merely deviate from the normal form (Morselli's "simple deviation"), and they may deviate either in the way of an excess (hyperplasia), or of a deficiency (hypoplasia), as, for example, macroglossia, microdontia, macro- and microphthalmia, etc.; or they may deviate in a true and actual sense (paraplasms), as, for example, in the various asymmetries (plagiocephaly, plagioprosopy, etc.). This whole group of above-mentioned stigmata, which seem to have a congenital origin, or, rather, to be connected in a general way with growth itself, are called *malformations,* to distinguish them from *deformations,* which evidently have an acquired origin, especially from pathological causes, such, for instance, as rachitis and forms of paralysis which arrest the development of a limb, etc., resulting in functional and morphological asymmetry.

Distribution of Malformations

Malformations (associated, as we have said, with individual development) may be found in all individuals who, through various causes (degeneration, disease, denutrition, defects of adaptment), have undergone any alteration in development. And, since we have not yet acquired a recognised standard of *morality of generation,* and the social environment, including the school, weighs heavily upon humanity in the plastic state, who is there without malformation? Complete normality is a *desideratum,* an ideal toward which we are progressing, and, we might add, it is the battle-flag of the teacher.

Accordingly, all men have malformations. It is interesting to see how they are affected by variations in age and social condition, and how they are distributed among normal persons and degenerates, in order to measure the extent of their contribution to the diagnosis between normal and abnormal man.

On the basis of notes taken from an important work by Rossi,*

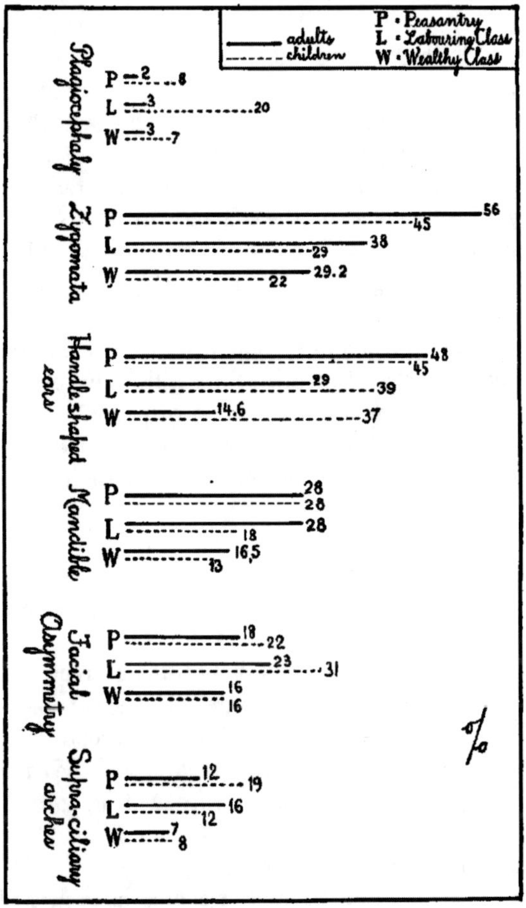

FIG. 138.—Percentage of stigmata among the peasantry, the labouring class and the wealthy class, for children and adults.

I have drawn up the following table, relating to malformations based upon a comparative study of children and adults, grouped under three different social conditions—peasants, city labourers and persons of the wealthy class.

*ROSSI, *Anthropological Anomalies in their relations to social conditions and to degeneration.*

At the further extremity of the horizontal lines will be found the figures recording the number of times that any one anomaly occurs in a hundred instances. The other indications are explained in the figure itself.

From this it is apparent that anomalies of the cranium are much more rare than those of the face, both in children and in adults.

But in children the anomalies of the cranium (and this includes the cases of plagiocephaly), are much more frequent than in adults in all social classes; this shows that in the course of growth the malformations of the cranium have to a great extent disappeared.

In regard to the face, on the contrary, or, at least, in regard to certain malformations of the face, the opposite holds good; the mandible and the zygomata, or, in general, that part of the face which grows rapidly during the period of puberty, show more anomalies in the case of adults than in the case of children.

This shows us that a face which is still beautiful in childhood may acquire malformations in successive periods of growth. In simpler words, the facts may be expressed as follows: that the cranium *corrects* itself and the face *spoils* itself in the course of growth.

But in the case of facial asymmetries the same thing occurs that we have already seen in regard to plagiocephaly; it is more frequent in children, hence asymmetries are infantile stigmata.

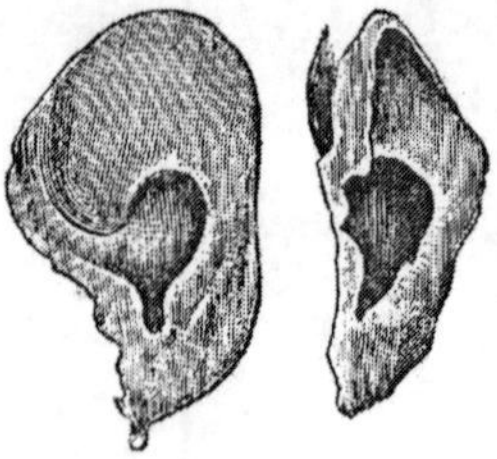

FIG. 139.—Two small examples of Morel's and Wildermuth's ear.

Some important characteristics are to be noted regarding the handle-shaped ear; all children have ears proportionally larger than those of adults and the *handle-shaped* form is very frequent in normal children, regardless of the social condition to which they belong. This malformation *corrects itself* in the course of growth, being far less frequent in adults of the wealthy class and even among the labouring classes; but among the peasantry it remains permanently, almost as though it were a *class stigma*. Although the mechanical theories are in disrepute as an interpretation of morphological phenomena, nevertheless it is worth while to note the singular frequency of this stigma in peasants, in connection with the habit of straining the ear to catch the faintest sounds, distant voices, echoes, etc., for which the *senses* of peasants are extremely acute.

The greater frequency of prominent superciliary arches in adult peasants and labourers may also be considered in relation to a defective cerebral development, connected, perhaps, with illiteracy, etc.; furthermore, the superciliary arches, together with a more than normal development of the jaw bones, are stigmata which usually occur together as determining factors of an *inferior morphological type.* The fact also that an excessive development of the mandible, unlike other malformations, is found with the same frequency among adults of the peasantry and the labouriug class, gives to this anomaly the significance of a *stigma of the poorer classes.* It should be remembered that children of inferior intelligence have a deeper mandible.

What is quite interesting to know, in addition to the frequency of stigmata at various ages and in the various social conditions, is the *number* of them that may coexist in the same individual. It was already asserted by Lombroso that a single undoubted malformation was not enough to prove degeneracy, but that it depended upon the number of stigmata existing simultaneously in the same individual. Now, confining our attention to *normal individuals,* we find, according to Rossi, that the individual number is less among the well-to-do than among the poor; and that it is less among the peasantry than among the working class. The working class in the cities are accordingly in the worst condition of physical development. Furthermore, children always show a greater number of individual malformations than adults.

INDIVIDUAL NUMBER OF MORPHOLOGICAL ANOMALIES

Number of anomalies	Adults: to every 100 individuals			Children: to every 100 individuals		
	Labourers	Peasants	Well-to-do	Labourers	Peasants	Well-to-do
....	4	18	14	....	....	12
1–2	56	36	68	18	16	44
3–4	31	26	18	52	68	38
5–6	9	....	....	27	13	6

From which it appears that only 4 per cent. of the labouring class are without malformations, while the peasantry and the well-to-do have from 18 to 14 per cent. Among normal adults there is a preponderance of persons having 1–2 stigmata; while those having 3–4 stigmata are more frequent than those without any at all.

Excepting for a few labourers, there are no normal persons with 5–6 malformations; in fact, this is the number of coexisting malformations that is held to be the *test of degeneration,* the sign of an abnormal morphological individuality.

Among children, on the contrary, this individual number of malformations (5–6) occurs, *even in the wealthy classes,* so that the child and the adult cannot be judged by the same standards.

The prevailing number of stigmata among children is 3–4. Therefore, in the course of growth, many of these malformations are eliminated. It should be noted that children without malformations are found only among the prosperous classes and in a rather small percentage (12 per cent.).

Accordingly, social conditions bring about a difference not only in robustness, stature, etc., but also in the degree of beauty which the individual is likely to attain. The social ideal of the establishment of justice for all mankind is consequently at the same time a *moral* and *æsthetic* ideal.

Another parallel that it is interesting to draw is that between the most unfortunate social class (the working class) and the degenerates. We have seen that the working class has the highest individual number of stigmata. Rossi compares them with two other categories of persons who are strongly suspected of being degenerates, or who at least must include a notable proportion of degenerates among their number, namely, *beggars,* as regards the adults, and *orphans,* as regards the children.

These classes differ in the general frequency of malformations; in fact, the chronic anomalies, taken collectively, give 17 per cent. for the labouring class and 25 per cent. for beggars. But the difference becomes strikingly apparent when we come to consider the *individual number* of stigmata.

Anomalies	Labourers (per cent.)	Beggars (per cent.)
3–4	31	41
5–6	9	21.3

And still greater is the difference between the children of labourers and the orphan children.

FREQUENCY OF ANOMALIES IN CHILDREN (PERCENTAGE)

Anomalies	Labouring class, pauperism	Orphans, degeneration
Cranial anomalies in general	32	39
Forehead very low	16	20.8
Alveolar prognathism	4	10
Enlarged mandible	20	25
Plagiocephaly	16	45.8
Prominent cheek-bones	16	41.6
Facial asymmetry	28	35.4
Anomalies of teeth	24	37.5

We see therefore that *degeneration* exerts a most notable influence upon morphological anomalies; it is far more serious than external (social) conditions.

Dr. Ales Hrdlicka, studying the distribution of malformations and deformations among poor children who were inmates of a large New York orphan asylum (634 males and 274 females) distinguishes the morphological anomalies into three categories: Those that are congenital (degeneration); those acquired through pathological causes (diseases), and those acquired through the circumstances of social adaptment, or, as the author expresses it, through *habit.* And to these he adds still another category of stigmata the causes of which remain uncertain.

If we examine the following extremely interesting table, we see at once that in the case of children the anomalies of form are associated with *degeneration* and with *disease,* because the anomalies *acquired* individually by the child as the result of personal habits are comparatively so few in number as to be quite negligible, and all of them are exclusively in reference to the trunk; in other words, a result of the position assumed on school benches.

As between degeneration and disease, the proportion of anomalies caused by the former is considerably more than double. Hence, the great majority of malformations have their origin, so to speak, *outside of the individual,* the responsibility resting on the parents.

Organs in regard to which the anomalies occur	Anomalies							
	Males				Females			
	Congenital	Pathological	Acquired through habit	Cause uncertain	Congenital	Pathological	Acquired through habit	Cause uncertain
Head		74		15		26		10
Periosteum					1			
Hair	26	2		1	17			
Forehead	15	25		1	1	8		1
Face	51	68		10	11	17		4
Eyes				15				6
Ears	221				88			
Teeth	67	20		37	19	4		27
Gums	51	7		104	41	3		23
Palate	88	59		81	30	40		44
Uvula	14			112	6			54
Body (bust)	5	54	72	2	3	18	9	1
Limbs	60	14		11	39	4		3
Genital organs	275	1		1				
Totals	873	324	72	390	256	120	9	173
Percentage	40	10	4	18	45	21	1	30

The greatest number of anomalies due to degeneration occur in connection with the *ear*, and the *genital organs*, and next in order come those of the *palate*, the *teeth* and the *limbs*. The maximum number of anomalies due to *pathological causes* are in connection with the *head*, and principally with the *face;* after that, with the *palate*, and then with the *bust.*

The anomalies most difficult to diagnose seem to be those relating to the gums, the palate and the uvula, in regard to which it is not easy to determine whether they are due to degeneration or to disease.

In order that we may have a clear understanding regarding *malformations*, it is well to insist upon still another point: Malformation does not signify *deviation* from a type of ideal beauty, but from *normality.*

Now, there are normal forms which are very far from beautiful and which are associated with race. For instance, prognathism, ultra-dolichocephaly, a certain degree of flat-foot, prominent cheek-bones, the Mongolian eye, etc., are all of them characteristics which are regarded by us as the opposite of beautiful, but they are normal in certain races (therefore practical experience is indispensable). These principles which, when thus announced, are perfectly clear, must be extended far enough to include that sum total of individuals whom we are in the habit of calling *our race.* That we are hybrids, still showing more or less trace of the racial stocks which originally concurred in our formation, is well known, but not clearly enough. The *primitive races* are more or less evident in different centres of population; for instance, in the large and promiscuous cities, hybridism tends more or less completely, to *mask* the *types* of race, producing individual uniformity through an intermixture of characteristics that renders all the people very much alike (civilised races). These are the individuals who form the majority of the population, and whom we are in the habit of regarding as being *normally formed.* But when we get away from the big centres it may happen, and indeed does happen, that the primitive racial forms or types become more apparent; thus, for example, I found in Latium almost pure racial types at Castelli Romani (dolichocephalics, brunette type, short stature), and at Orte (brachycephalics, blond type, tall stature); the nuclei of population at Castelli were especially pure. Now, as a result of a highly particularised series of observations I found *normal forms that were not beautiful* in each of these races; thus, for example, in the brunette race, while the face is extremely beautiful and delicate, the hands are coarse, the feet show a tendency toward flat-foot, the breasts are pear-shaped, pendent and abundantly hairy; in the blond type, on the contrary, while the facial lineaments are coarse and quite imperfect, the hands, feet and breasts are marvellously beautiful.

Accordingly, the marks of beauty are distributed in nature among the *different races;* there is no race in existence that is wholly beautiful, just as there is no individual in existence who is perfect in all his parts.

Furthermore, since there is for every separate characteristic a long series of individual variations, both *above* and *below* (see chapters on *Biometry* and *Statistical Methodology*), it is very easy to assume that we are on the track of a malformation, when it is really a matter of racial characteristic. And this is all the more likely to constitute a source of error, because the school of Lombroso promulgated the morphological doctrine that a degenerate sometimes shows an *exaggeration* of ethnical characteristics.

Thus, for example, we meet with ultra-brachycephalics and ultra-dolichocephalics among the criminal classes.

Let us suppose that a teacher who has made a study of anthropology receives an appointment in one or another of the Castelli Romani. Among the *normal* individuals studied by me, certain ones showed a cephalic index *of* 70. Now, a teacher accustomed to *examine* the crania of city children and to find that the limits range more or less closely around mesaticephaly, would be led to assume that he was in the presence of an *abnormal* individual.

Now, in the places where morphological characteristics of race are most persistent, the *social forms* are primitive, and so also are the sentiments, the customs and the *ethical level,* because *purity of race* means an absence of hybridism, *i.e.,* an absence of intimate communication with human society evolving in the flood-tide of civilisation. Consequently, in addition to the above-mentioned characteristic (ultra-dolichocephaly), the individual would probably show an intellectual inferiority, an inferiority of the ethical sense, etc., and this would serve to strengthen the teacher's first impression. But the normal *limits of growth* for a given age, the absence of real and actual malformations (for instance, in this case there is probability of facial beauty, etc.), would cause him very quickly to correct his first judgment with a more thoughtful diagnosis. Therefore a study of local ethnical characteristics would be very useful as a basis for pedagogical anthropology, as I have tried to show in one of my works (*Importanza della etnologia regionale nell'antropologia pedagogica,* "The importance of regional ethnology in pedagogical anthropology").

And this also holds good for the interpretation of true malformations.

We have hitherto been guided in our observation of so-called *stigmata* by analytical criteria, that is, we have been content with determining the single or manifold malformations in the individual without troubling ourselves to determine their *morphological genesis* or their *genesis of combination.*

For example, the *ogival palate* is a well-known anomaly of form, but in all probability it will occur in an individual whose family has the *high and narrow palate* that is met with, for instance, as the normal type among the dolichocephalics of Latium; the same may be said in regard to flat-foot, etc. Multifold diastemata and macrodontia will, on the contrary, be more easily met with in families whose palate is wide and low (brachycephalics). And just as certain normal forms or characteristics are found in combination in a single individual (for instance, brachycephaly, fair hair, tall stature, etc.), so it is also in the case of stigmata, which will be found occurring together in one individual, not *by chance,* but according to the laws of morphological combination, and probably as an *exaggeration* of (unlovely) characteristics which belong, as normal forms, to the family or race.

There are already a number of authorities on neuropathology, De Sanctis among others, who have noted that there is an *ugly family type* which sometimes reproduces itself in a sickly member of the family, in such a way as to exaggerate pathologically the unlovely but normal characteristics of the other members, and furthermore, that an exaggeration of unlovely characteristics may increase from generation to generation, accompanied by a disintegration of the psychic personality.

Consequently, a knowledge of the morphological characteristics which in all probability belong to the races from which the subjects to be examined are derived, has a number of important aspects. The literature of anthropology is certainly not rich in *racial* studies, consequently, I feel that it will not be unprofitable to summarise in the following table the characteristics that distinguish the two racial types encountered by me among the female population of Latium.

TABLE OF THE DIFFERENTIAL CHARACTERISTICS OF THE TWO RACIAL TYPES

Brunette Dolichocephalics and Blond Brachycephalics

Organs to which the characteristics refer	Dolichocephalic, brunette type of low stature	Brachycephalic, blond type of tall stature
Visage	Elongated ellipsoidal or ovoidal; fine, delicate lineaments, rounded curves, softly modeled.	Rounded, broad; coarse features; contour frequently angular, especially around the cheek-bones.
Eyes	Large, usually almond-shaped; pigmentation brown, shading from black to chestnut.	Not so large, the form frequently tending to the oblique; the contours of the inner angle of the eye less clear-cut, owing to the plica epicantica. Pigmentation light gray, blue.
Nose	Very leptorrhine; nostrils delicate and mobile.	Leptorrhine, tending toward mesorrhine; sometimes the nose is fleshy, nostrils thick and slightly movable only.
Mouth	Labial aperture small, lips finely modeled and very red.	Labial aperture wide, lips frequently fleshy, and not well modeled.
Teeth	Small, with curved surface, gleaming, almost as wide as long, not greatly dissimilar, "like equal pearls."	Teeth large and flat, enamel dull; difference between incisors, canines, etc., sharply marked.
Palate	Very high and narrow (ogival).	Flat and wide
Profile	Proopic	Platyopic
Ear	Finely modeled, small, delicate.	Often irregular, large, thick.
Frontal line of roots of hair.	Very distinct; forehead small.	Indistinct; forehead protuberant.
Neck	Long and slender, flexible	Short, more or less stocky
Thorax	Flattened in antero-posterior direction.	Projecting forward

TABLE OF THE DIFFERENTIAL CHARACTERISTICS OF THE TWO RACIAL TYPES.—*Continued*

Brunette Dolichocephalics and Blond Brachycephalics

Organs to which the characteristics refer	Dolichocephalic, brunette type of low stature	Brachycephalic, blond type of tall stature
Breasts............	Position low, form tending to pear-shape; nipples slightly raised, auerole broad; often hairy between the breasts.	Position high, breasts round; nipple prominent, aureole small and rose-colored; always hairless.
Pelvis and abdomen.	High and narrow; the abdomen becomes prominent toward the thirtieth year, even in unmarried women.	Low and broad; the abdomen does not become prominent.
Lumbar curve......	Slightly pronounced; position of buttocks low.	Quite pronounced; position of buttocks high.
Limbs..............	Distal port on slightly shorter (as compared with the proximal); limbs slender.	Distal portion slightly longer (as compared with the proximal); limbs well endowed with muscles.
Hands.............	Coarse; palm long and narrow; fingers short.	Delicate, palm broad, fingers long.
Fingers............	Short, thick, with flattened extremities; nails flat, not very pink nor very transparent.	Long, tapering; nails with deep placed quicks, rosy and shining.
Palmar and digital papillæ	Coarse; frequently with geometric figures on the finger tips; pallid.	Very fine, rosy, and with open designs.
Feet..............	Big; form tending to flatness...	Small, much arched..........
Body as a whole....	Slender; slight muscularity. Tendency toward stoutness in old age with deformation of the body.	Beautiful; strong muscles. No tendency toward too much flesh. Furthermore, the body preserves its contours.
Complexion........	Brunette and dark...........	White.......................
Color of hair.......	Black to chestnut............	Blond.......................
Form of hair.......	Short, always wavy or curly, fine with ellipsoidal section.	Long, straight, section slightly elliptical, and sometimes almost round.
Hair on body.......	Growth of hair sometimes found on thorax and on the legs.	The surface of the body is hairless.

The Origin of Malformations during Development.—Malformations are a morphological index, and we have already shown that there is a relation between the physical and the psychical personality. A defective physical development tells us that the psychic personality must also have its defects (especially in regard to the intelligence).

Not only degenerates, but even we normal beings, in the conflict of social life, and because of our congenital weaknesses, have felt that we were losing, or that we were failing to acquire the rich possibilities latent in our consciousness, and that vainly formed the height of our ambition. And when this occurred, the body also lost something of the beauty which it might have attained, or rather, it lacked the power to develop it. In the words of Rousseau, "Our intellectual gifts, our vices, our virtues, and consequently our characters, are all dependent upon our organism."

Nevertheless, this interrelation must be understood in a very wide sense, and is modified according to the period of embryonal or extrauterine life at which a lesion or a radical disturbance in development chances to occur. In a treatise entitled *The Problems of Degeneration*, in which the most modern ideas regarding degeneration are summed up, and new standards of social morality advocated, Brugia gives a most graphic diagram, which I take the liberty of reproducing.

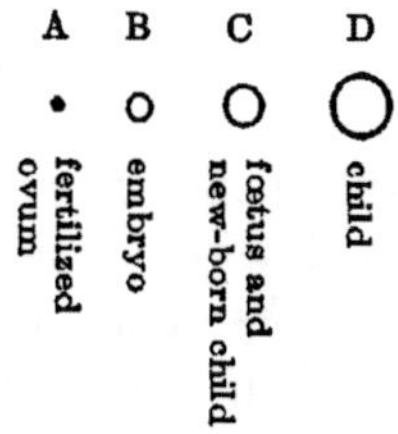

From the little black point to the big circle are represented the different stages of embryonal and fœtal development, until we reach the child. In A we have the fertilized ovum. Here it may be said that the new individual does not yet exist; we are at a transition point between two adults (the parents) and a new organism, which is *about to develop.* Now comes the embryo, which may be called the new individual in a *potential* state; then the fœtus, in which the human form is at last attained; and lastly the child, which will proceed onward toward the physical and spiritual conquests of human life. But so long as an individual has not completely developed, deviations may occur in his development; but these will be just so much the graver, in proportion as the individual is in a more plastic state.

We should reserve the term *degeneration*, real and actual, to that which presupposes an alteration at A, *i.e.*, at the time of conception. An alteration all the graver if it antedates A, that is to say, if it preexisted in the ovum and in the fertilizing spermatozoon, *i.e.*, in the parents. In this case, there is no use in talking of a direct educative and prophylactic intervention on behalf of the individual resulting from this conception; the intervention must be directed toward all adult individuals who have attained the power of procreation. And in this consists the greatest moral problem of our times—sexual education and the sentiment of responsibility toward the species. All mankind ought to feel the *responsibility* toward the posterity which they are preparing to procreate and they ought to lead a life that is hygienic, sober, virtuous, and serene, such as is calculated to preserve intact the treasures of the immortality of the species. There exist whole families of degenerates, whose offspring are precondemned to swell the ranks of moral monsters. These individuals, who result from a *wrongful conception*, carry within them malformations of the kind known as degenerative, and together with them alterations of the moral sense that are characteristic of degenerates, that is to say, they will be unbalanced (through inheritance) in their entire personality.

Something similar will happen if such a lesion befalls the embryo, *i.e.*, while the individual is still in the potential state (lacking human form). In the fœtus, on the contrary, *i.e.*, the individual who has attained the human form but is still in the course of intrauterine development, any possible lesion, and more especially those due to pathological causes, while they cannot alter the entire personality, may injure that which is already formed, and in so violent a manner as to produce a *physical monster*, whose deformities may even be incompatible with life (*e.g.*, cleft spine or palate, hydrocephaly, Little's disease, which is a form of paralysis of fœtal origin, and all the teratological (*i.e.*, monstrous) alterations). That is to say, in going from A to C we pass from *malformations* to *deformations;* from simple physical alterations of an æsthetic nature to physical monstrosities sometimes incompatible with life itself; while in regard to the psychic life, we find that the remoter lesions (in A) result for the most part in anomalies of the moral sense, while those occurring later (B, C) result for the most part in anomalies of the intellect. So that at one extreme we may have moral monsters, with malformations whose significance can be revealed only through observation guided by science and at the other extreme, physical monsters, whose moral sense is altered only slightly or not at all. Those who suffer injury at A may be intelligent, and employ their intelligence to the malevolent ends inspired by moral madness; those who suffer injury at C or D are harmless monsters, often idiots, or even foredoomed to die. The peril to society steadily diminishes from A to C, while the peril to the individual steadily augments.

Over all these periods so full of peril to human development and so highly important for the future of the species, we may place one single word:

Woman.—Throughout the period that is most decisive for its future, humanity is wholly *dependent upon woman.* Upon her rests not only the responsibility of preserving the integrity of the germ, but also that of the embryonal and fœtal development of man.

The respect and protection of woman and of maternity should be raised to the position of an inalienable social duty and should become one of the principles of human morality.

To-day we are altogether lacking in a sense of moral obligation toward the species, and hence lacking in a moral sense such as would lead to respect for woman and maternity—so much so, indeed, that we have invented a form of *modesty* which consists in concealing maternity, in not speaking of maternity! And yet at the same time there are sins against the species that go unpunished, and offenses to the dignity of woman that are tolerated and protected by law!

But even after the child is born and has reached the period of lactation, we should still write across it the words *Woman* and *Mother*. The education and the responsibility of woman and of society must be modified, if we are to assure the triumph of the species. And the teachers who receive the child into the school, after its transit through society (in the form of its parents' germs) and through the mother, cannot fail to be interested in raising the social standards of education and morality. Like a priesthood of the new humanity, they should feel it their duty to be *practitioners* of all those virtues which assure the survival of the human species.

Moral and Pedagogic Problems within the School.—Children when they first come to school have a personality already outlined. From the unmoral, the sickly, the intellectually defective to the robust and healthy children, the intelligent, and those in whom are hidden the glorious germs of genius; from those who sigh over the discomforts of wretchedness and poverty to those who thoughtlessly enjoy the luxuries of life; from the lonely hearted orphan to the child pampered by the jealous love of mother and grandmother:—they all meet together in the same school.

It is quite certain that neither the spark of genius nor the blackness of crime originated in the school or in the pedagogic method! More than that, it is exceedingly probable that the extreme opposite types passed unnoticed, or nearly so, in that environment whose duty it is to prepare the new generations for social adaptation. From this degree of blindness and unconsciousness the school will certainly be rescued by means of the scientific trend which pedagogy is to-day acquiring through the *study of the pupil.* That the teacher must assume the new task of *repairing* what is wrong with the child, through the aid of the physician, and of protecting the normal child from the dangers of enfeeblement and deformation that constantly overhang him, thus laying the foundations for a splendid human race, *free to attain* its foreordained development—all this we have already pointed out, and space does not permit us to expand the argument further.

But, in conclusion, there is one more point over which I wish to pause. If the Lombrosian theory rests upon a basis of truth, what attitude should we pedagogists take on the question of moral education? We are impotent in the face of the fact of the interrelation between physical and moral deformity. Is it then no longer a sin to do evil and no longer a merit to do good? No. But we have only to alter the *interpretation* of the facts, and the result is a high moral progress pointing a new path in pedagogy. There are, for example, certain individuals who feel themselves irresistibly attracted toward evil, who become inebriated with blood; there are others, on the contrary, who faint at the mere sight of blood and have a horror of evil. There are some who feel themselves naturally impelled to do good, and they do it in order to satisfy a personal desire (many philanthropists) thus deriving that pleasure which springs from the satisfaction of any natural need. In our eyes, all these individuals who act instinctively, though in opposite ways, deserve neither praise nor blame; they were born that way; one of them is physiologically a proletarian, the other is a capitalist of normal human ability. It is a question of birth. When the educator praised the one and punished the other, he was sanctioning the necessary effects of causes that were unknown to him:

> "But still, whence cometh the intelligence
> Of the first notions man is ignorant,
> And the affection of the first allurements
> Which are in you as instinct in the bee
> To make its honey; and this first desire
> Merit of praise or blame containeth not."
> (DANTE, *Longfellow's Translation.*)

The instinctive malefactor is not to blame, the blame should rest rather upon his parents who gave him a bad heredity; but these parents were in their turn victims of the social causes of degeneration. The same thing may be said if a pathological cause comes up for consideration in relation, for instance, to certain anomalies of character.

Analogously, he who is born good and instinctively does good deeds, deriving pleasure from them, deserves no praise. There is no vainer sight than is afforded by a person of this sort, living complacently in the contemplation of himself, praised by everyone, and to all practical intent, held up as a contrast to the evil actions of the degenerate and the diseased who act from instinct no more nor less than he does himself. The man who is born physiologically a capitalist assumes high moral obligations; he ought to discipline his nature as a normal man in order to make it serve the general good. And this is not to be accomplished through an *instinct* to do good, which acts at haphazard, but through the *deliberate will* to do good, even if the requisite actions bring no immediate satisfaction, but even involve a sacrifice. Society will be ameliorated and rendered moral through the harmonious efforts of good men, trained for the social welfare. Man will become good only when his goodness costs him a voluntary effort.

Hence it will be necessary not to limit ourselves, as has been done in the past, to admiring the man who is born good, but to educate him so as to render him thoughtful, strong and useful; not to condemn the sinner, but to redeem him through education and through a sense of fellowship in the common fault, which is the scientific form of pardon. The degenerate, who succeeds in conquering his sinful instinct and in ceasing to do harm, the normal man who renders himself morally sublime by dedicating his splendid physiological inheritance to the collective good, will be equally meritorious. But what a moral abyss gapes open to divide them! Because it is a short stride at best that the physiological proletariat can take, while for the soul of the normal man an untrammelled pathway lies open toward perfection.

Accordingly the new task of the teacher of the future is a multifold one. He is the artificer of human beauty, the new modeler of created things, just as the sublime chisel of Greek art was the modeler of marbles. And he prepares for greater utilisation the physiological and intellectual forces of the new man, like a Greek deity scattering broadcast his prolific riches.

But above all he prepares the souls for the sublime sentiment which awaits the humanity of the future, glorying in the attainment of peace, and then indeed he becomes almost a redeemer of mankind.

CHAPTER VII

TECHNICAL PART

In a book the technical part can serve only to point the way, because the acquirement of technique demands *practical experience.*

The technique of anthropology consists, essentially, of two principal branches: 1. the gathering of anthropological data by means of measurements (anthropometry) and by inspection (anthroposcopy); 2. the formulation of laws based on these anthropological data.

Anthropometry requires a knowledge: a. of anthropometric instruments; b. of the anatomical points of contact to which the instruments must be applied.

For beginners it will be found helpful to mark upon the subject the anthropometric points of contact by means of a dermographic pencil.

In anthropology so large a number of measurements are taken, both from life and from skeletons, that a minute description of them all would demand a separate treatise. We shall limit ourselves to indicating such measurements as it has been found of *practical utility* to take in school.

The Form

In the theoretic part of this work we emphasized the word *form,* representing the body as a whole and embodying the conception of relationship between the proportions of the body, tending to determine the morphological individuality.

From the normal point of view the two individualities which are most interesting and worthy of comparison are those of the *new-born child* and the *adult* (see Fig. 140 and its eloquent testimony). In these two individualities the greatest possible prominence is given to those differences of proportion between bust and limb on which all the various measurements of the form depend: the *standing and sitting stature; the total spread of the arms;* the *weight;* the *circumference of the thorax* (see "Theoretic Lessons on the Form"). With the theory recalled to mind we may now pass on to the *practical procedure for obtaining these various measures.* Among them the most important is the *stature,* whose cycle is represented in Fig. 141. The theoretic section of this book devotes special attention to the stature in a separate chapter following that on the Form. It is well to have in mind the general principals before taking up the technique of the separate measurements.

Stature.—The stature is the distance intervening between the plane on which the individual stands in an erect position and the top of his head.

Technical Procedure.—It is necessary to know how to place the subject in an erect position, heels together and toes turned

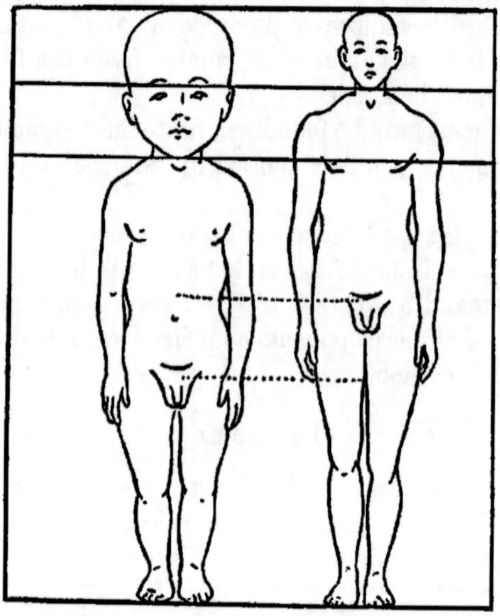

FIG. 140.—*New-born child* and *adult man* reduced to the same height and preserving their relative bodily proportions. The head of the new-born child is twice the height of that of the adult and extends downward to the level of the latters's nipples. The pubes of the adult correspond to the navel of the new-born child; and the pubes of the child to the middle of the adult's thigh.

out, shoulders square, arms pendent, head orientated, *i.e.*, occipital point touching the wall, gaze horizontal).

In measuring the individual stature it is customary to use an instrument called an anthropometer (Fig. 142).

It consists of a horizontal board on which the subject stands, a stationary vertical rod marked with the metric scale against which the subject rests his back, and another small movable rod perpendicular to the first and projecting forward from it; this is

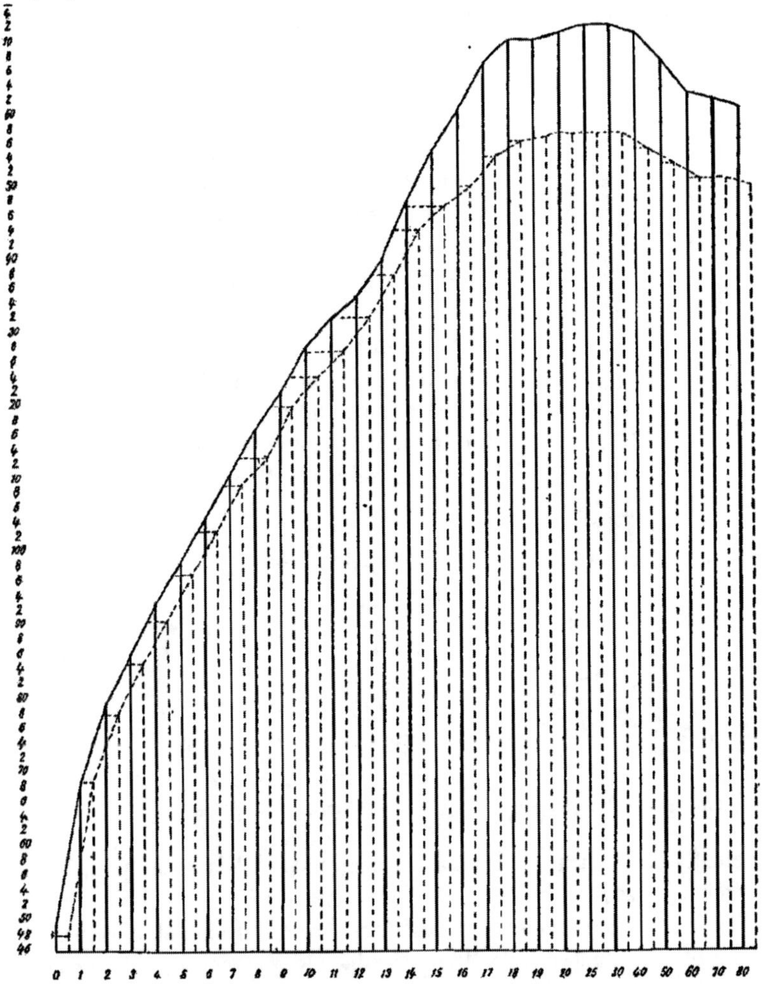

FIG. 141.—Diagram representing the cycle of stature of man (unbroken line) and woman (dotted line), from birth to the end of life.

lowered until it is tangent to the apex of the cranium; and the scale upon the upright rod gives the number corresponding to the stature.

Certain anthropologists are now trying to perfect the anthropometer (Mosso's school). And, indeed, how is it possible to bring the entire person posteriorly in contact with the vertical rod of the anthropometer? The rod is straight while the body follows the curves of the vertebral column and the gluteus muscles. Accordingly, Professor Monti, an assistant to Professor Mosso, has proposed a new anthropometer which, in place of the single rod at the back, has a pair of rods, so that the more prominent portions of the body may occupy the intermediate space; a similiar anthropometer was already in use for measuring kyphotics.

At the present day there are exceedingly complicated and accurate anthropometers which comprise, in addition, instruments for obtaining various other measurements, such as the thoracic and cephalic perimeters, etc. But these are very costly and not practical for use in schools. Their use is confined

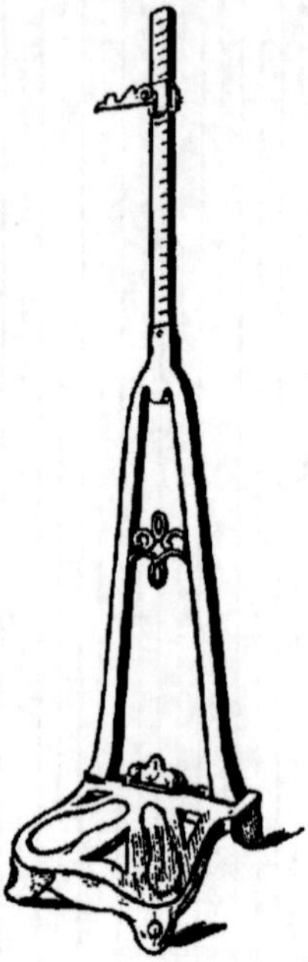

Fig. 142.—Anthropometer.

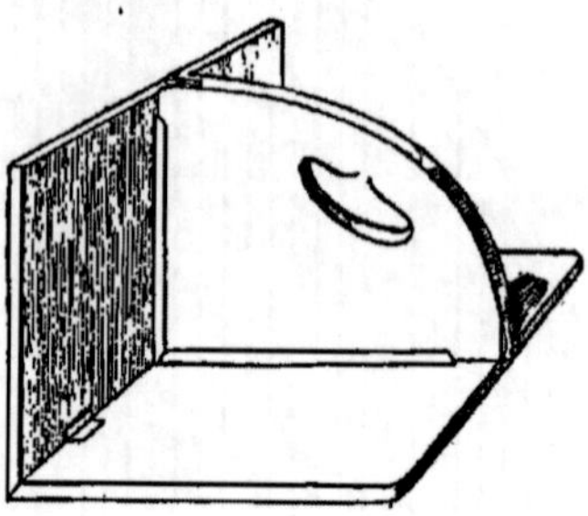

Fig. 143.—A square.

chiefly to medical clinics, as, for example, Viola's anthropometer, which is used in Professor De Giovanni's clinic.

Broca recommends to travelers an anthropometer consisting of a graduated rod with a movable index attached. By means of this a series of distances from the ground can be measured, and consequently various partial heights of the body, from the ground to the top of the head, from the ground to the chin, to the pubis, to the knee, etc., but grave errors may be committed and its use is not advisable so long as we have within reach a universal anthropometer.

The universal anthropometer consists essentially of two planes perpendicular to each other; now we may say that in every room, in the meeting of two planes, the floor and the wall, we have an anthropometer. There is no reason why we should not make use of this simple means! Placing the child in an erect position with the body touching the wall throughout its whole length, we place a perfectly horizontal rod tangent to the top of the head, we make a mark upon the wall, and then with a millimetric measure we take the distance between the mark and the floor, and this gives us the stature. Two difficulties are met with, first, that of holding the rod horizontally on the top of the head, and secondly, that of measuring the distance in a perfectly vertical line. In the first difficulty a carpenter's square may help us or, if there is a school of manual training within convenient reach it is easy to have a little instrument constructed (Fig. 143) consisting of two planes perpendicular to each other, one of which should be held tangent to the head while the other is pressed against the wall (carpenter's square).

As regards the vertical measurement, a plumb line may be used, but it is more practical to trace upon the wall that we mean to use for such measurements, a design consisting of a vertical line on which a mark may be made at the height of one metre from the floor in order to simplify the task of measuring.

It is better if the millimetric tape is made of metal, so that it will not vary in length; but even a tailor's measure of waxed tape may answer the purpose if it is new and has been tested with a metallic measure or an accurate metre rule.

The height of the stature is taken *without the shoes*, and it is necessary to state at what hour of the day the measurement is made, because in the morning we are taller (though by only a few millimetres) than we are in the evening. The stature may also be taken in a recumbent position (length of body), and in this case will be longer by about one centimetre.

Consequently in giving the measure of stature it is necessary to state in what position the subject was placed, by what method the measurement was taken (whether with an anthropometer or not) and at what hour of the day the measurement was made.

It is not necessary to say that the subject was required to remove his shoes, since that is taken for granted.

Sitting Stature.—Besides the stature taken on foot, the sitting stature (height of bust) is also taken by an analogous process.

It is the distance between the plane on which the individual is seated and the vertex of his head. The subject should be seated upon a wooden bench having a horizontal plane and should place his back in contact with the wall; just as in the case of the preceding measure the shoes had to be removed, in the present case the clothing is discarded, leaving only the light underwear (Fig. 144). With the aid of the square we find the point corresponding to the vertex of the head and with the millimetric measure we obtain the distance on the wall between this point and the plane of the bench.

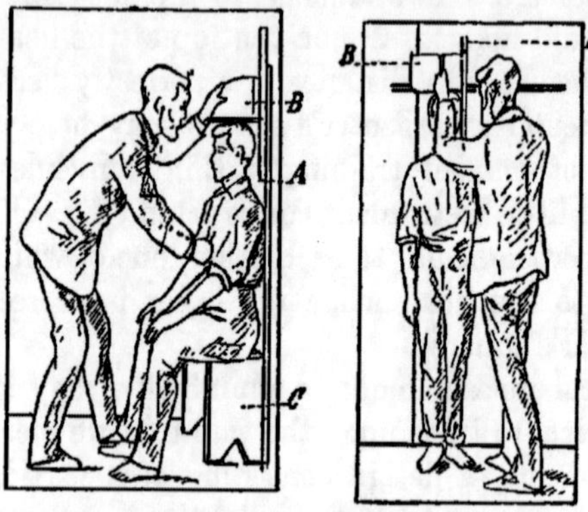

FIG. 144.—(1) Sitting stature. (2) Standing stature. (Method of taking measurements with the Anthropometer.)

Index of Stature.—We know that these two measures are extremely important for ascertaining the type of stature, *i.e.*, *macroscelia* and *brachyscelia*, determined by the proportion between the sitting stature and the total stature reduced to a scale of 100, that is, the relation of the bust to the total height of the individual. Let us remember in this connection that the bust should be a 52d or 53d part of the total stature and that below 52 down to 50, it is macroscelous, and that above 53, up to 55, it is brachyscelous.

Having obtained the two numbers corresponding to the two statures, *e.g.*, stature 1.60 m., bust 0.85 m., how are we to find out the percentual relation between the two measurements? First, we form an equation: $85:160 = x:100$.

$$\text{from which we obtain } x = \frac{100 \times 85}{160} = 53$$

This stature is of the normal average type, that is, it is mesatiscelous; but the mesatiscelia is high (in comparison with the other measurement that is also mesatiscelous, namely, 52), in other words, it is *brachy-mesatiscelous*.

Note the formula which gives us the value of x. If we substitute general symbols in place of the concrete values, we may say that x is equal to one hundred times the lesser measurement (m) divided by the greater measurement (M). If, in place of x, we substitute I, signifying index, we may draw up the following general formula of indices:

$$I = \frac{100 \times m}{M}$$

This formula of relations between measurements is of wide application in anthropology and is fundamental. Indices of every measurement are sought for. The one given above is the index of stature, and it determines the *type* of stature. All the other indices are calculated by similiar procedure.

Total Spread of the Arms.—This measurement is taken quite simply. The subject must place himself with his arms outstretched in a horizontal direction and on a level with his shoulders. The measurement corresponds to the distance intervening in a horizontal line from the tip of one middle finger to the other (Fig. 145). A specially constructed anthropometer may be used for this measurement. It has a long horizontal rod adjustable perpendicularly, so that it may be placed on a level with the shoulders of the subject to be measured. This rod forms a cross with the other vertical rod with which the subject should be in contact. The arms are then extended along the cross rod which is marked with a millimetric scale. But this greatly complicates the anthropometer, and hardly any anthropometer possesses this attachment. This measure may be successfully taken with the very simple aid of the wall. The only difficulty offered is that of securing a perfectly horizontal position for the arms. For this purpose horizontal lines, which either happen by chance to be upon the wall or which may be drawn on purpose, will be of assistance. In order to have guiding lines suited to different statures, several horizontal lines may be drawn intersecting the vertical line already traced for guidance of the millimetric tape measure used in taking the stature.

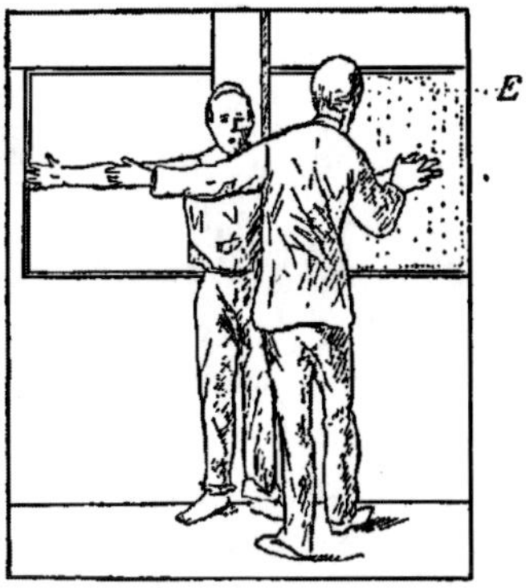

Fig. 145.—Method of measuring the total spread of arms.

Thoracic Perimeter.—The thoracic perimeter is taken on the nude thorax, in an erect position and with the arms hanging beside the bust, by applying the millimetric measure in such a way that its upper margin passes just below the nipples. The tape measure should completely encircle the thorax in a horizontal plane passing through the mammary papillæ. Since the thorax is in constant motion, we must observe the oscillations of the tape measure and obtain the average; or else we may take the measurements during the state of expiration (repose). In giving the figure it is necessary to specify the procedure followed.

Vital Index. Index of Life.—Index of life is the name given to the proportion between the stature and the thoracic perimeter. It ought to be equal to 50, *i. e.,* $Tp = \frac{S}{2}$

$$Vi = \frac{100 \times Tp}{S} = 50 \text{ (normal)}.$$

Weight.—The weight of an individual is taken by means of ordinary *scales*. In order to obtain the weight of the nude person, the clothing may be weighed separately and their weight subtracted from the total weight of the clothed person. The weight should be taken before eating, in order that unassimilated alimentary substances may not alter the real weight of the subject. If this method cannot be rigorously followed out, it should be specified how much clothing the subject retained, whether he had eaten, etc.

Ponderal Index.—Stature and weight are the most synthetic and comprehensive measurements of the form. But we need a clear proportion between these two measures to tell us whether an individual weighs more or less *relatively* to his *stature*. It may happen, for instance, that a stout person of short stature actually weighs less than another person who is tall and thin; but relatively to his stature he may on the contrary be heavier, that is, he may have a higher *ponderal index*. A robust and plump child will weigh in an absolute sense less than an adult who is extremely thin and emaciated; but relatively to the mass of his body he weighs more. Now this relative weight or index of weight (ponderal index) gives us precisely this idea of *embonpoint*, of the more or less flourishing state of nutrition in which an individual happens to be. But linear measurements such as the stature cannot be compared with volumetric measurements, such as the weight. Hence it is necessary to reduce the volumetric measure—the weight—to a linear measure, which is done by extracting the cube root from the number representing the weight. Then the root of the weight may be compared to the stature reduced to a scale of 100. By forming a general proportion, in which W represents the weight of a given individual, and S the corresponding figure of his stature, we obtain:

$$S : \sqrt[3]{W} :: 100 : x \text{ (where } x \text{ represents the ponderal index)}$$

$$\text{hence } Pi = \frac{100 \times \sqrt[3]{W}}{S}$$

The application of this formula would necessitate some rather complicated calculations, which it would be inconvenient to have to repeat for a large number of subjects.

But there are tables of calculations already compiled, which are due to Livi, and which are given, together with other tables, in Livi's own work, *Anthropometry* (Hoepli). These are numerical tables, to be read in the same manner as tables of logarithms. At the top, in a horizontal direction, the stature is given in centimetres, while in the vertical column the weight is given in kilograms. The calculation of all the ponderal indices has been worked out, in relation to every possible stature and weight. If we look up the ponderal index corresponding to the figures already cited in illustration (see p. 182), we find that for the adult the $Pi = 23.6$, and for the child the $Pi = 27.4$; *i.e.*, considered relatively the child weighs more in the given case. This is the true and accurate technical method of finding the relative proportion between weight and stature.

Accordingly, we have now learned to take all the measurements relative to the form, to calculate from them the more important indices (or proportions), such as the index of stature, the index of life, and the ponderal index. We have also learned to understand and to consult the tables of anthropological calculations.

THE CRANIUM

The Head and Cranium.—Let us bear in mind the fact that the word *head* is used in speaking of a living person, and *cranium*, of a skeleton.

The science which makes a study of the cranium is called craniology. The cranium and the head may be studied either by observing the external form—*cranioscopy* or *cephaloscopy;* or else by taking measurements—*craniometry* or *cephalometry.* Craniology makes use equally of cranioscopy and of craniometry: in fact, if cranioscopy alone were used, certain anomalies might escape attention, because we can recognise them only by measuring the head; and conversely, if we confined ourselves to craniometric researches, we might miss certain anomalies of form, which we become aware of only by attentively observing the cranium. Frequently craniometry serves to verify cranioscopy. For example, a cranium may appear to the eye too large or too small, but certainly if we measure the cranial circumference with a tape-measure we shall have an accurate decision of a case which may well be a simple optical illusion. Indeed, we all know how easy it is to give an erroneous judgment, relying only on our senses; for the personal equation enters very largely into judgments of this sort. For instance, a person of low stature easily judges that other men are tall, and *vice versa.* To the eye of the Italian or the Frenchman, the hair of young English girls is a pale blond; to the Scandinavians of the North it is a warm blond. If two men possessed of different æsthetic tastes and in different frames of mind wish to describe one and the same garden they will give two widely different descriptions which will reveal far more of their individual impressions and moods than of the actual characteristics of the garden described. It is easy to understand how important it is in scientific descriptions to exclude completely the influence of the observer's personality. In the cranioscopic study of a cranium, for instance, the precise characteristics of that cranium are what must be found and nothing else whatever, no matter who the student is nor in what part of the world he is working. But in order to achieve this result it is not enough to take observations; it is also necessary to know how to observe, and in observing to follow a scientific method.

Cranioscopy.—Cranioscopic methods require that the skull shall be observed from several sides. Blumenbach, who studied crania by observing them from the vertex, divided them into ovoid, rhomboid, etc., while Camper, on the other hand, studying them in profile, classified them as flat, elongated, etc., and the conclusions of the two scientists were irreconcilable.

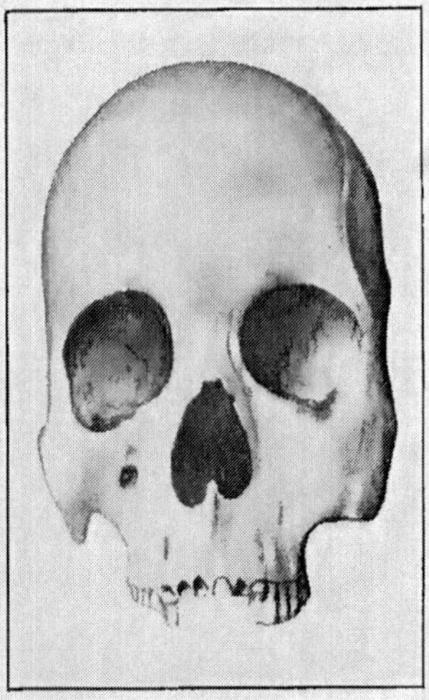

Fig. 146.—Facial norm.

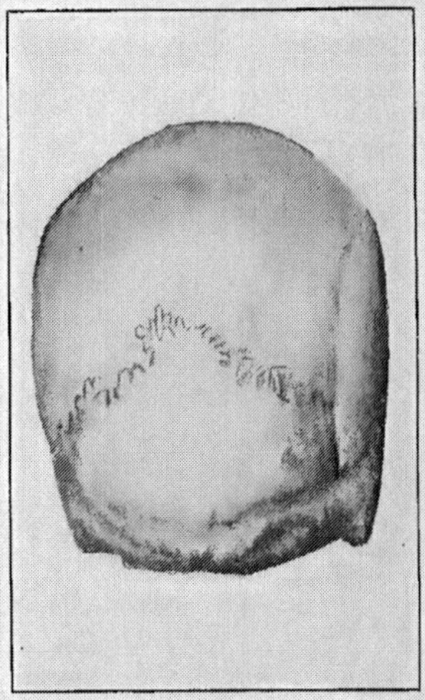

Fig. 147.—Occipital norm.

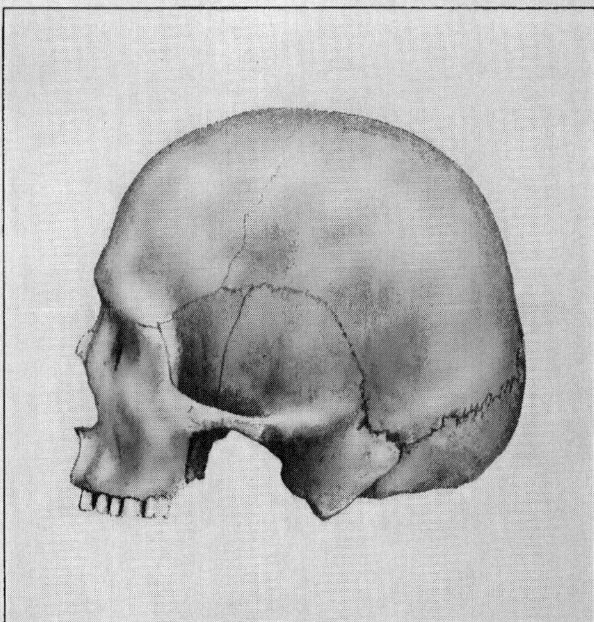

Fig. 148.—Lateral norm.

The cranium must be observed from above, from the front, in profile and from the occipital part; and in such a manner that the observer's glance shall fall perpendicularly upon whichever cranial side is under observation. Hence it is said that the observation is made according to the norm, *i.e.*, according to the perpendicular, and there are four *norms* in cranioscopy—*vertical*, *frontal*, *lateral*, and *occipital*. In this way we may be sure that no anomaly of form will escape the eye.

There are innumerable anomalies of form. We will indicate only the principal ones. In order to detect all the anomalies that may occur in a cranium it is necessary to observe it according to all the norms, each one of which may reveal a different set of anomalies.

A. *Vertical Norm.*—The word *norm*, as we have already said, has here the signification of perpendicular. To look at a cranium according to the vertical norm means to let our glance fall perpendicularly upon the vertex of the cranium. We may do this in one of two ways, either by raising our head above that of the subject of inspection, in such a way that our glance falls vertically upon it, or by bending back the head of the person to be observed until the crown of his head becomes perpendicular to our gaze. This norm is taken by placing oneself behind the person to be observed, who, if an adult, should be seated while the observer remains standing; and by taking the head to be examined between the two hands in such a way that the extended thumbs and index-fingers form a horizontal circlet around the cranial walls.

This is the most important of the norms, not only because it reveals the most important normal forms already described in the text, but also the greater number of anomalies such as are indicated below.

1. *Crania with Rectilinear Perimeter.*—It may happen that the line bounding the cranial vault is not curved but formed of broken straight lines from which various geometrical figures result, producing crania known as trigonocephalic, pentagonoid, parallelopepidoid, etc.

The most important among these and among all the abnormal forms is the trigonocephalic cranium, having the base of the triangle toward the occiput and the vertex toward the forehead. The result of such formation is that the frontal region is restricted, a circumstance of obvious gravity. The infantile cranium is normally pentagonoid; the persistence of this form in the adult is a sign of arrested development, but not serious. Sergi does not admit this form among the anomalies when the nodules are but slightly emphasised.

2. *Asymmetrical and Plagiocephalic Crania.*—The sagittal plane divides the cranium into two unequal halves. The asymmetry may be either frontal, in which case one frontal nodule is more prominent than the other—anterior plagiocephaly, or else parietal, in which case one of the parietal nodules is more prominent than the other—posterior plagiocephaly.

These are the two forms of simple plagiocephaly. It may happen that there is simultaneously an anterior and posterior asymmetry, and in such a case it generally happens that if the more prominent frontal nodule is on the right, the more prominent parietal nodule is on the left, so that the two more prominent nodules correspond in a diagonal sense. This is compound plagiocephaly.

Plagiocephaly is extremely common; if very apparent, it constitutes a grave defect, but not if only slight. For that matter, it would be difficult to find a cranium rigorously symmetrical, even among normal persons.

3. *Crania with curved and symmetrical lines*, but in which the perimeter consists not of a single ellipsoidal curve, but of two curves.

a. *Clinocephalic Cranium.*—The coronal suture has a girdle-like furrow, in such fashion that there result an anterior and a posterior curve which together form a sort of figure 8. This anomaly may be perceived also from the lateral norm.

b. *Cymbocephalic Cranium.*—There is a girdle-like furrow along the sagittal line, so that the cranium has the appearance of being divided into two pockets, one on the right hand and the other on the left.

B. *Lateral Norm.*—The observer must stand at the side of the subject to be observed and look at him perpendicularly to the profile.

We remain standing while we look if the subject is an adult and is standing up, but we sit down if the subject is a child and is standing; and we determine the vertical position by moving the subject's head as the occasion requires.

I note, as seen from this norm, two anomalies in which the ellipsoidal uniformity outlining the profile of the cranium is altered.

a. *Oxycephalic Cranium.*—The line of the profile is noticeably raised at the bregma, from which the anterior part of the cranium continues to rise, almost in the direction of the forehead, instead of curving backward. In its entirety this anomalous cranium has the form of a "sugar loaf."

b. *Acrocephalic Cranium.*—The line of the profile, on the contrary, is not raised until near the lambda.

C. *Occipital Norm.*—The observer places himself behind the subject and gazes perpendicularly at the occipital point.

D. *Frontal Norm.*—The observer stands in front of the subject and gazes at him on a level with the forehead.

I may point out only one very important anomaly seen from this norm.

a. *Scaphicephalic Cranium.*—The lateral parts of the cranium are flattened to such a degree that the vault is extremely narrow along the sagittal line (see Figs. 51 and 52).

Craniometry.—The *volume* of the cranium is of high importance because it bears a relation to that of the brain. In the studies which have been made relative to the correspondence between physical and intellectual development, the measurement of the cranial volume comes first in order.

In measuring the cranium it is necessary to use:

a. *the millimetric tape measure,* b. *the craniometric calipers,* c. *the compass with sliding branches,* d. *the double square.* In order to facilitate the task of measuring and to secure uniformity it is necessary first to locate the craniometric points to which it will be necessary to apply the instrument. These craniometric points are easily located on the cranium, where a great number of them have been studied. In the case of a living person, on the contrary, these points are reduced to a small number because of the difficulty of accurately locating them.

The points on the vault of the cranium, along the sagittal line, are:

1. The *nasion* (point of union of the nasal and frontal bones).

2. The *ophryon* (middle point of the line tangent to the two superciliary arches, a line corresponding to the horizontal drawn transversely across the forehead and passing through the two points on the temporal lines which are nearest to the median line. This point lies in an important region of the forehead, situated between the two eyebrows—the glabella. The central point of the middle region of the forehead above the glabella is called the *metopion*).

3. The *bregma* (point of juncture between the coronal and sagittal suture).

4. The *vertex.*

5. The *lambda* (point of juncture between the sagittal suture and the occipital or lambdoid suture).

6. The *occipital point.*

7. The *inion* (situated at a level midway between the occipital point and the occipital foramen).

Laterally we have these other craniometric points:

1. The *external orbital apophysis* (formed from the frontal bone).

2. The *supra-auricular point.*

3. The *auricular point* (corresponding to a little depression which may be felt just below the tragus and in correspondence with the zygomatic arches).

4. The *minimum frontal point* (a bony angle which may be felt about 1 centimetre above the external orbital apophysis, along the temporal line).

On a living person the following points can easily be located:

Along the sagittal line:

1. The *nasion.*
2. The *ophryon.*
3. The *vertex.*
4. The *occipital point.*

Laterally:

1. The *external orbital apophysis.*
2. The *supra-auricular point.*
3. The *auricular point.*
4. The *minimum frontal point.*

Now, with these points as guides it becomes practical to measure the various curves and diameters of the cranium. The curves are measured by means of the millimetric tape; the diameters by means of the calipers.

There are various curves; we shall confine ourselves to considering only the following:

The *maximum circumference*, which is obtained by passing the tape across the ophryon, the occipital points and the supra-auricular points, beginning to apply it at the ophryon. Its measure varies from 520 to 540 mm. in man and from 490 to 510 mm. in woman, if taken from the skull. In the case of a living person 20 mm. should be added.

If we find a circumference greater than normal, we are beginning to enter upon the anomaly which goes by the name of *macrocephaly.* If, on the other hand, the maximum circumference is notably smaller, we are entering upon the anomaly of *microcephaly.*

Measurement of Diameters.—Maximum Antero-posterior Diameter.—With the left hand place one branch of the calipers upon the glabella; the other extreme point is to be sought tentatively along a vertical line dividing the occiput in two halves. Partially close the calipers by means of the screw and then make trial by raising and lowering the posterior branch. It ought to move with a slight friction.

This is the classic diameter which measures the maximum length of the cranium and which, as we have seen, it is customary to compare with the width in order to obtain the cephalic index. In the adult man it normally oscillates between 170 and 180 mm.

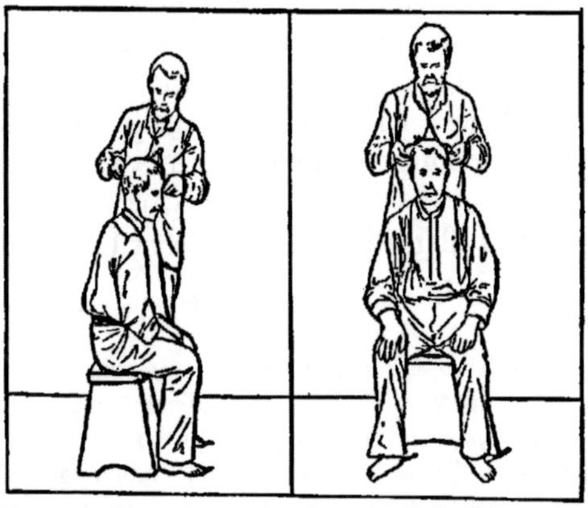

FIG. 149.—Inspecting cranium (lateral and vertical norms).

Maximum Transverse Diameter.—This measures the width of the cranium. The investigator places himself in front of the subject in order to keep the compass quite horizontal through the guidance of the eyes. The maximum distance is found by experimenting. It normally corresponds very nearly to the supra-auricular points. In children this diameter is frequently situated higher up toward the parietal nodules; in men of tall stature, in whom the cranial vault is generally slightly developed, this diameter may be found, on the contrary, lower down, near the mastoid apophyses. If this diameter occurs similiarly low down in children, a notable growth in stature may be prophesied (Manouvrier); and if inquiry is made it will be found that the parents are very tall. This diameter measures, in the adult, from 140 to 150 mm.

Vertical Diameter.—This measures the height of the cranium from the occipital foramen to the bregma. This diameter cannot be measured directly excepting on a skull; in the case of a living person its projection is taken, which, though far from accurate, is given by the distance between the vertex and the external auditory meatus.

It is necessary to use the double square. The horizontal branch is placed tangent to the vertex, its direction should be perceptibly parallel to the transverse orbital line, the graduated vertical branch should pass over the auricular foramen. The required number may be read, corresponding to the point of the tragus.

The height of the cranium is exceedingly important; its variations produce variations in the physiognomy.

In the first period of childhood, the cranium is very low in comparison to its width; this is also true of dwarfs. In these cases the width of the cranial vault is large in comparison to that of the base; a low cranium bulging above is distinctive of babies and dwarfs.

In the adult this diameter measures from 130 to 140 mm.

Among the other measurements which are taken on the cranium, the following may be cited:

The *antero-posterior metopic diameter:* from the metopic to the occipital point. In children it is sometimes the maximum longitudinal diameter.

The *ophryo-iniac diameter* from the ophryon to the inion.

The *minimum frontal diameter:* between the two minimum frontal points.

The *maximum frontal diameter:* between the two external orbital apophyses.

The *bistephanic diameter:* between the two stephanic points.

The *bitemporal diameter:* this is the greatest width of the cranium between the verticals passing through the base of the tragus.

The *biauricular diameter:* the craniometrical points are in front of, and a little below, but very near to the upper insertion of the auricle. They are little depressions that can be felt, as we have already said, by applying the finger along the upper edge of the root of the zygomatic arch.

Height of forehead: from the ophryon to the roots of the hair.

Circumferences and Curves:

Anterior Semicircle.—The tape is applied from one supra-auricular point to the other, passing through the ophryon; it corresponds to the anterior part of the maximum circumference. Manouvrier measures it in correspondence to the verticals erected from the tragus.

Posterior Semicircle.—This is obtained by subtracting the anterior semicircle from the whole circumference.

Vertical Curve of the Head.—The tape passes through a plane that is vertical to the orientated head, starting from the supra-auricular points or from the tragus, according to different authorities.

Cephalic Index.—This is the proportion between the *maximum transverse* and *longitudinal* diameters. It is obtained by applying the familiar formula:

$$Ci = \frac{100d}{D}$$

in which d represents the transverse diameter and D the longitudinal. The index represents the percentual relation between the two diameters, and is obtained from the formula by reducing the greater diameter to a scale of 100, as follows:

$$D : 100 = d : X, \textit{ whence } X = \frac{100d}{D}$$

Instead of working out the calculations, we may find the required index in the tables already compiled.

Volume.—The volume of the cranium cannot be taken directly, except in the case of a skull. After the various osseous foramina have been closed, the cranial cavity is filled through the occipital foramen with any one of a number of substances (millet, shot, water, etc.), which is afterward measured. The method of taking this measurement is practised on a facsimile of a cranium already calculated, and usually made of metal.

But in the case of a living person the direct calculation of the volume is impossible. Nevertheless various empirical methods have been sought for obtaining this measurement, even though imperfect and approximate. Recently renewed use has been made, especially in France, of an approximate calculation made by means of Broca's cubic index. The volume of the cranium is equal to half the product of the three diameters, divided by an index which varies according to age.

This index is as follows:

Adults from 25 years upward	men	1.20
	women	1.15
Young persons from 25 to 20 years	men	1.15
	women	1.10
Young persons from 20 to 16 years	men	1.10
	women	1.08
Children of both sexes	15–10 years	1.07
	10–5 years	1.06
	5 years and below	1.05

An index of cranial development is afforded by the maximum circumference. The average volume of the normal adult cranium is about 1,500 cubic centimetres: *mesocephalic cranium.*

When the cranium is much inferior in volume, it is called *microcephalic* (from 1,200 down to 700 cubic centimetres). When on the contrary it is much superior (from 1,900 up to 2,200 cubic centimetres), it is called *macrocephalic* or *megalocephalic.*

For the face, the following craniometric points should be noted:

Along a longitudinal line:

1. The *nasion* (point of meeting of the nasal and frontal bones).

2. Subnasal point (meeting of nasal septum with upper maxilla).

3. *Upper alveolar point* (between the two upper incisors at their point of insertion).

4. *Lower alveolar point* (point corresponding to the above, in the lower maxilla).

5. *Mental point* (middle point of the chin).

The following craniometric points are situated laterally.

6. *Auricular point* (corresponding to the auricular foramen; in living persons it is situated on the tragus).

7. *Malar point* (on the malar bones).

8. *Zygomatic point* (corresponding to the zygomatic arches).

9. Gonion or goniac point (angle of mandible).

The face also may be studied by inspection—*prosoposcopy;* and by measurement—*prosopometry.*

Prosoposcopy.—We proceed to inspection according to two norms: A. facial norm; B. lateral norm or norm of profile.

A. *Facial Norm.*—If it is a question of a living person, we make complete inspection of the visage, from the roots of the hair to the chin. First of all we direct attention to the forehead, which will give us an index of the development of the anterior region of the brain; next, we observe whether a plane passing longitudinally through the median line would divide the face into two equal halves (facial symmetry).

From an æsthetic point of view, the three following vertical distances ought to correspond in length:

Height of forehead (from the roots of the hair to the nasion).

Length of nose (from the nasion to the subnasal point).

Labio-mental height (from the subnasal point to the point of the chin). And in regard to width the three following horizontal distances ought, according to the æsthetic laws of art, *very nearly* to correspond (especially in the female face):

Width of forehead, between the two external orbital points.

Bimalar width, between the two malar points.

Bigoniac width, between the two gonia.

It should be remembered that the standards of *beauty* do not necessarily coincide with those of *normality*.

B. *Lateral Norm.*—In observing the face according to this norm, three facts should be chiefly noted:

1. The relative volumetric development between facial and cerebral cranium.

2. The direction of the forehead, which, in the normal profile, ought to be vertical.

3. Whether the facial profile protrudes or not beyond the extreme anterior limit of the forehead.

Prosopometry.—Many forms of measurements are taken on the skeleton of the face and many total and partial indices are obtained, such, for instance, as the facial index, the orbital index, the nasal index, etc.

Measurements of diameters and angles are also taken on the face of the living subject and indices are obtained.

We, however, shall limit ourselves to indicating only those measurements which are taken most frequently in our special field of application.

The diameters and the height of the face are obtained by the *craniometric calipers* and *Mathieu's compass with sliding branches;* the facial angle is measured in projection by means of the *double square;* and directly, by the *goniometer.*

One mode of measuring the facial angle in projection is that of drawing the facial profile with the help of special instruments; or else of taking a photograph in perfect profile and tracing and measuring the facial angle on the picture.

Principal Linear Measurements:

Total length of visage: from line of hair root to point of chin.

Total length of face: from the nasion to the point of the chin.

Length of the nose: from the nasion to the sub-nasal point.

Height of mandible: from the upper edge of the lower incisors to the lower edge of mandible.

Subnase-mental height: from the subnasal point to the point of the chin.

Bizygomatic diameter: between the two bizygomatic arches.

Bimalar diameter: between the two malar points.

Bigoniac diameter: between the two gonia.

Biorbital diameter: between the two external borders of the orbits.

Gonio-mental distance: from the goniac point to the point of the chin.

Auriculo-frontal radius: from the tragus or from the auricular point to the ophryon.

Auriculo-subnasal radius.

Auriculo-mental radius.

(The last four measurements, if compared right and left, give an index of facial *symmetry;* the radii when compared together serve as an indirect measure of prognathism.)

Width of nose between the external borders of the nostrils (the branches of Mathieu's compass are placed tangent to the nostrils).

(The index of the nose is obtained from the length and breadth, by applying the well-known formula of indices; the nose thereupon receives various names—leptorrhine, mesorrhine, platyrrhine).

Width of orbit: from the inner extremity of the ocular *rima* (eye-slit) to the external border of the orbit.

Width of the ocular rima: between the two extremities of the *rima.*

Width of the labial rima: between the two extremities of the *rima.*

Length of the ear: from the highest upper edge of the auricle to the lower extremity of the lobule.

Index of the ear: this is obtained, by the well-known formula, from the length and breadth. The normal index is 50; the types of ear above 50 are *low* types.

Anthropologists obtain the facial index from the skeleton, especially for the purpose of determining the proportion of the face in human remains found in the geological strata. In such crania the mandible is wanting, and the teeth are wanting. Consequently, there are several ways of computing the facial index, because, while the transverse or bizygomatic diameter, which is considered as the lesser diameter, always remains constant, the longitudinal, which is considered as the greater, varies. The longitudinal diameter is calculated sometimes from the ophryon to the chin, at others from the ophryon to the point of insertion of the two upper middle incisors. In the first case it is now less, and again greater than the bizygomatic diameter; in the second case, it is always less, and the resulting facial index is notably greater than 100.

The most usual formula for the facial index is the following:

$$Fi = \frac{\text{bizygomatic diameter} \times 100}{\text{ophryo-mental diameter}}$$

on the basis of which Pruner Bey gives the following mean averages according to race, for the general facial index:

Arabs	96.7
Chinese	101.7
Hottentots	105.7
Tasmanians	109.9
Laplanders	124.7

This index is not exact and constant, like that for the cranium; in fact, in case a person loses his teeth the index is altered. At the present day, especially in the French school, the anterior or total facial index is taken into consideration, in which the vertical diameter is measured from the vertex of the head to the chin (Collignon), and, consequently, the index is always less than 100. The following is the nomenclature that results for the anterior facial index:

Leptoprosopics	62 and below
Mesoprosopics	from 62 to 66
Chameprosopics	66 and above

If we take for the measure of *length* that of the *visage*, *i.e.*, the distance between the middle point of the frontal line of roots of the hair and the chin, we obtain indices that are higher by 5 than those of the French school, namely:

Leptoprosopics	67 and below
Mesoprosopics	from 67 to 71
Chameprosopics	71 and above

In many cases this index differs in the individual by as much as 10 from the cranial index, as I proved in my work on the population of Latium. Consequently, anyone who has a cranial index of 81 ought to have a *visage index* of 71, etc.

Contrary to what happens in the case of the cranium, the index of the face varies according to the age, the face being very short in childhood, and much longer in the adult.

Angles.—The angles distinguished by anthropologists are so numerous that it is impossible for us to take them all under consideration.

In the case of a living person, the angles may be measured

directly with the aid of Broca's *goniometer;* the transverse branch passes across the subnasal point; the two antero-posterior branches are inserted, with the buttons with which they terminate, into the external auricular canals; the vertical branch, swinging on a hinge, is adjusted in such a way that the little rod which it carries at the end rests upon the ophryon.

This complicated instrument resembles an instrument of torture and could not be applied to children; furthermore, it is difficult to adjust, and consequently the angles that it gives are inexact: every muscular contraction causes the angle to vary. For this reason the goniometer is impracticable.

If, by means of an instrument we trace the projection of the facial profile, the facial angle may be taken on such a drawing; it may also be traced and calculated on a photograph taken in profile.

Broca's angle is that included between the auricular foramen, the subnasal point and the ophryon.

Camper's angle is that included between the auricular foramen, the point of insertion of the upper incisors and the metopic point.

We, on the contrary, in *judging* of the facial angle, or rather of the existence and degree of prognathism, have resorted to *inspection,* aided by certain facial lines, namely (Fig. 104):

a. Vertical Facial Line.—If the subject holds his head level, with the occipital point in contact with a vertical rod, and his gaze fixed straight before him, then what we call the vertical line is the line perpendicular to the horizontal direction of the gaze, and tangent to the extreme anterior limit of the brain. This line, in the perfect human face, is perpendicular to the horizontal line uniting the auricular point with the subnasal point, and hence forms a right angle with it.

b. Line of Facial Profile.—This is the line uniting the nasal point with the subnasal point. This line is never vertical, and therefore cannot form a right angle with the auriculo-subnasal line, but forms an angle that approximates more or less nearly to a right angle (85°): this is the *facial angle.*

Transversely there is only one line for us to consider, and it has already been noted:

c. The *auriculo-subnasal line,* or *line of orientation.*

Facial Norm.—Our attention should be directed, as we have already said:

1. *To the forehead.*

This, if anomalous, may be:

Broad (if greater than 133 mm.).
Narrow (if less than 100 mm.).
High (if over 60 mm.).
Low (if under 50 mm.).

2. *To the Symmetry of the Face.*—If the face is notably asymmetrical, in respect to a plane dividing it longitudinally, the fact is at once perceptible. But a slight asymmetry may fail to be detected either by measurements (trago-mental diameters) or by inspection. Consequently, it will be well to follow certain practical rules in making this observation.

Observe first of all the median line of the face: the bridge of the nose, the nasal septum, the upper labial furrow and the point of the chin ought all to lie in the same vertical line; very often a slight deviation of the nasal septum above the upper labial furrow will betray the asymmetry; furthermore, the two naso-labial *plicæ* or folds should be noted, for they ought to be symmetrical in *direction* and in *depth;* lastly, we must observe the symmetry of the zygomatic prominences. We shall often discover three concurrent facts: a slight deviation in the median line of the face usually corresponding to the nasal septum; a greater depth of one of the naso-labial plicæ; and a greater prominence of the zygoma and the cheek on the same side.

Our attention should next be turned to the correspondence required by æsthetics between the following three diameters:

Minimum frontal.
Bizygomatic.
Bigoniac.

A very notable difference between these distances may also lead to the discovery of anomalies.

Sometimes we may discover, even by inspection alone, a notable narrowness of the frontal diameter, as compared with the other two.

The *bizygomatic* diameter may show an exaggerated development, and this is frequently accompanied by a hollowness in the temporal and upper maxillary regions and by a beak-like prognathism (prominence of the middle portion of the upper maxilla);

at other times this degenerative sign calls our attention to the mongoloid type.

The *bigoniac* diameter may also show an exaggerated development due to the enormous volume of the mandible (criminaloid type—Lombroso's assassin type). It is necessary to supplement our observation with the measurement of these three diameters, because it may very often appear to the eye that the minimum frontal diameter is below the normal, merely by comparison with the other two diameters which are overdeveloped; while when measured, it may turn out to be normal. Or, conversely, the other diameters, the bizygomatic or bigoniac, although actually normal, may appear overdeveloped, because of the shortness of the minimum frontal diameter (see "Faces of Inferior Type."

Meanwhile we must not forget that the following are signs of grave degeneration:

a. The minimum frontal diameter less than 100 mm. (the gravity of this is increased if at the same time the other two diameters are found as described in *b*).

b. The other two diameters greater than 110 mm. (Lombroso's born delinquents, assassin type).

Lateral Norm, or Norm of Profile.—Our attention ought to be directed, as we have already said:

1. To the direction of the forehead. If abnormal, this may be:

a. Receding;
b. Bombé.

The receding forehead is an indication of an incomplete or defective development of the frontal lobe of the brain; we find the forehead notably receding in the microcephalic type.

The *bombé* forehead is characteristic of hydrocephaly, but may occur also in the scaphoid cranium. When the forehead is bombé, the facial angle becomes equal to or greater than a right angle, because the face recedes beneath the extreme anterior boundary of the brain; in this case we have the opposite case to prothognathism, namely, *orthognathism.*

2. Our attention should next be directed to the facial profile, in order to observe the form and degree of *prognathism.*

The authorities distinguish three principal forms of prognathism:

a. Prognathism properly so-called: prominence of the upper maxilla as a whole.

b. Prophatnia.—Prominence of the alveoli.

c. Progeneism.—Prominence of the mandible—the lower dental arch projects in front of the upper.

Measurements of the Thorax

Principal anthropometric points: *acromial* point; *sternal fossa; xiphoid* point; *mammillary* points.

Measurements.—*Thoracic Circumference.*—Already described among the measurements of the form.

Recording instruments are now made that are exceedingly complicated and quite costly, that register the movements of respiration; they are used in medical clinics, but would be of little practical use in our schools.

Axillary and Submammary Circumference.—Taken as above, but at different levels.

Biacromial Diameter.—This is taken by means of special calipers called a *thoracimeter* or *pelvimeter,* because it is used to obtain the big measurements of the body (thorax and pelvis). The two buttons at the ends of the branches are applied to the acromial points, while the measurer occupies a position in front of the subject to be measured.

Transverse Thoracic Diameter.—The buttons of the thoracimeter are applied on a level with the mammary papillæ, along the axillary lines (vertical lines descending from the centre of the arm-pits.

Antero-posterior Thoracic Diameter.—This is also taken at the level of the nipples: the branches are applied anteriorly on the sternum and posteriorly on the vertebral channel.

These two diameters serve to furnish the thoracic index:

$$\text{Ti} = \frac{100d \text{ (antero-posterior)}}{\text{D (transverse)}}$$

Spirometer.—The subject takes a maximum inspiration and retains his breath until he has exactly fitted his mouth to the apparatus; then he emits all his breath in a forced expiration. This causes the index to rise, and the amount may be read upon it.

Sternal Length.—From the xiphoid point to the sternal fossa.

Bimammillary Diameter.—Distance between the two nipples.

Abdomen.—It would be really difficult to take measurements of the abdomen in the school. The principal anthropometric points to remember are the *umbilical* point, the two *antero-superior iliac* points, the *pubis.*

The distances which it would be useful to take are the following: *xipho-umbilical* and *umbilico-pubic* distances, which give an idea of the upper development (liver) and lower development (intestines) of the abdomen, and the *biacromial* diameter which measures the width of the pelvis.

Limbs.—In the case of the limbs also it is by no means easy or practicable to take many measurements. Consequently it should

FIG. 150.

be sufficient to indicate that there are a great number of different measurements for every different segment of the limbs.

There are two principal instruments needed for this: a large compass with adjustable branches, for the long segments, and a small compass for the short segments. With the large compass we measure the length of the upper arm and forearm, the length of the thigh and shin, the length of the foot. With the small compass we measure the total length of the hand, its width, the length of the fingers and of the digital segments, etc.

The circumference of the limbs is taken with the ordinary metallic tape.

In order to fulfil the present-day scope of pedagogic anthropology, it is sufficient to take only a few measurements (the form and the head), but it is necessary to take them with great accuracy, and above all, to *verify* one's personal ability as a measurer, so that everyone who wishes to try the experiment may have a reliable method of testing himself. To this end it is necessary to know how to calculate one's own special *personal error*.

THE PERSONAL ERROR

In anthropometry, a knowledge of the anthropometric points, the instruments to apply to them, their use and their interpretation, is not sufficient. There is need of prolonged experience in accordance with the accepted method and under a practical guide.

As a matter of fact, the degree of accuracy with which a measurement is taken is always relative, no matter who takes it, but in the case of a person who has had no practice this relativity may present so wide a margin as to be practically useless.

To obtain an approximate figure of a measurement means nothing, unless the figure is supplemented not only by a statement as to which of the *accepted methods* was used in taking it, but also by a minute description of the manner in which this method was carried out.

It is necessary to bear in mind:

1. That the ability to find the anthropometric points implies a certain knowledge of anatomy; it is a practical research, to be made under the guidance of a teacher, while the actual finding of the points as well as the taking of the measurements, should be left to the learner.

2. That the manner of applying the instruments is not without effect upon the resulting figure: for example, if the compass is held horizontally in measuring the frontal diameter, the result is different from what it would be if the instrument were held vertically. If the compass is held by the extremities of the branches, the diameter is slightly different from what it would be if the compass was held by the handle. Accordingly, it is necessary to describe minutely how we are accustomed to hold the instruments.

3. That the resulting figure differs according to whether or not the screw has been turned, or whether it has been read *in position,* or by approaching the instrument to the eye.

4. That when an instrument is old, it registers different results from those it gave when new; consequently, it is necessary to *verify it,* before proceeding to take a series of measurements. Hence it is proper to state not only precisely what instrument is used, but also that the precaution has been taken to verify it.

But what is still more important is to find out one's own *personal data.*

If the same measurement is taken twice under precisely similar conditions, the same figure is hardly ever obtained both times; everyone, even the most experienced, has his own *personal error.* By practice the amount of this error may be steadily lowered, but cannot be eliminated. Constant figures are an evidence of dishonesty, of mere *copying;* they are almost certainly not authentic.

It is important to know one's own *average error.*

It is calculated as follows:

Let us suppose that successive attempts have resulted in the following figures relative to the same measurement:

9, 10, 11, 12, 8

The mean average of these numbers is

$$\frac{9+10+11+12+8}{5}=10$$

Let us see how the values obtained differ in respect to 10:

9 10 11 12 8
10

−1, 0, +1, +2, −2 = differences from the mean average figure. We now take the average of these differences, disregarding the plus and minus signs:

$$\frac{1+0+1+2+2}{5}=\frac{6}{5}=1.2=\text{mean average error}$$

The personal mean error is a datum that it is necessary to know in order to give value to any measurements that we may wish to give forth.

In taking the various test measurements for the purpose of calculating one's personal error, it is well to use the precaution of not taking them twice at the same sitting, but after an interval of time, not only so that all marks will have disappeared that may have been left upon the skin by the instrument in the act of measuring, but also that the preceding figure will have faded from our memory. Accordingly, the measurements should be repeated on successive days and if possible under the same conditions of *time* and *place.*

It is well to make a careful choice of the time and place, because these also have their effect upon the figures.

It will be observed that if the measurements are made in a well-appointed place, with a steady light, without noises, in short, without disturbing causes, the personal error is much more easily decreased, *i.e.*, the measurements are more exact, because the measurer can better concentrate his attention.

Even the hour of the day has an influence upon the figures. It is known that none of us has the same ability to perform our various tasks at all the different hours of the day; for instance, it is not a matter of indifference whether we ask the pupils in a school to solve a problem at one hour of the day rather than at another. This is true of all occupations, and hence also of anthropometry; there are certain hours of the day at which fewer errors in measurement will be made, independently of the state of fatigue.

Consequently, it is well to know this individual datum, and to tell at what hour and in what environment the measures have been taken.

The figures are of more value if they have been compared with the results of other observers; it is necessary, after we have found our own average error, to select, for the purpose of verifying our results, some other observer, of similar experience to our own, and whose personal error is also known.

Here it is necessary to take into consideration still another factor—one's personal susceptibility to suggestion. If we have confidence in the person through whom we verify our figures, we are inclined to obtain figures equal to his own. We have only to compare our earlier figures with those since we began to use him as a test, in order to see *whether*, and *to what extent* we are influenced by suggestion. Hence, to obviate this danger it is necessary to obtain our respective figures without communicating them to each other.

It will also be necessary to take precautions not to be influenced by suggestion under any other circumstances. For instance, we are in hopes, while taking a series of measurements of school children, that we shall be able to prove that the heads of the more intelligent are larger than those of the less intelligent. In order that the figures shall be free from alterations due to suggestion, it is necessary that the measurer, while actually taking the measurements, shall be unaware which children are better and which are worse, from the intellectual point of view.

The personal error cannot be calculated in regard to a single measurement and then applied to all the others, but it must be worked out anew for every separate measurement; it oscillates variously, as a matter of fact, in relation to the longer and shorter diameters, the cranial measurements, and the measurements of the trunk and the limbs.

We are sufficiently skilled to take measurements when we have attained for measurements of cranial diameters a mean error of from 1 to 2 mm., for the vertical cranial diameter one of 4 mm., and for the stature, one of from 5 to 6 mm.

Finally, in anthropometry, theory is of no value without a long and intelligent practice, constituting an actual and personal education in anthropometric technique.

All anthropometric figures have a relative value dependent upon the extent of this education in the individual investigator.

This is a case in which it may be said that the figures are worthless without the *signature*.

CHAPTER VIII

STATISTICAL METHODOLOGY

HAVING taken measurements with the rigorous technical precision that is to-day demanded by anthropometry, we should know how to extract from these figures certain *laws*, or at least certain statistical conclusions.

There are two principal methods of regrouping the figures:—*mean averages* and *seriations*.

Mean Averages.—Averages are obtained, as is a matter of common knowledge and practice, by taking the sum of all the figures and dividing the result by the number of data. The general formula is as follows:

$$\frac{a+b+c+d}{1+1+1+1}$$

When comparative figures are given, as, for example, those recorded by Quetélét for the stature, the diameters of the head, etc., such figures are always mean averages.

Such averages may be more or less general. We might, for example, obtain a mean average of the stature of Italians, and this would be more general than the mean stature for a single region of Italy, and this again more general than the mean stature for a city, or for some specified social class, etc.

It is interesting to know how the mean will be affected, according to the number of individuals examined, because it is obvious that the mean stature of Italians cannot be based upon measurements of *all* Italians, but upon a larger or smaller number of individuals. Now, if we take various different numbers of individuals, shall we obtain different mean statures? And if so, what number of subjects must we have at our disposal in order to obtain a constant medial figure, and hence the one that represents the *real mean average?* It has been determined that a relatively small number will suffice to give the mean, if the measurements are taken with uniform method and from the same class of subjects (sex, age, race, etc.); for the cranium, 25 subjects are sufficient, and for the stature, 100 subjects.

This method furnishes us with an abstract number, insofar as it does not correspond to any *real individual*, but it serves to give us the synthetic idea of an entirety. In anthropology we need this sort of fundamental synthesis before proceeding to individual analysis for the purpose of interpreting a specified person.

Now, it is evident that the figures representing the mean stature for each region in Italy give us a basis for judging of the distribution of this important datum, while an accumulation of a hundred thousand individual figures would lead to nothing more profitable than confusion and weariness.

The following table, however, is quite clear and instructive:

MEAN STATURE IN ITALY

(According to Departments)

Departments	Stature in centimetres
Piedmont	162.7
Liguria	163.7
Lombardy	163.6
Venetia	165.4
Emilia	164.0
Tuscany	164.3
Marches	162.4
Umbria	162.7
Latium	162.5
Abruzzi and Molise	160.6
Campania	161.3
Apulia	160.4
Basilicata	158.9
Calabria	159.4
Sicily	161.1
Sardinia	158.9

Yet the interpretation of such a table is not simple; it is necessary to read the numbers, to remember them in their reciprocal relation; and it demands effort and time to acquire a *clear and synthetic* idea of the distribution in Italy of this one datum, *stature*.

On the other hand, we must lose as little time and spare our forces as far as possible. The value of positive methodology lies in the extent to which it accomplishes these two subjects.

Geographical charts serve the purpose of this desired simplification. Let us take an outline map of Italy, divide it into regions, and *colour* these different regions darker or lighter, in proportion as the stature is higher or lower.

The gradations and shadings in colour will tell us at a single glance, and without any fatigue on our part, what the table of figures reveals at the cost of a very perceptible effort. Little squares must be added on the margin of the chart, corresponding to the gradations in colour, and opposite them the figures which they respectively indicate—after the fashion in which the scale of reduction is given in every geographical map. In this way we may *study* these charts, and their examination is pleasant and interesting, while it successfully associates the two ideas of an "anthropometric datum" and of a "region," a result which a series of figures, pure and simple, could not achieve.

We have seen Livi's charts of Italy, both for stature and for the cephalic index. Analogous charts may be constructed for all the different data, for example, the colour of the hair, the shape of the nose, the facial index, etc. In the same manner we may proceed to a still more analytical distribution of anthropometric data among the different provinces of a single *region*. For example, I myself prepared charts of this sort for the stature, the cephalic index and the pigmentation of the population of Latium.

Sometimes we want to see in one single, comprehensive glance, the *progress* of some anthropological datum; for instance, in its development through different ages. Quételet's series of figures for growth in stature, in weight, in the diameters of the head, the cranial circumference, etc., offer when read the same difficulty as the similar tables of distribution according to regions. On the contrary, we get a synthetic, sweeping glance in *diagrams*, such as the one which shows the growth of stature in the two sexes. The method of constucting such diagrams is very simple, and is widely employed. When we wish to represent in physics certain phenomena and laws; or in hygiene, the progress of mortality through successive years, etc., we make use of the method of diagrams.

Let us draw two fundamental lines meeting in a right angle at A (Fig. 151): AS is known as the *axis of the abscissæ; AO*, the *axis of the ordinates*. We divide each of these lines into equal parts. Let us assume that the divisions of AS represent the years of age, and those of AO the measurements of stature in centimetres; and since the new-born child has an average height of 50 cm., we may place 50 as the initial figure. From the figure O (age) and from 50 cm. (measure), we erect perpendiculars meeting at a, where we mark the point. At the age of one year the average stature is about 70 cm., accordingly we erect perpendiculars from 1 (age) and from 70 (measure), obtaining the point c. Since the stature at two years is about 80 cm. the same procedure gives us the point e. Since the stature at the age of three is about 86 cm., I erect the perpendicular from a level slightly higher than half-way between 80 and 90, obtaining the point i; and so on, for the rest.

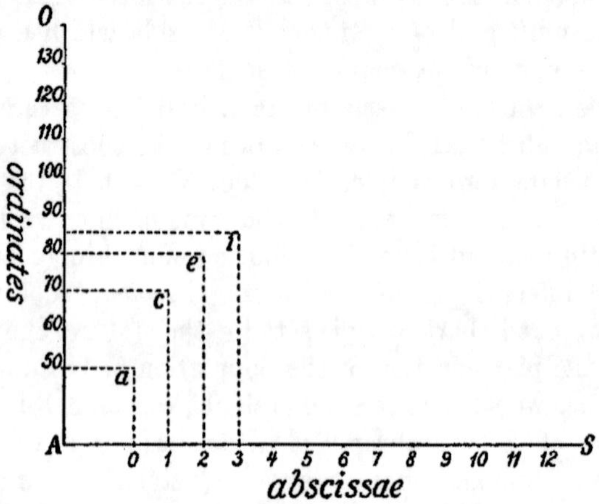

FIG. 151.

Meanwhile we begin to be able to see at a glance that the stature increases greatly in the first year and that thereafter the intensity of its growth steadily diminishes.

If we unite the points thus constructed, the line of representation is completed.

The verticals Oa, $1c$, $2e$, etc., are the *ordinates*, and the horizontals $50a$, $70c$, etc., are the abscissæ of the line of representation; and since it is constructed along the intersections of these lines, they are for that reason collectively called *coordinates*. It is usual in constructing these diagrams to mark the coordinates in such a way that they will not be apparent, instead of which only the axes and the line representing the development of the phenomenon are shown (Fig. 152).

Sometimes a different method of representing the phenomenon graphically is followed, namely, by tracing the successive series of distances developed on the ordinates (Fig. 153); in which case the characteristic arrangement of the lines causes this to be known as the *organ-pipe* method.

The diagram for the growth in stature, given earlier in this volume, is constructed according to the method shown in Fig. 151. When there are a great number of data to represent, which overlap and interweave, this method of graphic representation still lends itself admirably to the purpose; in such a case we shall have a number of broken lines, either parallel or intersecting, which may

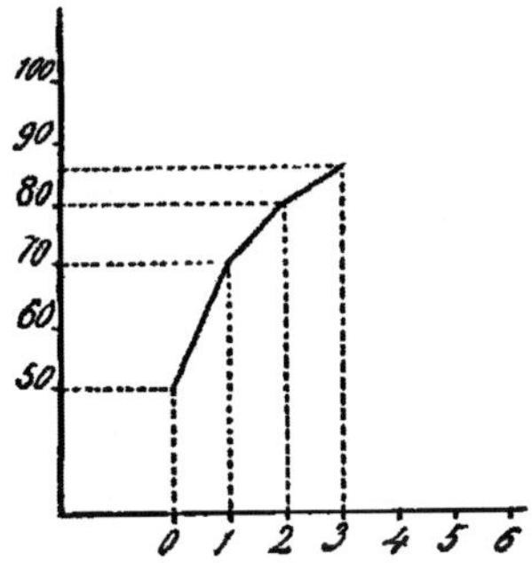

Fig. 152.

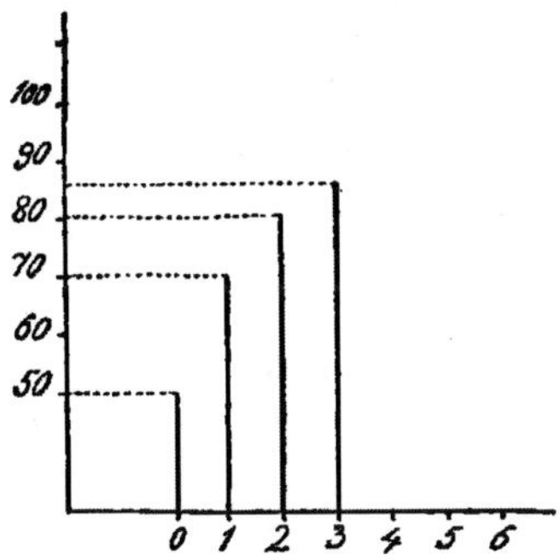

Fig. 153.

be distinguished by different colours or different methods of tracing (dots, stars, etc.), so that they may interweave without becoming confused, thus giving us at a glance the development of several phenomena at once (for example, total stature and sitting stature, length of upper and lower limbs, in one and the same diagram).

For the purpose of practice, a graphic representation of the changes in ponderal weight through the different ages may be constructed in class. The figures for stature and weight at each age should be read aloud; one student can find the corresponding *ponderal index* in the tables, while another constructs the graphic line upon the blackboard.

In this manner we can see better than by reading the figures, how the ponderal index increases during the first year and becomes much higher during early infancy; and then how it diminishes up to the age of puberty, holding its ground with slight oscillations during the puberal period; after which it again increases when the individual begins to *fill out* after the seventeenth year, and once again later when he takes on flesh, to fall off again during the closing years, when old age brings lean and shrunken limbs.

Seriation.—Another method of rearranging the figures is that of *seriation.* Let us assume that we are taking the average of a thousand statures, or of hundreds of thousands. We will try to find some means of simplifying the calculation. Since the individual oscillations of stature are contained within a few centimetres and the individuals amount to thousands, large numbers will be found to have the same *identical* statures. Accordingly, let us rearrange the individuals according to their stature, obtaining the following result:

Stature in metres	Number of individuals
1.50	20
1.55	80
1.60	140
1.61	200
1.62	300
1.63	450
1.70	100
1.75	80
1.80	10

By multiplying the 1.50 by 20, 1.55 by 80, etc., and by adding the results, we shall have simplified the process for obtaining the sum total which must then be divided by the number of individuals.

Well, while doing this for the purpose of simplifying the calculation, we have hit upon the method of distributing the individuals in a *series,* that is, we have regrouped the corresponding figures according to *seriation.*

Seriation has been discovered as a method of *analysing* the mean average, and it demonstrates three things: first, the extent of oscillations of anthropologic data, a thing which the mean average completely hides,—indeed, we have seen in the case of the cephalic index the mean averages oscillate between 75 and 85, when calculated for the separate regions, while, in the case of individuals, the oscillations extend from 70 to 90; secondly, it shows the numerical prevalence of individuals for the one or the other measurement; third, and finally, seriation reveals a *law*, to us, namely, that the distribution of individuals, according to anthropological data, is not a matter of chance; there is a prevalence of individuals corresponding to certain average figures, and the number of individuals diminishes in proportion as the measurements depart from the mean average, equally whether they increase or diminish.

I take from Livi certain numerical examples of serial distribution:

Stature in inches	Number of observations
60	6
61	26
62	32
63	26
64	160
65	154
66	191
67	128
68	160
69	89
70	45
71	7
72	6
73	3
74	1

Although these figures are not rigorously exact, there is a certain numerical prevalence of individuals in relation to the stature of 66 inches, and above and below this point the number of individuals diminishes, becoming very few toward the extremes.

The lack of exactness and of agreement in serial distribution is due to the numerical scarcity of individuals. If this number were doubled, if it were centupled, we should see the serial distribution become systematised to the point of producing, for example, such symmetrical series as the following:

1	1	1
12	16	15
66	120	105
220	560	455
495	1,820	1,365
792	3,368	3,003
924	8,008	5,005
—	11,440	6,435
792	12,870	—
495	—	6,435
220	11,440	—
66	8,008	5,005
12	3,368	3,003
1	1,820	1,365
	560	455
	120	105
	16	15
	1	1

This law of distribution is one of the most wide-spread laws; it ordains the way in which the characteristics of animals and plants alike must behave; and the statistical method which is beginning to be introduced into botany sheds much light upon it.

This law may be represented graphically by arranging the anthropologic data on the abscissæ (*e.g.*, those of stature), and the number of individuals on the ordinates.

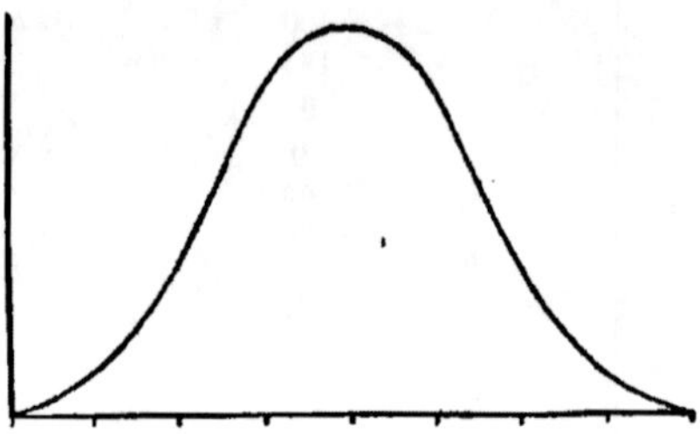

FIG. 154.

In such cases we have a curve with a maximum central height and a symmetrical bilateral diminution (Fig. 121): this is the curve of Quételet.

Or better yet, it is known as *Quételet's binomial curve,* because this anthropologist was the first to represent the law graphically and to perceive that its development was the same as that so well known in mathematics for the coefficients in Newton's binomial theorem.

Newton's binomial theorem is the law for raising any binomial to the *n*th power, and is expanded in algebra as follows:

$$(a+b)^n = a^n + na^{n-1}b + \left(\frac{n(n-1)}{2}\right)a^{n-2}b^2 +$$

$$+\left(\frac{n(n-1)\ (n-2)}{2.3}\right)a^{n-3}b^3+$$

$$+\left(\frac{n(n-1)(n-2)\ (n-3)}{2.3.4}\right)a^{n-4}b^4+$$

$$+\left(\frac{n(n-1)\ (n-2)\ (n-3)\ (n-4)}{2.3.4.5}\right)a^{n-5}b^5+\ldots+b^n$$

substituting for n some determined coefficient, for example, 10, the binomial would develop, in regard to its coefficients, after the following fashion:

$$(a+b)^{10}=a^{10}+10a^9b+\left(\frac{10.9}{2}\right)a^8b^2+$$

$$+\left(\frac{10.9.8}{2.3}\right)a^7b^3+\left(\frac{10.9.8.7}{2.3.4}\right)a^6b^4+$$

$$+\left(\frac{10.9.8.7.6}{2.3.4.5}\right)a^5b^5+\left(\frac{10.9.8.7.6.5}{2.3.4.5.6}\right)a^4b^6+$$

$$+\left(\frac{10.9.8.7.6.5.4}{2\ 3.4.5.6.7}\right)a^3b^7+\left(\frac{10.9.8.7.6.5.4.3}{2.3.4.5.6.7.8}\right)a^2b^8+$$

$$+\left(\frac{10.9.8.7.6.5.4.3.2}{2.3.4.5.6.7.8.9}\right)ab^9+b^{10}.$$

Whence it appears that, after performing the necessary reductions, the coefficients following the central one diminish symmetrically in the same manner as they increased: that is, according to the selfsame law that we meet in the anthropological statistics of seriations.

Indeed, here is the binomial theorem with the reductions made:

$$(a+b)^{10}=a^{10}+10a^9b+\left(\frac{10.9}{2}\right)\ a^8b^2+$$

$$+\left(\frac{10.9.8}{2.3}\right)a^7b^3+\left(\frac{10.9.8.7}{2.3.4}\right)a^6b^4+$$

$$+\left(\frac{10.9.8.7.6}{2.3.4.5}\right)a^5b^5+$$

$$+\left(\frac{10.9.8.7}{2.3.4}\right)a^4b^6+\left(\frac{10.9.8}{2.3}\right)a^2b^7+$$

$$+\left(\frac{10.9}{2}\right)a^2b^8+10ab^9+b^{10}.$$

And after calculating the coefficients, we obtain the following numbers in a symmetrical series:

10
45
120
210
252
210
120
45
10

This is why the curve of Quételet is called *binomial.*

Let us assume that we wish to represent by means of Quételet's curves, two seriations, for instance in regard to the stature of children of the same race, sex and age, but of opposite social conditions: the poor and the rich.

These two curves of Quételet's, provided that they are based upon an equal and very large number of individuals, will be identical, because the law itself is universal. Only, the curve for the rich children will be shifted along toward the figures for high statures, and that for the poor children toward the low statures.

At a certain point *A* the two curves meet and intersect, each invading the field of the other: so that within the space *ABC* there are individual rich children who are shorter than some of the poor, and individual poor children who are taller than some of the rich: *i.e.,* the conditions are contrary to those generally established by the curve as a whole. This rule also, of the intersection of binomial curves, is of broad application; whenever a general principle is stated, *e.g.* that the rich are taller than the poor, it is necessary to understand it in a liberal sense, knowing that wherever we should descend to details, the opposite conditions could be found (superimposed area *ABC*). For all that, the principle as a whole does not alter its characteristic, which is a differentiation of diverse types (for example, the tall rich and the short poor). The same would hold true if we made a comparison of the stature of men and women; the curve for men would be shifted toward the higher figures and that for women toward the lower, but there would be a point where the two curves would intersect, and in the triangle *ABC* there would be women taller than some of the men, and men shorter than some of the women. The differences have reference to the numerical *majority* (the high portions of the curves) which are clearly separated from each other, like the tops of cypress trees which have roots interlacing in the earth. Now, it is the *numerical prevalence* of individuals, in any mixed community, that gives that community its distinctive type, whether of class or of race. If we see gathered together in a socialistic assemblage a proletarian crowd, suffering from the affects of pauperism, the majority of the individuals have stooping

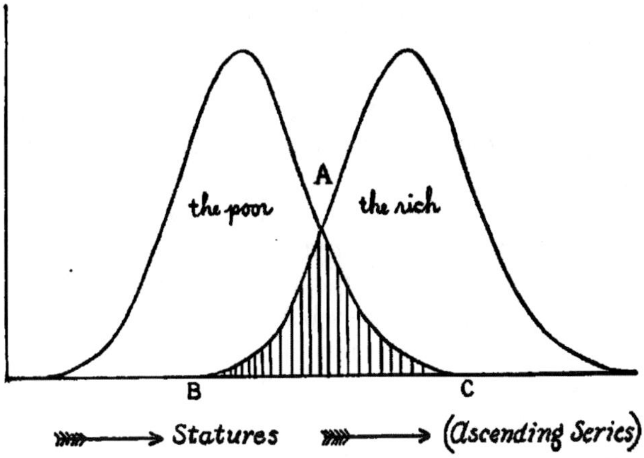

Fig. 155.

shoulders, ugly faces and pallid complexions; all this gives to the crowd a general aspect, one might say, of physical inferiority. And we say that this is the type of the labouring class of our epoch in which labour is proletarian—a type of caste. On the other hand, if we go to a court ball, what strikes us is the numerical prevalence of tall, distinguished persons, finely shaped, with velvety skin and delicate and beautiful facial lineaments, so that we recognise that the assemblage is composed of privileged persons, constituting the type of the aristocratic class. But this does not alter the fact that among the proletariat there may be some handsome persons, well developed, robust and quite worthy of being confounded with the privileged class; and conversely, among the aristocrats, certain undersized individuals, sad and emaciated, with stooping shoulders and features of inferior type, who seem to belong to the lower social classes.

For this same reason it is difficult to give *clear-cut* limits to any law and any distinction that we meet in our study of life. This is why it is difficult in zoology and in botany to establish a system, because although every species differs from the others, in the salience of its characteristics and the numerical prevalence of individuals very much alike, none the less every species grades off so insensibly into others, through individuals of intermediate characteristics, that it is difficult to separate the various species sharply from one another. It is only the treetops that are separate, but at their bases life is intertwined; and in the roots there is an inseparable unity. The same may be said when we wish to differentiate normality from pathology and degeneration. The man who is clearly sane differs beyond doubt from the one who is profoundly ill or degenerate; but certain individuals exist whose state it would be impossible to define.

Now, while seriations analyse certain particularities of the individual distribution, by studying the actual truth, mean averages give us only an abstraction, which nevertheless renders distinct what was previously nebulous and confused in its true particulars. The synthesis of the mean average brings home to us forcibly the true nature of the characteristics in their general effect. The analysis of the seriation brings home to us forcibly the truth regarding this effect when we observe it in the actuality of individual cases.

"When, from the topmost pinnacle of the Duomo of Milan or from the hill of the Superga," says Levi in felicitious comparison, "we contemplate the magnificent panorama of the Alpine chain, we see the zone of snow distinguished from that free from snow by a line that is visibly horizontal and that stretches evenly throughout the length of the chain. But if we enter into the Alpine valleys and try to reach and to touch the point at which the zone of snow begins, that regularity which we previously admired disappears before our eyes; we see, at one moment, a snow-clad peak, and at the next another free from snow that either is or seems to be higher than the former."

Now, through the statistics of mean averages, we are able to see the general progress of phenomena, like the spectator who gazes from a distance at the Alpine chain and concludes that the zone of snow is above and the open ground is below; while, by means of seriation, we are in the position of the person who has entered the valley and discovers the actuality of the particular details which go to make up the uniform aspect of the scene as a whole. Both aspects are true—just as both of those statistical methods are useful—for they reciprocally complete each other, concurring in revealing to us the laws and the phenomena of anthropology.

CHAPTER IX

BIOGRAPHICAL HISTORY OF THE PUPIL AND HIS ANTECEDENTS

The child, like every other individual, represents an *effect* of multifold causes: he is a product of *heredity* (biological product) and a product of society (social product). The characteristics of his ancestors, their maladies, their vices, their degeneration, live again in the result of the conception which has produced a new indivdual: and this individual, whether stronger or weaker, must pass through various obstacles in the course of his intra-uterine life and his external life. The sufferings and the mistakes of his mother are reflected in him. The maladies which attack him may leave upon him permanent traces. Finally, the social environment receives the child at birth, either as a favoured son or as an unfortunate, and leads him through paths that certainly must influence his complex development.

All of the preceding and theoretic parts of this volume which took up each characteristic for separate consideration, have already explained all that it is necessary to know in order to interpret the characteristics present in a given individual, and the more or less remote causes which contributed to them.

We may now *apply* our acquired knowledge to individual study, by making investigations into the antecedents of the child and recording his *biographic history*. It forms a parallel to the *clinical history* which is recorded in medicine: and it leads to a diagnosis, or at least to a scientific judgment regarding the child.

Although this biographic part is eminently practical, certain principal points of research may be indicated for the purpose of guiding the student. But no one will ever make a successful study of medical pedagogy unless he will *follow* the practical lessons dedicated to the individual study of the scholar, and make a practice of personal observation. In the Pedagogical School of Rome, we provide *subjects*, taken from the elementary schools or from the Asylum School of De Sanctis for defective children. And we read their biographical history in regard to their antecedents, and then make an objective examination of them, frequently extending it to an examination of their sensibility and their psychic conditions and enquiring into their standard of scholarship. From these lessons based upon theory, profitable discussions often result; and they certainly are the most profitable lessons in the course.

A biographical history is essentially composed of three parts: the *antecedents,* which comprises an investigation of the facts antedating the individual in question; *the objective examination,* which studies the individual personally; and the *diaries, i.e.,* the continued observation of the same individual who has already been studied in regard to himself and his antecedents.

The objective examination and the diaries cannot be considered solely in the light of anthropology, because they chiefly require the aid of psychology. But even anthropology makes an ample and important contribution, first, in the form of an objective morphological examination, the vast importance of which has already been shown; secondly, because it gives us a picture of the biologico-social personality which it is necessary to compare with the *reactions* of the subject in question, with his psychic manifestations, his degree of culture, etc.; and upon this comparison depends the chief importance of the individual study of the pupil.

Accordingly, in addition to an examination of the individual, anthropology ought to concern itself also with the conditions antedating the individual; therefore, it traces back to the *origins* (antecedents), while psychology reserves for itself the principal task of *following the psychological development* of the subject in his school life (diaries); a task in which it will nevertheless go hand in hand with anthropology since the latter must follow at the same time the physiomorphological development of the subject himself.

Accordingly, the gathering of *antecedent* statistics is the task of anthropology. The antecedent statistics may be called the *history of the genesis* of the individual; the manner of collecting them is by means of *enquiries* that are generally made of the child's nearest relations (the mother) or of the teachers who have superintended his previous education. The enquiries are conducted under the guidance of a certain system of which we give the following outline:

- anamnesis
  - biopathological..
    - remote
      - ascendant
      - collateral
    - near
      - mother
        - conception
        - pregnancy
        - delivery
        - lactation
      - child...
        - first development of
          - dentition
          - locomotion
          - speech
        - maladies incurred
        - maternal opinions of child
          - character
          - intelligence
          - etc.
  - sociological......
    - vocation of parents
    - their morality
    - their culture
    - their care of their children
  - school record ...
    - opinions of teachers, history of previous schooling.

We may distinguish biopathological antecedents, which have regard to the organism of the child as a living individual; sociological antecedents, having regard to the social environment in which the child has grown up and which contributes to the formation of his psychophysical personality; and scholastic antecedents or *scholarship*, regarding the previous schooling of the child under examination. The biopathological antecedents are certainly of fundamental importance. They are called *remote* when we refer to the hereditary antecedents of the subject, and *near* when we have reference to his personal antecedents.

Remote Antecedents.—These include an investigation regarding the ancestors, the brothers and sisters, and the collateral relations. The age of the parents (since we know that too immature or too advanced an age, or a disparity in age between the parents may result in the birth of weak children). Degree of relationship between the parents (since we know that the offspring of parents related to each other may be weak). Maladies incurred by them or prevalent in their families, incidental vices of the parent (since we know that constitutional maladies, such as syphilis, tuberculosis, gout, pellagra, malaria, mental and nervous diseases, etc., *alcoholism* or an irregular life of excesses, may lead to the procreation of degenerates). Furthermore, since it is known that according to the laws of collateral heredity, maladies may reappear in nephews which previously occurred in uncles and not in the parents, information should be sought, so far as possible, from all members of the family. Information regarding the brothers of the subject offers an interest of a very particular kind, because this gives us an insight into the generative capacity of the parents: for instance, if there were abortions, children who died at an early age of convulsions, meningitis, etc., this argues unfavourably for the normality of the subject.

Near Biopathological Antecedents: *Mother, Child.*—Our inquiries should centre first of all upon the mother, in order to know the conditions of conception, pregnancy, delivery and lactation, in the case of the child under examination, because we know that frequently an error at the time of conception may produce a degenerate or a weakling. For example, a child generated in a state of physical or mental exhaustion—*e.g.*, after a long trip on a bicycle, or after passing an examination—may be born feeble, predisposed to nervous diseases (idiocy, meningitis), just as he may be born abnormal (epilepsy, anomalies of character, criminal tendencies) if generated by the father during an alcoholic excess, or by the mother while suffering from hypocondria, illness, etc. The history of the pregnancy is also of interest: whether it proceeded regularly to the close of the nine months, whether the mother suffered especially from mental anxiety, illness or received any blow on the abdomen.

Other causes which may affect the health of the child have reference to birth and to lactation. If the delivery requires an operation, it may, for instance, deform the skull; while a hired wet-nurse, or artificial feeding are more or less apt to cause deterioration in the child.

Having completed this first enquiry, we pass on to consider the child itself, from the time of birth onward, lingering especially over its early development and more particularly over the *cutting of the teeth*, *learning to walk* and *learning to speak*, which are the three first obstacles to infantile development. The healthy child overcomes them according to normal laws, while the child of tardy development shows the first characteristic anomaly in these three fundamental points of its early existence (tardiness of development, incomplete and defective development, development accompanied by diseases, etc.).

Usually a tardiness in the development of the teeth denotes general weakness and more especially skeletal weakness (rachitis, syphilis); tardiness in learning to walk may occur in connection with the above-named causes (weakness of the lower limbs); or with difficulty in attaining an equilibrium (of cerebral origin; witness the case of idiots who, without being paralytic, cannot walk, because they cannot *learn how to walk*); or with paresis, more or less partial or diffused, of the muscles controlling the act of walking (infantile paralysis, Little's disease, etc.). A tardy development of speech is sometimes found together with a notable intellectual development and the child will not begin to speak until he can express thoughts and speak well; but more frequently such delayed development is due to partial *deafness;* or it originates in the association centres of the brain (the idiot child cannot *learn* to speak).

It will also be helpful to know whether the child was ever ill. It is very important in this connection to find out whether the child ever suffered from infantile eclampsia in early life (convulsions, or "fits" as the mothers of the lower classes call them). This is an indication of a cerebral malady which leaves behind it permanent alterations of the brain and of its functions. The child may be an idiot, or may belong to one of the various catagories of children who go under the name of defectives; or he may be abnormal in character (cerebroplegic forms). Another important fact to record is nocturnal *enuresis* (loss of urine during sleep subsequent to the normal age); this is considered by some authorities as a pre-epileptic state—that is, a child that suffers such losses may in the future become subject to epilepsy, and quite probably, if studied, will show various anomalies of the nervous system, such, for example, as too deep sleep, slowness of intelligence, etc. Repeated attacks of *infective diseases*, even though they are survived, also denote organic weakness, with facile predisposition to infective agencies—in other words, deficient powers of immunity.

Prolonged intestinal maladies or typhus in the early months (denutrition from pathological causes, exhaustive diseases) may, in themselves, be the cause of the child's enfeeblement and its consequent arrest in development.

But in the interpretation of such observations, the physician should be the guide and the direct judge.

The most salient symptoms in regard to the child—intelligence, conduct, character, endurance, etc.—are, for the most part, expressed with great clearness by the mothers. Prof. De Sanctis, for example, has noted that the mother's first words might serve the purpose of a diagnosis; for instance, the mother says of an idiot child: "he doesn't understand," of a child retarded in development, "he is stupid," of an abnormal child, "he understands but he is bad." Accordingly, Prof. De Sanctis begins his diagnostic researches by registering the *maternal judgments,* because the mother is *struck* by the salient characteristics of her child; and even if she is uneducated she always finds concise and effective phrases to express her judgment.

To the end of rendering the research into antecedents surer and more complete so far as regards the personal antecedents of the child, certain anthropological tablets are being introduced to serve as *maternal diaries.* In this way the mothers have a guide for studying their children, and this forms one of the first practical attempts toward the "education of the mothers."

Here is a form of chart for keeping a record of the dentition. The significance of the letters is as follows:

U. r.: upper right, *i.e.,* the right half of the upper jaw.

U. l. : upper left.

L. r.: lower right.

L. l. : lower left. (The fact must be borne in mind that in the first dentition there are twenty teeth.)

FIRST DENTITION

Teeth	Dates: of first appearance	Dates: of complete development	Dates: of shedding	Observations
U. r. 1				
2				
3				
4				
5				
U. l. 1				
2				
3				
4				
5				
L. r. 1				
2				
3				
4				
5				
L. l. 1				
2				
3				
4				
5				

In this way we have an analytical and exact chart of the development of the teeth. Analogous tables are made for the second dentition, for the growth of the stature, for increase in weight, for certain physiological notes, etc. When the first period of growth is ended, the mother's note-books contain annual notes, like the following:

YEAR 190....

Date	January	February	March	April	May	June	July	August	September	October	November	December
Weight..............												
Stature..............												

Special annual diaries are now employed for keeping a minute record of maladies incurred, symptoms, treatment, etc.

These note-books, similar to those hitherto kept by ladies for their house accounts, or for sentimental notes, would be of great service and aid to pedagogic anthropology, even though their use could not be extended to all mothers (the mothers of the proletariat, immoral women, etc., either could not or would not give similar contributions). The institution of "Children's Houses," if more widespread, could easily facilitate the *education of the mothers* and the diffusion of "Maternal Note-books" throughout all grades of society. But at most these mother's diaries furnish us only with notes of the near antecedents and not of the remote, which are of extreme importance.

Sociological Antecedents: *Vocation, Morality, Culture.*—Before all else, in inquiring into the sociological antecedents, it is necessary to know in what sort of an environment the child has grown, and whether it is an environment favorable, or otherwise, to his physical, psychic, intellectual and moral development. This is an exceedingly important matter to determine for the purposes of a clinical history, since the child's moral conduct and the profit derived from study depend to a large extent upon the environment in which the child has grown and lived. To this end inquiries should be made into the economic circumstances of the child's parents, their vocation, moral standards and degree of education, and also into the child's mode of life, whether with the parents or other relations, or with persons not related to him, whether he plays in the street, keeps company with street children, etc.

School Record: *Judgments of Teachers.*—This is the history of the pupil as made by his teachers, beginning with the first day that he enters school. The judgments of teachers, although not always so precise and so fair as those of mothers, nevertheless have an importance of their own. Inquiry should be made into the child's conduct in school and the profit he derives from his studies.

Illustrative Cases.—There are, for example, certain families so infected with a degenerative or pathological taint that the remote antecedents are sufficient in themselves to stigmatise the biological condition of an abnormal subject. This may be seen in the genealogy of the Misdea family (taken from Lombroso's work):

Grandfather: **MICHELE MISDEA**
(Not very intelligent, but very active)

1st uncle Guiseppe (imbecile)	**2nd uncle Domenico (eccentric and violent)**	**3d uncle Cosimo (quick-tempered, killed in a quarrel)**	**4th uncle Michele (semi-imbecile)**	**Misdea the father (alcoholic, spendthrift, married to an hysterical woman, one of whose brothers was a brigand and another a thief).**
1st cousin (idiot)	**2d cousin (madman)**	**3d cousin (imbecile)**	**4th cousin (imbecile)**	
1st brother Cosimo (obscene, epileptic, drunkard, convicted of assault).	**2d brother Salvatore Misdea**	**3d brother (sane)**	**4th brother (alcoholic)**	**5th brother (incorrigible)**
grandson (obscene)				

Similarly extraordinary is the genealogy of Ada Türcker, an alcoholic, thief and vagabond, born in 1740, a large part of whose numerous descendants it has been possible to trace. Out of the 834 individuals derived from this degenerate woman, the lives of no less than 709 have been followed up, and among these are included 143 mendicants, 64 inmates of asylums, 181 prostitutes, 69 criminals, and 7 murderers, who altogether cost the state upward of seven million francs!

Besides families like these there are others infected with a pathological taint, in which phthisis and gout alternate with epilepsy and insanity. Then again there are other families in which the pathological taint is scarcely perceptible, as for example, the family of an epileptic child with criminal tendencies, personally studied by me; all the members of this family are long-lived and enjoy good health; the father alone is a sufferer from articular rheumatism. Lastly there are families in which there is no sign of pathological or degenerative weakness; and in such cases we say that there is nothing noteworthy in the genealogy, and the near antecedents assume the highest degree of importance.

The study of antecedents not only has a scientific importance, in so far as it contributes to a knowledge of anthropological varieties of mankind (due to adaptation); but it also has an immediate pedagogic importance through its useful application to the school.

Lino Ferriani is the first jurist to investigate the antecedents of juvenile delinquents, by gathering notes not only regarding their parents, but also in regard to their own *school standing* (by consulting the teachers in the schools where these juvenile criminals received their education!). I have extracted from his volume on "Precocious and senile delinquency" the following statistics of the physico-moral condition of the parents:

Convicted of crimes against property	1,237
Convicted of crimes against the person	543
Addicted to wine	2,006
Women leading meretricious lives	581
Doubtful reputation	1,500
Very bad reputation	670
Good reputation	210
Industrious	1,888
Semi-idle	4,000
Idle	2,000
Sentenced for drunkeness	1,590
Sentenced for offences against public morals	240
Alcoholics	1,001
Confined in lunatic asylums	48
Mothers deflowered before the age of 15	1,560
Couples separated through fault of the husband	59
Couples separated through fault of the wife	69
Couples separated through fault of both parties	135

Among these notes there is a numerical preponderance of *idlers* (the idle and semi-idle: degenerates are weaklings who cannot work and who shun work; their only form of work is crime, which is an attempt to reap the fruit of other people's industry) and alcoholism (addicted to wine, alcoholics, and those sentenced for drunkenness; this also is a stigma of degeneration: weaklings have recourse to alcohol, because it gives them an illusion of strength). Furthermore, the majority show, through crime and prostitution, that they belong to the class of social parasites.

In regard to the psycho-physical characteristics of juvenile offenders, Ferriani gives these principal notes:

Nervous	1,250
Habitual liars	3,000
Fond of wine and gluttonous	2,501
Proud of delinquency	2,700

Blasphemers	3,900
Cruel to animals	2,100
Excessive emaciation	1,648
Long hands	1,650
Unreliable workers	2,195
Without interest in life	1,347
Desirous of authority	1,000
Scrofulous	700
Rachitic and syphilitic	500
Vindictive	842
Timid and cowardly	900
Obscene	900
Cruel to parents	700
Cruel to companions	700

And now we come to the most interesting part of all, namely, the notes taken by teachers where these children went to school.

Boys.—Age from ten to twelve years. Characteristic notes on 100 children in regard to bad conduct:

Humiliating poorer companions	2
Absolute refusal to obey	4
Corrupting companions	4
Mutilating books of poor companions	2
Spirit of rebellion	1
Malicious and headstrong	1
Resentful of routine	1
Stealing food at expense of companions	6
Abnormally spiteful	4
Impertinent answers	7
Proud of inventing misdeeds	2
Stealing from companions and teacher (school stationary, etc.)	10
Calumniating companions	6
Desire to play the spy	8
Obscene writings in toilet room	2
Obscene writings in copy-books	6
Obscene actions in the shcool-room	9
Obscene writings on the benches	3
Violence with a weapon (pen-knife)	2
Bullying smaller boys	12
Feigning loss of speech for a month, to avoid reciting lessons	1
Blaspheming	1
Afraid of everything and savagely vindictive	1
Frequently absent from school, to play games of chance	3
Spirit of destruction	1
Spirit of contradiction	1

Girls.—Age from ten to twelve years. Characteristic notes on 50 children in regard to bad conduct:

Soiling the clothing of their companions	3
Abnormally spiteful	2
Intense envy	4
Frequent absence from school, to play games of chance	4
Tyranny	3
Immoderate vanity	2
Spirit of rebellion	1
Insolent answers	1
Absolute intolerance of supervision	1
Damaging the school furniture	2
Slandering the teacher	4
Slandering school-mates	6
Theft, limited to pens	1
Lascivious love-letters	4
Constantly speaking ill of her mother	1
Attempts to make school-mates unhappy	1
Unkindness toward animals	1
Unkindness toward old persons	1
Unkindness toward small children	1
Obscene writings in the toilet room	1
Harmful anonymous letters	1
Hatred of beautiful things	1
Spirit of contradiction	1
Corrupting companions	1
Thefts in school	1
Mutilating the clothing of companions	1

The prevailing faults among the boys are: theft, obscene actions, tyranny over the weak; and among the girls: slander, extreme envy and lascivious love-letters.

If we compare the notes regarding the parents with those relating to the children, we find a connection amounting to that of cause and effect. We might almost say that the phenomenon revealed to us in school through the teachers' notes concerns not so much the pupil himself as his past history. To keep this sort of record of misconduct, so damnatory to the pupils in question, would be worse than useless, if we were unable to trace back their source to the presumable causes which determined them. There is an intimate relation between the environment and the products of that environment. If we should read the notes relating to the children who receive prizes for good conduct, and who are held up as moral examples, we could trace back and find the cause of these notes in a favourable family environment; hence, the qualities which we praise in the child are not a merit peculiar to the child, but are due to causes, of which the pupil himself is merely the fortunate epilogue.

And passing from studies taken from works of criminal anthropology to examples contained in works of pedagogic anthropology (these works all being based upon the same scientific standards), I am happy to cite a work which has even earned the praise of Lombroso: *Notes on Infantile Psycho-physiology,* written by Professor Calcagni.

Notwithstanding that this book of Menotti Calcagni's is inspired by the most advanced pedagogic conceptions, so that it well deserves to be cited in its entirety with much profit, I shall avail myself only of the part which particularly interests me at the present moment. It is the part containing the data collected and arranged by the author in a series of tables, in the form of a brief clinical history, of each pupil in the class studied by the author.

I shall pass over the statistical tables concerning the personal examination of the pupils (anthropological, physiological, etc.), and confine myself to just two tables: one in regard to the examination into the pupil's antecedents (name and surname; day of birth; place of birth; age of father; age of mother; vocation of father; vocation of mother; conditions of home environment, hygienic, economic and moral; conditions of other members of the family; maladies and casualties incurred by the parents before and after the procreation of the child; defects and vices of parents, and details regarding their psychic constitutions; conditions and accidents during pregnancy, birth and puerperal period; illnesses incurred by the child); the other in regard to the pupil's previous school record (name and surname; pupils enrolled at beginning of the year; those transferred to other classes; those promoted without examination; those promoted after examination; those permitted a second trial; those not admitted to examination; those dropped from their class, and for how many different years). I select from these the notes referring to the children *promoted without examination* and those *not admitted to examination; i.e.,* the privileged ones before whom an obstacle has been withdrawn which the majority must surmount before continuing on their path in life: go forward in peace, you favoured ones! and those who are not even allowed a chance to overcome the obstacle: turn back, you to whom the path of other men is closed!

And I read these notes relative to those *promoted without examination:* "Father shoemaker, Mother dress-maker, home orderly, frugal and clean; brothers labourers;"—"F. professor of chemistry, M. housekeeping, condition of environment excellent, brothers studious;"—"F. assistant engineer, M. keeps house, conditions of environment good, deaths in family from acute diseases;"—"F. country tradesman, M. keeps house, conditions of environment excellent, very religious family;"—"F. man of means, M. housekeeping, conditions of environment excellent, brothers studious;"—"F. machinist, M. keeps the house, home somewhat damp because of adjoining garden; much anxiety on the part of the mother regarding the children, because her first husband was a consumptive, and the seven children she had by him all died. Children of second marriage all healthy; but the pupil in question frequently had attacks of fever;"—"F. cab-driver, M. keeps house, economic and moral conditions satisfactory;"—"F. antiquarian, M. keeps house, condition good;"—"F. manager of a lottery office, M. keeps house, economic conditions of the very best, moral conditions good," etc.

And here are a few notes on the pupils *not admitted to the examinations:* "Father itinerant vendor, Mother keeps house, home exceedingly dirty, utmost indifference regarding the children and their education. Insufficient nutriment for the mother both before and after the child's birth;"—F. cobler, M. wash-woman, poverty, squalor, and indifference, dwelling gloomy and cramped;" —"F. mason, M. dead, dwelling gloomy and unhealthy, through lack of supervision, Giacinto often runs away from home and goes to play on the banks of the Tiber; the mother died of tuberculosis; the father is an alcoholic; the child was brought up by a wet-nurse, etc."

To recapitulate: in the case of children promoted without examination there is an absolute prevalence of the most favourable social and biologico-moral conditions, while the opposite holds true of the children excluded from examinations.

Finally, in my own modest work on children adjudged to be the highest and the lowest in their classes, I arrived at some very eloquent conclusions.

In the case of children who stand at the foot of their class, the prevailing conditions are not only an unhealthy home but an over-crowded one, with ten or twelve persons sleeping in a single room. On the contrary, in the case of the children standing at the head of their class, the homes are for the most part roomy, comfortable, well-aired and hygienic.

In regard to nutrition, the children who have the lowest standing are those who go to school without their breakfast and who go from the school to the street without having had their luncheon. Those who stand first, on the contrary, bring with them a luncheon that is sufficient and sometimes over-lavish; and after school, they return home, with the assurance that food, care and comfort await them.

The parents of these leaders of their class belong nearly all of them to the liberal professions or the more favoured crafts and trades; consequently the pupils enjoy a more comfortable and respectable environment, a higher standard of culture, a mother who can aid them in their lessons, and who, equally with the father, watches with solicitous care over her children's education.

The others, the dullest pupils, go at the close of school into the street, or else—although fortunately very few of them do so—return directly to the wretchedly cramped quarters that they call home.

Consequently it is not enough to recognise the fact that in school we have to deal with the more intelligent pupil and the less intelligent, with the moral and the immoral, the highest and the lowest; these are effects, the causes of which it is our duty to discover; and that is what the study of antecedents does for us.

Here begins the far-sighted task of the teacher, who no longer praises the pupil who is a product of fortunate causes, nor blames the unfortunate one heavily handicapped by a destiny which is in no way his fault; but he gives to all an affectionate and enlightened care, designed to correct and reform the reprobates and raise them to the level of the chosen few, thus working for the brotherhood and the amelioration of all mankind, and devoting special attention to those that need it most.

The study of antecedents is what contributes most to the interpretation of personality. It is needful, however, that it should be sufficiently thorough; and to this end a certain order of interrogation should be followed. Physicians are well acquainted with this order, from the habit they have acquired of taking the antecedents of the patient in their clinical practice; but for making biographic charts for schools, a *guide* is needed for the use of whoever puts the questions. Besides, the biographical history is based on different principles from those of the clinical history (*e.g.*, the moral status of the parents, their degree of culture, etc., which are not taken into consideration, in treating a patient). Consequently, the blank forms of biographic charts contain suggestions that are likely to prove helpful in conducting an inquiry into antecedents. Among such models, I have selected that of Pastorello, because it is one of the most complete, and also because it was compiled by an educator (see page 420).

Nevertheless, the inquiry into his antecedents is only a preparation for the scientific study of the pupil in his *present state;* a study which should *follow* the pupil through his daily life (diaries) and thus constitute his complete *Biographical History.*

Having collected the antecedent details, we pass on to the objective anthropological and psychic examination of the pupil: beginning with the anthropological, which it is more important to secure first; since the psychic examination will produce better results after a *prolonged observation of the subject* (diaries, school records).

In the anthropological examination it is customary to begin by taking the principal measurements (total stature, sitting stature, weight, thoracic perimeter, perimeter of the head, and its two maximum diameters) which furnish the data needed to give a fundamental idea of the child's physiological constitution and racial type, and to determine the normality of his growth. Many other measurements may be taken (spirometry, dynamometry), according to the custom of the school, and, in private schools, according to the object which the Principal has in view, in the way of contributions to science. For instance, in a school for defectives the examinations as to general sensibility, speech, muscular strength have an importance of the first order, and equally important is the accurate and minute inspection of the different organs, for the purpose of discovering possible malformations. There are various special objects to be attained by gathering anthropological data, and accordingly every school based upon modern scientific principles has its own "Biographical Chart" drawn up according to special forms containing the necessary measurements and observations, and the examiner has only to follow the directions of this guide and to fill in the required information obtained from the individual pupil.

INQUIRY INTO ANTECEDENTS IN PASTORELLO'S BIOGRAPHIC CHART

General Information Regarding Pupil's Family

Name and Surname of Parents

Father ....

Mother ....

What degree of relationship, if any, exists between the parents? ....

....

At what age did the parents contract marriage? ....

....

How old were the parents at the time of the child's birth? ....

....

State of Health

Father. ....

Mother ....

From what diseases have the relatives of the pupil died? ....

....

Have there been any predominant diseases in the family? ....

....

Education

Father. ....

Mother. ....

Employment

Father ....

Mother ....

Ancestry

Father ....

....

....

....

Mother ....

....

....

....

Moral and Financial Condition of the Pupil's Family

....

....

Is the family interested in the education of the children? ....

....

....

....

Family Habits, Eccentricities and Vices

....

....

Here, for instance, is the anthropological form used in the great orphan asylum in New York:

NEW YORK JUVENILE ASYLUM

ANTHROPOLOGICAL EXAMINATION AND MEASUREMENTS.—*No. of page*

Date of entrance	Minimum frontal diameter
Sex	Height of head
Age	Inspection: cranium
Date of birth	Face
Name	Eyes
Total stature	Ears
Sitting stature	Gums
Total spread of arms	Teeth
Weight	Palate
Prehensile strength, right hand	Uvula
Prehensile strength, left hand	Strabismus
Power of traction	Limbs
Thorax { Antero-posterior diameter	Body
Thorax { Transverse diameter	Genitals
Maximum circumference of head	Lung
Maximum antero-posterior diameter	Heart
Maximum transverse diameter	Special notes

This form has signs of *modernity:* in fact, it concedes the greater part of the research that is to be made in the first objective examination to anthropological observations, limiting the observations of a physiological nature to those of muscular strength—it being well known that all *functions* in general, and especially the *psychic functions,* cannot be determined with reliable accuracy except after repeated and prolonged observations. Furthermore, the modern tendency in anthropologic research is revealed by the preference given to measurements of the body in its entirety, giving first place to those of the *bust* and *limbs,* from which the important ratio of their development is obtained (standing and sitting stature, total spread of the arms), and the *weight.* Furthermore, there is a notable *absence of measurements of the face,* measurements which it is the modern tendency to abandon where the subjects of research are children, since in this case they have no physiological or ethnical importance, because the face of the child *varies from year to year,* and has no *fixed* index like that of the cranium. A study of the facial measurements might be of importance as contributing to a knowledge of the evolution of the face through successive years; but such knowledge can be obtained, so far as is needed, from "special studies and researches," without making *obligatory* a form of research that is both troublesome and dangerous (the application of pointed instruments to the faces of children). The best method of examining the face is by photographing the full face and the profile at intervals of one year. Accordingly, the biographic form used in the "Children's Houses" contains only questions of an anthropologic nature of importance in relation to growth (see the form of the Biographic Chart of the "Children's Houses," page 423).

The greatest importance attaches to the *stature* and *weight.* Indeed, while all the required measurements are taken *once a year* on the occasion of the child's birthday, the total stature and the weight are taken once a month upon the day of that month corresponding to the child's birthday. The numerous other physiopathological and psychic notes, the examination in regard to speech, etc., are obtained partly from the diaries and partly from the physician, according to the necessities of individual cases.

The photograph should complete the examination of the pupil. The methods of observation adopted in the "Children's Houses" represent, I think, the ideal method for the accurate recording of individual characteristics. Since the pedagogical methods there employed are themselves founded upon the "spontaneity" of the manifestations of children, it may be said that they represent the technical and rational means of proceeding to a psychic examination of the child.

I cannot linger upon this point, because the question deserves a special investigation; but it must suffice to point out that in order to render biographic charts a necessary adjunct to the management of schools, so as to offer a real aid to the teacher and not to have them mean to her (as happens to-day only too frequently!), "just so much more work," the immediate utility of which is doubtful, it is essential that the *pedagogic methods of instruction* should be changed.

So long as a child is required to perform certain definite acts, he will reveal nothing of himself beyond responding, in so far as he is capable, to the requirements of his environment; and any attempt to make psychological deductions from such response would contain profound errors.

ANTHROPOLOGICAL FORM

USED IN THE "CHILDREN'S HOUSES," IN ROME AND MILAN

No.............. *Date of Enrollment*..............

Name and Surname...*Age*...........
Name of Parents..*Age: M*........*F*.....
Vocation...
Hereditary Antecedents...
....
....
....
Personal Antecedents..
....
....
....

ANTHROPOLOGICAL NOTES

Total stature	Weight	Thoracic circumf.	Essential stature	Index of stature	Ponderal index	Cranium			
						Circumf.	a.-p. diam.	Transv. diam.	Cephalic index

....
Physical constitution...
Muscular development...
Color of complexion...
Color of hair..

NOTES

....
....

Nevertheless, the earlier forms of biographic charts, and even the modern ones *in general use in Italy* (!) frequently contain minute requirements for psychic examination in relation to such points as memory, attention, perception and intelligence.

And even less satisfactory are the requirements in the charts regarding the examination for *sensibility*—namely, ability to distinguish colours, sense of touch, smell, etc.; because the pedagogic methods in vogue in school (and this applies to-day to all our schools) make no provision for a rational exercise of the senses, nor for instruction in the nomenclature relating to them. An examination of the senses for the purposes of the biographic chart should at most be limited to a test of their *acuteness*, forming an inquiry analogous to that of *sensibility to pain*. For an inquiry into the power to discriminate between various sensations ceases to be a simple examination of the senses, and becomes a combined test of psychic powers and of the degree of culture attained (the degree to which the senses have been trained). Furthermore, it is well known that a psychical examination demands preparation on the part of the person to be examined, complete repose from all emotion, isolation of the senses, etc., the preparation depending upon the special research which it is desired to make; all of which is absolutely opposed to the *aggressiveness* of the tumultuous examination conducted by an investigator whose chief aim is to fill in the blanks upon the biographic charts. The psychic examination of a pupil is a task to be accomplished slowly, by watching the child's behaviour, in the course of its *daily life* under the eye of an intelligent and trained observer.

Nevertheless, it is sometimes necessary, especially in schools for defective children, to form at once a comprehensive first impression of the psychic condition of a given child; it furnishes the observer with a needed point of departure, and abridges the long and difficult task of a psychological study of the pupil, to be made in the course of the ensuing year. In such a case, the biographical form should not contain such general topics as the following:

Memory,
Sense of place and time,
Judgment,
Moral sense, etc.,

but a series of very simple *questions* to be put by the examiner to the pupil, the replies to which must be recorded *accurately*, without alteration in any manner, but reproducing their incorrectness of speech, their hesitations, etc. In this way such a form of inquiry constitutes not only a first psychical examination, but also a first examination as to defects of speech, which is of much value and reproduces quite exactly the state of the subject at a given moment.

On the contrary, the sort of results obtained according to the older method, *e.g.*:

Memory, poor;
Intelligence, sufficient;
Attention, easily aroused, etc.;

were practically worthless, especially in absence of any knowledge of the competence of the person who formulated these judgments.

Here is an example of a series of questions to be used as a psychic test, prepared by Professor Sante de Sanctis, and included in the Biographic charts of the Asylum-School for Defective Children at Rome:

1. What is your name?
2. How old are you?
3. What is your mamma's name?
4. Have you any brothers?
5. Have you any sisters?
6. What is your father's business?
7. Is your father (or mother) old or young?
8. At what age is one old?
9. How do you know that a man is old?
10. What is this? (a couch in the corridor).
11. What is it for?
12. What is this? (a table).
13. What is it for?
14. Do you always feel well?
15. Are you hungry?
16. When are you hungry?
17. Do you ever dream at night?
18. What do you dream?
19. What time is it now, more or less?
20. What year is it?
21. What month is it?
22. What season of the year?
23. What day of the month is it?
24. What day of the week?
25. Where do you live?
26. Where are you at the present moment?
27. What are these? (two books or two pictures) and which of the two is the larger?
28. Which of these three glasses has the most water in it?
29. Which will weigh the most and which the least of the three?
30. How many persons are there in your home?
31. Is your home large or small?
32. How many rooms are there?
33. Whom do you love most?
34. What would you do if (the person named) were hungry?
35. What would you do if he were very sick?
36. Or if he died?
37. Do you love some playmate, or some friend? Why do you love him?
38. Do you hate anyone? Why?
39. Do you know the meaning of right and wrong?
40. Do you know the meaning of rewards and punishments?

Out of all the existing forms of biographic charts I have selected four in their entirety; two are historical: 1. the first form for the individual examination of the pupil ever published in any treatise on pedagogy; and 2. the first form printed in Italy by the city authorities with the intention of having it introduced into the elementary schools.

The first of these is the biographic chart proposed by Séguin in his pedagogic treatise relating to the education of idiots (*Traitement moral, hygiene, et éducation des idiots*, 1846); the second is the one proposed by Sergi for the communal schools of Rome, and printed by the Commune with the intention (1889), never actually carried out, of introducing it into the schools; at all events, this is the first historic document representing an idea twenty years in advance of the time when the idea itself was destined to begin to be popularised.

Here are the two forms in question:

Séguin's Form.—This follows out all of Séguin's pedagogical ideas, and all of his didactic methods; it is a guide for the physician, and a minute guide for the teacher who intends to adopt the Séguin methods of education. Séguin calls his biographic chart a "Monographic Picture," and divides it into five paragraphs, the fifth of which deals with the pupil's antecedents.

Monographic Picture (*Sèguin*)

I. *Portrait* (*Objective Morphological Examination*)

Age.
Sex.
Temperament, health.
Illnesses, accessory infirmities.
Detailed configuration of the cranium.
Configuration of the face.
Proportional relation between cranium and face.
Inequality of the two sides of cranium and face.
Hair, skin.
Proportional relation between the trunk and the limbs.
Inequality of the two sides of the trunk and limbs.
General attitude of the body.
Attitude of the head.
Attitude of the trunk.
Attitude of the lower limbs.
Attitude of the upper limbs.
Attitude of the hand and fingers.
Configuration of the organs of speech, and their possible relation to the organs of generation; dentition.
Configuration of the thorax.
State of the vertebral column.
State of the abdomen.

II. *Physiological Examination*

Activity, general and applied.
Apparent state of the nervous system.
General irritability of the nervous system.
Irritability of special groups of nerves.
Cries, groans, singing, muttering, etc.
The change which certain stimulants such as cold, heat, electricity, odours, etc., produce upon irritability and sensibility, general or special.
Probable state of the brain.
Voluntary articular flexions.
Locomotion.
Positions, recumbent, seated, standing, walking, ascending, descending.
Running.
Jumping.
Grasping objects.
Dropping objects.
Catching objects.
Throwing objects.
Ability to dress, eat, etc., without aid.

Probable state of the spinal marrow.
Probable state of the organic nerves.
Probable state of the sensory nerves.
Probable state of the motor nerves.
Difference of action between the sensory nerves and the motor nerves.
Inequality of action of the motor nerves and sensory nerves on the two sides of the body.
The muscular system, contractibility of muscles, and condition of sphincter muscles in particular.
Muscular movements.
Voluntary movements.
Automatic movements depending on the condition of the sympathetic nerve.
Automatic movements depending on the state of the central nervous system.
Spasmodic movements.
Coordinated and disassociated movements.
Sense of touch.
Sense of taste.
Sense of smell.
Sense of hearing.
Sense of sight.
Erectility.
The voice, abnormal tones.
Speech.
Assimilative functions.
Unnatural appetites.
Manner of taking food.
Mastication.
Swallowing.
Digestion.
Evacuation of fæces and urine, voluntary or involuntary; other excretions, saliva, nasal mucus, tears, sebaceous humor, sweat, perspiration, etc.
Pulse.
Respiration.
Sleep.

III. *Psychic Examination*

Attention.
Sensorial perception.
Intellectual perception.
Deduction.
Coordination.
Inventiveness.
Unrelated memories.
Foresight and forethought.
To what extent are these intellectual operations, when they exist, applied to concrete phenomena, mixed phenomena (*i.e.*, concrete and abstract) and to ideas of a moral nature?
Are the general ideas of time, space, conventional measurements, relative value, intrinsic or arbitrary, understood and applied in actual daily life?
Comparison.
Judgment.
Reflection.
Have the ordinary rudiments, such as the alphabet, reading, writing, drawing, arithmetic, been taught to the pupil or not, and can they be taught in his present state?
Have his attitude toward music and mathematics, enjoyment of singing, irresistible desire to sing, been brought about naturally?
Has he a perception of the physical proportion of bodies, such as colour, form, dimensions, relations between the parts to form a whole?

IV. *Examination Regarding Instincts and Sentiments*

Instinct of self-preservation.

Instincts of order, readjustment, preservation and destruction of objects.

Aggressiveness, cruelty.

Instinct of assimilation and possession.

Is the child obedient or rebellious, respectful or impertinent, affectionate or cold, rude or courteous, grateful, jealous, merry or sad, proud, vain or indifferent, courageous or cowardly, timid or venturesome, circumspect or thoughtless, credulous or suspicious?

Has the child a sense of abstract right and wrong or only in relation to a small number of acts that concern himself?

Does the child show spontaniety or an active will—the kind of will which is the initial cause of all human actions producing intellectual or social results?

Has the child only a negative will associated with instincts and does he protest energetically against any extraneous will that tends to compel the idiot to concern himself with social or abstract phenomena?

Finally, in what direction and within what limits has the idiot passed beyond the boundaries of his *ego* in order to enter into physcial, instinctive, intellectual and moral communication with the phenomena which surround him?

V. *Etiology*

Origin of father and mother.

Their constitution.

Hereditary diseases.

Place of residence at the time of the child's conception, gestation, birth and lactation.

Possible causes of idiocy.

Circumstances worthy of note during conception.

Circumstances worthy of note during gestation, delivery, lactation.

Serious illnesses of the child during the first year.

Infirmities and illnesses from the first year down to the first symptoms of idiocy. Progress, retrogression or stationary state from the child's birth down to the time of examination.

If we realise that this model for a biographic chart was proposed more than one-half a century ago, it makes us marvel at the modern spirit of its concepts: it actually considers the relation between the development *of the trunk and of the limbs*, the *mimic attitudes of the body*, the *constitution*, etc., all of which concepts are foreign to the studies of the medical clinics from which Séguin must have drawn his inspiration, since even to the present day the tendency in the clinics is toward purely analytical investigation, with the exception of Professor De Giovanni's clinic.

In the model proposed by Sergi, the examination was required to be made twice: first upon the reception of the pupil, and again at his departure with the modifications shown below:

BIOGRAPHICAL CHART FOR SCHOOLS (SERGI)

TABLE I.—*Physical Observations*

On entering school Class............ Year..............	On leaving school Class............ Year................
1. Name.	1. Name.
2. Age.	2. Age.
3. Birthplace.	3. Birthplace.
4. Parentage (father and mother).	4. Parentage (father and mother).
5. Vaccination.	5. Vaccination.
6. Stature.	6. Stature.
7. Weight.	7. Weight.
8. Pulmonary capacity.	8. Pulmonary capacity.
9. Muscular force.	9. Muscular force.
10. General state of health.	10. General state of health.
11. Past illnesses.	11. Past illnesses.
12. Anomalies, deformities.	12. Anomalies, deformities.
13. Head, horizontal circumference.	13. Head, horizontal circumference.
14. Head, maximum length.	14. Head, maximum length.
15. Head, maximum width.	15. Head, maximum width.
16. Cephalic index.	16. Cephalic index.
17. Face, length.	17. Face, length.
18. Face, width.	18. Face, width.
19. Facial index.	19. Facial index.
20. Hair, colour, form.	20. Hair, colour, form.
21. Eyes, colour.	21. Eyes, colour.
22. Skin, complexion.	22. Skin, complexion.
23. Incidental remarks.	23. Incidental remarks.

BIOGRAPHICAL CHART FOR SCHOOLS (SERGI)

TABLE II.—*Psychological Observations*

On entering school Class............ Year..............	On leaving school Class............ Year...............
1. Sight, acuteness, far- or near-sighted.	1. Sight, acuteness, far- or near-sighted.
2. Sense of colour, normal, defective.	2. Sense of colour, normal, defective.
3. Hearing, acuteness.	3. Hearing, acuteness.
4. Sense of touch, acuteness.	4. Sense of touch, acuteness.
5. Intelligence, quick or slow.	5. Intelligence, quick or slow.
6. Perception, rapid or gradual.	6. Perception, rapid or gradual.
7. Memory, tenacious or short.	7. Memory, tenacious or short.
8. Attention, easily aroused or not.	8. Attention, easily aroused or not.
9. Speech, rapid or slow.	9. Attention, how long sustained.
10. Speech, pronunciation perfect or imperfect.	10. Attention, progressive weariness.
11. Speech, stammering.	11. Speech, rapid or slow.
12. Emotional sensibility, dull or easily assumed.	12. Speech, pronunciation perfect or imperfect.
13. Conduct and character at home.	13. Speech, stammering.
14. Affection for parents.	14. Emotional sensibility, dull or easily assumed.
15. Taciturnity or loquacity.	15. Conduct and character in school.
16. Preferences during free hours.	16. Friendships in school.
17. Caprices, eccentricities.	17. Taciturnity or loquacity.
18. Unusual incidental occurrences.	18. Preferences during free hours.
	19. Caprices, eccentricities.
	20. Unusual incidental occurrences.

The two other biographic charts that deserve specific mention are, unlike the above, charts in actual use, since they have both been recently introduced into practical service.

The first, which I reproduce in entirety, is the one adopted by the Commune of Bologna for its schools; the second is the one introduced, for the purpose of studying the inmates, into the government reformatories, of Italy, that have recently been transformed into educational institutions, into which a number of important reforms have been introduced, through the influence of scientific pedagogy—among others, these biographical charts and the anthropological researches connected with them.

Biographic chart for elementary schools:

DISTRICT OF .... *Year* 191....

Class...........

COMMUNE OF BOLOGNA

OFFICE X.—HYGIENE

Biographic Chart of the Pupil

Name and Surname...

Age...

Place of birth and residence..

Parents' Place of birth and vocation..................................

THE TEACHER.

....

State of skin, of the subcutaneous tissue, the muscles, the lymphatic glands

Head { horizontal circumference / maximum width / maximum length

Celphalic index

Face { height / width

Facial index

Hair { colour / form

Eyes { keenness of sight / hypermetropia / myopia / colour sense / colour of iris

Hearing, acuteness

Teeth { form / number decayed / number missing

Anomalies of development

Weight of body { at the beginning, / at the end of the year

Total spread of arms

Stature

Pulmonary capacity

THE PHYSICIAN

....

Illnesses incurred during the school year

....

....

Total number of absences

....

Number of absences on account of illness

....

Profit derived from instruction

....

Conduct and character in school

....

Affection toward parents and schoolmates

....

Special observations

....

....

....

THE MASTER

....

The biographic chart of the reformatories is among the most complete; nevertheless, it is based upon antiquated methods for the study of the individual, including, for instance, the facial index and ignoring that of the stature; and limiting the psychic examination to abstract notes (reflection, attention, etc.). It constitutes, however, an anthropological *record*, for it follows the child throughout his whole residence in the reformatory.

What is called, in the chart in question, the *moral account*, corresponds to our *third subdivision* in biographic histories, in so far as it represents a summary of the daily records. Under this head mention is made of the moral balance, and the notes tell us that it is founded upon "*punishments*" and "*rewards.*" In so far as they treat of disciplining children, these notes are not to be taken as a model; they are evidently a relic of antiquated educative methods that have survived amid the efforts of a new scientific movement. There is no mention made of medical treatment bestowed upon the children, who may very often owe their so-called *moral* anomalies to a pathological condition which must frequently be *aggravated* by punishments. It is well known that many normal children have periods of agitation which is manifested by the most various kinds of action (impulsiveness, sexual excesses, rebellion), followed by periods of calm during which the child exhibits the opposite characteristics (industriousness, obedience, etc.). The biographic chart is quite likely to show a record of punishments and rewards corresponding to these contrasted periods; and in this respect it follows antiquated pedagogic methods, which are precisely what need to be reformed under the light of science.

An illustration of this is contained in the biographic history of an idiot boy in the asylum of the *Bicêtre*, a report of which is given below: the periodic *anomalies of character* in the boy should be noticed. Many epileptic children do not have convulsions, but exhibit instead anomalies of character which become permanent and are naturally aggravated by fatigue and punishment; and the great majority of such children pass eventually into reformatories.

In the forms customarily used for biographic charts, there is liberal provision for daily notes. Accordingly, in the biographic chart of the child in question there are a number of blank pages on which *casual notes* have been entered (diary). Every fact deserving of notice has been entered; facts of a physio-pathological nature, such as illnesses, strength, endurance in running, appetite, outbursts of anger without cause; school-notes regarding the progress attained by the child in school, especially when he has overcome serious difficulties, correction of incidental defects of speech, etc., and notes of a psycho-moral nature regarding acts committed by the child, tending to show the state of his feelings.

The master has a general register which may be compared to the *daily entry book* used in book-keeping, and in which all the *notes of the day* are entered. Days and even months frequently pass without any entry being made in regard to some particular child. From this general register the master later draws up individual *summaries* which are then transcribed into the corresponding biographic history of each child.

Once in so many years all the measurements and observations are repeated in their entirety (*e.g.*, at the most important periods of growth with especial study of the epoch of puberty). When the child is definitely discharged from the school, a general summary is drawn up; in such a case the *biographic chart* represents that individual's *own personal history;* a human and social document of the highest interest to anyone who wishes to *know himself*, and continue his own self-education! It might serve as a useful guide to a man of intelligence.

These registers and biographic charts may be compared to the record of points and the report cards that are in use to-day in the schools. Even the report cards which are obtained through a fatiguing process of *averages* represent a summary of notes taken every day by the teacher (although not every day for *every* pupil). But the report card is of no practical use to the man who wishes to draw up a faithful record of the education he has received that will serve to *guide him through life.*

Since there do not yet exist any complete biographic histories relating to normal children, I shall reproduce one of an idiot boy who was received into the great Paris hospital for defectives; this history is interesting because it is the result of the methods of Séguin who was the founder of the anthropological movement in pedagogy; it would be still more interesting if we could offer the complete history of a normal man or of a wayward boy redeemed by education. But let us hope for this in the near future!

The summary of the history which I here reproduce does not

contain the objective examination of the boy at the time of his reception; because that would only be a repetition of what has already been described, while the part which it now interests us to illustrate is that containing the summaries of the diaries. The antecedents, however, are given because they are indispensable for an understanding of the patient's personality.

SUMMARY OF THE BIOGRAPHIC HISTORY OF AN IDIOT BOY

Admitted at the Age of 3 Years, and Dismissed at the Age of 17

OUTLINE: Father an alcoholic.—Mother subject to migraine.—No consanguinity between the parents. Equality of ages (difference of two years).—A sister died of convulsions.—Conception during an alcoholic excess on the part of the father.—Albuminuria during pregnancy.—The child cried both night and day.—Twitchings of the body and head.—Did he ever have convulsions?—Fits of anger.—At the time of admission, he could neither speak nor walk (July 30, 1881, age 3 years).—The child has involuntary emissions of fæces and urine (is uncleanly).

September, 1884.—The child has learned to walk.

1885.—Development of speech.—The child is beginning to give notice of its natural necessities.

1886.—The child is no longer uncleanly.—The twitchings of head and body and the fits of anger have diminished.

1887–1890.—Progressive improvement, with alternate progressive and stationary periods.

1891.—Description of the patient.

1892–1897.—Physical and intellectual evolution.—Progress in studies.—Acquirement of a trade.—Results.

Remote Antecedents. (Notes furnished by the mother.)—*Father:* 35 years old, tailor's cutter, large, strong, of calm temperament, a smoker; numerous *excesses of alcoholic beverages*, especially absinthe—as many as eleven a day; venereal excesses; came home intoxicated almost every day; never had convulsions in infancy, nor any nervous shock; suffered only from eczema. No syphilis.—*Father's Family:* Paternal grandfather a mason, sober, died of heart disease. Paternal grandmother, of calm temperament, enjoyed good health. No other information regarding paternal ancestry.—*Mother:* 33 years old, seamstress, good health, regular features; no convulsions in infancy. Menstruated at age of 13 years, married at 20. Suffered from migraine since she was nine years old. These headaches lasted three days and occurred at the menstrual periods, ceasing throughout pregnancy and lactation. The symptoms were: headache, buzzing in the ears, to the point of deafness, and vision of sparks before the eyes. The attacks terminated with vomiting. *Mother's Family:* Father sober and in good health; mother died of influenza. No information regarding either the ascendant or collateral branches; but there seem to have been no other cases of nervous disease in the family. No consanguinity, no disparity in ages. *Brothers and Sisters of the Patient:* The mother of D—— had five children; the first, a boy ten years and a half old, intelligent, no convulsions; the second, a girl, died at fourteen months, after having convulsions that continued for eight days; the third, a girl, seven years old, intelligent, no convulsions; the fourth, the patient in question; the fifth, a girl, born after D——'s admission to the asylum; she is intelligent and healthy, no convulsions.

Near Antecedents. The child's mother is convinced that the conception took place during *alcoholic* intoxication. Pregnancy was accompanied by generalised œdema from the fifth month onward, due to albuminuria. No *eclampsia.* No fainting fits, etc. Delivery timely, difficult, but accomplished naturally. The child at birth was strong and not asphyxiated. Was nursed by the mother for the first two months, after which he depended upon hired nurses and artificial feeding (was sent to the country where he was fed chiefly from the bottle). Was returned to the mother at the age of eleven months; could not walk; would eat anything within reach of his hands, coal, excrements. Cried continually, day and night, to the great disturbance of the neighbours. Cut his first tooth at five months; and at the age of three years the first dentition was not yet completed. Has a habit of swaying his body forward and backward; beats his head against the wall, the chairs, etc., and strikes his forehead with his clenched fist. Has habitual constipation. Is extremely affectionate, loves to be caressed. Yet he will bite anyone who approaches him, including his brothers and sisters. It cannot be learned whether when he was staying with the wet-nurse he ever had convulsions. It is certain that he had none after his return to the family. The habit of *onanism* dates from the time of his return from the nurse. Vaccinated at 13 months, slight attack of varioloid at the age of two years; no other infectious diseases. No manifestation of scrofula; no traumatism.

Objective Examination of the Patient (omitted).—The *history* is accompanied by eight photographs of the boy, taken respectively at the ages of 3, 4, 6, 8, 11, 15, and 16 years, three of which, namely, those taken at the ages of 6, 11 and 16, are reproduced on page 278.

Diaries

July 2.—He is uncleanly (emissions of fæces and urine). Does not know how to behave at table; when he eats he spills his food over his clothing. Is gluttonous but not voracious; he does not steal the food of his companions, but he protests when he sees food given to others and not to him. Is mistrustful, hides his bread for fear that it will be taken from him; and if any one takes notice of this, he utters a cry of rage. He is affectionate, very timid, jealous, obstinate, grumbling, somewhat sullen, seldom laughs. Although weak, he fights his companions and frequently falls into *fits of anger;* then he flings himself on the floor and beats his head against the furniture. He sways his body forward and backward. His *power of speech* is limited to three words: *papa, mamma,* and *no.* He is able to make himself understood when he wants anything.

August–September.—Two slight attacks of ophthalmia. The child has now learned to walk.

January–March, 1885.—Otitis (inflammation of the ear).

August.—The ability to speak is developing progressively. He has begun to give notice of his natural necessities; is seldom uncleanly, so that it is now possible to let him wear trousers. The habit of balancing his body back and forth is tending to disappear. The accesses of anger have become rarer. He is less jealous and plays indiscriminately with his companions.

January, 1886.—The improvement continues. D—— is now very attentive in school. When out walking he takes an interest in the things he sees and asks for explanations. Is doing well in the first gymnastic exercises. Makes a good appearance.

March.—D—— has now become altogether cleanly. Furthermore, he knows how to wash, dress and undress himself alone. At table, can handle his spoon and fork quite properly, but cannot yet manage his knife. Is less gluttonous; his speech is fully developed. Although he cannot keep still in school and constantly changes his position, he has succeeded in learning to know his letters, the different colours, etc., can count up to 50, and can name the greater part of the objects contained in the boxes used for object lessons. The balancing of the body has completely disappeared. D—— has a tendency toward onanism. Accesses of anger are still noted, during which he is very vulgar.

December.—Condition stationary. Misconduct in class, frequent fits of anger, during which he abuses everyone and strikes his smaller comrades.

March, 1887.—D—— is calmer and does better work. Can count up to sixty. His general knowledge has increased. Can tell his age, his name, the name of his parents, what their employment is, where they live, etc.

April, 1888.—The improvement continues. His behavior is better. Has learned the names of materials, of plane surfaces, of solids; can distinguish vowels from consonants. It has been impossible to induce him to trace simple strokes even upon the blackboard.

December.—Is more diligent and has taken a fancy to writing.

January–June, 1889.—Is in the infirmary on account of anal ulcers.

December.—Notable improvement in general knowledge. Has begun to write certain letters in his copybook.

December, 1890.—D——'s conduct is good. He is no longer disorderly; and if at times it is necessary to reprove him, he recognises his fault, cries, and promises to do better. He fears above all that his misconduct will be reported to his mother. Has a fairly accurate notion of right and wrong, is no longer so extremely jealous and shows affection for his comrades. Has learned to write syllables well; is able to copy short paragraphs; can do simple sums in addition; gives clear answers to questions. Walking, running, jumping, going up and down stairs have become easy for him. The child uses his fork and knife at table; chews his food well, does not suffer from any digestive disturbance. Is orderly, and attends to himself in all details of his toilet.

April 21, 1891: *Objective Examination.*—The child's face has a uniformly ruddy complexion; lips full-blooded; skin smooth, without scars or eruptions, excepting a slight scaliness due to eczema. Two small ganglia in the left submaxillary region, but no others in any other locality. Cranium symmetrical; volume and form normal. Frontal and parietal nodules slightly prominent; occipital nodule quite prominent (pentagonoid cranium). Hair light blonde, abundant, fine, growing low upon the forehead. Posterior vortex normal, forehead wide, but not high. Visage oval; with a slight depression of the nostril and corner of the mouth on the right side; has on the whole an intelligent express on; it is mobile and reflects the moods and feelings natural to boyhood. The superciliary arches are only slightly arched. The eyebrows are chestnut in colour and scanty; the lashes are abundant and long. Iris dark blue; pupils equal in size and react under the influence of light. No functional disturbance, and no lesion in regard to the eyes. Field of vision normal. D—— recognises all the colours. Nose small, and straight, with a pronounced aperture of the nostrils. Zygomata regular, without exaggerated prominences; naso-labial furrows barely indicated. Aperture of mouth very wide and habitually half open. Lips thick and slightly drooping. Tongue normal. Palatine vault distinctly ogival. Tonsils enlarged; the boy is subject to tonsillitis. All these parts show quite a blunted sensibility, which permits of an examination of the pharynx, without causing nausea. Chin rounded, without indentation. Ears long and thick, the outer edge is normal, including the fold of the helix; the ears protrude conspicuously from the cranium and are very peculiar in shape; namely, the upper two-thirds of the external ear form with the lower one-third an obtuse angle of such nature that the *concha* or shell really represents the outline of a very deep and almost hemispherical sea-shell. The lobule is thick, regular, and notably detached. The ear is the seat of frequent attacks of erythema, complicated by swelling. Neck rather short and quite stout; circumference 26 centimetres. The lobes of the thyroid glands are plainly palpable to the touch.

Thorax and Abdomen.—No notable peculiarities. Auscultation and percussion show that the internal organs are normal. Body is hairless. Genital organs are normal. The upper and lower limbs are normal in all their segments.

Icthyosis of the skin on thighs and knees. General sensibility normal; usual physiological reflex actions.

Treatment.—Regular application of the medico-pedagogical method: tonics during the winter; hydrotherapy annually, from the first of April to the first of November.

April 24.—The mother, finding the child much improved, takes him home on leave (March) and later (end of April) requests his dismissal, which is granted reluctantly, in the fear that the boy may lose part of what he has so laboriously gained.

May 19, 1892.—The boy, having become insubordinate and not making satisfactory progress in the public school (to which he was sent, so that he would not be present at the scenes between the mother and the father, who is habitually intoxicated), has been sent back to the asylum.

June.—The physical evolution continues. The child is very timid and sensitive, cannot bear to be reproved and cries when he is corrected. Reads fluently, but without expression Has begun to write familiar words from dictation. During his absence from the asylum he learned to know the numbers and to do simple examples in addition and subtraction.

Treatment: School work; gymnastics; hydrotherapy.

July.—D—— is at present conducting himself in a way difficult to control; he plays ill-natured jests upon his companions; places needles and tacks in seats; during the assembly he amuses himself by sticking little pins into the backs of the girls who sit in front of him.

December.—The boy is very lazy, and often refuses to read or to do his tasks; he grins and sneers if he is corrected. But he carries out very well all the movements in the lower gymnastic course. Has been sent to the *tailor's work-shop* and seems to have taken a fancy to the trade.

April, 1893.—D—— has become quite reasonable, does good work in school, does not like to be inactive, has ceased to grin and sneer. His writing has improved; his reasoning power is good; he is careful of his clothes to the point of vanity; eats with propriety, has ceased to bolt his food; yet it is still noticed that he has a tendency to appropriate the wine of his companions.

June.—D—— is passing through a bad period; he laughs at everything that is said to him, is very obstinate, annoys his comrades, tears up copy-books, breaks pens, etc. Is careless regarding his clothing; makes a disturbance at night in the dormitory.

December.—Same state. Tries to smoke; is unwilling to do any work; laughs at everybody; dresses with great carelessness; it is necessary to compel him to wash his hands and face. No sign of *puberty.*

December, 1894.—Notable improvement; D—— reads quite readily, writes quite well, recognises all ordinary objects, their use, and their colour; has a conception of time. Is docile, neat, industrious in school work, is attentive to explanations and understands them. In the work-shop he continues to show progress.

January–June, 1895.—The improvement continues; D—— has begun to learn the multiplication table; he is well-mannered and scrupulous in his behaviour; excellent in gymnastics. In the tailor's work-shop he makes marked progress; he has already learned to put together an entire garment by himself, and he knows how to use the machine. From time to time he has periods of indolence; and this happens more often in the work-shop than in the class.

Puberty.—A slight down has begun to appear upon his upper lip.

July 8.—According to the night nurse, D—— had an attack of epilepsy during the night; he never had one before, and he has not had one since.

July 10.—Troubled sleep, nightmare, unintelligible and threatening words.

January, 1896.—Very notable improvement in class. The boy profited above all from the *lessons about natural objects,* in which he takes much interest. From time to time he shows a tendency to dissipation and gambling. Is docile, cleanly, and neat in personal appearance to the point of vanity. The master of the work-shop is very much pleased with him; he works well with the machine. Is doing well in gymnastics and in singing.

Puberty.—His beard has begun to grow even on his cheeks.

June.—Hand-writing, far from improving, seems to be growing worse. On the contrary, it is noticed that he has made progress in arithmetic. Can perform all four primary operations and has begun to solve easy problems. His general knowledge has improved. Has become a good tailor's workman.

January–June, 1897.—The boy prefers the work-shop to the school and for some time the mistake has been made of leaving him wholly in the work-shop.

December.—Same state from point of view of his studies; character docile, conduct good, personal care and neatness satisfactory. Works well and rapidly in the work-shop; can make complete suits of clothing; uses the machine dexterously; is beginning to cut out garments.

Puberty complete, no onanism. The right eyelids are less widely open than the left by nearly a quarter. The patient says that he does not see so well with the right eye as with the left, and cannot distinguish with it even large letters unless they are very near.

TABLE OF WEIGHT AND STATURE

Measurements	1890	1894		1895		1896		1897		1898
	January	January	July	January	July	January	July	January	July	January
Weight in kilograms.	25	34.700	35.200	35	37.800	39.800	44	46	51	53.700
Stature in metres.	1.22	1.39	1.42	1.42	1.50	1.53	1.58	1.61	1.66	1.69

MEASUREMENTS OF THE HEAD IN CENTIMETRES

	1891	1893	1894	1895		1896		1897		1898
	January	January	January	January	July	January	July	January	July	January
Maximum horizontal circumference.	50.2	50.2	50.2	52	52	52	52	52	52	54
Anterior semi-circumference......	33	33	33	33	33	33	33	33	33	34
Distance from the occipito-atlantoid articulation to the root of nose.	36	36	36	36	36	36	36	36	36	37
Maximum antero-posterior diameter.	17.5	17.8	17.8	18	18	18	18	19	19	19
Maximum biauricular diameter...	11	12	12	12.5	12.5	12.5	12.2	12.5	12.5	13
Maximum biparietal diameter....	13.5	14	14	14.5	14.5	14.5	14.5	14.5	14.5	14.5
Maximum bitemporal diameter...	—	—	—	—	11	11	11	11.5	11.5	12
Medial height of forehead........	5	5	5	5	5	5	5	5	6	6

In the antecedents of this patient, the only suggestions of degeneration are the *alcoholism* of the father and the fact that conception took place in a state of intoxication. The mother's migraine might also be considered as a nervous malady amounting to a family taint, but cannot be held responsible for so grave an abnormality as idiocy.

Consequently, it remains beyond doubt that the most interesting antecedent fact to be considered in this case is the *conception during alcoholic intoxication.*

The individual we are studying is a sick person; this is shown by *ptosis* (drooping eye-lid), the recurrent periods of agitation, the epileptic convulsion in the night detected by the night nurse.

It is interesting to observe in the photographs of the child, the alteration of expression between the periods of calm and those of agitation; in the latter the face is asymmetrical and shows contractions in the left facial region, while the right side is paretic; the paresis is also manifested by *ptosis* (drooping lids). During the periods of calm, on the contrary, the left side also is atonic.

In the course of the history the differences in the child's conduct in the two states are well described.

During the periods of calm, the child is attentive, docile, careful of his dress, timid, and makes progress in his studies; during the periods of agitation he is unstable, rebellious, careless, unkind to his comrades, and makes no progress whatever. At the beginning, there were no periods of calm at all; furthermore, the child had every appearance of being an idiot; medico-pedagogic treatment rendered longer and more frequent, and finally permanent, these periods of calm, during which the child's intellectual redemption became possible. The treatment did not consist solely in the *education of an idiot,* but also in the *cure of a sick child.* "At the time of admission," according to the *observations* in the record, "the diagnosis was *retarded mentality,* and that only in relation to primary instruction, because in regard to matters of common knowledge and manual work, the patient comes very near to a normal lad of average intelligence."

Such a surprising *transformation* of an individual is certainly deserving of admiration; but this diligently compiled study is not yet quite completed. As a matter of fact, when the education of D—— was begun, observations regarding types of stature were not yet made; but his photographs show that he was an exaggerated macroscelous type. The trade adopted by D—— which will oblige him to sit with his chest bowed over the machine, or in a kneeling position while he sews, will in all probability drive him straight along the road to tuberculosis, a malady to which his organism has singularly predisposed him. It would be interesting to follow further the history of this patient, who has been transformed from an idiot into a skilful and industrious workman.

The society, which under the guidance of science, achieved his difficult redemption, has perhaps at the same time condemned him to death.

The modern standards of pedagogical anthropology would have furnished a more far-sighted guidance in the choice of a vocation.

Meanwhile, however, this history reported by Thulié is a luminous demonstration of the folly of rewards and punishments; the only forms of intervention during the periods of agitation, which lasted for entire months, during which the boy was continually unruly, impulsive, malicious, reckless, and incapable of work, were tonics, hydrotherapy and kindly treatment.

"Punishments" would have cruelly wrecked the life of a human being who was naturally gentle, affectionate, and capable of diligent work and permanent improvement.

Something similar ought to be attempted in the reformatories. The boys who are regarded as incorrigible are frequently *sick* boys, with an hereditary degenerative taint, and need to live in a tranquil environment and to receive medical treatment.

The biographic charts of the reformatories give no evidence that this educative movement has as yet been understood. They show that *punishments* are still regarded as possessing a corrective efficacy, because the conception that the so-called delinquent children may be a pathological product and a result of disastrous family and social conditions, has not yet penetrated with sufficient clearness.

But progress along this path is surely bound to come as a result of the experience which this principle of reform has made possible.

The biographic charts have unquestionably laid the foundations of a new edifice in pedagogy.

Scientific Pedagogical Advantages of Biographic Histories:

1. The biographic chart takes the place of the report cards and records of the relative marks of merit and demerit; for while

these records and reports constituted a statement of *effects,* altogether empirical, the biographic chart *investigates the causes* and in this way furnishes pedagogy with a scientific basis. There is no need of further demonstration. The principal consequences of the above indicated progress are two in number.

2. The biographic chart, replacing the earlier classifications, raises the teacher's standard of culture by directing him along a scientific path, associates the teacher's work with that of the physician, and makes the teacher a far-sighted director of the development and perfectioning of the new generations.

3. The biographic chart includes a new educative movement which abolishes rewards and punishments.

On this third point much might be said, since it touches upon one of the fundamental doctrines of pedagogical progress. But since this is not a treatise upon scientific pedagogy, it is necessary to limit the exposition to a few fundamental points.

In fact, it will be sufficient to speak of cases in which education is most difficult and where the rewards and punishments are unavailing—for these will include all simpler cases. A luminous example is furnished by the education of *new-born infants.* Of all human beings they used to be the most troublesome because of the impossibility of educating them by the old-fashioned methods. They cried at all hours of the day and night, making a slave of the mother or whoever took her place.

To-day, babies are quiet; it is marvelous to go through the infant ward in the Obstetrical Clinic of Rome; absolute silence reigns there, and yet if we lift up the white curtains of the cribs, we see the little ones lying with their eyes wide open. A deeper knowledge than was formerly had of the *hygiene of the child* has enabled us to interpret his needs, and when these are satisfied, the child is tranquil. Bodily cleanliness, liberty of movement, prolonged repose in the crib, and *rational feeding* have obtained this remarkable result of silencing the baby, of rendering it more robust and of liberating the mother from the slavery of her mission. The classic cry of the child in swaddling bands was a protest against the suffering which ignorance imposed upon him. To-day the little one, lying tranquilly in his crib, begins to exercise his senses earlier and more easily, a ray of light strikes him and attracts his attention, and with this his education has begun, while formerly the suffering due to indigestion kept him for a much longer time a stranger to the external world.

The same thing may be repeated for every year of childhood. Often what we call *naughtiness* on the part of the individual child is *rebellion* against our own mistakes in educating him. The coercive means which we adopt toward children are what destroy their natural tranquility. A healthy child, in his moments of freedom, succeeds in escaping from the toys inflicted upon him by his parents, and in securing some object which arouses the investigating instinct of his mind; a worm, an insect, some pebbles, etc.; he is silent, tranquil and attentive. If the child is not well, or if his mother obliges him to remain seated in a chair, playing with a doll, he becomes restless, cries, or gives way to convulsive outbursts ("bad temper"). The mother believes that educating her child means forcing him to do what is pleasing to her, however far she may be from knowing what the child's real needs are, and unfortunately we must make the same statement regarding the school-teachers! Then, in order to make him yield to coercion, she punishes the child when he rebels and rewards him when he is obedient. By this method we *drive a child by force* along paths that are not natural to him. In the same way, absolute governments employed public entertainments and the gallows, in order to compel the people to act and think according to the will of their sovereign; indeed, they were considered as indispensable means of good government. To-day we have come to realise that such means are more or less adapted to the successful crushing of a people's spirit, but not to governing them well. The reign of *liberty*, which leaves men the opportunity to give expression to their own powers and above all to their own thoughts, is doing away with festivals and executions; and it is not until this is accomplished that men can be really *well governed.*

Something similar is going to take place in the schools. But here, since the children are incapable of understanding *what they ought to do* for their own best good, science *studies them* in order to assist their natural needs.

I believe that we must greatly modify our ideas regarding infant psychology, as soon as trained psychologists begin to observe the spontaneous manifestations of children, to the end of encouraging their tendencies.

Having applied scientific methods in the "Children's Houses," we were amazed at the behaviour of those little children; for instance, they showed contempt for toys, while they loved objects on which they could exercise their free powers of reason.

Intellectual exercise is the most pleasing of all to the small child if he is in good health. Indeed, we already know that children break their toys in order to see how they are made inside; this shows that the exercise of their intellect interests them more than playing with an object that is often irrational. But children are not, as is generally believed, naturally destructive; on the contrary, their instinct is to *preserve.* This is seen in the way in which they save little objects that they have acquired by themselves; and in the "Children's Houses," we have also seen it in the way that they preserve unharmed even the most trivial scrap of paper, although free to tear it up, so long as that scrap of paper helps them to exercise their thoughts.

Here we see the great difference between the healthy, normal child who employs himself in the way that pleases him, and is attentive and tranquil; and another child who, equally healthy and normal, is obliged to do what other people wish him to do, and is restless, and troublesome and cries.

To aid the physical development of the child under the guidance of natural laws is to favour his health and his growth; to aid his natural psychic tendencies is to render him more intelligent.

This principle has been intuitively recognised by all pedagogists, but the practical application of it was not possible, excepting under the guidance of scientific pedagogy, founded upon a direct knowledge of the human individual.

To-day it is possible for us to establish a régime of liberty in our schools, and consequently it is our duty to do so.

Whenever a child exhibits anomalies of character that do not signify rebellion against irrational methods of education, and are not expressions of a struggle for liberty, he represents the unhappy effect of some *pathological cause*, or of some *social error*, that has only too fatally accomplished its corruptive task.

This is what the biographic history will reveal!

As a general rule, a *bad* child should be taken to see a *physician*, because it is almost certain that he is a sick child.

But the *treatment* of such maladies is very often mainly pedagogical; curative pedagogy, however, must absolutely abolish *punishment*.

We now know as a fact absolutely established in sociology that the fear of punishment, of torture and even of death does not avail to diminish crime, nor the imperious manifestation of human passions.

Brigandage is not repressed by cutting off heads, but by civilization in all its forms of industry, intercommunication, etc.

And this principle is especially true in the case of children; harshness of methods and severity of punishment will not avail to inculcate, and still less to create, goodness. Man is conquered through kindness and gentleness; among all the beatitudes, that of inheriting the earth (*i.e.*, of winning over their fellow-men) is given to the *meek: blessed are the meek, for they shall inherit the earth.*

We know that hypocrisy, adulation and seduction are criminal means by which man seeks to deceive his fellow men to his own profit; but they are based upon gentleness; it would never occur to anyone to seduce and to conquer hypocritically, with the help of violence. Because the weak point in man, that to which he is most susceptible, is gentleness, praise, caresses. We have seen that the psychic stimulus needed to augment human activity, to arouse an apathetic person to action, and even to produce a condition of flourishing growth in a child, is the pleasant stimulus of kindness and caresses. The mother's caress, like the mother's milk, is a means of stimulating the child to a more complete nutrition and vitality. And the entire category of physiological weaklings, such as the defectives, epileptics and criminals, have a proportionately greater need of such stimulus than normal individuals; consequently, how can coercion ever be expected to restore such unbalanced personalities to their proper equilibrium? Those whom we have been in the habit of oppressing with severity and punishment are the very ones most in need of the stimulus of affection. Indeed, it is only the strong man and the hero who can pass unscathed through persecution; the weak are left broken, down-trodden, or slain.

Sursum Corda.—Always strive to uplift, never to depress.

A beautiful theory and a humane idea. But is it practicable, and to what extent? In short, what can be done practically, for instance, in the exceedingly difficult case of juvenile delinquents, in order to correct their evil tendencies and save them from their waywardness, without coercion?

But what are evil tendencies of the mind? With that one phrase we are trying to embrace and ostensibly bind together a quantity of widely different effects.

The study of the individual should suggest to us the particular method of education required by him. Meanwhile, in regard to the question of juvenile delinquents, a wide road leading straight back to first causes, has been opened by the *pathological* factor. Who, for instance, does not know that the conduct and the sentiments of an individual may become unbalanced through the effects of poison or disease? This takes us at once into the field of nervous or mental pathology: the first symptom of *paralytic dementia* is not the trembling, or alteration of speech, or interruption of certain reflex actions, or muscular weakness, nor the real and actual delirium. The symptom which first manifests itself as an indication of profound disturbance in the personality of the unfortunate victim of this cruel disease is an almost unheralded alteration of the natural character and conduct. The man who hitherto has been a good husband and father, becomes a profligate, spendthrift and gambler; the man who has hitherto been most scrupulous in his language and in his sexual conduct becomes foul-mouthed and obscene; the man who was a kind and affectionate husband becomes violent and aggressive toward his wife. Anyone wishing to consider these preliminary symptoms of paralytic dementia as *evil tendencies of the mind*, would strive in vain with appropriate sermons, reproofs and punishments to make the sick man *repent* and come back to his former state!

Let us pass on to another example. There is no one who is not aware of the effects of alcohol. There are persons who, when in a state of intoxication, commit actions that are worse than reprehensible, even criminal; actions which the individual himself deplores as soon as the poisonous effects have passed away. Kind-hearted persons go so far as to maltreat their own children, even when they are little babies; they commit violent and degrading acts that often make them shed tears of repentance as soon as they become aware of them. Well, if we should try to make such a person understand, while he is still in a state of intoxication, that his actions are improper, it would be wasted effort. It is better to let the matter pass, or else to give him treatment for his alcoholic condition, which is the cause of his misconduct.

And passing on to another class of cases, does not everyone know that when people are afflicted with a diseased liver, their character alters, they become jealous, quarrelsome, hypochondriac, melancholy? It would be useless to tell such persons that they were formerly more tractable and morally superior; they are already sufficiently afflicted without having us, who are in good health, aggravate them with our useless preaching. And analogously, it is well known that when hysteria attacks a woman it may transform her from a virtuous and modest person to an unhappy creature, compelled by her physical condition to forget herself and compromise the unquestioned propriety of her past life; or again, it may change her from a gentle soul to an insupportable fury, or it may actually develop into such pronounced delirium as to necessitate her confinement in an insane asylum. In this case also, it is the malady that demands treatment, since it is the sole cause of the sad manifestations of a change in character.

Now, the pathological cause most frequently associated with criminal manifestations, is undoubtedly epilepsy. Lombroso himself attributed a vast influence to this etiological factor of criminality; and every day this far-sighted intuition of the master is confirmed and made clearer. The epileptic is not always a criminal, nor does the criminal always show the classic convulsive symptoms. There are cases of epilepsy in which the symptoms are attenuated or latent or replaced by different but equivalent symptoms. It is frequently necessary to diagnose an *epileptic character* from impulsive tendencies and from long protracted nocturnal *enuresis* in childhood. De Sanctis has lately been able to prove in his hospital practice that there are many children who have unmistakable epilepsy of the classic type, with violent accesses, but without criminal tendencies; at a certain age the convulsions cease, the patient is apparently cured: but he has become a criminal. On the other hand, there are children with immoral tendencies, destructive, violent, incorrigible; one would say that these were clear cases of predisposition to crime; all at once a genuine epileptic attack occurs, followed by other repeated attacks; the criminal tendencies disappear; the patient is simply an epileptic. In these cases, we have successive forms of epileptic equivalence. In the majority of cases, therefore, the proper course would be to *treat* the patient for epilepsy, as being the cause of the apparent "evil tendencies of mind." And hence one notable side of the great problem of the moral education of juvenile criminals is transformed fundamentally into this other problem: "Can epilepsy be treated and cured?"

Up to the present, the treatment of epilepsy is a problem. While therapeutics prescribe bromides and warm baths, pedagogy is to-day following a very different course with a combined treatment of hygiene and education. Benedickt, and following him, the principal authorities among medical specialists, are at present condemning the use of depressing bromides, which hide the attacks as an anesthetic hides pain, but do not cure them. The cure, says Benedickt, depends upon hygienic life in the open air in order to absorb the poisons, and upon graded work, provided, however, that the malady is still recent and has not assumed a chronic form. Two principles of much importance: the malady must be of recent occurrence! Consequently, it is only in the *period of childhood* that we can attempt the treatment of the great majority of those predisposed to crime, with any hope of effecting a cure! A declaration of tremendous interest for the defense of society. But the treatment must be *pedagogic*. Accordingly, we have returned to the point of departure. We began by asking: "How are we to educate them"? A course of reasoning led us along this different road, "it is necessary to give them treatment." But the treatment consists in educating them. Well, from all this we can so far extract one unassailable principle; in their education all coercive measures must be absolutely abolished, because nervous and convulsive maladies are most successfully treated with gentleness and quiet; it is evident that all emotion, all fear, all nervous exhaustion, all punishment in short, no matter how mild or just it may be, would seem to be *prohibited* in pedagogic treatment.

Accordingly, it is necessary to approach the question anew; what is needed is to set the nervous system in order, to calm it, to restore its equilibrium. Benedickt says: this is to be achieved *through work*, rationally measured and graded; hence, manual training, as organised, for example, in the Reformatory of San Michele, constitutes of itself a moral cure; it concurs in readjusting the nervous system by reinforcing it.

However, we must not generalise over such complex questions; if the pathological factor, and more especially epilepsy, constitutes a great centre of *biologic causes* producing individuals predisposed to crime, we cannot conclude that there is a constant correspondence between epilepsy and criminality. But there is no doubt that among these predisposed we shall almost always find some who are suffering from a taint, or from dystrophy, due to tuberculosis or syphilis; in short, the *minus habens*, the physiological proletariat.

The benefit wrought by education consists not only in contributing to the real and actual cure, as in the case of epilepsy; but also in the corrective, as well as curative, effect upon the personality. The abnormal mentality which generally accompanies degenerate or epileptic conditions requires special methods of education, which in many cases must absolutely exclude all forms of coercion. Mental hygiene, an abundance of psychic stimulus, partly intellectual (chiefly through objective demonstration) and partly moral (in the form of praise and gentle caressing treatment), are indispensable accompaniments of such education. An abnormal mentality almost always accompanies defects of the mind; from the hypochondriac or the epileptic to the imbecile and the idiot, the abnormal mentality builds itself up from inaccurate perceptions, and hence more or less from illusions; a deficiency of reasoning power or a half delirious condition completes the fatal organisation of a mode of thought which renders such an individual unfitted for his environment. We have seen an example of this in the boy whose clinical history was read in class; his perceptions were inexact, consequently colours, odours, and sounds reached him in a manner somewhat different from our perception of them; his mental world must therefore be differently constructed from ours. Defectives frequently pass by objects without obtaining any impression of them, or else transform what impression they do get into a false idea. Even their sensations of touch and pain are different from the normal. Hence, they do not feel as we do, and are often inaccessible to the anguish of pain which refines human nature by sometimes raising it to the point of heroism. And because we have learned through our own sufferings to understand the meaning of pity, altruism and solidarity, these unhappy beings differ from us even in their relation to society. Their scanty powers of logic lead them to fall openly into errors, which provoke vindictive retaliation on our part that tends in the ultimate analysis to isolate these unfit beings from social intercourse.

To us, their whole conversation is a series of falsehoods, because it does not correspond to what we ourselves see and feel. An understanding between them and us becomes steadily more difficult, in proportion as we continue to perfect ourselves in our individual evolution, while their unhappy state is steadily aggravated through the formidable struggles and persecutions which they meet in an environment to which they are unadaptable. For instance, we saw that one of the boys who has been studied in class, had committed his most reprehensible acts as a result of false logic. "Why do you kill all the pigeons?" "To make them keep still." "Why do you beat your little sister?" "Because she won't work like the others." (The sister in question was only eighteen months old!) Well, he showed in this way that he had learned something from the corrections that he had received. They had punished him so much for being restless, and so much because he did not want to work, that he finally applied his acquired zeal to correcting others in the way that his defective logic dictated. And similarly, after seeing how they weigh objects with a steel-yard—also a form of work—it occurred to him to stick the hook into his little sister, in order to weigh her; and having learned that useful work is paid for in money, which serves to buy the necessities of life, he stole all the money that he could find at home, and gave it to the motormen on the tram-cars, who in his opinion perform the most useful work in the world.

I once had occasion to study a paranoiac patient in the asylum for the criminal insane, who had spent twenty years in prison before his insanity became so pronounced as to cause his removal from one place of restraint to the other. He had killed his betrothed, out of jealousy, so he said, but he narrated the tragic deed with a fullness of detail and a readiness of phrase—his lurking in ambush, the unfortunate girl's approach, her fall under the blows of the cobbler's knife—that proved the cold-blooded calculation with which the crime was committed.

This man was convinced that he possessed such oratorical gifts that if he had pleaded his own case in place of his attorney, the persuasive magic of his eloquence would have resulted in his acquittal. The lawyer had advised him not to speak and the prisoner was sentenced to a term of thirty years. The appeal to the Court of Cassation was denied. The result was that in his desperation at the failure of his defence, and more particularly because he had lost the chance of showing his oratorical powers in public, he conceived the idea that the only way by which he could come into court again, and speak for himself, and *force them to acquit him*, was to commit another murder. And he actually sprang at his lawyer's throat, armed with a nail, meaning to kill him. Thus we see how paranoiac delirium, and defective reasoning powers, sad evidences of pathological conditions, combined to create the most cynical and repellant of all criminal types.

Accordingly the *treatment* of the pathological condition, and the education of the *mentality* in children who are thus predisposed, constitute a great work on behalf of the defence of society.

Well, this is precisely what scientific pedagogy is trying to do, through a rational education of the senses: to correct false perceptions and straighten out the warped and twisted mentality of abnormal children; and little by little, through repetition of the same lessons under different forms, and the establishment of a cooperation of all the senses, the perception of objects tends to approach nearer and nearer to the normal. Meanwhile, hygienic or medical treatment may be used to correct the accompanying physical defects.

Accordingly, we are able to modify an abnormal personality by means of rational medico-pedagogic treatment; and it is by this means alone, and not through destructive coercion, that we may hope to approach the greatly desired goal.

Lastly, it is also necessary, in the etiology of crime, to take into consideration the environment, the bad example, the brutality, the absence of affection, all of which are things which might well pervert the mind of even a normal individual; and when such conditions exist, the removal of the transgressor to a different environment where he may have the benefit of physical, intellectual and moral hygiene, may result in completely transforming him. In these sad cases nothing short of the profoundest love will serve to redeem and even transform into a hero the man who has fallen into evil ways through misfortune.

No one can any longer believe that coercive measures should be added to the cruelty of the environment which oppresses the *transgressor*. If he has gone astray in the midst of sorrow it will be only through consolation that he can be born again to a new life; if he lost the straight path amid arid wastes, nothing short of a purifying and assuaging spiritual water will enable him to recover his path. As a sign of our humanity let us keep a smile upon our lips and our hearts free of all harshness of offense or defense; our weapons are intelligence and love and it is only by these weapons that we can become conquerors.

But, it may be answered, granted that the education of abnormal persons, and more especially juvenile delinquents, constitutes a complex work in which medicine, a special environment, and the methods of scientific pedagogy contribute harmoniously through diverse ways to the ultimate goal: yet in actual practice how are we to intervene to render docile these rebels whom society itself, with all the forces at its disposal, recognises as dangerous and condemns to isolation? In short, it is argued, a more direct method will be required for their moral education; a clear-cut method to offset that equally direct form consisting of coercion and punishment that are now the consequence of the reprehensible act. Under all the conditions to be considered in regard to the biopathological factors and the social environment, there still remains another element and the most evident of all, namely, the immediate and practical influence exerted directly upon the minds of wayward children. We may say quite truly that beneath the pathological facts and the social injustices, there exists something more profound which, for the sake of simplicity we may call the *soul of humanity*. Something which responds from soul to soul, which may be aroused from the depths of subconsciousness like a surprise, which may be touched and reveal itself in an outburst of affection previously hidden and unsuspected. Unknown profoundities of the spirit, that seem to merge into the eternity of the universe itself and unexpectedly produce new forms as in a chemical reaction. And this is what we really mean by "moral education."

Well, in order to accomplish such a lofty work, we do not need to find a *method*. Method is always more or less mechanical. Here, on the contrary, is the supreme expression of human life—an evocation of the superman. What we need to find is not a method, but a *Master*.

Séguin, in his glorious treatise on scientific pedagogy, dedicates a chapter to the training of the teacher of defective children. The teacher of abnormal pupils is not an educator, he is a *creator;* he must have *been born* with special gifts, as well as to have perfected himself for this high task. He ought, says Séguin, to be handsome in person, and strong as well, so that he may attract and yet command; his glance should be serene, like that of one who has gained victories through faith and has attained enduring peace; his manner should be imperturbable as that of one not easily persuaded to change his mind. In short, he ought to feel beneath him the solid rock, the foundation of granite on which his feet are planted and his steps assured. From this solid base, he should rise commandingly, like a magician. His voice should be gentle, melodious, and flexible, with bursts of silvery and resounding eloquence, but always without harshness. Séguin describes the methods by which the teacher should educate his own voice, speech and gesture; he should take a course in facial expression and declamation, like a great actor who is preparing to win favor of the select and critical public of the proudest capital.

For, as a matter of fact, he must attract the minds and souls of human beings who are almost inaccessible, beings who form whole armies in the world, entire peoples, they are so numerous; powerful human armies that threaten society with terrible punishment and bring about cruel executions.

But the perfect teacher must possess something more than physical beauty and acquired art; he must have the loftiness of a soul ardent for its mission; yet even this may be cultivated and perfected. The, teacher must "perfect himself" in his moral nature. There are men, who from the moment they make their appearance, exert a sort of fascination; everyone else becomes silent in their presence. It is almost as though some natural fluid emanated from them and spread to the others, so profoundly does everyone feel the attraction. When such a man speaks, the words seem, as if by magic, to touch the profoundest recesses of the heart. Hypnotists and magicans! Conquerers of souls! Valient souls themselves; souls with a great mission!

Well, this is more or less what is demanded of the teacher of abnormal children. He ought to be conscious of his personal dignity and human virtue, and of a sincere love for the children whom it is his task to redeem; his own greatness must overcome their wretchedness. And if he continues to perfect himself and to mount toward the moral altitudes, cultivating at the same time a love for his own mission, he will, as if by magic, become an educator; he will feel that a magic power of suggestion goes forth from him and conquers; the work of redemption will then seem to accomplish itself like a conflagration which has been kindled from some central point and spreads in rolling flames through the dried undergrowth.

Undoubtedly, the guidance of science is not everything to a teacher; the better part is given him through his own moral perfectionment.

4. The biographic history completes the individual study of the pupil and prepares for his diagnosis: combining, to this end, the work of the school with that of the home.

Sergi, in his memorable work, *First Steps in Scientific Pedagogy*, expresses himself as follows: "*the biographic chart is a methodical means for learning to know the body and spirit of the pupil through direct observations*. . . . And, since pupils may be classified according to tendencies, character and intelligence, the master may rationally divide them into various groups, to which he will give varied treatment, according to the direction in which each group shows the greatest need of education. . . . And he will place himself in closer association with *the pupils' families*, who should communicate to him their earliest observations regarding the physical and psychological nature of their children."

As a matter of fact, the anthropological movement, through

the inquiries necessitated by the compilation of biographic charts, often proves illuminating to the members of the family, in regard to facts and conditions of which they had hitherto remained ignorant (sexual hygiene); in regard to the view they should take of their own children (those who had been regarded as "bad," and who were really illl), in regard to the way they should watch over them and take care of them, etc. Hence it has made a beginning of the practical application of a pedagogic principal that hitherto has only been abstractly visioned, of coordinating the educative work of the family with that of the school. A pedagogic institution which practically realizes this conception, which was hitherto only a utopian dream of pedagogy, is the "Children's House;" because by having school in the home and by having teachers and mothers living together, it results in harmonizing the environment of the family with that of the school, for the furtherance of the great mission of education.

5. The biographic chart will furnish everyone with a document capable of guiding him in his own subsequent self-education.

Sergi says further in the work above quoted:

"The biographic chart should become a *precious document to every man*, if the sort of record of which I speak were continued through a series of years, from the kindergartens upward through the entire course of the secondary schools, because it would contain, in compact and methodical form, the history of his physical and mental life, and he would find it of inestimable advantage both in practical life and in his various social relations."

6. Lastly, the biographic chart with its gathering of positive data, prepares a great body of scientific material which will be useful, not alone to pedagogy, but also to sociology, medicine, and jurisprudence."

And in the same aforesaid work, Sergi adds: "If, for example, we should gather" (under the guidance of his biographic chart) "biographic notes in the city of Rome alone and in the elementary schools for both sexes, we should have for a single year, an average of fifty thousand observations, taken on entering and leaving school; if we could have them throughout the whole course of elementary instruction, the number of observations would amount to two hundred and fifty thousand.

"Then we should be able to see *in every social class all the individual variations in physical and physiological condition which contribute to the development of the intelligence and to the manifestations of sentiments which play an active part in practical life. And all this would have a value of a sociological character."*

This conception of Sergi's is precisely one of the scientific aspects of biographic histories that is of the highest importance, provided that they could be recorded in so simple a manner as to render the researches practically possible, and provided, also, that they could be gathered *with a scientific uniformity of method* designed to render international researches harmonious. We are certainly still very far removed from the time when international pedagogical congresses will be held for the purpose of establishing a single model form of biographic chart for each of the various grades in school; and also an agreement as to the technical method of taking the anthropological measurements! Before arriving at this point it will be necessary to make many tentative efforts and experiments.

But a truly scientific sociology, as well as pedagogy, ought to emanate from such a study of *human beings in the course of formation*, because such an enormously large number of observations as could be gathered in school, will reveal to us the biologico-social mechanism through which those activities are formed that are destined to promote the progress of humanity and civilisation (the new generations).

Medicine and the biological sciences in general entered upon a new era of exceedingly rapid progress when the microscope made possible the study of *histology* and *bacteriology;* well, the researches *in regard to the individual* constitute the histology and bacteriology of social science! When Le Play, in his great work, *Les Ouvriers Européens,* instituted the "family monograph," *i.e.,* the study of household accounts as a basis for "positive sociology," he was considered as the founder of a true *social science.* Because the true needs of men, the mechanism through which are determined the various personalities that afterward *react upon society* as *creative or destructive* forces, can be discovered only through studying minutely such needs and mechanisms, individual by individual, family by family. If Le Play's method, and consequently *positive social science,* have not as yet made much progress, this is because of the *difficulty of penetrating within the family in order to study it.*

From the bio-psychological point of view, if not from that of the family account book, the biographic chart of the schools is nevertheless a practical means of contributing to social histology; it is a field open to research and one which must be crossed by *every one* of the individuals who constitute society. Furthermore, it constitutes a foundation for social embryogeny; because in the school we may study the *genesis of separate individuals;* the causes which molded their congenital personality, and those which brought about its definitive formation. In the words of Le Play, indorsed by Bodio, this is the only positive material from which the *legislator* may draw his inspiration in order to become a true dispenser of justice to the people and to conduct the far-sighted reforms that are really necessary for the welfare of society.

Consequently, the anthropologic movement in pedagogy marks an aspect of scientific reform which is universal.

A direct contribution to pedagogy and at the same time to scientific sociology is given by the biographic charts in the "Children's Houses." Since this is a case of *school within the home,* where the mistress, being domiciled with her scholars, has them under her charge from the age of two or three years, and where there is a permanent resident physician to aid in the compilation of the biographic charts, it is evident that there is a chance of practically applying both the pedagogic plans for studying the pupil, and the social plans of Le Play, who by means of family monographs based upon the family account book, proposed to obtain nothing more nor less than an index of morality, culture, and individual needs! And as a matter of fact, the *manner of spending the salary,* the savings, the squanderings, the purpose for which money is spent, whether it is for low vices, or for vanity, or for æsthetic or intellectual pleasures in general, etc., reveal the state *of civilisation and morality* in which people *live.* In the "Children's Houses" such a study of the family is easy because it *is revealed of its own accord,* since the families are in contact with the school; consequently, these "Children's Houses" may serve to lay a true and practical foundation for *embryogenesis* and social histology. In short, the importance of research regarding the individual goes far beyond the school; it leads the way to every kind of social reform.

Even medicine, like every other science, is going to build up a firmer scientific basis through the help of the biographic charts of the schools: Professor De Sanctis has drawn up models for examinations, mainly of a medical nature, to be used in his asylum-schools for defectives; and by thus following the development of the pupils, he has succeeded in throwing positive light upon the biopathological mechanism through which an abnormal psycopathic or neuropathic personality develops; while psychiatry or neuropathology formerly recorded nothing more of such an abnormal personality than the episode of the moment at which the adult patient presented himself at the clinic. Even the individual criminal has now come to be studied in relation to his genesis, and jurists who are seeking a scientific basis for their enactments, should not neglect the individual studies that are being compiled in the schools for defectives. The biographic chart introduced into the government reformatories in Italy will also furnish a direct contribution to social histology, in regard to the genesis of criminal personalities.

Consequently, the reform which has begun with the introduction of an anthropological movement into the school and the establishment of biographic charts, is nothing less than a reform of science as a whole. Medicine, jurisprudence, and sociology as well as pedagogy, are laying new foundations upon it.

CHAPTER X

THE APPLICATION OF BIOMETRY TO ANTHROPOLOGY FOR THE PURPOSE OF DETERMINING THE MEDIAL MEN

Theory of the Medial Man.—Measurements are used not only in anthropology but in zoölogy and botany as well; that is, they are applied to all living creatures; therefore anthropometry might to-day be regarded as a branch of *biometry.* The measurements obtained from living beings, and the statistical and mathematical studies based upon them, tend to determine the *normality* of characteristics; and when the biometric method is applied to man, it leads to a determination of the normal dimensions, and hence of the *normal* forms, and to a reconstruction of the *medial man* that must be regarded as the man of perfect development, from whom all men actually existing must differ to a greater or less extent, through their infinite normal and pathological variations.

This sort of touch-stone is of indisputable scientific utility, since we cannot judge of *deviations* from the norm, so long as normality is unknown to us. In fact, when we speak of normality and of anomalies, we are using language that is far from exact, and to which there are no clear and positive corresponding ideas.

Whatever has been accomplished in anthropology up to the present time in the study of the morphology of degenerates and abnormals, has served only to illustrate this principle very vaguely —that the *form* undergoes alteration in the case of pathological individuals. It is only now that we are beginning to give definite meaning to this principle, by seeking to determine what the *form* is, when it has not undergone any alteration at all. From this fundamental point a new beginning must be made, on more certain and positive bases, of the study of *deviations from normality* and their etiology.

As far back as 1835, Quételet, in his great philosophical and statistical work, *Social Physics or the Development of the Faculties of Man,* for the first time expounded the theory of the "medial man," founded on statistical studies and on the mathematical laws of errors. He reached some very exact concepts of the morphology of the medial man, based upon measurements, and also of the intellectual and moral qualities of the medial man, expounding an interesting theory regarding *genius*.

But inasmuch as Quételet's *homme moyen* was, so to speak, at once a mathematical and philosophical reconstruction of the *non-existent perfect man*, who furthermore could not possibly exist, this classical and masterly study by the great statistician was strenuously combatted and then forgotten, so far as its fundamental concepts were concerned, and remembered only as a scientific absurdity. The thought of that period was too analytical to linger over the great, the supreme synthesis expounded by Quételet.

Mankind must needs grow weary of anatomising bodies and tracing back to origins, before returning to an observation of the whole rather than the parts, and to a contemplation of the future. In fact, the thought of the nineteenth century was so imbued with the evolutionary theories as set forth by Charles Darwin, that it believed the reconstruction of the *Pithecanthropus erectus* from a doubtful bone a more positive achievement than that of the *medial man* from the study of millions of living men.

But to-day the researches that we have accomplished in the biological field regarding evolution, regarding natural heredity, regarding individual variability, are leading biology as a whole toward eminently synthetic conclusions; and studies which remained neglected or which were combatted in the past, are beginning to be brought into notice and properly appreciated: such studies, for instance, as Mendel's theory and that of Quételet. Galton, Pearson, Davenport, Dunker, Heinke, Ludwig, and above all others De Vries, are in the advance guard of modern biological thought. But beyond all these scientists, there is one who has an interest for us not only because he is an Italian, but because he has reestablished Quételet's ancient theory of the *medial man*, under the present-day guidance of biometry: I mean Prof. Giacinto Viola.

The Importance of Seriation.—Under the statistical method, the basis of biometry is furnished by a regrouping of measurements in the form of series. We have seen that Quételet's binomial curve represents the symmetrical distribution of subjects in relation to some one central anthropometric measurement.

Let us suppose, for instance, that the curve here described represents the distribution of the stature. If we mark upon the abscissæ the progressive measurements, 1.55; 1.56; 1.57; 1.58; 1.59; 1.60, etc. . . . . 1.75; 1.76; 1.77; 1.78; 1.79; 1.80, and on the axis of the ordinates the number of individuals having a determined stature, the path of the curve will show that there is a majority of individuals possessing a mean central measurement; and that the number of individuals diminishes gradually and symmetrically above and below, becoming extremely few at the extremes (exceptionally tall and low statures). When the total number of individuals is sufficiently large, the curve is perfect (curve of errors): Fig. 156.

In such a case, the *general mean* coincides with the *median*, that is, with the number situated at the centre of the basal line, because, since all the other measurements, above and below, are perfectly symmetrical, in calculating the mean average they cancel out. There is still another centre corresponding to the mean: the *centre of density* of the individuals grouped there, because the maximum number corresponds to that measurement. Accordingly, if, for example, in place of half a million men whose measurements of stature, when placed in seriation, produced a perfect binomial curve, we had selected only ten men or even fewer from those corresponding to the median line; the general mean stature obtained from those half million men and that obtained from the ten individuals would be identical. For we would have selected *ten individuals* possessing that mean average stature which seems to represent a *biological tendency*, from which many persons deviate to a greater or less extent, as though they were erroneous, aberrant, for a great variety of causes; but these aberrant statures are still such that by their excess and their deficiency they perfectly compensate for each other; so that the mean average stature precisely reproduces this *tendency*, this centre actually attained by the maximum number of individuals. Supposing that we could see together all these individuals: those who belong at the centre being

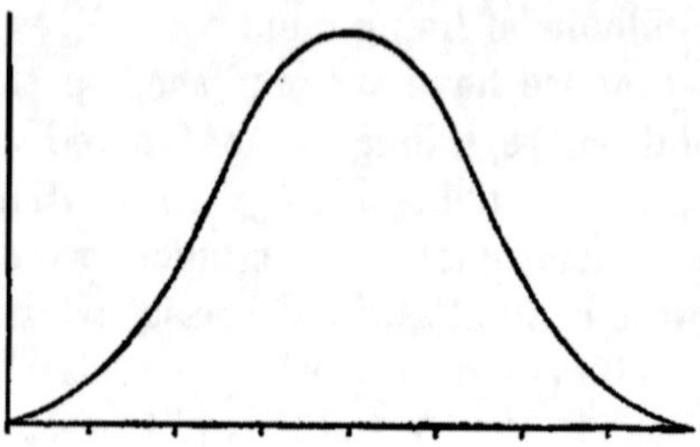

FIG. 156.—The highest part of this curve corresponds to the medial centre of density.

numerically most *prevalent*, will give a definite *intonation* to the whole mass. Anyone having an eye well trained to distinguish differences of stature could mentally separate those prevalent individuals and estimate them, saying that they are of *mean average stature.* This curve is the mathematical curve of errors; and it corresponds to that constructed upon the exponents of Newton's binomial theorem and to the calculation of *probability.* It corresponds to the curve of errors in mathematics: for example, to the errors committed in measuring a line; or in measuring the distance of a star, etc. Whoever takes measurements (we have already seen this in anthropometrical technique and in the calculation of personal error) commits errors, notwithstanding that the *object to be measured* and the individual making the measurements remain the same. But the most diverse causes; nerves, the weather, weariness, etc., causes not always determinable and perhaps actually more numerous than could be discovered or imagined, all have their share in producing errors of too much and too little, which are distributed in gradations around the *real measurement* of the object. But since among all these measurements taken in the same identical way we do not know which is the true one; the seriation of errors will reveal it to us, for it causes a maximum number of some one definite measurement (the true one) to fall in the centre of the aberrations that symmetrically grade off from the centre itself.

Viola gives some very enlightening examples in regard to errors. Suppose, for instance, that an artist skilled in modeling wished to reproduce in plaster a number of copies of a leaf, which he has before his eyes as a model.

The well-trained eye and hand will at one time cause him to take exactly the right quantity of plaster needed to reproduce the actual dimensions of the leaf; at another, on the contrary, he will take more and at another less than required.

By measuring or superimposing the real leaf upon the plaster copies, the sculptor will be able to satisfy himself at once which of his copies have proved successful.

But supposing, on the contrary, that the real leaf has disappeared and that a stranger wishes to discover from the plaster copies which ones faithfully reproduce the dimensions of the leaf? They will be those that are numerically most prevalent.

The same thing holds true for any attempt whatever to attain a *predetermined object.* For example, shooting at a mark. A skilful marksman will place the maximum number of shots in the centre, or at points quite near to the centre; he will often go astray, but the number of errors will steadily decrease in proportion as the shots are more aberrant, *i.e.*, further from the centre. If a marksman wished to practise in like manner against some wall, for example, on which *he* has chosen a point that is not marked, and hence not recognisable by others, this point *thought of* by the marksman, may be determined by studying the cluster of shots left upon the wall.

In the same way an observer could determine the hour fixed for a collective appointment, such as a walking trip, by the manner in which the various individuals arrive in groups; some one will come much ahead of time because he has finished some task which he had expected would keep him busy up to the hour of appointment; then in increasing numbers the persons who come a few minutes ahead of time because they are provident and prompt; then a great number of people who have calculated their affairs so well as to arrive precisely on time; a few minutes later come those who are naturally improvident and a little lazy; and lastly come the exceptional procrastinators who at the moment of setting forth were delayed by some unexpected occurrence.

Causes of error in the individual and in the environment interfere in like manner with the astronomer who wishes to estimate the distance of the stars and it is necessary for him to repeat his measurements and calculations on the basis of those which show the greatest probability of being exact.

Accordingly, such *distribution* of errors is *independent* of the causes which produce them and which, whatever they are, remain practically the same at any given time, and consequently produce constant effects and symmetrical errors; but it is dependent upon the fact of the existence of some pre-established thing (a measurement, the dimensions of an object to be copied, an appointed hour, the centre of a target, etc.). In short, whenever a *tendency* is established the *errors* group themselves around the objective point of this tendency.

In the case of anthropometry, as for instance, in the curve of stature given above, we find that the resulting medial stature was *pre-determined, e.g., for a given race;* but many individuals, for various causes, either failed to attain it or surpassed it to a greater or less extent; and therefore in the course of their development they have acquired an erroneous stature.

Consequently, this medial stature which still corresponds to the mean average of a very large number of persons, is the stature that is biographically pre-established, the normal stature of the race.

If we select individuals presumably of the same race and in sound health, the serial curve of their statures ought to be very high and with a narrow base, because these individuals are *uniform.* When a binomial curve has a *very wide* basis of oscillations in measurements, it evidently contains elements that are not uniform; thus, for example, if we should measure the statures of men and women together, we should of course obtain a curve, but it would be very broad at the base and quite low at the centre of density; and a similar result would follow if we measured the statures of the rich and the poor without distinguishing between them. Since normal stature, including individual variations, has an exceedingly wide limit of oscillation (from 1.25 m. to 1.99 m.), if we should measure all the men on earth, we should obtain a very wide base for our binomial curve, which nevertheless would have a centre of density corresponding to the median line and to the general mean average.

Now this mean stature, according to Quételet, is the mean stature of the European; and it is that of the *medial man.* But if we should take the races separately, each one of them would have its own binomial curve, which would reveal the respective mean stature for each race. In the same way, if we took the complex curve of all the individuals of a single race, and separated the men from the women, the two resulting groups would reveal the *mean average male stature* and the *mean average female stature* of the race in question. An analogous result would follow if we separated the poor from the rich, etc.

Every time that we draw new distinctions, the base of the *curves,* or in other words the limits of oscillation of measurements, will contract, and the *centre of density* will rise; while the intermediate gradations (due, for example, to the intermixture of tall women and short men; or to the overlapping standards of stature of various kindred races, etc.), will diminish. In short, if we construct the binomial curve from individuals who are uniform in sex, race, age, health, etc., it not only remains symmetrical around a centre but the eccentric progression of its groups is steadily determined in closer accordance with the order and progression of the exponents of Newton's binomial.

However, a *symmetrical grading off* from the centre is not the same thing as a symmetrical grading off from the centre *in a predetermined mode, i.e.*, that of the binomial exponents. The binomial symmetry is obtained through calculations of mathematical combinations. Now, if the *fact* of the centrality of a prevailing measurement is to be proved in relation to the predetermination of the measurement itself: for example, in regard to *racial heredity*, and hence is a fact that reveals *normality*, the manner of distribution of errors—namely, in accordance with calculations of *probability*—might very well be explained by Mendel's laws of heredity, which serve precisely to show how the prevailing characteristics are distributed according to the mathematical calculation of probabilities.

Accordingly, the *normal characteristic of race* would coincide with the dominant characteristic of Mendel's hereditary powers. The characteristic which has been shown as the stronger and more potent is victorious over the recessive characteristics that are latent in the germ. Meanwhile, however, there are various errors which, artificially or pathologically, cause a characteristic, which would naturally have been recessive, to become dominant, or, in other words, most prevalent.

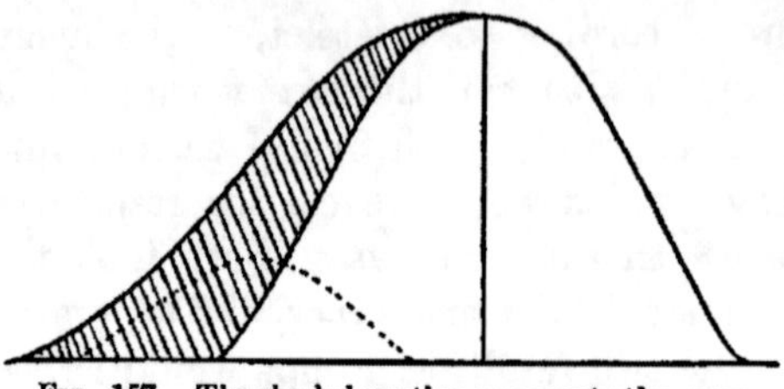

FIG. 157.—The shaded portion represents the eccentricity of the curve, due to the presence of cretins.

Whenever a binomial curve constructed from a large number of individuals is found to be *eccentric;* and shows, *e.g.*, in the case of stature, a deviation toward the low statures, it reveals (see De Helguero's curves) the presence of a heterogeneous intermixture of subjects, for example, of children among adults, or, as in the case demonstrated by De Helguero, an intermixture of *pathological individuals* with normal persons (Fig. 157).

The binomial curve obtained by De Helguero from the inhabitants of Piedmont included, as a matter of fact, a great number of *cretins;* they formed within the great normal mass of men, a little mass of individuals having a stature notably inferior to the normal.

By correcting the eccentric curve on the left of the accompanying figure, and by tracing a dotted line equal and symmetrical to the right side, we obtain a normal binomial curve; well, this curve will actually be reproduced if we subtract all the cretins from the whole mass of individuals.

The section distinguished by parallel lines represents that portion of the curve which departs from the normal toward the low statures, and is due to the cretins; it may be transformed into a small dotted binomial curve at the base, which is constructed from the statures of the cretins alone.

Accordingly, the symmetrical binomial curve gives us a *mean average value* in relation to a specified measurement.

What has been said regarding stature serves as an example; but it may be repeated for *all the anthropometric measurements,* as Viola has proved by actual experiment.

The sitting stature, the thoracic perimeter, the dimensions of an entire limb or of each and every segment of it; every particular which it has seemed worth while to take into consideration, comports itself in the same manner; and this is also true of all the measurements of the head and face.

That is to say, if we make a seriation of measurements relating to the sitting stature of an indeterminate number of individuals, we find a numerical prevalence of those corresponding to the medial measurement marked upon the axis of the abscissæ; and the number of individuals will continue to decrease with perceptible symmetry on each side of the centre, *i.e.*, toward the higher and lower statures. If we take into consideration the significance of the sitting stature, this binomial curve relates to individuals who possess a normal physiological mass (the bust; centre of density) and to individuals who fall below or exceed that mass. We have already, in speaking of the types of stature, taken the bust under consideration in relation to the limbs, in order to judge the more or less favourable reciprocal development; but here we obtain an *absolute datum of normality,* independent of proportional relations to the body as a whole; *in other words, there exists a physiological mass* for the human body which is *normal* in itself. The individuals whose sitting stature corresponds to the medial measure of the binomial curve, are precisely those who have the normal development of bust.

The same thing repeats itself in the case of the thoracic perimeter, or the weight, or the length of the leg, or the cranial circumference, etc.

Hence we have a means of obtaining the *normal medial measurements* by the seriation of a number of measurements actually obtained from living individuals the number of whom should be sufficiently large to enable us to construct a perceptibly symmetrical and regular binomial curve.

Such medial measurements, although they correspond to the true mean average (as we have already seen), are not for this reason *unreal*, like arithmetical means which represent a synthetic entirety that does not correspond to the single individuals actually existing; the medial measurements obtained by seriation are, on the contrary, measurements that really belong to living individuals; namely, to that group of individuals that possess this particular measurement. Therefore, it is not a combination, or fusion, or abstraction.

***

But individuals who have one medial measurement, do not necessarily have all the other medial measurements; that is to say, the individuals who find that they belong on the medial abscissæ in relation to stature, do not find themselves similarly placed in relation to the sitting stature, or the thoracic perimeter, or the weight, or the cranial circumference, etc. Indeed, it is *impossible* that all the bodily measurements of the same individual should be *medial measurements:* or, to express it better, there has not been found up to the present among living individuals, in the whole wide world, a man so constructed.

Such a man would represent anthropologically the *medial man.*

It is also very rare to find a man quite lacking in medial measurements: everyone has a few central measurements and certain others that are eccentric.

At the same time it must be admitted that there are men who have many, and even a large majority, of the central measurements; while the rest of their measurements are eccentric or paracentral.

One of the objections which used to be made was that if we

should wish to unite all the medial measurements, they would not fit together, or rather, that a man could not be constructed from them; but that the result would be a monstrosity. Nevertheless, this assertion or objection has proved to be absolutely fantastic and contrary to the actual fact.

Professor Viola has observed that men who have a very large number of medial measurements are singularly *handsome.*

More than that: the medial man reconstructed from medial measurements really gathered from living persons, has the identical proportions of the famous statues of Greek art.

Here, for example, in Figs. 158 and 159, facing page 464, we have the medial man and the Apollo; even to the eye of the observer, they show a marked similarity in proportions. The medial man is very nearly the portrait of an exceedingly handsome young Roman, studied by Viola; this person possessed a great majority of the mean average measurements; but some of his measurements did not correspond to the normal averages, and accordingly Viola had them corrected by an artist under the guidance of anthropological biometry; and the figure thus corrected is represented in the drawing here given. Well, this drawing corresponds perfectly to the proportions of the Apollo.

Consequently, the mean average measurements do not pass unnoticed; it is not alone the anthropological instrument or mathematical reconstruction that reveals them; when presented to the eye of the intelligent man, they *notify him that* they exist, they arouse in him an *æsthetic emotion,* they give him the alluring impression of the *beautiful.*

When the mean average measurements are found accumulated in large numbers in the same person, they render that person the centre of a mysterious fascination, the admiration of all other men.

Now, this coincidence of the *beautiful* with the average is equivalent to a coincidence of the beautiful with *normality.* "This unforeseen demonstration," says Viola, "throws a vivid light upon the hitherto obscure problem of the æsthetic sense. . . . If a man evolves according to normal laws, his proportions arouse an exceptional æsthetic enjoyment."

Anyone having an eye trained to recognise the *beautiful,* is able through his æsthetic sensations, to pick out *normality* from the great crowd of biological errors, which is precisely what the scientist does with great weariness of measurements and calculations. In fact, the great artists recognise the *beautiful parts* of a number of beautiful individuals, and they unite them all together in a single work of art. The Greeks did this, they reconstructed the medial man, on a basis of actual observation, and by extracting all the normalities, all the measurements most prevalent in individuals, and forming from them a single ideal man. The Greek artists were observers; we might call them the positivists in art. Their art is supreme and immortal, because they simultaneously interpreted what is *beautiful* and what is *true* in life.

In short, medial measurements are true measurements, actually existing in individuals. No one can acquire a true æsthetic taste by contemplating works of art. The æsthetic sense is trained and refined by observing the truth in nature and by learning to separate instinctively the normal from the erroneous.

No other form of art reproduces the *subject* so faithfully as the Greek; medieval and modern artists have incarnated their own personal inspiration, without training themselves to that accurate observation which refines the sense of the *beautiful*, when we are in the presence of the *truth*, represented by normality, which is the triumph of life.

Accordingly, we may reconstruct the *medial man* from the truth as found in nature. Within the wide scale of individual variations we pass from men possessing few medial measurements (ugly men) to men possessing many of them (handsome men), and even a majority of such measurements (extremely handsome). Our sensation in the presence of the ugly man is repulsion, *biological pain;* in the presence of the handsome man we feel an æsthetic contentment, *biological pleasure.* In this way we take part in the mysterious failures and triumphs of nature, as children in the great family of life.

Now, as Viola says, the individual variations that group themselves symmetrically around the medial measurement may be divided into *groups* or *types, e.g.*, central, paracentral and eccentric, both above and below the mean.* Such types are considered by Viola chiefly from the *pathological* point of view, or rather, that of the *physical constitution* and relative predisposition to disease. It is only the *central* type that has such perfect harmony of parts as to embody the perfection of strength and physical health; as

* Viola, *The Laws of Morphological Correlation of the Individual Types.*

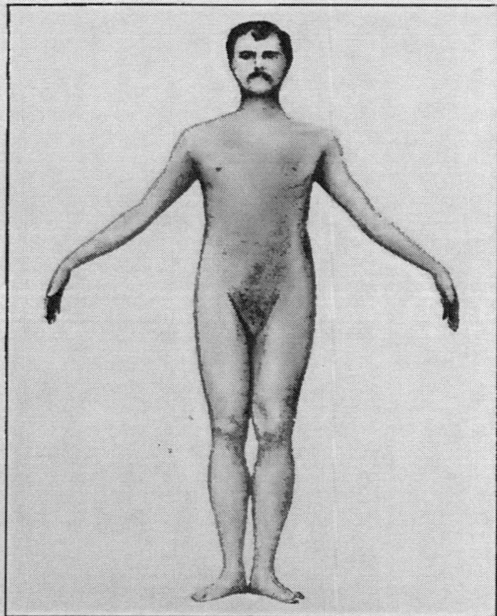

FIG. 158.—Viola's medial man.

FIG. 159.—Apollo.

the type diverges from the centre, it steadily loses its power of resistance and becomes less capable of realising a long life.

Since the measurements are extremely numerous, it is necessary, in order to proceed to a separation of types, to select some one measurement to be regarded as fundamental, and in respect to which all others have a secondary importance; and such a measurement is found in the one which is associated with the development of the physiological man; namely, the *sitting stature.* In the centre there is the medial measurement; little by little, as we withdraw from the centre, we approach on the one side toward macroscelia and on the other side toward brachyscelia. It is possible to determine to within a millimetre the *normality* of any measurement whatever. When this fundamental datum has once been accepted as a *basis* for the construction of *types,* let us assume that we next add another and secondary measurement; for instance, that of the lower limbs. By the method of seriation we obtain a measurement that is *absolutely normal when considered by itself;* it is the central measurement. A perfectly formed and healthy man ought to possess both the medial sitting stature and the medial length of lower limbs; in actual cases, however, it is difficult ot find so favourable a union, and the two series of measurements *combine* in various ways; showing a tendency, however, to unite in such a way that a short bust goes with long legs, and *vice versa.* The degree to which this rule is carried out produces two types that steadily tend to become more eccentric; they are the macroscelous and brachyscelous types, or, as De Giovanni calls them, *morphological combinations.* We have only to calculate the *type of stature,* and that also groups itself according to the binomial curve; and thus gives us a gradation of the *combinations of parts.* Viola notes that the paracentral individuals show characteristics quite different from those of the eccentrics; their constitution is more favourable, and they differ in respect to their characteristic proportions between thorax and abdomen, and in certain other physiological particulars that are of pathological importance.

In this way a *method* has been built up for determining mathematically the one absolute normality; as well as the anomalies in all their infinite variety, which may, however, be regrouped under *types,* on the basis of their eccentricities.

Here then we have, thanks to Viola, and under the guidance of the glorious school of De Giovanni, a pathway indicated, that is exceedingly rich in its opportunities for research, and that may advance the importance of anthropometry side by side with that of biometry, the development of which is to-day so earnestly pursued, especially in England.

***

One of the objections which may be raised to the theory of the medial man is that there cannot be any one perfect, human model because of the diverse races of mankind, each with its own established biological characteristics.

For instance, I believe that I have proved that what we consider as *beautiful* is distributed among *different races;* in other words, perfect beauty of all the separate parts of the body is never found united in any one race, any more than it is in any one person.

The women of Latium who are dark and dolicocephalic have most beautiful faces, but their hands and feet are imperfect; the brachycephalic blondes, on the contrary, are coarse-featured, while their hands and feet are extremely beautiful. The same may be said regarding their breasts and certain other details. Furthermore, the stature of the dolicocephalics is too low as compared with what is shown to be the *average stature,* while the brachicephalics are similarly too tall. Nevertheless, it is *extremely difficult* to discover racial types of such comparative purity as to establish these differences: it was by a lucky chance that I succeeded in tracing out, at Castelli Romani and at Orte, certain groups of the races that were very nearly pure. The rest of the population are, for the most part, hybrids showing a confused intermingling of characteristics.

In fact, pure *types of race* no longer exist, least of all where civilisation is most intense. In order to speak of *types of race,* it is necessary to go among barbaric tribes; and even this is a relative matter, because all the races on earth are more or less the result of intermixture. Yet in civilised countries an occasional group of pure racial stock may be discovered in isolated localities, as though they had found refuge, so to speak, from the vortex of civilisation which is engulfing the races. Throughout the history of humanity we may watch this absorption of racial and morphological characteristics, and the formation of more and more intimate intermixtures, leading to the final disappearance of the original *types of race*.

When a primitive race emigrated, when men crossed over from Africa to the European coast of the Mediterranean, or Aryans from oriental Asia traversed the mountains and steppes of Russia and the Balkan countries, they were on their way to conquer territory and to subjugate peoples, but they were also on their way to lose their own type, the characteristics of their race. Yet even this sacrifice of *race* was not without compensation: indeed, it seems as though the *race* loses through hybridism a large part of its *ugly* characteristics, but retains and transmits for the most part the characteristics that are pleasing. Unquestionably, the more civilised peoples are better looking than the barbarians, although the history of emigration would seem to indicate an almost common racial origin.

When we remember that in human hybridism the result is not always a true and complete *fusion* of characteristics, but for the most part an intermixture of them—so that, for example, the hybrid has the type of cranium belonging to one race, and the stature belonging to another race—we have the explanation of the fact that throughout thousands of years certain morphological characteristics have remained fixed, to such an extent as to permit anthropologists to use them as a basis upon which to trace out the origins of races. But these characteristics, while fixed in themselves, are *interchanged* among individual hybrids, who form more or less felicitous *combinations* of characteristics belonging to several races.

When we recall what was said in this regard concerning heredity (general biological section) it is necessary to conclude that Mendel's law must be invoked to explain the phenomenon.

Human hybridism, like all hybridism throughout the whole biological field, falls under this law.

But there is still another phenomenon that should be noted: civilised men, who are the most hybrid of all hybrids upon earth, have formed a *new type* that is almost unique, the *civilised race,* in which one and all resemble one another. It is only logical to believe that, in proportion as facilities of travel become easier and intermarriage between foreign countries more widespread, it will become less and less easy to distinguish the Englishman from the Frenchman, or the Russian or the Italian; provided that the various hybridisms in the respective countries have developed an almost uniform local type, so that the general characteristics of

French hybridism may be distinguished from those of English hybridism, etc.

Even these local hybrid types, determining, as it were, the physiognomy of a people, will disappear when Europe finally becomes a single country for civilised man.

In short, we are spectators of this tendency: a fusion or intermixture of characteristics that is tending to establish one single human type, which is no longer an original racial type, but the *type of civilisation.* It is the unique race, the *resultant human race,* the product of the fusion of races and the triumph of all the elements of beauty over the disappearance of those ugly forms which were characteristic of primitive races.

Are the dominant forces in the human germinative cells those which bring a contribution of beauty? One would say "yes," on the strength of the morphological history of humanity.

There is no intention of implying by this that humanity is tending toward the incarnation of perfectly beautiful human beings, all identical in their beauty; but they will be harmonious in those skeletal proportions that will insure perfect functional action of their organism. Harmony is fundamental; the soft tissues, the colour of hair and eyes, may upon this foundation give us an infinite *variety* of beauty. "Even in music," says Viola, "so long as the laws of harmony are respected, there are possibilities of melodic thoughts of infinite beauty in gradation and variety; but the first condition is that the aforesaid laws shall be respected."

The soft and plastic tissues are like a *garment* which may be infinitely varied: because life is richer in normal forms than in abnormal; richer in triumphs than in failures; and hence more impressive in the varieties of its beauties than in its monstrosities.

Such philosophic concepts of the *medial man* are exceedingly fertile in moral significance. The ugly and imperfect races have gone on through wars, conquests, intellectual and civil advancement unconsciously preparing new intermarriages and higher forms of love, which eliminated all that is harsh and inharmonic, in order to achieve the triumph of human beauty. In fact, quite aside from the heroic deeds of man, the constructor of civilisation, we are witnessing the coming of the unique man, the man of perfect beauty, such as Phidias visioned in a paroxysm of æsthetic emotion.

A living man who incarnates supreme beauty, supreme health,

supreme strength: almost as though it were Christ himself whom humanity was striving to emulate, through a most intimate brotherhood of all the peoples on earth.

***

On the analogy of the medial morphological man, Quételet also conceived of the *medial intellectual man* and the *medial moral man*.

The medial intellectual man is closely bound to the thoughts of his century; he incarnates the prevailing ideas of his time; he vibrates in response to the majority. He is to his nation and century, says Quételet, "what the centre of gravity is to the body—namely, the one thing to be taken into consideration in order to understand the phenomena of equilibrium and movement." Considered from the ideal side, the medial man ought to centralise in himself and keep in equilibrium the movement of thought of his period, giving it harmonic form, in works of art or of science. And it is the capacity for accomplishing this work of synthesis that constitutes the *inborn quality* in the man of genius.

He does not create; he reassembles in one organism the *scattered members*, the medial vibrations of the crowd; he feels and expresses all that is new and beautiful and great that is in process of formation in the men who surround him, who are frequently unconscious of the beauty which is in them, just as they are unconscious of having those normal predetermined measurements of their bodies. But whenever they discover in a creation of thought *something of themselves*, they are stirred to enthusiasm at recognising this something belonging to them as forming part of a harmonious whole: and they applaud the work of art or of science which has stirred their enthusiasm. The medial intellectual man who has produced it is a beneficent genius to humanity because he aids its upward progress by appealing to the better part in each individual.

Now, there has never existed a medial intellectual man who sums up all the thought of his time: just as there does not exist a living man so beautiful as to incarnate all the medial measurements. But the man of genius is he who does embody the greater part of such ideas: and he produces a masterpiece when he succeeds in shedding his own individuality in order to assume what is given him from without. Goethe said that it was not he who composed

Faust, but a spirit which invaded him. And the same thought is expressed in the autobiographies of many men of genius.

A well-known writer told me that it sometimes happened to him, while he was writing, to forget himself completely; at such times he no longer wrote the truth as he saw and felt it consciously, but transmitted pure and unforeseen inspiration.

Such portions, said this author, are judged by the public as containing the greatest degree of beauty and truth.

When a great orator thrills a crowd, he certainly does nothing more than repeat what is already in the thoughts of each member of that crowd; every individual present had, as it were, in his subconsciousness, the same thought that is expressed by the orator, which was taking form within him but had not yet *matured* and which he would not have had the knowledge or the ability to express. The orator, as it were, matures and extracts from him that new thought which was taking shape within him; his better part, which after light is shed upon it will have the power to elevate him. But no orator could ever persuade a crowd with ideas that do not already exist in that crowd, and which consequently, are not part of the truth of their age.

The orator is like the centre of gravity, inasmuch as he gives form and equilibrium to the scattered and timid thought of the crowd.

Carducci* says "the art of the lyric poet consists in this: to express what is common to all in the form in which he has created it anew and specially in his mind; or rather to give to the thought which is peculiar to himself an imprint of universal understanding, so that each one looking into it may recognise himself."

***

When we think of the brilliant concept of the medial man, we behold a fundamental and profound principle: the necessity of hybridism and consequently of a profound intermixture of races; all of which goes side by side with the spread of civilisation, and the increased facilities of traveling and of communication between different communities. Connected with these material advantages is the moral progress which leads to a realisation of perfect brotherhood between men that is rendered steadily more possible by environment, and is sanctioned little by little by laws and customs; whereas at the start it was only an ethical or mystical theory.

* Cited by Viola.

While the physical formations of the races are becoming merged, the racial customs are also blending and disappearing in a single civilisation, in one sole form of thought. If, at one time, the powerful race was the one united to its territory, faithful to its customs, adhering to its moral code and its religion, all this melts away in the presence of universal hybridism which actually means the birth of a new generation of men and a new outlook upon life.

When we contemplate the morphologically medial man, he seems to stand as a symbol of unlimited universal progress. His realisation seems to demand very lofty standards of morality and civilisation.

Whereas, on the contrary, the survival of types and of customs and sentiments peculiar to separate races, is the expression of local conditions that are inferior both in morality and in civil progress. As for the innumerable *paracentral errors* which form to-day a large proportion of individual varieties, they are due directly to the imperfection of the environment, which does not permit of the natural development of human life, and consequently interferes through a wide range of methods and degrees with the development of ideal normality.

Hence, the extreme eccentric errors are the consequence of diseases and far-reaching social imperfections which lead to genuine deviations from the normal, including *pathological* and *degenerate malformations*, and associated with them the lowest forms of individual degradation, both intellectual and moral.

All the paracentral errors and malformations are a physical burden which retards the perfectionment of man. Admitting that hybridism will eventually result in complete beauty, it will be greatly delayed in its attainment through the accumulation of errors that surround the characteristics of race. They form a heavy ballast, if the phrase may be permitted, that impedes the progress of its ascension.

Consequently, the long awaited social progress which is gradually bringing about the "brotherhood of man" is not in itself sufficient for the attainment of the ideal mean.

There are certain errors that must more or less necessarily be encountered along the pathway of humanity; and that act either directly or indirectly upon posterity, deforming and destroying its resistance to life; and it is these that must be taken under consideration, because they delay the normal progress of human society.

They are conscious and well recognised errors; hence up to a certain point the *active* agency of man may combat them and succeed little by little in mitigating them and overcoming their disastrous influence upon biological humanity.

There are, in general, two influences developing and promoting that improvement which leads toward the *medial man:* in proportion as the real and practical intermarriage of races approaches its realisation, social errors diminish; and as the brotherhood of humanity is promoted, it leads to social reforms by which the "sins of the world" are little by little overcome.

But these may also be *actively* combated; and in this direction education has a task of inestimable importance to civilisation. We ought to know not only the thought of our century, which is the luminous torch in the light of which we advance along the path of progress; but also the *moral needs* of our time, and the errors which may be conquered through our conscious agency.

To know "the faults of our century," which are destined to be conquered in the coming century, and to make preparation for the victory—such is our moral mission. The ethical movement of human society has continued to advance from conquest to conquest, and in looking backward the more civilised part of mankind have been horrified at the conditions that have been outgrown and have called them "barbarous."

Thus, for example, slavery was an unsurmountable obstacle to progress, and had to be crushed out by civilisation; the license to *kill* is also a form of barbarism which to-day we are boasting of having just outgrown—or, at least, of having reached the final limit of its duration. In early times it was not only permissible to kill, but in many of its forms murder was considered honourable, as, for instance, in wars and in duels; it was also one form of justice to kill for vengeance, either social or individual; the condemnation to death of a criminal, the murder of an adulterous wife, the murder of anyone who has attacked the *honour* of the family, all this seemed just in the past. Lastly, murder was committed for pure diversion, as in the auto-da-fè and in the games of the circus.

Our civic morality seems to have attained its extreme altitude in having sanctioned the inviolability of human life; and the present-day struggle against the death penalty, against war, against revolutions, against uxoricide, in the case of adultery, and against duelling, shows us the triumph of a new and loftier conception of humanity in the upward progress of man.

The intermixture of races and the intermingling of national interests, have aroused a sort of collective sentiment actually existing as a normal form of conscience, namely, "human solidarity."

But we are still in a state of complete *barbarity*, still sunk in the most profound unconsciousness, all of us partners in the same great sin that threatens the overthrow of so-called civilised humanity; namely, *barbarity toward the species.*

We are ignorant, we are almost strangers, in regard to our *responsibility* toward those who are destined to issue from us as the continuation of humanity downward through the centuries; those who form the ultimate scope of our biological existence, inasmuch as each one of us is merely a connecting link beween certain portions of past and future life. We are all so engrossed with the progress of our environment and of the ideas embodied in it, that we have not yet turned our attention inward toward ourselves: toward *life.*

This solidarity which we recognise as existing among men at the present moment, ought to be extended to the men of the future. And since the species is closely bound up in the individual who is destined to reproduce it, this gives us at once the basis for a code of *individual moral conduct*, such as would assure to everyone the integrity of the fruit of his own reproduction. Sexual immorality which is the stigma of the barbarity of our times, entails the most ignominious form of slavery; the slavery of women through prostitution. And emanating from this form of barbarity, the slavery has expanded and spread to all women, more or less oppressive, more or less conscious. The wife is a slave, for she has married in ignorance and has neither the knowledge nor the power to avoid being made the instrument for the birth of weakly, diseased or degenerate children; and still more deeply enslaved is the mother who cannot restrain her own son from degradations that she knows are the probable source of ruin of body and soul. We are all silently engaged in an enormous crime against the species and against humanity; and like accomplices we have made a tacit agreement not to speak of it. Indeed, the mysterious silence regarding sexual life is absolute; it is as though we feared to compromise ourselves in the sight of that great and powerful judge, our own posterity; we hide under an equal silence the good and the bad in relation to sexual life. This sort of terror goes by the name of shame and modesty. Such an excuse for silence certainly sounds like pure irony, coming as it does in the full midst of the orgy, at a time when we all know that every man is laden with his sins, and that we are all either accomplices or slaves in the common fault. It would seem that a race so modest as to blush at the mere mention of sexual life ought to be eminently chaste, and far removed from the age of foundling asylums and houses of ill fame; the age in which infanticide exists as proof of absolute impunity in regard to sexual crimes.

What we call shame and modesty, is in reality not shame or modesty in regard to sexual acts and phenomena, but only in regard to *sins* against them.

These acts and phenomena, being directly related to *creation* and the eternity of the species, ought to be regarded by men as in the nature of a lofty religious culte, equally, for instance, with that which from the earliest prehistoric times placed the symbol of maternity, *the mother and the child*, side by side with the *scythe*, symbol of labour, in places of worship. We cannot admit that *love*, sung by the poets as a divine sentiment, is the moral exponent of unworthy and shameful acts. It is the error, the perversion of sexual life, the source of degeneration, of degradation and of the death of the species, that makes us keep silent, conceal and blush with shame.

In reality, all this ought to stir us, not to embarrassment and shame, but to a formidable rebellion, a sharp awakening of conscience, a redemption from a state of inferior civilisation.

It was a barbarous sovereign who, in the delusive hope that it would cure him of eczema, caused the throats of little children to be cut, so that he might immerse himself in the warm bath of their blood.

To-day anyone who would sacrifice the lives of children to allay the itching of his own skin, would be in our eyes a monster of criminality.

And yet almost equally criminal are the men of our time, lords, in a barbaric sense, of sexual life; and we silently acquiesce in customs which in the future centuries will perhaps be remembered as a monstrous barbarism.

The whole moral revival which awaits us, revolves around the struggle against the sexual sins. The emancipation of woman, the protection of maternity and of the child, are its most luminous exponents; but no less efficacious evidences of such progress are all the efforts directed against alcoholism and the other vices and diseases which are reflected in their unhappy consequences to posterity. There is just one side of the question that has hitherto been scarcely touched at all, and that is the chastity of man and his responsibility as a father; but even this has already come to be felt as an imperative necessity for progress. In place of reducing other human beings to slavery and prostituting them; instead of betraying them and shattering their lives by seduction and the desertion of their offspring, the man of the future will choose to *become chaste.* He will feel that otherwise he is dishonoured; morally lost. Man will not be willing to be so weak as to confess himself dragged down to degradation and crime because unable to conquer his own instincts; man who has nothing but victories on the credit side of his history, and who even succeeded in overcoming the greatest of all his irresistible instincts, that of self-preservation, in showing himself capable of going into combat and dying for the ideals of his fatherland.

Man is capable of every great heroism; it was man who found a means of conquering the formidable obstacles of his environment, establishing himself lord of the earth, and laying the foundations of civilisation. He will also teach himself to be chaste, within sufficiently narrow limits to guarantee the dignity of the human race and the health of the species; and in this way he will prescribe the ethics for the centuries of the near future: *sexual morality.* There are customs and virtues, lofty ethical doctrines that stand in direct accord with the conservation and the progress of life. Bodily cleanliness, temperance in drink, the conquest of personal instincts, human brotherhood in the full extent of the thought, the feeling, and the practice, chastity; all these are just so many forms of the defense of life, both of the individual and of the species. To-day, in hygiene, in pathology and in anthropology, science is showing us the truth through positive proofs, through experiments and statistics. But these virtues which are paths leading to *life,* are simply being reconfirmed by science; just as they are being little by little attained by civil progress, which prepares their practical elements; but they were always intuitively recognised by the human heart: nothing is older in the ethics of mankind than the principal of brotherhood, of victory over the instincts, of chastity. Only, these virtues, *intuitively perceived,* could not be universally *practised,* because universal practice demanded time for preparation. But they survived partly as affirmations of absolute virtue and partly as *prophesies* of a future age and were considered as constituting the *highest good.* Just as the esthetic sense led to the recognition of *normality* at a time when this scientific concept was very far from being understood as it is to-day; in the same way the ethical and religious sense was able to feel intuitively and to separate from customs and from sentiments belonging to an evanescent form of transitory civilisation or from the temporary racial needs, those others that relate fundamentally to the biological preservation of the individual and the species and the practical attainment of human perfection. And while the medial intellectual man or the artistic genius combines wholly or in part the thoughts of his time, the medial moral or religious man sums up the guiding principles of life which everyone feels profoundly in the depth of his heart; and when he speaks to other men it seems as though he instilled new vigour into the very roots of their existence, and he is believed, when he speaks of a happier future toward which humanity is advancing. If the intellectual genius is almost a reader of contemporaneous thought as it vibrates around him, the religious genius interprets more or less completely and perfectly the universal and eternal spirit of life in humanity.

Accordingly, the medial men incarnate the *beautiful,* the *true,* and the *good:* in other words, the theories of positivism arrive at the self-same goals as idealism, those of poetry, philosophy and art.

By following the path of observation, we reach a goal analogous to that sought along the path of intuition.

The theory of the medial man constructed fundamentally upon positive bases of *measurements* and *facts,* represents the limit* of perfection of the human individual associated with the limit of perfection of *human society,* which is formed in a two-fold way: a close association between all human beings, or the formation of a true social organism (complete hybridism in body; human brotherhood in sentiment), and the steadily progressive emancipation, of every individual member from anxiety concerning the *defense of life,* in order to enjoy the triumph of the *development of life.* All that was formerly included under *defense* will assume

* Limit, in the mathematical sense.

collective forms of a high order (repressive justice replaced by more varied forms of prevention: which have for their final goal a widespread education and a gradual amelioration of labour and social conditions); and in this *reign of peace* there will arise the possibility *of developing all* the forces of life (biological liberty).

In such a conception, the individual organism depends more and more upon the social organism: just as the cells depend upon the multicellular organism; and we may almost conceive of a new living entity, a *super-organism* made up of humanity, but in which every component part is allowed the maximum expansion of its personal activity emancipated from all the obstacles that have been successively overcome. This conception of *biological liberty,* in other words, the triumph of the free and peaceful development of life, through the long series of more or less bitter *struggles and defenses of life,* constitutes, in my opinion, the very essence of the new pedagogy. And the evolution of modern thought and of the social environment can alone prepare for its advent, perhaps at no distant day.

TABLES SUMMARIZING

THE MEAN PROPORTIONS OF THE BODY ACCORDING TO AGE

Useful for judging of normal development and incidentally for diagnosing forms of infantilism:

Preceded by figures (from QUÉTÉLET) giving the *growth of stature in man and in woman (it being well known that the stature is the fundamental measurement for forming the aforesaid judgments).*

Age	Males	Females
0	0.496	0.483
1	0.696	0.690
2	0.797	0.780
3	0.860	0.850
4	0.932	0.910
5	0.990	0.974
6	1.046	1.032
7	1.112	1.096
8	1.170	1.139
9	1.227	1.200
10	1.282	1.248
11	1.327	1.275
12	1.359	1.327
13	1.403	1.386
14	1.487	1.447
15	1.559	1.475
16	1.610	1.500
17	1.670	1.544
18	1.700	1.562
19	1.706	1.566
20	1.711	1.570
25	1.722	1.577
30	1.722	1.579
40	1.713	1.555
50	1.674	1.536
60	1.639	1.516
70	1.623	1.514

New-born child....	Length of body....................	0.50 m.
	Weight..........................	3 kg.
	Maximum cranial circumference......	335 mm.
	Circumference of thorax...........	350 mm.
	Index of stature..................	68
	Ponderal index....................	28.8 —

Age in years	1	2	3
Stature in metres....................	0.696	0.797	0.860
Index of stature.....................	65	63	62
Weight in kilograms..................	10	12	13.21
Ponderal index.......................	30.9	28.7	27.5
Maximum circumference of head in millimetres.	440	471	486

Age in years	4	5	6
Stature in metres	0.932	0.990	1.046
Index of stature	60	59	57
Weight in kilograms	15	16.70	18.04
Ponderal index	26.5	25.8	25.1
Maximum circumference of head in millimetres.	496	503	508

Age in years	7	8	9
Stature in metres	1.112	1.170	1.227
Index of stature	56	55	55
Weight in kilograms	20.16	22.26	24.09
Ponderal index	24.4	24	23.5
Maximum circumference of head in millimetres.	513	519	523

Age in years	10	11	12
Stature in metres	1.282	1.327	1.359
Index of stature	54	53	53
Weight in kilograms	26.12	27.85	31
Ponderal index	23.1	22.8	23.1
Maximum circumference of head in millimetres.	527	531	535

Age in years	13	14	15
Stature in metres	1.403	1.487	1.559
Index of stature	52	52	51
Weight in kilograms	35.32	40.50	46.41
Ponderal index	23.4	23.1	23.1
Maximum circumference of head in millimetres.	539	543	547

Age in years	16	17	18
Stature in metres	1.610	1.670	1.700
Index of stature	51	52	52
Weight in kilograms	53.39	57.40	61.26
Ponderal index	23.4	23.1	23.2
Maximum circumference of head in millimetres.	551	555	561

TABLES OF CALCULATIONS

I

TABLES FOR CALCULATING THE CEPHALIC INDEX

CALCULATIONS OF THE CEPHALIC INDEX

Antero-posterior diameters from 160 to 174 mm.; bilateral diameters from 120 to 159 mm.

Bi-lateral diameters in millimetres	Antero-posterior diameters, in millimetres														
	160	161	162	163	164	165	166	167	168	169	170	171	172	173	174
120	75	75	74	74	73	73	72	72	71	71	71	70	70	69	69
121	76	75	75	74	74	73	73	72	72	72	71	71	70	70	70
122	76	76	75	75	74	74	73	73	73	72	72	71	71	71	70
123	77	76	76	75	75	75	74	74	73	73	72	72	72	71	71
124	77	77	77	76	76	75	75	74	74	73	73	73	72	72	71
125	78	78	77	77	76	76	75	75	74	74	74	73	73	72	72
126	79	78	78	77	77	76	76	75	75	75	74	74	73	73	72
127	79	79	78	78	77	77	77	76	76	75	75	74	74	73	73
128	80	80	79	79	78	78	77	77	76	76	75	75	74	74	74
129	81	80	80	79	79	78	78	77	77	76	76	75	75	75	74
130	81	81	80	80	79	79	78	78	77	77	76	76	76	75	75
131	82	81	81	80	80	79	79	78	78	78	77	77	76	76	75
132	82	82	81	81	80	80	80	79	79	78	78	77	77	76	76
133	83	83	82	82	81	81	80	80	79	79	78	78	77	77	76
134	84	83	83	82	82	81	81	80	80	79	79	78	78	77	77
135	84	84	83	83	82	82	81	81	80	80	79	79	78	78	78
136	85	84	84	83	83	82	82	81	81	80	80	80	79	79	78
137	86	85	85	84	84	83	83	82	82	81	81	80	80	79	79
138	86	86	85	85	84	84	83	83	82	82	81	81	80	80	79
139	87	86	86	85	85	84	84	83	83	82	82	81	81	80	80
140	87	87	86	86	85	85	84	84	83	83	82	82	81	81	80
141	89	88	87	87	86	85	85	84	84	83	83	82	82	82	81
142	89	88	88	87	87	86	86	85	85	84	84	83	83	82	82
143	89	89	88	88	87	87	86	86	85	85	84	84	83	83	82
144	90	89	89	88	88	87	87	86	86	85	85	84	84	83	83
145	91	90	90	89	88	88	87	87	86	86	85	85	84	84	83
146	91	91	90	90	89	88	88	87	87	86	86	85	85	84	84
147	92	91	91	90	90	89	89	88	87	87	86	86	85	85	84
148	92	92	91	91	90	90	89	89	88	88	87	87	86	86	85
149	93	93	92	91	91	90	90	89	89	88	88	87	87	86	86
150	94	93	93	92	91	91	90	90	89	89	88	88	87	87	86
151	94	94	93	93	92	92	91	90	90	89	89	88	88	87	87
152	95	94	94	93	93	92	92	91	90	90	89	89	88	88	87
153	96	95	94	94	93	93	92	92	91	91	90	89	89	88	88
154	96	96	95	94	94	93	93	92	92	91	91	90	90	89	89
155	97	96	96	95	95	94	93	93	92	92	91	91	90	90	89
156	97	97	96	96	95	95	94	93	93	92	92	91	91	90	90
157	98	98	97	96	96	95	95	94	93	93	92	92	91	91	90
158	99	98	98	97	96	96	95	95	94	93	93	92	92	91	91
159	99	99	98	98	97	96	96	95	95	94	94	93	92	92	91

CALCULATIONS OF THE CEPHALIC INDEX

Antero-posterior diameters from 175 to 189 mm.; bilateral diameters from 125 to 164 mm.

Bilateral diameters in millimetres	Antero-posterior diameters, in millimetres														
	175	176	177	178	179	180	181	182	183	184	185	186	187	188	189
125	71	71	71	70	70	69	69	69	68	68	68	67	67	66	66
126	72	72	71	71	70	70	70	69	69	68	68	68	67	67	67
127	73	72	72	71	71	71	70	70	69	69	69	68	68	68	67
128	73	73	72	72	72	71	71	70	70	70	69	69	68	68	68
129	74	73	73	72	72	72	71	71	70	70	70	69	69	69	68
130	74	74	73	73	73	72	72	71	71	71	70	70	70	69	69
131	75	74	74	74	73	73	72	72	72	71	71	70	70	70	69
132	75	75	75	74	74	73	73	73	72	72	71	71	71	70	70
133	76	76	75	75	74	74	73	73	73	72	72	72	71	71	70
134	77	76	76	75	75	74	74	74	73	73	72	72	72	71	71
135	77	77	76	76	75	75	75	74	74	73	73	73	72	72	71
136	78	77	77	76	76	76	75	75	74	74	74	73	73	72	72
137	78	78	77	77	77	76	76	75	75	74	74	74	73	73	72
138	79	78	78	78	77	77	76	76	75	75	75	74	74	73	73
139	79	79	79	78	78	77	77	76	76	76	75	75	74	74	74
140	80	80	79	79	78	78	77	77	77	76	76	75	75	74	74
141	81	80	80	79	79	78	78	77	77	77	76	76	75	75	75
142	81	81	80	80	79	79	78	78	78	77	77	76	76	76	75
143	82	81	81	80	80	79	79	79	78	78	77	77	76	76	76
144	82	82	81	81	80	80	80	79	79	78	78	77	77	77	76
145	83	82	82	81	81	81	80	80	79	79	78	78	78	77	77
146	83	83	82	82	82	81	81	80	80	79	79	78	78	78	77
147	84	84	83	83	82	82	81	81	80	80	79	79	79	78	78
148	85	84	84	83	83	82	82	81	81	80	80	80	79	79	78
149	85	85	84	84	83	83	82	82	81	81	81	80	80	79	79
150	86	85	85	84	84	83	83	82	82	82	81	81	80	80	79
151	86	86	85	85	84	84	83	83	83	82	82	81	81	80	80
152	87	86	86	85	85	84	84	84	83	83	82	82	81	81	80
153	87	87	86	86	85	85	85	84	84	83	83	82	82	81	81
154	88	87	87	87	86	86	85	85	84	84	83	83	82	82	81
155	89	88	88	87	87	86	86	85	85	84	84	83	83	82	82
156	89	89	88	88	87	87	86	86	85	85	84	84	83	83	83
157	90	89	89	88	88	87	87	86	86	85	85	84	84	84	83
158	90	90	89	89	88	88	87	87	86	86	85	85	84	84	84
159	91	90	90	89	89	88	88	87	87	86	86	85	85	85	84
160	91	91	90	90	89	89	88	88	87	87	86	86	86	85	85
161	92	91	91	90	90	89	89	88	88	87	87	87	86	86	85
162	93	92	92	91	91	90	90	89	89	88	88	87	87	86	86
163	93	93	92	92	91	91	90	90	89	89	88	88	87	87	86
164	94	93	93	92	92	91	91	90	90	89	89	88	88	87	87

CALCULATIONS OF THE CEPHALIC INDEX

Antero-posterior diameters from 190 to 204 mm.; bilateral diameters from 130 to 169 mm.

Bi-lateral diam-eters in milli-metres	Antero-posterior diameters in millimetres														
	190	191	192	193	194	195	196	197	198	199	200	201	202	203	204
130	68	68	68	67	67	67	66	66	66	65	65	65	64	64	64
131	69	69	68	68	68	67	67	66	66	66	65	65	65	65	64
132	69	69	69	68	68	68	67	67	67	66	66	66	65	65	65
133	70	70	69	69	69	68	68	68	67	67	66	66	66	66	65
134	71	70	70	69	69	69	68	68	68	67	67	67	66	66	66
135	71	71	70	70	70	69	69	69	68	68	67	67	67	67	66
136	72	71	71	70	70	70	69	69	69	68	68	68	67	67	67
137	72	72	71	71	71	70	70	70	69	69	68	68	68	67	67
138	73	72	72	72	71	71	70	70	70	69	69	69	68	68	68
139	73	73	72	72	72	71	71	71	70	70	69	69	69	68	68
140	74	73	73	73	72	72	71	71	71	70	70	70	69	69	69
141	74	74	73	73	73	72	72	72	71	71	70	70	70	69	69
142	75	74	74	74	73	73	72	72	72	71	71	71	70	70	70
143	75	75	74	74	74	73	73	73	72	72	71	71	71	70	70
144	76	75	75	75	74	74	73	73	73	72	72	72	71	71	71
145	76	76	76	75	75	74	74	74	73	73	72	72	72	71	71
146	77	76	76	76	75	75	74	74	74	73	73	73	72	72	72
147	77	77	77	76	76	75	75	75	74	74	73	73	73	72	72
148	78	77	77	77	76	76	76	75	75	74	74	74	73	73	73
149	78	78	78	77	77	76	76	76	75	75	74	74	74	73	73
150	79	79	78	78	77	77	77	76	76	75	75	75	74	74	74
151	79	79	79	78	78	77	77	77	76	76	75	75	75	74	74
152	80	80	79	79	78	78	78	77	77	76	76	76	75	75	75
153	80	80	80	79	79	78	78	78	77	77	76	76	76	75	75
154	81	81	80	80	79	79	79	78	78	77	77	77	76	76	75
155	82	81	81	80	80	79	79	79	78	78	77	77	77	76	76
156	82	82	81	81	80	80	80	79	79	78	78	78	77	77	76
157	83	82	82	81	81	81	80	80	79	79	78	78	78	77	77
158	83	83	82	82	81	81	81	80	80	79	79	79	78	78	77
159	84	83	83	82	82	82	81	81	80	80	79	79	79	78	78
160	84	84	83	83	82	82	82	81	81	80	80	80	79	79	78
161	85	84	84	83	83	83	82	82	81	81	80	80	80	79	79
162	85	85	84	84	84	83	83	82	82	81	81	81	80	80	79
163	86	85	85	84	84	84	83	83	82	82	81	81	81	80	80
164	86	86	85	85	85	84	84	83	83	82	82	82	81	81	80
165	87	86	86	85	85	85	84	84	83	83	82	82	82	81	81
166	87	87	86	86	86	85	85	84	84	83	83	83	82	82	81
167	88	87	87	87	86	86	85	85	84	84	83	83	83	82	82
168	88	88	87	87	87	86	86	85	85	84	84	84	83	83	82
169	89	88	88	88	87	87	86	86	85	85	84	84	84	83	83

II

TABLES FOR CALCULATING THE PONDERAL INDEX

CALCULATIONS OF THE PONDERAL INDEX

Statures from 46 to 60 centimetres; weights from 2 to 16 kilograms

Weights in kilograms	Statures in centimetres														
	46	47	48	49	50	51	52	53	54	55	56	57	58	59	60
2 —	27 4	26 8	26 2	25 7	25 2	24 7	24 2	23 8	23 3	22 9	22 5	22 1	21 7	21 4	21 0
2 10	27 8	27 3	26 7	26 1	25 6	25 1	24 6	24 2	23 7	23 3	22 9	22 5	22 1	21 7	21 3
2 20	28 3	27 7	27 1	26 6	26 0	25 5	25 0	24 5	24 1	23 7	23 2	22 8	22 4	22 1	21 7
2 30	28 7	28 1	27 5	26 9	26 4	25 9	25 4	24 9	24 4	24 0	23 6	23 2	22 8	22 4	22 0
2 40	29 1	28 5	27 9	27 3	26 8	26 2	25 7	25 3	24 8	24 3	23 9	23 5	23 1	22 7	22 3
2 50	29 5	28 9	28 3	27 7	27 1	26 6	26 1	25 6	25 1	24 7	24 2	23 8	23 4	23 0	22 6
2 60	29 9	29 3	28 6	28 1	27 5	27 0	26 4	25 9	25 5	25 0	24 6	24 1	23 7	23 3	22 9
2 70	30 3	29 6	29 0	28 4	27 8	27 3	26 8	26 3	25 8	25 3	24 9	24 4	24 0	23 6	23 2
2 80	30 6	30 0	29 4	28 8	28 2	27 6	27 1	26 6	26 1	25 6	25 2	24 7	24 3	23 9	23 5
2 90	31 0	30 3	29 7	29 1	28 5	28 0	27 4	26 9	26 4	25 9	25 5	25 0	24 6	24 2	23 8
3 —	31 3	30 7	30 0	29 4	28 8	28 3	27 7	27 2	26 7	26 2	25 7	25 3	24 9	24 4	24 0
3 10	31 7	31 0	30 4	29 8	29 2	28 6	28 0	27 5	27 0	26 5	26 0	25 6	25 1	24 7	24 3
3 20	32 0	31 4	30 7	30 1	29 5	28 9	28 3	27 8	27 3	26 8	26 3	25 9	25 4	25 0	24 6
3 30	32 4	31 7	31 0	30 4	29 8	29 2	28 6	28 1	27 6	27 1	26 6	26 1	25 7	25 2	24 8
3 40	32 7	32 0	31 3	30 7	30 1	29 5	28 9	28 4	27 9	27 3	26 9	26 4	25 9	25 5	25 1
3 50	33 0	32 3	31 6	31 0	30 4	29 8	29 2	28 6	28 1	27 6	27 1	26 6	26 2	25 7	25 3
3 60	33 3	32 6	31 9	31 3	30 7	30 1	29 5	28 9	28 4	27 9	27 4	26 9	26 4	26 0	25 5
3 70	33 6	32 9	32 2	31 6	30 9	30 3	29 7	29 2	28 6	28 1	27 6	27 1	26 7	26 2	25 8
3 80	33 9	33 2	32 5	31 8	31 2	30 6	30 0	29 4	28 9	28 4	27 9	27 4	26 9	26 4	26 0
3 90	34 2	33 5	32 8	32 1	31 5	30 9	30 3	29 7	29 1	28 6	28 1	27 6	27 1	26 7	26 2
4 —	34 5	33 8	33 1	32 4	31 7	31 1	30 5	29 9	29 4	28 9	28 3	27 8	27 4	26 9	26 4
4 10	34 8	34 1	33 4	32 7	32 0	31 4	30 8	30 2	29 6	29 1	28 6	28 1	27 6	27 1	26 7
4 20	35 1	34 3	33 6	32 9	32 3	31 6	31 0	30 4	29 9	29 3	28 8	28 3	27 8	27 3	26 9
4 30	35 3	34 6	33 9	33 2	32 5	31 9	31 3	30 7	30 1	29 6	29 0	28 5	28 0	27 6	27 1
4 40	35 6	34 9	34 1	33 4	32 8	32 1	31 5	30 9	30 4	29 8	29 3	28 8	28 3	27 8	27 3
4 50	35 9	35 1	34 4	33 7	33 0	32 4	31 7	31 2	30 6	30 0	29 5	29 0	28 5	28 0	27 5
4 60	36 2	35 4	34 6	33 9	33 3	32 6	32 0	31 4	30 8	30 2	29 7	29 2	28 7	28 2	27 7
4 70	36 4	35 6	34 9	34 2	33 5	32 8	32 2	31 6	31 0	30 5	29 9	29 4	28 9	28 4	27 9
4 80	36 7	35 9	35 1	34 4	33 7	33 1	32 4	31 8	31 2	30 7	30 1	29 6	29 1	28 6	28 1
4 90	36 9	36 1	35 4	34 7	34 0	33 3	32 7	32 0	31 4	30 9	30 3	29 8	29 3	28 8	28 3
5 —	37 2	36 4	35 6	34 9	34 2	33 5	32 9	32 3	31 7	31 1	30 5	30 0	29 5	29 0	28 5
5 25	37 8	37 0	36 2	35 5	34 8	34 1	33 4	32 8	32 2	31 6	31 0	30 5	30 0	29 5	29 0
5 50	38 4	37 6	36 8	36 0	35 3	34 6	33 9	33 3	32 7	32 1	31 5	31 0	30 4	29 9	29 4
5 75	39 0	38 1	37 3	36 6	35 8	35 1	34 5	33 8	33 2	32 6	32 0	31 4	30 9	30 4	29 9
6 —	39 5	38 7	37 9	37 1	36 3	35 6	34 9	34 3	33 6	33 0	32 4	31 9	31 3	30 8	30 3
6 25	40 0	39 2	38 4	37 6	36 8	36 1	35 4	34 8	34 1	33 5	32 9	32 3	31 8	31 2	30 7
6 50	40 6	39 7	38 9	38 1	37 3	36 6	35 9	35 2	34 6	33 9	33 3	32 7	32 2	31 6	31 1
6 75	41 1	40 2	39 4	38 6	37 8	37 1	36 3	35 7	35 0	34 4	33 7	33 2	32 6	32 0	31 5
7 —	41 6	40 7	39 9	39 0	38 3	37 5	36 8	36 1	35 4	34 8	34 2	33 6	33 0	32 4	31 9
7 50	42 5	41 6	40 8	39 9	39 1	38 4	37 6	36 9	36 2	35 6	34 9	34 3	33 7	33 2	32 6
8 —	43 5	42 6	41 7	40 8	40 0	39 2	38 5	37 7	37 0	36 4	35 7	35 1	34 5	33 9	33 3
8 50	44 4	43 4	42 5	41 7	40 8	40 0	39 2	38 5	37 8	37 1	36 4	35 8	35 2	34 6	34 0
9 —	45 2	44 3	43 3	42 4	41 6	40 8	40 0	39 2	38 5	37 8	37 1	36 5	35 9	35 3	34 7
10 —	46 8	45 8	44 9	44 0	43 1	42 2	41 4	40 6	39 9	39 2	38 5	37 8	37 1	36 5	35 9
11 —	48 3	47 3	46 3	45 4	44 5	43 6	42 8	42 0	41 2	40 4	39 7	39 0	38 3	37 7	37 1
12 —	49 8	48 7	47 7	46 7	45 8	44 9	44 0	43 2	42 4	41 6	40 9	40 2	39 5	38 8	38 1
13 —	51 1	50 0	49 0	48 0	47 0	46 1	45 2	44 4	43 5	42 7	42 0	41 2	40 5	39 8	39 2
14 —	52 4	51 3	50 2	49 2	48 2	47 3	46 3	45 5	44 6	43 8	43 0	42 3	41 6	40 8	40 2
15 —	53 6	52 5	51 4	50 3	49 3	48 4	47 4	46 5	45 7	44 8	44 0	43 3	42 5	41 8	41 1
16 —	54 8	53 6	52 5	51 4	50 4	49 4	48 5	47 5	46 7	45 8	45 0	44 2	43 4	42 7	42 0

CALCULATIONS OF THE PONDERAL INDEX

Statures from 61 to 75 centimetres; weights from 2 to 16 kilograms.

Weights in kilograms	Statures in centimetres														
	61	62	63	64	65	66	67	68	69	70	71	72	73	74	75
2 —	20 7	20 3	20 0	19 7	19 4	19 1	18 8	18 5	18 3	18 0	17 7	17 5	17 3	17 0	16 8
2 10	21 0	20 7	20 3	20 0	19 7	19 4	19 1	18 8	18 6	18 3	18 0	17 8	17 5	17 3	17 1
2 20	21 3	21 0	20 7	20 3	20 0	19 7	19 4	19 1	18 9	18 6	18 3	18 0	17 8	17 6	17 3
2 30	21 6	21 3	21 0	20 6	20 3	20 0	19 7	19 4	19 1	18 9	18 6	18 3	18 1	17 8	17 6
2 40	22 0	21 6	21 3	20 9	20 6	20 3	20 0	19 7	19 4	19 1	18 9	18 6	18 3	18 1	17 9
2 50	22 2	21 9	21 5	21 2	20 9	20 6	20 3	20 0	19 7	19 4	19 1	18 8	18 6	18 3	18 1
2 60	22 5	22 2	21 8	21 5	21 2	20 8	20 5	20 2	19 9	19 6	19 4	19 1	18 8	18 6	18 3
2 70	22 8	22 5	22 1	21 7	21 4	21 1	20 8	20 5	20 2	19 9	19 6	19 3	19 1	18 8	18 6
2 80	23 1	22 7	22 4	22 0	21 7	21 3	21 0	20 7	20 4	20 1	19 8	19 6	19 3	19 0	18 8
2 90	23 4	23 0	22 6	22 3	21 9	21 6	21 3	21 0	20 7	20 4	20 1	19 8	19 5	19 3	19 0
3 —	23 6	23 3	22 9	22 5	22 2	21 8	21 5	21 2	20 9	20 6	20 3	20 0	19 8	19 5	19 2
3 10	23 9	23 5	23 1	22 8	22 4	22 1	21 8	21 4	21 1	20 8	20 5	20 2	20 0	19 7	19 4
3 20	24 2	23 8	23 4	23 0	22 7	22 3	22 0	21 7	21 4	21 1	20 8	20 5	20 2	19 9	19 7
3 30	24 4	24 0	23 6	23 3	22 9	22 6	22 2	21 9	21 6	21 3	21 0	20 7	20 4	20 1	19 9
3 40	24 7	24 3	23 9	23 5	23 1	22 8	22 4	22 1	21 8	21 5	21 2	20 9	20 6	20 3	20 1
3 50	24 9	24 5	24 1	23 7	23 4	23 0	22 7	22 3	22 0	21 7	21 4	21 1	20 8	20 5	20 2
3 60	25 1	24 7	24 3	24 0	23 6	23 2	22 9	22 5	22 2	21 9	21 6	21 3	21 0	20 7	20 4
3 70	25 4	25 0	24 6	24 2	23 8	23 4	23 1	22 7	22 4	22 1	21 8	21 5	21 2	20 9	20 6
3 80	25 6	25 2	24 8	24 4	24 0	23 6	23 3	22 9	22 6	22 3	22 0	21 7	21 4	21 1	20 8
3 90	25 8	25 4	25 0	24 6	24 2	23 8	23 5	23 1	22 8	22 5	22 2	21 9	21 6	21 3	21 0
4 —	26 0	25 6	25 2	24 8	24 4	24 0	23 7	23 3	23 0	22 7	22 4	22 0	21 7	21 4	21 2
4 10	26 2	25 8	25 4	25 0	24 6	24 3	23 9	23 5	23 2	22 9	22 5	22 2	21 9	21 6	21 3
4 20	26 4	26 0	25 6	25 2	24 8	24 4	24 1	23 7	23 4	23 0	22 7	22 4	22 1	21 8	21 5
4 30	26 7	26 2	25 8	25 4	25 0	24 6	24 3	23 9	23 6	23 2	22 9	22 6	22 3	22 0	21 7
4 40	26 9	26 4	26 0	25 6	25 2	24 8	24 5	24 1	23 8	23 4	23 1	22 8	22 5	22 1	21 9
4 50	27 1	26 6	26 2	25 8	25 4	25 0	24 6	24 3	23 9	23 6	23 3	22 9	22 6	22 3	22 0
4 60	27 3	26 8	26 4	26 0	25 6	25 2	24 8	24 5	24 1	23 8	23 4	23 1	22 8	22 5	22 2
4 70	27 5	27 0	26 6	26 2	25 8	25 4	25 0	24 6	24 3	23 9	23 6	23 3	22 9	22 6	22 3
4 80	27 7	27 2	26 8	26 4	26 0	25 6	25 2	24 8	24 4	24 1	23 8	23 4	23 1	22 8	22 5
4 90	27 8	27 4	27 0	26 5	26 1	25 7	25 3	25 0	24 6	24 3	23 9	23 6	23 3	22 9	22 6
5 —	28 0	27 7	27 1	26 7	26 3	25 9	25 5	25 1	24 8	24 4	24 1	23 7	23 4	23 1	22 8
5 25	28 5	28 0	27 6	27 2	26 7	26 3	25 9	25 6	25 2	24 8	24 5	24 1	23 8	23 5	23 2
5 50	28 9	28 5	28 0	27 6	27 2	26 7	26 3	26 0	25 6	25 2	24 9	24 5	24 2	23 9	23 5
5 75	29 4	28 9	28 4	28 0	27 6	27 2	26 7	26 3	26 0	25 6	25 2	24 9	24 5	24 2	23 9
6 —	29 8	29 3	28 8	28 4	28 0	27 5	27 1	26 7	26 3	26 0	25 6	25 2	24 9	24 6	24 2
6 25	30 2	29 7	29 2	28 8	28 3	27 9	27 5	27 1	26 7	26 3	25 9	25 6	25 2	24 9	24 6
6 50	30 6	30 1	29 6	29 5	28 7	28 3	27 9	27 4	27 0	26 7	26 3	25 9	25 6	25 2	24 9
6 75	31 0	30 5	30 0	29 5	29 1	28 6	28 2	27 8	27 4	27 0	26 6	26 3	25 9	25 5	25 2
7 —	31 4	30 9	30 4	29 9	29 4	29 0	28 6	28 1	27 7	27 3	26 9	26 6	26 2	25 9	25 5
7 50	32 1	31 6	31 1	30 6	30 1	29 7	29 2	28 8	28 4	28 0	27 6	27 2	26 8	26 4	26 1
8 —	32 8	32 3	31 7	31 2	30 8	30 3	29 9	29 4	29 0	28 6	28 2	27 8	27 4	27 0	26 7
8 50	33 5	32 9	32 4	31 9	31 4	30 9	30 5	30 0	29 6	29 2	28 7	28 3	28 0	27 6	27 2
9 —	34 1	33 5	33 0	32 5	32 0	31 5	31 0	30 6	30 1	29 7	29 3	28 9	28 5	28 1	27 7
10 —	35 3	34 7	34 2	33 7	33 1	32 6	32 1	31 7	31 2	30 8	30 3	29 9	29 5	29 1	28 7
11 —	36 5	35 9	35 3	34 7	34 2	33 7	33 2	32 7	32 2	31 8	31 3	30 9	30 5	30 1	29 7
12 —	37 5	36 9	36 3	35 7	35 2	34 7	34 2	33 7	33 2	32 7	32 2	31 8	31 4	30 9	30 5
13 —	38 5	37 9	37 3	36 7	36 2	35 6	35 1	34 6	34 1	33 6	33 1	32 7	32 2	31 8	31 3
14 —	39 5	38 9	38 3	37 7	37 1	36 5	36 0	35 4	34 9	34 4	33 9	33 5	33 0	32 6	32 1
15 —	40 4	39 8	39 1	38 5	37 9	37 4	36 8	36 3	35 7	35 2	34 7	34 2	33 8	33 3	32 9
16 —	41 3	40 6	40 0	39 4	38 8	38 2	37 6	37 1	36 5	36 0	35 5	35 0	34 5	34 1	33 6

CALCULATIONS OF THE PONDERAL INDEX

Statures from 76 to 90 centimetres; weights from 4 to 37 kilograms

Weights in kilograms	Statures in centimetres														
	76	77	78	79	80	81	82	83	84	85	86	87	88	89	90
4 —	20 9	20 6	20 3	20 1	19 8	19 6	19 4	19 1	18 9	18 7	18 5	18 2	18 0	17 8	17 6
4 50	21 7	21 4	21 2	20 9	20 6	20 4	20 1	19 9	19 7	19 4	19 2	19 0	18 8	18 6	18 3
5 —	22 5	22 2	21 9	21 6	21 4	21 1	20 9	20 6	20 4	20 1	19 9	19 7	19 4	19 2	19 0
5 50	23 2	22 9	22 6	22 3	22 1	21 8	21 5	21 3	21 0	20 8	20 5	20 3	20 1	19 8	19 6
6 —	23 9	23 6	23 3	23 0	22 6	22 4	22 2	21 9	21 6	21 4	21 1	20 9	20 6	20 4	20 2
6 50	24 6	24 2	23 9	23 6	23 3	23 0	22 8	22 5	22 2	22 0	21 7	21 4	21 2	21 0	20 7
7 —	25 2	24 8	24 5	24 2	23 9	23 6	23 3	23 0	22 8	22 5	22 2	22 0	21 7	21 5	21 3
7 50	25 7	25 4	25 1	24 8	24 5	24 2	23 9	23 6	23 3	23 0	22 8	22 5	22 2	22 0	21 7
8 —	26 3	26 0	25 6	25 3	25 0	24 7	24 4	24 1	23 8	23 5	23 3	23 0	22 7	22 5	22 2
8 50	26 9	26 5	26 2	25 8	25 5	25 2	24 9	24 6	24 3	24 0	23 7	23 5	23 2	22 9	22 7
9 —	27 4	27 0	26 7	26 3	26 0	25 7	25 4	25 1	24 8	24 5	24 2	23 9	23 6	23 4	23 1
9 50	27 9	27 5	27 2	26 8	26 5	26 1	25 8	25 5	25 2	24 9	24 6	24 3	24 1	23 8	23 5
10 —	28 3	28 0	27 6	27 3	26 9	26 6	26 3	26 0	25 6	25 3	25 0	24 8	24 5	24 2	23 9
10 50	28 8	28 4	28 1	27 7	27 4	27 0	26 7	26 4	26 1	25 8	25 5	25 2	24 9	24 6	24 3
11 —	29 3	28 9	28 5	28 2	27 8	27 5	27 1	26 8	26 5	26 2	25 9	25 6	25 3	25 0	24 7
11 50	29 7	29 3	28 9	28 6	28 2	27 9	27 5	27 2	26 9	26 6	26 2	25 9	25 6	25 4	25 1
12 —	30 1	29 7	29 3	29 0	28 6	28 3	27 9	27 6	27 2	26 9	26 6	26 3	26 0	25 7	25 4
12 50	30 5	30 1	29 8	29 4	29 0	28 7	28 3	28 0	27 6	27 3	27 0	26 7	26 4	26 1	25 8
13 —	30 9	30 5	30 1	29 8	29 4	29 0	28 7	28 3	28 0	27 7	27 3	27 0	26 7	26 4	26 1
13 50	31 3	30 9	30 5	30 1	29 8	29 4	29 0	28 7	28 3	28 0	27 7	27 4	27 1	26 8	26 5
14 —	31 7	31 3	30 9	30 5	30 1	29 8	29 4	29 0	28 7	28 3	28 0	27 7	27 4	27 1	26 8
14 50	32 1	31 7	31 3	30 9	30 5	30 1	29 7	29 4	29 0	28 7	28 3	28 0	27 7	27 4	27 1
15 —	32 4	32 0	31 6	31 2	30 8	30 4	30 1	29 7	29 4	29 0	28 7	28 3	28 0	27 7	27 4
15 50	32 8	32 4	32 0	31 6	31 2	30 8	30 4	30 0	29 7	29 3	29 0	28 7	28 3	28 0	27 7
16 —	33 2	32 7	32 3	31 9	31 5	31 1	30 7	30 4	30 0	29 6	29 3	29 0	28 6	28 3	28 0
16 50	33 5	33 1	32 6	32 2	31 8	31 4	31 0	30 7	30 3	30 0	29 6	29 3	28 9	28 6	28 3
17 —	33 8	33 4	33 0	32 5	32 0	31 7	31 4	31 0	30 6	30 2	29 9	29 6	29 2	28 9	28 6
17 50	34 2	33 7	33 3	32 9	32 4	32 0	31 7	31 3	30 9	30 5	30 2	29 8	29 5	29 2	28 8
18 —	34 5	34 0	33 6	33 2	32 8	32 4	32 0	31 6	31 2	30 8	30 5	30 1	29 8	29 4	29 1
18 50	34 8	34 4	33 9	33 5	33 1	32 7	32 3	31 9	31 5	31 1	30 8	30 4	30 1	29 7	29 4
19 —	35 1	34 6	34 2	33 8	33 3	32 9	32 5	32 1	31 8	31 4	31 0	30 7	30 3	30 0	29 6
19 50	35 4	35 0	34 5	34 1	33 6	33 2	32 8	32 4	32 0	31 7	31 3	30 9	30 6	30 2	29 9
20 —	35 7	35 2	34 8	34 4	33 9	33 5	33 1	32 7	32 3	31 9	31 6	31 2	30 8	30 5	30 2
21 —	36 3	35 8	35 4	34 9	34 5	34 1	33 6	33 2	32 8	32 5	32 1	31 7	31 4	31 0	30 7
22 —	36 9	36 4	35 9	35 5	35 0	34 6	34 2	33 8	33 4	33 0	32 6	32 2	31 8	31 5	31 1
23 —	37 4	36 9	36 5	36 0	35 5	35 1	34 7	34 3	33 9	33 5	33 1	32 7	32 3	31 9	31 6
24 —	37 9	37 5	37 0	36 5	36 0	35 6	35 2	34 7	34 3	33 9	33 5	33 2	32 8	32 4	32 0
25 —	38 5	38 0	37 5	37 0	36 5	36 1	35 7	35 2	34 8	34 4	34 0	33 6	33 2	32 9	32 5
26 —	39 0	38 5	38 0	37 5	37 0	36 6	36 1	35 7	35 3	34 8	34 4	34 0	33 7	33 3	32 9
27 —	39 5	39 0	38 5	38 0	37 5	37 0	36 6	36 1	35 7	35 3	34 9	34 5	34 1	33 7	33 3
28 —	40 0	39 4	38 9	38 4	38 0	37 5	37 0	36 6	36 2	35 7	35 3	34 9	34 5	34 1	33 7
29 —	40 4	39 9	39 4	38 9	38 4	37 9	37 5	37 0	36 6	36 1	35 7	35 3	34 9	34 5	34 1
30 —	40 9	40 4	39 8	39 3	38 8	38 4	37 9	37 4	37 0	36 6	36 1	35 7	35 3	34 9	34 5
31 —	41 3	40 8	40 3	39 8	39 3	38 8	38 3	37 8	37 4	37 0	36 5	36 1	35 7	35 3	34 9
32 —	41 8	41 2	40 7	40 2	39 7	39 2	38 7	38 3	37 8	37 4	36 9	36 5	36 1	35 7	35 3
33 —	42 2	41 7	41 1	40 6	40 1	39 6	39 1	38 7	38 2	37 7	37 3	36 9	36 5	36 0	35 6
34 —	42 6	42 1	41 5	41 0	40 5	40 0	39 5	39 0	38 6	38 1	37 7	37 2	36 8	36 4	36 0
35 —	43 0	42 5	41 9	41 4	40 9	40 4	39 9	39 4	38 9	38 5	38 0	37 6	37 2	36 8	36 3
36 —	43 4	42 9	42 3	41 8	41 3	40 8	40 3	39 8	39 3	38 8	38 4	38 0	37 5	37 1	36 7
37 —	43 8	43 3	42 7	42 2	41 6	41 1	40 6	40 1	39 7	39 2	38 7	38 3	37 9	37 4	37 0

CALCULATIONS OF THE PONDERAL INDEX

Statures from 91 to 105 centimetres; weights from 4 to 37 kilograms

Weights in kilograms	Statures in centimetres														
	91	92	93	94	95	96	97	98	99	100	101	102	103	104	105
4 —	17 4	17 2	17 0	16 9	16 7	16 5	16 4	16 2	16 0	15 9	15 7	15 6	15 4	15 3	15 1
4 50	18 1	17 9	17 8	17 6	17 4	17 2	17 0	16 8	16 7	16 5	16 3	16 2	16 0	15 9	15 7
5 —	18 8	18 6	18 4	18 2	18 0	17 8	17 6	17 4	17 3	17 1	16 9	16 8	16 6	16 5	16 3
5 50	19 4	19 2	19 0	18 8	18 6	18 3	18 2	18 0	17 8	17 6	17 5	17 3	17 1	17 0	16 8
6 —	20 0	19 7	19 5	19 3	19 1	18 9	18 7	18 5	18 4	18 2	18 0	17 8	17 6	17 5	17 3
6 50	20 5	20 3	20 1	19 9	19 6	19 4	19 2	19 0	18 8	18 7	18 5	18 3	18 1	17 9	17 8
7 —	21 0	20 8	20 6	20 4	20 1	19 9	19 7	19 5	19 3	19 1	18 9	18 8	18 6	18 4	18 2
7 50	21 5	21 3	21 1	20 8	20 6	20 4	20 2	20 0	19 8	19 6	19 4	19 2	19 0	18 8	18 6
8 —	22 0	21 7	21 5	21 3	21 1	20 8	20 6	20 4	20 2	20 0	19 8	19 6	19 4	19 2	19 0
8 50	22 4	22 2	22 0	21 7	21 5	21 3	21 0	20 8	20 6	20 4	20 2	20 0	19 8	19 6	19 4
9 —	22 9	22 6	22 4	22 1	21 9	21 7	21 4	21 2	21 0	20 8	20 6	20 4	20 2	20 0	19 8
9 50	23 3	23 0	22 8	22 5	22 3	22 1	21 8	21 6	21 4	21 2	21 0	20 8	20 6	20 4	20 2
10 —	23 7	23 4	23 2	22 9	22 7	22 4	22 2	22 0	21 8	21 5	21 3	21 1	20 9	20 7	20 5
10 50	24 1	23 8	23 5	23 3	23 1	22 8	22 6	22 3	22 1	21 9	21 7	21 5	21 3	21 1	20 9
11 —	24 4	24 2	23 9	23 7	23 4	23 2	22 9	22 7	22 5	22 2	22 0	21 8	21 6	21 4	21 2
11 50	24 8	24 5	24 3	24 0	23 8	23 5	23 3	23 0	22 8	22 6	22 3	22 1	21 9	21 7	21 5
12 —	25 2	24 9	24 6	24 4	24 1	23 8	23 6	23 4	23 1	22 9	22 7	22 4	22 2	22 0	21 8
12 50	25 5	25 2	25 0	24 7	24 4	24 2	23 9	23 7	23 4	23 2	23 0	22 8	22 5	22 3	22 1
13 —	25 8	25 6	25 3	25 0	24 7	24 5	24 2	24 0	23 7	23 5	23 3	23 0	22 8	22 6	22 4
13 50	26 2	25 9	25 6	25 3	25 1	24 8	24 5	24 3	24 1	23 8	23 6	23 3	23 1	22 9	22 7
14 —	26 5	26 2	25 9	25 6	25 4	25 1	24 8	24 6	24 3	24 1	23 9	23 6	23 4	23 2	23 0
14 50	26 8	26 5	26 2	25 9	25 7	25 4	25 1	24 9	24 6	24 4	24 1	23 9	23 7	23 4	23 3
15 —	27 1	26 8	26 5	26 2	26 0	25 7	25 4	25 2	24 9	24 7	24 4	24 2	23 9	23 7	23 5
15 50	27 4	27 1	26 8	26 5	26 2	26 0	25 7	25 4	25 2	24 9	24 7	24 4	24 2	24 0	23 7
16 —	27 7	27 4	27 1	26 8	26 5	26 2	26 0	25 7	25 5	25 2	25 0	24 7	24 5	24 2	24 0
16 50	28 0	27 7	27 4	27 1	26 8	26 5	26 2	26 0	25 7	25 5	25 2	25 0	24 7	24 5	24 2
17 —	28 3	27 9	27 6	27 4	27 1	26 8	26 5	26 2	26 0	25 7	25 5	25 2	25 0	24 7	24 5
17 50	28 5	28 2	27 9	27 6	27 3	27 0	26 8	26 5	26 2	26 0	25 7	25 5	25 2	25 0	24 7
18 —	28 8	28 5	28 2	27 9	27 6	27 3	27 0	26 7	26 5	26 2	26 0	25 7	25 4	25 2	25 0
18 50	29 1	28 7	28 4	28 1	27 8	27 6	27 3	27 0	26 7	26 4	26 2	25 9	25 7	25 4	25 2
19 —	29 3	29 0	28 7	28 4	28 0	27 8	27 5	27 2	26 9	26 7	26 4	26 2	25 9	25 7	25 4
19 50	29 6	29 3	28 9	28 6	28 3	28 0	27 8	27 5	27 2	26 9	26 7	26 4	26 1	25 9	25 6
20 —	29 8	29 5	29 2	28 9	28 6	28 3	28 0	27 7	27 4	27 1	26 9	26 6	26 3	26 1	25 8
21 —	30 3	30 0	29 7	29 4	29 0	28 7	28 4	28 2	27 9	27 6	27 3	27 0	26 8	26 5	26 3
22 —	30 8	30 5	30 1	29 8	29 5	29 2	28 9	28 6	28 3	28 0	27 7	27 5	27 2	26 9	26 7
23 —	31 2	30 9	30 6	30 3	29 9	29 6	29 3	29 0	28 7	28 4	28 2	27 9	27 6	27 3	27 1
24 —	31 7	31 3	31 0	30 7	30 4	30 0	29 7	29 4	29 1	28 8	28 6	28 3	28 0	27 7	27 5
25 —	32 1	31 8	31 4	31 1	30 8	30 5	30 1	29 8	29 5	29 2	28 9	28 7	28 4	28 1	27 8
26 —	32 5	32 2	31 8	31 5	31 2	30 9	30 5	30 2	29 9	29 6	29 3	29 0	28 8	28 5	28 2
27 —	33 0	32 6	32 3	31 9	31 6	31 2	30 9	30 6	30 3	30 0	29 7	29 4	29 1	28 8	28 6
28 —	33 4	33 0	32 7	32 3	32 0	31 6	31 3	31 0	30 7	30 4	30 1	29 8	29 5	29 2	28 9
29 —	33 8	33 4	33 0	32 7	32 3	32 0	31 7	31 3	31 0	30 7	30 4	30 1	29 8	29 5	29 3
30 —	34 1	33 8	33 4	33 1	32 7	32 4	32 0	31 7	31 4	31 1	30 8	30 5	30 2	29 9	29 6
31 —	34 5	34 1	33 8	33 4	33 1	32 7	32 4	32 1	31 7	31 4	31 1	30 8	30 5	30 2	29 9
32 —	34 9	34 5	34 1	33 8	33 4	33 1	32 7	32 4	32 1	31 7	31 4	31 1	30 8	30 5	30 2
33 —	35 3	34 9	34 5	34 1	33 8	33 4	33 1	32 7	32 4	32 1	31 8	31 5	31 1	30 8	30 6
34 —	35 6	35 2	34 8	34 5	34 1	33 7	33 4	33 1	32 7	32 4	32 1	31 8	31 5	31 2	30 9
35 —	35 9	35 6	35 2	34 8	34 4	34 1	33 7	33 4	33 0	32 7	32 4	32 1	31 8	31 5	31 2
36 —	36 3	35 9	35 5	35 1	34 8	34 4	34 0	33 7	33 4	33 0	32 7	32 4	32 1	31 7	31 4
37 —	36 6	36 2	35 8	35 4	35 1	34 7	34 4	34 0	33 7	33 3	33 0	32 7	32 3	32 0	31 7

CALCULATIONS OF THE PONDERAL INDEX

Statures from 106 to 120 centimetres; weights from 11 to 60 kilograms

Weights in kilograms	Statures in centimetres														
	106	107	108	109	110	111	112	113	114	115	116	117	118	119	120
11	21 0	20 8	20 6	20 4	20 2	20 0	19 9	19 7	19 5	19 3	19 2	19 0	18 8	18 7	18 5
12	21 6	21 4	21 2	21 0	20 8	20 6	20 4	20 3	20 1	19 9	19 7	19 6	19 4	19 2	19 1
13	22 2	22 0	21 8	21 6	21 4	21 2	21 0	20 8	20 6	20 4	20 3	20 1	19 9	19 8	19 6
14	22 7	22 5	22 3	22 1	21 9	21 7	21 5	21 3	21 1	21 0	20 8	20 6	20 4	20 3	20 1
15	23 3	23 0	22 8	22 6	22 4	22 2	22 0	21 8	21 6	21 4	21 3	21 1	20 9	20 7	20 6
16	23 8	23 6	23 3	23 1	22 9	22 7	22 5	22 3	22 1	21 9	21 7	21 5	21 4	21 2	21 0
17	24 3	24 0	23 8	23 6	23 4	23 2	23 0	22 8	22 6	22 4	22 2	22 0	21 8	21 6	21 4
18	24 7	24 5	24 3	24 0	23 8	23 6	23 4	23 2	23 0	22 8	22 6	22 4	22 2	22 0	21 8
19	25 2	24 9	24 7	24 5	24 3	24 0	23 8	23 6	23 4	23 2	23 0	22 8	22 6	22 4	22 2
20	25 6	25 4	25 1	24 9	24 7	24 5	24 2	24 0	23 8	23 6	23 4	23 2	23 0	22 8	22 6
21	26 0	25 8	25 5	25 3	25 1	24 9	24 6	24 4	24 2	24 0	23 8	23 6	23 4	23 2	23 0
22	26 4	26 2	25 9	25 7	25 5	25 2	25 0	24 8	24 6	24 4	24 2	23 9	23 7	23 5	23 3
23	26 8	26 6	26 3	26 1	25 9	25 6	25 4	25 2	24 9	24 7	24 5	24 3	24 1	23 9	23 7
24	27 2	27 0	26 7	26 5	26 2	26 0	25 7	25 5	25 3	25 1	24 9	24 6	24 4	24 2	24 0
25	27 6	27 3	27 1	26 8	26 6	26 3	26 1	25 9	25 6	25 4	25 2	25 0	24 8	24 6	24 4
26	27 9	27 5	27 4	27 2	26 9	26 7	26 4	26 2	26 0	25 8	25 5	25 3	25 1	24 9	24 7
27	28 3	28 0	27 8	27 5	27 3	27 0	26 8	26 5	26 3	26 1	25 9	25 6	25 4	25 2	25 0
28	28 7	28 4	28 1	27 9	27 6	27 4	27 1	26 9	26 6	26 4	26 2	26 0	25 7	25 5	25 3
29	29 0	28 7	28 4	28 2	27 9	27 7	27 4	27 2	26 9	26 7	26 5	26 3	26 0	25 8	25 6
30	29 3	29 0	28 8	28 5	28 2	28 0	27 7	27 5	27 3	27 0	26 8	26 6	26 3	26 1	25 9
31	29 6	29 4	29 1	28 8	28 6	28 3	28 0	27 8	27 6	27 3	27 1	26 8	26 6	26 4	26 2
32	30 0	29 7	29 4	29 1	28 9	28 6	28 3	28 1	27 9	27 6	27 4	27 1	26 9	26 7	26 5
33	30 3	30 0	29 7	29 4	29 2	28 9	28 6	28 4	28 1	27 9	27 7	27 4	27 2	27 0	26 7
34	30 6	30 3	30 0	29 7	29 5	29 2	28 9	28 7	28 4	28 2	27 9	27 7	27 5	27 2	27 0
35	30 9	30 6	30 3	30 0	29 7	29 5	29 2	28 9	28 7	28 4	28 2	28 0	27 7	27 5	27 3
36	31 2	30 9	30 6	30 3	30 0	29 7	29 5	29 2	29 0	28 7	28 5	28 2	28 0	27 7	27 5
37	31 4	31 1	30 9	30 6	30 3	30 0	29 7	29 5	29 2	29 0	28 7	28 5	28 2	28 0	27 8
38	31 7	31 4	31 1	30 8	30 6	30 3	30 0	29 7	29 5	29 2	29 0	28 7	28 5	28 3	28 0
39	32 0	31 7	31 4	31 1	30 8	30 5	30 3	30 0	29 7	29 5	29 2	29 0	28 7	28 5	28 3
40	32 3	32 0	31 7	31 4	31 1	30 8	30 5	30 3	30 0	29 7	29 5	29 2	29 0	28 7	28 5
41	32 5	32 2	31 9	31 7	31 3	31 1	30 8	30 5	30 2	30 0	29 7	29 5	29 2	29 0	28 7
42	32 8	32 5	32 2	31 9	31 6	31 3	31 0	30 8	30 5	30 2	30 0	29 7	29 5	29 2	29 0
43	33 0	32 7	32 4	32 1	31 8	31 6	31 3	31 0	30 7	30 5	30 2	29 9	29 7	29 4	29 2
44	33 3	33 0	32 7	32 4	32 1	31 8	31 5	31 2	31 0	30 7	30 4	30 2	29 9	29 7	29 4
45	33 6	33 2	32 9	32 6	32 3	32 0	31 8	31 5	31 2	30 9	30 7	30 4	30 1	29 9	29 6
46	33 8	33 5	33 2	32 9	32 6	32 3	32 0	31 7	31 4	31 2	30 9	30 6	30 4	30 1	29 9
47	34 0	33 7	33 4	33 1	32 8	32 5	32 2	31 9	31 7	31 4	31 1	30 8	30 6	30 3	30 1
48	34 3	34 0	33 6	33 3	33 0	32 7	32 4	32 2	31 9	31 7	31 3	31 1	30 8	30 5	30 3
49	34 5	34 2	33 9	33 6	33 3	33 0	32 7	32 4	32 1	31 8	31 5	31 3	31 0	30 7	30 5
50	34 8	34 4	34 1	33 8	33 5	33 2	32 9	32 6	32 3	32 0	31 8	31 5	31 2	31 0	30 7
51	35 0	34 7	34 3	34 0	33 7	33 4	33 1	32 8	32 5	32 2	32 0	31 7	31 4	31 2	30 9
52	35 2	34 9	34 6	34 2	33 9	33 6	33 3	33 0	32 7	32 5	32 2	31 9	31 6	31 4	31 1
53	35 4	35 1	34 8	34 5	34 1	33 8	33 5	33 2	32 9	32 7	32 4	32 1	31 8	31 6	31 3
54	35 7	35 3	35 0	34 7	34 4	34 1	33 7	33 5	33 2	32 9	32 6	32 3	32 0	31 8	31 5
55	35 9	35 5	35 2	34 9	34 6	34 3	34 0	33 7	33 4	33 1	32 8	32 5	32 2	32 0	31 7
56	36 1	35 8	35 4	35 1	34 8	34 5	34 2	33 9	33 6	33 3	33 0	32 7	32 4	32 2	31 9
57	36 3	36 0	35 6	35 3	35 0	34 7	34 4	34 1	33 8	33 5	33 2	32 9	32 6	32 3	32 1
58	36 5	36 2	35 8	35 5	35 2	34 9	34 6	34 3	34 0	33 7	33 4	33 1	32 8	32 5	32 3
59	36 7	36 4	36 0	35 7	35 4	35 1	34 8	34 5	34 1	33 9	33 6	33 3	33 0	32 7	32 4
60	36 9	36 6	36 2	35 9	35 6	35 3	35 0	34 6	34 3	34 0	33 7	33 5	33 2	32 9	32 6

CALCULATIONS OF THE PONDERAL INDEX

Statures from 121 to 135 centimetres; weights from 11 to 60 kilograms

Weights in kilograms	Statures in centimetres														
	121	122	123	124	125	126	127	128	129	130	131	132	133	134	135
11	18 4	18 2	18 1	17 9	17 8	17 7	17 5	17 4	17 2	17 1	17 0	16 8	16 7	16 6	16 5
12	18 9	18 8	18 6	18 5	18 3	18 2	18 0	17 9	17 7	17 6	17 5	17 3	17 2	17 1	17 0
13	19 4	19 3	19 1	19 0	18 8	18 7	18 5	18 4	18 2	18 1	17 9	17 8	17 7	17 5	17 4
14	19 9	19 8	19 6	19 4	19 3	19 1	19 0	18 8	18 7	18 5	18 4	18 3	18 1	17 9	17 9
15	20 4	20 2	20 0	19 9	19 7	19 6	19 4	19 3	19 1	19 0	18 8	18 7	18 5	18 4	18 3
16	20 8	20 7	20 5	20 3	20 2	20 0	19 8	19 7	19 5	19 4	19 2	19 1	18 9	18 8	18 7
17	21 2	21 1	20 9	20 7	20 6	20 4	20 2	20 1	19 9	19 8	19 6	19 5	19 3	19 2	19 0
18	21 6	21 5	21 3	21 1	21 0	20 8	20 6	20 5	20 3	20 2	20 0	19 9	19 7	19 6	19 4
19	22 0	21 9	21 7	21 5	21 3	21 2	21 0	20 8	20 7	20 5	20 4	20 2	20 1	19 9	19 8
20	22 4	22 2	22 1	21 9	21 7	21 5	21 4	21 2	21 0	20 9	20 7	20 6	20 4	20 3	20 1
21	22 8	22 6	22 4	22 2	22 1	21 9	21 7	21 6	21 4	21 2	21 1	20 9	20 7	20 6	20 4
22	23 2	23 0	22 8	22 6	22 4	22 2	22 1	21 9	21 7	21 6	21 4	21 2	21 1	20 9	20 8
23	23 5	23 3	23 1	22 9	22 8	22 6	22 4	22 2	22 0	21 9	21 7	21 5	21 4	21 2	21 1
24	23 8	23 6	23 4	23 3	23 1	22 9	22 7	22 5	22 4	22 2	22 0	21 8	21 7	21 5	21 4
25	24 2	24 0	23 8	23 6	23 4	23 2	23 0	22 8	22 7	22 5	22 3	22 2	22 0	21 8	21 7
26	24 5	24 3	24 1	23 9	23 7	23 5	23 3	23 1	23 0	22 8	22 6	22 4	22 3	22 1	21 9
27	24 8	24 6	24 4	24 2	24 0	23 8	23 6	23 4	23 3	23 1	22 9	22 7	22 6	22 4	22 2
28	25 1	24 9	24 7	24 5	24 3	24 1	23 9	23 7	23 5	23 4	23 2	23 0	22 8	22 7	22 5
29	25 4	25 2	25 0	24 8	24 6	24 4	24 2	24 0	23 8	23 6	23 5	23 3	28 1	22 9	22 8
30	25 7	25 5	25 3	25 1	24 9	24 7	24 5	24 3	24 1	23 9	23 7	23 5	23 4	23 2	23 0
31	26 0	25 7	25 5	25 3	25 1	24 9	24 7	24 5	24 3	24 2	24 0	23 8	23 6	23 4	23 3
32	26 2	26 0	25 8	25 6	25 4	25 2	25 0	24 8	24 6	24 4	24 2	24 1	23 9	23 7	23 5
33	26 5	26 3	26 1	25 9	25 7	25 5	25 3	25 1	24 9	24 7	24 5	24 3	24 1	23 9	23 8
34	26 8	26 6	26 3	26 1	25 9	25 7	25 5	25 3	25 1	24 9	24 7	24 5	24 4	24 2	24 0
35	27 0	26 8	26 6	26 4	26 2	26 0	25 8	25 6	25 4	25 2	25 0	24 8	24 6	24 4	24 2
36	27 3	27 1	26 8	26 6	26 4	26 2	26 0	25 8	25 6	25 4	25 2	25 0	24 8	24 6	24 5
37	27 5	27 3	27 1	26 9	26 7	26 4	26 2	26 0	25 8	25 6	25 4	25 2	25 1	24 9	24 7
38	27 8	27 6	27 3	27 1	26 9	26 7	26 5	26 3	26 1	25 9	25 7	25 5	25 3	25 1	24 9
39	28 0	27 8	27 6	27 3	27 1	26 9	26 7	26 5	26 3	26 1	25 9	25 7	25 5	25 3	25 1
40	28 3	28 0	27 8	27 6	27 4	27 1	26 9	26 7	26 5	26 3	26 1	25 9	25 7	25 5	25 3
41	28 5	28 3	28 0	27 8	27 6	27 4	27 1	26 9	26 7	26 5	26 3	26 1	25 9	25 7	25 5
42	28 7	28 5	28 3	28 0	27 8	27 6	27 4	27 2	26 9	26 7	26 5	26 3	26 1	25 9	25 7
43	29 0	28 7	28 5	28 2	28 0	27 8	27 6	27 4	27 2	26 9	26 7	26 5	26 3	26 1	25 9
44	29 2	28 9	28 7	28 5	28 2	28 0	27 8	27 6	27 4	27 2	26 9	26 7	26 5	26 3	26 1
45	29 4	29 2	28 9	28 7	28 5	28 2	28 0	27 8	27 6	27 4	27 2	26 9	26 7	26 5	26 3
46	29 6	29 4	29 1	28 9	28 7	28 4	28 2	28 0	27 8	27 6	27 4	27 1	26 9	26 7	26 5
47	29 8	29 6	29 3	29 1	28 9	28 6	28 4	28 2	28 0	27 8	27 5	27 3	27 1	26 9	26 7
48	30 0	29 8	29 5	29 3	29 1	28 8	28 6	28 4	28 2	28 0	27 7	27 5	27 3	27 1	26 9
49	30 2	30 0	29 7	29 5	29 3	29 0	28 8	28 6	28 4	28 1	27 9	27 7	27 5	27 3	27 1
50	30 4	30 2	30 0	29 7	29 5	29 2	29 0	28 8	28 6	28 3	28 1	27 9	27 7	27 5	27 3
51	30 6	30 4	30 1	29 9	29 7	29 4	29 2	29 0	28 7	28 5	28 3	28 1	27 9	27 7	27 5
52	30 9	30 6	30 3	30 1	29 9	29 6	29 4	29 2	28 9	28 7	28 5	28 3	28 1	27 9	27 7
53	31 0	30 8	30 5	30 3	30 0	29 8	29 6	29 3	29 1	28 9	28 7	28 5	28 2	28 0	27 8
54	31 2	31 0	30 7	30 5	30 2	30 0	29 8	29 5	29 3	29 1	28 9	28 6	28 4	28 2	28 0
55	31 4	31 2	30 9	30 7	30 4	30 2	29 9	29 7	29 5	29 3	29 0	28 8	28 6	28 4	28 2
56	31 6	31 4	31 1	30 9	30 6	30 4	30 1	29 9	29 7	29 4	29 2	29 0	28 8	28 6	28 3
57	31 8	31 5	31 3	31 0	30 8	30 5	30 3	30 1	29 8	29 6	29 4	29 2	28 9	28 7	28 5
58	32 0	31 7	31 5	31 2	31 0	30 7	30 5	30 2	30 0	29 8	29 5	29 3	29 1	28 9	28 7
59	32 2	31 9	31 7	31 4	31 1	30 9	30 7	30 4	30 2	29 9	29 7	29 5	29 3	29 1	28 8
60	32 4	32 1	31 8	31 6	31 3	31 1	30 8	30 6	30 3	30 1	29 9	29 7	29 4	29 2	29 0

CALCULATIONS OF THE PONDERAL INDEX

Statures from 136 to 150 centimetres; weights from 26 to 75 kilograms

Weights in kilograms	Statures in centimetres														
	136	137	138	139	140	141	142	143	144	145	146	147	148	149	150
26	21.8	21.6	21.5	21.3	21.2	21.0	20.9	20.7	20.6	20.4	20.3	20.1	20.0	19.9	19.7
27	22.1	21.9	21.7	21.6	21.4	21.3	21.1	21.0	20.8	20.7	20.5	20.4	20.3	20.1	20.0
28	22.3	22.2	22.0	21.8	21.7	21.5	21.4	21.2	21.1	20.9	20.8	20.7	20.5	20.4	20.2
29	22.6	22.4	22.3	22.1	21.9	21.8	21.6	21.5	21.3	21.2	21.0	20.9	20.8	20.6	20.5
30	22.8	22.7	22.5	22.4	22.2	22.0	21.9	21.7	21.6	21.4	21.3	21.1	21.0	20.9	20.7
31	23.1	22.9	22.8	22.6	22.4	22.3	22.1	22.0	21.8	21.7	21.5	21.4	21.2	21.1	20.9
32	23.3	23.2	23.0	22.8	22.7	22.5	22.4	22.2	22.0	21.9	21.7	21.6	21.5	21.3	21.2
33	23.6	23.4	23.2	23.1	22.9	22.8	22.6	22.4	22.3	22.1	22.0	21.8	21.7	21.5	21.4
34	23.8	23.6	23.5	23.3	23.1	23.0	22.8	22.7	22.5	22.3	22.2	22.0	21.9	21.7	21.6
35	24.1	23.9	23.7	23.5	23.4	23.2	23.0	22.9	22.7	22.6	22.4	22.3	22.1	22.0	21.8
36	24.3	24.1	23.9	23.8	23.6	23.4	23.3	23.1	22.9	22.8	22.6	22.5	22.3	22.2	22.0
37	24.5	24.3	24.1	24.0	23.8	23.6	23.5	23.3	23.1	23.0	22.8	22.7	22.5	22.4	22.2
38	24.7	24.5	24.4	24.2	24.0	23.8	23.7	23.5	23.3	23.2	23.0	22.9	22.7	22.6	22.4
39	24.9	24.8	24.6	24.4	24.2	24.0	23.9	23.7	23.5	23.4	23.2	23.1	22.9	22.8	22.6
40	25.1	25.0	24.8	24.6	24.4	24.3	24.1	23.9	23.7	23.6	23.4	23.3	23.1	23.0	22.8
41	25.4	25.2	25.0	24.8	24.6	24.5	24.3	24.1	23.9	23.8	23.6	23.5	23.3	23.1	23.0
42	25.6	25.4	25.2	25.0	24.8	24.7	24.5	24.3	24.1	24.0	23.8	23.6	23.5	23.3	23.2
43	25.8	25.6	25.4	25.2	25.0	24.8	24.7	24.5	24.3	23.2	24.0	23.8	23.7	23.5	23.4
44	26.0	25.8	25.6	25.4	25.2	25.0	24.9	24.7	24.5	24.3	24.2	24.0	23.9	23.7	23.5
45	26.2	26.0	25.8	25.6	25.4	25.2	25.0	24.9	24.7	24.5	24.4	24.2	24.0	23.9	23.7
46	26.3	26.2	26.0	25.8	25.6	25.4	25.2	25.1	24.9	24.7	24.5	24.4	24.2	24.0	23.9
47	26.5	26.3	26.2	26.0	25.8	25.6	25.4	25.2	25.1	24.9	24.7	24.6	24.4	24.2	24.1
48	26.7	26.5	26.3	26.1	26.0	25.8	25.6	25.4	25.2	25.1	24.9	24.7	24.6	24.4	24.2
49	26.9	26.7	26.5	26.3	26.1	26.0	25.8	25.6	25.4	25.2	25.1	24.9	24.7	24.6	24.4
50	27.1	26.9	26.7	26.5	26.3	26.1	25.9	25.8	25.6	25.4	25.2	25.1	24.9	24.7	24.6
51	27.3	27.1	26.9	26.7	26.5	26.3	26.1	25.9	25.7	25.6	25.4	25.2	25.1	24.9	24.7
52	27.4	27.2	27.1	26.9	26.7	26.5	26.3	26.1	25.9	25.7	25.6	25.4	25.2	25.1	24.9
53	27.6	27.4	27.2	27.0	26.8	26.6	26.5	26.3	26.1	25.9	25.7	25.6	25.4	25.2	25.0
54	27.8	27.6	27.4	27.2	27.0	26.8	26.6	26.4	26.2	26.1	25.9	25.7	25.5	25.4	25.2
55	28.0	27.8	27.6	27.4	27.2	27.0	26.8	26.6	26.4	26.2	26.0	25.9	25.7	25.5	25.4
56	28.1	27.9	27.7	27.5	27.3	27.1	26.9	26.8	26.6	26.4	26.2	26.0	25.9	25.7	25.5
57	28.3	28.1	27.9	27.7	27.5	27.3	27.1	26.9	26.7	26.5	26.4	26.2	26.0	25.8	25.7
58	28.5	28.3	28.1	27.8	27.6	27.5	27.3	27.1	26.9	26.7	26.5	26.3	26.2	26.0	25.8
59	28.6	28.4	28.2	28.0	27.8	27.6	27.4	27.2	27.0	26.8	26.7	26.5	26.3	26.1	26.0
60	28.8	28.6	28.4	28.2	28.0	27.8	27.6	27.4	27.2	27.0	26.8	26.6	26.5	26.3	26.1
61	28.9	28.7	28.5	28.3	28.1	27.9	27.7	27.5	27.3	27.1	27.0	26.8	26.6	26.4	26.2
62	29.1	28.9	28.7	28.5	28.3	28.1	27.9	27.7	27.5	27.3	27.1	26.9	26.7	26.6	26.4
63	29.3	29.0	28.8	28.6	28.4	28.2	28.0	27.8	27.6	27.4	27.3	27.1	26.9	26.7	26.5
64	29.4	29.2	29.0	28.8	28.6	28.4	28.2	28.0	27.8	27.6	27.4	27.2	27.0	26.8	26.7
65	29.6	29.4	29.1	28.9	28.7	28.5	28.3	28.1	27.9	27.7	27.5	27.4	27.2	27.0	26.8
66	29.7	29.5	29.3	29.1	28.9	28.7	28.5	28.3	28.1	27.9	27.7	27.5	27.3	27.1	26.9
67	29.9	29.6	29.4	29.2	29.0	28.8	28.6	28.4	28.2	28.0	27.8	27.6	27.4	27.3	27.1
68	30.0	29.8	29.6	29.4	29.2	29.0	28.8	28.6	28.4	28.2	28.0	27.8	27.6	27.4	27.2
69	30.2	29.9	29.7	29.5	29.3	29.1	28.9	28.7	28.5	28.3	28.1	27.9	27.7	27.5	27.3
70	30.3	30.1	29.9	29.6	29.4	29.2	29.0	28.8	28.6	28.4	28.2	28.0	27.8	27.7	27.5
71	30.4	30.2	30.0	29.8	29.6	29.4	29.2	29.0	28.8	28.6	28.4	28.2	28.0	27.8	27.6
72	30.6	30.4	30.1	29.9	29.7	29.5	29.3	29.1	28.9	28.7	28.5	28.3	28.1	27.9	27.7
73	30.7	30.5	30.3	30.1	29.8	29.6	29.4	29.2	29.0	28.8	28.6	28.4	28.2	28.0	27.9
74	30.9	30.6	30.4	30.2	30.0	29.8	29.6	29.4	29.2	29.0	28.8	28.6	28.4	28.2	28.0
75	31.0	30.8	30.6	30.3	30.1	29.9	29.7	29.5	29.3	29.1	28.9	28.7	28.5	28.3	28.1

CALCULATIONS OF THE PONDERAL INDEX

Statures from 151 to 165 centimetres; weights from 26 to 75 kilograms

Weights in kilograms	Statures in centimetres														
	151	152	153	154	155	156	157	158	159	160	161	162	163	164	165
26	19 6	19 5	19 4	19 2	19 1	19 0	18 9	18 7	18 6	18 5	18 4	18 3	18 2	18 1	18 0
27	19 9	19 7	19 6	19 5	19 4	19 2	19 1	19 0	18 9	18 7	18 6	18 5	18 4	18 3	18 2
28	20 1	20 0	19 8	19 7	19 6	19 5	19 3	19 2	19 1	19 0	18 9	18 7	18 6	18 5	18 4
29	20 3	20 2	20 1	19 9	19 8	19 7	19 6	19 4	19 3	19 2	19 1	19 0	18 8	18 7	18 6
30	20 6	20 4	20 3	20 2	20 0	19 9	19 8	19 7	19 5	19 4	19 3	19 2	19 1	18 9	18 8
31	20 8	20 7	20 5	20 4	20 3	20 1	20 0	19 9	19 8	19 6	19 5	19 4	19 3	19 2	19 0
32	21 0	20 9	20 8	20 6	20 5	20 4	20 2	20 1	20 0	19 8	19 7	19 6	19 5	19 4	19 2
33	21 2	21 1	21 0	20 8	20 7	20 6	20 4	20 3	20 2	20 0	19 9	19 8	19 7	19 6	19 4
34	21 5	21 3	21 2	21 0	20 9	20 8	20 6	20 5	20 4	20 2	20 1	20 0	19 9	19 8	19 6
35	21 7	21 5	21 4	21 2	21 1	21 0	20 8	20 7	20 6	20 4	20 3	20 2	20 1	19 9	19 8
36	21 9	21 7	21 6	21 4	21 3	21 2	21 0	20 9	20 8	20 6	20 5	20 4	20 3	20 1	20 0
37	22 1	21 9	21 8	21 6	21 5	21 4	21 2	21 1	21 0	20 8	20 7	20 6	20 4	20 3	20 2
38	22 3	22 1	22 0	21 8	21 7	21 6	21 4	21 3	21 1	21 0	20 9	20 8	20 6	20 5	20 4
39	22 5	22 3	22 2	22 0	21 9	21 7	21 6	21 5	21 3	21 2	21 1	20 9	20 8	20 7	20 6
40	22 6	22 5	22 4	22 2	22 1	21 9	21 8	21 6	21 5	21 4	21 2	21 1	21 0	20 9	20 7
41	22 8	22 7	22 5	22 4	22 2	22 1	22 0	21 8	21 7	21 5	21 4	21 3	21 2	21 0	20 9
42	23 0	22 9	22 7	22 6	22 4	22 3	22 1	22 0	21 9	21 7	21 6	21 5	21 3	21 2	21 1
43	23 2	23 0	22 9	22 7	22 6	22 5	22 3	22 2	22 0	21 9	21 8	21 6	21 5	21 4	21 2
44	23 4	23 2	23 1	22 9	22 8	22 6	22 5	22 3	22 2	22 1	21 9	21 8	21 7	21 5	21 4
45	23 6	23 4	23 2	23 1	22 9	22 8	22 7	22 5	22 4	22 2	22 1	22 0	21 8	21 7	21 6
46	23 7	23 6	23 4	23 3	23 1	23 0	22 8	22 7	22 5	22 4	22 3	22 1	22 0	21 8	21 7
47	23 9	23 7	23 6	23 4	23 3	23 1	23 0	22 8	22 7	22 6	22 4	22 3	22 1	22 0	21 9
48	24 1	23 9	23 8	23 6	23 4	23 3	23 1	23 0	22 9	22 7	22 6	22 4	22 3	22 2	22 0
49	24 2	24 1	23 9	23 8	23 6	23 5	23 3	23 2	23 0	22 9	22 7	22 6	22 4	22 3	22 2
50	24 4	24 2	24 1	23 9	23 8	23 6	23 5	23 3	23 2	23 0	22 9	22 7	22 6	22 5	22 3
51	24 6	24 4	24 2	24 1	23 9	23 8	23 6	23 5	23 3	23 2	23 0	22 9	22 7	22 6	22 5
52	24 7	24 6	24 4	24 2	24 1	23 9	23 8	23 6	23 5	23 3	23 2	23 0	22 9	22 8	22 6
53	24 9	24 7	24 5	24 4	24 2	24 1	23 9	23 8	23 6	23 5	23 3	23 2	23 0	22 9	22 8
54	25 0	24 9	24 7	24 5	24 4	24 2	24 1	23 9	23 8	23 6	23 5	23 3	23 2	23 0	22 9
55	25 2	25 0	24 9	24 7	24 5	24 4	24 2	24 1	23 9	23 8	23 6	23 5	23 3	23 2	23 0
56	25 3	25 2	25 0	24 8	24 7	24 5	24 4	24 2	24 1	23 9	23 8	23 6	23 5	23 3	23 2
57	25 5	25 3	25 2	25 0	24 8	24 7	24 5	24 4	24 2	24 1	23 9	23 8	23 6	23 5	23 3
58	25 6	25 5	25 3	25 1	25 0	24 8	24 7	24 5	24 3	24 2	24 0	23 9	23 7	23 6	23 5
59	25 8	25 6	25 4	25 3	25 1	25 0	24 8	24 6	24 5	24 3	24 2	24 0	23 9	23 7	23 6
60	25 9	25 8	25 6	25 4	25 3	25 1	24 9	24 8	24 6	24 5	24 3	24 2	24 0	23 9	23 7
61	26 1	25 9	25 7	25 6	25 4	25 2	25 1	24 9	24 8	24 6	24 4	24 3	24 1	24 0	23 9
62	26 2	26 0	25 9	25 7	25 5	25 3	25 2	25 1	24 9	24 7	24 6	24 4	24 3	24 1	24 0
63	26 4	26 2	26 0	25 8	25 7	25 5	25 3	25 2	25 0	24 9	24 7	24 6	24 4	24 3	24 1
64	26 5	26 3	26 1	26 0	25 8	25 6	25 5	25 3	25 2	25 0	24 8	24 7	24 5	24 4	24 2
65	26 6	26 5	26 3	26 1	25 9	25 8	25 6	25 4	25 3	25 1	25 0	24 8	24 7	24 5	24 4
66	26 8	26 6	26 4	26 2	26 1	25 9	25 7	25 6	25 4	25 3	25 1	24 9	24 8	24 6	24 5
67	26 9	26 7	26 5	26 4	26 2	26 0	25 9	25 7	25 5	25 4	25 2	25 1	24 9	24 8	24 6
68	27 0	26 9	26 7	26 5	26 3	26 2	26 0	25 8	25 7	25 5	25 4	25 2	25 0	24 9	24 7
69	27 2	27 0	26 8	26 6	26 5	26 3	26 1	26 0	25 8	25 6	25 5	25 3	25 2	25 0	24 9
70	27 3	27 1	26 9	26 8	26 6	26 4	26 2	26 1	25 9	25 8	25 6	25 4	25 3	25 1	25 0
71	27 4	27 2	27 1	26 9	26 7	26 5	26 4	26 2	26 0	25 9	25 7	25 6	25 4	25 3	25 1
72	27 5	27 4	27 2	27 0	26 8	26 7	26 5	26 3	26 2	26 0	25 8	25 7	25 5	25 4	25 2
73	27 7	27 5	27 3	27 1	27 0	26 8	26 6	26 4	26 3	26 1	26 0	25 8	25 6	25 5	25 3
74	27 8	27 6	27 4	27 3	27 1	26 9	26 7	26 6	26 4	26 2	26 1	25 9	25 8	25 6	25 4
75	27 9	27 7	27 6	27 4	27 2	27 0	26 9	26 7	26 5	26 4	26 2	26 0	25 9	25 7	25 6

CALCULATIONS OF THE PONDERAL INDEX

Statures from 166 to 180 centimetres; weights from 46 to 95 kilograms

Weights in kilograms	Statures in centimetres														
	166	167	168	169	170	171	172	173	174	175	176	177	178	179	180
46	21 6	21 5	21 3	21 2	21 1	21 0	20 8	20 7	20 6	20 5	20 4	20 2	20 1	20 0	19 9
47	21 7	21 6	21 5	21 4	21 2	21 1	21 0	20 9	20 7	20 6	20 5	20 4	20 3	20 2	20 1
48	21 9	21 8	21 6	21 5	21 4	21 3	21 1	21 0	20 9	20 8	20 6	20 5	20 4	20 3	20 2
49	22 0	21 9	21 8	21 7	21 5	21 4	21 3	21 2	21 0	20 9	20 8	20 7	20 6	20 4	20 3
50	22 2	22 1	21 9	21 8	21 7	21 5	21 4	21 3	21 2	21 1	20 9	20 8	20 7	20 6	20 5
51	22 3	22 2	22 1	21 9	21 8	21 7	21 6	21 4	21 3	21 3	21 1	20 9	20 8	20 7	20 6
52	22 5	22 4	22 2	22 1	22 0	21 8	21 7	21 6	21 5	21 4	21 3	21 1	21 0	20 9	20 7
53	22 6	22 5	22 4	22 2	22 1	22 0	21 8	21 7	21 6	21 5	21 4	21 3	21 1	21 0	20 9
54	22 8	22 6	22 5	22 4	22 2	22 1	22 0	21 9	21 7	21 6	21 5	21 4	21 3	21 1	21 0
55	22 9	22 8	22 6	22 5	22 4	22 2	22 1	22 0	21 9	21 7	21 6	21 5	21 4	21 3	21 1
56	23 0	22 9	22 8	22 6	22 5	22 4	22 2	22 1	22 0	21 9	21 7	21 6	21 5	21 4	21 3
57	23 2	23 0	22 9	22 8	22 6	22 5	22 4	22 2	22 1	22 0	21 9	21 7	21 6	21 5	21 4
58	23 3	23 2	23 0	22 9	22 8	22 6	22 5	22 4	22 2	22 1	22 0	21 9	21 7	21 6	21 5
59	23 5	23 3	23 2	23 0	22 9	22 8	22 6	22 5	22 4	22 2	22 1	22 0	21 9	21 7	21 6
60	23 6	23 4	23 3	23 2	23 0	22 9	22 8	22 6	22 5	22 4	22 2	22 1	22 0	21 9	21 7
61	23 7	23 6	23 4	23 3	23 2	23 0	22 9	22 8	22 6	22 5	22 4	22 2	22 1	22 0	21 9
62	23 8	23 7	23 6	23 4	23 3	23 1	23 0	22 9	22 7	22 6	22 5	22 4	22 2	22 1	22 0
63	24 0	23 8	23 7	23 5	23 4	23 3	23 1	23 0	22 9	22 7	22 6	22 5	22 4	22 2	22 1
64	24 1	24 0	23 8	23 7	23 5	23 4	23 3	23 1	23 0	22 9	22 7	22 6	22 5	22 3	22 2
65	24 2	24 1	23 9	23 8	23 6	23 5	23 4	23 2	23 1	23 0	22 8	22 7	22 6	22 5	22 3
66	24 3	24 2	24 1	23 9	23 7	23 6	23 5	23 4	23 2	23 1	23 0	22 8	22 7	22 6	22 4
67	24 5	24 3	24 2	24 0	23 9	23 7	23 6	23 5	23 3	23 2	23 1	22 9	22 8	22 7	22 6
68	24 6	24 4	24 3	24 2	24 0	23 9	23 7	23 6	23 5	23 3	23 2	23 1	22 9	22 8	22 7
69	24 7	24 6	24 4	24 3	24 1	24 0	23 8	23 7	23 6	23 4	23 3	23 2	23 0	22 9	22 8
70	24 8	24 7	24 5	24 4	24 2	24 1	24 0	23 8	23 7	23 6	23 4	23 3	23 2	23 0	22 9
71	24 9	24 8	24 6	24 5	24 4	24 2	24 1	23 9	23 8	23 7	23 5	23 4	23 3	23 1	23 0
72	25 1	24 9	24 8	24 6	24 5	24 3	24 2	24 0	23 9	23 8	23 6	23 5	23 4	23 2	23 1
73	25 2	25 0	24 9	24 7	24 6	24 4	24 3	24 2	24 0	23 9	23 7	23 6	23 5	23 3	23 2
74	25 3	25 1	25 0	24 8	24 7	24 5	24 4	24 3	24 1	24 0	23 9	23 7	23 6	23 5	23 3
75	25 4	25 3	25 1	25 0	24 8	24 7	24 5	24 4	24 2	24 1	24 0	23 8	23 7	23 6	23 4
76	25 5	25 4	25 2	25 1	24 9	24 8	24 6	24 5	24 3	24 2	24 1	23 9	23 8	23 7	23 5
77	25 6	25 5	25 3	25 2	25 0	24 9	24 7	24 6	24 4	24 3	24 2	24 0	23 9	23 8	23 6
78	25 7	25 6	25 4	25 3	25 1	25 0	24 8	24 7	24 6	24 4	24 3	24 1	24 0	23 9	23 7
79	25 8	25 7	25 5	25 4	25 2	25 1	24 9	24 8	24 7	24 5	24 4	24 2	24 1	24 0	23 8
80	26 0	25 8	25 6	25 5	25 3	25 2	25 1	24 9	24 8	24 6	24 5	24 3	24 2	24 1	23 9
81	26 1	25 9	25 8	25 6	25 5	25 3	25 2	25 0	24 9	24 7	24 6	24 4	24 3	24 2	24 0
82	26 2	26 0	25 9	25 7	25 6	25 4	25 3	25 1	25 0	24 8	24 7	24 5	24 4	24 3	24 1
83	26 3	26 1	26 0	25 8	25 7	25 5	25 4	25 2	25 1	24 9	24 8	24 6	24 5	24 4	24 2
84	26 4	26 2	26 1	25 9	25 8	25 6	25 5	25 3	25 2	25 0	24 9	24 7	24 6	24 5	24 3
85	26 5	26 3	26 2	26 0	25 9	25 7	25 6	25 4	25 3	25 1	25 0	24 8	24 7	24 6	24 4
86	26 6	26 4	26 3	26 1	26 0	25 8	25 7	25 5	25 4	25 2	25 1	24 9	24 8	24 7	24 5
87	26 7	26 5	26 4	26 2	26 1	25 9	25 8	25 6	25 5	25 3	25 2	25 0	24 9	24 8	24 6
88	26 8	26 6	26 5	26 3	26 2	26 0	25 9	25 7	25 6	25 4	25 3	25 1	25 0	24 8	24 7
89	26 9	26 7	26 6	26 4	26 3	26 1	26 0	25 8	25 7	25 5	25 4	25 2	25 1	24 9	24 8
90	27 0	26 8	26 7	26 5	26 4	26 2	26 1	25 9	25 8	25 6	25 5	25 3	25 2	25 0	24 9
91	27 1	26 9	26 8	26 6	26 5	26 3	26 2	26 0	25 9	25 7	25 6	25 4	25 3	25 1	25 0
92	27 2	27 0	26 9	26 7	26 6	26 4	26 2	26 1	25 9	25 8	25 6	25 5	25 4	25 2	25 1
93	27 3	27 1	27 0	26 8	26 7	26 5	26 3	26 2	26 0	25 9	25 7	25 6	25 5	25 3	25 2
94	27 4	27 2	27 1	26 9	26 7	26 6	26 4	26 3	26 1	26 0	25 8	25 7	25 5	25 4	25 3
95	27 5	27 3	27 2	27 0	26 8	26 7	26 5	26 4	26 2	26 1	25 9	25 8	25 6	25 5	25 3

CALCULATIONS OF THE PONDERAL INDEX

Statures from 181 to 195 centimetres; weights from 46 to 95 kilograms

Weights in kilograms	Statures in centimetres														
	181	182	183	184	185	186	187	188	189	190	191	192	193	194	195
46	19 8	19 7	19 6	19 5	19 4	19 3	19 2	19 1	19 0	18 9	18 8	18 7	18 6	18 5	18 4
47	19 9	19 8	19 7	19 6	19 5	19 4	19 3	19 2	19 1	19 0	18 9	18 8	18 7	18 6	18 5
48	20 1	20 0	19 9	19 7	19 6	19 5	19 4	19 3	19 2	19 1	19 0	18 9	18 8	18 7	18 6
49	20 2	20 1	20 0	19 9	19 8	19 7	19 6	19 5	19 4	19 3	19 2	19 1	19 0	18 9	18 8
50	20 4	20 2	20 1	20 0	19 9	19 8	19 7	19 6	19 5	19 4	19 3	19 2	19 1	19 0	18 9
51	20 5	20 4	20 3	20 2	20 0	19 9	19 8	19 7	19 6	19 5	19 4	19 3	19 2	19 1	19 0
52	20 6	20 5	20 4	20 3	20 2	20 1	20 0	19 9	19 8	19 6	19 5	19 4	19 3	19 2	19 1
53	20 8	20 6	20 5	20 4	20 3	20 2	20 1	20 0	19 9	19 8	19 7	19 6	19 5	19 4	19 3
54	20 9	20 8	20 7	20 5	20 4	20 3	20 2	20 1	20 0	19 9	19 8	19 7	19 6	19 5	19 4
55	21 0	20 9	20 8	20 7	20 6	20 4	20 3	20 2	20 1	20 0	19 9	19 8	19 7	19 6	19 5
56	21 1	21 0	20 9	20 8	20 7	20 6	20 5	20 4	20 2	20 1	20 0	19 9	19 8	19 7	19 6
57	21 3	21 1	21 0	20 9	20 8	20 7	20 6	20 5	20 4	20 3	20 2	20 0	19 9	19 8	19 7
58	21 4	21 3	21 2	21 0	20 9	20 8	20 7	20 6	20 5	20 4	20 3	20 2	20 1	20 0	19 9
59	21 5	21 4	21 3	21 2	21 0	20 9	20 8	20 7	20 6	20 5	20 4	20 3	20 2	20 1	20 0
60	21 6	21 5	21 4	21 3	21 2	21 0	20 9	20 8	20 7	20 6	20 5	20 4	20 3	20 2	20 1
61	21 7	21 6	21 5	21 4	21 3	21 2	21 0	20 9	20 8	20 7	20 6	20 5	20 4	20 3	20 2
62	21 9	21 7	21 6	21 5	21 4	21 3	21 2	21 1	20 9	20 8	20 7	20 6	20 5	20 4	20 3
63	22 0	21 9	21 7	21 6	21 5	21 4	21 3	21 2	21 1	20 9	20 8	20 7	20 6	20 5	20 4
64	22 1	22 0	21 9	21 7	21 6	21 5	21 4	21 3	21 2	21 1	20 9	20 8	20 7	20 6	20 5
65	22 2	22 1	22 0	21 9	21 7	21 6	21 5	21 4	21 3	21 2	21 1	20 9	20 8	20 7	20 6
66	22 3	22 2	22 1	22 0	21 8	21 7	21 6	21 5	21 4	21 3	21 2	21 0	20 9	20 8	20 7
67	22 4	22 3	22 2	22 1	22 0	21 8	21 7	21 6	21 5	21 4	21 3	21 2	21 0	20 9	20 8
68	22 6	22 4	22 3	22 2	22 1	21 9	21 8	21 7	21 6	21 5	21 4	21 3	21 2	21 0	20 9
69	22 7	22 5	22 4	22 3	22 2	22 1	21 9	21 8	21 7	21 6	21 5	21 3	21 3	21 1	21 0
70	22 8	22 6	22 5	22 4	22 3	22 2	22 0	21 9	21 8	21 7	21 6	21 5	21 4	21 2	21 1
71	22 9	22 8	22 6	22 5	22 4	22 3	22 1	22 0	21 9	21 8	21 7	21 6	21 5	21 3	21 2
72	23 0	22 9	22 7	22 6	22 5	22 4	22 2	22 1	22 0	21 9	21 8	21 7	21 6	21 4	21 3
73	23 1	23 0	22 8	22 7	22 6	22 5	22 3	22 2	22 1	22 0	21 9	21 8	21 7	21 5	21 4
74	23 2	23 1	22 9	22 8	22 7	22 6	22 4	22 3	22 2	22 1	22 0	21 9	21 8	21 6	21 5
75	23 3	23 2	23 0	22 9	22 8	22 7	22 6	22 4	22 3	22 2	22 1	22 0	21 8	21 7	21 6
76	23 4	23 3	23 1	23 0	22 9	22 8	22 7	22 5	22 4	22 3	22 2	22 1	21 9	21 8	21 7
77	23 5	23 4	23 2	23 1	23 0	22 9	22 8	22 6	22 5	22 4	22 3	22 2	22 0	21 9	21 8
78	23 6	23 5	23 3	23 2	23 1	23 0	22 9	22 7	22 6	22 5	22 4	22 3	22 1	22 0	21 9
79	23 7	23 6	23 4	23 3	23 2	23 1	22 9	22 8	22 7	22 6	22 5	22 3	22 2	22 1	22 0
80	23 8	23 7	23 5	23 4	23 3	23 2	23 0	22 9	22 8	22 7	22 6	22 4	22 3	22 2	22 1
81	23 9	23 8	23 6	23 5	23 4	23 3	23 1	23 0	22 9	22 8	22 7	22 5	22 4	22 3	22 2
82	24 0	23 9	23 7	23 6	23 5	23 4	23 2	23 1	23 0	22 9	22 7	22 6	22 5	22 4	22 3
83	24 1	24 0	23 8	23 7	23 6	23 5	23 3	23 2	23 1	23 0	22 8	22 7	22 6	22 5	22 4
84	24 2	24 1	23 9	23 8	23 7	23 5	23 4	23 3	23 2	23 1	22 9	22 8	22 7	22 6	22 5
85	24 3	24 2	24 0	23 9	23 8	23 6	23 5	23 4	23 3	23 1	23 0	22 9	22 8	22 7	22 5
86	24 4	24 3	24 1	24 0	23 9	23 7	23 6	23 5	23 4	23 2	23 1	23 0	22 9	22 8	22 6
87	24 5	24 3	24 2	24 1	24 0	23 8	23 7	23 6	23 4	23 3	23 2	23 1	23 0	22 8	22 7
88	24 6	24 4	24 3	24 2	24 0	23 9	23 8	23 7	23 5	23 4	23 3	23 2	23 0	22 9	22 8
89	24 7	24 5	24 4	24 3	24 1	24 0	23 9	23 7	23 6	23 5	23 4	23 3	23 1	23 0	22 9
90	24 8	24 6	24 5	24 4	24 2	24 1	24 0	23 8	23 7	23 6	23 5	23 3	23 2	23 1	23 0
91	24 9	24 7	24 6	24 4	24 3	24 2	24 1	23 9	23 8	23 7	23 5	23 4	23 3	23 2	23 1
92	24 9	24 8	24 7	24 5	24 4	24 3	24 1	24 0	23 9	23 8	23 6	23 5	23 4	23 3	23 1
93	25 0	24 9	24 8	24 6	24 5	24 4	24 2	24 1	24 0	23 8	23 7	23 6	23 5	23 4	23 2
94	25 1	25 0	24 8	24 7	24 6	24 4	24 3	24 2	24 1	23 9	23 8	23 7	23 6	23 4	23 3
95	25 2	25 1	24 9	24 8	24 7	24 5	24 4	24 3	24 1	24 0	23 9	23 8	23 6	23 5	23 4

INDEX

(*A.—Names*)

INDEX

(B.—Subjects)

Published by

Facsimile Publisher
Ashok Vihar, Delhi-110052 (India)
Website: www.facsimilepublisher.com

Distributed by

Gyan Books Pvt. Ltd.
5, Ansari Road, Daryaganj, New Delhi-110002 (India)
E-mail: books@gyanbooks.com, Website: www.gyanbooks.com

2 222000 013363